ASIAN DEVELOPMENT Outlook 2013

Asia's Energy Challenge

Asian Development Bank

ISBN 978-92-9254-022-7 (Print), 978-92-9254-023-4 (PDF)
ISSN 0117-0481
Publication Stock No. FLS135622

Cataloging-in-Publication Data

Asian Development Bank.
Asian development outlook 2013. Asia's energy challenge.
Mandaluyong City, Philippines: Asian Development Bank, 2013.

1. Economics. 2. Finance. 3. Asia. I. Asian Development Bank.

The annual *Asian Development Outlook* provides a comprehensive economic analysis of 45 economies in developing Asia and the Pacific.

6 ADB Avenue, Mandaluyong City
1550 Metro Manila, Philippines
Tel +63 2 632 4444
Fax +63 2 636 2444
www.adb.org

For orders, please contact:
Department of External Relations
Fax +63 2 636 2648
adbpub@adb.org

Printed on recycled paper

Contents

Foreword

Developing Asia's economies are returning to healthy growth. In the face of continued sluggishness in the United States, the euro area, and Japan, the region is finding ways to bolster its resilience. The *Asian Development Outlook 2013* estimates regional growth will pick up to 6.6% in 2013 and reach 6.7% in 2014. While this is a distinct improvement on 2012, when growth stood at just over 6%, it is far from the heady double-digit pace before the global financial crisis.

But in many ways this new Asian reality is a positive development. Leading regional economies are settling into a pattern of more moderate, more sustainable growth, founded on new opportunities nearer to home. Asia's contributions to global imbalances—its persistent current account surpluses—are smoothly winding down. Muted demand from wealthy countries is providing the impetus for the region to turn to internal sources and trade with its neighbors. With the major industrial economies expected to grow by only 1% in 2013, the roles of domestic demand and intra-Asian trade will continue to expand.

Yet growth has been uneven, as the region recovers at different speeds. Growth acceleration in the People's Republic of China (PRC) is supporting the rebound of the region. The PRC will expand by 8.2% in 2013 and 8.0% in 2014, up from 7.8% in 2012. India looks set to improve its growth rate from 5.0% in fiscal year 2012 to 6.0% in 2013 and further to 6.5% in 2014, but it must assiduously break down the barriers inhibiting investment.

The rising importance of intraregional trade is most evident in Southeast Asia. Economies in the Association of Southeast Asian Nations (ASEAN) will maintain their robust growth supported by increasingly strong trade ties within Asia. The vision of the Regional Comprehensive Economic Partnership is a broader free trade area with ASEAN as the hub. Making this vision a reality will further enhance Asia's dynamism.

One effect of regional economies returning to their production potential in the midst of rising global liquidity is that inflation has begun to pick up. Though inflation is expected to remain in check, helped by stable global commodity prices, authorities must carefully watch for pressures on consumer prices and financial markets and take action where necessary.

The immediate horizon presents a number of challenges that could derail developing Asia's recovery. Political squabbling is creating tensions within the region and beyond. Passions must be kept in check while long-term solutions are sought.

Looking further ahead, Asia must secure sufficient energy to drive economic expansion in the decades to come. The region already consumes roughly a third of global energy, and this is set to rise to over half by 2035. But Asia remains home to two-thirds of the world's poor, and many of its megacities are mired in polluted air and water. Therefore, securing adequate physical energy supplies must be achieved while preserving the environment and extending the benefits of electricity to the millions who still live without it.

The related set of energy goals will be challenging and require creativity and commitment from policy makers. Action is urgently needed on multiple fronts. Asia must find ways to restrain its energy demand by making the most efficient use of scarce energy resources. Replacing inefficient subsidies with support targeting the poor will send the right signal. Investment in new technology and infrastructure, along with a healthy dose of creativity, will be needed to achieve cleaner transport and greener cities. Asia must also prioritize renewable energy supplies and new technologies that can make conventional power cleaner and more efficient.

A bold vision of a regionwide market in energy is needed to bring together all the demand and supply solutions. Asia can achieve the degree of energy system integration currently enjoyed in Europe if its leaders take urgent action. The region has enjoyed immense gains from intraregional trade and cross-border production schemes. Applying these lessons to energy markets will help usher in the "Clean Asian Century."

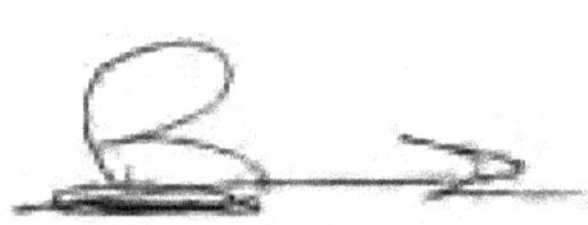

BINDU N. LOHANI
Ranking Vice President
Asian Development Bank

Acknowledgments

The *Asian Development Outlook 2013* was prepared by the staff of the Asian Development Bank (ADB) in the Central and West Asia Department, East Asia Department, Pacific Department, South Asia Department, Southeast Asia Department, and Economics and Research Department, as well as the resident missions. Representatives of these departments and the Office of Regional Economic Integration constituted the Regional Economic Outlook Task Force, which met regularly and coordinated closely to develop consistent forecasts for the region.

The authors who contributed the sections are bylined in each chapter. The subregional coordinators were Tatsuji Hayakawa for Central and West Asia, Yolanda Fernandez Lommen for East Asia, Sabyasachi Mitra for South Asia, Pradeep Srivastava for Southeast Asia, and Christopher Edmonds for the Pacific.

A team of economists in the Economics and Research Department, led by Joseph E. Zveglich, Jr., assistant chief economist, Macroeconomics and Finance Research Division, assisted by Edith Laviña, coordinated the overall production of the publication. Technical and research support was provided by Arnelyn May Abdon, Shiela Camingue, Cindy Castillejos-Petalcorin, Gemma Esther Estrada, Nedelyn Magtibay-Ramos, Pilipinas Quising, Aleli Rosario, and Lea Sumulong. The economic editorial advisors Robert Boumphrey, Joshua Greene, Richard Niebuhr, Anthony Patrick, and Reza Vaez-Zadeh made substantive contributions to the country chapters and regional outlook.

Support and guidance from members of the ADB Energy Community of Practice is gratefully acknowledge, notably from Anthony Jude, Gil-Hong Kim, Jong-Inn Kim, Kee-Yung Nam, Pradeep Perera, and Pil-Bae Song. Special thanks to Jun Tian, advisor in the Regional and Sustainable Development Department, who provided the Asia and Pacific energy consumption forecasts used in the theme chapter. Anil Terway provided editorial advice on the theme chapter.

Peter Fredenburg did the style and manuscript editing. Alvin Tubio was responsible for typesetting, as well as graphics generation in which he was assisted by Maria Susan Torres. Art direction of the cover design was by Anthony Victoria, with artwork from Design Muscle. Critical support for the printing and publishing of the report was provided by the Logistics Management Unit of the Office of Administrative Services. Fermirelyn Cruz, Elenita Pura, and Rhia Bautista-Piamonte provided administrative and secretarial support.

The Department of External Relations, led by Ann Quon, Omana Nair, and Sean Crowley, planned and coordinated the dissemination of the *Asian Development Outlook 2013*.

C. Rhee

Changyong Rhee
Chief Economist
Economics and Research Department

Definitions

The economies discussed in the *Asian Development Outlook 2013* (*ADO 2013*) are classified by major analytic or geographic group. For purposes of this publication, the following apply:

- **Association of Southeast Asian Nations (ASEAN)** comprises Brunei Darussalam, Cambodia, Indonesia, the Lao People's Democratic Republic, Malaysia, Myanmar, the Philippines, Singapore, Thailand, and Viet Nam.
- **Developing Asia** refers to the 45 developing member countries of the Asian Development Bank.
- **Central Asia** comprises Armenia, Azerbaijan, Georgia, Kazakhstan, the Kyrgyz Republic, Tajikistan, Turkmenistan, and Uzbekistan.
- **East Asia** comprises the People's Republic of China; Hong Kong, China; the Republic of Korea; Mongolia; and Taipei,China.
- **South Asia** comprises Afghanistan, Bangladesh, Bhutan, India, the Maldives, Nepal, Pakistan, and Sri Lanka.
- **Southeast Asia** comprises Brunei Darussalam, Cambodia, Indonesia, the Lao People's Democratic Republic, Malaysia, Myanmar, the Philippines, Singapore, Thailand, and Viet Nam.
- **The Pacific** comprises the Cook Islands, Fiji, Kiribati, the Marshall Islands, the Federated States of Micronesia, Nauru, Papua New Guinea, Palau, Samoa, Solomon Islands, Timor-Leste, Tonga, Tuvalu, and Vanuatu.
- Unless otherwise specified, the symbol "$" and the word "dollar" refer to US dollars.

ADO 2013 is generally based on data available up to **15 March 2013**.

Abbreviations

ADB	Asian Development Bank
ASEAN	Association of Southeast Asian Nations
CCS	carbon capture and storage
CNG	compressed natural gas
CO_2	carbon dioxide
ECB	European Central Bank
EU	European Union
FDI	foreign direct investment
FY	fiscal year
GDP	gross domestic product
GHG	greenhouse gas
Gtoe	gigatons of oil equivalent
GW	gigawatt (1 billion watts)
IEA	International Energy Agency
IMF	International Monetary Fund
kW	kilowatt (1,000 watts)
Lao PDR	Lao People's Democratic Republic
Mtoe	million tons of oil equivalent
MW	megawatt (1 million watts)
OECD	Organisation for Economic Co-operation and Development
OPEC	Organization of the Petroleum Exporting Countries
PM_{10}	airborne particulate matter less than 10 microns in diameter
PRC	People's Republic of China
TWh	terawatt-hour (1 trillion watts expended for 1 hour)
US	United States of America

ADO 2013—Highlights

Developing Asia is bouncing back from the slowdown of the previous year. Robust domestic demand and greater reliance on regional trade will accelerate growth from 6.1% in 2012 to 6.6% in 2013 and 6.7% in 2014.

Though still relatively stable, inflation is forecast to pick up as regional economies return to their production potential in the midst of rising global liquidity from advanced economies. Consumer prices are expected to rise by 4.0% in 2013 and 4.2% in 2014, up from 3.7% last year.

Developing Asia's recovery phase remains vulnerable to shocks. Strong capital inflows could feed asset bubbles. Political discord surrounding fiscal debates in the United States, austerity fatigue in the euro area, and border disputes in Asia could jeopardize macroeconomic stability.

The region needs an ample supply of clean, affordable energy to continue its rapid growth in the coming decades. To achieve energy security, developing Asia must actively contain its rising demand, aggressively explore new supply sources and technology, and progressively integrate regional energy markets and infrastructure.

Key messages

- Developing Asia's growth is gathering speed after declining somewhat in 2012. Gross domestic product is forecast to expand by 6.6% in 2013 and 6.7% in 2014, following the slower 6.1% pace in 2012. The expected acceleration is occurring broadly across the region, but there are notable differences in the pace.

- Growth will rebound in the People's Republic of China (PRC), from 7.8% in 2012 to 8.2% in 2013 and 8.0% in 2014, driven by strong consumption and investment. The more moderate pace reflects a shift in focus from the growth rate alone toward its quality in terms of being more inclusive and environmentally friendly. India's growth has the potential to pick up from 5.0% in 2012 to 6.0% in 2013 and 6.5% in 2014, but the South Asian giant must create a more favorable environment for investment if it is to sustain this higher rate.

- Southeast Asia is benefiting from robust domestic demand and greater trade with its neighbors in the region. The subregion can reap considerable benefits from further integration among the economies of the Association of Southeast Asian Nations (ASEAN) and with its regional trading partners.

- Continued sluggishness in the United States (US), euro area, and Japan suggests that developing Asia must continue to shift toward more domestic demand and trade with emerging markets. Together, the major industrial economies are expected to manage 1.0% growth in 2013 and 1.9% in 2014. The further narrowing of the region's current account surplus—from 2.0% of gross domestic product (GDP) in 2012 to 1.9% in 2013 and 1.8% in 2014—indicates that the shift to internal sources of growth is progressing.

- Capital flows into the region bounced back rapidly after the crisis, in part because of the unconventional monetary policies pursued by central banks in major industrial economies. Advanced economies will likely continue their accommodative monetary stance, and authorities in developing Asia must safeguard the soundness of the financial sector to avoid the emergence of disruptive asset bubbles.

- Price pressures must be closely monitored in this environment of continued global liquidity expansion. Robust growth has largely eliminated slack productive capacity in many regional economies such that loose monetary policy risks reigniting inflation. Inflation is expected to tick up from 3.7% in 2012 to 4.0% in 2013 and 4.2% in 2014.

- Developing Asia's favorable fiscal position cannot be taken for granted, as longer-term structural issues need to be addressed to ensure inclusive growth in the future. Improved revenue efficiency is needed to finance public investment, while better governance can enhance public service delivery.

- Political risks are emerging as the main threats to the region's continued robust growth over the forecast horizon. Political contention is calling into question the ability of authorities to find compromise solutions to nagging fiscal problems in the US, deepening austerity fatigue in the euro area, and simmering border disputes in Asia.

- With its rising prominence in the global economy, developing Asia has become a major player in commodity markets. The business cycles of the larger regional economic blocks affect commodity prices and their producing economies—India mostly within Asia but the PRC globally. Asia's growing thirst for oil imports makes the region more vulnerable to shocks from geopolitical tensions that may affect the production of this key commodity.

- The region faces a threefold energy challenge. Developing Asia's energy needs will expand in tandem with its growing economic influence, but its own endowment is insufficient. Further, scaling up its current energy mix would be devastating to the environment. Yet, for growth to be truly inclusive, the poor must also have affordable access to energy.

- Policies to restrain demand—such as replacing wasteful general subsidies with targeted ones and planning for cleaner transport and green cities—are part of the solution. Meanwhile, expanded supply must draw more from renewable resources such as wind and solar. Asia is already staking out a leadership position in renewables, but expanding these sources will not be enough to fill the gap. Consequently, Asia needs to invest in making conventional power cleaner and more efficient.

- Asia must aspire to the degree of regional cooperation and integration in energy by 2030 that currently prevails in Europe. Cooperation among the region's leaders at the highest levels is needed to expedite the benefits. It will take action on all fronts—reducing demand, increasing supply, and integrating systems—to realize the future envisioned as the "Clean Asian Century."

Asia builds momentum amid global doldrums

Developing Asia's growth prospects

- **Growth in developing Asia is picking up.** The expansion of GDP in the region is forecast to pick up to 6.6% in 2013 from 6.1% in 2012. Resilient private consumption demand will help maintain that pace into 2014 as the region grows by an expected 6.7%. The rebound is supported by recovery in the PRC and robust growth in the economies of the ASEAN. As economic activity gains strength, so will upward pressure on prices. This will lift the region's inflation to a forecast 4.0% in 2013, up from 3.7% last year, with a further tick to 4.2% in 2014.

  » **Meanwhile, growth in the major industrial economies languishes.** Collectively, the advanced economies managed to grow by only 1.2% in 2012, the same pace as in the previous year, with Japan's rebound from disaster offsetting contraction in the euro area. Though the hazards emanating from the advanced economies—a euro area breakdown or a US fiscal shock—have abated, fiscal consolidation, high unemployment, and austerity fatigue will continue to make their recovery uncertain. Forecasts for 2013 point to a period of consolidation in the first half of the year before growth slowly picks up in the remainder of the forecast period. Overall, GDP is expected to expand by 1.0% in 2013 and 1.9% in 2014.

» **The process of global rebalancing continues.** Strong domestic demand and intraregional trade, coupled with weak demand from advanced economies, have further narrowed developing Asia's current account surplus. The surplus dropped from 2.5% of GDP in 2011 to 2.0% in 2012. Although exports are projected to pick up, imports will likely rise even more quickly, tightening the overall current account surplus further to 1.9% of GDP in 2013 and 1.8% in 2014.

- **The region's giants are showing different speeds of recovery.** The PRC will expand by 8.2% in 2013 and 8.0% in 2014, compared with 7.8% in 2012, as strong domestic demand continues and export performance picks up. India has considerable potential, but its future performance relies on resolving contentious structural and policy issues that inhibit investment. Strong consumption will continue to drive India's recovery from 5.0% in fiscal year 2012 to 6.0% in 2013 and further to 6.5% in 2014 if reform can build momentum.

- **Robust domestic demand and greater intraregional trade underlie Southeast Asia's recent resilience.** ASEAN was the only subregion to enjoy faster growth in 2012, rising to 5.5% from 4.7% in 2011. Reform-oriented economies less dependent on exports, like the Philippines and Indonesia, relied on their own domestic demand to compensate for soft demand from the major industrial economies. Larger trade with other regional countries—particularly within ASEAN and with the PRC—also helped cushion the impact of the slow recovery in advanced economies. ASEAN's resilience is expected to extend through the forecast horizon, with its member economies averaging growth of 5.4% in 2013 and 5.7% in 2014.

- **Deeper and broader ASEAN economic integration after 2015 can further boost members' income.** The proposed Regional Comprehensive Economic Partnership between ASEAN and its other free trade agreement partners would enlarge trade volumes within a large block of dynamic economies, helping the subregion diversify its export markets. More integration would, however, also expose these economies to stronger spillover from shocks, which would have to be managed properly.

Managing capital flows under quantitative easing

- **The advanced economies will continue the loose monetary policies begun during the global downturn.** As the crisis intensified and policy rates neared zero in 2008, advanced economy central banks resorted to unconventional monetary policy. The US Federal Reserve and others used so-called quantitative easing (QE), expanding their balance sheets with direct purchases of less-liquid assets than their traditional holdings, to support financial markets and prop up economic activity. Recent central bank announcements suggest these measures are likely to continue in the near term in response to lagging recovery.

- **QE seems to have prevented a deeper decline of advanced economies and contributed to the sharp rebound of capital flows into Asia.** In the depth of global financial turmoil, as bank liquidity dried up everywhere, aggregate inflows to 10 large regional economies—the PRC; Hong Kong, China; India; Indonesia; Japan; the Republic of Korea; the Philippines; Singapore; Taipei,China; and Thailand—plummeted to 1.7% of GDP in 2008–2009 from an average of 8.4% the previous 3 years. But inflows rebounded nearly as sharply, returning to an average of 7.4% of GDP in 2010–2012.

- **Asian economies with more open and developed capital markets experienced greater swings in capital inflows.** In particular, large capital flows were manifest more in portfolio investment and other investment such as bank loans than in foreign direct investment. Empirical analysis shows QE, in particular the interventions during the worst of the global crisis, contributed to appreciating local currencies, lowering domestic interest rates, and containing sovereign risk premiums in Asia. Analysis also shows a tradeoff between exchange rates and real estate prices, suggesting that monetary easing in advanced economies can affect Asian economies through either currency appreciation or asset price inflation.

Macroeconomic policy to maintain stability

- **Inflation is expected to remain in check, but price pressures should be closely monitored.** In general, inflation in developing Asia remains contained, partly because food prices are stable throughout the region. But tame inflation does not translate at this juncture into a free hand to wield monetary policy to stimulate economic activity. In an environment of excess global liquidity, central banks in economies where forecast output is close to long-term trend must monitor the potential for price pressures to build up and stand ready to intervene to avoid accelerating inflation. Several countries are already dealing with higher inflation or structural imbalances. Stabilization should be their priority.

- **Potentially volatile capital flows remain a risk to stability.** The spillover of liquidity from further QE raises the concern that asset market bubbles may build up. Moreover, unconventional monetary policy in advanced economies will eventually end, so the region's policy makers must be prepared. They must watch cross-border financial transactions to protect banking sector soundness. Where necessary, macroprudential policy must be reinforced.

- **Fiscal policy should be directed to strengthen future growth.** Current economic conditions in most economies in the region do not warrant using fiscal policy to stimulate demand. The focus of fiscal policy should shift toward supporting long-term structural change for inclusive growth. Governments should prioritize financing longer-term public investments and ensuring the efficient delivery of public goods, while making revenue mobilization more effective to maintain a healthy fiscal balance.

- **Political risk in many forms has emerged as the main threat to the global and regional outlook.** The probability of a US fiscal shock or a euro area breakdown has faded. However, political wrangling over raising the US debt ceiling remains likely, reprising the brinksmanship in 2011 that pummeled global financial markets. Austerity-induced recession in the euro area could undermine the political support needed to continue moving vulnerable countries' sovereign debt back onto a sustainable path. Border disputes in Asia spilled over into the economic arena in 2012. The heated rhetoric has since cooled but could be reignited for political gain. Geopolitical risks in oil-producing countries could shock prices for this critical commodity, spilling over into the region as inflation.

Commodity markets and developing Asia

- **Rising consumption and investment demand has turned developing Asia into a net importer of commodities.** While the major industrial economies have struggled to recover from the global financial crisis, resilient growth has made Asia a heavyweight in markets for commodities such as copper, iron, coal, oil, and cotton. In 2011, the PRC's share of global commodity consumption was 20% for nonrenewable energy resources, 23% for major agricultural crops, and 40% for base metals. The region's expanded role in commodity markets makes it an important "shock emitter" to resource-rich countries through commodity prices.

- **The PRC sources commodities globally, while India looks to its neighbors.** Because its demand for commodities is so large, the PRC cannot limit itself to regional markets. In fact, 9 of the 10 countries that rely the heaviest on PRC commodity purchases are outside of developing Asia. India, on the other hand, tends to rely on regional resource exporters for commodities other than petroleum products. As such, fluctuations in PRC demand have global consequences, while India's impacts are largely contained within the region. The large ASEAN economies are generally net commodity exporters but, like the PRC and India, source petroleum products from outside the region.

- **Developing Asia's energy needs have risen in tandem with its economic expansion.** The region consumes roughly a third of global primary energy. Coal remains the dominant energy source, fueling more than half of the region's production, followed by petroleum. Natural gas consumption is still limited but rising quickly. The price volatility of energy complicates efforts to maintain macroeconomic stability. Looking past this short-term issue, developing Asia's sustainable growth will depend critically on securing adequate energy supply. This issue is explored in depth in the theme chapter.

Outlook by subregion

- **Developing Asia's pickup from 2012 is largely shared in its subregions but with some distinct differences.** The aggregate pace of growth in East and South Asia is forecast to accelerate in 2013, as movements in the larger economies dominate subregional averages. Southeast Asia, which did not experience a slowdown in 2012, and Central Asia will maintain their pace into 2013. The Pacific stands out for its sharp deceleration forecast for 2013, held back by natural resource issues. Inflation is projected to quicken in 2013 in all subregions except South Asia, where average inflation is well above the developing Asia average.

- **Growth in East Asia is set to bounce back in 2013, setting the pace among the subregions.** Emerging from a trough of 6.5% growth in 2012, East Asia's GDP will expand this year and next by 7.1%, the most rapid rate among the subregions. Rising domestic demand and improved export performance are spurring expansion in the PRC, with positive spillovers across East Asia, especially in Taipei,China and Hong Kong, China. The PRC growth rate is forecast to moderate to 8.0% in 2014 from 8.2% this year, as more stringent environmental standards and policies to make growth inclusive may slow the pace of investment. The PRC's inflation rate will trend moderately upward in 2013 and 2014, while Mongolia's rate declines but not out of double digits. Inflation in the subregion is forecast to rise from 2.6% in 2012 to 3.1% this year and 3.3% in 2014.

- **South Asia's growth will turn around after 2 years of softening.** Growth in the region slowed to 5.0% in 2012 from 6.0% in 2011, marking the second year of weaker performance. This mainly reflects India's economic downdraft marked by faltering investment, persistently high inflation, and tight monetary policy that was compounded by weaker export demand. Weaker exports were also a factor in growth slipping in Bangladesh and Sri Lanka. Growth in South Asia is forecast to rise to 5.7% in 2013 and 6.2% in 2014, as India's growth edges up (assuming continued reforms there) to 6.0% and then 6.5%. Pakistan's lack of political consensus prevents it from dealing effectively with its acute economic problems, and the economy will likely again require urgent structural reform and liquidity support to avert balance-of-payments problems. Afghanistan is also at a critical juncture, as it will need to adjust to the withdrawal of international security forces by the end of 2014. South Asia's inflation eased substantially to 8.0% in 2012, aided by relatively stable global commodity prices. Inflation should edge down to 7.4% and then 7.1% over the next 2 years.

- **Southeast Asia will maintain its growth pace in 2013.** The only subregion to record accelerating growth in 2012 owes this distinction largely to Thailand's recovery from floods in 2011 and the Philippines' rebound in public investment. Meanwhile, robust private consumption and investment have offset the impact of soft external demand in many ASEAN economies. Southeast Asia's momentum is forecast to continue in 2013, with growth at 5.4%, and quicken slightly to 5.7% in 2014 as the outlook improves for the industrial economies. Indonesia, the largest ASEAN economy, is set to expand by about 6.5% in both years. Better harvests and more stable global food and oil prices brought down inflation in the subregion in 2012 to an average of 3.9%. But strong domestic demand and wage pressures in several countries will push inflation up to 4.2% in 2013. Inflation is expected to ease again in 2014 but could be higher if Indonesia and Malaysia reduce fuel subsidies as planned.

- **Higher public investment will lift Central Asia's growth in 2013.** Central Asia saw growth slip to 5.6% in 2012 and can expect to roughly maintain that pace, with 5.5% growth in 2013. Higher public investment spending is projected to raise industrial production, oil aside, in both Azerbaijan and Kazakhstan. The more rapid pace of growth in these two economies will offset deceleration in most other countries in 2013. Slower agricultural expansion is projected to hold down growth in Uzbekistan, while less rapid expansion in the hydrocarbon sector will do the same in Turkmenistan. Average regional growth is expected to rise to 6.0% in 2014, as higher public investment catalyzes growth in Azerbaijan, Kazakhstan, and Uzbekistan. Inflation slowed notably in 2012, from 8.9% to 5.3%, largely because of much smaller increases in food prices. Adjustments in administered prices in Kazakhstan, along with higher public spending and the return of more normal inflation affecting food and other items in most countries, are expected to raise average inflation to 6.7% in 2013 and 2014.

- **The Pacific is slowing in 2013 from its rapid pace last year.** The Pacific was the fastest growing subregion in 2012, with natural resource investments in Papua New Guinea—the subregion's largest economy by far—boosting the overall growth rate to 7.3%. But growth in the Pacific is expected to slow to 5.2% in 2013 before rising slightly to 5.5% in 2014. Following the completion of construction on its liquefied natural gas project, Papua New Guinea should expect slower economic activity until gas exports commence at the end of 2014. Timor-Leste will continue its double-digit growth led by oil and gas. The growth outlook for the rest of the subregion is mixed. Inflation in the Pacific is expected to increase to 6.1% in 2013 and 6.3% in 2014 from 5.3% in 2012, despite forecast softness in international food and fuel prices. Again, developments are largely driven by Papua New Guinea, where inflation is forecast to rise in both 2013 and 2014 on high government spending and rising local prices for imports.

Special theme: Asia's energy challenge

Critical energy needs for the Asian Century

- **Energy systems will be challenged to satisfy developing Asia's economic aspirations.** With 6% annual growth, developing Asia could produce 44% of global GDP by 2035. This Asian Century scenario would see the region's share of world energy consumption rise rapidly from barely a third in 2010 to 51%–56% by 2035. With insufficient energy, developing Asia would need to scale back its growth ambitions.

- **Securing adequate energy is a serious challenge because Asia cannot rely solely on its endowment.** The region has abundant coal but currently commands only 16% of the world's proven conventional gas reserves and 15% of technically recoverable oil and natural gas liquids. More renewable energy and nuclear power generation are planned, but not enough to keep pace with demand. To fill the gap, oil imports would have to rise from the current 11 million barrels per day to more than 30 million barrels per day by 2035, making Asia more vulnerable to external energy shocks.

- **On its current energy path, Asia's emissions would soon swamp global targets.** Without radical changes to the region's energy mix, its consumption of fossil fuels would climb, doubling oil consumption and tripling natural gas consumption. Even highly polluting coal consumption would rise by a whopping 81%. This would double carbon dioxide (CO_2) emissions to over 20 billion tons by 2035. Asia alone would then emit almost all of the 22 billion tons that climate change experts see as that year's maximum sustainable CO_2 emissions for the whole world. Locally, expanded fossil fuel use would foul air and water.

- **Ensuring affordable energy for the poor is a key to inclusive growth.** Nearly half of the people in the world without electricity live in Asia. Traditional fuels supply primary energy for 2.8 billion people, who suffer the health risks, paltry energy services, and environmental damage these fuels entail. Universal access to electricity and clean cooking fuel would have high social and economic returns, but getting connections to people without access would require a fivefold increase in annual energy investments globally.

- **The multidimensional energy challenge demands a multipronged approach.** Supply security depends on tapping new energy sources and technology. Environmental sustainability entails aggressively exploring all options to curb burgeoning energy demand. Affordable access will require more inclusive energy policies. Technological developments and policy reforms to integrate regional energy markets will need to be mobilized to realize the Asian Century.

Containing burgeoning energy demand

- **Asia has an array of options by which to check its energy appetite.** But tackling outmoded subsidies requires political will, and green innovation takes imagination.

  » **Energy prices that reflect true costs will send the right signals to households and firms.** Consumer subsidies artificially reduce the price of energy, diverting it from more efficient uses and disproportionately benefiting the nonpoor. Subsidies impose a tremendous burden on public budgets, exceeding 2% of GDP in India, Indonesia, and Viet Nam, and 4% in Bangladesh and Pakistan. If countries around the world eliminated wasteful subsidies, global CO_2 emissions would be an estimated 2.6 billion tons lower in 2035. However, those who benefit from wasteful subsidies invariably resist removing them, despite the large economywide gains.

  » **Urban planning, clean transport, and fuel switching can radically reduce demand.** Green, smart cities and clean transportation offer the promise of affordable, environmentally sustainable ways of powering Asia's growing urbanization. Switching consumers and firms from electricity to gas for applications such as cooking can achieve enormous efficiency gains over time.

- **Behavioral change is essential to reap energy efficiency benefits.** Cost savings from using more efficient technologies can induce people to use more energy, offsetting some of the gains from these initiatives. Avoiding this rebound effect fundamentally requires changing people's behavior. After the Fukushima accident, Japan has succeeded in curbing electricity demand through the Setsuden ("saving electricity") movement, lowering peak usage by 15% during the summer of 2012.

Tapping cleaner energy supplies

- **Expanded clean energy supply must augment demand management to bridge the gap.** Asia's future energy supply must be bigger and its mix much cleaner than it is today. Greater use of renewable energy will play a key role.

  » **Developing Asia can realize the promise of renewable energy from wind and solar.** The region has significant potential for renewable energy. In less than a decade, generating capacity rose from negligible to 82 gigawatts (GW) for wind and to 20 GW for solar, with great potential to further expand both. Asian countries are among the world leaders in the manufacture of renewable energy plants, which already power microgrids commercially in some remote communities. Wind and solar are becoming cheaper and are expected to reach grid parity in some countries in a few years, but in the meantime they require favorable policy and financial incentives.

- **Hydropower is a well-established renewable energy source in Asia.** The region has 542 GW of hydropower capacity installed or under construction, with potential to quadruple it to 2,204 GW. The costs of large hydropower projects are huge, and addressing their environmental and social impacts a challenge, but these initiatives can have strongly positive outcomes if they are well planned and executed.

- **Biofuels can dramatically lower CO_2 emissions from transport.** Production technologies under development will avoid pitting fuel against food by using materials such as algae.

- **Renewable energy sources alone are not enough.** The energy mix will evolve slowly as older investments in plant and equipment are retired, but environmental needs are urgent. Asia needs its new conventional power plants to be cleaner and more efficient.

  - **Asia's substantial reserves of shale gas have potential to offset coal use.** Asia's geology is incompletely investigated, but indications are that the PRC has as much as 20% of global reserves of shale gas. India's technically recoverable reserves are much smaller at an estimated 1% of the global total but still substantial at 1.6 billion tons of oil equivalent. As shale gas recovery uses emergent technology, the environmental impacts of drilling and production need to be evaluated for potential risks.

  - **Nuclear power contributes to lowering greenhouse gas emissions.** If nuclear power were phased out of the region's energy mix, CO_2 emissions from Asia's power sector would be 8%–13% higher in 2035. But expanding nuclear energy in Asia requires addressing three remaining challenges: proliferation, waste management, and, above all, safety.

  - **Emerging technologies make carbon-based fuels cleaner to use.** Carbon capture and storage has potential to lower CO_2 emissions, and Asia is starting to invest in this technology. International support can hasten progress.

Fostering regional market synergies

- **Integrated energy markets can multiply gains from curbed demand and clean energy supply.** Integrating power transmission in the Greater Mekong Subregion would save $14 billion over 20 years by substituting hydropower for power generation using fossil fuels. By 2020, this would avoid 14 million tons of CO_2 emissions annually. Well-designed, unified regional electricity systems can efficiently cover supply failures with integrated regional backup capacity.

- **Political and regulatory barriers inhibit market integration.** Cross-border power and gas grids require standardized regulations, pricing, and contracts. These technical requirements demand in turn that participants be confident, open, and equitable about sharing benefits. To seal multilateral grid agreements and bring plans to fruition, neighboring countries must share information and allay one another's concerns about the reliability of supply.

Achieving a brighter Asian energy future

- **Asia must aspire to create a pan-Asia energy market by 2030.** When it comes to regionally integrated electricity and gas markets, thinking big maximizes benefits. The degree of regional cooperation and integration in energy that currently prevails in Europe should be achievable by 2030. The region must advance the interconnection of electric grids across borders to realize maximum efficiency in power generation and delivery. The first step is to get together and agree on the way forward. Asia should set up a ministerial task force to study the European experience and promote the political will to share more openly information on national power sectors, toward better harmonizing regulations, standards, and pricing policies.

- **Asia must immediately take concrete steps to curb demand.** Replacing inefficient general fuel subsidies with targeted subsidies, such as the system Indonesia is currently setting up, can be a politically acceptable approach to eliminating broad inefficiencies without excluding the poor. Second-generation greenhouse gas emission taxes recycle tax proceeds to help reduce the cost of cleaner inputs, thereby limiting their adverse impact on economic activity while mitigating global warming. Planning for "green cities" is crucial for an increasingly urban Asia.

- **Expanding the supply of clean energy needs to be broadly pursued.** As energy sources vary across the region, options to augment energy supplies depend on country endowments. Each potential source has merits and shortcomings, but every drop—every watt—counts! Developing future technologies requires government support in the beginning. If each country exerts effort on all fronts according to its comparative advantage, then Asia will be able to expand its energy supply. As the biggest energy user, Asia must marshal research and development capacity equal to the task. Technology transfer from developed countries can accelerate the deployment of new technologies.

- **Asia must address the needs of countries with energy deficiencies and low incomes.** Concrete steps to support Energy for All include establishing income policies to secure an adequate energy floor for the poor, selecting appropriate technologies for distributed and off-grid power generation, and promoting community participation. Narrowing differences between countries is critical. Low-income countries need international aid to help them build equitable energy infrastructure that protects the poor.

- **Action is needed on all fronts to secure Asia's energy future.** Curbing demand growth while aggressively exploring cleaner supply options should be part of the larger vision of a regional energy market. The region's leaders must find the political will to realize the future envisioned as the "Clean Asian Century."

Growth rate of GDP (% per year)

Subregion/Economy	2010	2011	2012	2013	2014
Central Asia	**6.8**	**6.8**	**5.6**	**5.5**	**6.0**
Azerbaijan	5.0	0.1	2.2	3.1	4.8
Kazakhstan	7.3	7.5	5.0	5.2	5.6
East Asia	**9.8**	**8.2**	**6.5**	**7.1**	**7.1**
China, People's Rep. of	10.4	9.3	7.8	8.2	8.0
Hong Kong, China	6.8	4.9	1.4	3.5	3.8
Korea, Rep. of	6.3	3.7	2.0	2.8	3.7
Taipei,China	10.8	4.1	1.3	3.5	3.9
South Asia	**8.5**	**6.0**	**5.0**	**5.7**	**6.2**
Bangladesh	6.1	6.7	6.3	5.7	6.0
India	9.3	6.2	5.0	6.0	6.5
Pakistan	3.1	3.0	3.7	3.6	3.5
Sri Lanka	8.0	8.2	6.4	6.8	7.2
Southeast Asia	**7.9**	**4.7**	**5.5**	**5.4**	**5.7**
Indonesia	6.2	6.5	6.2	6.4	6.6
Malaysia	7.2	5.1	5.6	5.3	5.5
Philippines	7.6	3.9	6.6	6.0	5.9
Singapore	14.8	5.2	1.3	2.6	3.7
Thailand	7.8	0.1	6.4	4.9	5.0
Viet Nam	6.8	5.9	5.0	5.2	5.6
The Pacific	**5.5**	**8.3**	**7.3**	**5.2**	**5.5**
Fiji	0.1	1.9	2.5	2.0	2.3
Papua New Guinea	7.4	11.1	9.2	5.5	6.0
Developing Asia	**9.2**	**7.3**	**6.1**	**6.6**	**6.7**

Notes: Developing Asia refers to the 45 developing member countries of the Asian Development Bank. East Asia comprises the People's Republic of China; Hong Kong, China; the Republic of Korea; Mongolia; and Taipei,China. Southeast Asia comprises Brunei Darussalam, Cambodia, Indonesia, the Lao People's Democratic Republic, Malaysia, Myanmar, the Philippines, Singapore, Thailand, and Viet Nam. South Asia comprises Afghanistan, Bangladesh, Bhutan, India, the Maldives, Nepal, Pakistan, and Sri Lanka. Central Asia comprises Armenia, Azerbaijan, Georgia, Kazakhstan, the Kyrgyz Republic, Tajikistan, Turkmenistan, and Uzbekistan.

(continued on the next page)

Inflation (% per year)

Subregion/Economy	2010	2011	2012	2013	2014
Central Asia	7.0	8.9	5.3	6.7	6.7
Azerbaijan	5.7	7.9	1.1	6.0	7.0
Kazakhstan	7.1	8.3	5.1	6.7	6.5
East Asia	3.1	5.0	2.6	3.1	3.3
China, People's Rep. of	3.3	5.4	2.6	3.2	3.5
Hong Kong, China	2.3	5.3	4.1	3.9	4.3
Korea, Rep. of	3.0	4.0	2.2	2.5	2.8
Taipei,China	1.0	1.4	1.9	1.6	1.8
South Asia	9.4	9.3	8.0	7.4	7.1
Bangladesh	7.3	8.8	10.6	7.8	7.0
India	9.6	8.9	7.5	7.2	6.8
Pakistan	10.1	13.7	11.0	9.0	9.5
Sri Lanka	6.2	6.7	7.6	7.5	6.5
Southeast Asia	4.1	5.5	3.9	4.2	4.1
Indonesia	5.1	5.4	4.3	5.2	4.7
Malaysia	1.7	3.2	1.7	2.2	3.0
Philippines	3.9	4.6	3.2	3.6	3.8
Singapore	2.8	5.3	4.5	3.8	3.0
Thailand	3.3	3.8	3.0	3.2	3.1
Viet Nam	9.2	18.6	9.2	7.5	8.2
The Pacific	5.1	8.5	5.3	6.1	6.3
Fiji	5.5	8.7	4.3	4.5	4.0
Papua New Guinea	6.0	8.4	4.1	6.5	7.5
Developing Asia	4.4	5.9	3.7	4.0	4.2

(continued from the previous page)

The Pacific comprises the Cook Islands, Fiji, Kiribati, the Marshall Islands, the Federated States of Micronesia, Nauru, Papua New Guinea, Palau, Samoa, Solomon Islands, Timor-Leste, Tonga, Tuvalu, and Vanuatu.

Data for Bangladesh, India, and Pakistan are recorded on a fiscal-year basis. For India, the fiscal year spans the current year's April through the next year's March. For Bangladesh and Pakistan, the fiscal year spans the previous year's July through the current year's June.

1

Asia builds momentum amid global doldrums

Asia builds momentum amid global doldrums

Through the depths of the 2008–2009 global financial crisis, developing Asia managed to maintain a respectable pace of gross domestic product (GDP) expansion. Despite continued weakness in the advanced economies, the region looks set to maintain its momentum, bolstered by robust spending for private consumption. Deepening trade links within the region are partly offsetting the tardy return of demand from industrial country consumers.

This evolution is reflected in the narrowing of the region's current account surplus. While it is too early to claim victory over the persistent global imbalances of the previous decade, which aggravated the weaknesses that led to the global downturn, steady progress suggests that the region is adjusting to the new realities.

Recognition of change in the world's growth drivers is what must underlie the region's macroeconomic policy responses. This is not simply a cyclical slowing that should be met with monetary and fiscal stimulus. Signs suggest the region has moved back to its potential growth path. The uptick in inflation hints at the potential for price pressures ahead, which need close monitoring. The low deficits and debt enjoyed by many regional economies should not be squandered; rather, fiscal policy should be directed to lay the groundwork for future growth that is more inclusive.

Asia is emerging as an important global consumer, and this is nowhere more evident than in commodity markets (Figure 1.1.1). The region's energy demand, in particular, is expanding more rapidly than its economic might. Looking ahead, policy makers must meet the challenge of securing adequate energy to support its growth, in a way that safeguards the environment and provides to populations broad access to affordable energy.

1.1.1 Petroleum and copper consumption, developing Asia

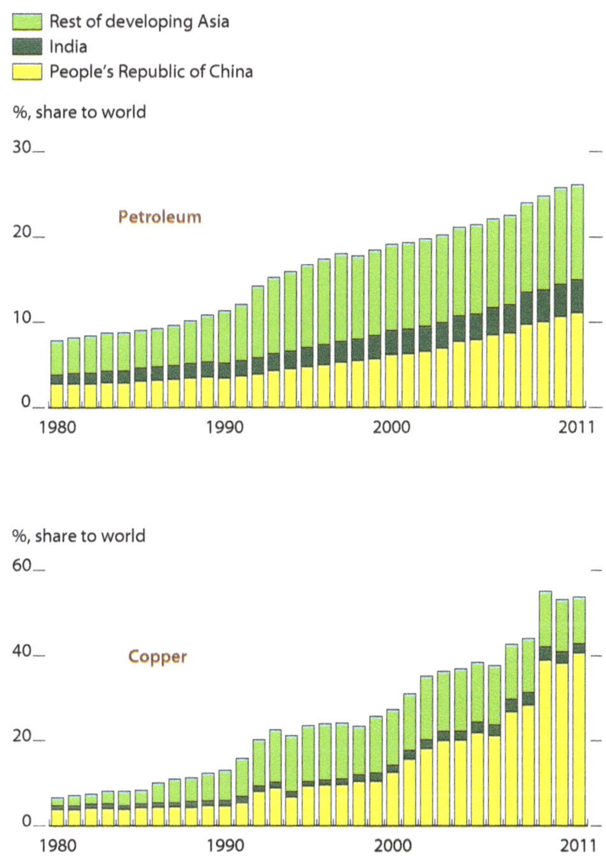

Note: For petroleum consumption, developing Asia covers 39 economies. For copper, it covers the People's Republic of China, India, the five largest economies in the Association of Southeast Asian Nations (Indonesia, Malaysia, the Philippines, Singapore, and Thailand), and seven other economies.

Sources: ADB estimates using data from the *Asian Development Outlook* database; World Bank. World Development Indicators and Global Development Finance database. http://databank.worldbank.org/ddp/home.do (both accessed 15 March 2013).

Click here for figure data

This chapter was written by Arief Ramayandi, Akiko Terada-Hagiwara, Changyong Rhee, Lea Sumulong, Benno Ferrarini, Shikha Jha, Madhavi Pundit, Pilipinas Quising, and Joseph E. Zveglich, Jr., of the Economics and Research Department, ADB, Manila. Background materials from Dongchul Cho, Donghyun Park, and Ganeshan Wignaraja are gratefully acknowledged.

Regaining growth at different speeds

After moderating in 2012, growth is starting to recover across developing Asia. It is forecast to accelerate in the next 2 years, driven largely by domestic factors this year and by external demand and a strengthening global economy next year. Developing Asia is forecast to grow by 6.6% in 2013 and 6.7% in 2014, up from 6.1% last year (Figure 1.1.2). As economic activity gains strength, inflation is also expected to rise gradually, reaching 4.1% during the forecast period from 3.7% last year.

The advanced economies continued to be weak in 2012, growing by only 1.2% as a group (Box 1.1.1). Though uncertainties remain, forecasts for 2013 point to a period of consolidation for the advanced economies in the first half of the year, then GDP rising slowly during the rest of the forecast period. GDP growth is expected to moderate to 1.0% in 2013 before strengthening to 1.9% in 2014.

Most subregions of developing Asia anticipate growth picking up. However, the speed of recovery differs by region. The growth rebound will be supported by the People's Republic of China (PRC) and continued resilience in the Association of Southeast Asian Nations (ASEAN). The PRC will expand by 8.2% in 2013 and 8.0% in 2014, up from 7.8% in 2012, as strong domestic demand continues and export performance picks up. ASEAN is expected to post resilient growth during the forecast period. Larger trade with other regional countries—particularly within ASEAN and with the PRC—will help cushion the impact of slow recovery in the advanced economies. ASEAN members are projected to grow by 5.4% in 2013 and 5.7% in 2014. India's strong consumption will support its growth, which is expected to recover from 5.0% in FY2012 (ended 31 March 2013) to 6.0% in FY2013 and further to 6.5% in FY2014. Attaining these goals will require reforms that resolve contentious structural and policy issues inhibiting investment.

In 2012, the main factor depressing growth in developing Asia was the larger-than-expected slowdown in the PRC and India. Growth in the PRC slid from 9.3% in 2011 to 7.8% in 2012, the lowest rate in 13 years, driven by a cooled real estate sector and slower exports. India's economic growth in FY2012 is believed to have slowed to 5.0%, its lowest rate in a decade, from 6.2% in FY2011. Overall, regional factors explained about half of the growth slowdown in developing Asia, the main external drags being unexpectedly severe contraction in the euro area and elevated oil prices (ADB 2012).

1.1.2 GDP growth and inflation, developing Asia

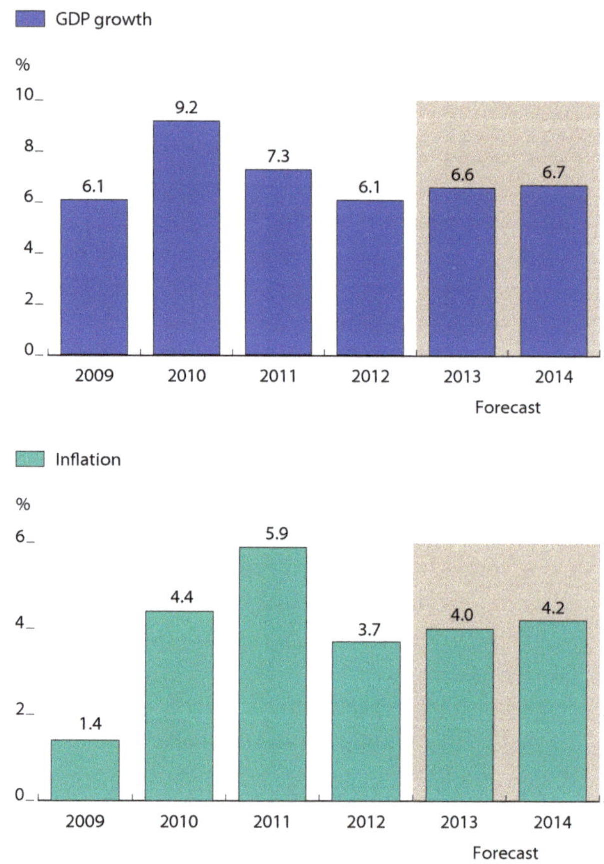

Source: Asian Development Outlook database.
Click here for figure data

1.1.1 Industrial economies continue to consolidate

Growth in the major industrial economies was subdued and somewhat mixed in 2012. Relatively strong GDP growth in the third quarter in the United States (US) and the euro area was followed by a slowdown in the last quarter. Japan slipped back into a recession in the middle of the year, but growth turned positive in the fourth quarter. For the group as a whole, 2013 is likely to be a year of consolidation, with expected growth of only 1%, slightly less than in 2012. While fiscal tightening may constrain growth in the US and the euro area in the short term, Japan's spending plans are expected to boost its growth.

GDP growth in major industrial economies (%)

	2011	2012	2013	2014
Area	Actual		*ADO* projection	
Major industrial economies	1.2	1.2	1.0	1.9
United States	1.8	2.2	2.0	2.6
Euro area	1.4	−0.6	−0.3	1.2
Japan	−0.6	2.0	1.2	1.4

Notes: Average growth rates are weighted by gross national income using the Atlas method. More details in Annex table A1.1.

Sources: US Department of Commerce, Bureau of Economic Analysis. http://www.bea.gov; Eurostat. http://epp.eurostat.ec.europa.eu; Economic and Social Research Institute of Japan. http://www.esri.cao.go.jp; ADB estimates.

In the US, GDP grew by 2.2% in 2012, exceeding the 1.8% increase in 2011. In 2013, the start of budget sequestration in March, along with other fiscal tightening, could inhibit growth. The Congressional Budget Office estimates the spending cuts from sequestration will total $85.4 billion in 2013. While the markets have not reacted adversely to these cuts, there may be a lagged effect on consumer spending and on employment. However, positive signs in consumer spending, investment, and housing and labor markets suggest that the economy is strengthening, though only gradually. House prices began to rise in 2012, as did the number of housing units authorized, started, and under construction. Labor market indicators closely watched by policy makers, such as the unemployment rate and the number of people filing for unemployment benefits, also improved for the first time since the downturn in 2008–2009. Provided that the fiscal drag phases out and monetary policy continues to be supportive, output in the US is expected to pick up gradually and the economy to expand by 2.6% in 2014.

Japan's economy grew by 2.0% in 2012 after declining in 2011. However, GDP contracted in the second and third quarters of 2012 for many reasons: a strong yen, territorial tensions with the People's Republic of China, Europe's debt crisis, and surging energy imports. Investment and exports remained sluggish, and the balance of trade remained in deficit for 8 consecutive months. Deflation persisted in 2012 without any sign of ending. In response to the bleak outlook, the Shinzō Abe administration has instituted a set of expansive policies referred to as Abenomics. The government announced an economic stimulus package amounting to over ¥23 trillion, or 4.8% of GDP, and hopes to encourage private sector investment. To battle deflation, the Bank of Japan has adopted an inflation target of 2% and announced further easing of monetary policy. Recent data show some gains in manufacturing, mainly in auto sales and machinery orders. Positive policy measures should spur growth to 1.2% in 2013 and 1.4% in 2014.

Unlike the US and Japan, the euro area saw output decline by an estimated 0.6% in 2012. While German industrial production and economic growth are starting to improve, the other large euro economies remain weak. Most other countries in the euro area saw their economies shrink. Low private consumption and fixed capital formation have hampered growth. Youth unemployment reached 24% in the euro area. The recession in the euro area is seen extending into the first half of 2013 before slow recovery begins in the second half of the year. For the whole year, GDP is expected to contract by 0.3%.

Several euro area peripheral economies remain ridden by crisis. Greece continues to face unsustainable debt, despite international rescue efforts led by the European Commission, European Central Bank, and International Monetary Fund. In mid-March, Cyprus became the latest country to be offered a bailout package, in this case for €10 billion, by the International Monetary Fund and European authorities. Concerns about the viability of the euro area remain, as austerity measures are deepening unemployment, social unease, and economic contraction. The European Central Bank will have to uphold its firewall against speculative attacks until fundamental structural and institutional reforms start addressing deep-rooted euro area flaws. It is unclear whether European and national politics will withstand this important test.

Euro area countries have begun to introduce fiscal tightening, as the European Union Fiscal Compact requires that fiscal deficits be less than 3% of GDP by the end of 2013. This may depress domestic demand and employment. On the other hand, an easing of financial tensions and improvements in external demand may boost the region's exports and thereby support growth. Monetary policy will likely remain accommodative as inflation stays under control, in line with the declining trend in international commodity prices. GDP growth is projected to pick up to 1.2% in 2014.

Boost from domestic consumption

With weakened demand from the PRC and India added to dim global demand from the major industrial economies, only domestic factors remained as drivers of growth for many economies in developing Asia. The external slowdown affected open, trade-oriented economies in East and Southeast Asia most severely, with growth plunging to less than 2% in the Republic of Korea; Taipei,China; and Singapore (Figure 1.1.3).

Despite anemic external demand, some economies, mainly in Southeast Asia, managed to maintain growth momentum on the back of growth in private consumption and investment. Economic reforms after the Asian financial crisis, a better-balanced economic structure, and natural resources all contributed to the robust performance of the ASEAN economies in 2012.

Among domestic factors, private consumption continued to be the key driver of growth in 2012, contributing more than half of growth across the economies in developing Asia. By comparison, growth in other factors, such as investment and exports, varied considerably across countries. Unemployment rates kept declining in most countries, however, and labor markets continued to improve, lifting consumer confidence at least during the first half of last year.

Nonetheless, retail sales weakened in the second half of 2012, slowing sharply in the third quarter (Figure 1.1.4). Of the 9 economies, only Thailand and Indonesia showed relatively resilient retail sales, while, toward the end of the year, Singapore and Viet Nam joined the economies in East Asia that were showing weaker retail sales. Some signs indicate that the soft patch is ending, and consumption should pick up again in the second half of 2013.

Investment, both private and public, was uneven across countries. Investment was generally resilient in Southeast Asian economies, with both private and public investment rising in Thailand and Malaysia. But it declined in a few economies such as the Republic of Korea and Taipei,China, due largely to sluggish export performance (Figure 1.1.5). In the Philippines, buoyant economic activity fueled a large decline in inventories, which exceeded relatively robust fixed investment. As a result, gross investment declined.

On average, inventories rose in 2012, particularly in Southeast Asia, driven by robust domestic activity, after declining in 2011. However, economies in East Asia were left out of this trend, as investors remained cautious about the global and regional outlook, and for the PRC in particular. Taipei,China and the Republic of Korea may continue to wait for a clearer signal of global recovery before private investment picks up this year.

1.1.3 Demand-side contributions to growth, selected developing Asia, 2012

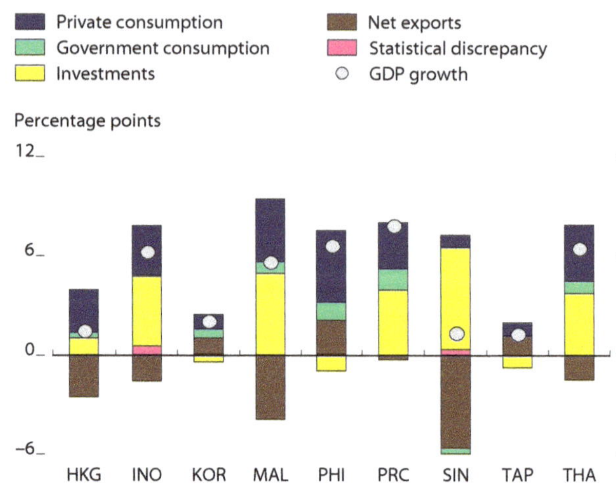

HKG = Hong Kong, China, INO = Indonesia, KOR = Republic of Korea, MAL = Malaysia, PHI = Philippines, PRC = People's Republic of China, SIN = Singapore, TAP = Taipei,China, THA = Thailand.

Source: CEIC Data Company (accessed 5 March 2013).

Click here for figure data

1.1.4 Retail sales, selected developing Asia

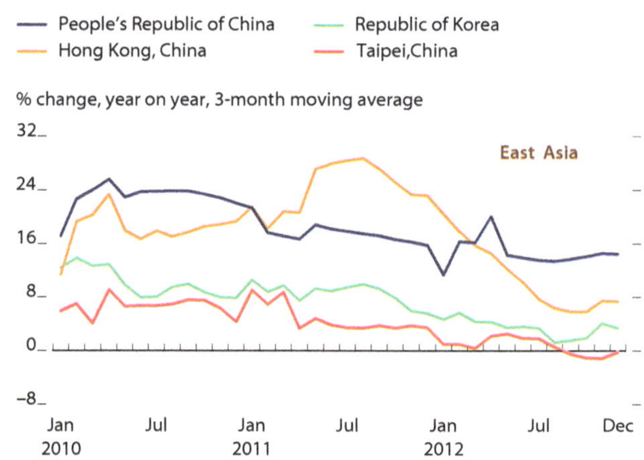

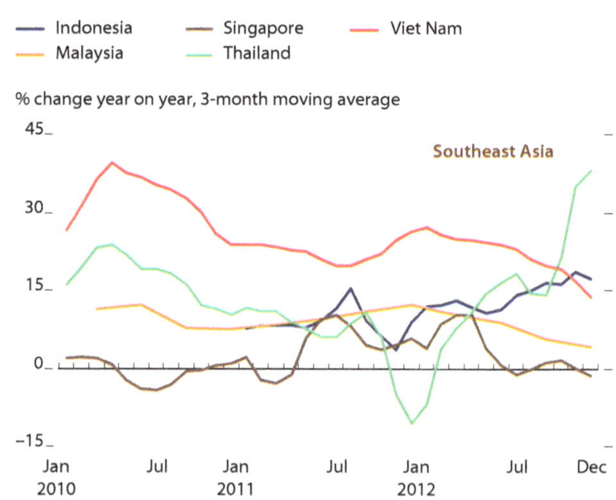

Note: Data for Malaysia are quarterly.

Source: CEIC Data Company (accessed 5 March 2013).

Click here for figure data

Drag from weak export demand

On the external front, global economies remained sluggish, particularly with the euro area contracting by 6% in 2012, during which the growth forecast for major industrial economies for 2013 was revised down by almost 1 percentage point. The sharp slowdown in the PRC and India added to the already dim external prospects. Although the PRC's growth started to stabilize late in 2012, boosted by stimulus measures, the economies with strong trade ties with the PRC still felt a sharp downturn over the entire year. The slowdown in India also contributed to weak exports in Sri Lanka and Bangladesh, but the slowdown was felt mainly within India.

Weakened external demand sharply decelerated merchandise export growth in developing Asia from 18.5% in 2011 to 4.4% in 2012 (Figure 1.1.6)—much lower than the 10.5% forecast earlier, in April 2012. In two of the five Asian subregions—South Asia and the Pacific—exports contracted in 2012. The weakening of exports was particularly severe in South Asia, where all countries except Bangladesh and Nepal experienced a contraction. Import demand also diminished, and import growth slowed from 21.6% in 2011 to a mere 3.9% in 2012, far below the 12.8% forecast in April 2012.

Southeast Asia bucked the trend toward plunging imports, as imports to the subregion remained fairly resilient, growing at almost 7% more quickly than exports, to satisfy strong domestic demand. As a result, net exports declined, subtracting from growth in five of the six Southeast Asian developing economies, and the merchandise trade surplus narrowed by more than 26% in Southeast Asia. In the Republic of Korea and Taipei,China, by comparison, merchandise imports fell much more steeply than exports, reflecting weak demand for capital goods in particular. Thus, net exports contributed to growth in these two economies.

The external environment is expected to improve gradually in 2013. Although the global economy as a whole is forecast to begin recovering only later this year, growth in the PRC has already begun accelerating, with economic activity showing signs of turnaround in the last quarter of 2012, as industrial and electricity production both started to grow more quickly (Figure 1.1.7). Growth is expected to continue accelerating in the first half of 2013 and then stabilize for the rest of this year and next, as the impact of the mid-2012 stimulus fades and greater efforts are made to comply with more stringent environmental targets.

External demand in developing Asia generally is rising because of growth acceleration in the PRC and, to a lesser extent, in India. Export growth in developing Asia economies is expected to accelerate to 8.3% this year from the low base last year and to rise further to 9.7% in 2014. Imports are expected to grow at a slightly faster rate than exports, by 8.3% this year and 10.1% in 2014, on relatively

1.1.5 Contributions to investment growth, selected developing Asia

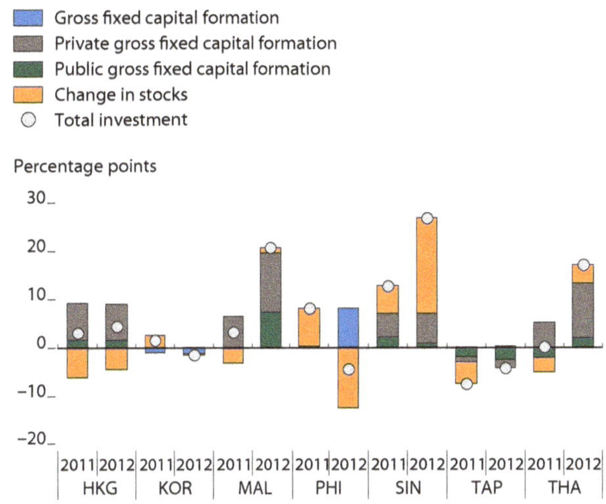

HKG = Hong Kong, China, KOR = Republic of Korea, MAL = Malaysia, PHI = Philippines, SIN = Singapore, TAP = Taipei,China, THA = Thailand.

Source: CEIC Data Company (accessed 5 March 2013).

Click here for figure data

1.1.6 Export and import growth, by subregion

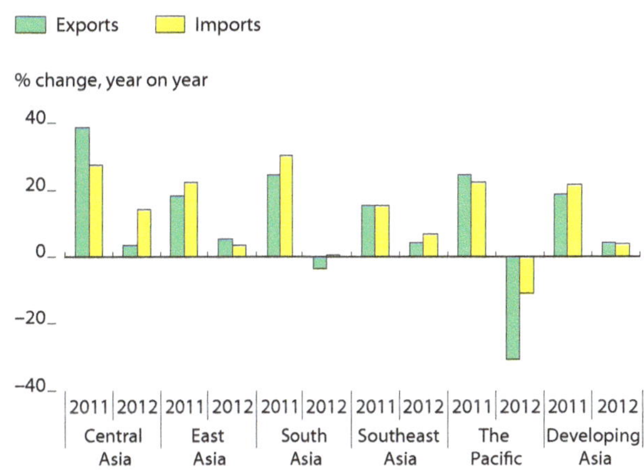

Source: Asian Development Outlook database.

Click here for figure data

1.1.7 People's Republic of China GDP growth, industrial production index, and electricity production

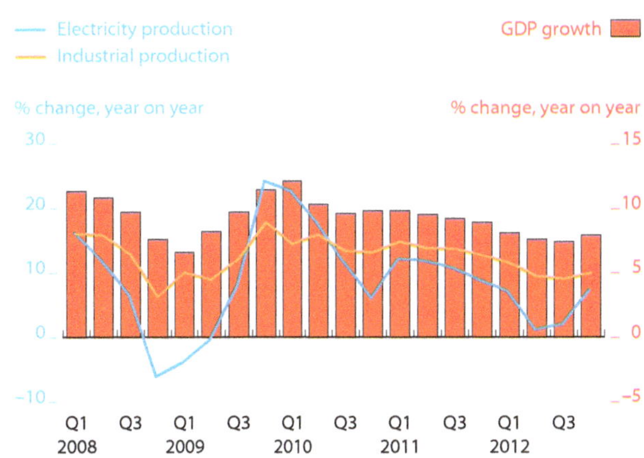

Source: CEIC Data Company (accessed 6 March 2013).

Click here for figure data

resilient domestic consumption and an expected pickup in investment. Weak demand from advanced economies, along with strong domestic demand, helped shrink developing Asia's combined current account surplus from 2.5% of GDP in 2011 to 2.0% in 2012. Import growth outpacing export growth to support robust domestic demand will further shrink the overall current account surplus to 1.9% of GDP in 2013 and to 1.8% in 2014 (Figure 1.1.8). This trend is expected to be shared across most subregions except for South Asia, where exports are expected to grow more quickly than imports in 2014.

The global current account balance, measured as a share of global GDP, also shows a narrowing trend. The global current account balance shrank to 1.3% of world GDP in 2012 from 1.5% in 2011, well down from its peak of 2.2% in 2007 (Figure 1.1.9). Developing Asia as a whole continued to show a surplus, contributing nearly 0.5% of world GDP to the surplus, of which more than half was from the PRC. Developing Asia's surpluses are still large, but the region's share of the world surplus has been declining, from almost 60% in 2009 to 41% in 2011 and to 37% in 2012.

Aside from developing Asia, the dominant supply-side contributors continue to be the Middle East (mainly oil exporters), Japan, and the Russian Federation. As the oil price has stayed elevated over the past 2 years, the Middle East's current account surplus remained above 0.5% of world GDP. On the deficit side, the US is the dominant player, with a deficit of nearly 0.7% of world GDP. Stable growth in overseas markets, particularly emerging markets, has helped underpin demand for US-made goods, keeping the US current account gap from expanding as sustained spending in the US drives import growth. The figures underscore US dependence on foreign investors for funding.

1.1.8 Current account balance, developing Asia

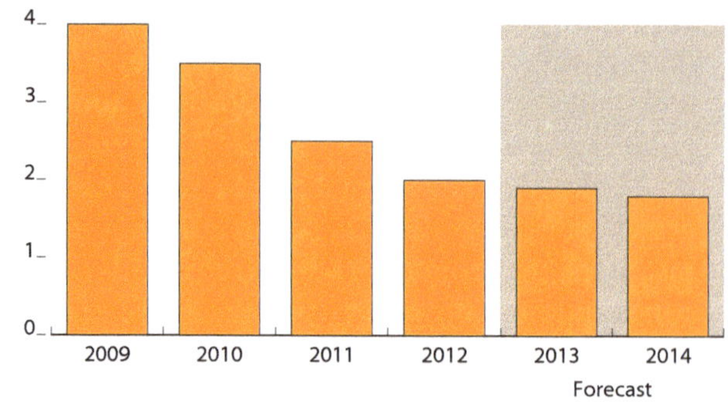

Source: Asian Development Outlook database.

Click here for figure data

1.1.9 World current account balance

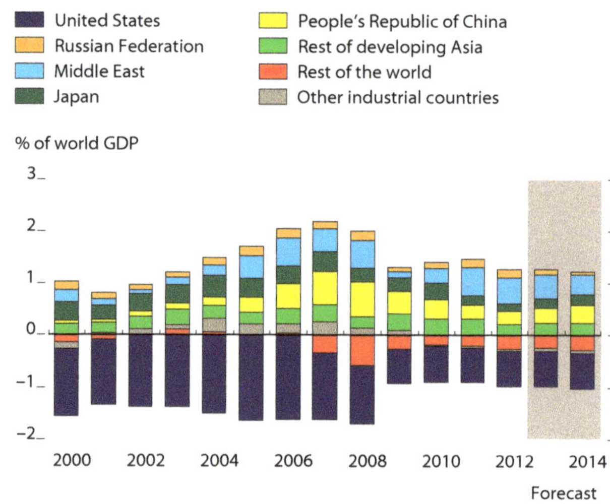

Sources: ADB estimates using data from International Monetary Fund; World Economic Outlook database (October 2012); *Asian Development Outlook* database.

Click here for figure data

Varying growth prospects across subregions

With the improving external environment, economic growth in East Asia as a whole is forecast to accelerate from 6.5% last year to above 7.0% this year and the next, surpassing once again the expansion in the other subregions of developing Asia (Figure 1.1.10).

The positive spillover effects of more rapid expansion in the PRC—which reflects both rising domestic demand and improved export performance—will contribute to more robust growth in all East Asian economies, especially Taipei,China and Hong Kong, China (where the growth rate will likely more than double in 2013) and, to a lesser extent, in the Republic of Korea and Mongolia.

As Southeast Asian economies are also tightly linked with the PRC, higher growth in the PRC in 2013 will support growth momentum in Southeast Asia. This subregion is forecast to grow by 5.4% in 2013, little changed from last year's robust growth despite sluggish growth in the major industrialized economies. Factors that helped explain the region's growth acceleration in 2012 were two rebounds, in Thailand from the impact of severe floods in 2011 and in the Philippines from a slump in government investment. In 2013, growth will benefit from generally accommodative fiscal and monetary policies supporting consumption and investment. Indonesia, the biggest economy in Southeast Asia, is seen expanding by 6.5% in the forecast period, a slight gain from 6.2% last year. In 2014, subregional growth as a whole is expected to accelerate slightly, to 5.7%, as the outlook improves for the industrial economies.

Economies in South Asia will depend on the turnaround in India, which is contingent on reform in the South Asian giant. Growth in the subregion is seen as rising to 5.7% in 2013 and 6.2% in 2014. The subregion's anemic growth of 5.0% in 2012 was due to India's slowdown, marked by faltering investment, persistently high inflation, and tight monetary policy, compounded by weakening export demand during the year. Weaker exports also helped explain slower growth in Bangladesh and Sri Lanka. In Pakistan, a recovery from earlier severe floods helped raise growth despite a decline in exports.

Signs of recovery are still weak in India. The economy is expected to improve in FY2013 but post only modest growth, as constraints on domestic investment and low optimism among investors will continue (Figure 1.1.11). A normal monsoon and monetary easing would help raise GDP growth to 6% in FY2013. Better global prospects, an easing of commodity prices, and progress in resolving structural bottlenecks are seen allowing growth to increase to 6.5% in FY2014.

Unlike in other subregions, economic performance in Central Asia and in the Pacific largely reflects the production cycles of major export commodities, their economies less influenced by developments in external demand. Commodity exports, therefore, dominate developments in these two subregions.

In 2012, the Pacific was the fastest-growing subregion in Asia and the Pacific. This mainly reflected strong growth in Papua New Guinea, by far the largest economy in the subregion. However, once construction on a liquefied natural gas project is completed, economic activity in Papua New Guinea is expected to slump until gas exports commence at the end of 2014. Thus, growth in Papua New Guinea is forecast to slow from 9.2% in 2012 to 5.5% this year. In the rest of the subregion, performance is expected to be mixed, with growth in Timor-Leste continuing to be notably high because of its oil and gas resources. Given the strong weight of Papua New Guinea, growth in the subregion as a whole is expected to slow from 7.3% in 2012 to 5.2% in 2013 before rebounding slightly to 5.5% in 2014.

Growth in Central Asia slipped to 5.6% in 2012, mainly because of a poor harvest and virtual stagnation in industry in Kazakhstan, which cut growth to 5.0% from 7.5% in 2011, and less rapid growth in Turkmenistan.

1.1.10 GDP growth by subregion

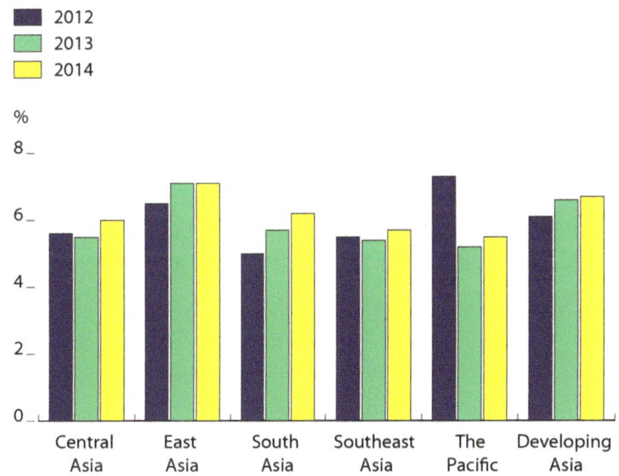

Source: Asian Development Outlook database.
Click here for figure data

1.1.11 India GDP, industrial production index, and electricity production

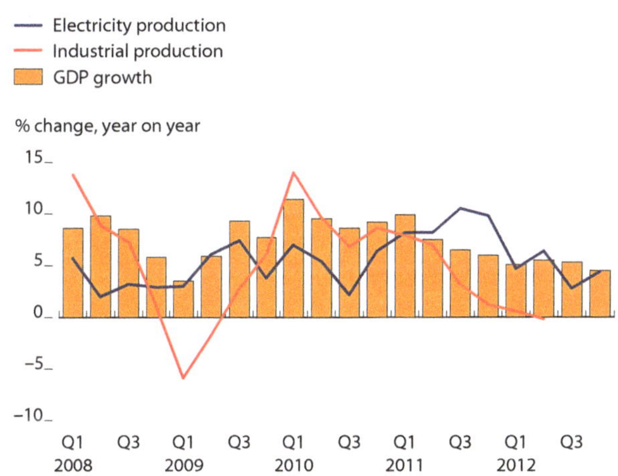

Source: CEIC Data Company (accessed 6 March 2013).
Click here for figure data

Growth also slowed in Georgia, as uncertainty linked to parliamentary elections curbed investment, and decelerated into negative territory in the Kyrgyz Republic, where gold production fell.

Slower economic activity across the subregion is expected to outweigh higher public investment in Azerbaijan and Kazakhstan, keeping Central Asia's growth flat in 2013. In 2013, projected growth acceleration in Kazakhstan to 5.2%, Azerbaijan to 3.1%, and the Kyrgyz Republic to 5.5% will not completely offset forecast deceleration in most other countries. Higher public investment spending is expected to raise industrial production aside from oil in both Azerbaijan and Kazakhstan. Slower agricultural expansion is projected to drag on growth in Uzbekistan, while less rapid expansion in the hydrocarbon sector will do the same in Turkmenistan. Armenia, Georgia, and Tajikistan also anticipate lower growth rates, while higher gold production should boost growth in the Kyrgyz Republic. In 2014, the average regional growth rate is expected to rise to 6.0% as higher public investment outlays spur growth in Azerbaijan, Kazakhstan, and Uzbekistan.

Differences in country circumstances lie behind the divergent outcomes in the region. While oil producers are buoyed or buffeted by global markets, and agricultural producers are subject to the whims of the weather, the export manufacturing economies have had to adjust to weakness in the advanced economies. That said, Southeast Asia's recent robustness raises a question: Has regional integration helped it to adjust to the new global realities?

Integration for a resilient Southeast Asia

ASEAN economies weathered the recent global financial crisis relatively well. The region's economic growth plummeted during the worse of the crisis in 2009 but quickly rebounded in the following year.

ASEAN countries currently supply 15% of total output in developing Asia and 25% of the region's total trade. Robust domestic demand is a key reason for the region's resilience under the recent crisis. Countries with large domestic consumer markets, like Indonesia, managed to weather the crisis well by relying on domestic demand. In addition, more prudent fiscal management in the aftermath of the Asian financial crisis in 1997–1998 has given ASEAN countries more scope to stimulate domestic economies through fiscal expansion (ADB 2010). Other advantages, such as abundant natural resources and slower wage growth than in the PRC, have contributed to the dynamism of the region's economies. All of these factors helped ASEAN countries avoid a collapse in GDP during the global financial crisis and contributed to the region's sharp recovery immediately afterward.

This analysis does not mean that international trade is no longer important to the region. As global trade rebounded in 2010, the larger ASEAN members—Indonesia, Malaysia, the Philippines, and Thailand—saw their exports grow sharply, fueling stronger consumption and investment that supported growth (ADB 2011).

A change in trade structure has also helped secure trade for the region. Since 2000, total trade within ASEAN and with the PRC and India has grown much more quickly than trade with ASEAN's traditional partners among the advanced economies (Figure 1.2.1). Greater trade within developing Asia helped cushion the impact of soft export demand from traditional markets during the recent crisis.

Rapidly increasing trade within developing Asia reflects the heavy involvement of ASEAN countries in global value chains, which has made them important parts of the global factory. In the production of durable goods such as electronics, most ASEAN economies occupy the middle reaches of value chains, where they specialize in processing intermediate goods (Ma and Van Assche 2012). The processed intermediate goods are exported to countries such as the PRC and Thailand, which specialize in the downstream assembly of final durable goods that are eventually shipped for final sale in Europe and the US. Given weak demand in these latter markets, higher trade within Asia can support export demand in ASEAN countries only temporarily.

Nevertheless, economic ties between ASEAN and other countries in Asia have grown rapidly in the first decade of this century. The PRC is now ASEAN's most important single trading partner. India may not be

1.2.1 Trade between ASEAN countries and their major trading partners

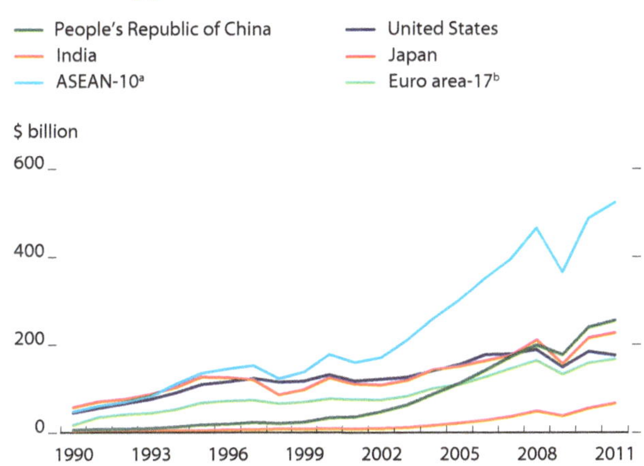

[a] The Association of Southeast Asian Nations (ASEAN)-10 are Brunei Darussalam, Cambodia, Indonesia, the Lao People's Democratic Republic, Malaysia, Myanmar, the Philippines, Singapore, Thailand, and Viet Nam.

[b] The euro area-17 are Austria, Belgium, Cyprus, Estonia, Finland, France, Germany, Greece, Ireland, Italy, Luxembourg, Malta, Netherlands, Portugal, Slovakia, Slovenia, and Spain.

Source: United Nations. Comtrade database. http://comtrade.un.org (accessed 4 March 2013).

Click here for figure data

as important to ASEAN as the association's traditional markets but has grown significantly more important in recent years and now provides a share of export demand for ASEAN that is no longer negligible. The share of exports from ASEAN to the PRC and India increased rapidly in the 2000s, marking stronger economic ties (Figure 1.2.2).

Deepening economic ties between ASEAN and the two giants of developing Asia propel greater synchronization of business cycles. Thus, events in the PRC and India will more directly affect economic activity in the ASEAN countries. Slower growth in either the PRC or India, for example, could be a drag on output growth in ASEAN. In other words, a shock in either of the giants will likely have spillover implications for ASEAN.

Although the PRC and India are still achieving enviable GDP growth rates, their pace of expansion is now projected to be slower than that achieved during the high growth years preceding the global financial crisis. Output in the two economies will therefore tend to be lower than what it would be if GDP grew at historical rates. Closer economic ties will mean slowdown in the PRC and India will have greater implications for ASEAN's growth outlook.

1.2.2 Trade shares of ASEAN countries' major trading partners

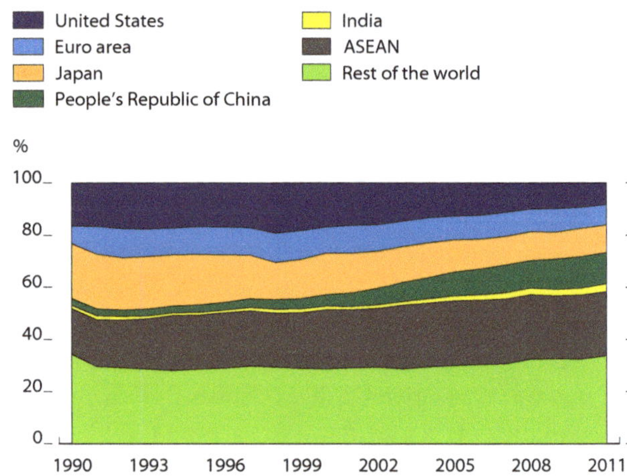

ASEAN = Association of Southeast Asian Nations.

Source: United Nations. Comtrade database. http://comtrade.un.org (accessed 4 March 2013).

Click here for figure data

How strong is the spillover from the two giants to the ASEAN economies? Precisely answering this question is a challenge. Figure 1.2.3 provides the likely reduction in the level of output of the larger ASEAN economies relative to their baseline forecast in response, during the same year, to PRC and India GDP being 1 percentage point lower than their baselines.

The spillover into ASEAN of a GDP shock in the PRC is twice as large as one from India. Absent any other distortion, GDP being 1 percentage point less than baseline in the PRC tends to reduce ASEAN's output by almost 1/3 of a percent from its baseline in the same year. The spillover into ASEAN from a shock in India is only about 1/6 of the shortfall in India. Looking at the impact on larger ASEAN countries, spillover from the PRC has the largest effect in Malaysia, where it is almost 1/2 as large as in the PRC, followed by Indonesia and Singapore at about 1/3. Spillover from India into these countries is only 1/2 that from the PRC. In Thailand, a 1 percentage point GDP drop coming from either the PRC or India has a similar impact, causing the Thai GDP to decline by about 1/5 of a percent. The Philippines appears to be the least-integrated country in the group, suffering no significant spillover from the PRC and only 1/10 of a shock emanating from India.

The magnitude of the spillover can also be used to gauge the implications of a lower growth rate in either of the two giants on ASEAN's GDP growth. For example, absent any policy response from ASEAN authorities, the PRC's growth dropping below its potential would induce a roughly proportional drop in ASEAN's growth below its potential. The spillover magnitudes calculated above are the approximate proportionality factor.

To illustrate the median effect of a slowdown in the PRC on ASEAN growth, the likely GDP growth reduction in ASEAN is computed on the assumption that GDP historically grew in the PRC at 10% annually and in ASEAN at 6%. Growth at 1 percentage point lower than the historical rate in the PRC could, absent any other distortion, reduce ASEAN GDP growth by about 1/4 of a point less than its historical rate. This predicts future growth at less than historical potential. If the future potential growth rate of the PRC declines 2 percentage points to 8% per annum, future potential growth in ASEAN could be 0.5 percentage points lower, or 5.5% per annum.

In reality, the PRC economy is not slowing much, and ASEAN authorities can take measures to offset the blow. As such, the effect of any slowdown on the ASEAN economies will likely be contained. Spillover from India to ASEAN economies is much smaller, limiting the impact on the region caused by slower growth in India. In sum, although the two giants are expected to grow more slowly to the forecast horizon, the effect on ASEAN will likely be limited and amenable to mitigation.

1.2.3 Impact on ASEAN members of GDP growth 1 percentage point lower than the baseline

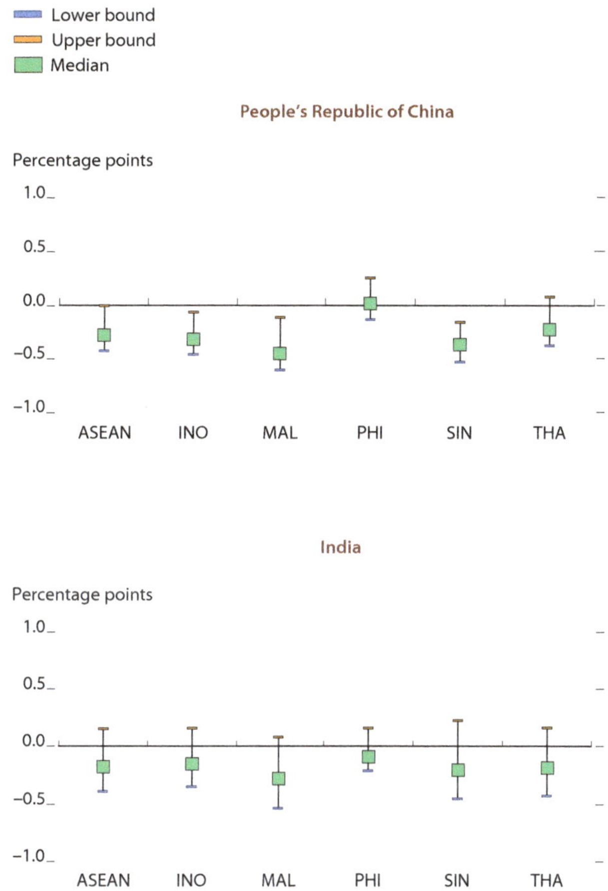

ASEAN = Association of Southeast Asian Nations, INO = Indonesia, MAL = Malaysia, PHI = Philippines, SIN = Singapore, THA = Thailand.

Source: Ramayandi, forthcoming.

Click here for figure data

A more integrated ASEAN

To capitalize on ASEAN's intensive production network, the region is moving to intensify its regional integration. ASEAN countries aim to achieve the ASEAN Economic Community (AEC) by 2015, fulfilling the goal laid out in its Vision 2020 (ASEAN Secretariat 1997). The statement envisages ASEAN as a highly competitive single market and production base that is fully integrated into the global economy and pursues equitable economic development. Under the AEC, ASEAN will promote the free flow of goods and services, investments, and skilled labor among its member countries. A single market and production base should enable ASEAN to gain more from its contributions to value chains by improving its efficiency and economies of scale. Rashid et al. (2009) suggest that ASEAN income would be 5.3% higher with the AEC and that benefits would spread through all ASEAN countries as trade in goods and services expanded.

By December 2011, ASEAN had progressed considerably toward implementing the AEC. The ASEAN Secretariat detailed in 2012 the progress made (ASEAN Secretariat 2012). Toward the first pillar of the AEC, 66% of the measures leading to a single market and production base that were slated for completion by the end of 2011 had been completed. So had 68% of the measures toward the second pillar, the competitive economic region base; 67% toward the third pillar, equitable economic development; and 86% toward the fourth pillar, integration into the global economy. That implementation progress fell short of fully achieving any of the targets highlights the difficulty of fully implementing the AEC.

Beyond the AEC, ASEAN is also considering several international economic partnership frameworks that would enhance its further integration into the global economy, notably the Regional Comprehensive Economic Partnership. This aims to join ASEAN with six nations enjoying bilateral free-trade partnerships with ASEAN members (Box 1.2.1).

1.2.1 Toward the Regional Comprehensive Economic Partnership

At the East Asia Summit on 20 November 2012 in Phnom Penh, leaders agreed to formally launch negotiations to establish the proposed Regional Comprehensive Economic Partnership (RCEP). Led by ASEAN, RCEP negotiations will include all 10 ASEAN members and their 6 partners in free trade agreements (FTAs): Australia, the PRC, India, Japan, the Republic of Korea, and New Zealand. An eventual RCEP trade deal would create the world's largest free trade bloc, with profound economic implications for the world economy.

Origins and scope of negotiations

The RCEP concept was first mooted at the November 2011 ASEAN leaders summit in Bali. While strengthening ASEAN's central role in the regional trade architecture, the key purpose of the partnership is to reconcile two long-standing proposals for a large region-wide trade agreement: the East Asia Free Trade Agreement, which focused on ASEAN members plus the PRC, Japan, and the Republic of Korea, and the Comprehensive Economic Partnership, which added Australia, India, and New Zealand. The RCEP bridges the two proposals by adopting open accession. Negotiations among the 16 current parties began in early 2013 with the aim of concluding talks by the end of 2015.

The RCEP seeks to achieve a modern and comprehensive trade agreement. It is comprehensive in that its negotiating agenda will cover trade in goods, trade in services, investment, economic and technical cooperation, and dispute settlement. Negotiations adopt as principles that the RCEP will

- be consistent with World Trade Organization (WTO) rules on trade in goods and services,
- seek to improve on existing ASEAN+1 FTAs,
- take into account participating countries' different stages of development and allow for special concessions to least-developed countries, and
- enshrine open accession to enable other external economic partners (including other ASEAN FTA partners) to participate at a future date if they agree to comply with the group's trade rules and guidelines.

Economic benefits

The size and economic importance of the RCEP free trade bloc is striking (box table). The RCEP promises to be a powerful vehicle for the spread of sophisticated global production networks underlying the rise of Asia as the world's factory and reducing the risk of an Asian "noodle bowl" of multiple trade rules in overlapping Asian FTAs (Kawai and Wignaraja 2013). Implementing a comprehensive, high-quality RCEP will provide open and simplified trade rules consistent with WTO agreements on goods and services. Rules of origin can be rationalized, made more flexible, and better administered through electronic means. In the area of investment rules—for which the WTO has no agreements—the RCEP will go beyond existing multilateral rules and promote easier flows of foreign direct investment and technology transfer by multinational corporations.

It is noteworthy that the RCEP will provide other economic benefits such as freer market access for goods, services, skills, and technology; large markets that offer economies of scale and scope for specialization; and insurance against protectionist sentiments. Additionally, the RCEP will provide a blueprint for Asia's emerging regional trade architecture toward achieving a free-trade area across Asia and the Pacific.

Simulation modeling suggests that the RCEP will bring significant economic benefits to the global economy in the long run. An exercise using a computable general equilibrium model showed the RCEP offering income gains reaching $644 billion in 2025, equal to 0.6% of world GDP (Petri, Plummer, and Zhai 2012). The box figure shows the percentage of income gained by anticipated RCEP members. All economies party to an RCEP agreement are projected to gain.

Regional Comprehensive Economic Partnership Scale

Measure	Magnitude	World share (%)
Population[a]	3.4 billion	49
Gross domestic product[a]	$21.4 trillion	30
Trade in goods and services[b]	$12.0 trillion	29
Foreign direct investment (inflows)[b]	$402.8 billion	26
Foreign direct investment (outflows)[b]	$378.9 billion	22

[a] Population and gross domestic product figures are International Monetary Fund (IMF) estimates for 2012.

[b] 2011.

Sources: International Monetary Fund. World Economic Outlook database; World Bank. World Development Indicators database. http://databank.worldbank.org; United Nations Conference on Trade and Development (all accessed 20 February 2013).

1.2.1 (*continued*)

Challenges and way forward

Realizing these benefits hinges on rising to several challenges during negotiations and afterwards (Hiebert and Hanlon 2012, Das Basu 2012, Kawai and Wignaraja 2013). First is the political challenge of ensuring that participants, including the regional giants, respect the central role of ASEAN in RCEP negotiations. Second is overcoming the risk, arising from the divergent interests of more- and less-developed economies, that the RCEP achieves little trade and investment liberalization and is encumbered by many protectionist exclusions. Third is for the RCEP to gradually improve its coverage of new trade issues, such as competition policy and environmental and labor standards, which are increasingly a feature in the most comprehensive regional trade agreements in Asia and internationally. Fourth is the risk that businesses fail to avail themselves of the RCEP because they insufficiently understand its legal provisions, particularly as they affect small and medium-sized enterprises.

The way forward for RCEP negotiations is to use the best features of existing Asian FTAs, including existing ASEAN+1 FTAs, as the bases for negotiations toward the best possible RCEP; to establish a clear timetable for concluding RCEP negotiations; and to actively involve the private sector in negotiations. Significant outreach and business services need to be provided to small and medium-sized enterprises to maximize the benefits they will enjoy and lower the costs of using the RCEP.

Income gains from the Regional Comprehensive Economic Partnership in 2025

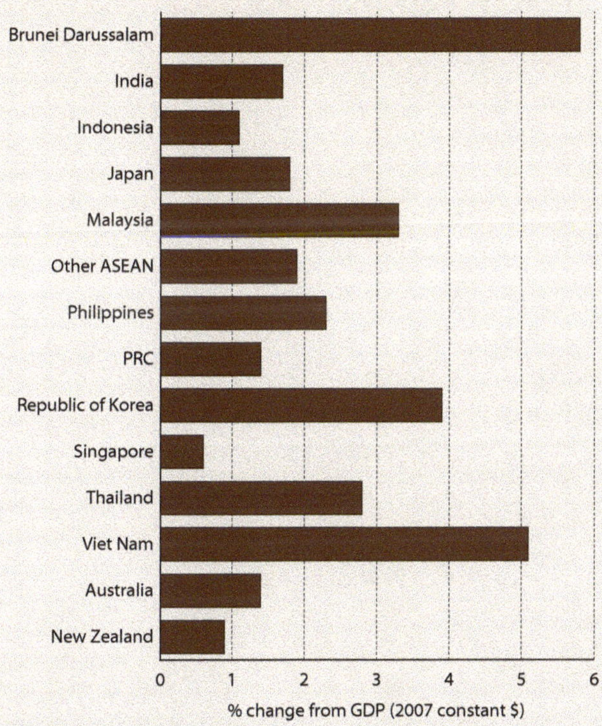

PRC = People's Republic of China, Other ASEAN = Cambodia, Lao People's Democratic Republic, and Myanmar.

Source: Petri, P., G. Plummer, and F. Zhai. 2012. *Note on Alternative Asian Track Scenarios.* http://asiapacifictrade.org/wp-content/uploads/2012/11/Asian-track-alternatives.pdf

Click here for figure data

References

Das Basu, S. 2012. *RCEP: Going Beyond ASEAN+1 FTAs.* ISEAS perspective, 17 August. http://www.iseas.edu.sg/documents/publication/ISEAS%20Perspective_4_17aug12.pdf

Hiebert, M. and L. Hanlon. 2012. *ASEAN and Partners Launch Regional Comprehensive Economic Partnership.* http://csis.org/publication/asean-and-partners-launch-regional-comprehensive-economic-partnership

Kawai, M. and G. Wignaraja. 2013. Patterns of FTAs in Asia: A Review of Recent Evidence. *Policy Studies No. 65.* Honolulu: East West Center. http://www.eastwestcenter.org/publications/patterns-free-trade-areas-in-asia

Petri, P., G. Plummer, and F. Zhai. 2012. *Note on Alternative Asian Track Scenarios.* http://asiapacifictrade.org/wp-content/uploads/2012/11/TPP-track-alternatives.pdf

Realizing further economic integration, both within and beyond ASEAN, has the potential to improve income and welfare in ASEAN economies still further. More integration will, however, subject ASEAN countries to stronger spillover from shocks that must be carefully managed to mitigate higher risks in future crises.

Historically, external factors have affected output fluctuations in the ASEAN countries (Ramayandi, forthcoming). Consistent with the "factory Asia" model of cross-border supply chains, shocks originating from the advanced economy markets—the ultimate destination for the final goods—have generated considerable output fluctuation in ASEAN economies. Yet links within ASEAN also play a role in transmitting shocks among its members. Because most intra-ASEAN activities are through the production network, shocks emanating from one ASEAN country can disrupt the region's supply chain and, hence, destabilize output in other members.

Further integrating the region with the global economy exposes ASEAN countries to being more directly affected by external events. Therefore, to advance and manage economic integration, ASEAN countries must advance regional cooperation and policy coordination. This is particularly important to improve the region's macroeconomic surveillance capacity, toward minimizing contagion from possible future crises.

Avoiding the middle-income trap

The AEC and the RCEP promise to build on ASEAN's current strong growth prospects to stimulate progress toward higher per capita income in each member country. At present, almost all of the 10 ASEAN countries have graduated from low-income status. Singapore and Brunei Darussalam are ASEAN's two high-income countries as defined by the World Bank. Malaysia and Thailand are now categorized as upper-middle income countries, while Indonesia, the Philippines, Viet Nam, and the Lao People's Democratic Republic are lower-middle income.

The climb to middle income poses perils. Once countries reach certain income thresholds they face the risk of structural stagnation, making it hard for them to achieve higher incomes per capita (Box 1.2.2). To reduce the risk of a future growth slowdown gelling as the so-called middle-income trap, ASEAN countries must continue progressing from lower to higher value-added activity. Doing so requires ASEAN countries to keep improving their human capital and shifting their production up the technological ladder. ASEAN countries should develop their education systems and guarantee adequate infrastructure and energy supply to support these improvements. These steps may give ASEAN members a better chance of avoiding the middle-income trap.

Greater regional integration and reform are required to sustain ASEAN's growth and avoid the middle-income trap in the medium to long run. In the shorter term, however, spillovers caused by the abundance of global liquidity and the resulting volatility in capital flows remain a worry for ASEAN and other emerging economies in Asia.

1.2.2 Education and the middle-income trap

Rapid growth in developing countries is an eye-catching feature of the world economy. The question is how long this rapid growth can continue. Attempts to answer it have given rise to a literature on growth slowdowns that have become known collectively as the middle-income trap. The economic outlook since the global financial crisis of 2008–2009 has further intensified interest in the middle-income trap. The issue is of great interest to the ASEAN-4: Indonesia, Malaysia, the Philippines, and Thailand, all of which are middle-income economies aiming to make the jump to high-income status.

Eichengreen, Park, and Shin (2012) analyzed the historical experience of growth slowdowns to shed light on future prospects. They considered post-1956 cases of fast-growing countries that did or did not seem to fall into the middle-income trap, defined as sustaining GDP per capita at an average annual rate of 3.5% for 7 years or longer but then slowing significantly by at least 2 percentage points between successive 7-year periods. The authors found that growth slowed at a mean GDP per capita of $16,540 in 2005 constant US dollars adjusted for purchasing power parity. At this income, per capita income growth slowed on average from 5.6% to 2.1%. By comparison, per capita GDP in the PRC was $8,511 in 2007, when the source data, Penn World Tables 6.3, ended. Slowdowns most likely affect economies with high growth in the earlier period, high old-age dependency ratios, very high investment ratios, and undervalued currencies.

Eichengreen, Park, and Shin (2013) revisited these questions, updating and extending earlier results. There are several reasons for doing so. Concerns about slowdowns have continued to grow, as has the literature on the subject. The PRC's growth rate has decelerated from more than 10% in 2010 to less than 8% in 2012. In addition, more and better data are available through 2010, courtesy of Penn World Tables 7.1. The paper revises earlier estimates of per capita GDP for a number of countries, not least for the PRC, whose 2010 per capita GDP at 2005 prices purchasing power parity is now estimated to have been somewhat lower at $7,129.

The new data illuminates a slightly different list of growth slowdowns. The results are broadly consistent with the earlier findings but not entirely. While slowdowns are still most likely when per capita GDP reaches about $15,000, the new data point to two modes, one at around $15,000 and the other at around $11,000 (box figure).

A valuable finding is that the share of the population with at least a secondary education correlates positively with dodging the middle-income trap, other things being equal. Education in general has the same effect, holding constant the share of secondary school and university. The quality of human capital matters in avoiding growth slowdowns. In addition, slowdowns are less likely in countries with high-tech products accounting for a large share of exports. This highlights the importance of moving up the technology ladder.

Frequency distribution of growth slowdowns

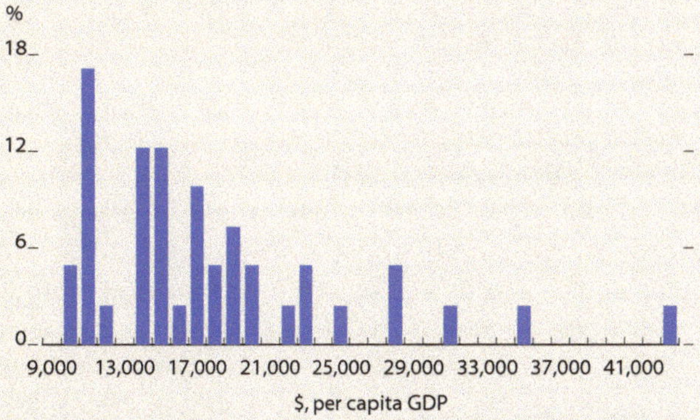

Note: The bars indicate the frequency of actual growth slowdowns by per capita income.

Source: Eichengreen, B., D. Park, and K. Shin. 2013. Growth Slowdowns Redux: New Evidence on the Middle-Income Trap. *National Bureau of Economic Research Working Paper* No. 18673.

Click here for figure data

The finding that high-quality human capital reduces the probability of a slowdown is especially relevant for ASEAN. Skilled workers and professionals are needed to move up the global value chain. High-quality human capital is especially important for modern services with high value added like business services (ADB 2012). It matters for moving up the technological ladder and the global value chain in manufacturing, as the experience of newly industrialized economies clearly shows. Yet the lack of skilled workers and professionals is the single biggest business concern for employers in ASEAN (ADB 2008).

Whether or not the ASEAN-4 can avoid the middle-income trap thus depends largely on whether they develop education systems that successfully produce graduates with the skills that employers require. A highly skilled workforce holds the key to the region's quest to produce and export more sophisticated high-tech goods.

References

ADB. 2008. Asia's Skills Crisis, In *Asian Development Outlook 2008: Workers in Asia.* Manila: ADB.

______. 2012. *Asian Development Outlook 2012 Update: Services and Asia's Future Growth.* Manila: ADB.

Eichengreen, B., D. Park, and K. Shin. 2013. Growth Slowdowns Redux: New Evidence on the Middle-Income Trap. *National Bureau of Economic Research Working Paper* No. 18673.

______. 2012. When Fast Growing Economies Slow Down: International Evidence and Implications for China. *Asian Economic Papers* 11. pp. 42–87.

Managing capital flows under quantitative easing

As the global financial crisis unfolded, advanced economies relied heavily on expansionary monetary and fiscal policy to stabilize markets. However, with credit constraints so severe and nominal interest rates nearing the zero lower bound, traditional monetary policy proved inadequate. Central banks in advanced economies resorted to several unconventional measures to increase money supply. This involved not only increasing the size and adjusting the composition of their balance sheets, but also expanding the variety of their holdings to include assets with longer maturities or higher risk than traditional short-term treasury securities. In particular, the US has launched three rounds of historically unprecedented quantitative easing (QE) since the crisis erupted in 2008, enormously expanding the Federal Reserve's balance sheet by almost threefold in 3 years. The impacts of such unconventional monetary policy have attracted a lot of attention from economists and political pundits.

The authorities in the advanced economies take the view that QE stabilizes financial markets, promotes growth, and therefore must have positive effects globally. Some observers in emerging economies, on the other hand, have voiced concern about the negative spillover effects of such policies on their capital flows, exchange rates, and asset prices. This has prompted the International Monetary Fund to issue regular spillover reports to G20 meetings. With the Government of Japan recently announcing an aggressive, unconventional monetary policy, emerging economies' fears have resurfaced. Japan's QE is intended to help spur inflation to the central bank's 2% target and reignite growth, an outcome that would benefit economies in developing Asia. But emerging market policy makers are concerned that the policy may cause their currencies to appreciate, undermining their competitiveness.

While it is generally accepted in the literature that QE was effective in lowering US long-term yield rates and stimulating economic activity, evidence of international spillover effects is mixed. Neely (2010) and Chen et al. (2012) found that the first round of QE, in particular, substantially affected global yield rates, exchange rates, and capital flows. Morgan (2011) also found some evidence of impacts of US capital outflows on exchange rates and interest rates. The International Monetary Fund (2012) found instead no significant traces of US liquidity leaking out of the US.

The analysis of the empirical impact of QE on Asian economies, which draws on Cho and Rhee (forthcoming), looks only at US QE, as Japan's QE has only recently been announced. It first analyzes trends of capital flow aggregates and their composition, and then uses regression analysis to examine more directly the effects on domestic financial variables.

Recent trends in capital inflows

To understand whether US expansionary monetary policy has increased capital flows into Asia or changed their composition, the first step is to compare trends before and after the global financial crisis. Extraordinary movements in capital flows, if any are found, cannot be attributed solely to QE, as they can be driven by a multitude of other factors. The trend analysis simply identifies noticeable changes after QE that policy makers may need to be concerned about, though they may not have clearly identified causes.

Figure 1.3.1 shows aggregate private capital inflows since 2005 into 10 Asian economies: the PRC; Hong Kong, China; India; Indonesia; Japan; the Republic of Korea; the Philippines; Singapore; Taipei,China; and Thailand. Capital inflows shown as aggregate amounts in Figure 1.3.1a are notable for their volatility. Inflows rapidly increased to over $1.4 trillion in 2007, collapsed with the crisis in 2008 and 2009, sharply rebounded to the pre-crisis level in 2010 and 2011 as the global economy recovered along with QE, and then slowed after the second half of 2011, when the European crisis escalated. While Figure 1.3.1a shows that approximately half of the aggregate capital inflows were accounted for by the PRC and Japan, Figure 1.3.1b proves that the volatility of capital inflows was perceptible in most Asian countries. By presenting average ratios of capital inflow to GDP, Figure 1.3.1b suppresses the dominating effects of the PRC and Japan, exaggerating instead the influence of the regional financial hubs—Singapore and Hong Kong, China—as their capital inflows are extremely large relative to their GDP. In the depth of global financial turmoil, the capital inflows to these 10 economies plummeted to 1.7% of GDP in 2008–2009 from an average of 8.4% in the previous 3 years. But inflows rebounded nearly as sharply, returning to an average of 7.4% of GDP in 2010–2012. The same pattern is observed even excluding Singapore and Hong Kong, China. Capital inflows collapsed from 8.1% of GDP on average in 2007 to 1.9% in 2008, and then recovered to about 7% in 2010, close to the pre-crisis level.

1.3.1 Private capital inflows to Asia

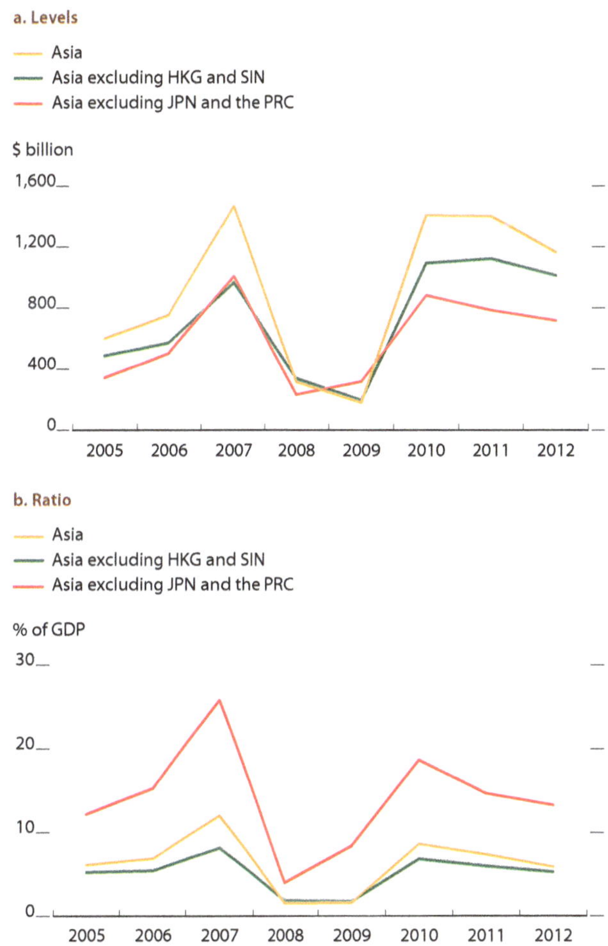

HKG = Hong Kong, China, JPN = Japan, PRC = People's Republic of China, SIN = Singapore.

Notes: As data for 2012 are available only to the third quarter for Hong Kong, China; India; and the Philippines, and to the first half for the PRC, they are annualized by multiplication. Ratios are weighted averages of the GDP ratios for individual countries.

Source: ADB estimates from CEIC Data Company (accessed 15 March 2013).

Click here for figure data

Figure 1.3.2 presents the composition of capital inflows for all economies excluding Singapore and Hong Kong, China. It is noticeable that while FDI was robust up to the crisis, portfolio investment was most volatile, collapsing from 2.2% of GDP in 2007 to –2.9% of GDP in 2008, as foreigners sold off Asian equities and bonds. Another noteworthy observation is that other inflows, which are mostly bank loans, exceeded the pre-crisis level and became the main source of capital inflows after the crisis. Meanwhile, the ratio of FDI has been slipping, and the ratio of portfolio investment has not fully recovered to the pre-crisis level.

Figure 1.3.3 shows the composition of capital inflows by individual country. For the two financial hubs, capital inflows easily exceed 10% of GDP, mainly driven by the category *Others*. Patterns of capital inflows

1.3.2 Components of private capital inflows to Asia (excluding Singapore and Hong Kong, China)

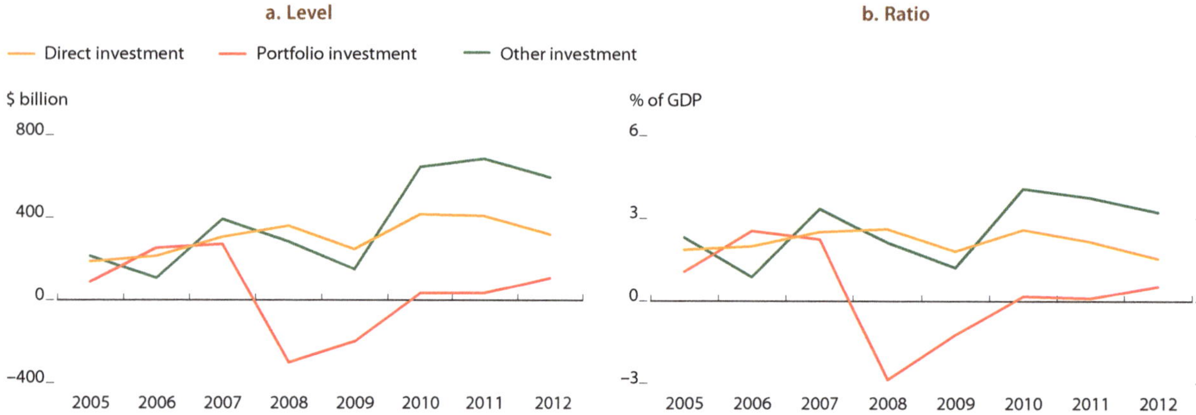

Note: As data for 2012 are available only to the third quarter for India and the Philippines, and to the first half for the PRC, they are annualized by multiplication. Ratios are weighted averages of the GDP ratios for individual countries.

Source: ADB estimates from CEIC Data Company (accessed 15 March 2013).

Click here for figure data

to the PRC and Japan are stark contrasts: Whereas capital inflows to the PRC are mainly foreign direct investment (FDI) and have been relatively smooth, the main component of capital inflow fluctuations in Japan are portfolio investment. This difference between the PRC and Japan seems to reflect their differing degree of financial market liberalization. The relatively open financial markets of the Republic of Korea and Taipei,China experienced patterns similar to Japan's, in that portfolio investment drove the wild swings in capital inflows around the crisis. In other Asian economies (except India), the role of portfolio investment was relatively weak, the amplitude of fluctuation relatively small, and the patterns similar.

In sum, capital inflows to Asia went through drastic fluctuations around the global financial crisis, driven mainly by portfolio investments into countries with relatively open financial markets. In particular, the quick rebound of capital inflows in 2009 and 2010, despite the heightened uncertainties and massive credit constraints in the advanced economies, suggests that QE contributed to the sharp rebound of capital flows to Asia.

As capital outflows from Asia have not been as volatile as inflows, net capital flow movements generally resemble inflow movements. Excluding Singapore and Hong Kong, China, the average ratio of net capital flows to GDP fell to –0.8% in 2008 but recovered to 2.0% by 2010, driven mostly by fluctuations in portfolio and other investments, from –1.2% of GDP in 2008 to 0.8% of GDP in 2010. As for reserve accumulation, the PRC has been a dominant player, accounting for 70%–80% of the total accumulated by the 10 sample economies from 2007 to 2011. This pace appears, however, to have significantly slowed in 2012. In terms of net aggregate financial account that includes reserve accumulation as well as private inflows and outflows, most Asian economies were capital exporters prior to the crisis, with outflows larger than inflows (India excepted). After the crisis, however, capital export is shrinking in most countries, which may be related to global rebalancing.

1.3.3 Components of private capital inflows to individual countries

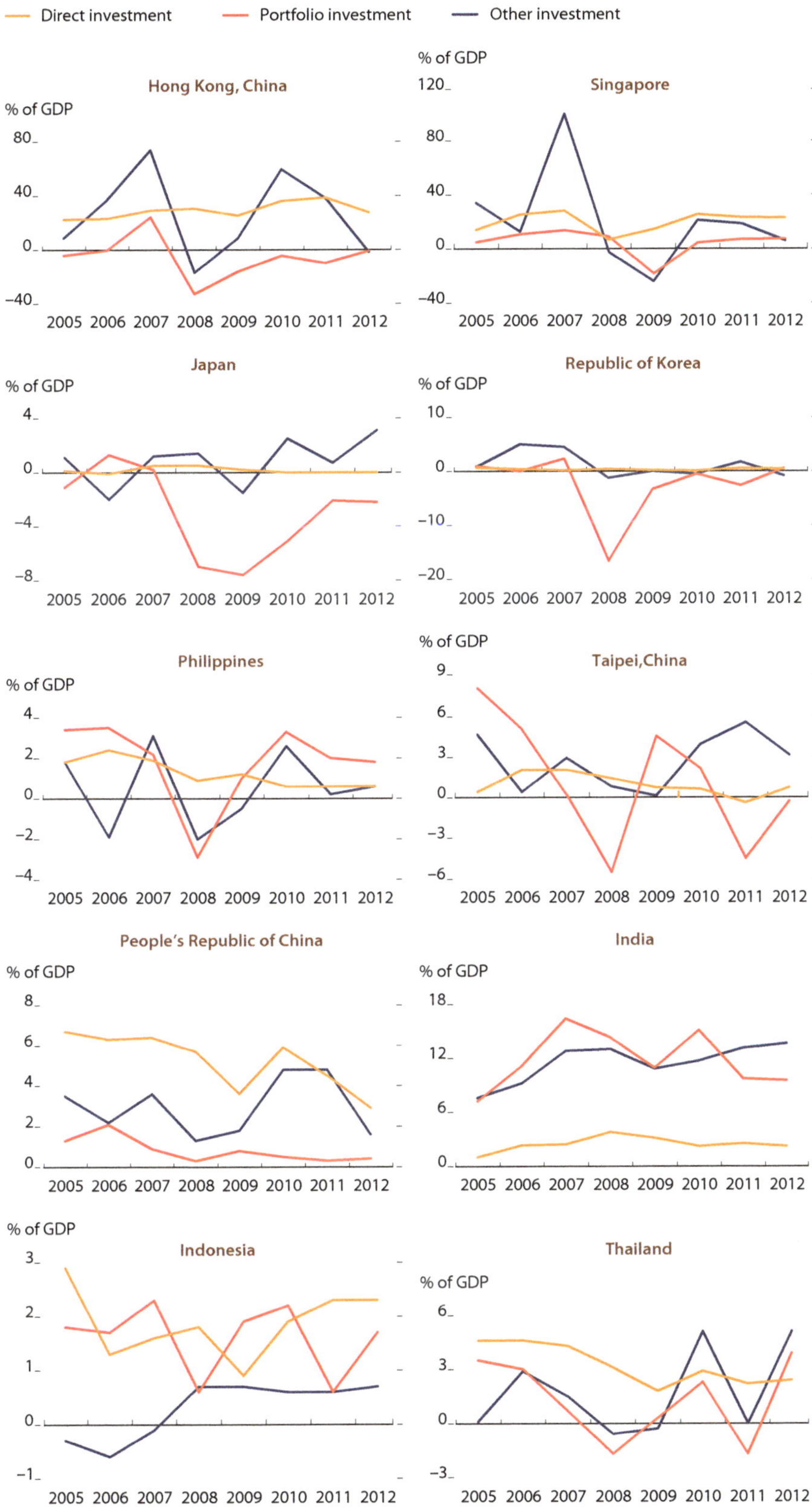

Note: As data for 2012 are available only to the third quarter for Hong Kong, China; India; and the Philippines, and to the first half for the PRC, they are annualized by multiplication.

Source: ADB estimates from CEIC Data Company (accessed 15 March 2013).

Click here for figure data

Modeling the impact of quantitative easing

The review of trends before and after the crisis has severe limitations because the impact of QE cannot be clearly identified. Regression analysis was used to isolate the QE impacts while controlling for other contemporaneous factors. As proxies for QE, 10 dummy variables were constructed indicating the weeks of important QE announcements (Table 1.3.1).

To examine the effects of QE variables on Asia, regressions were carried out for three major domestic financial variables: the credit default swap premium on 5-year sovereign debt (CDS); the yield rate on a 5-year government bond denominated in local currency (BOND); and the exchange rate vis-à-vis the US dollar (EXR) in eight Asian economies (the PRC; Hong Kong, China; Japan; the Republic of Korea; Malaysia; the Philippines; Singapore; and Thailand). Included with QE event dummies were explanatory variables assumed to be exogenous to Asian financial markets: the yield rate on 5-year US Treasuries (USRATE) and an index of global investor sentiment and market volatility (VIX). Weekly data from 2003 to 2012 were compiled using Wednesday, Thursday, or Tuesday quotes, in that order of priority depending on availability for US data, and quotes 1 day later for Asian country data.

The three domestic financial variables from each country might, however, be simultaneously determined. An implicit assumption was that causality ran CDS→BOND→EXR, i.e., CDS was included in BOND and EXR regressions, and BOND was included in EXR regressions. The results from the eight country regressions are summarized in Table 1.3.2.

Although results differ across countries, QE1 events had pronounced effects on domestic financial variables, especially on exchange rates, while QE2 and QE3 effects were relatively mute. Despite some exceptions, QE1 events generally lowered CDS and BOND and appreciated EXR.

1.3.1 Event dummies

	Event date	Event
QE1	2008 Nov 25	The Federal Reserve announces purchases of $100 billion in debt of housing-related government-sponsored enterprises (so-called federal agency debt) and up to $500 billion in MBS.
	2008 Dec 1	Federal Reserve Chairman Ben Bernanke mentions that the Federal Reserve could purchase long-term Treasuries.
	2008 Dec 16	An FOMC statement first mentions the possible purchase of long-term Treasuries.
	2009 Jan 28	An FOMC statement says that it is ready to expand federal agency debt and MBS purchases, as well as to purchase long-term Treasuries.
	2009 Mar 18	The FOMC announces that it will purchase an additional $750 billion in federal agency MBS and increase its purchases of federal agency debt by $100 billion and of long-term Treasuries by $300 billion.
QE2	2010 Nov 3	The Federal Reserve announces the purchase of $600 billion of Treasury securities by the end of the second quarter of 2011.
	2011 Jul 13	Bernanke says, "The Federal Reserve is ready to ease monetary policy further if economic growth and inflation slow much more."
QE3	2012 Aug 31	Bernanke mentions that the Federal Reserve is ready to do more, including purchase long-term Treasuries.
	2012 Sep 12	The Federal Reserve announces the launch of a new, open-ended program to purchase every month $40 billion in federal agency MBS and its decision to maintain extremely low policy rates until at least mid-2015.
	2012 Dec 12	The FOMC announces its decision to continue its purchases of federal agency MBS at a monthly pace of $40 billion and longer-term Treasury securities at $45 billion.

FOMC = Federal Open Market Committee, MBS = mortgage-backed securities.

Sources: For QE1, Neely, C. J. 2010. The Large Scale Asset Purchase Had Large International Effects. *Working Paper Series* No. 2010-018D. Missouri: Federal Reserve Bank of St. Louis; for QE2 and QE3, the Federal Reserve Board. http: www.federalreserve.gov

1.3.2 Summary of local variable regressions

		CDS	BOND	EXR
Domestic variables	BOND			"0"
	CDS		"0"	++
Global variables	USRATE	"0"	+++	"0"[a]
	VIX[b]	+++	"0"	+++[c]
QE1 (5 Events)		-	-	--
QE2 (2 Events)		"0"	"0"	"0"
QE3 (3 Events)		"0"	"0"	"0"

+++ = coefficients positive and statistically significant at 1%, ++ = at 5%, + = at 10%, --- = coefficients negative and statistically significant at 1%, -- = at 5%, - = at 10%, "o" = coefficients not statistically significant, BOND = yield rate on a 5-year government bond denominated in local currency, CDS = credit default swap premium on 5-year sovereign debt, EXR = local Asian exchange rate vis-à-vis the US dollar, QE = quantitative easing, USRATE = the yield rate on 5-year United States Treasuries, VIX = index of global investor sentiment and market volatility.

[a] +++ for Japan and Singapore.

[b] The Chicago Board Options Exchange Market Volatility Index, which provides "a key measure of market expectations of near-term volatility conveyed by S&P500 stock index option prices" (http://www.cboe.com/micro/VIX/vixintro.aspx).

[c] "o" for the People's Republic of China and --- for Japan.

Sources: For QE1, Neely, C. J. 2010. The Large Scale Asset Purchase Had Large International Effects. *Working Paper Series* No. 2010-018D. Missouri: Federal Reserve Bank of St. Louis; for QE2 and QE3, the Federal Reserve Board. http: www.federalreserve.gov

The magnitudes of some QE impacts were sizable: For example, the 16 December 2008 statement from the Federal Open Market Committee first mentioning the possible purchase of long-term Treasuries caused Asian currencies (except in the PRC and Hong Kong, China) to appreciate by 2%–5%, with Japan being the most sensitive (though, notably, the impacts of QE events were smaller when VIX is included, suggesting that QE events lessened global uncertainty). The finding that only QE1 had a significant impact on Asian currency appreciation aligns with the observation that capital inflows recovered quickly after 2008 but did not show any further sign of increasing after 2010.

The QE events were likely to have influenced Asia's financial markets as well through their impacts on global variables. Without exception, Asia's CDS premiums significantly dropped along with VIX, by more than double the rate in most economies, and Asia's BONDs fell along with USRATE, generally by 0.2–0.3 as much. To the extent that the QE events have lowered VIX and USRATE, therefore, they must have positively contributed to easing financial conditions in Asia.

The impacts of global variables on Asia's exchange rates differ across countries depending on their exchange rate regimes and their degree of financial market liberalization. Asia's exchange rates are generally insensitive to variations in USRATE, except in Japan and Singapore, where financial markets are fully liberalized. But these rates are extremely sensitive to the variations in VIX, with the Republic of Korea being the most sensitive, followed by Singapore. The PRC's exchange rate is not sensitive to VIX. The Japanese yen strengthens on the increase of VIX, reflecting its role as a safe haven during the crisis.

In relation to the different responses of exchange rates to capital flows across countries, an interesting observation is their relationship with asset price inflation. After the global financial crisis, housing prices in some economies increased sharply, raising cautionary flags to regional policy makers. It is particularly notable that housing prices have spiked largely where exchange rates have been stable or rigid and have been relatively steady where local currencies have appreciated. Figure 1.3.4 demonstrates the tradeoff between exchange rates and house prices, with a correlation coefficient −0.64, suggesting that QE may have affected Asian countries through *either* currency appreciation *or* higher prices for real estate, the most important household asset in many Asian countries.

These findings suggest that QE events affected Asia's financial markets through at least three channels: They stabilized the global financial market, calming sentiment and volatility to stabilize capital inflows, which lowered credit default swap premiums and strengthened currency values in Asia. They lowered the long-term interest rate, which brought down Asian domestic interest rates. And they changed market expectations through direct announcements.

1.3.4 Changes in REER and real house price index: December 2008 versus September 2012

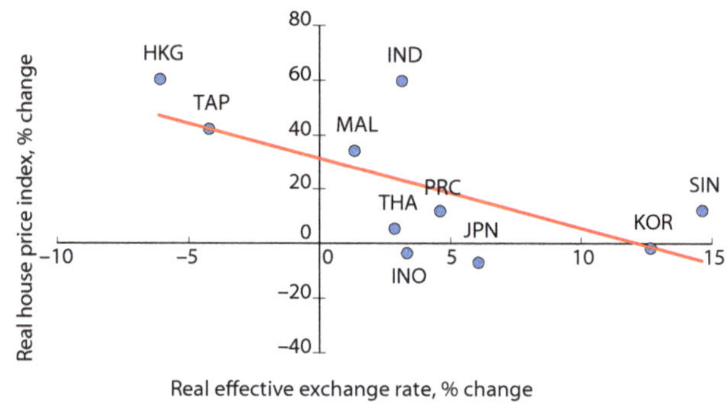

HKG = Hong Kong, China, IND = India, INO = Indonesia, JPN = Japan, KOR = Republic of Korea, MAL = Malaysia, PRC = People's Republic of China, REER = real effective exchange rate, SIN = Singapore, TAP = Taipei,China, THA = Thailand.

Sources: Government Housing Bank of Thailand; CEIC Data Company (accessed 15 March 2013).

Click here for figure data

Implications for policy

QE generally contributed to arresting the free fall of the advanced economies after the collapse of Lehman Brothers in 2008. The trend and regression analyses conducted before and after the global financial crisis provided some insights on the impacts of QE on Asia. The results of the analyses highlight three ways Asian policy makers can manage the spillover effects of QE in the advanced economies.

Strengthened macroprudential policies. Although QE has been extensive in the advanced economies, these unprecedented and unconventional policies will inevitably end at some point. To the extent that QEs have affected Asia's financial markets, future unwinding will also have impacts, and effects could be magnified in countries that have not prepared for them. It is imperative to closely monitor cross-border financial transactions—in particular portfolio investment, which was most volatile around the crisis—and their implications on banking sector soundness. Where necessary, macroprudential policy must be strengthened.

Improved monitoring of asset markets. In some Asian economies, housing prices have risen sharply enough to cause concern to policy makers. As proven by the recent crisis, bubbles in real estate markets undermine financial and macroeconomic stability. Policy makers thus need to closely monitor potential risks in the banking sector that may trigger instability when asset price trends reverse.

Reserves maintained in line with increasingly volatile financial flows. While it is not optimal for central banks to target exchange rates through extensive foreign exchange purchases, it is prudent for them to maintain foreign reserve holdings sufficient to counter increasingly volatile financial flows—all the more so if their currencies are not reserve currencies. This will give them sufficient buffer to cope with sudden reversals in financial flows.

Macroeconomic policy to maintain stability

The advanced economies are expected to continue expanding liquidity, which has repercussions for developing Asia in its current macroeconomic situation. Where recovery has progressed to the point that output is approaching full capacity, strong capital inflows would have potential to put upward pressure on the prices of goods or assets. Authorities will need to adjust to the changing environment to maintain macroeconomic stability.

Monetary policy alert to price pressures

The continuing economic recovery across developing Asia lifted production nearly back to its long-term trend. By 2012, actual GDP was very close to its potential in a broad range of economies—a situation that is expected to prevail through the forecast horizon (Figure 1.4.1). This is an important change from recent years, when slack capacity meant there was little risk of inflation accelerating.

Stable food prices are so far helping to keep consumer price pressures largely in check. Inflation for the region as a whole is expected to pick up slightly, from 3.7% in 2012 to 4.0% in 2013 and further to 4.2% in 2014. Some exceptions are India and Viet Nam, which are still coping with high inflation from their previously overheated domestic economies. Throughout developing Asia, inflation is projected to pick up slightly in 2013–2014 (Figure 1.4.2), driven mainly by rising inflation in East Asia. The inflation trend is not uniform across the region, however, and some easing is foreseen in 2014 in South and Southeast Asia.

Some economies in developing Asia have cautiously resorted to easing their monetary policy in an effort to counter the downward cycle caused by weak global demand in 2012. After an episode of monetary tightening to stem rising inflationary pressure in 2010–2011, central banks cautiously reversed their policy stance in 2012 to prod domestic demand and thus compensate for slower global economic activity caused by renewed concerns about the debt crisis in Europe (Figure 1.4.3).

The major industrial economies are likely to continue their ultra-accommodative monetary policy, as they are not expected to enjoy a rapid turnaround within the forecast horizon (see Annex: Consolidation in advanced economies). In the meantime, the central banks of the industrial economies will keep their policy rates near zero and continue pouring

1.4.1 Output gap

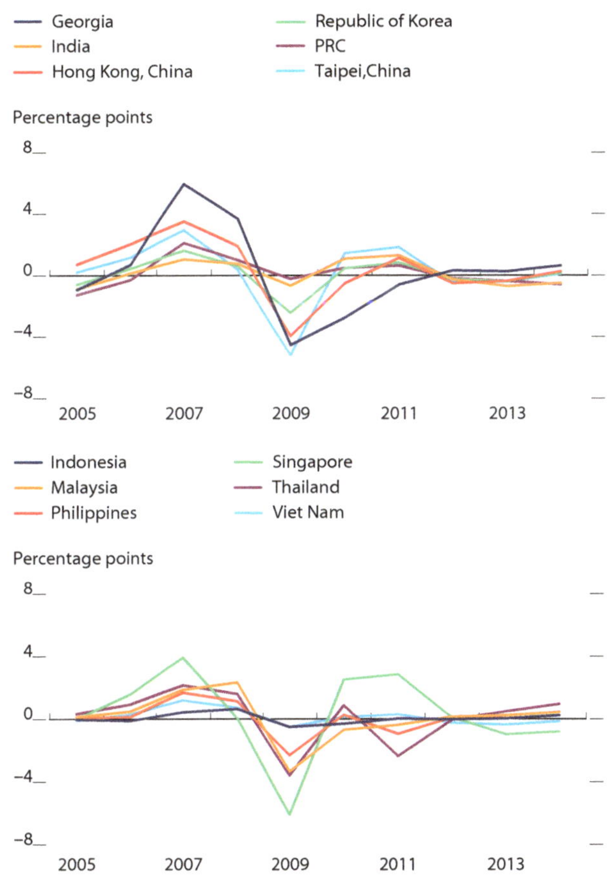

PRC = People's Republic of China.

Source: ADB estimates based on data from CEIC Data Company (accessed 15 March 2013).

Click here for figure data

1.4.2 Inflation forecasts by subregion

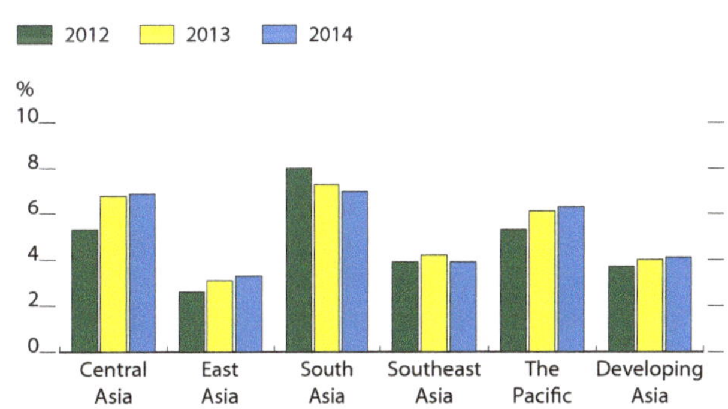

Source: Asian Development Outlook database.

Click here for figure data

liquidity to their economies. The global spillover of this excess liquidity raises concerns of asset bubbles building up in Asia.

During the forecast period, monetary policy is expected to have a limited role to play in stimulating economic activity in developing Asia. With output gaps hovering around zero and global liquidity expanding, the authorities should instead monitor their short-term economic development carefully and stand ready to stabilize aggregate demand should the economy tip toward overheating. Although inflation still looks benign, a slow buildup of inflationary pressure is anticipated, in particular in the PRC, Indonesia, the Philippines, and Thailand. Monetary policy is better kept neutral at this juncture, but central banks should be vigilant against the sudden return of inflation. Some fine-tuning in monetary management may be required to avoid overheating in economies that are already close to their long-term trend growth. Countries with high inflation and structural imbalance should prioritize stabilization.

Governments in Asia need to be careful that the surge in capital inflows does not fuel excessive rises in asset prices while, at the same time, being prepared for a possible reversal in monetary flows should investor sentiment reverse. The current global environment of excess liquidity demands that the authorities watch cross-border financial transactions closely and consider their implications for the soundness of the banking sector. Macroprudential policy should be tightened when necessary.

1.4.3 Benchmark policy rates, selected countries in developing Asia

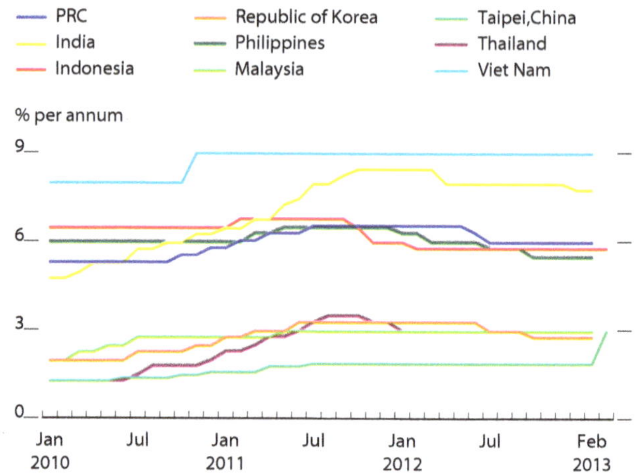

PRC = People's Republic of China.
Source: CEIC Data Company (accessed 13 March 2013).
Click here for figure data

Fiscal policy for future growth

With growth sputtering in 2012, some authorities engineered short-term fiscal boosts. This caused fiscal balance to worsen in general across the region in 2012 (Figure 1.4.4). However, further fiscal stimulus to prop up demand is, like expansionary monetary policy, unwarranted in the current environment. Many economies have sufficient fiscal latitude—as indicated by ratios of debt to GDP that are sustainable and trending down—but the authorities should not overestimate their fiscal strength. Favorable fiscal balances could quickly evaporate in a severe macroeconomic shock caused by an interest rate spike, liquidity squeeze, or growth slowdown (Ferrarini, Jha, and Ramayandi 2012). Rather, the region's current fiscal resources should be directed toward enhancing its potential for future growth that is inclusive.

Governments throughout the region should pay more attention to strengthening public infrastructure, which will improve their economies' capacity to grow more quickly and inclusively. Building human capital requires upgraded public physical infrastructure to improve connectivity, efficient spending on health care and education, and better-targeted social protection programs.

1.4.4 Fiscal balance of the central government

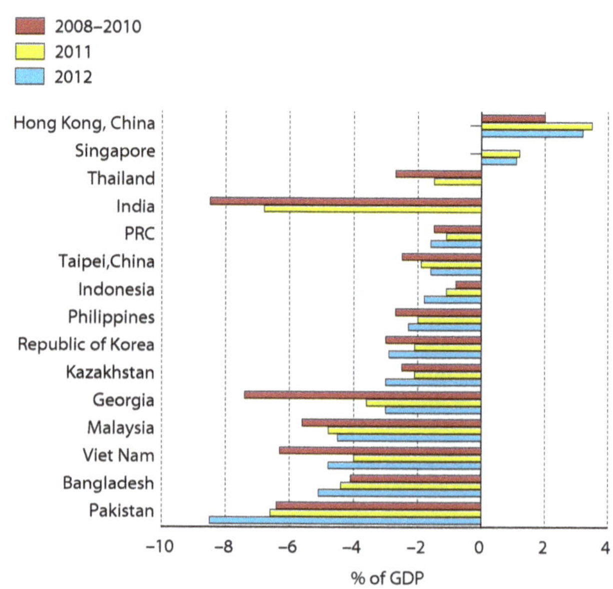

PRC = People's Republic of China.
Source: Asian Development Outlook database.
Click here for figure data

To ensure adequate financing for infrastructure priorities, governments need to allocate their budgets more efficiently, which will entail minimizing inefficient subsidies, especially those that encourage wasteful fuel consumption, and redirecting these funds to more productive public investments. In tandem, revenues must be mobilized more effectively to maintain a healthy fiscal balance and avert the buildup of public debt. As income tax typically contributes very little to government revenues in Asia, broadening the tax base is an urgent task for many countries in developing Asia, to effectively enlarge government's capacity to generate future revenues (Figure 1.4.5).

1.4.5 Personal income tax and central government revenues, latest year

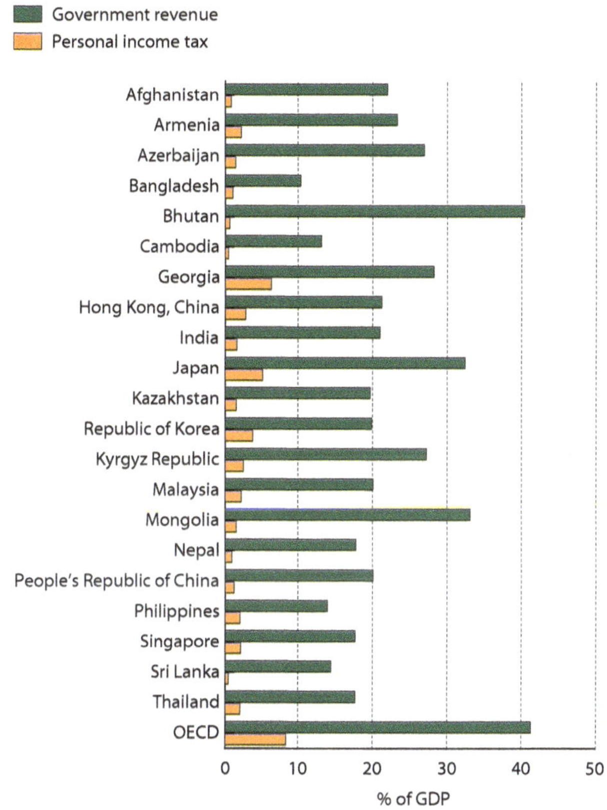

OECD = Organisation for Economic Co-operation and Development.

Notes: Data for developing Asian economies are between 2008 and 2011. Data for OECD refer to simple average in 2010.

Source: Asian Development Outlook database.

Click here for figure data

Risks to the outlook

Political risk has emerged as the main threat to the global and regional outlook. In 2012, the two risks that grabbed attention were a fiscal shock from the US and a financial shock from the euro area, either of which could have derailed global growth. These risks have receded. Yet political tensions in the US and the euro area remain, preventing the compromise needed to reach long-term solutions to both problems. Meanwhile, border disputes in Asia spilled over into the economic arena in 2012. The heated rhetoric has since cooled but could be reignited for political gain. Finally, geopolitical risks in oil-producing countries could shock prices for this critical commodity, spilling over into the region as inflation.

Unresolved fiscal drag in the US. Despite the fragility of the US economic recovery, lawmakers there have been unable to forge a compromise on important fiscal policy issues. Even the last minute deal to avert the "fiscal cliff"—a convergence on 1 January 2013 of the expiration of temporary tax reductions and the beginning of across-the-board spending cuts—provided only momentary respite. The deal had delayed the automatic spending cuts for 2 months to allow further negotiations, but no compromise was reached, leaving the so-called sequester to take effect from 1 March 2013. The Congressional Budget Office estimates that the combined effect of the tighter fiscal policy under current legislative mandates could reduce US GDP growth by 1.5 percentage points in 2013. The administration and Congress will also need to reach an agreement to raise the debt ceiling, which in January 2013 was temporarily suspended until 18 May 2013. Further political wrangling over the debt ceiling remains likely, reprising the brinksmanship in 2011 that pummeled global financial markets.

Austerity fatigue in the euro area. It seems that the heightened anxiety underlying the sudden swings in euro area financial markets since the crisis in Greece erupted has calmed somewhat. Market reaction was surprisingly muted when negotiations on the terms of the rescue package for Cypriot banks severely strained that country's relations with the European Commission, European Central Bank, and International Monetary Fund in March 2013. This confrontation underscores the political obstacles ahead to achieving a long-term solution to euro area weaknesses. A failure to consolidate the path for economic recovery in 2013 could send the euro area into another round of financial tensions as budget deficits in its member countries are likely to be again above target. For example, the fiscal consolidation plan for Greece, signed November 2012, left out many details on the precise mechanisms for bringing down Greece's ratio of debt to GDP on time. As austerity fatigue deepens, the debate intensifies over whether fiscal consolidation, and the consequent drag on growth throughout the euro area, is the right approach to getting beyond the crisis. The inconclusive election result in Italy—in part because of a protest vote against further fiscal tightening—highlights the difficult times ahead trying to build political consensus around reforms. As the currency zone struggles to gather growth momentum, the potential remains for a sharp financial shock emanating from Europe.

Border disputes in Asia. Asia's long history and the upheavals of the 20th century have left a number of national boundaries in dispute. Lingering contention over borders rarely obstructs cooperative relations within the region. However, when disputes heat up, the sharp political rhetoric can spill over into the economic arena. The dispute over the islands that the PRC calls the Diaoyu and Japan the Senkaku reached a fevered pitch in late 2012. Although the islands themselves are uninhabited, sovereignty over them confers rights to aquatic and undersea natural resources such as fishing grounds and natural gas reserves. The angry exchange of words escalated into a PRC boycott of Japanese goods, causing a sharp drop in trade and engulfing Japanese investment in a cloud of uncertainty. The region has similar flashpoints between the PRC and several ASEAN nations, the PRC and India, India and Pakistan, and the Republic of Korea and Japan, among others. The potential for nationalistic passions—as happened in the PRC and Japan in 2012—is a clear risk to the outlook.

Potential spikes in oil prices. The moderate inflation outlook is supported by the forecast decline in oil prices. Brent crude is expected to drop from an average price of $112 per barrel in 2012 to $110 in 2013 and $105 in 2014 (see Annex: Consolidation in advanced economies). But, as past experience demonstrates, geopolitical tensions involving major oil producers can demolish supply assumptions. Geopolitical risks stemming from the ongoing civil unrest in the Middle East and North Africa, even when not in a major oil producer (e.g., Syria and Egypt), has the potential to push up prices. Possible supply disruptions in Venezuela and Nigeria, and international sanctions imposed on Iran over its nuclear program, could also bid up international oil prices. In addition, oil price projections assume a slow recovery in major consuming countries tempering oil demand. Stronger-than-expected growth in these economies would put upward pressure on oil prices. If any of these risks materialized, an oil price spike would add to consumer price pressures and, depending on its magnitude, might even shake the region's growth momentum.

Asia's growing thirst for oil imports makes the region more vulnerable to shocks from geopolitical tensions with potential to affect the production of this key commodity. Asia's rising economic importance is giving the region a bigger presence in commodity markets generally. How is this change affecting commodity market price dynamics?

Developing Asia's rising demand for commodities

Commodity price cycles in the past decade have synchronized, taking in oil, metals, and many agricultural products (Figure 1.5.1). While supply shocks such as bad harvests account for commodity price spikes, they do not explain why such a broad range of prices have moved nearly in unison. This suggests that the commodity boom–bust cycle has a strong demand element. To what extent does demand from developing Asian economies—particularly larger economies like the PRC and India—affect global commodity price trends?

1.5.1 Price movements of selected commodities

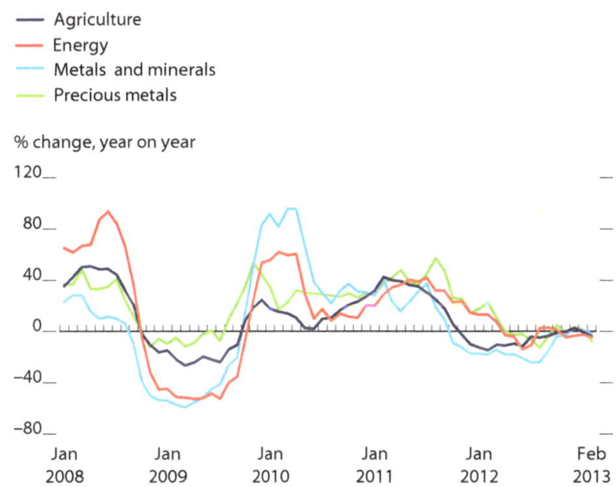

Source: World Bank. Commodity Price Data (Pink Sheet). http://www.worldbank.org (accessed 25 March 2013).

Click here for figure data

Asia's growing presence in commodity markets

Developing Asia became a major commodity-consuming region during the last decade (Table 1.5.1), turning the region into a net commodity importer. Its relative importance has increased even more since the 2008–2009 global financial crisis started, as the economies of the major industrial countries slowed significantly. Asian demand for some commodities has made many resource exporters heavily dependent on Asian consumers and subject to demand fluctuations in Asia. Rising vulnerability to shocks originating in Asian commodity consumers has become a serious concern, particularly for open economies endowed with rich natural resources both inside and outside of the region.

The PRC is Asia's largest commodity consumer by far. It even overtook the US in the consumption of major metals and agricultural commodities in the late 2000s, making it the world's largest consumer of many commodities. The PRC consumed in 2011 about 20% of nonrenewable energy resources, 23% of major agricultural crops, and 40% of base metals.

The PRC's share of consumption of agricultural products, such as oilseed soybeans, doubled over the past decade, driven by a change in diet to foods richer in oil. Yet, the PRC has historically been a major consumer of quite a few agricultural crops such as rice, maize, and cotton. Change has been more significant in nonagricultural commodities. The PRC's surging share of base metal consumption has been particularly noticeable, rising from 10% during the 1990s to over 40% today.

In tandem with its rapid economic growth, the PRC's energy needs have risen. Its use of primary energy has doubled since the 1990s, and it now accounts for nearly 20% of global consumption. The PRC's petroleum consumption—including gasoline, jet fuel, kerosene, distillate fuel oil, residual fuel oil, and liquefied petroleum gas—now occupies about 10% of world consumption, despite being less important in the PRC's energy

1.5.1 Consumption share of selected commodities, average of 2009–2012

	PRC	India	ASEAN-5[a]	Total Asia	US	Rest of the world
	Share of world consumption					
Agriculture						
Milled rice	30.7	20.1	14.6	65.4	0.9	33.7
Palm oil	12.4	15.1	24.3	51.7	2.2	46.1
Sugar	9.2	15.0	7.0	31.1	6.4	62.5
Cotton[b]	38.4	18.4	3.6	60.4	3.2	36.4
Energy[c]						
Total energy	19.4	5.7	3.8	28.8	18.2	52.9
Petroleum	10.6	3.7	5.2	19.6	21.9	58.6
Natural gas	3.2	1.9	4.0	9.1	21.5	69.4
Coal	44.9	8.8	1.8	55.5	13.4	31.1
Electricity	19.3	3.8	2.6	25.7	21.2	53.0
Renewable energy (biofuels)	2.5	0.3	1.6	4.4	48.2	47.4
Metals[c]						
Refined aluminum	40.7	3.9	2.9	47.5	10.4	42.2
Refined copper	39.3	2.6	3.6	45.5	9.0	45.5
Stainless steel	32.5	5.6	...	38.1	8.4	53.5

... = data not available, ASEAN = Association of Southeast Asian Nations, PRC = People's Republic of China, US = United States.

[a] ASEAN-5 are Indonesia, Malaysia, the Philippines, Singapore, and Thailand.

[b] Domestic consumption of cotton in ASEAN-5 excludes Singapore.

[c] Data for energy and metals are up to 2010/11 only.

Sources: ADB estimates using data from Haver Analytics; International Energy Agency. http://www.iea.org/stats/index.asp; World Bureau of Metal Statistics; World Bank. World Development Indicators database. http://databank.worldbank.org (accessed 11 February 2013).

mix than other forms of primary energy, particularly coal. The PRC has accounted for 45% of the world's coal usage on average during the past 4 years. Its use of natural gas and biofuels, on the other hand, remains limited.

Although the PRC has a greater global presence than India as a commodity consumer, India can transmit powerful shocks within Asia, all the more so because it relies on regional resource exporters to meet most of its needs. India's role as a commodity consumer is more significant for agriculture products than for metals or petroleum. One of the largest importers and consumers of edible oils, India consumes more palm oil than either the US or the PRC and relies on imports for over 25% of its annual requirement, as domestic production is meager. The country also consumes more sugar than the PRC or the US.

India's energy consumption is still only about a third of what the PRC or the US consumes. It relies largely on coal for primary energy and has accounted for about 9% of world coal consumption over the past 4 years. India's metal use is much smaller than the PRC's, but its share of world consumption generally exceeds the total for the ASEAN-5: Indonesia, Malaysia, the Philippines, Singapore, and Thailand.

The presence of ASEAN-5 as a commodity consumer is notable for only a few items, primarily rice, palm oil, and stainless steel. This country

1.5.2 Commodity intensity of copper and petroleum

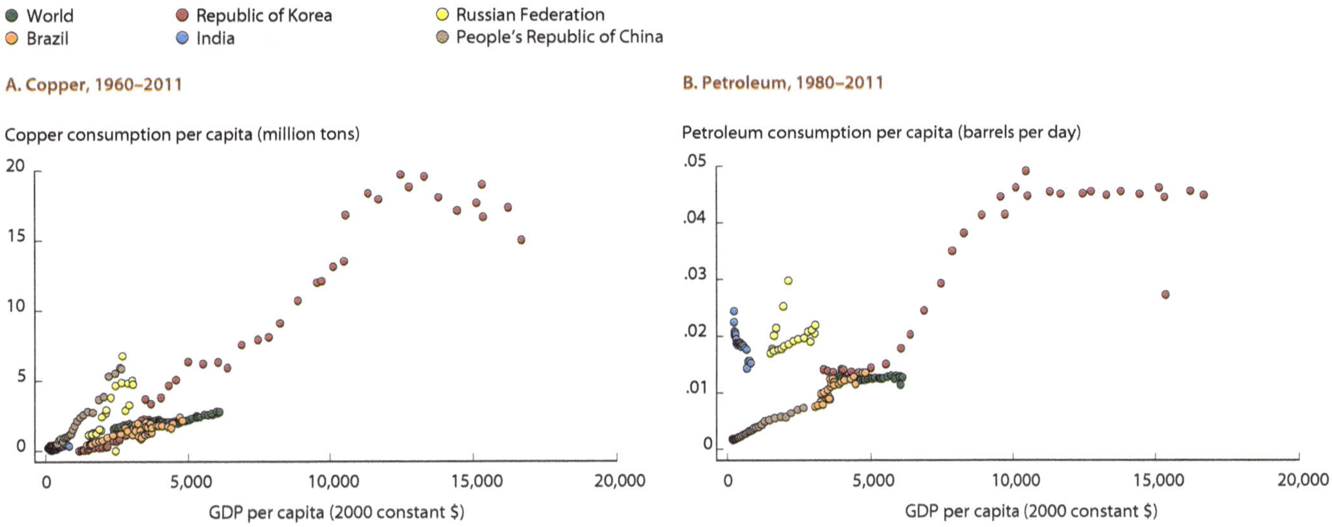

Sources: ADB estimates using data from International Energy Agency. http://www.iea.org/stats/index.asp; World Bureau of Metal Statistics; World Bank. World Development Indicators database. http://databank.worldbank.org (all accessed 11 February 2013).

Click here for figure data

grouping is a net commodity exporter and a major producer of palm oil, which over the past decade has relegated soybean oil, once the most popular vegetable oil, to second place. As palm is generally the cheapest vegetable oil, it is an important component in the developing world's higher intake of oils and fats.

The long-term trend of rising commodity consumption in the PRC is illustrated by demand notable for very high commodity intensity (Figure 1.5.2). The PRC's commodity intensity, measured as commodity consumption per capita, has soared over the last decade, rising far above the historical experience of other countries. Its energy consumption is high for its stage of economic development. The same is true for its copper consumption. The PRC consumed 5.5 tons of copper per capita in 2010, more than three times the world average in 1960 or eight times higher than what the Republic of Korea consumed in 1970, when its per capita income roughly equaled the PRC's today.

The picture is slightly different for petroleum. The average person in India used 2.43 liters of petroleum products daily in 2011, or five times the 0.48 liters recorded in the PRC in 1998, when its per capita income matched India's current per capita income of just above $800. India's high consumption may reflect the subsidies provided for some petroleum products, notably diesel and liquefied petroleum gas.

The PRC's unusually fast-growing commodity intensity likely reflects the rapid expansion of its tradable export sector and its massive fixed asset investment, particularly since 2000. Both are commodity intensive, making the PRC's economic cycles likely have strong bearing on aggregate import demand for commodities and hence their prices.

1.5.2 Production–consumption ratios of primary commodities, average of 2004–2012

	PRC	India	ASEAN-5[a]
Agriculture			
Milled rice	0.71	0.41	1.08
Oilseed soybean	0.27	1.00	0.19
Palm oil	...	0.00	3.88
Sugar	0.90	1.04	1.14
Cotton[b]	0.76	1.27	0.01
Energy[c]			
Petroleum	0.91	1.13	0.91
Natural gas	0.98	0.80	1.47
Coal	1.02	0.92	2.44
Metals[c]			
Refined aluminum	1.03	1.03	0.25
Refined copper	0.67	1.37	0.64
Stainless steel	1.33	1.82	...

... = data not available, ASEAN = Association of Southeast Asian Nations, PRC = People's Republic of China.

[a] ASEAN-5 are Indonesia, Malaysia, the Philippines, Singapore, and Thailand.

[b] Domestic consumption for cotton of ASEAN-5 excludes Singapore.

[c] Data for energy and metals are up to 2010/11 only.

Sources: ADB estimates using data from Haver Analytics; International Energy Agency. http://www.iea.org/stats/index.asp; World Bureau of Metal Statistics; World Bank. World Development Indicators database. http://databank.worldbank.org (accessed 11 February 2013).

Asia's consumption of a number of commodities significantly exceeds its own supply, forcing the region to rely on external suppliers. The production–consumption gap is particularly large in metals and edible oil, demand for which is growing rapidly to support industrial development and richer diets (Table 1.5.2). The ASEAN-5 countries help fill the production–consumption gap of the PRC and India for some agricultural products, but these countries are themselves net importers of metals and major energy products. Commodity prices are driven in the short-run mainly by the business cycle of the main consumers (not to disregard seasonality and unanticipated transitory changes in the supply–demand balance). Because developing Asia has become a heavyweight in commodity demand, the ups and downs of its demand make waves for commodity-exporting economies.

Asia's impact on commodity exporters

If a commodity exporter depends heavily on one commodity or export destination, it is especially vulnerable to demand fluctuations. The effects can be partly offset if the commodity exporter can influence prices. An index to measure the degree of dependency on commodity markets in the PRC, India, and the five ASEAN countries (Indonesia, Malaysia, the Philippines, Singapore, and Viet Nam) can be computed for each commodity and each importer by taking into account concentrations in a specific commodity and export destination, as well as the exporter's pricing power (Box 1.5.1).

1.5.1 Computing export dependency ratio

Commodity exporters' vulnerability to changeable Asian demand can be measured using the export dependency index. The index is a geometric mean of three components: how concentrated a country's exports are in one commodity, how dependent the country is on a specific national market, and the buying and selling countries' relative power to set the price.

$$Index_{i,j} = \sqrt[3]{\frac{EXP_{i,j}}{EXP_j} \times \frac{EXP_{i,j,k}}{EXP_{i,j}} \times avg\left[\frac{IMP_{i,k}}{IMP_i}, \left(1 - \frac{EXP_{i,j}}{EXP_i}\right)\right]}$$

where

$\frac{EXP_{i,j}}{EXP_j}$ = country *j*'s exports of commodity *i* as a share of its total exports;

$\frac{EXP_{i,j,k}}{EXP_{i,j}}$ = country *j*'s exports of commodity *i* to country *k* divided by its total export of that commodity; and

$avg\left[\frac{IMP_{i,k}}{IMP_i}, \left(1 - \frac{EXP_{i,j}}{EXP_i}\right)\right]$ = the average of 2 components:

$\frac{IMP_{i,k}}{IMP_i}$ is the share of country *k*'s imports of commodity *i* in the global market;

$\left(1 - \frac{EXP_{i,j}}{EXP_i}\right)$ is 1 minus country *j*'s export market share of commodity *i*.

The index is scaled from 0 (no dependence) to 1 (complete dependence). The higher the score, the more vulnerable an exporter is to disrupted trade. As the index shows, a commodity exporter is not vulnerable just because it ships a huge share of a particular commodity to one market. It is highly vulnerable only if its export performance depends heavily on that commodity and its pricing power is limited.

Reference

BBVA. 2013. How dependent is Latin America's Economy on China? *Economic Watch*, BBVA Research.

The export dependency index shows quite a few countries around the globe heavily reliant on PRC import demand because of its sheer size (Table 1.5.3). They include the PRC's neighbors, exporters further afield in Latin America and Africa, and industrial economies such as Australia. Within the region, Solomon Islands is the most PRC-dependent economy for its exports of wood. It shipped more than 90% of its total squared wood exports to PRC in 2011, a share that has tripled in the past decade. India and Kazakhstan depend heavily on the PRC for their exports of metal. Southeast Asia has several countries exporting several commodities that rely heavily on PRC demand: Indonesia for

1.5.3 Top commodity exporters to the People's Republic of China, average of 2009–2012

Rank	Exporter	Commodity (excluding petroleum)	Export dependency
Top 10 of all exporters			
1	Solomon Islands	Wood in the rough or roughly squared	0.69
2	Mauritania	Iron ore	0.51
3	Australia	Iron ore	0.47
4	Benin	Cotton	0.45
5	Zambia	Copper	0.44
6	Chile	Copper	0.42
7	Togo	Cotton	0.40
8	Brazil	Iron ore	0.36
9	South Africa	Iron ore	0.34
10	Gabon	Wood in the rough or roughly squared	0.32
Top 5 Asian exporters			
1	Solomon Islands	Wood in the rough or roughly squared	0.69
2	India	Iron ore	0.25
3	Indonesia	Coal	0.24
4	Kazakhstan	Copper	0.23
5	Kazakhstan	Iron ore	0.21

Source: ADB estimates using United Nations, Comtrade database. http://comtrade.un.org (accessed 11 February 2013).

coal, natural gas, and palm oil; Malaysia for natural gas and palm oil; Thailand for rice and rubber; Viet Nam for rubber, sugar, cement, coal, and wood; and Myanmar for rubber and maize.

Outside of Asia, many Latin American and African commodity exporters are subject to fluctuations in PRC demand for metals and agricultural products, notably Chile for copper and Brazil for soybeans. PRC imports of iron ore and soybeans comprise roughly 60% of global import demand for these commodities, including 60%–70% of Australian iron ore exports and US soybean exports. The dependency index is much higher for Australia than for the US, as iron ore occupies a concentrated 20% of all Australian exports and soybeans only 1% of US exports. Australia is therefore more vulnerable than the US to commodity shocks from the PRC.

India's import demand is much smaller but rising quickly (Table 1.5.4). So far, only a few countries rely heavily on Indian demand, mainly for minerals and metals such as coal, iron ore, and steel. However, a few commodities can make India a shock emitter to its neighbors, as India tends to rely on neighboring countries for its commodity needs. Nepal and Bhutan are particularly exposed to Indian demand through exports of steel, copper, and construction materials such as cement and aggregate. Their export dependency ratios have increased over the past decade.

By contrast, very few commodity exporters rely on demand from the five ASEAN countries (Table 1.5.4), and the largest of these economies, Indonesia, is itself a net commodity exporter. While the five ASEAN countries seem to emit lesser shocks than India or the PRC, there are exceptions. For example, like the PRC, the five ASEAN countries import substantial amounts of cotton, mainly from African economies that are thus subject to shocks originating in ASEAN.

How have resource exporters managed demand shocks so far?

A growth slowdown hitting commodity importers affects exporters through multiple channels but mainly through exports and terms of trade. Resource-dependent economies' terms of trade—i.e., the price of exportable goods relative to the price of importable goods—fluctuated substantially in response to shifting demand in importing economies and the gyrating commodity prices often associated with macroeconomic volatility.

Not all nations have felt the same impact from demand shifts. Mendoza (1995) estimates that roughly half of the variation in aggregate output in a sample of the Group of Seven industrialized nations and 23 developing economies is attributable to terms-of-trade shocks.

1.5.4 Top 10 commodity exporters to India and five ASEAN countries, average of 2009–2012

Rank	Exporter	Commodity (excluding petroleum)	Export dependency
India			
1	Bhutan	Steel	0.55
2	Nepal	Steel	0.42
3	Bhutan	Copper	0.33
4	Qatar	Natural gas	0.23
5	South Africa	Coal	0.23
6	Australia	Coal	0.22
7	Bahrain	Iron ore	0.21
8	Indonesia	Palm oil	0.21
9	Nepal	Tea	0.21
10	Nepal	Copper	0.20
ASEAN			
1	Burundi	Coffee	0.27
2	Benin	Cotton	0.20
3	Togo	Cotton	0.20
4	Namibia	Zinc	0.20
5	Burkina Faso	Cotton	0.17
6	Mali	Cotton	0.15
7	Indonesia	Natural gas	0.14
8	Uganda	Cotton	0.12
9	Zimbabwe	Cotton	0.12
10	Bahrain	Iron ore	0.12

ASEAN-5 = Association of Southeast Asian Nations.

ASEAN-5 here refers to Indonesia, Malaysia, the Philippines, Singapore, and Viet Nam.

Sources: ADB estimates using United Nations, Comtrade database. http://comtrade.un.org (accessed 11 February 2013).

Similarly, Kose (2002) finds that terms-of-trade shocks explain almost all of the variance in output in small, open developing economies. These findings suggest that small, open economies possessing limited policy levers and exposed to external shocks are more severely affected than are the industrial economies.

The economies heavily dependent on Asian demand for commodities have experienced severe volatility during the past 5 years. Export prices dropped sharply across commodities in 2008–2009 in response to the widening output gap both globally and in emerging Asia (the PRC; Hong Kong, China; India; Indonesia; the Republic of Korea; Malaysia; the Philippines; Singapore; Taipei,China; and Thailand). But the terms of trade did not always fall. Among exporters to Asia, the terms of trade for Solomon Islands and Chile were more severely affected than those for Bhutan and Australia (Figure 1.5.3). The different impacts reflected the differences in policy levers available to each country.

Fiscal policy is an important concern for commodity exporters, as procyclical fiscal policy in countries heavily dependent on commodities for government revenue amplifies commodity shocks. The exchange rate regime is also important. When prices are slow to adjust, a flexible exchange rate, as in Australia, helps stabilize the economy in response to terms-of-trade shocks with rapid adjustments to the nominal

1.5.3 Asia's output gap versus commodity export price and terms of trade

Sources: ADB estimates using data from United Nations, Comtrade database. http://comtrade.un.org; World Bank. World Development Indicators database. http://databank.worldbank.org (accessed 11 February 2013).

Click here for figure data

exchange rate (Broda 2004, Edwards and Levy Yeyati 2005, Aghion et al. 2009). Countries that peg their currencies—such as Bhutan to the Indian rupee and Solomon Islands to the US dollar—have less flexibility in their response to price shocks. Maintaining flexible fiscal and monetary policies can help counter commodity price fluctuations and mitigate their impacts.

An exercise quantifying the effects of a growth slowdown originating in Asia suggests that Latin America would, as a supplier of agricultural crops and metals, immediately feel a slowdown about a quarter as large. South America would also be exposed to volatile price overshooting until supply adjusted and commodity prices stabilized (Box 1.5.2).

These analyses confirm that developing Asia is increasingly important as a commodity consumer and emitter of demand shocks. Meanwhile, its energy needs have been rising in tandem with its rapid economic growth. As energy prices—for petroleum, in particular—are very sensitive to demand fluctuations and often overshoot, securing energy supply becomes critical to support developing Asia's growth and avoid creating excessive macroeconomic volatility. Developing Asia must rationalize its energy use and supply or else resign itself to scaling down its hopes for the coming Asian Century.

1.5.2 Asia and Latin America: the commodity market connection

How would a lower growth path for developing Asia affect natural resource exporters such as Latin America? The overall impact depends on the importance of several different effects.

Trade and commodity prices are the main channels for transmitting shocks. Regarding trade, lower growth in developing Asia reduces demand for exports from Latin America. This is partly offset by depreciation in the real effective exchange rates of Latin American currencies, which improves the competitiveness of the export sector in Latin America and of local firms competing with imports. In the commodities channel, reduced import demand from developing Asia lowers world commodity prices, generally worsening the terms of trade for Latin America. Commodity prices fluctuate in response to changes in demand, but to varying degrees. Oil prices are much more responsive to a change in global output—about three times more elastic than metal prices and nine times more than food prices.

A slowdown in developing Asia would have less impact on world metal and food prices than on oil prices, as the region's share of global metal and food imports is lower than of oil (box figure). In 2011, developing Asia's oil trade deficit was 3.6% of GDP, three times the 1.2% deficit in metals (the deficit in food is near zero). In addition, world metal and food prices tend to be much less sensitive to changes in demand.

The impact of lower commodity prices on growth in Latin America is determined by two main factors: the supply response of commodity sectors and a wealth effect stemming from worse terms of trade. The supply response, a decline in production, is larger for metals and food than for oil, because metal and food occupy a larger share of Latin America's production and exports. The negative wealth effect curbs consumption and tax revenues.

A global projection model is used to simulate the overall impact a slowdown in developing Asia would have on Latin America. The model includes three aggregate commodities (oil, metals, and food) and seven country blocks (the US, the euro area, Japan, emerging Asia, the PRC, Latin America, and the rest of the world). The emerging Asia block comprises Hong Kong, China; India; Indonesia; the Republic of Korea; Malaysia; the Philippines; Singapore; Taipei,China; and Thailand—with the PRC as a separate block, the Asia-10.

To gauge the net impact a persistent slowdown in the Asia-10 would have on Latin America, a model scenario is estimated assuming a series of negative shocks to aggregate supply that lower the Asian economies' potential output growth by half a percentage point throughout the simulation period. The drop in potential output growth has a more pronounced impact on the Asia-10's actual output growth—a 1.3% contraction in the first year—as economies adjust to their lower potential output, with negative spillovers to the other economies. Commodity prices drop sharply in the immediate aftermath of the shock, as short-term price elasticities are much greater than long term. Lower commodity prices stimulate a modest rebound in the Asia-10 economies that use those commodities. This initial overshooting of commodity prices leads to greater output volatility in the short run.

The output response of commodity-exporting Latin America is quite different. The initial sharp drop in commodity prices compounds the effect of lower output, reducing growth in the region by 0.3% in the first year. The subsequent recovery in commodity prices then supports Latin American growth, offsetting the negative effects from the trade channel caused by lower external demand from the Asia-10. Output in Latin America stabilizes at 0.1% below its initial level by the 5th year.

The simulation results indicate that the overshooting response of commodity prices drives the short-run output dynamics. The initial sharp decline in commodity prices partly offsets the decline in output in the Asia-10 but actuates through the trade channel the contraction in output in Latin America. A decline in Asia's growth sharply reduces growth in Latin America in the short run, largely through a steep drop in world commodity prices. The impact is mitigated over time, however, as lower commodity prices spur demand across regions and commodity prices stabilize slightly below the initial level.

Net trade balance for commodities

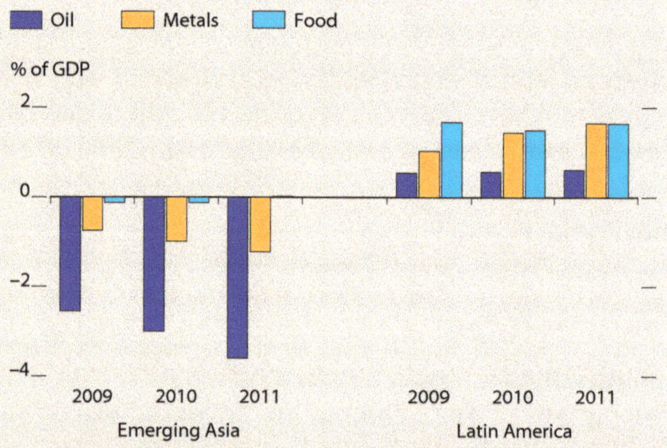

Sources: United Nations. Comtrade database. http://comtrade.un.org; World Bank. World Development Indicators database. http://databank.worldbank.org (accessed 11 February 2013).

Click here for figure data

Reference

Carabenciov, I., C. Freedman, R. Garcia-Saltos, O. Kamenik, D. Laxton, and P. Manchev. Forthcoming. GPM6—The Global Projection Model with 6 Regions. *International Monetary Fund Working Paper*.

References

Aghion, P., P. Bachetta, R. Ranciere, and K. Rogoff. 2009. Exchange Rate Volatility and Productivity Growth: The Role of Financial Development. *Journal of Monetary Economics.* 56(4). pp. 494–513.

ASEAN Secretariat. 1997. ASEAN Vision 2020. Kuala Lumpur (adopted in 1997).

______. 2012. ASEAN Economic Community Scorecard, http://www.asean.org/resources/publications/asean-publications/item/asean-economic-community-scorecard-3

Asian Development Bank. 2010. Macroeconomic Management Beyond the Crisis. *Asian Development Outlook 2010: Macroeconomic Management Beyond the Crisis.* Manila.

______. 2011. Asia in the Uneven Global Recovery. *Asian Development Outlook 2011: South–South Economic Links.* Manila.

______. 2012. Dimming Global Growth Prospects. *Asian Development Outlook 2012 Update: Services and Asia's Future Growth.* Manila.

Broda, C. 2004. Terms of Trade and Exchange Rate Regimes in Developing Countries. *Journal of International Economics.* 63. pp. 31–58.

Chen, Q., A. Filardo, D. He, and F. Zhu. 2012. International Spillovers of Central Bank Balance Sheet Policies. *BIS Papers* No. 66. Basel: Bank for International Settlements.

Cho, D. and C. Rhee. Forthcoming. *Effects of Quantitative Easing on Asia: Focus on Capital Inflows and Financial Market Variables.* Manila: Asian Development Bank.

Edwards, S. and E. Levy Yeyati. 2005. Flexible Exchange Rates as Shock Absorbers. *European Economic Review.* 49(8). pp. 2079–2105.

Ferrarini, B., S. Jha, and A. Ramayandi, eds. 2012. *Public Debt Sustainability in Developing Asia.* Manila: Asian Development Bank, and Oxfordshire: Routledge.

International Monetary Fund (IMF). 2012. *2012 Spillover Report.* Washington, DC: IMF.

Kose, M. A. 2002. Explaining Business Cycles in Small Open Economies 'How Much Do World Prices Matter?' *Journal of International Economics.* 56. pp. 299–327.

Ma, A. and A. Van Assche. 2012. Is East Asia's Economic Faith Chained to the West? *ADB Economics Working Paper Series* No. 239. Manila: ADB.

Mendoza, E. G. 1995. The Terms of Trade, the Real Exchange Rate, and Economic Fluctuations. *International Economic Review.* 36. pp. 101–137.

Morgan, P. 2011. Impact of US Quantitative Easing Policy on Emerging Asia. *Asian Development Bank Institute (ADBI) Working Paper* No. 321. Tokyo: ADBI.

Neely, C. J. 2010. The Large Scale Asset Purchase Had Large International Effects. *Working Paper Series* No. 2010–018D. Missouri: Federal Reserve Bank of St. Louis.

Ramayandi, A. Forthcoming. *Near-term Impact of Slower China and India on Asia: A GVAR Perspective.* A background paper for the *ADO 2013.* Manila: ADB.

Rashid, Z., F. Zhai, P. A. Petri, M. G. Plummer, and S. Y. Chia. 2009. Regional Market for Goods, Services, and Skilled Labor. *Realizing the ASEAN Economic Community: A Comprehensive Assessment.* Singapore: ISEAS Publishing.

Annex: Consolidation in advanced economies

The year is likely to be one of consolidation for the major industrial economies as a whole, but with diverging fortunes for the United States (US) and the euro area. Enthusiasm following strong gross domestic product (GDP) growth in the third quarter of 2012 (Q3 2012) in the US and the euro area was tempered somewhat by a weak fourth quarter. Japan slipped back into recession after a promising start to the year. As 2013 opened, economic activity in these economies remained weak. Continued fiscal tightening in the US and the euro area will act as a drag on growth there, while spending plans in Japan should help its economy back to modest growth. Collectively, the major industrial economies are expected to manage GDP growth of only 1.0% in 2013, slightly off the pace of the previous 2 years, with an uptick to 1.9% in 2014.

Moderate inflation of less than 2% is expected to prevail in 2013–2014, providing scope for continued monetary easing. The benign inflation environment is supported by slight declines in food and fuel prices as boosted supplies more than offset the rise in demand expected from increased economic activity. Prices are seen to pick up moderately in 2014 as production rises closer to its potential (Table A1.1).

A1.1 Baseline assumptions on the international economy

	2011	2012	2013	2014
	Actual		*ADO 2013*	*ADO 2013*
		Estimate	*projection*	*projection*
GDP growth (%)				
Major industrial economies[a]	1.2	1.2	1.0	1.9
United States	1.8	2.2	2.0	2.6
Euro area	1.4	−0.6	−0.3	1.2
Japan	−0.6	2.0	1.2	1.4
World trade (% change)				
Merchandise exports	5.0	2.5	4.0	5.0
Prices and inflation				
Brent crude spot prices (average, $ per barrel)	111.0	112.0	110.0	105.0
Energy price index (% change)	30.1	−0.4	−0.2	−3.0
Food index (% change)	23.9	0.7	−2.0	−0.5
Consumer price index inflation (major industrial economies' average, %)	2.4	1.8	1.2	1.7
Interest rates				
United States Federal funds rate (average, %)	0.1	0.1	0.1	0.1
European Union refinancing rate (average, %)	1.2	1.0	0.9	0.9
Japan interest rate (average, %)	0.1	0.1	0.1	0.1
$ Libor[b] (%)	0.2	0.3	0.2	0.2

[a] Average growth rates are weighted by gross national income, Atlas method.

[b] Average interbank quotations on 1-month loans.

Sources: US Department of Commerce, Bureau of Economic Analysis, http://www.bea.gov; Eurostat, http://epp.eurostat.ec.europa.eu; Economic and Social Research Institute of Japan, http://www.esri.cao.go.jp; World Trade Organization, http://www.wto.org; Consensus Forecasts; Bloomberg; International Monetary Fund, Primary Commodity Prices, http://www.imf.org; World Bank, Global Commodity Markets, http://www.worldbank.org; ADB estimates.

Recent developments in major industrial economies

United States

GDP growth dropped to just 0.1% at a seasonally adjusted annualized rate in Q4 2012, after showing an increase of 3.1% in the third quarter. The slowdown in the last quarter mainly reflected falls in inventory investment and federal government spending on defense. The declining inventory investment suggests that businesses are still reluctant to hold stocks and expand production in an uncertain environment. On the positive side, private consumer spending remained strong throughout 2012, and fixed investment picked up in the end. Although export growth slowed in 2012 from the previous year, it outpaced import growth. Despite the slowdown in the final quarter, GDP increased by 2.2% for the year, higher than the 1.8% increase in 2011 (Figure A1.1).

Although the consumer confidence index dropped in the last 2 months of 2012 and in January 2013, it recovered somewhat in February 2013 as fiscal uncertainty was partly resolved and the shock from the expiration of payroll tax cuts waned (Figure A1.2). While the February reading of 67.3 points is well below the 2007 average (100 on the index), let alone the 2007 highs almost bumping 110, it recovered from the nadir below 25 points in February 2009 and has averaged about 65 in 2012. Retail sales and industrial production rose gradually from the trough in May 2009. Purchasing managers' index values for the first 2 months of 2013, compiled by the Institute for Supply Management, are 53.1 for January and 54.2 for February, both above 50 and therefore indicating that the manufacturing economy is expanding.

Some positive signs in housing and labor markets suggest the recovery in the US is strengthening. House prices, measured by the housing affordability index median price, declined in Q3 2012 but rose slightly in the last 2 months of the year. Looking at the 3-month moving average to smooth out monthly volatility shows prices trending upward in 2012. In terms of quantities, the number of housing units under construction and of housing starts rose in 2012. For houses under construction, in fact, the 3-month moving average of monthly growth rates measured year on year finally returned to positive territory in January 2012 (Figure A1.3). In addition, the number of housing units authorized, which gives an indication of things to come, increased in 2012. In February 2013, the year-on-year 3-month moving average of the growth rate was 31.9%.

Unemployment, which tends to lag recovery, fell below 8% in September 2012 for the first time since early 2009. Declines have been slow to materialize, with February 2013 unemployment still at 7.7% and well above its long-run

A1.1 Demand-side contributions to growth, United States

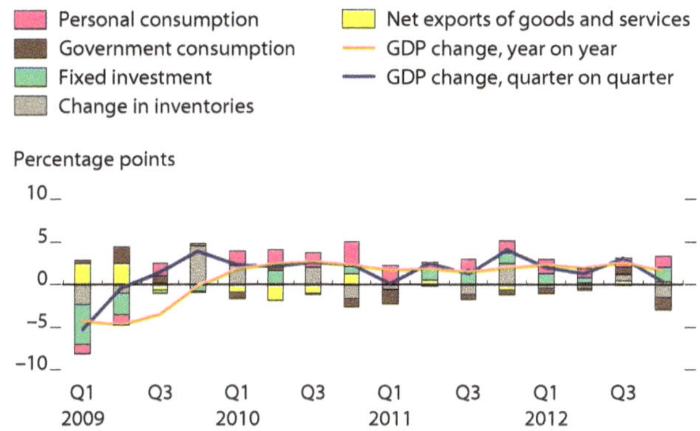

Source: US Department of Commerce. Bureau of Economic Analysis. http://www.bea.gov (accessed 7 March 2013).

Click here for figure data

A1.2 Business activities and consumer confidence indicators, United States

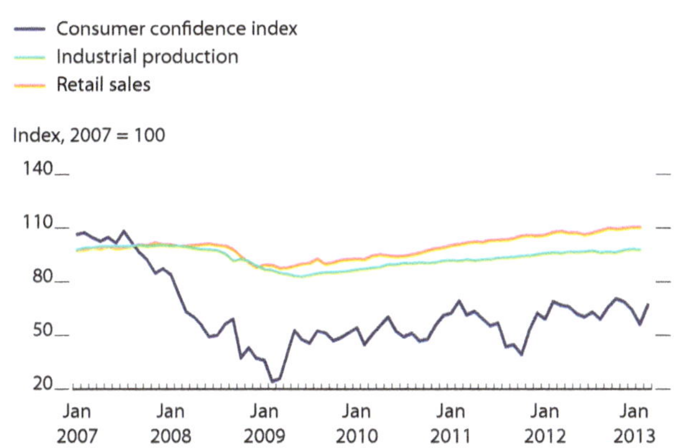

Source: CEIC Data Company (accessed 7 March 2013).

Click here for figure data

A1.3 Changes in number of housing units (seasonally adjusted), United States

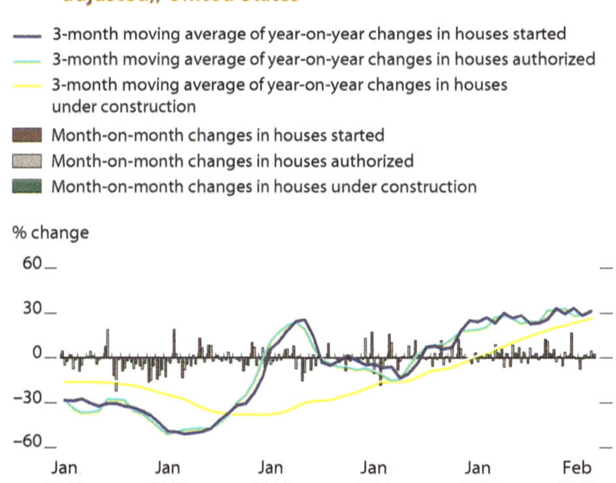

Source: CEIC Data Company (accessed 21 March 2013).

Click here for figure data

average of 6%, which is causing worries that no new jobs are being added (Figure A1.4). Looking at a broader measure of underutilized workers—one that sums the number of unemployed with those working part time for economic reasons and those who want work but have quit searching—tells a similar story. While the broader measure has dropped from its peak of just over 17% in 2009–2010, the February 2013 rate of 14.3% was still higher than before the global economic downturn. However, the number of people filing claims for unemployment benefits fell to a 4-week seasonally adjusted average of 339,750 in the week ending 16 March 2013, the lowest since March 2008, suggesting further strengthening in the labor market is likely in the coming months.

Inflation, both overall and core, remains under control (Figure A1.5). Since the US Federal Reserve plans to link interest rate changes to the state of the labor market and the inflation rate, an accommodative monetary policy is likely to continue. Credit from commercial banks grew steadily in 2012. The 3-month moving average of credit from commercial banks rose by 5.4% in January 2013 over a year earlier. Higher credit growth denotes increased lending by commercial banks.

To avoid the fiscal cliff on 1 January 2013, US authorities reached agreement on some revenue enhancements. However, the deal only delayed the implementation of automatic spending cuts by 2 months. Because lawmakers were unable to reach consensus on a compromise deficit-reduction package, across-the-board spending cuts through so-called sequestration took effect on 1 March 2013. The temporary reduction in employee Social Security contributions, from 6.2% of earnings to 4.1%, was allowed to expire on 1 January 2013 as scheduled. With continued uncertainty in the economy, the mix of tax increases and spending cuts will likely slow output and suppress consumer demand, and hence growth, in the short term. The Congressional Budget Office estimated in February 2013 that the combined impact of the fiscal policy changes would be a 1.5 percentage point reduction in US growth in 2013 (Box A1.1).

The cut in public demand will need to be balanced by continued private sector strength to avoid a slip back into recession. The positive signs in investment, consumption, housing, employment, and credit point in the direction of a gradually strengthening economy. The US should grow by 2.0% in 2013, slightly slower than in 2012. Assuming that the fiscal drag phases out but that monetary policy continues to be supportive, output in the US is expected to pick up gradually and the economy to expand by 2.6% in 2014.

A1.4 Unemployment rate, United States

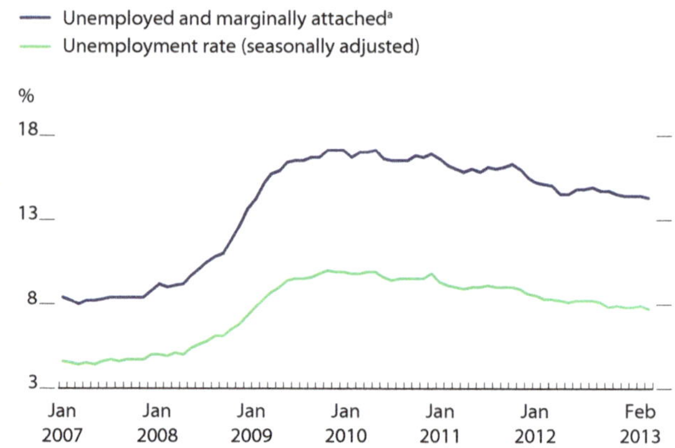

[a] As share of labor force plus people marginally attached to the labor force.

Source: US Department of Labor. Bureau of Labor Statistics. http://www.bls.gov/ (accessed 19 March 2013).

Click here for figure data

A1.5 Inflation, United States

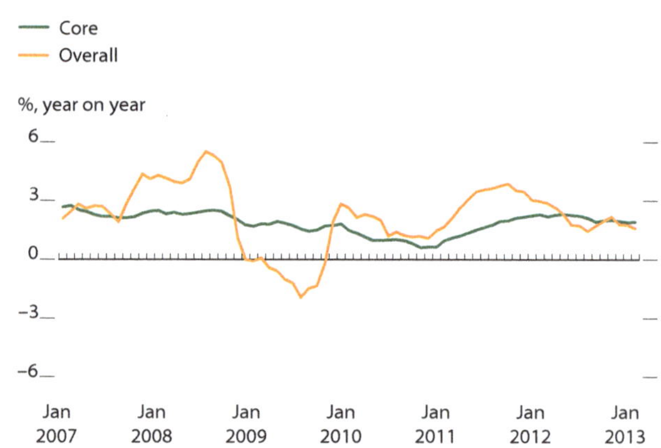

Source: CEIC Data Company (accessed 8 March 2013).

Click here for figure data

Euro area

The euro area's output contracted by an estimated 0.6% in 2012. The last quarter of 2012 saw a decline in Germany's GDP, but there are signs that German industrial production and economic growth have since improved. In any case, the strength of the German economy is offset by weakness

A1.1 Fiscal tightening in the United States

In August 2011, the United States Congress passed the Budget Control Act as part of the compromise to raise the US debt ceiling and avoid a technical default. The act called on lawmakers to approve a plan to reduce the fiscal deficit by $1.2 trillion over 10 years or face automatic across-the-board cuts to certain categories of defense and nondefense spending: budget sequestration. The idea was that the untargeted nature of sequestration would be so unpalatable that leaders of both parties would be motivated to find a compromise deal to reach the deficit goal.

However, the frantic deal to avoid the so-called fiscal cliff—expenditure reductions and tax increases that were set to take effect on 1 January 2013—only delayed sequestration by 2 months. As no deal was reached on 1 March 2013, and no further extensions were approved, affected agencies have begun to implement the cuts. Accordingly, after accounting for interest savings from the spending cuts, the remaining amount of $984 billion would have to be cut over 9 years from 2013 to 2021. This amounts to about $109 billion per year. In each category, the cuts affect discretionary and mandatory spending.

The Congressional Budget Office estimates the automatic spending cuts will total $85.4 billion in 2013—split evenly between defense and other spending. This is equivalent to a 7.8% reduction in defense spending and a 4.6% cut to other programs. With regard to the $42.7 billion in cuts to nondefense spending, the mandatory cuts include $11.35 billion to Medicare payments and $5.52 billion to other programs. Key mandatory programs such as Social Security, Medicaid, the Children's Health Insurance Program, the Earned Income Tax Credit, and veterans' compensation are exempt from sequestration. Most of the remaining $25.8 billion in spending cuts will be to discretionary programs on health, education, research, security, and housing assistance.

Taken together, the budget sequester, increase in payroll taxes, and increased tax rate on high earners present considerable tightening of fiscal policy in the US. But the shock to the macroeconomy has been muted as financial markets have largely taken the changes in stride. This is partly because the lagged effects of fiscal tightening will be felt only over time. In particular, consumers tend to respond to lower income by first drawing down their savings then adjusting their spending habits. Meanwhile, across-the-board spending reductions will be phased in over the course of the year as public agencies begin to cut expenses and reduce their payrolls. So, while the overall impact should be a drag on growth—by up to 1.5 percentage points in 2013 according to the Congressional Budget Office—it will not deliver an immediate shock to the US economy.

in the other large euro area economies, notably France and Italy. The euro area recession is seen extending into the first half of 2013 before slow recovery begins in the second half of the year, with the year as a whole showing contraction by 0.3%. In 2014, the region is expected to continue recovering slowly. Assuming that financial tensions do not intensify further, improvements in external demand during the year could gradually lift the euro area's exports to support growth. Monetary policy will likely remain accommodative as inflation remains in check, in line with the declining trend in the international commodity prices. GDP growth is projected to pick up to 1.2% in 2014.

In Q4 2012, the euro area's output shrank by 0.6% quarter on quarter, following a 0.1% decline in the third quarter, which was the weakest euro area performance since the slump in Q1 2009. At a seasonally adjusted annualized rate, GDP contracted by 2.3% in the fourth quarter (Figure A1.6). Economic contraction during Q4 2012 accelerated to 0.9% in Italy and 0.8% in Spain. In Germany, fourth-quarter GDP dropped by 0.6% and in France by 0.3%. Most other countries in the euro area saw their economies shrink.

The unemployment rate rose to 11.9% in January 2013. Youth unemployment reached 24.2% in the euro area. This aggregate masks considerable disparity among member states,

A1.6 Demand-side contributions to growth, euro area

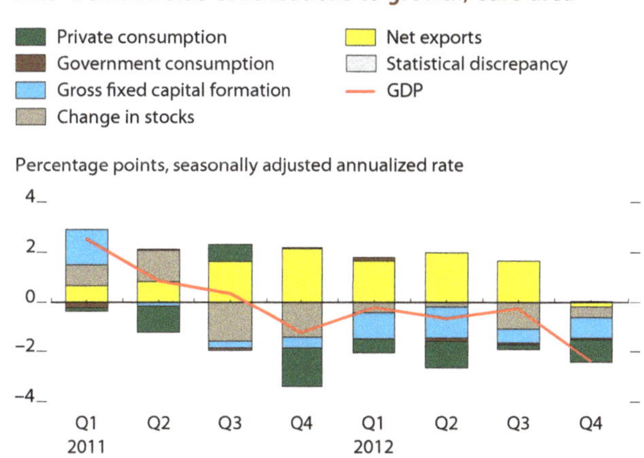

Source: Eurostat. http://epp.eurostat.ec.europa.eu (accessed 8 March 2013).

Click here for figure data

with youth unemployment highest in Spain at 55.5% and in Italy at 38.7%, and lowest in Austria, Germany, and the Netherlands at 8%–10% (Figure A1.7).

Throughout 2012, net exports were the major contributor to GDP growth. Euro area trade in goods with the rest of the world recorded a sizeable surplus, as exports to most of the region's major trading partners expanded while demand for imports from these countries was either anemic or shrinking (Figure A1.8). The euro area current account, reflecting also services, incomes, and transfers, recorded a surplus of 1.2% of GDP in 2012, up from 0.1% in 2011.

Fixed capital formation subtracted 0.6–1.2 percentage points from GDP growth in each quarter of 2012. This reversal comes after almost 2 years of persistently positive investment growth from Q2 2010 to Q4 2011. Throughout 2012, changes in inventories continued to weigh down on GDP growth. Industrial production contracted throughout 2012, at a year-on-year monthly rate of 1.6%–3.8%. The decline continued at 2.1% in January 2013. Based on the latest purchasing managers' index, manufacturing production in Germany fell in March after growing for 2 consecutive months, while manufacturing remained unchanged in France. Ireland and Spain recorded positive growth in their manufacturing production in February 2013, month on month, benefiting from rising export orders. Rates of contraction accelerated in Italy and the Netherlands (Figure A1.9).

Private consumption imposed a substantial drag on GDP growth, constrained by high unemployment and low consumer confidence. Retail trade shrank by 1.7% in 2012, falling by 0.8% from November to December 2012, but slightly picked up in January 2013.

Widespread austerity and weakening economies have undermined retailers' ability to increase prices. Consequently, price pressures remain subdued. Having peaked at 3.0% in September 2011, consumer price inflation fell from 2.7% in January 2012 to 2.2% in November and December, decelerating further to 1.8% in February 2013. This reflects a significant slowdown of oil price inflation in Q4 2012, from 8.0% in October 2012 to 5.2% in December, and further to 3.9% in February 2013.

The European Central Bank has been maintaining the interest rate on its main refinancing operations at 0.75%. However, monetary transmission and banks' onlending to firms remain impaired, as banks in several countries face capital constraints combined with the need to further adjust their balance sheets.

Looking ahead, the March 2013 manufacturing purchasing managers' index reading below 50 signals the continuing deterioration in euro area business conditions. The index improved to an 11-month high in January but relapsed in February and March. A similar trend was visible in the services index (Figure A1.10).

A1.7 Unemployment rates, euro area

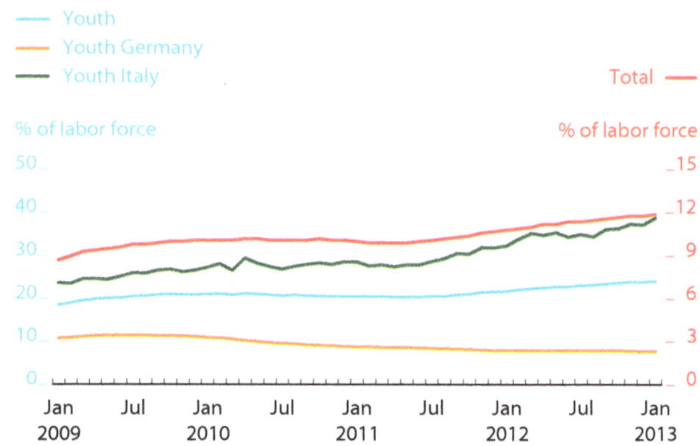

Source: Eurostat. http://epp.eurostat.ec.europa.eu (accessed 8 March 2013).

Click here for figure data

A1.8 Trade in goods, euro area

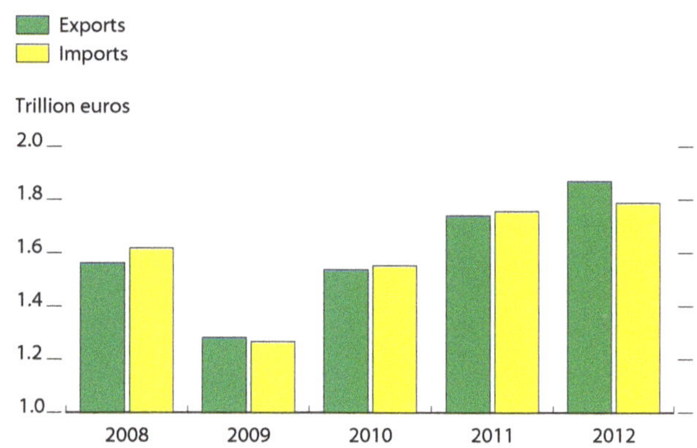

Note: Extra euro area trade.

Source: Eurostat. http://epp.eurostat.ec.europa.eu (accessed 24 March 2013).

Click here for figure data

A1.9 Manufacturing purchasing managers' indexes, euro area

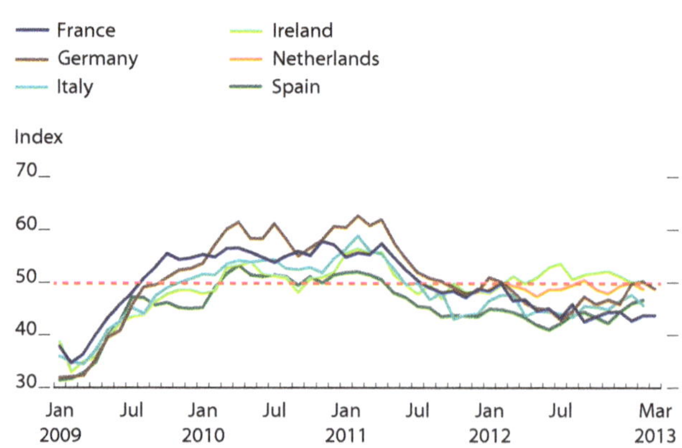

Note: A reading <50 signals deterioration in manufacturing activity; >50 means improvement.

Source: Bloomberg (accessed 24 March 2013).

Click here for figure data

Germany is showing some signs of weakness, notably the recent contraction in the purchasing managers' index as new export orders fell again, dampening expectations of Germany's economy returning to growth in Q1 2013. In any case, Germany's capacity to spur euro area manufacturing is countered by French slippage, Italy and Spain mired in deep recession, and continuing weaknesses and debt overhangs in some smaller euro area economies.

France, the euro area's second-largest economy, has seen its competitiveness slip quickly and, with it, industrial activity and exports of manufactured goods and services alike (Figure A1.11). The decline of the French economy has caused government budgets to fall short of expectations. The EU Fiscal Compact requires that fiscal deficits be less than 3% of GDP by the end of 2013, and compliance leaves the Government of France with few options other than to adopt a tighter fiscal stance in 2013, though this will weigh down domestic demand and labor markets. There have been signs, however, that euro area policy makers are willing to press for less austerity and more leniency regarding Fiscal Compact compliance, which is likely to heat up political debates in the months ahead.

Italy, the euro area's third-largest economy, is in its seventh consecutive quarter of recession, facing its deepest economic and political crisis in postwar history. Contractionary fiscal policy may have appeased international financial markets, but Italy certainly paid the price of exacerbating the economic downturn and with it the burden of the country's huge stock of public debt. Private sector lending and spending remain subdued and unemployment rampant. Italy's deep lack of competitiveness requires overdue reforms to the country's bureaucracy, judicial system, tax system, and public sector. The implementation of difficult reform is further delayed by the outcome of Italian elections in February 2013, which gave no single party or coalition control over both chambers of parliament. The governability of the country has not been assured, making new elections in the latter half of 2013 likely. Italy's economic and political crises sharpen uncertainty surrounding the euro area outlook for 2013.

Several of the euro area's peripheral economies remain ridden by crisis. Greece's economy continues to struggle, and its public finances have yet to prove sustainable, despite repeated international rescue efforts led by the European Commission, European Central Bank, and International Monetary Fund. After a long debate, Cyprus became in mid-March the latest country to be offered a bailout by the International Monetary Fund and European authorities. The bailout package is set at €10 billion, with losses imposed on large deposits in Cypriot banks. The country's second-largest financial institution will be closed and its deposits over €100,000 will be placed in an asset-managing institution.

A1.10 Purchasing managers' indexes, euro area

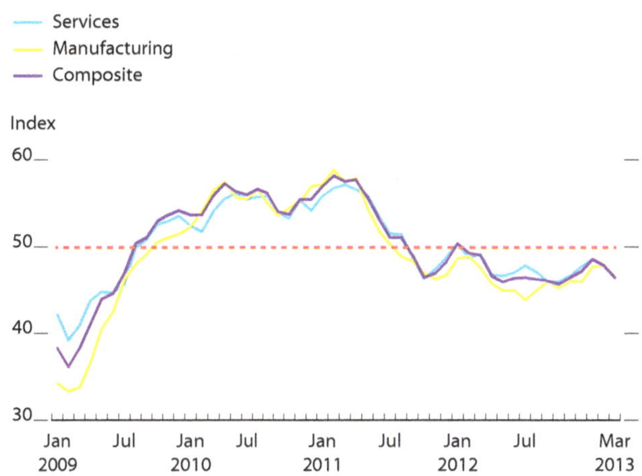

Note: A reading <50 signals deterioration in business conditions; >50 means improvement.

Source: Bloomberg (accessed 24 March 2013).

Click here for figure data

A1.11 Unit labor costs and external trade balances

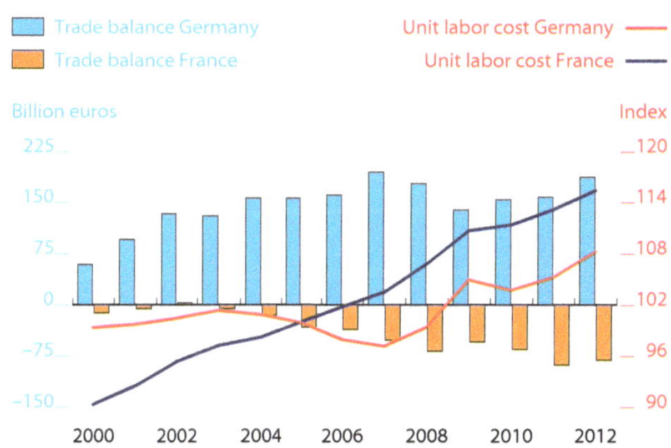

Source: Eurostat. http://epp.eurostat.ec.europa.eu (accessed 24 March 2013).

Click here for figure data

A1.12 Ten-year government bonds, selected euro area countries

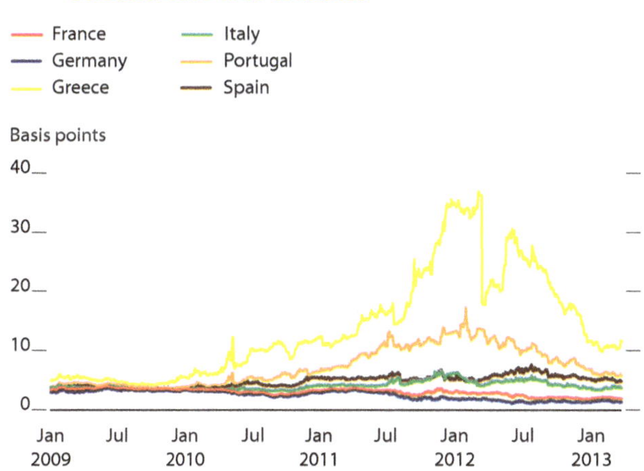

Source: Bloomberg (accessed 24 March 2013).

Click here for figure data

The bailout leaves the island's economy with a large debt overhang, and the sustainability of its public finances remains in question.

Perceptions about an imminent euro area shake up have subsided since July 2012, when the European Central Bank announced its bond-buying program in defense of the euro. As a result, bond yields against German government bonds declined considerably (Figure A1.12). Beyond market perceptions, deep concerns about the viability of the euro area remain, as austerity measures are sharpening unemployment, social unease, and economic contraction. The euro area's salvation continues to rest in the determination of the European Central Bank to uphold its firewall against speculative attacks until deep structural and institutional reforms have addressed the most fundamental euro area flaws. It remains unclear whether European and national politics will stand up to this important test.

Japan

While Japan grew at 2.0% in 2012 as a whole, driven by strong first quarter growth, the economy experienced a technical recession, with GDP contracting in Q2 and Q3 2012. However, with solid growth in private consumption, GDP growth edged up into a positive territory in the final quarter (Figure A1.13). Japan's trade deficit nearly tripled to a record ¥6.9 trillion ($78.3 billion or 1.2% of GDP) for 2012 as a whole. A strong yen, territorial tensions with the People's Republic of China (PRC), Europe's debt crisis, and surging energy imports were among the factors that contributed to this deterioration. Given general weakness in domestic demand, deflation persisted in 2012 without showing any sign of letting up (Figure A1.14).

Nonetheless, the depressed mood in Japan before the Lower House election last December seems to have receded substantially, reflecting the success of the Shinzo Abe administration in lifting sentiment. The Business Survey Index about the economic outlook, particularly for large firms, improved noticeably. The new administration has instituted a set of policies referred to as Abenomics to spur growth. The strategy includes aggressive monetary policy, flexible short-term fiscal policy with medium-term consolidation, and institutional and regulatory measures to strengthen the competitiveness.

To battle stubborn deflation, the Bank of Japan has adopted an inflation target of 2% and announced on 22 January that it will begin open-ended asset purchases in 2014, while leaving the size of its current asset purchase program unchanged for 2013. In anticipation of further easing of monetary policy, financial markets reacted strongly, and the currency started a sharp depreciation. Since September, the yen fell from ¥78.1 per US dollar to about ¥95, a depreciation of nearly 20% in only 7 months (Figure A1.15). During the same period, the Nikkei 225 index has soared by 40%, reaching a 4-year high exceeding 12,000 in March.

A1.13 Demand-side contributions to growth, Japan

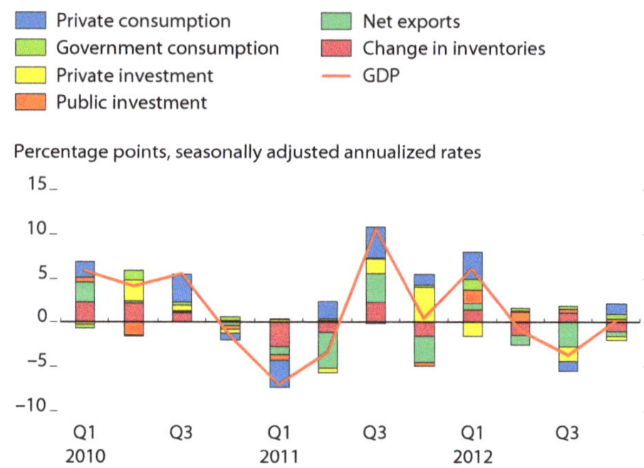

Source: Economics and Social Research Institute, Cabinet Office, Government of Japan. http://www.esri.cao.go.jp/en (accessed 12 March 2013).

Click here for figure data

A1.14 Inflation, Japan

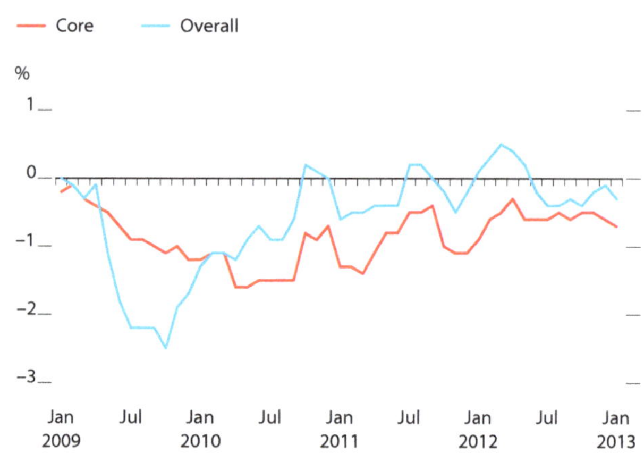

Note: Core inflation excludes food and energy.

Source: CEIC Data Company (accessed 12 March 2013).

Click here for figure data

A1.15 Exchange rate, Japan

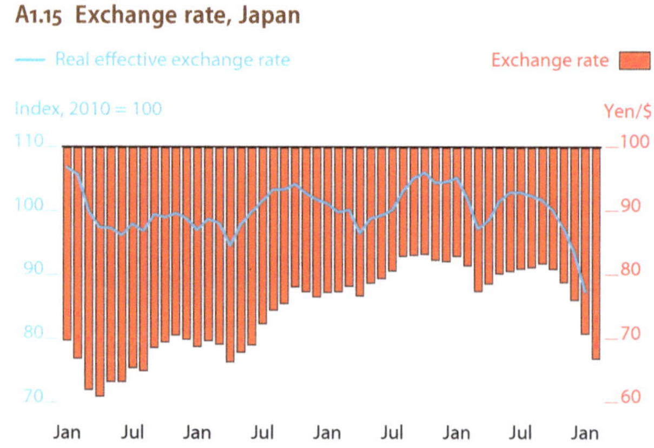

Source: CEIC Data Company (accessed 12 March 2013).

Click here for figure data

The new Japanese administration announced an economic stimulus package amounting to over ¥23 trillion, or 4.8% of GDP—one of the largest ever packages of its kind. Yet the impact of the package is uncertain as more than half of it consists of, first, about ¥10 trillion in noncash measures such as easing the credit environment for farmers and small and medium-sized enterprises and, second, about ¥3 trillion to cover the state pension deficit. The surplus carried over from the previous budget because of difficulty in spending appropriations will cover most of the new stimulus package, only 34% of which relies on new bond issuance.

Recent hard data indicators are starting to support a positive outlook. After declining in November last year, manufacturing resumed its upward trend in December and January. Auto sales continued to recover from the September slump, which was driven by the expiration of the eco-car subsidy program (Figure A1.16). Yet exports and investments remain sluggish. Machinery orders, a leading indicator for private investment, continued to recover, though still at a much lower level than recorded before the global financial crisis. Trade figures in February continue to show weak exports and strong imports tipping the balance of trade in goods into deficit for the eighth straight month—the longest run of such deficits since 1980.

A1.16 Manufacturing industrial production index, car sales, and goods exports, Japan

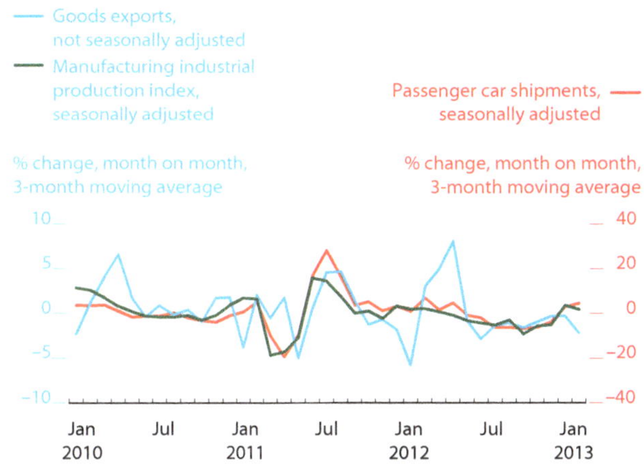

Sources: CEIC Data Company; Ministry of Economy, Trade and Industry. http://www.meti.go.jp/english/ (accessed 20 March 2013).
Click here for figure data

All in all, expansionary policies, yen depreciation, and consumers' advance purchases in anticipation of an increase in the consumption tax from 5% to 8% scheduled for April 2014 should lift Japan's domestic demand. GDP growth is forecast to reach 1.2% in 2013 and 1.4% in 2014. This growth is expected to be buoyed by resilient private consumption accompanying public spending, with the sizable supplementary budget adding to growth. The contribution of external demand is problematic. Yen depreciation should help reverse export weakness in the coming months. However, sluggish bilateral trade between Japan and the PRC continued through the first two months of 2013, even as tensions between the two sides have calmed down. The main risk to this outlook is insufficient labor supply to reconstruct areas hit by the 2011 tsunami, which has delayed reconstruction and hence held down public investment. Consumer price index inflation is forecast to pick up gradually this year and surpass 2% in 2014 because of the consumption tax increase planned in April 2014.

International trade

In light of continued weakness in global demand, global merchandise trade expanded at a moderate 2.5% in 2012 (Figure A1.17). Softer-than-expected growth in the PRC and other emerging markets helped restrain the pace of expansion. Given a modest outlook for growth in the advanced industrialized economies, the expansion of merchandise exports will likely pick up somewhat to 4.0% in 2013, remaining well below its 10-year average growth rate of 10.8%. As global economic activity firms, trade is expected to accelerate to 5.0% in 2014.

A1.17 Growth in merchandise world trade

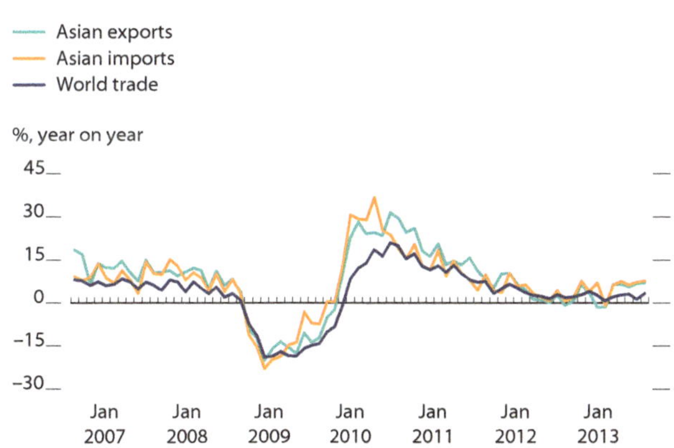

Source: CPB Netherlands Bureau for Economic Policy Analysis. CPB World Trade Monitor. http://www.cpb.nl/en/world-trade-monitor (accessed 25 March 2013).
Click here for figure data

Commodity prices

Average commodity prices in 2012 were similar to those of the previous year. Nonetheless, developments in the global economic and political arena, as well as natural disturbances, created wide fluctuations in prices. Improved conditions for oil supply in the face of subdued growth in demand are keeping oil prices in check, though continuing geopolitical tensions hold the potential to disturb the balance. Food prices remain stable as adequate supplies calm the markets, but the risk of price spikes persists amid low food stocks.

Recent oil price movements

International benchmark Brent crude averaged $112 per barrel in 2012, just a dollar higher than the previous year's average. Crude prices edged higher as the year drew to a close because of higher seasonal demand in December and persistent geopolitical tensions. Ending 2012 at $113 per barrel, oil prices continued to strengthen in the first 2 months of 2013 to reach levels close to what they reached the year before. Brent crude spot prices hit $120.50 in mid-February, for an increase of 6% in less than 2 months from the year-end figure and just $7.50 below the February 2012 peak of $128 (Figure A1.18).

The run-up in oil prices was propelled by the continued reduction in oil production by Saudi Arabia, early optimism about the economic prospects of the PRC, geopolitical tensions, and strong financial market activity. Saudi Arabia reduced production from an average of 9.8 million barrels per day in September to 9.1 million in January 2013, largely on account of lower seasonal demand in its domestic market. On the other hand, positive economic news improved the outlook for the PRC as its GDP growth climbed to 7.9% in Q4 2012 and the purchasing managers' index remained positive since October 2012, indicating sustained expansion in manufacturing. Geopolitical risks heightened as terrorists attacked an Algerian oil facility, Israel launched a series of airstrikes on Syria, and the US implemented additional sanctions on Iran. The upsurge in crude oil spot prices mirrored the gains in financial markets as the Standard and Poor's 500 index breached the 1,500 mark on 25 January for the first time since December 2007, while—in another first in more than 5 years—the Dow Jones Industrial Average index rose above 14,000 on 1 February (Figure A1.19). The broader financial market rally was supported by US jobs and manufacturing data that were better than expected. Consequently, spot oil and futures prices reacted positively to the signal of increased demand.

A1.18 Price of Brent crude

Source: Bloomberg (accessed 16 March 2013).

Click here for figure data

A1.19 Oil and stock prices

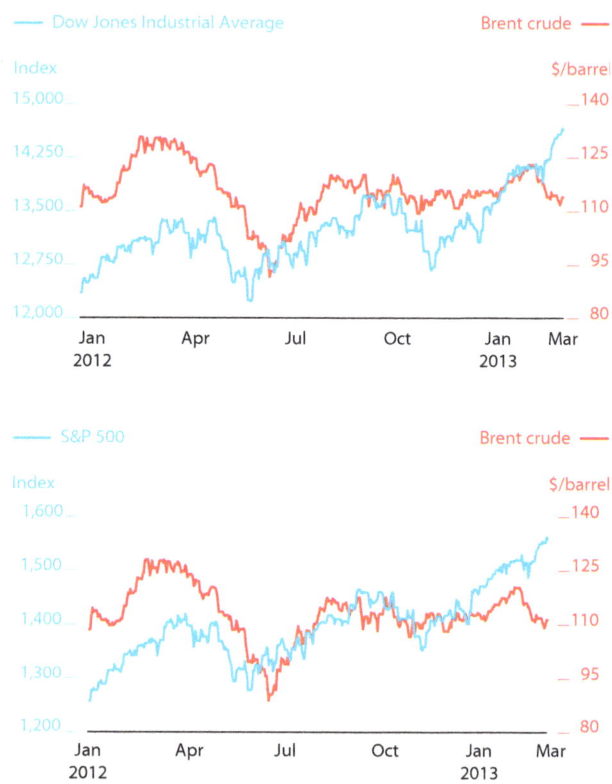

Source: Bloomberg (accessed 16 March 2013).

Click here for figure data

However, after reaching the initial peak, Brent crude prices started to decline, wiping out the initial 2-month price increase with a price decline of 8.5% in 1 month down to $110 per barrel on 12 March 2013. Weak economic statistics from Europe and the PRC dampened earlier optimism. The euro area January unemployment rate climbed to 11.9% from 11.8% in the previous month, while the PRC's purchasing managers' index unexpectedly declined further in February to just slightly above the manufacturing expansion–contraction divide.

Theoretically, the futures market should be more stable than spot prices, as futures prices are based on long-run fundamentals while spot prices reflect short-run shifts in demand and supply. However, the two have been moving together, and futures prices have been as volatile as spot prices amid intensifying and lingering political and economic risks (Figure A1.20). The front-month futures price, for example, jumped from $111.10 at the end of December to $118.90 in February, before subsiding to $109.80 in mid-March.

A1.20 Daily spot and futures price of Brent crude

Source: Bloomberg (accessed 16 March 2013).

Click here for figure data

Oil price prospects

The March report of the International Energy Agency showed growth in world oil supply outpacing growth in demand. Supply increased by 2.8% to reach 90.9 million barrels per day (mbd), while demand increased by 1% to reach 89.8 mbd in 2012. In February, supply continued to inch up, largely from rising oil production in Iraq and Saudi Arabia.

Supply conditions are forecast to improve in the short term. The March US Energy Information Administration report forecasts the global supply of oil to increase by 0.8 mbd in 2013 and 1.9 mbd in 2014 as countries outside of the Organization of the Petroleum Exporting Countries (OPEC), largely the US and Canada, recover from unplanned outages and scheduled maintenance. The global consumption forecast was revised downward from the February report, to a slight increase to 90.1 mbd in 2013 on higher demand expected in the PRC. In 2014, consumption is expected to further increase, albeit at a still-tepid rate, to 91.5 mbd. The small increase in demand is in line with the ADO forecasts of 1.2% growth in 2013 and 2.0% growth in 2014 in the major industrial economies—rates that are much lower than the pre-crisis average of 2.5% in 2003–2007 and so indicate a global economy that remains weak and fragile. OPEC members notionally bound by the group's 30 mbd target are expected to continue to produce more than their quotas to accommodate the projected rise in world oil consumption and counterbalance supply disruptions. Increases in production are expected from other OPEC members such as Iraq, Nigeria, and Angola.

Notwithstanding these developments, periodic disruptions will likely continue in light of political tensions in major producer economies and a new wave of political unrest in Africa. Tensions are still high in Syria, Sudan, and Iraq, where payment disputes between Baghdad and the Kurdistan regional government will likely reduce output from Iraq's northern oil fields. With no resolution in sight to the issues confronting Iran, its oil production is forecast to continue to fall.

Although concerns about the persisting fragility of the global economy are tempering oil price spikes, global oil prices are projected to stay close to 2012 levels and average $110 per barrel in 2013. Changes in the regional distribution of oil demand and supply, sociopolitical upheavals, speculation, and the financialization of commodities will amplify price shifts in the short run. In 2014, prices are forecast to soften and average $105 per barrel on account of better-supplied markets and easing geopolitical tensions.

Recent food price developments

From their peak in February 2011, agricultural prices fell by 16.7% as of the end of 2012. All sub-indexes exhibited this downward trend, with food prices showing the least decline (Figure A1.21). Food prices firmed up in the second half of 2012, as the heat wave in the US affected maize production and drought in Eastern Europe and Central Asia affected prospects for wheat. Wheat and maize prices vacillated within a narrow band in the first half of 2012. Then, as bad weather affected production prospects in major production areas, second-half prices jumped by close to 20% for maize and 30% for wheat over the first half. Rice prices, on the other hand, were more stable, riding below $600/ton for most of 2012. This is mainly because the market for rice remains better supplied than those for maize and wheat. In sum, food prices remained elevated in 2012.

This year, food prices are starting to ease. February food inflation, as measured by the World Bank food index, was still positive but more than 3 percentage points moderated from the previous month (Figure A1.22). Edible oil prices declined by only 1% from a year earlier, primarily reflecting the fall in palm and soybean oil prices. The price index for other food continued its downward trend, showing deflation since the end of 2011. This largely reflects the price of sugar, which has been on a downtrend and is almost 25% lower than a year ago. According to the Food and Agriculture Organization of the United Nations, sugar prices have been declining in anticipation of higher world production, notably from Brazil and Thailand. For the second consecutive month, grain prices registered lower rates of growth year on year. Grain prices rose by 9% over a year earlier, 3 percentage points lower than in January 2013. The recent decline was mainly from easing wheat prices as crop prospects improved in the US. The average price of maize in February 2013 was only slightly lower than a month earlier because supply was still tight. The increase in rice prices since late 2012 is generally attributed to Thailand's rice-pledging scheme and some tightening of supply from the US.

Food price prospects

Weather permitting, harvests in most major grain-producing countries are expected to at least match those of 2012, more likely increase, especially in areas affected by drought last year. The March cereal report of the Food and Agriculture Organization revised upwards its 2012/13 crop year production estimates for cereals by 4 million tons from the February figure of 2,301 million tons. The report said the upward revision mainly accommodated positive adjustments in rice production, which in Asia is expected to reach 443 million

A1.21 Agriculture price indexes

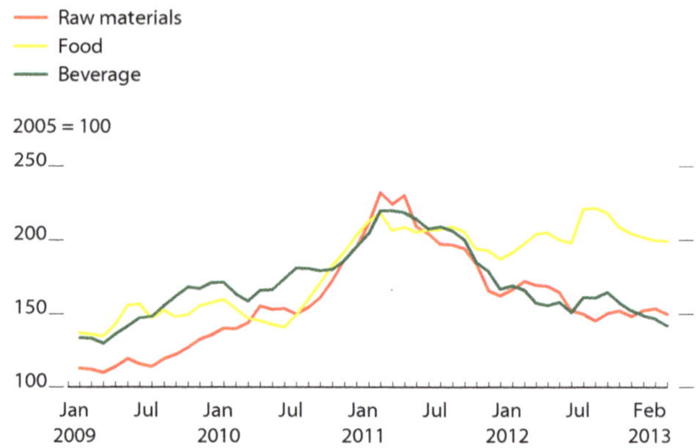

Source: World Bank. Commodity Price Data (Pink Sheet). http://www.worldbank.org (accessed 15 March 2013).

Click here for figure data

A1.22 Food inflation

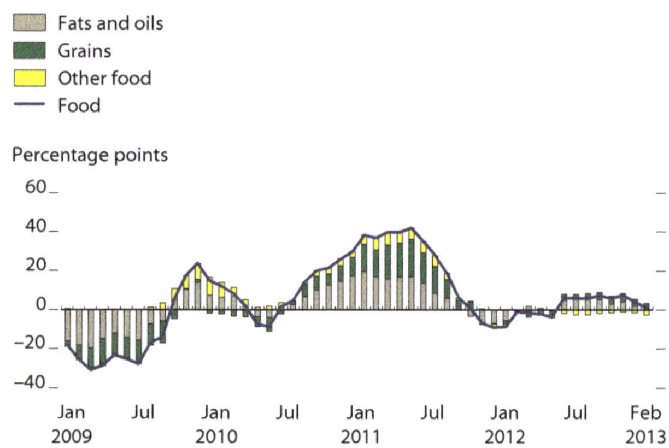

Source: World Bank. Commodity Price Data (Pink Sheet). http://www.worldbank.org (accessed 16 March 2013).

Click here for figure data

A1.23 World cereal situation

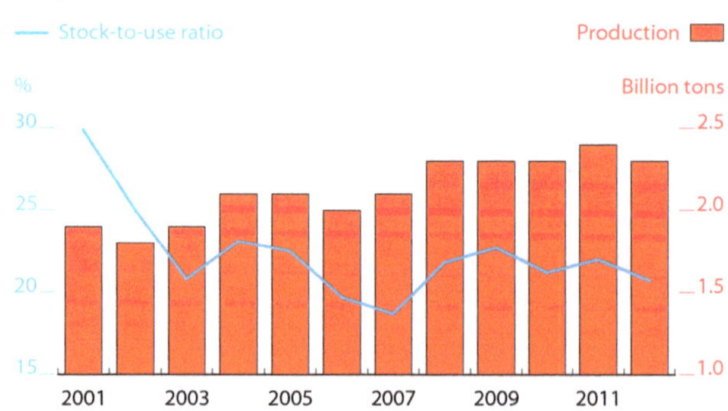

Source: Food and Agriculture Administration of the United Nations. http://www.fao.org (accessed 16 March 2013).

Click here for figure data

tons, 4.2 million tons more than in 2011/12. As an early indication, grain prices have been declining since December.

Utilization is still expected to exceed production, keeping the demand–supply balance tight (Figure A1.23). However, better international coordination should give countries the confidence not to use export bans and thus maintain more calm than in 2008 and temper price spikes. Lower crude oil prices forecast in the next 2 years should dampen food price increases by reducing the costs of major inputs and demand for biofuels, which compete for food crops. Given these projections and the high base in 2012, food prices are forecast to fall in 2013 and 2014. Nevertheless, as low stocks of major grains provide little cushion to fluctuations in supply and demand, small movements in the supply–demand equation may translate into large price adjustments. Indeed, the volatility of key grain commodities in the 2000s has been higher than in the 1990s (Figure A1.24).

A1.24 Price volatility of selected grain commodities

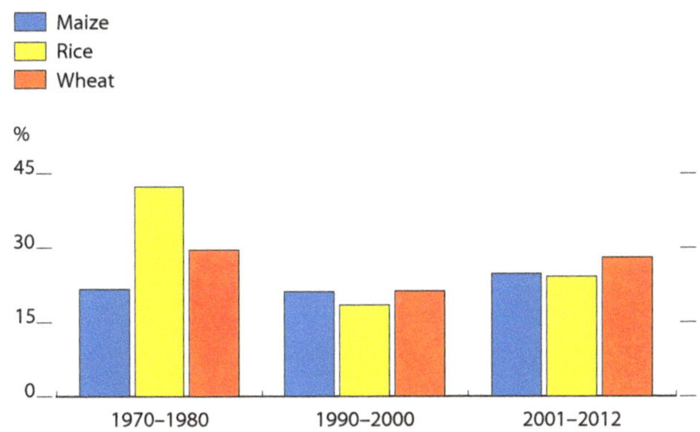

Note: Volatility is measured as the standard deviations of the logarithmic changes in monthly average prices at an annual rate.

Source: ADB estimates.

Click here for figure data

External environment in sum

Developing Asia should continue to expect soft demand for its exports from the major industrial economies. Even with the slight rise in growth expected in the US, the euro area, and Japan in 2014, these economies will continue to operate below their potential. With fiscal tightening the main theme for all but Japan, advanced country central banks are likely to continue accommodative monetary policy. Prices of food and fuel should remain subdued overall, though further volatility is expected. As a result, external price pressures should remain muted.

2

Asia's energy challenge

Asia's energy challenge

Critical energy needs for the Asian Century

Rapid growth has transformed developing Asia's presence in the world economy. The region will likely continue to grow rapidly, further weighing, for better or worse, on global developments. Developing Asia's gross domestic product (GDP) will more than quadruple from 2010 to 2035, and by 2050 the region will generate over half of global GDP. This promising vision of Asia's 21st century is often called the Asian Century growth scenario, articulated in *Asia 2050: Realizing the Asian Century* (ADB 2011). Past growth has dramatically improved Asia's living standards, lifting millions out of poverty. Future growth will do the same.

But, crucially, can developing Asia secure the energy it needs to fuel this dramatic economic expansion? Energy security rests on three pillars: the adequacy and reliability of physical energy supply, environmental sustainability, and affordable access. Where will this energy come from? Can the region expand its energy infrastructure to support its growing needs? Even if the adequate supply of energy is available, will it be environmentally sustainable and widely accessible and affordable? Failure on any of these fronts would hinder efforts to realize the environmentally sustainable, inclusive growth that lies behind the Asian Century ideal.

2.1.1 Developing Asia's growing share of GDP and primary energy consumption, 2010–2035

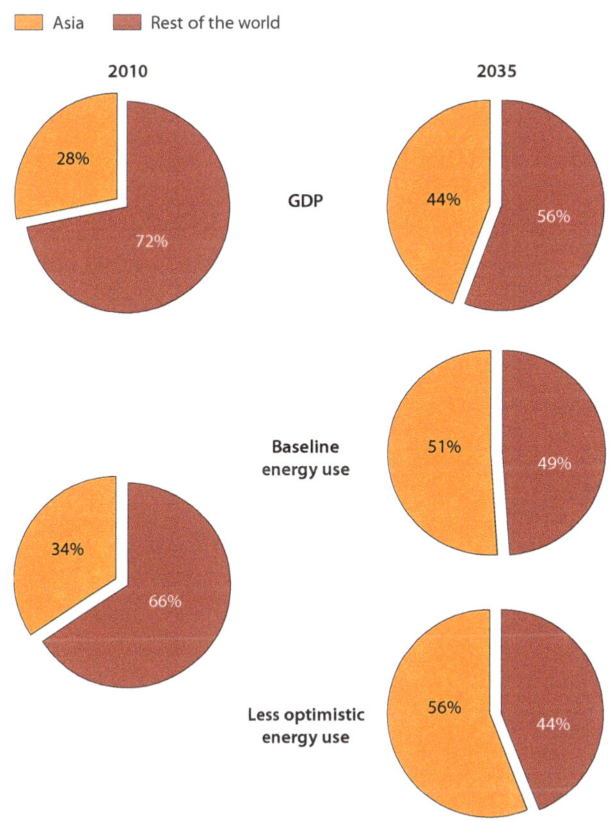

Sources: IEA 2012a; Lee, Park, and Saunders, forthcoming.
Click here for figure data

Energy and economic growth

In 2010, Asia contributed 28% of global GDP. If Asia follows the expected growth trajectory, by 2050 its per capita GDP will reach Europe's current level, and its share of global GDP will nearly double to 52%, making about 3 billion additional Asians affluent (ADB 2011). Asia will already account for 44% of global GDP by 2035 (Figure 2.1.1).

This chapter was written by Minsoo Lee and Donghyun Park of the Economics and Research Department, and Harry Saunders of Decision Processes Incorporated. It draws on the background papers listed at the end of the chapter. Changyong Rhee, chief economist, provided guidance at various stages.

2.1.1 The Asian Century scenario: energy consumption projections

Energy consumption forecasts derive from econometric analyses by country and sector. Demand equations are estimated using historical data of standard explanatory variables such as GDP, population, industrial production, and vehicle stocks. The model incorporates changes in the structure of output and energy efficiency improvements. Future values of energy demand are then projected using the explanatory variables. The model thus takes into account the historical correlation between explanatory variables and energy consumption (box figure).

Broadly speaking, the econometric strategy begins by deriving final energy demand projections, from which it derives primary energy demand projections. "Final energy demand" refers to the consumption of final energy goods such as electricity and gasoline, and "primary energy demand" to the implicit demand for energy sources such as oil and coal required to meet final energy demand.

For all countries, data on key macroeconomic indicators such as GDP, population, and crude oil price are used as the bases for future projections of final energy demand. In addition, some countries have data on more detailed socioeconomic variables such as industrial production, vehicle stocks, number of households, and floor space, which provide additional inputs for these countries' projections.

Transformation analysis examines the transformation of primary energy into final energy. Examples of transformation include electricity generation, oil refining, and gas processing. Primary energy demand projections can be derived by energy type by combining final energy demand and transformation analysis. Net imports of final energy are also factored into primary energy demand projections, as are changes in energy policy.

Modeling framework

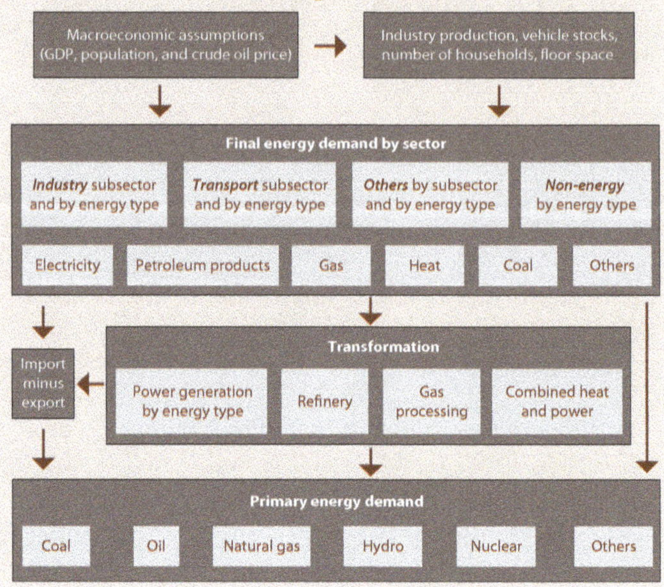

Such economic expansion requires huge amounts of energy. Already in 2010, Asia accounted for 34% of world energy consumption. The link between the final energy used by firms and households, which rises as GDP expands, and an economy's demand for primary energy depends on a complex host of factors (Box 2.1.1). But assumptions on the evolution of energy intensity—changes in the physical energy used to generate each unit of GDP—have big effects on forecast demand.

For example, if economic expansion raises, by the middle of the 21st century, energy consumption per capita for Asia's 5 billion people to the level found today in industrialized economies, the region's share of global energy use is projected to increase to 51% by 2035 (Figure 2.1.1, baseline). This is a conservative estimate, reflecting an optimistic projection of energy intensity trends. This baseline model endogenously projects energy intensity declining by 3.2% per year on average over the forecast horizon. This would bring energy intensity in 2035 down to 45% of its 2010 value—an improvement by better than half.

This compares with the historical trend from 1990 to 2000 of 2.47% improvement per year, which is used in the less optimistic scenario. If energy intensity follows its historical trend, Asia's share of world energy consumption would be as high as 56% by 2035 (Figure 2.1.1, less optimistic).

Energy intensity trends are hard to predict as they are driven by many factors beyond improved technical efficiency. The faster decline of energy intensity in the baseline scenario assumes improvements supported by changes in industry structure, slower industrialization in the People's Republic of China (PRC), and productivity gains for non-energy inputs. This forecast is subject to greater uncertainty than the less optimistic scenario based on historical trend. Figure 2.1.2 shows the growth of energy consumption under the two scenarios. Asia's energy consumption is projected to double from 2010 to 2035 even under the optimistic baseline scenario.

Note that this report's baseline forecast shows the primary energy growth rate to be 2.82% annually from 2010 to 2035. This is quite consistent with the forecasts of other organizations (Table 2.1.1). Energy consumption grows despite substantial improvement in energy intensity because of sharply increased per capita GDP. While Asia's population is forecast to grow only modestly by 0.7% annually, Asians will drive more and air-condition more as they become richer.

2.1.2 Sensitivity of energy consumption to projected energy intensity

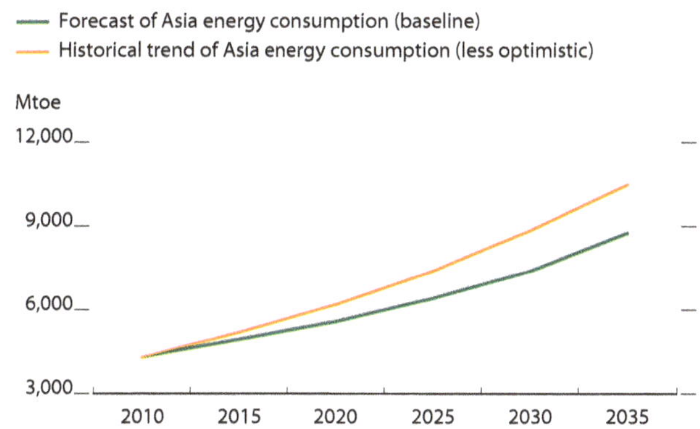

Mtoe = million tons of oil equivalent.
Source: Lee, Park, and Saunders, forthcoming.
Click here for figure data

Composition of Asia's energy demand

Aside from becoming higher, energy demand poses many challenges for developing Asia in terms of its composition. In particular, what is the mix of primary sources that will satisfy Asia's growing thirst for energy? The current composition of Asia's energy demand holds some important clues (Figure 2.1.3).

Under the baseline scenario in Box 2.1.1, most of the twofold (202%) increase in energy consumption from 2010 to 2035 will come from fossil fuels. Coal use is expected to increase by 81% as oil consumption approximately doubles and natural gas use more than triples. The use of renewables is set to increase but will make a relatively small contribution to 2035 energy requirements. The same goes for nuclear power.

Subregional differences in energy demand and the energy mix will be substantial by 2035. Following the Asia 2050 study's forecasts (ADB 2011), the scenarios allow for large differences in subregional growth rates in the next 2 decades. Regional GDP growth will likely be dominated by South and East Asia—South Asia because of its high potential growth rate and East Asia because its growth at about 6% builds on its existing large share of developing Asia's GDP (the two subregions will jointly account for 83% of developing Asia's GDP by 2035).

Aside from these different growth rates, different subregions rely on different energy mixes (Figure 2.1.4). Coal plays a much larger role in East and South Asia than in Central Asia, Southeast Asia, or the Pacific. Natural gas occupies a markedly bigger share of the energy mix in Central Asia than in the four other subregions. Relatively low demand in the Pacific islands will be met by oil and natural gas in most countries. On the other hand, across all subregions coal, oil,

2.1.1 Comparison of organizations' energy consumption forecasts

	Primary energy growth rate (%)	Time horizon
Energy Information Administration (non-OECD Asia)	2.90	2008–2035
BP (Asia–Pacific)	2.72	2010–2030
International Energy Agency (New Policies Scenario, Asia)	2.20	2010–2035
Asian Development Bank	2.82	2010–2035

OECD = Organisation for Economic Co-operation and Development.
Sources: EIA 2011a, BP 2013, IEA 2012a.

2.1.3 Fuel composition for Asia's energy requirements

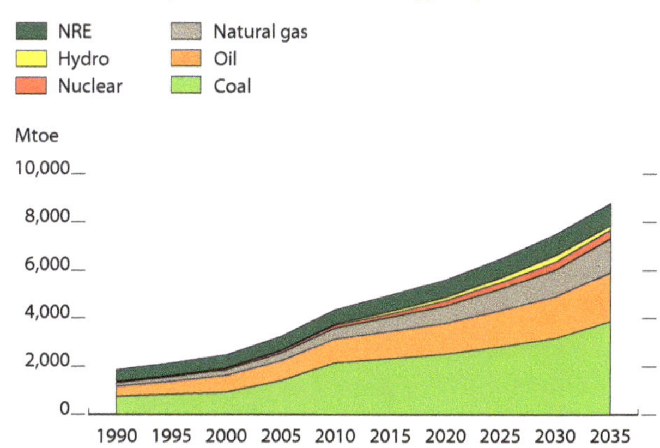

Mtoe = million tons of oil equivalent, NRE = new and renewable energy.
Source: Lee, Park, and Saunders, forthcoming.
Click here for figure data

and natural gas dominate while renewables and nuclear occupy only a limited share of the energy mix.

An achievable energy future for Asia

Energy consumption that more than doubles under the Asian Century vision poses a colossal challenge. Can it be achieved? Where will Asia find so much energy—over half the energy needed by the entire world in 2035? If the answer is that Asia cannot find it, the region will not realize the Asian Century. Asia faces a stark reality: Either it secures adequate energy supply or economic growth suffers accordingly. Even if Asia is able to secure enough physical energy supply, there remains the question of whether it can do so while safeguarding environmental sustainability and ensuring affordable energy for all. The three pillars of energy security are examined below, one by one.

Adequacy and reliability implications

Coal is abundant in Asia, which has a 35% share of the world endowment (Table 2.1.2). Asia can reasonably expect to source coal from other regions if need be.

Less abundant than coal in Asia is conventional natural gas, of which Asia has 16% of proven global reserves. The gas trade is widely distributed in terms of sources, though, and international trade in gas is growing. As such, Asia can expect to have relatively unfettered access to gas (Table 2.1.3).

Oil is different. And it poses the greatest threat to the adequacy of Asia's physical energy supply. Proven reserves of crude oil in the region amount to a mere 9% of the world total. When combined with natural gas liquids, the Asian share is 15% of world reserves (Table 2.1.4).

Crude oil supply is by no means the only element of energy supply security, but it is the most problematic for Asia because of the region's limited endowment and how it compensates. In 2010, Asia imported nearly half of all crude oil traded on international markets. If crude oil demand grows as projected in Figure 2.1.3, developing Asia's oil imports will expand dramatically (Figure 2.1.5). Taking into account Asian production, Asia's oil imports are expected to almost triple from 11 million to over 31 million barrels per day by 2035, growing annually by 4.2%.

Control over Asia's oil supply has steadily shifted toward Middle East suppliers. In 1990, 33% of developing Asia's oil imports came from the Middle East; by 2010, this figure had risen by half to 48%. As this accelerating trend will likely continue, Asia's high and growing dependence on a single region poses a risk to adequate and reliable energy supply. Disrupted flow of crude oil from the Middle East for an extended period would hit Asia hard. Worse, Asia's refineries

2.1.4 Primary energy demand, by Asian subregion

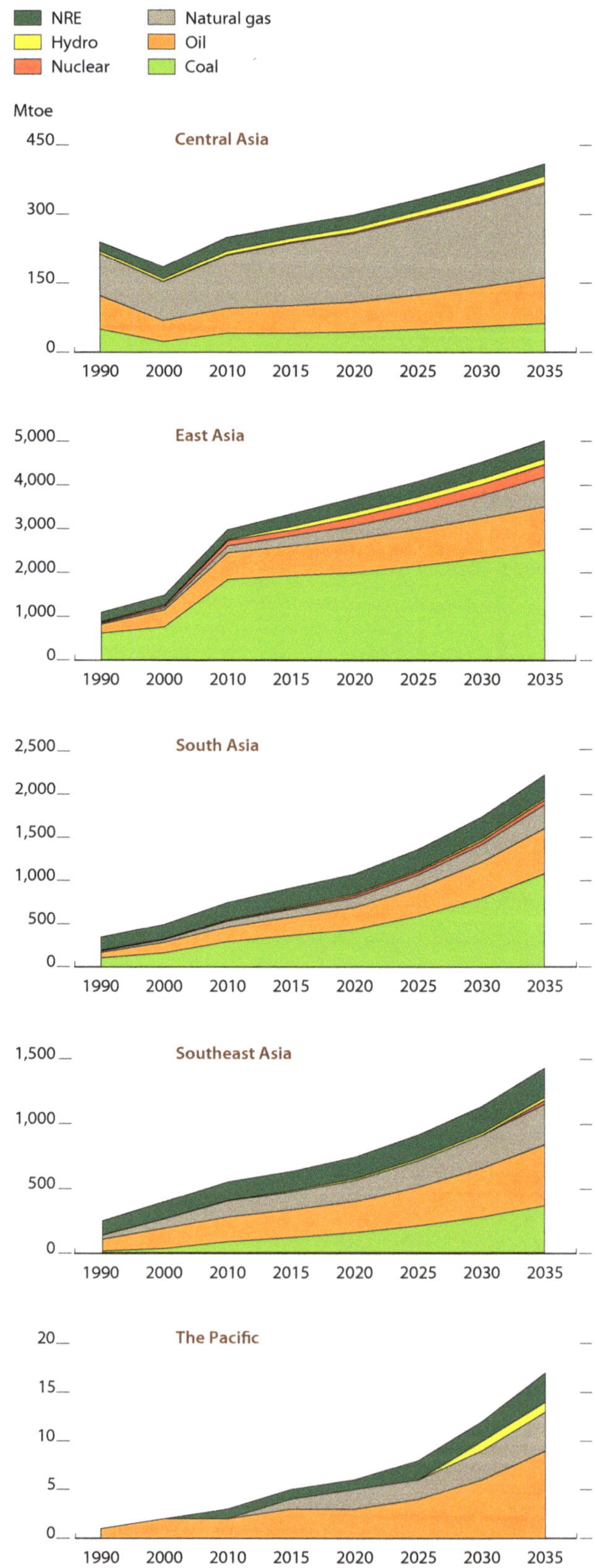

Mtoe = million tons of oil equivalent, NRE = new and renewable energy.

Source: Lee, Park, and Saunders, forthcoming.

Click here for figure data

2.1.2 Proven reserves of coal, 2011 (billion tons)

	Anthracite and bituminous[a]	Sub-bituminous and lignite[a]	Total[a]	Share of Total (%)
Total North America	112.80	132.30	245.10	28.5
Total South and Central America	6.90	5.62	12.52	1.5
Total Europe and Asia	93.00	211.60	304.60	35.4
Total Middle East and Africa	32.70	0.17	32.87	3.8
Australia	37.10	39.30	76.40	8.9
DPRK	0.30	0.30	0.60	0.1
India	56.10	4.50	60.50	7.0
Indonesia	1.50	4.01	5.51	0.6
Japan	0.34	0.01	0.35	0.04
Kazakhstan	21.50	12.10	33.60	3.9
New Zealand	0.03	0.54	0.57	0.1
Pakistan	...	2.07	2.07	0.2
PRC	62.20	52.30	114.50	13.3
Republic of Korea	...	0.13	0.13	0.01
Thailand	...	1.24	1.24	0.1
Viet Nam	0.15	...	0.15	0.02
Other Asia and Pacific	1.58	2.13	3.71	0.4
Total Asia and Pacific	180.80	118.62	299.42	34.8
of which:				
Developing Asia	143.35	78.77	222.12	25.7
Developed Asia	37.47	39.85	77.32	9.0

... = data not available, DPRK = Democratic People's Republic of Korea, PRC = People's Republic of China.

[a] measured in billion metric tons.

Notes: Anthracite is hard, high-energy coal; bituminous, sub-bituminous, and lignite are progressively softer kinds of coal with progressively less energy.

Source: BP 2012.

2.1.3 Undiscovered technically recoverable gas

Region	Mean estimate (trillion cubic meters)	Share (%)
Arctic + former Soviet Union	57	29
Middle East and North Africa	33	17
Asia and the Pacific	32	16
Europe	5	3
North America	20	10
South America and Caribbean	24	12
Sub-Saharan Africa	26	13
Total	198	100

Source: US Geological Survey 2012.

2.1.4 Undiscovered technically recoverable oil and natural gas liquids

Region	Mean estimate (thousand MMBO)	Share (%)	Mean estimate (thousand MMBNGL)	Share (%)
Arctic + former Soviet Union	66	12	40	24
Middle East and North Africa	111	20	31	18
Asia and Pacific	53	9	25	15
Europe	10	2	3	2
North America	83	15	19	12
South America and Caribbean	126	22	21	13
Sub-Saharan Africa	115	20	28	17
Total	565	100	167	100

MMBNGL = million barrels of natural gas liquids, MMBO = million barrels of oil.

Source: US Geological Survey 2012.

are configured to process mostly light Middle Eastern crudes and, unlike refineries in other regions, cannot immediately handle very heavy crudes. If the Middle East tap closed, Asia would be poorly equipped to switch to heavy crudes available from elsewhere.

Long-term oil security can be enhanced by substituting other fuels, but the short run lacks options. Asia uses oil largely for transportation (48% in 2010), which almost always requires readily portable energy. The convenience of liquid fuels for this purpose, the well-developed supply chain, and superior economics give petroleum products a huge advantage over alternatives. Biofuels offer some potential as substitutes for oil products, but they are unlikely to be commercially competitive within the forecast horizon.

Much of the projected surge in oil imports reflects the rapid expansion of motor traffic expected in Asia. The PRC's vehicle fleet for passengers and goods is forecast to grow

2.1.5 Projected Asian oil import requirements

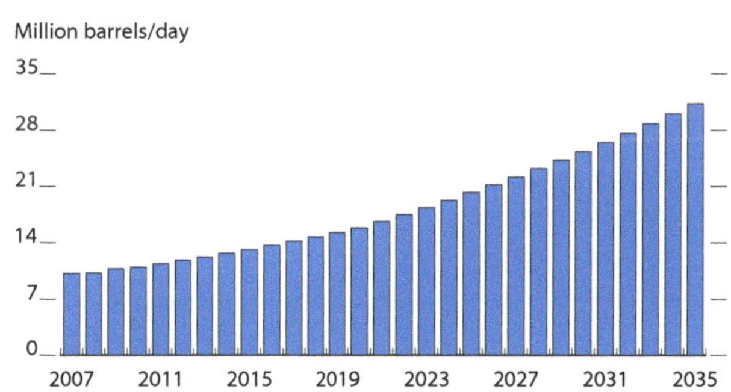

Source: Isaak, Park, and Lee, forthcoming.

Click here for figure data

at over 6% annually (Figure 2.1.6). Rapid economic growth means that more Asians can now afford cars. Trading public transport for private cars is a natural consequence of Asia's growing affluence and middle class, and it will further whet the region's thirst for imported oil.

In addition to oil supply disruptions, threats to supply adequacy arise from potential interruptions of electricity and gas supply. Unreliable electric and gas systems can leave households without power and stymie industrial and commercial activity, causing heavy losses. India has experienced serious interruptions to electricity supply, with the July 2012 blackout in India affecting some 670 million people. In 2009, a dispute between the Russian Federation and Ukraine over pricing and transit costs for gas prompted the former to cut off all gas supplies to and passing through Ukraine, imposing wintertime supply disruptions on 18 European countries—and this dispute remains unresolved.

By 2035, most Asian countries will produce less than half the energy they need, and many will produce only a tiny fraction. This means that Asia will remain heavily dependent on energy imports, in particular of oil, for the foreseeable future. More generally, securing adequate and reliable energy supply will persist as a difficult challenge across the region.

Figure 2.1.7 ranks Asian economies according to an index of energy self-sufficiency, in which a value of 1 indicates all primary energy demand is met with indigenous resources and a value of 0 indicates complete reliance on energy imports. The index is calculated based on each country's projected primary energy mix until 2035 (e.g., how much it will use coal to generate electricity), its current proved indigenous reserves of fossil fuel, and its projected consumption until 2035 (Fueyo, Gómez, and Dopazo, forthcoming).

Only three countries in developing Asia—Azerbaijan, Brunei Darussalam, and Kazakhstan—are energy self-sufficient. Some economies have minimal self-sufficiency. Singapore and Hong Kong, China both have high demand for fossil fuels but no supply. As their energy sources were entirely imported even in 2010, their situation will change little by 2035. The Republic of Korea has limited fuel reserves—some coal and nuclear fuels, the latter perhaps largely uranium processed from imports. In 2010, the Republic of Korea imported about 80% of its primary energy (IEA 2012a). Indigenous reserves will be depleted by 2035. The share of hydropower will be negligible at 0.06% of primary energy consumption, and other renewables' share will be only 2.02% (Lee, Park, and Saunders, forthcoming).

Japan's trends for economic growth and energy demand are unique in Asia, reflecting its economic maturity. Its GDP will grow very slowly between 2010 and 2035. Its primary energy consumption will fall by 15%, but hydropower's share of primary energy will remain more or less constant at 1.5%, while that of other renewables will rise substantially from 2.1% to 15.7%.

2.1.6 Vehicle population forecast for the PRC, 2005–2035

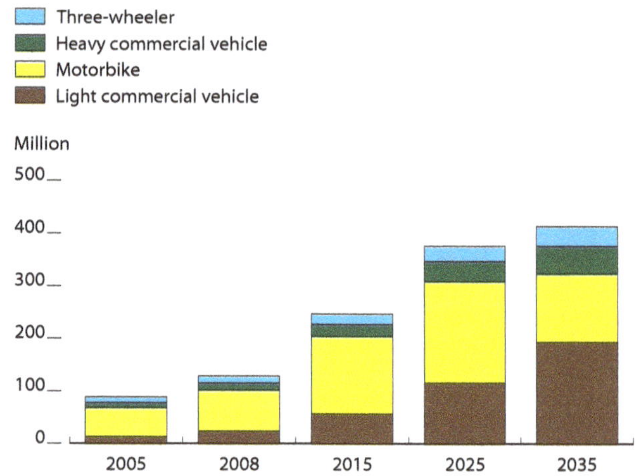

PRC = People's Republic of China.

Source: ADB 2006.

Click here for figure data

2.1.7 Energy self-sufficiency in Asia and the Pacific, 2035

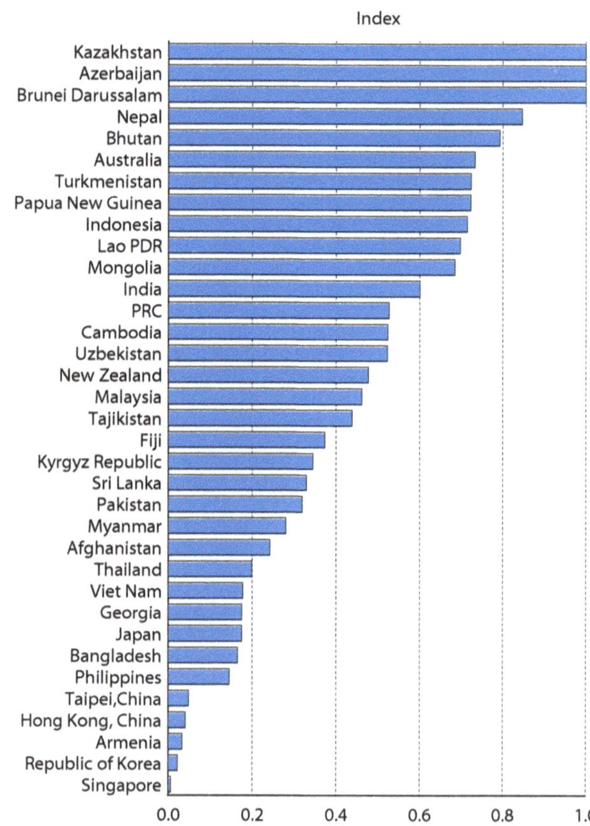

Lao PDR = Lao People's Democratic Republic, PRC = People's Republic of China.

Note: The self-sufficiency index formula accounts for the share of renewable resources projected to be available, projected demand for conventional fuels, and corresponding depletion of conventional fuels given the country's endowment.

Source: Fueyo, Gomez, and Dopazo, forthcoming.

Click here for figure data

Thailand, the Philippines, and Viet Nam will have self-sufficiency rates in 2035 similar to Japan's. A major reason is that their energy consumption will grow much more quickly to fuel their faster economic growth. Country-specific factors matter. Thailand has considerable known reserves of coal and gas, but they will be depleted by 2035. The share of renewables remains constant at about 20%. In the Philippines, the contribution of renewables will shrink from 43% in 2010 to 14% in 2035, by which time proven indigenous gas and coal reserves will be depleted. While Viet Nam is endowed with significant oil and gas reserves and was a net energy exporter in 2010, rapid growth and a shift from traditional to modern energy sources will deplete its reserves by 2035. The share of renewables is projected to shrink from 43% to 17%.

Focus on environmental sustainability

If Asia does find the physical energy supply it needs to fuel its growth, what would be the impact on the environment? Expanding the region's primary energy mix as currently projected would have serious consequences for the environment, both in Asia and globally. Local air and water quality, water availability, land use, and global climate all stand to suffer greatly if projected energy demand is met mostly by fossil fuels.

Local impacts on air, water, and land

The current picture of Asia's energy future entails significant damage to the local environment. Toxic emissions from fossil fuels are already a serious problem. Air pollution degrades human health and drives up hospital admissions, and indoor air pollution causes premature death in women and children. Air pollution is caused largely by energy production and use. The energy and transport sectors generate 70% of nitrogen oxide emissions and 80% of emissions of sulfur dioxide and particulate matter (PM_{10}, referring to particles that are less than 10 microns in diameter and therefore able to penetrate deep into the respiratory tract).

Sulfur dioxide emissions have grown in Asia, even per capita. Sulfur dioxide is responsible for the damage acid rain does to lakes and forests, and it poses serious human health risks. PM_{10} is an especially problematic air pollutant, its inhalation strongly associated with heart and chronic lung disease. Roughly half of PM_{10} pollution comes from power plants, 30% from transportation, and most of the remainder from wildfires and dust storms. Air pollution is projected to cause more than 3.6 million deaths per year by 2030 throughout the region, mostly in the PRC and India. With coal use projected to grow by over 50% during the forecast period, air quality problems associated with sulfur dioxide and PM_{10} are likely to continue, absent aggressive limits placed on

2.1.8 Cities with high particulate concentrations, 2008–2009

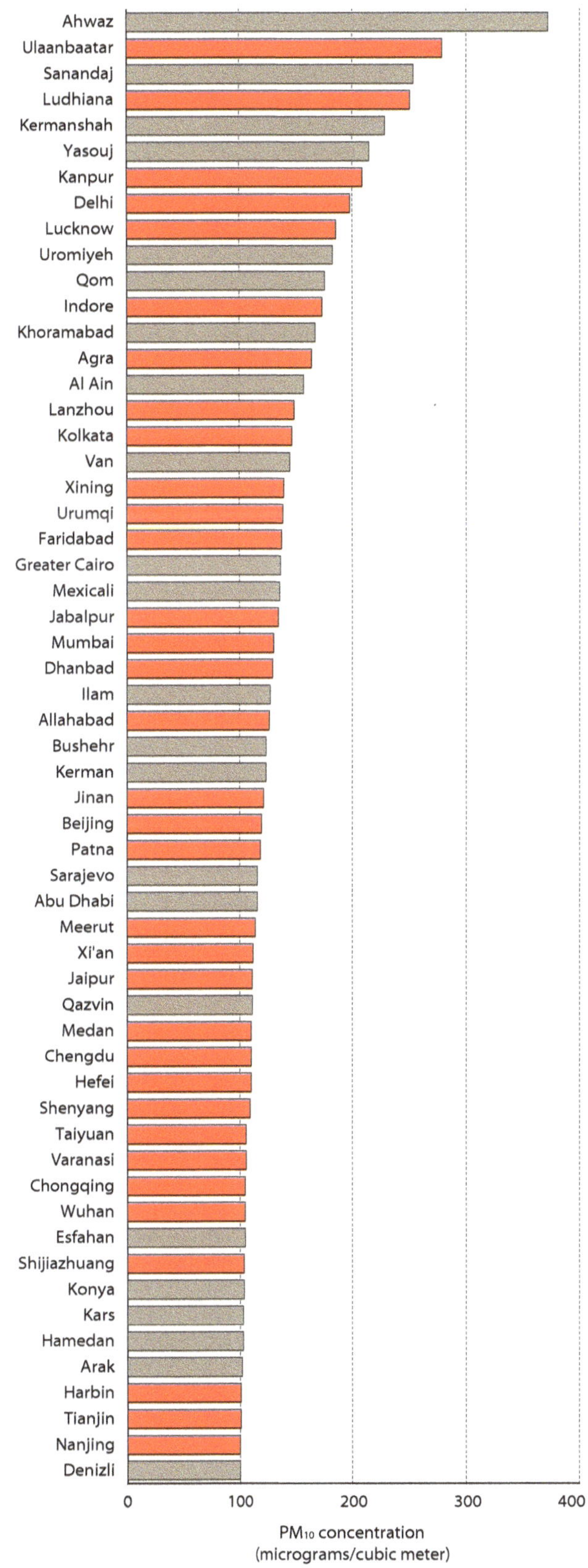

PM_{10} = particulate matter less than 10 microns in diameter.
Note: Red bars denote cities in Asia.
Source: ADB 2012.
Click here for figure data

toxic emissions. Further, more cars portend ever-deeper concerns about air quality, especially in urban areas.

Clean Air Asia, the regional network on air-quality management, aggregated data from more than 300 Asian cities in 2012 and found that PM10 concentrations were within safe targets in only 16 cities, most of them in Japan. This means that more than 94% of the cities sampled have air unsafe to breathe. Setting an air quality guideline of 20 micrograms of PM10 per cubic meter as safe for long-term exposure (WHO 2008), the World Health Organization ranks cities that average 100 micrograms per cubic meter or worse and finds 34 of the world's 57 most polluted cities in Asia (Figure 2.1.8).

Like air quality, water availability fares poorly under Asia's projected energy future. Burning fossil fuels to generate electricity requires lots of water for cooling. Further, oil, gas, and biofuel all require significant quantities of water to produce. Asia is already notably vulnerable to water scarcity, second only to Africa.

Fuelwood and biofuels present additional problems because the resulting deforestation causes social dislocation and the loss of natural carbon sinks and biodiversity. Present and projected demand for fuelwood exceeds the capacity of the natural ecosystem to supply it. Biofuels derived from maize, oil palm, and other crops displace food crops on farmland. Forests harvested for fuelwood or cleared to cultivate biofuels account for much of current change in land use.

Consequences for global climate change

The damage inflicted by Asia's projected energy future affects not only the local environment but the global climate. If developing Asia continues to rely on fossil fuels, its energy-related carbon emissions (ignoring other greenhouse gas emissions) will more than double over the forecast period. By 2035 Asia will contribute nearly half of global carbon dioxide (CO_2) emissions (IEA 2012a). The International Energy Agency (IEA) calls the pathway under current worldwide policies unsustainable and emphasizes the need to build an energy pathway to limit global warming to 2 degrees Celsius above preindustrial levels, the target agreed under the United Nations Framework Convention on Climate Change. The *World Energy Outlook*, published annually by the IEA, refers to three scenarios of energy growth: the current policies scenario, with no change to policies in place; the new policies scenario, which includes countries' commitments and plans even if specific measures are not yet announced; and the so-called 450 scenario, which the IEA proposes as the threshold for preventing dangerous climate change. The 450 scenario calls for limiting CO_2 emissions in the atmosphere to 450 parts per million. Figure 2.1.9 shows that under current forecasts developing Asia alone would emit more CO_2 than is sustainable for the entire world.

2.1.9 Projected energy-related carbon dioxide emissions from developing Asia

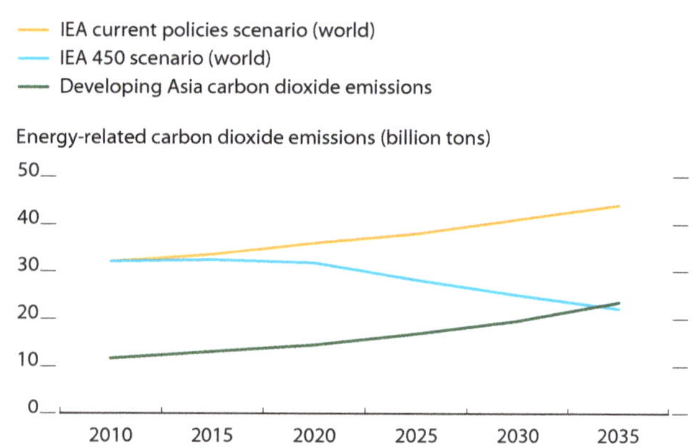

IEA = International Energy Agency.

Sources: IEA 2012a; Lee, Park, and Saunders, forthcoming.

Click here for figure data

This would have very serious consequences for Asia's many countries that are particularly vulnerable to climate change. Geography, climatology, low per capita income, and patterns of urbanization put Indonesia, the Philippines, Thailand, and Viet Nam at risk of losing 6.7%

of their combined GDP by 2100 if temperatures change as the Intergovernmental Panel on Climate Change predicts. This is more than twice the global average of losses linked to climate change. Cambodia, the Lao People's Democratic Republic (Lao PDR), the Philippines, the Mekong Delta, central Thailand, and Sumatra and Java in Indonesia are more at risk than wealthier countries such as Brunei Darussalam and Singapore. The PRC and India could use up 1%–12% of their annual GDP coping with climate refugees, altered disease vectors, and failing crops.

Bangladesh, where 15% of the population lives within 1 meter of sea level at high tide, is prone to flooding, tropical cyclones, and storm surges—not to mention drought. In Cambodia, substantial human and crop losses are attributed to worsening drought and flooding that are likely preludes to more extreme weather.

According to the Organisation for Economic Co-operation and Development (2010), 7 of the world's 10 cities most exposed to climate change are in developing Asia (Table 2.1.5).

Cities are not the only places under threat. Large swathes of rural coastal areas in Asia are vulnerable to climate change. Parts of South Asia, including virtually all of Bangladesh and large parts of Nepal, are at very high risk from climate change.

2.1.5 Cities most exposed to climate change

Rank	Country	City	Current assets exposed ($ billion)	Future assets exposed ($ billion)
1	USA	Miami	416	3,513
2	PRC	Guangzhou	84	3,357
3	USA	New York–Newark	320	2,147
4	India	Kolkata	32	1,961
5	PRC	Shanghai	73	1,771
6	India	Mumbai	46	1,598
7	PRC	Tianjin	30	1,231
8	Japan	Tokyo	174	1,207
9	PRC	Hong Kong, China	36	1,163
10	Thailand	Bangkok	39	1,117
11	PRC	Ningbo	9	1,074
12	USA	New Orleans	234	1,013
13	Japan	Osaka–Kobe	216	969
14	Netherlands	Amsterdam	128	843
15	Netherlands	Rotterdam	115	826
16	Viet Nam	Ho Chi Minh City	27	653
17	Japan	Nagoya	109	623
18	PRC	Qingdao	3	602

PRC = People's Republic of China, USA = United States of America.
Source: OECD 2010.

The imperative of affordable access

Assuming Asia can secure adequate physical energy supply to power growth and safeguard the environment, the challenge remains to ensure that energy is accessible and affordable. Energy is one of the most basic human needs, and therefore true energy security necessarily entails universal access to affordable energy. Affordable access to energy is a prerequisite for inclusive growth and the political support that makes policy effective.

Asia has the unfortunate distinction of harboring most of the world's energy poor. Energy poverty perpetuates hunger by forcing women and children to gather fuel for hours on end that they would rather spend earning incomes or studying. Nearly half of the world's people without electricity live in Asia, as do the majority of people who rely on traditional fuels such as wood, charcoal, and dung. In 2010, 2.8 billion Asians, or 79% of the world population, relied on such traditional fuels, which provide low-quality energy while often destroying natural ecosystems (Figure 2.1.10).

Affordable access to modern energy is shockingly deficient in Asia. In 2010, some 18% of Asians, or 628 million

2.1.10 Asian proportion of those in energy poverty

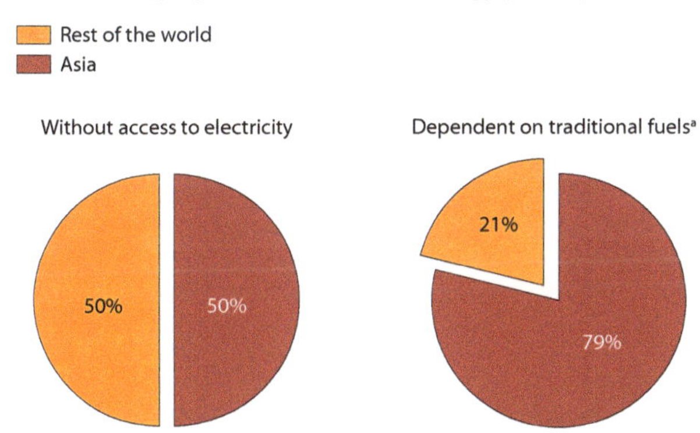

[a] The traditional fuels category includes all types of solid fuels and kerosene, not just biomass.

Notes: Electrification numbers for Asia were taken from 2012 Rapid Assessment and Gap Analyses and United Nations Development Programme Energy Country Briefs supplemented with World Bank population data for 2011. Global electrification and solid fuels numbers for non-Asian countries were taken from IEA (2011a).

Sources: IEA 2012a; Sovacool 2012.

Click here for figure data

individuals, had no electricity. In that year, the percentage of population continent-wide without electricity and reliant on biomass for cooking was higher in Africa than in Asia, but some Asian countries such as Bangladesh approached the African average (Table 2.1.6).

2.1.6 Number and share of population without modern energy services, 2010

	Without access to electricity		Dependent on biomass for cooking	
	Population (million)	Share of total population (%)	Population (million)	Share of total population (%)
Africa	**590**	**57**	**698**	**68**
Congo	58	85	63	93
Ethiopia	65	77	82	96
Kenya	33	82	33	80
Nigeria	79	50	117	74
Tanzania	38	85	42	94
Uganda	29	92	31	96
Other sub-Saharan Africa	286	66	328	75
North Africa	1	1	2	1
Developing Asia	**628**	**18**	**1,814**	**51**
Bangladesh	88	54	149	91
People's Republic of China	4	0	387	29
India	293	25	772	66
Indonesia	63	27	128	55
Pakistan	56	33	111	64
Philippines	16	17	47	50
Viet Nam	2	2	49	56
Rest of developing Asia	106	34	171	54
Latin America	**29**	**6**	**65**	**14**
Middle East	**18**	**9**	**10**	**5**
Developing countries	**1,265**	**24**	**2,588**	**49**
World	**1,267**	**19**	**2,588**	**38**

Source: IEA 2012a.

Energy is a basic human need. It is required to heat and cool, prepare and preserve food, provide light, communicate, and operate modern conveniences, as well as to enable the delivery of social services like education, health, and recreation. Expanding access to energy for Asia's legions of energy poor is a priority made all the more urgent because failure would perpetuate substantial public health hazards. Yet traditional fuels like kerosene, fuelwood, dung, charcoal, and coal still supply much of the energy used in Asia. Solid fuels dominate, with fuelwood claiming the largest share in most Asian countries (Figure 2.1.11).

Rapid growth can make the future better than the present. The IEA's new policies scenario (including countries' commitments and plans regarding energy use) projects that developing Asia's population without electricity will decline substantially to 334 million by 2030, which translates into a decline from 18% to 8%. The IEA is more pessimistic about movement away from traditional fuels, estimating that the number of people without clean cooking facilities in India in 2030 will still be more than twice the population of the US today (IEA 2012a). It further estimates that achieving its vision of Energy for All, or universal access to modern energy by 2030, will require 3.5 times more investment to this end than is contemplated in the new policy scenario and 5.3 times investment in 2009. The current outlay is less than $10 billion globally. The additional investment will extend supply to heretofore unserved populations and build capacity to meet the additional demand.

ADB projections show every Asian subregion having to spend less of its income on electricity in 2035 than in 2012. Figure 2.1.12 shows that electricity expenditure as a fraction of GDP per capita (wealth per capita) will be lower in 2035 (vertical axis) than it was in 2012 (horizontal axis) for all subregions because they all lie below the solid line that indicates equal shares of income spent on electricity in both years (expenditure will be unchanged but low in developed Asia). While this analysis does not directly indicate that all energy sources will be more affordable or accessible, it does show a key component of energy becoming more affordable for the poor. Importantly, however, improved energy access

2.1.11 Traditional fuel use by type for selected Asian economies

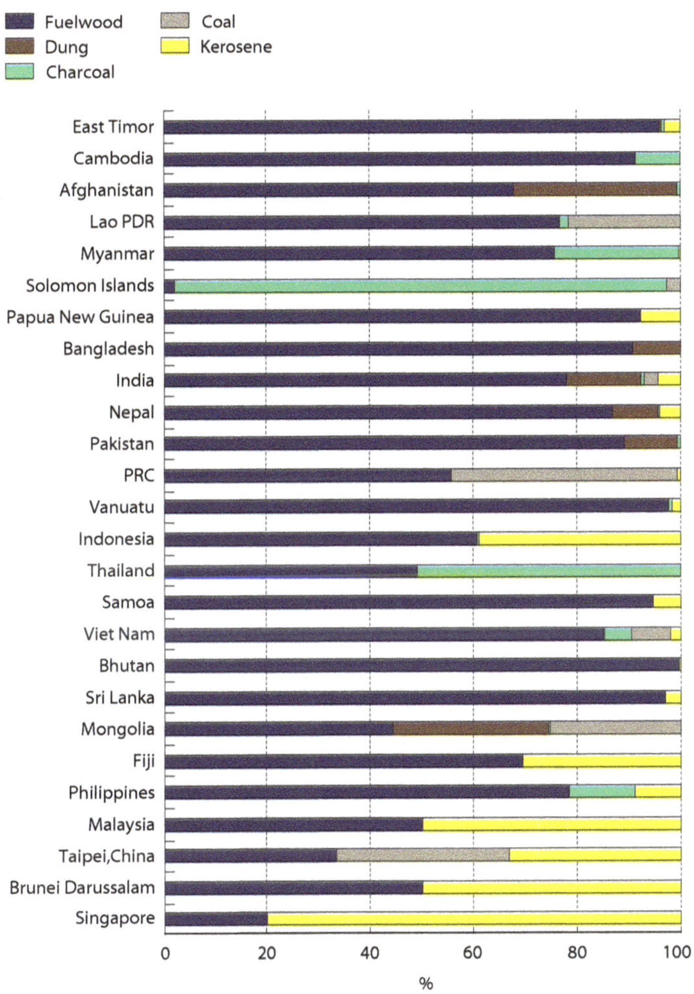

Lao PDR = Lao People's Democratic Republic, PRC = People's Republic of China.

Source: Sovacool 2012.

Click here for figure data

2.1.12 Projected energy affordability in Asia

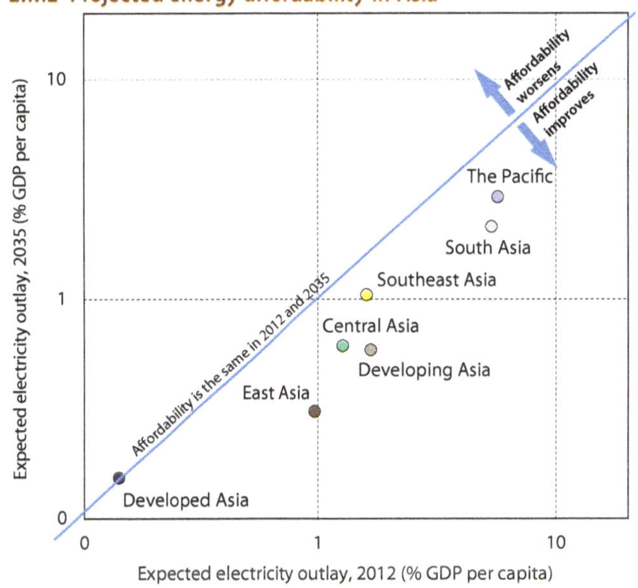

Source: Fueyo, Gomez, and Dopazo, forthcoming.

Click here for figure data

and affordability is not preordained, as these projections assume that the cost of electricity reflects the forecast mix of primary energy used to generate it. As we have seen, this mix creates a number of thorny environmental problems, as well as broadly worsening energy security (Box 2.1.2).

The less-optimistic scenario for Asia's energy future, based on current trends, paints a stark picture. It suggests that Asia will be hard pressed to secure enough energy supply to achieve the rapid growth required for widespread poverty reduction. Further, high growth in energy supply needs to be accompanied by significant quality changes to protect the environment and ensure affordable access. This threefold challenge of energy supply adequacy, environmental sustainability, and affordable access requires a multipronged approach. The region needs to aggressively explore all options by which to curb its burgeoning energy demand, tap new energy supply, and foster regional market synergies that maximize the gains achieved on both sides of the demand–supply equation.

2.1.2 Recent trends in energy security: some evidence from an index

Sovacool et al. (2011) ominously points to stagnant or declining energy security in Asia and the Pacific. The study assessed the performance of 18 countries in the region on energy security based on 20 indicators spread broadly across energy supply, affordability, efficiency and innovation, environmental stewardship, and governance. The assessment informed an energy security index that included all Southeast Asian nations, as well as the PRC, India, Japan, and the Republic of Korea. Australia, the European Union, the US, and New Zealand were included as benchmarks. This study then assessed national progress in 5-year increments from 1990 to 2010 in two ways: The first rated the country's average overall or absolute performance for 1990–2000. The second took a temporal perspective that looked at how each country improved or regressed.

1 Energy and environmental performance absolute score for selected countries, 1990–2010

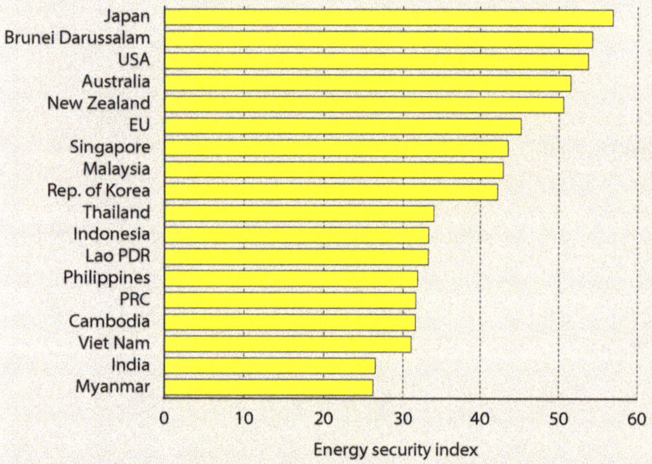

EU = European Union, Lao PDR = Lao People's Democratic Republic, PRC = People's Republic of China, USA = United States of America.

Source: Sovacool et al. 2011.

Click here for figure data

Box figure 1 shows that the top three performers were Japan, Brunei Darussalam, and the US. The worst were Viet Nam, India, and Myanmar. Higher score refers to better energy security performance. The bar shows the energy security index for each country and the value ranges from 0 to 100. Box figure 2 shows that Myanmar suffered the largest deterioration of energy and environmental security, a 63% decline, between 1990 and 2010. The best improvers were Malaysia, Australia, and Brunei Darussalam.

This study raises three main points. First, most countries have improved their energy security only marginally or else regressed. Interestingly, even the best performers fell far short of a perfect score of 100. Japan and Brunei Darussalam scored favorably on barely more than half of the metrics, and the fourth-placed US scored favorably on only one-third. This conclusion is discouraging in light of all the apparent progress that has been made since the 1970s: the creation of the IEA, the rapid growth of renewable energy, the rise of energy efficiency and demand management, and research on cutting-edge technologies. Despite these frenetic efforts, the index suggests that energy security in most countries has stagnated or even weakened.

Second, the index reveals great disparity. Japan, a strong leader, did not leave improving energy security to the marketplace. Its experience underscores the importance of government intervention. The success of Japanese energy policy arose from coordinated and consistent political support for policy and aggressive investments to achieve ambitious targets.

Third, the study reveals the difficult tradeoffs among components of energy security. Japan achieved its low energy intensity, advanced technology, and mitigation of greenhouse gas emissions only with large government subsidies and comparatively high prices for energy services. The Lao PDR has a small carbon footprint and high penetration of hydroelectricity but has prioritized exporting energy rather than expanding domestic access, though it is now seeking to expand hydropower supply to the domestic market. Dam construction continues to erode environmental quality, and the country remains completely dependent on imported oil to fuel transport. Myanmar's extreme export-oriented energy strategy can leave its population literally in the dark, its favorable score on environmental indicators reflecting only limited capacity and poor access. The fundamental problem is that some elements of energy security, such as affordability, apparently come only at the expense of others, such as sustainability and efficiency. Perhaps in recognition of this, Myanmar is beginning to change its export-oriented strategy.

2 Change in energy and environmental performance score of selected countries, 1990–2010 (%)

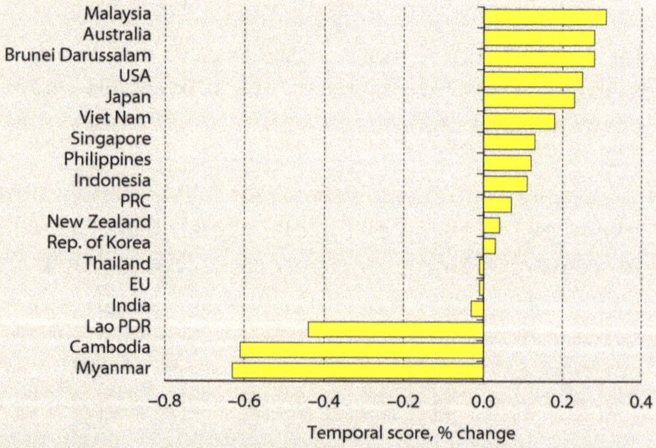

EU = European Union, Lao PDR = Lao People's Democratic Republic, PRC = People's Republic of China, USA = United States of America.

Source: Sovacool et al. 2011.

Click here for figure data

Containing burgeoning energy demand

Asia enjoys an array of promising options to check its energy appetite. Regional governments do not have to look far for a compelling example of the potential for demand management. Japan depends almost entirely on imported energy, especially oil but also coal and liquefied natural gas, to power its huge economy, the third largest in the world. Yet Japan's energy intensity is low—the lowest in the world, lower than in the European Union, the US, Latin America, or the developing world. Spurred by the oil shocks of the 1970s, Japan has worked hard to improve its economic output per unit of energy. Despite temporary bumps perversely enabled by the collapse of oil prices in the 1980s and 1990s, Japan's energy intensity in 2010 was 25% lower than in 1980.

The broader lesson that developing Asia can draw from the Japanese experience is that managing energy demand more efficiently can make a big difference to the energy pathway, and there is every reason for others to try to emulate Japan's success. Effective government leadership can mobilize behavior change in firms and households. The lesson for Asian governments is that they must take the lead in changing the mindset and culture of their citizens so that they use energy more efficiently and thus do their part to promote Asia's energy security.

Several strategies offer promise toward more efficient demand management even in the short term. Broadly speaking, these strategies can be grouped into three groups. First, eliminating consumer subsidies and taxing greenhouse gas emissions will move the price of energy toward its true cost. Second, green innovation such as smart cities and clean transportation will improve energy efficiency and environmental sustainability. Third, changing behavior can curtail wasteful energy consumption. Demand management is promising but presents various challenges. Tackling outmoded subsidies requires political will, green innovation takes investment in technology, and changing behavior entails instilling fundamentally new attitudes.

Energy prices that reflect true costs

One obvious channel for managing demand more efficiently is to remove distortions that artificially reduce the price of energy to below its true cost. Sometimes government policy such as consumer subsidies are the source of such distortions, which encourage energy overconsumption. In other cases, government intervention such as greenhouse gas taxes are required to bridge the gap between the true cost of energy, including its environmental cost, and its purchase price.

Eliminating consumer subsidies

Consumer subsidies designed to guarantee affordability and protect households from the potentially large shocks of fuel price increases end up artificially reducing the price of energy and thus encouraging overconsumption. Simulation results from Del Granado, Coady, and Gillingham (2012) show that a $0.25 per liter increase in fuel prices causes a 4.5% decline in household real incomes in Asia and Pacific (Table 2.2.1). This impact is partly direct, forcing households to spend more on fuel, and partly indirect, as prices paid for goods and services swell with higher embedded energy costs.

2.2.1 Direct and indirect welfare impacts of fuel price increases (%)

	Direct impact, by product				Direct impact	Indirect impact	Total impact
	Gasoline	Kerosene	LPG	Electricity			
Africa	0.2	1.2	0.2	0.1	1.7	3.7	5.4
South and Central America	0.2	0.2	0.3	0.2	0.8	2.4	3.3
Asia and the Pacific	0.3	1.6	0.3	0.3	2.5	2.0	4.5
Middle East and Central Asia	1.4	0.7	1.0	0.5	3.6	3.7	7.4
All regions	0.4	1.1	0.3	0.2	2.0	3.3	5.4

LPG = liquefied petroleum gas.
Note: Welfare impacts are caused by increasing the price of fuels by $0.25 per liter.
Source: Del Granado, Coady, and Gillingham 2012.

Most Asian countries provide some form of subsidy to offset harm to welfare, with subsidies varying widely from country to country (Figure 2.2.1). Subsidies in developing Asia are larger than elsewhere except the Middle East, and they are increasing (Table 2.2.2).

A lot of attention has been paid to fossil fuel subsidies globally, as overconsumption damages energy supply adequacy and the environment. Member countries of the Group of 20 and Asia–Pacific Economic Cooperation have declared that such subsidies will be phased out. According to the IEA (2012a), oil-exporting countries offer the highest subsidies in terms of their share of GDP. Among non-oil-exporting countries in Asia, Bangladesh and Pakistan have the highest GDP shares—though estimates vary from year to year with fluctuations in international prices for liquefied petroleum gas, natural gas, and oil.

Such subsidies are well-intentioned, or at least popular, but they increase energy consumption, distort energy development planning, and, when applied unevenly, provide incentives for adulteration and illegal cross-border sales. Worse, the main beneficiaries of energy subsidies are not the poor. If the intent is to make energy more affordable to the poor, only the poorest 20 percentile should benefit from the subsidy. In fact, the poor in Asia benefit little from subsidized fuel prices because many lack electricity and gas connections, few own vehicles, and most use public transport sparingly. The IEA (2011a) surveyed nine Asian countries with the highest fossil fuel subsidies, along with two countries in Africa, and found that only 15% of the benefit of kerosene subsidies—and a paltry 5% of subsides for liquefied petroleum gas—went to the poorest 20th percentile (Figure 2.2.2).

As the stated intent of energy subsidies is to provide affordable energy to the disadvantaged, the better solution would be to give the target populations direct cash benefits or energy coupons. Poor households are identified for benefits like food distribution, education support, and medical treatment. The energy subsidy could be similarly targeted.

2.2.1 Fossil-fuel subsidy, 2011

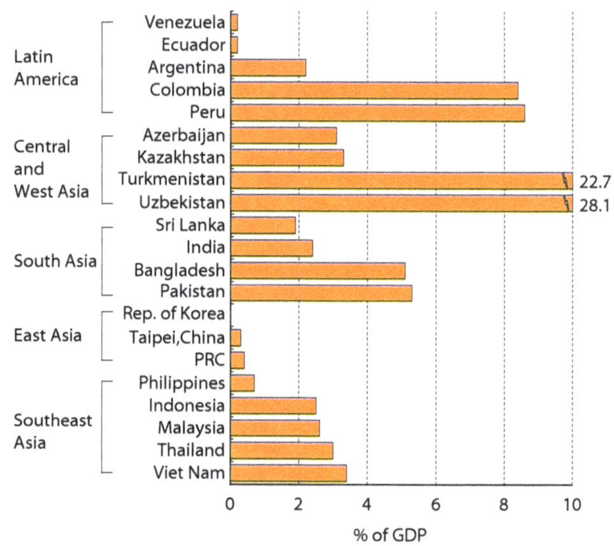

PRC = People's Republic of China.
Source: IEA 2012a.
Click here for figure data

2.2.2 Fossil fuel consumption subsidies ($ billion)

	2007	2008	2009	2010	2011
Developing Asia	90.6	177.0	94.6	113.7	161.7
Latin America	51.7	71.0	25.5	40.2	59.5
Middle East	124.0	193.9	124.7	170.4	204.2
Africa	36.5	51.5	26.7	41.2	48.1
Eastern Europe	39.4	61.3	39.7	46.9	49.5

Note: Countries surveyed were Angola, Bangladesh, the People's Republic of China, India, Indonesia, Pakistan, the Philippines, South Africa, Sri Lanka, Thailand, and Viet Nam.
Source: IEA 2011a.

2.2.1 Replacing general price subsidies with targeted transfers in Indonesia

A fuel subsidy puts pressure on the budget and external account. The Government of Indonesia still administers fuels prices, which lag far behind international price increases and cause unsustainably high fiscal spending. In 2012, the government spent $22 billion on fuel subsides—at 2.6% of GDP, they were 0.6 percentage points higher than the government's infrastructure spending. As Indonesia now imports fuel, the policy weighs on the country's external account.

Although reducing the fuel subsidy will remain politically difficult, domestic debate is moving in the right direction. Cutting the fuel subsidy increases prices and is thus politically very unpopular. However, the public recognizes that the general fuel subsidy disproportionately benefits the rich and middle class, disregarding any question of need. A household survey found the richest 10% of households consuming 40% of all subsidized gasoline (World Bank 2011). In addition, the policy encourages overconsumption. As reallocating fiscal resources to infrastructure, health, and education would spur growth and make it more inclusive, the administration and parliament agreed in the 2013 budget to allow higher fuel prices.

Switching from general price subsidies to targeted transfers is the best option. The government is planning to establish in 2014 a national social security system through which the government will pay insurance premiums for poor families. Discussion is under way to use the new social security system to target energy subsidy transfers to the poor.

For example, a cash payment scaled for the energy used by a typical energy-poor household, not tied to the household's energy consumption, would extend access without encouraging wasteful use. In fact, a beneficiary household would have incentive to use less energy and keep the surplus from the payout to pay for other needs. This achieves the objective of restraining energy use without creating the perverse incentives that so frequently drive energy systems off track.

Replacing general energy subsidies with subsidies targeting the energy poor can immediately restrain energy demand without denying those in need. It can go a long way toward laying the foundation for Asian energy security. Box 2.2.1 shows the Indonesian government's efforts to reduce subsidies despite political difficulties.

2.2.2 Share of fossil-fuel subsidies received by the poorest 20th percentile, 2010

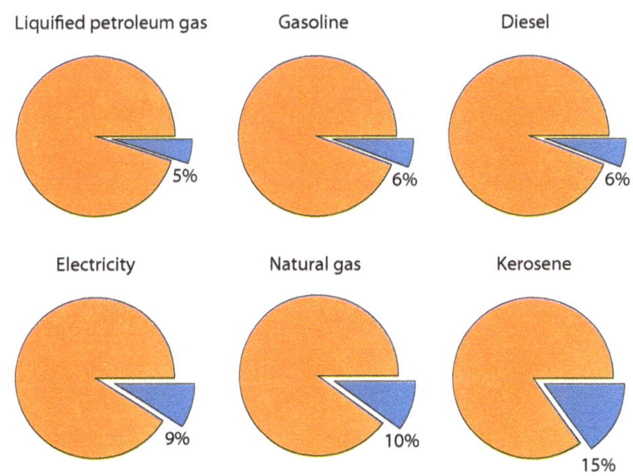

Note: Countries surveyed were Angola, Bangladesh, the People's Republic of China, India, Indonesia, Pakistan, the Philippines, South Africa, Sri Lanka, Thailand, and Viet Nam.

Source: IEA 2011a.

Click here for figure data

Taxing greenhouse gas emissions

Market energy prices rarely reflect the true price of energy when such negative externalities as pollution are factored in. A widely touted option is the so-called carbon tax on emissions of greenhouse gases (GHGs). The argument in favor of such a tax is that the price of energy should cover such externalities as GHG emissions. This inclusive price would create incentives to reduce energy consumption and develop new clean technologies, which would strengthen two of the three pillars of Asian energy security: energy supply adequacy and environmental sustainability. However, carbon taxes face two primary difficulties.

First, the so-called "free rider" problem is that countries benefit from others' adoption of a carbon tax whether or not they themselves adopt one and shoulder the competitive trade disadvantage it imposes through higher costs. Second, a carbon tax raises energy prices and thus undercuts affordability, compromising that pillar of Asian energy security. It also slows economic activity.

Addressing the free rider problem requires international policy coordination, but little progress has been made in international dialogue to impose a carbon tax. Some countries with caps on GHG emissions have considered imposing a duty on import of goods from countries that do not have caps. Consensus has so far been elusive, even for extending the Clean Development Mechanism toward capping emissions from fossil fuels mostly in developed economies and encouraging clean energy use in developing economies. This reflects failure to evaluate the impact of a carbon tax beyond the short term. In the long run, a carbon tax will encourage new technologies for tapping clean and renewable energy sources, lowering fossil fuel use in transportation, and developing other ways to mitigate GHG emissions. Developing countries in Asia could direct the revenues raised from a carbon tax toward accelerating clean energy technologies. In the long run, innovators would outperform free riders.

In addition, ways exist to mitigate the harm done by carbon taxes to energy affordability and economic growth. Tax proceeds can fund targeted subsidies to make affordable energy available to the poor, as described above. Keeping a carbon tax from inhibiting economic activity is trickier but possible. One solution is for governments to use tax proceeds to reduce the cost of another production input to offset firms' higher energy costs. The European Commission has evaluated this kind of revenue recycling (Kouvaritakis et al. 2005).

The United Kingdom introduced a "climate change levy," which compensated corporate payers of a carbon tax by reducing their contributions to employees' social insurance, essentially giving firms a break on their payroll taxes to offset increased energy costs. However, the government reneged on the promised reduction a few years later by returning social insurance contributions to the previous rate.

A general lesson from this experience is that governments can be tempted to use proceeds from a carbon tax and similar schemes for unintended purposes when a fiscal shortfall arises. But it also shows that such a program can be implemented if the political will exists. In 2003, the Council of Ministers of the European Union issued a directive that allowed member states to "offer companies tax incentives in return for specific undertakings to reduce emissions" (European Commission 2004). Such initiatives are voluntary at the moment, but the decision points to a growing perception that GHG taxation with revenue recycling may offer a powerful tool for policy makers.

Gains from green innovation

There is a lot of scope for technological innovation that can promote energy efficiency as well as environmental sustainability. Good city planning and design can lower individual and aggregate energy requirements by, for example, expanding the role of public transport. Gaseous transportation fuels such as compressed natural gas can mitigate the environmental impact of urban transportation. Substituting gas for electricity in end-use applications saves gas and displaces coal and other dirtier types of energy. Green innovation requires large investments in new technology and infrastructure, but the benefits are potentially huge.

Smart cities that save energy

A fast-growing body of research supports the idea that clever planning and design can enable new urban centers to deliver significant environmental and energy savings. As Asia grows, new cities will emerge, and this relatively clean slate provides the opportunity to substantially redefine urban design. Industrialized countries in which rural-to-urban migration has largely run its course lack this opportunity.

Urbanization itself offers evident benefits in energy efficiency and environmental protection. In the industrialized world, residents of compact urban centers individually consume less energy and water than their suburban and rural counterparts. They live in smaller spaces, consume less, discard less trash, and rely far less on cars for transportation, as walking, cycling, or public transportation are practical options that use energy far more efficiently than do private cars (Owen 2009).

The benefits can be multiplied. Careful urban design can apply knowledge of mobility patterns to create compact, walkable neighborhoods. Shared-use mobility and thoughtfully agglomerated office buildings can reduce transportation energy demands. Well-designed communication and control systems can provide real-time information on energy, water, and other resource use that can help consumers alter consumption and movement patterns to maximize their efficient use. Asian urban centers are taking the form of megacity hubs with suburban satellite cities. Rapid transportation systems like bus mass transit systems in the PRC and subways in India help lower energy use and improve the environment and quality of life (ADB 2012).

Careful urban planning can take advantage of cogeneration opportunities, in which waste heat from power generation can serve the heating and cooling needs of commercial buildings and households if the geographic configuration is compact enough. Ulaanbaatar, Mongolia, is procuring a combined heat-and-power plant to replace aging counterparts. Similarly, several cities in Central Asia have rehabilitated and upgraded their heating supply systems to be fed by combined heat-and-power plants. Large waste collection and disposal systems in urban centers can generate electricity from waste, as is done in Incheon, Republic of Korea. Malaysia has installed gas district cooling systems that boast system efficiency at 75%, or almost double the 40% for systems driven by electric motors.

Smart cities may rely on telecommuting and telepresence to minimize travel costs, design work flows that allow teams to work asynchronously toward flexible work hours, provide real-time information to enable more efficient consumption and travel patterns, establish on-demand and real-time control of materials and energy flows to residences and businesses, and remotely control industrial and commercial processes.

In Asia, moving toward this new growth paradigm is a matter of considerable urgency if its promise is to be realized. Whereas Europe needed 150 years from the beginning of serious urbanization to shift a majority of its population into urban centers, North America took only 105 years and Asia will need only 95 years (ADB 2012). From 1980 to 2010, Asia added more than a billion people to its cities, pushing urban densities higher than in the rest of the world. Asia has 8 of the 10 most densely populated large cities in the world, including the top three: Mumbai, Kolkata, and Karachi, in that order. In 2010, Asia was home to 12 of the world's 23 megacities, or just over half. This rapid urbanization is expected to continue, bringing Asia's urban population from the current 43% to 50% in 2025. Considering Asia's large population, the strong urbanization trend will continue thereafter, opening the door to a new growth paradigm if the process is properly managed.

Canada has established the Green Municipal Fund to support green cities studies and pilot projects through grants and low-cost loans. It has so far committed to disbursing $613 million to support 934 green initiatives in more than 460 communities across Canada. The benefits from 70 completed projects include reduced GHG emissions and water consumption.

The implementation of green and smart cities in Asia will require a major shift in urban planning. Additional public finance will be needed for the higher upfront capital and maintenance costs.

Clean, green transportation

Compressed natural gas (CNG) and other gaseous fuels have been introduced into urban transport mainly to address the pollution caused by gasoline and diesel internal combustion engines. Recognizing the contribution natural gas can make to better air quality and other benefits, the Republic of Korea and India, among others, have stepped up efforts to promote transport using CNG (Box 2.2.2). Two studies in California modeled the lifecycle impacts of this use of gaseous fuel, including its preparation, distribution, and use in various types of light- and heavy-duty vehicles. The main findings were that it would reduce energy use and GHG emissions by 6%–11%, local pollution by 20%–80%, and petroleum use by more than 90%. The model pertains to Californian patterns of vehicle use and processes of fuel delivery and electricity generation, and the magnitude of savings will vary across countries, but petroleum would undoubtedly be saved and local pollution reduced. Both reductions would make using CNG and other gaseous fuels beneficial in Asia, especially toward the goals of energy supply adequacy and local environmental sustainability.

Plug-in hybrid electric vehicles (PHEVs) and battery electric vehicles (BEVs) both reduce local air pollution. PHEVs run on a combination of conventional fossil fuels and a battery that is recharged by regenerative braking, which captures the energy otherwise lost when the vehicle slows. This allows PHEVs to use about 35% less fuel than a conventional vehicle. BEVs also use regenerative breaking but rely mostly on the grid power supply to recharge their batteries, so their lifecycle energy and GHG savings depend on the mix of the sources powering the grid. The result is primarily a shift of pollution away from where the vehicles are operated to where the electricity is generated. If the grid electricity is generated using coal, both lifecycle energy use and GHG emissions are higher from BEVs than from PHEVs. If the electricity is primarily from hydropower, however, emissions are very low.

Both options shift pollution out of urban centers. The PRC is aggressively deploying electric vehicles in line with a strategy of co-evolution between electric vehicles and the development of grid

2.2.2 Compressed natural gas transporting Koreans

Motor vehicles are responsible for 23% of energy-related carbon dioxide emissions (IEA 2010a). Using natural gas for transport can play an important role in reducing these emissions. Compressed or liquefied natural gas can power transport by land, sea, or air. The benefits of using natural gas range from immediate cost, noise, and emissions reduction to longer-term improvements in local air quality and energy security. Studies show emissions reduction in carbon dioxide equivalent averaging 25% when CNG replaces gasoline in passenger cars and light commercial vehicles. In more heavily used vehicles such as buses and trucks, CNG also offers significant emissions reduction (IEA 2010b).

The use of natural gas for transport in the Republic of Korea became significant with the introduction in 2000 of CNG buses to replace diesel-powered city buses, as mandated by the country's Clean Air Conservation Act. The government provides financial assistance for the purchase of natural gas vehicles and part of their fuel. In 2006, the government planned to set aside $100 million to support the program and provide bus operators with $24,000 for every CNG bus (Green Car Congress 2006). In Seoul, the city government restricted buses operating in the city to CNG, starting in 2010. The city government provided subsidies to bus operators for each CNG bus purchased to cover part of the cost differential. In other major cities, diesel buses at the end of their useful life (9 years by law) are being replaced by CNG buses. The use of CNG buses accelerated in the country in 2006–2010, when over 3,000 CNG buses were added each year (box figure). As of 2010, the country had 25,996 CNG buses in operation. One-third of them are in Seoul, where improved air quality is convincing proof that government support was a wise investment.

Number of buses using compressed natural gas in the Republic of Korea

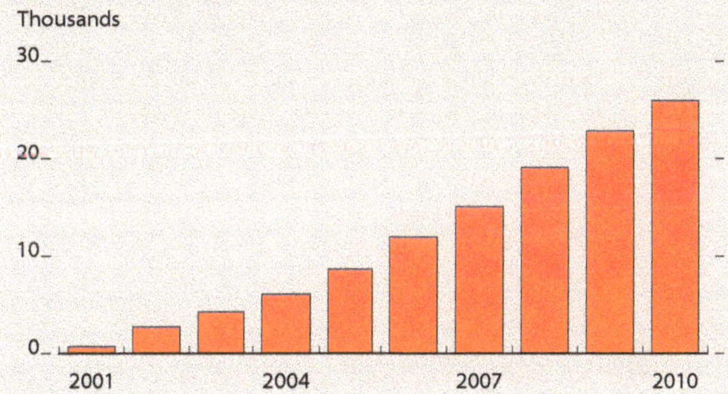

Source: Environmental Statistics Yearbook 2011, Republic of Korea.

Click here for figure data

generation using renewable energy (IEA 2011b,c). The country has begun with a three-stage pilot project dubbed the Ten Cities Ten-Thousand Vehicles Program, though it actually covers 25 cities, 12 in the first stage: Beijing, Changchun, Changsha, Chongqing, Hangzhou, Heifei, Jinan, Kunming, Nanchang, Shanghai, Shenyang, and Shenzhen.

Most electric vehicles currently in use in the pilot cities are public buses, taxis, official vehicles, and service vehicles, but five of the cities offer support for private electric vehicles. According to the IEA, Beijing delivered 1,000 neighborhood electric vehicles in 2009 and planned to develop 30,000 electric vehicles by 2012, 23,000 of them BEVs and 7,000 PHEVs. The Shanghai government set a target of 20,000 private electric vehicle purchases by the end of 2012, and Shenzhen expects to have 100,000 electric vehicles by 2015. The cities have invested in charging stations and other infrastructure and have enlisted major auto manufacturers in the program (IEA 2011b).

The IEA cites the Ministry of Industry and Information Technology as reporting that the plan includes promoting the widespread commercialization of BEVs, with vehicle batteries either recharged or swapped out. Personal BEV and PHEV ownership is slated to reach 500,000, as the deployment of medium and heavy PHEVs reaches 1 million, all by 2015. Thereafter, the plan calls for BEV and PHEV ownership by 2020 to reach 5 million, accounting for 5% of total vehicle ownership (IEA 2011b).

This strategy is rightly called "co-evolution" as the development of electric vehicle fleets and power generation using renewable energy reinforce each other. The introduction to the power grid of intermittently available renewables creates challenges to reliability and stability, which can be mitigated by connecting a fleet of electric vehicles through a "smart grid" (a technological advance discussed below on pages 104–105). Batteries in electric vehicles can store renewable power that is produced in excess of system load. Two-way charging infrastructure can allow electric vehicle batteries to feed back into the grid during peak demand. Such "spinning reserves" for power systems provide backup power that is immediately available and potentially reduce the cost of investment in generating capacity, strengthen the stability of the system, and provide backup against system failures. Meanwhile, electric vehicle owners can earn rebates by providing these services to the grid, thus reducing their operating costs.

Clean transport requires a major shift in services. Mass road transit systems can operate fleets with gaseous fuels, and private ownership can move toward electric vehicles. Close collaboration and partnership among municipal governments, carmakers, and fuel suppliers is essential. Initially, public finance can promote research and development and help build the critical mass of vehicles that brings the cost of gas and electricity distribution per vehicle down to manageable levels. Clean transport becomes more competitive as it grows.

Switching electricity for gas

Energy efficiency can be improved by replacing electricity with gas for end use. Consider using a cubic meter of gas two ways for cooking. One option is to burn the gas in a gas-fired power plant, which converts about 40% of the energy in the gas into electric energy (EIA 2013a) that a family can use to power an electric cooktop. If that same cubic meter of gas were instead delivered directly to power a gas cooktop, the same cooking energy would require only 40% of the original cubic meter of gas. The family would still have 60% of the cubic meter with which to prepare the next meal and half of the meal after that.

It is apparent that the energy supply system is better used if households purchase gas cooktops instead of electric ones. It makes little sense to burn gas in a power plant to boil water to generate electricity with which to boil water on an electric cooktop, when, instead, you can burn gas to boil water right in your kitchen. Replacing electricity with gas in many households and businesses would extend the useful life of natural gas reserves, thus enhancing energy supply adequacy by conserving gas resources. Further, using gas instead of electricity for cooking substantially reduces emissions.

The story is even more compelling if the power plant uses coal instead of gas. Coal is a much dirtier fuel for power generation than is natural gas, producing more emissions that are more problematic. To the extent that electric power is generated with coal, replacing electricity with gas for end uses offers even greater emissions benefits (Figure 2.2.3).

Much of the industrialized world is locked into existing electric and natural gas transmission and distribution systems. These systems are highly developed but shaped more by historical happenstance than by comprehensive planning to minimize investment cost and maximize energy efficiency. By contrast, as Asian societies expand their gas and electricity systems into new areas—as they will with urbanization and efforts to serve the energy poor—they will often build from scratch.

Asians will therefore enjoy more freedom of choice and potential for investment savings. Electricity generation, transmission, and distribution infrastructure is much more expensive to build than gas delivery infrastructure. While it may not be possible to replace electricity with gas for all new end uses in the foreseeable future, it is possible to reshape electricity and gas delivery systems in new ways that minimize redundancies and save capital costs.

And Asians will have more freedom to be energy efficient. Electricity and gas systems in the industrialized world arose at a time when energy efficiency was a low priority and utility regulators had little incentive to work with energy suppliers to find efficiency measures that could benefit from careful coordination between gas and electricity delivery. In contrast, Asia has the advantage of being able to pursue such coordination for future benefit.

2.2.3 The benefits of replacing electricity with gas

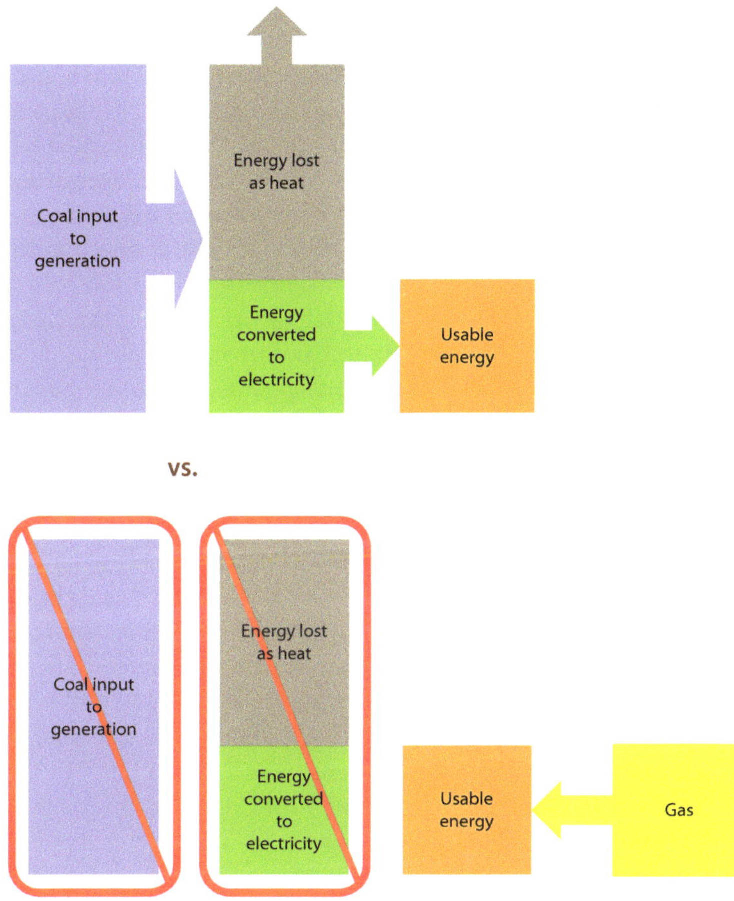

Source: Lee, Park, and Saunders, forthcoming.

If gas supplies become more abundant in Asia through, for example, the aggressive development of unconventional sources, the natural and immediate inclination is to use it as much as possible to replace dirty coal in generating electricity. This strategy seems obvious, but a broader view points a different direction. Natural gas has more value for environmental protection and energy conservation if it is used instead to replace electricity in end uses—2.5 times the value as the cooking illustration showed.

Such replacement may be practical only where energy supply systems expand into newly built-up areas. In the meantime, using gas to generate electricity may be the sensible alternative in established cities, at least for the time being. And, in a few countries, notably Bhutan, the Kyrgyz Republic, and Tajikistan, most electricity supplied to end users is generated from clean hydropower. In these cases—or where small, isolated grids are supplied by solar or wind power—switching from electricity to gas would be ill-advised as the electricity is from cleaner, renewable sources. These caveats do not apply, however, in most Asian locations that will experience dramatic economic and infrastructure expansion in the coming years and decades.

Gas can replace electricity for a number of end uses, among them certain industrial processes; space heating and cooling; and powering kitchen appliances such as cooktops, ovens, and refrigerators. Manufacturers of appliances, home heating and cooling equipment, and industrial capital equipment can be encouraged to promote gas over electric designs. Doing so will gradually reshape the fuel demand profile. If end users demand gas, energy providers will respond. In any case, the future development of gas and electricity transmission and distribution systems should be coordinated. Gas and electric utilities generally operate within regulatory frameworks, but sometimes the frameworks are only loosely coordinated. The economic advantages of minimizing infrastructure duplication combine with energy savings and emissions reduction to provide strong motivation for better coordinating gas and electricity systems in new infrastructure. Low international gas prices and investment in liquefied natural gas terminals mean that even energy-importing countries can benefit. Coordinated planning of new electricity and gas infrastructure should be augmented by building local firms' capacity to successfully enter the gas supply business, which has relatively few players in most of developing Asia.

Changing energy consumer behavior

Energy prices that reflect the true cost of energy will induce Asian households and firms to use energy more efficiently. But there is much more that can and should be done to promote more efficient energy use. Above all, there is a need to change the general public's energy use behavior by instilling a recognition that energy is a scarce, valuable resource. The impact of new energy efficiency technologies will depend on the scale and speed of their uptake. Conservation programs can induce individuals to refrain from purely wasteful energy consumption. Changing behavior ultimately requires a fundamental shift in the general public's attitudes. The government should act as a catalyst in this endeavor, as the Japanese experience shows.

Energy efficiency available on demand

Asian governments must take the lead in changing Asians' energy use behavior. More aggressive policies to promote to consumers cost-effective energy efficiency will enhance Asia's economic growth, private consumption, government expenditure, and investment. Further, energy efficiency gains reduce the effective price of energy, thus advancing the cause of affordability and access. Similarly, lower energy consumption reduces emissions, thus furthering environmental sustainability.

In addition, if programs encouraging investment in improved energy efficiency make energy services more economical, they will likely be accompanied by net increases in productive labor employment. Especially during times of economic slowdown, programs that improve energy efficiency by, for example, retrofitting buildings can employ otherwise idle labor to add value to the economy.

Other benefits flow from how energy efficiency gains expand producer and consumer surpluses and strengthen economic welfare. Evidence from Europe shows such gains directly improving public budgets when firms hire workers to retrofit aging, energy-inefficient buildings and pay associated payroll taxes, and when workers pay income and social insurance taxes rather than claim unemployment benefits

(Naess-Schmidt 2012). The IEA has recognized and identified how energy efficiency gains help alleviate poverty.

Several technologies to improve energy efficiency are now in use and well-established in developed economies but lack penetration across Asia. For example, consumers' use of compact fluorescent lamps and light-emitting diodes can save up to 70% of the electricity used by incandescent, sodium vapor, or halogen lamps. Active solar thermal systems to heat water and interiors are popular in the PRC, which has 39% more active solar thermal systems installed than the rest of the world combined (IEA 2011a).

Solar tubes can bring daylight into rooms without windows, and special solar paints can reflect most heat from the sun to lower the energy needed for cooling. Similarly, proper building insulation conserves heat during the winter. Hybrid electric vehicles reduce fuel consumption with brakes that capture energy from a decelerating vehicle for charging batteries that run the motor. High-efficiency electric motors are used extensively in industry. Such new technologies entail high upfront fixed costs, however, because their developers need to recoup research and development investments. Further, they initially may not be as reliable as existing efficient technologies. Encouraging more investment would accelerate their commercialization.

A very large market like Asia is conducive to the rapid deployment and commercialization of new technologies. Establishing and supervising efficiency standards can reinforce consumer demand for energy-efficient technologies, and the ready availability of loans can expand their adoption in firms and households. Government programs that create incentive for developing better technologies and designs in a concerted way can accelerate the progress of innovation.

The proposition that more aggressive policies toward energy efficiency can strengthen all three pillars of Asian energy security is extremely seductive. Unfortunately, though, the seduction of energy efficiency cuts both ways.

On the lookout for rebound effects

A large and growing body of research has shown that energy efficiency gains do not bring one-for-one reductions in energy consumption because of the so-called "rebound effect." In extreme cases, improved efficiency can backfire, spurring outright increases in energy consumption. It appears that energy efficiency improvements act much as energy price reductions or energy subsidies, encouraging higher energy use (Box 2.2.3).

What is particularly troublesome for Asia is that rebound effects appear to be larger in developing economies than in industrialized economies. Even with rebound effects, energy efficiency gains advance the cause of affordable access by reducing the effective cost of energy and spur economic growth by making energy cheaper for producers. If rebound falls short of backfire, efficiency gains improve environmental sustainability and energy supply adequacy by reducing energy use. Careful attention paid to managing rebound effects can ensure that investments in energy efficiency strengthen all pillars of Asian energy security.

2.2.3 Energy efficiency rebound effects: technical background

Measuring rebound effects compares the technical potential for energy savings from energy efficiency improvements with the energy savings actually realized. Formally, rebound magnitude is defined according to the following equation:

$$R = 1 - \frac{ES_A}{ES_P}$$

where ES_A is the actual energy savings realized and ES_P is the potential energy savings as estimated from engineering calculations.

If actual energy savings equal potential savings, rebound is zero. If there are no actual savings, rebound is unity, or 100%. If energy use rises, rebound is greater than 100%—a backfire.

Potential energy savings are calculated assuming that energy efficiency gains reduce energy use, in households and businesses alike, in direct proportion to the magnitude of the energy efficiency improvement. If every light bulb, television, refrigerator, or air conditioner were replaced by a more efficient counterpart, whether existing or new, energy use would be reduced correspondingly while the same end uses are served—perhaps even better served. Production using new energy-efficient technologies would reduce the energy required to produce and transport any given good or service, correspondingly reducing energy use—with outsized potential benefits, as the production side of the economy uses two-thirds of energy globally (ExxonMobil 2009).

However, energy efficiency gains lower the effective cost of energy, so users respond by using more. The magnitude of these effects depends on how flexibly consumers can adjust their consumption and how flexibly producers can substitute cheaper energy for other production inputs. Accordingly, actual energy savings will fall short of potential energy savings.

Energy intensity can be favorably reduced despite large rebound effects because energy efficiency is only one factor affecting energy intensity.

A large and growing empirical literature pioneered by Brookes (1979) and Khazzoom (1980) assesses the magnitude of the rebound effect. Recent studies include Saunders (1992, 2008, in press), Sorrell (2007, 2009), Turner (forthcoming), Tsao et al. (2010), and Jenkins, Nordhaus, and Shellenberger (2011).

Roy (2000) first suggested that rebound effects in developing countries may be larger than in industrialized countries. Li and Han (2012) showed energy efficiency rebound in the PRC to have been very large from 1997 to 2008, backfiring in 3 of those years. Lin and Liu (2013) analyzed passenger transportation in the PRC from 1994 to 2010 and found rebound at 107%—another backfire. Chakravarty, Dasgupta, and Roy (2013) provide a good survey of the literature.

Awareness and conservation programs

Potential exists to reduce energy use that is purely wasteful by altering individual behavior. Lights that burn when no one is present, trains that run on schedule but without passengers, individual car trips where pooling is possible, machinery idled instead of shut down during a production stoppage—all are examples of energy used for no constructive purpose. Programs designed to raise public awareness of the social value of eliminating energy waste can have positive impact despite their reliance on altruism and social pressure rather than proven market signals.

As with demand management generally, Japan provides a good example of the potential of conservation programs in its Setsuden ("saving electricity") movement (Box 2.2.4). The movement, which emerged following the Fukushima Daiichi nuclear accident, helped lower peak usage by 15% during the summer of 2012. The success of the Setsuden movement in preventing power outages in post-tsunami Japan attests to the potential of media awareness campaigns to change the behavior of firms and households. However, in light of the extreme circumstances under which the program was initiated, the jury is out on the degree to which Japan's experience can be replicated elsewhere. Although the exact

2.2.4 Japan's Setsuden initiative post-Fukushima

The Setsuden ("saving electricity") movement dramatically highlights Japan's ability to promote energy security through demand management. Nuclear power supplied 27% of Tokyo's energy needs before the March 2011 earthquake and tsunami that crippled the Fukushima nuclear power plant. The meltdown at Fukushima prompted stress tests and safety checks at other plants, mandating further shutdowns. Japanese firms and households consequently faced looming power shortages, and Setsuden arose as an unofficial, grassroots national movement to conserve electricity in response. Media campaigns encouraged firms and households to cut back. Workers moved their shifts to off-peak hours and weekends. Commercial establishments turned off air-conditioning.

The movement became official on 1 July 2011, when the government mandated reduced electricity use by large firms and prescribed reduction targets for households and small businesses. The restrictions were rescinded in September 2011, but only after the Setsuden movement succeeded in helping to prevent blackouts during the summer, when electricity use typically surges. Japan's peak usage fell by 15% from a year earlier.

The Setsuden movement built on earlier success. Throughout the last half century, the Government of Japan has catalyzed and led energy conservation. Its efforts have been rewarded with widespread voluntary compliance, the efforts of firms and households creating a virtuous cycle of energy efficiency improvements. The government's initiatives entail both regulation and support. Regulations based on the Law Concerning the Rational Use of Energy, 1979 set out energy efficiency standards for buildings, appliances, and other equipment. Government support consists of budgetary, tax, and financial measures. In addition to setting aside a budget for energy efficiency measures, the government provides tax breaks and subsidies.

Sources: EIA Country Analysis (www.eia.gov/countries/cab.cfm?fips=JA, updated 4 June 2012), Institute of Energy Economics, Japan 2011, Tokyo Electric Power Company 2012.

magnitude of energy savings obtainable by eliminating purely wasteful energy use is uncertain, they would come at virtually no cost.

In sum, better demand management can bring Asia significantly closer to the goal of energy security. It can do so by reducing the risk of inadequate supply and promoting environmental sustainability. But while better demand management is absolutely necessary for energy security, it cannot cover the whole distance. The journey requires solving the supply side of the equation, by augmenting the supply of clean, affordable energy. Fortunately, like the demand side, the supply side is as full of promising options.

Tapping cleaner energy supply

Asia's current energy picture contemplates some degree of energy supply enhancement: introducing new unconventional gas supplies, deploying renewable energy supplies, and modestly expanding nuclear power. As noted, however, meeting the needs of the Asian Century scenario would mean a tremendous increase in energy imports based on current plans to enhance indigenous supplies. Expanding its energy supply in a way that is environmentally sustainable will require Asia to pursue a combination of renewable energy, cleaner nonrenewable sources, and technologies to make carbon-based fuels cleaner to use.

Expansion of renewables

The current forecast shows the use of renewables increasing by half over the forecast period. Hydropower more than quadruples, but all renewables together still account for only 13% of the power generation mix in 2035. Is there an opportunity to substantially strengthen the role of renewables beyond forecasts?

Wind, solar, and other renewable energy technologies directly harness naturally available energy sources. They thus help to insulate the energy price from the ups and downs of fossil fuel production, thereby strengthening future energy security. These technologies can substitute for the fossil fuels used to generate electricity, reducing harmful emissions and improving environmental sustainability. Biofuels can potentially substitute for oil-based transportation fuels and so reduce the need for oil imports and enhance energy supply adequacy.

However, several difficulties prevent expanding renewables enough to make a major difference in Asia's energy future any time soon. Perhaps most fundamental is the need for renewable sources to be cost-competitive with the fuels they seek to replace. While various renewables have enjoyed significant cost reductions and are already economic in certain locales and remote areas, renewable energy generally remains too costly to be competitive. This is likely to change but how quickly is unclear.

Uncompetitive cost is not the only difficulty. Biofuels pose the risk of usurping agricultural land used to grow food if their production is to expand by the magnitude required to make a significant contribution. Using solar and wind to replace coal or oil in power generation is technically tricky, primarily owing to their intermittency. This complicates integrating large-scale solar and wind generation into power systems in a way that maintains system reliability, stability, and ability to quickly adjust output to minute-by-minute changes in system demand.

Many argue that being cost-competitive should be understood as factoring in environmental and other social costs that are external to the standard equations of microeconomics. However, capturing these "externalities" with subsidies or the imposition of taxes and mandates runs up energy prices and cramps economic activity. Also, the more expensive electricity derived from renewables undermines affordability, the third pillar of energy security. Policymakers have to consider such tradeoffs.

Nonetheless, one can argue that the long-term economic benefits garnered from the large-scale use of renewable energy outweigh short-term costs. Instruments such as feed-in tariffs during the introductory years of high-cost renewable technologies assure suppliers a reasonable price per kilowatt-hour to mitigate their commercial risk and thereby stimulate investment in larger capacity. Some policies directly promote renewables. One such is the renewable portfolio standard, which requires electricity distributors to source an increasing share of their primary energy from renewables. Renewable energy certificates create marketable instruments that producers can sell to distribution companies toward meeting the target renewable portfolio standard. Tax incentives like investment allowances and accelerated depreciation also help compensate for initially higher costs.

Pushing up capacity to generate electricity using renewables, by whatever means, accelerates the learning process and starts to bring down costs so that the longer-term economic benefits of cleaner energy supply can be realized sooner. The costs consequent of climate change could be very large, and public health costs associated with burning fossil fuels are bound to grow with their expanded use. There is economic benefit to be had by avoiding these costs sooner rather than later. Further, the massive energy market in Asia provides opportunity and room to introduce and develop new energy technologies that can be profitably sold to other countries wanting to expand their renewable energy sectors. Asia is already a world leader in the manufacture of state-of-the-art equipment for renewable technologies. The PRC, the Republic of Korea, and Taipei,China together produce most of the world's photovoltaic equipment for solar generation.

Wind power

Wind power has been rapidly expanding throughout the world, including in India and the PRC. The potential in Asia is enormous. According to one study (Shah 2012), Mongolia and the PRC could each install over 1 terawatt (1 million megawatts or 1,000 gigawatts) of wind capacity, which together would generate more than 3,000 terawatt-hours annually. This is over 60% of the PRC's total electricity consumption of 4,937 TWh in 2012. Kazakhstan, Afghanistan, and Viet Nam could each install over 100 gigawatts (GW). The only country currently exploiting more than 5% of its potential is India, its 30% exploitation driven largely by an accelerated depreciation allowance. However, the wind resource is distributed unevenly across Asia, endowing a handful of countries with huge potential but leaving many with little.

According to World Wind Energy Council, a leading industry association, the installed capacity of wind power in Asia in 2011 was 82.0 GW, or 36% of the total world capacity of 237.5 GW and comparable to Europe's 96.5 GW. By the end of 2012, global capacity had increased by 19% to 282.5 GW. With 75.5 GW, the PRC leads the world, and India is ranked fifth with 18.5 GW.

Figure 2.3.1 shows the distribution of wind resources and installed capacity across Asia. Unlike the solar resource, the wind resource varies significantly from site to site. In addition, at low winds and during storm conditions, turbines do not generate power. Sites need to have a mean wind speed of at least 6 meters per second (22 kilometers per hour) or higher, measured at the height of the rotor, to be viable. Improvements in design allow modern wind turbines to start generating power at a wind speed of 3 meters per second and cut off at 25 meters per second. Larger rotors, with diameters up to 127 meters, and higher turbines, with hub heights up to 135 meters, enable turbines to generate significant electricity even at sites with low wind, improving economics. Large turbines are also used offshore.

Wind is commercially more competitive than photovoltaic generation but not yet competitive enough to compete commercially with conventional forms of generation because it is too intermittent, hobbling wind with low capacity factors. Forecasts show the levelized cost of wind power falling by 20%–30% from current levels by 2030, making it nearly competitive with other forms of generation (Figure 2.3.2). The levelized cost is determined considering all operational costs, using a discount rate to spread the capital and financing cost over the life of the project, and including a reasonable return on investment.

If coal and gas prices were to escalate over this time frame, the relative economics of wind would improve accordingly. Challenges remain, however, to integrating this intermittent resource into the power grid. These challenges are complicated by wind resources' often being most bountiful in locations distant from demand centers, requiring lengthy connections with power grids.

In sum, wind power has numerous advantages over conventional power. Renewable resources are naturally available, so the primary energy resource costs nothing. Wind is virtually free of GHG emissions and emits no other air pollutants. Yet the prospects of wind power becoming cost effective within the forecast horizon is uncertain. If wind technologies are further developed at an accelerated pace, the day they become cost competitive can be brought forward. Small wind turbines are available that can provide electricity to small communities in remote locations cost-effectively because the locale makes other options expensive. They can thus help expand access to energy, but making it affordable to poor households requires public financing. As wind turbines require regular maintenance, this option also requires skilled maintenance staff.

2.3.1 Installed capacity and technical potential for wind

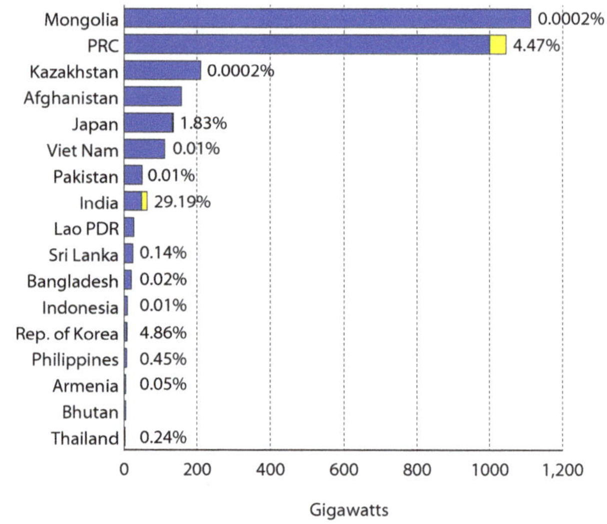

Lao PDR = Lao People's Democratic Republic, PRC = People's Republic of China.
Source: Shah 2012.
Click here for figure data

2.3.2 Projected levelized cost for wind electricity compared with conventional generation in the People's Republic of China

Levelized cost of energy, $/kilowatt-hour

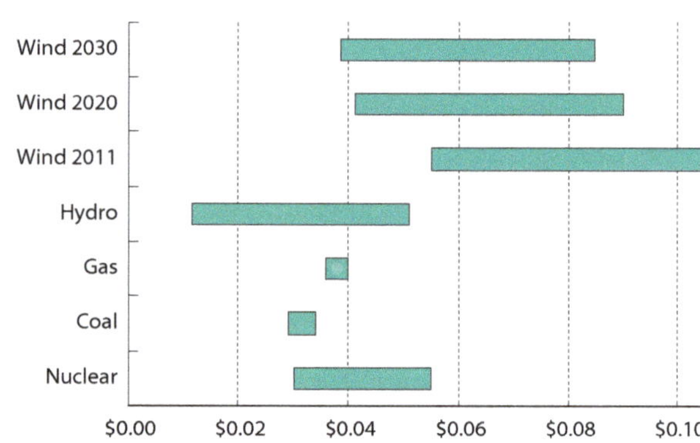

Source: Ross, forthcoming.
Click here for figure data

Solar power

Solar power has been developed in two main directions, one using photovoltaic (PV) technology and the other concentrating the sun's rays to provide heat for a turbine.

PV cells convert solar energy into electricity using semiconductors of two types. The more common crystalline silicon type is 14%–20% efficient. The other type, which uses a thin film, is less than 12% efficient but is cheaper to make. A panel's capacity factor is a measure of its effective utilization. A solar panel rated for 1 kilowatt (kW) can theoretically produce 8,760 kilowatt-hours (kWh) annually. However, actual output depends on the amount of energy in the sunlight, which depends on the location, daylight hours, cloud cover and how it reflects light, and ambient temperature. Considering these uncontrollable nature-linked parameters, the actual output of a 1 kW solar panel may be only 1,300 kWh in a year. That works out to a capacity factor of 15%, which is typical.

Concentrated solar power uses an array of mirrors to cause the sun's rays to converge on a central tower to heat fluid and raise steam to run a turbine, much as in a conventional thermal power plant. This technology has the option, with added cost, to store solar energy in salt solution and use it to generate electricity at night. Several configurations are used to concentrate the solar energy, their efficiencies ranging from about 10% for flat mirrors to over 30% for centralized towers and parabolic dishes.

Photovoltaic technology has been applied various ways since the 1960s. Despite being safe, clean, and extremely reliable, and its requiring no fuel and little maintenance, it has always been too expensive to achieve grid parity, or the ability to compete commercially on the grid without subsidies. This drawback may be changing, however, as the decades-long decline in PV module prices has accelerated in the last 5 years, leading some to speculate that grid parity is likely by the mid-2010s.

Should grid parity be achieved, it will have immense implications for all Asian countries, as they all need more power sources and have solar resources ranging from good to excellent. However, availability only during daylight hours, combined with the challenges of finding large tracts of land to accommodate large PV capacity, may limit penetration unless cheaper storage is developed. Meanwhile, PV is already the cheapest way to electrify small communities remote from the grid and thus has a potential role in providing electricity to hundreds of millions of Asians currently without power.

Asia's solar resource is shown in Figure 2.3.3. Lighter, more energetic colors indicate areas with more sunlight. Places close to the Equator have more hours of sunshine annually, but islands and coastal areas have more cloudy days that diffuse the sunlight. The sun is weaker at higher latitudes and never directly overhead, requiring that PV panels be fixed at an incline to capture the most solar energy. PV panels that track the sun as it rises and sets every day capture more sunlight than do fixed ones but with higher capital and maintenance costs for the tracking device.

Tilting and tracking even out spatial variation in the solar resource. From the worst site to the best site in Asia, the capacity factor even for fixed arrays varies from 10% to 20%, and most sites across the continent can achieve at least a capacity factor close to 16%. Tracking can improve on this. Thus, tilting and tracking makes solar energy accessible virtually anywhere in Asia.

PV technology has become cheaper over the decades it has been commercially available, and recently at an accelerated pace. The cost of crystalline silicon modules fell from about $80/watt in 1977 to less than $10/watt by the late 1980s and $4/watt in early 2008 (Economist 2012). At this point the price dropped off a cliff, halving in 2008–2009. Suppliers ramped up production to obtain subsidies offered to renewable energy

2.3.3 Solar resource in Asia

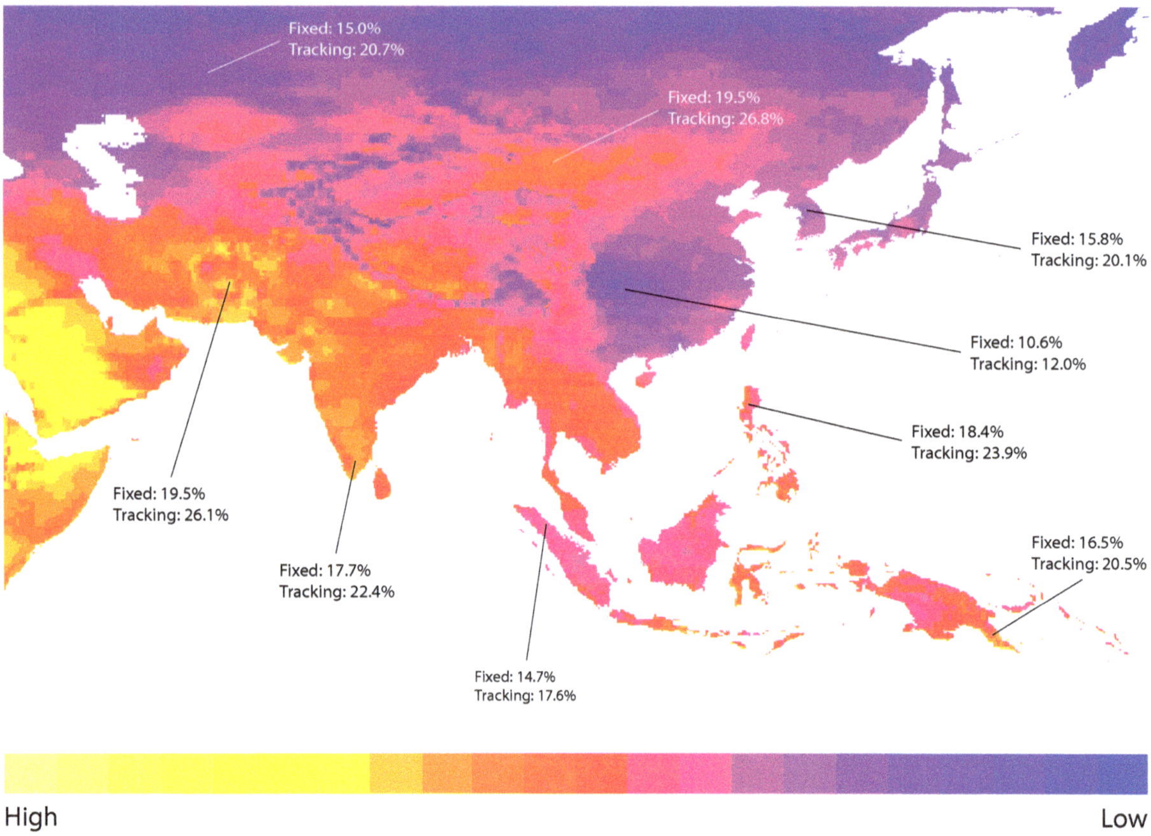

Notes: Color bar shows average global radiation on the horizontal in kilowatt-hours per square meter. For selected locations, the capacity factors for fixed arrays and tracking photovoltaic systems have been calculated with RETScreen 4 software. The capacity factor—the actual average power output as a percentage of the rated system power—is given for some locations; there are two values, one for a fixed system and another for tracking system.
Source: Map adapted from www.meteonorm.com

installations in Canada, Germany, and Spain, and they shifted manufacturing to lower-cost producers in the PRC that already had the skills for manufacturing semiconductors. Rapid cost declines have continued since then—recently reaching $0.70/watt—with radical implications for the PV industry. Module manufacturers have expressed some concern about overcapacity and low price, but production continues to expand as they find new ways to cut costs and learn from experience.

By the end of 2011, the global installed capacity of grid-connected PV systems was over 69 GW, which could annually produce 85 terawatt-hours (TWh), enough to power more than 20 million households (European Photovoltaic Industry Association 2013a). Preliminary estimates indicate that the installed capacity crossed the 100 GW threshold by the beginning of 2013, assuming additions in 2012 at the same pace as in 2011 (European Photovoltaic Industry Association 2013b). Notably, six countries in Asia and the Pacific have over 100 MW of grid-connected PV systems: the PRC with 7,000 MW, Japan 6,914 MW, Australia 2,200 MW, India 1,461 MW, the Republic of Korea 963 MW, and Thailand 360 MW.

How will PV prices evolve over time? Figure 2.3.4 compares the levelized cost of solar power from utility-scale plants (generally with capacity above 10 MW) with some conventional technologies. It suggests that even by 2030 PV-generated electricity will struggle to compete with large hydropower, cheap coal, nuclear, and cheap gas at today's prices. However, if coal and gas prices were to escalate significantly over this time horizon, solar could become more competitive.

PV installations can be integrated into the grid from a central plant, as with conventional power plants, or distributed around many locations on the grid. Distributed systems can be mounted on roofs and facades, minimizing land use and providing power close to where it is consumed, which reduces losses in transmission.

Concentrated solar power also has potential to contribute. Investment costs for concentrated solar power systems range from \$3,800/kW without storage to \$7,700/kW with storage, for an estimated levelized cost of electricity in 2009 ranging from \$0.18–\$0.27/kWh. Continued development is expected to halve the cost by 2025. US and European research and development programs envision even more dramatic cost reductions, targeting \$0.05–\$0.06/kWh by 2020 (Arvizu et al. 2011), which is cost-competitive with conventional alternatives.

2.3.4 Projected levelized cost for utility-scale photovoltaic systems compared with conventional generation in the People's Republic of China

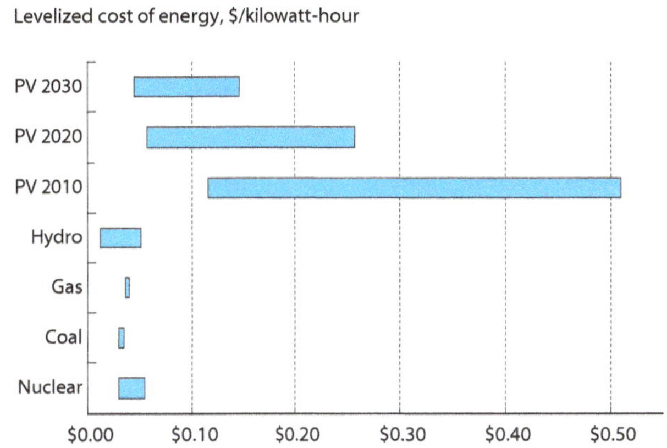

PV = photovoltaic.
Source: Ross, forthcoming.
Click here for figure data

In the meantime, governments have offered subsidies to spur the development of solar power by the private sector. Many governments hope that such subsidies, while costly in the short run, will accelerate the development of cost-competitive technologies and provide net economic and environmental gains over the long term.

In sum, solar power has numerous advantages over conventional power. The solar PV system is modular, so little technological change is needed for fitting individual homes, including even PV lanterns. It is virtually free of GHG emissions, and the primary energy source—sunlight—is freely available and widely distributed, notably in remote locales with no access to the grid.

PV is already cost competitive in many remote areas where the cost of extending electricity grids would be prohibitive: remote islands in the Pacific, the Philippines, and Indonesia; the mountains of Bhutan and the PRC; and the sparsely populated plains of Mongolia. These installations use public finance and international aid, but, as PV system costs decline, so will the need for subsidies. Improvements in battery technology will enable households to tap PV systems at night, making it an attractive investment. The Energy and Resources Institute in India has led the global distribution of solar lanterns that provide basic but clean light to poor households.

However, the prospects of utility-scale solar power becoming cost effective within the forecast horizon are uncertain unless more investment is forthcoming to further develop the technology. Satellites can assist evaluation of solar potential in a particular region, but assessments of capacity factor at specific locations, and thus of commercial solar potential, requires gathering data on the ground.

Hydropower

Hydropower has a number of attractive attributes. It is a clean resource with few GHG emissions and virtually no other pollutants emitted during operation. It is renewable, and once initial capital costs have been borne it provides energy extremely cheaply. In addition, large hydropower projects are commercially viable and do not require financial support from governments. Hydropower plants that reliably store energy behind a dam complement intermittent solar and wind energy and can respond quickly to variations in power demand to help maintain reliable electricity supply.

Hydropower technology is well established, and projects can be flexibly designed for an array of conditions. Some tap high volumes of water flow with little difference in height between the turbine intake and outlet, while others tap low volume falling greater distances. Some use reservoirs with several months of storage to allow power generation during dry seasons, while others depend on continuous water flow. Some pump water up to the higher reservoir when power demand is low to use it to generate electricity during peak demand hours. Micro hydro can serve the needs of a small community. A cascade of several dams can be built on a single watershed to generate power from the same water repeatedly.

Asia has substantial undeveloped hydro resources, only 20% of which have been developed (IEA 2013). As Asia's developed hydropower capacity in 2010 was 337 GW (EIA 2011d), total hydro potential approaches 1,700 GW (Table 2.3.1).

The aggressive expansion of hydro would entail some problems. Local opposition to hydropower development can be strong, as is clear in India. Conflicts often arise over the loss of agriculturally productive land and the need to resettle communities. Further, the communities that lose their land and homes to a new reservoir often do not benefit when water is diverted into canals for irrigation downstream. Tensions run higher when rivers cross international frontiers or even provincial boundaries. Environmental concerns extend to the loss of scenic valleys, habitat destruction, and fishery disruption.

A wild card is climate change. It may alter precipitation and thus river flows in a developed catchment, rendering reservoir storage capacity far from optional. Interestingly, the more violent storms and extended droughts that global warming is expected to cause will require greater water storage capacity for irrigation and flood prevention. This could make building dams for hydropower simultaneously part of a larger strategy to address climate change.

The capital cost of a hydropower project is site-specific and varies a lot depending on the civil works needed to build the dam and the reservoir. The levelized cost of energy similarly varies a lot but is generally \$0.04–\$0.10/kWH, which makes it very cost-competitive.

In the end, all renewables escape the fate common to oil, gas, coal, and fission-based nuclear—the potential of being consumed to exhaustion. In the long run, absent the successful development of truly breakthrough technologies, only renewables can sustain future generations indefinitely. Therefore, the question is not whether Asia should invest in renewable energy but how quickly and how much. The primary obstacle to renewables—that they are for the most part not yet

2.3.1 Top 10 hydropower producers

Country	Hydro electricity (TWh)	Share of electricity generation (%)
PRC	694	14.8
Brazil	403	80.2
Canada	376	62.0
United States	328	7.6
Russian Federation	165	15.7
India	132	13.1
Norway	122	95.3
Japan	85	7.8
Venezuela	84	68.0
Sweden	67	42.2

PRC = People's Republic of China, TWh = terawatt-hour.

Note: These numbers do include electricity imports such as those from the Itaipu hydropower plant of Paraguay to Brazil, which represent almost half of this hydropower plant generation (36 Twh).

Source: IEA 2012b.

cost-competitive with alternative sources—will inevitably diminish with time and technological progress.

Biofuels

Biofuels emit greenhouse gases, as do such conventional fuels as gasoline and diesel. However, they are produced from biomass, which sequester carbon dioxide from the atmosphere for photosynthesis while growing. Therefore, in principle, burning such fuels does not cause a net increase in atmospheric concentrations of carbon dioxide. Accordingly, their development and use can, in principle, advance environmental sustainability. Further, biofuels are liquids and therefore a convenient substitute for oil-based transportation fuels that can reduce the need for oil imports and enhance energy supply adequacy.

World production of biofuels in 2011 was mostly concentrated in the US and Brazil. Asia accounted for only 6% of total biofuel production, though it accounted for 13% of biodiesel production (Table 2.3.2).

The technical process for transforming biomass to biofuels is shown in Figure 2.3.5. The first generation of biofuels were made from the oil, starch, and sugar contained in cultivated crops. More recently, the technology is being developed to exploit cellulose from non-edible vegetation—a second generation of biofuels—which minimizes competition with food production. The latest, third-generation technology, still at a pilot stage, uses algae grown on land unsuitable for crops to avoid land-use competition. Ethanol and biodiesel are the main biofuels and can be added to gasoline and diesel.

It has been about 10 years since the US and Europe implemented various policies and incentives to promote biofuel production. According to *Agriculture Outlook 2012*, co-published by the Organisation for Economic Co-operation and Development and the Food and Agriculture Organization of the United Nations, 65% of EU vegetable oil, 50% of Brazilian sugarcane, and about 40% of US maize production is used as feedstock for biofuel production. During 2009–2011, global production of ethanol averaged 98.2 billion liters (equal to 8.6% of gasoline use by volume) and of biodiesel 21.3 billion liters (3.1% of diesel). High global oil prices have been a major factor behind such high production, which is projected to double by 2021. The leading Asian producers of ethanol are the PRC at 8,094 million liters, India at 1,976 million liters, and Thailand at 777 million liters, and of biodiesel Thailand at 664 million liters, Malaysia at 563 million liters, and Indonesia at 397 million liters.

However, the current generation of biofuels has three significant problems. First, biomass cultivation, transportation, and processing requires energy that must be subtracted from biofuel energy content to arrive at net energy output. The net energy ratio, or energy available in biofuel per unit of energy used to produce it, is lowest converting maize to ethanol.

2.3.2 Global biofuel production, 2011

	Percent of world production, 2011		
	Fuel ethanol	Biodiesel	Total biofuels
North America	62.9	16.3	53.0
United States	60.8	15.6	51.2
Central and South America	27.8	25.6	27.4
Brazil	26.2	11.4	23.1
Europe	4.9	44.0	13.2
Asia and Oceania	4.3	13.2	6.2
People's Republic of China	2.6	1.9	2.5
India	0.4	0.5	0.4
Thailand	0.6	2.5	1.0
Indonesia	0.0	5.0	1.1

Source: EIA 2011d.

2.3.5 Technology pathways to transform biomass into biofuel

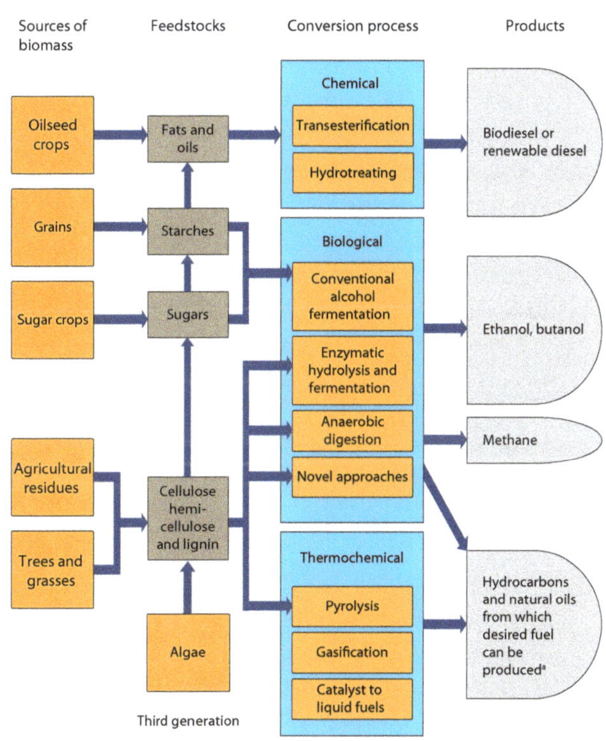

[a] e.g., gasoline or diesel equivalents, syngas, and hydrogen.
Source: Pena 2008.

Depending on the production process, the ratio is four times or more for cellulosic biomass and biodiesel. Second, the first-generation biofuels compete with food production by directly using food crops or land used to grow them. With its large poor population, Asia already faces challenges producing enough affordable food. Food security could be jeopardized if too many farmers chose to switch to biofuel crops. Third, biofuels are not yet cost-competitive with traditional transportation fuels, typically requiring significant subsidies.

Research is under way worldwide to address the first two issues by producing biofuels from materials that do not compete with food production, using the so-called "cellulosics" in crop residues, plants with high-energy content that grow well on degraded land, and algae. At this point these technologies are not yet cost-competitive, but if they reach fruition they could make a substantial contribution. In the meantime, according to the IEA, ethanol from sugarcane currently being produced in Brazil and Thailand shows significant potential to mitigate GHG emission, if no indirect land-use change occurs (IEA 2011c). The analysis shows lifecycle net GHG gains from using biofuels made from palm oil produced in Indonesia and Malaysia, the world's largest producers. However, other analyses conclude that net gains from biofuel production are illusory owing to land-use changes to support their production (Environmental Protection Agency 2012).

As with solar and wind, biofuels other than ethanol are not yet cost-competitive. The IEA shows the cost of producing conventional biodiesel in 2011 at nearly double that of gasoline and projects it remaining more expensive than gasoline for the foreseeable future. On the other hand, the IEA projects ethanol costs falling below gasoline costs before 2020 because of scale expansion and efficiency improvements. Second-generation biofuels from cellulosics, both ethanol and biodiesel, are not projected to become cost-competitive with gasoline until sometime around 2030 (IEA 2011c).

In lieu of cost-competitiveness, the rapid growth of biofuel production in Asia and elsewhere has been driven by biofuel subsidies. In Asia, the governments of the PRC, Indonesia, and Malaysia in particular provide subsidies. One study estimated that biofuels subsidies in the PRC in 2006 amounted to $115 million, or roughly $0.40/liter, and projected that such subsidies would reach about $1.8 billion by 2020 (International Institute for Sustainable Development 2008). The study found comparably large biofuels subsidies for Indonesia in 2006–2008.

In sum, the prospects of biofuels improving energy supply adequacy and environmental sustainability depend heavily, as with solar and wind, on aggressive investment in new technologies that will reduce their cost and overcome land-use conflicts.

Other renewables

Other renewable energy sources will supply clean energy in locales where natural conditions enable their deployment. While their contribution to Asian energy supply will be limited, geothermal energy and perhaps the expanded use of tidal and ocean current power will bring advantages where they can be implemented cost-effectively, helping to leave no stone unturned in Asia's quest for clean energy (Box 2.3.1).

2.3.1 Other emerging technologies

Geothermal energy. The installed capacity of geothermal plants in the Philippines is second only to the US, contributing 17% of the country's electricity supply (Government of the Philippines, Department of Energy 2011). Further, the Philippines plans to expand geothermal capacity by 75% by 2027 (Remo 2011). It is also used in Indonesia.

Geothermal has minor and manageable environmental impacts (Goldstein et al. 2011). Some consider geothermal a renewable resource, but if production exceeds rates of heat replenishment, geothermal reservoirs deplete much as do conventional oil and gas reserves. As these resources are exploitable only where the earth's mantle has intruded far enough into the crust to allow access—normally at the boundaries of tectonic plates—their general potential is limited.

Tidal and ocean current power. Ocean currents are used to drive turbines similar to wind turbines, or small dams are constructed to take advantage of tidal rise and fall. Without major policy changes, worldwide generation is forecast at around 12 TWh/year in 2030 and 25 TWh/year in 2050. This is less than 0.1% of developing Asia's projected electricity requirement. When it is commercially available, this technology can be used to provide cheap and clean energy needed by communities living on small islands in the Pacific, the Philippines, and Indonesia.

Landfill gas. Organic matter in municipal solid waste produces this gas, largely methane, as it decomposes. Capturing landfill gas for use in homes or power plants converts waste into energy and reduces emissions of this methane, a potent source of GHG. While capturing landfill gas is logical, environmentally sound, and in many cases economically attractive, it is a very small source that cannot contribute greatly to Asia's energy requirements.

Expansion of non-renewables

While renewables offer considerable promise, fossil fuels will continue to play a key role in the time horizon considered here. The current forecast shows natural gas use increasing over the forecast period along with coal, and a modest increase in nuclear power. But is there an opportunity to expand these fuels in a way that is clean and safe? Gas is cleaner than coal, and existing and emerging technologies may enable the use of coal in a more environmentally sustainable way. These questions are examined next.

Unconventional gas

The current forecast shows natural gas production more than tripling over the forecast period, increasing its share of supply from about 10% to 16%. But might this picture be improved with more aggressive development of unconventional gas supplies? Recent experience in the industrialized world shows that unconventional gas has the potential to come online quickly and to significantly change the energy supply picture.

The appeal of this idea is great. Unconventional gas resources such as shale gas and coal bed methane offer the promise of replacing coal in power generation (whether directly or indirectly) and oil in producing certain petrochemicals. Shale gas and coal bed methane are chemically equivalent to conventional natural gas.

The conventional way to produce natural gas is to drill and extract it out of "traps," or folds and pockets in underground sedimentary layers. Natural gas also exists in deeper layers, typically shales, from which the gas found today in the shallower traps migrated in geologic time (Figure 2.3.6). This "source rock" is much easier to find than traps and contains much larger quantities of gas. Traps are sparsely distributed compared with the source rock that extends over large areas in a basin.

2.3.6 Natural gas formations: conventional versus unconventional gas

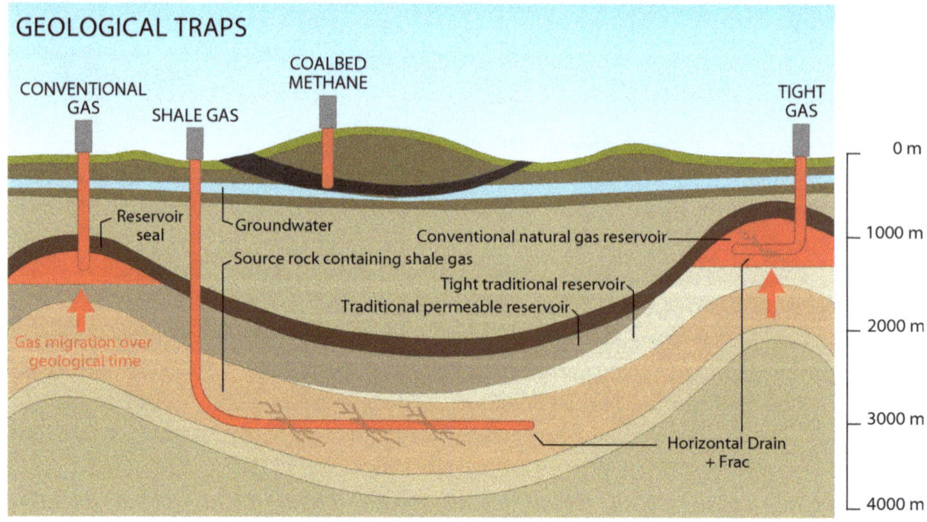

Source: Ross, forthcoming. Reprinted from Department of Mines and Petroleum 2013, with permission of the Department of Mines and Petroleum of Western Australia.

This resource has long been known to be large, but it was harder to exploit because the rock is impermeable and thus resistant to fluid flows. Further, the productive sedimentary layers span a thin vertical distance, meaning a vertical well cannot access much of the formation's resource. The recent revolution in shale gas production arose as two technologies came together. Horizontal drilling allows operators to drill down to the deeper shale and then drill horizontally across the formation to efficiently access a rich vein of the shale. In hydraulic fracturing, or "fracking," explosive charges first fracture the shale seam and then hydraulic fluid is pumped in to expand the fractures and allow gas to flow freely to the surface when the fluid is removed. These technologies have rendered accessible large volumes of gas. In the US, the shale gas share of all gas production exploded from 8% in 2007 to 30% in 2011 (EIA 2013b).

Many coal seams and surrounding rocks are also rich in methane, the main constituent of natural gas. As with shale gas, horizontal drilling provides access to rich underground coal seams, and the methane flows out because it is under pressure.

Other types of unconventional gas are not yet technically viable or commercially competitive. "Deep gas" existing in deposits at depths of 5 kilometers or more is exploitable with current technology but more expensive than conventional gas. Gas under extreme pressure in geopressurized zones may be abundant but is technically difficult to extract owing to these zones' extreme depth and pressure. Methane hydrates are icy materials containing gas that are found in marine sediments and Arctic regions. The US Geological Survey (2013) conservatively estimates the carbon bound in gas hydrates globally to be twice as abundant as in all other known fossil fuels. They are highly volatile, however, and the technology to exploit them safely is not yet developed.

To the degree that natural gas, whether from a conventional or unconventional source, can replace coal in power generation, GHG emissions will fall because gas burns more cleanly than coal. Distributed directly for end use, the ability of gas to mitigate GHG emissions is even higher. What is more, to the extent that gas can replace electricity in end uses, it can multiply its benefits in terms of energy efficiency and environmental protection compared with any fossil fuel used to produce electricity—including itself. To the degree gas can replace oil, it can enhance energy supply adequacy. The significant quantities of unconventional gas coming online can keep prices low, thus advancing affordability. But realizing any of these benefits requires more gas than is foreseen in the current forecast.

Asia's unconventional gas potential

Asia almost certainly has significant reserves of unconventional gas. What is uncertain is where it is and how much of it is technically recoverable (IEA 2012a,b, Rogner 1997, McGlade, Sorrell, and Speirs 2012). Regional assessments of unconventional gas have existed for over a decade, but there is only one publicly available basin-by-basin study for shale gas using a consistent methodology across countries (EIA 2011d). The study is based on work performed by Advanced Resources International (Kuuskraa 2009). Within Asia, the EIA study identified three promising countries—the PRC, India, and Pakistan—and compared the estimate of their technically recoverable shale gas resource with their proven conventional natural gas resources (Table 2.3.3). The PRC has the largest shale gas resources in the world, nearly 20% of the global total. The US, Argentina, Mexico, and South Africa complete the top five.

The PRC's coal bed methane resources are likely the largest in Asia outside of the Russian Federation, with gas "in place" (i.e., identified but not necessarily technically or economically recoverable) at depths within 2 kilometers measuring 34 gigatons of oil equivalent (Gtoe); this is comparable to the PRC's conventional gas resources and places it second not only in Asia but in the world. These resources are spread widely throughout the country (Figure 2.3.7).

Shale gas resources in India and Pakistan have received less attention than those in the PRC and, in the light of conflicting studies, are less certain. The EIA–Advanced Resources International study identified five priority basins (in orange in Figure 2.3.8), including one in Pakistan, and identified several other basins (in yellow) that were either unsuitable for gas production or lacked the data required for a resource assessment (EIA 2011b). The gas in place is estimated to be 7,536 Mtoe in basins in India, 1,653 Mtoe of it technically recoverable, and 5,346 Mtoe in basins in Pakistan, 1,323 Mtoe of it technically recoverable. Uncertainty points to the need to better characterize these resources.

India's coal bed methane in place has been estimated to be as high as 4.2 Gtoe (Ojha et al. 2011) or even 5.2 Gtoe (Dart Energy 2013). The most promising area is the Damodar Basin (Figure 2.3.8), particularly the Jharia Coalfield (Ojha et al. 2011).

Shale gas resources in Indonesia may be substantial but have not been subject to much independent assessment. One study by the Bandung Technical University estimated the country's "resource" at 26 Gtoe (Wah 2011). The Indonesian government Ministry of Energy and Mineral Resources advertises 8.7 Gtoe of "shale gas potential" (Focus Reports 2012). Indonesia's coal bed methane resources appear to be large, exceeding those of the PRC, but have seen little development because of policy restrictions and are surrounded by uncertainty. One study suggests that the technically recoverable resource spread throughout the archipelago might be 1,300 Gtoe, an amount equal to one-third of the country's conventional gas reserves. The most promising area is South Sumatra, where 4,800 Mtoe of gas in place was estimated to exist in coal bed seams at depths of 300–1,000 meters. The Barito and Kutei coal beds of Kalimantan are estimated to contain similar quantities of gas (Figure 2.3.9).

2.3.3 Shale gas resources in 34 countries

	Proven conventional gas reserves		Technically recoverable shale gas resources		Fraction of total shale resources of 34 countries studied[a]	Shale gas rank among 34 countries studied[a]
	TCF	Gtoe	TCF	Gtoe	%	
Europe						
France	0.2	0.01	180	4.67	2.7	12
Germany	6.2	0.16	8	0.21	0.1	31
Netherlands	49	1.27	17	0.44	0.3	27
Norway	72	1.87	83	2.15	1.3	13
United Kingdom	9	0.23	20	0.52	0.3	23
Denmark	2.1	0.05	23	0.6	0.3	21
Sweden	...	...	41	1.06	0.6	20
Poland	5.8	0.15	187	4.85	2.8	11
Turkey	0.2	0.01	15	0.39	0.2	28
Ukraine	39	1.01	42	1.09	0.6	19
Lithuania	...	...	4	0.1	0.1	33
Others	2.71	0.07	19	0.49	0.3	24
North America						
United States	272.5	7.07	862	22.37	13	2
Canada	62	1.61	388	10.07	5.9	7
Mexico	12	0.31	681	17.67	10.3	4
Asia and the Pacific						
PRC	107	2.78	1,275	33.09	19.3	1
India	37.9	0.98	63	1.63	1	15
Pakistan	29.7	0.77	51	1.32	0.8	17
Australia	110	2.85	396	10.28	6	6
Africa						
South Africa	...	...	485	12.59	7.3	5
Libya	54.7	1.42	290	7.53	4.4	8
Tunisia	2.3	0.06	18	0.47	0.3	26
Algeria	159	4.13	231	5.99	3.5	9
Morocco	0.1	0	11	0.29	0.2	29
Western Sahara	...	...	7	0.18	0.1	0.32
Mauritania	1	0.03	0	0	0	34
South America						
Venezuela	178.9	4.64	11	0.29	0.2	30
Colombia	4	0.1	19	0.49	0.3	25
Argentina	13.4	0.35	774	20.09	11.7	3
Brazil	12.9	0.33	226	5.86	3.4	10
Chile	3.5	0.09	64	1.66	1	14
Uruguay	...	...	21	0.54	0.3	22
Paraguay	...	...	62	1.61	0.9	16
Bolivia	26.5	0.69	48	1.25	0.7	18

... = data not available, Gtoe = giga ton of oil equivalent, PRC = People's Republic of China, TCF = trillion cubic feet.

[a] Includes Western Sahara and a grouping of countries in Europe (Others: Romania, Hungary, and Bulgaria).

Source: EIA 2011d.

2.3.7 People's Republic of China's unconventional gas resources

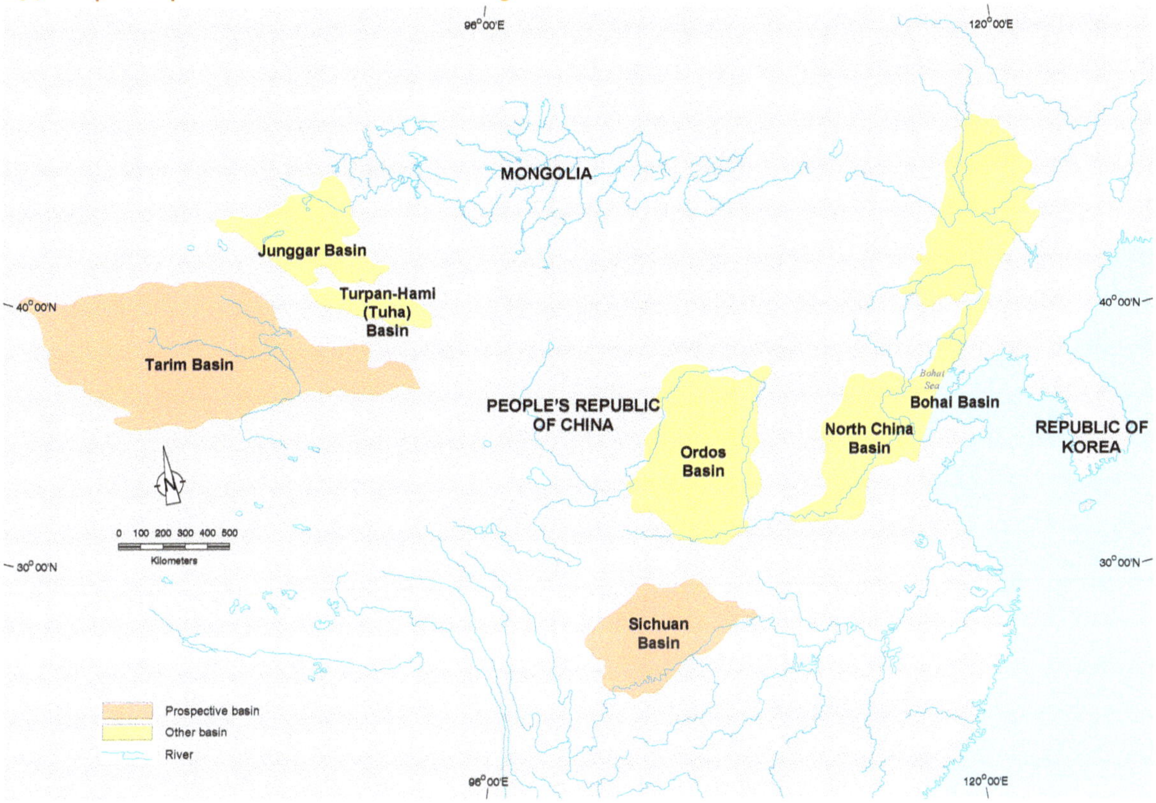

Source: Approximation based on EIA 2011b.

Were Indonesia to achieve a reserves-to-production ratio comparable to the PRC's, it would be producing about 50 Mtoe/year of coal bed methane gas by 2030.

Challenges to shale gas production

The rapid expansion of shale gas production in the US prompted predictions that the country would become a net exporter of liquefied natural gas by 2016 and a net exporter of natural gas overall by 2020 (EIA 2012c). This prediction is contentious.

Uncertainty is even greater for Asia. The ambitious shale gas targets set by the Government of the PRC and the interest expressed by the governments of India, Indonesia, Kazakhstan, and Pakistan in exploiting their shale gas resources reflect the enthusiasm of the last several years. Many in government and industry expect to see an Asian echo of the North American shale gas boom.

But the North American shale gas revolution may not be easy to repeat in Asia. The Asian situation differs from that in North America in a number of ways that may challenge shale gas production. And the cost of extracting shale gas may be higher in Asia than in North America, compromising its ability to supplant other fuels or sources of gas.

The challenges facing Asian shale gas development include the following:

- **More challenging geological conditions.** Relative to gas shales in North America, many in the PRC appear to be smaller, deeper,

2.3.8 India and Pakistan's unconventional gas resources

Source: Approximation based on EIA 2011b.

more complex, and higher in clay content, which makes fracturing difficult (Lelyveld 2012, Kim and Yu 2012, Katakey, Sethuramån, and Guo 2012).

- **Lack of geological data.** Successfully producing shale gas requires a good understanding of regional geology. In North America, good data covering large prospective areas has accumulated through decades of conventional drilling and seismic surveys (Butkiewicz 2012). Not so in Asia.
- **Development on densely populated land.** Unlike in North America, many prospective shale gas production areas in the PRC, India, and other parts of Asia are heavily populated. This means more involuntary resettlement and environmental impact in Asia. Even when the required land area is minimized by drilling only one wellhead, from which sprout multiple horizontal wells, each wellhead may require a thousand truck trips over a period of several weeks to transport water and equipment for the drilling. Pipelines for collecting the gas from wellheads and roads for moving heavy vehicles will require space.

Exporting the shale gas revolution to Asia will require creative policy approaches that attend to these challenges.

2.3.9 Indonesia's unconventional gas resources

Source: Approximation based on ADB 2003.

While natural gas produces lower GHG emissions than coal when burned to generate electricity, it is not as clean as nuclear or most renewables. A concern is that leakage of methane, a powerful GHG, can occur during production, separation, transmission, and distribution. A further concern is that shale gas development risks groundwater contamination if not prudently undertaken, including the proper treatment and disposal of water and debris from boreholes. The land used for drilling and surface works needs to be restored after drilling, which could become a contentious issue with the local populations who see restoration as incomplete. High disclosure standards and effective enforcement capacity will have to be built before the large-scale production of shale gas can start.

Moreover, current shale gas production technology uses copious amounts of water. Competition for water to meet local agricultural and domestic needs may place serious constraints on the rate at which shale gas can be developed.

In 2012, the IEA published its golden rules for a golden age of gas, outlining the standards and protocols they believe will permit the environmentally sustainable development of unconventional gas.

If available in sufficient quantities, natural gas from shale and coal bed methane could replace a certain portion of naphtha used for petrochemicals, thus reducing the need for oil imports and advancing energy supply adequacy. However, unless these supplies also contain sufficient quantities of readily separable natural gas liquids—heavier substances extracted from "wet" gas prior to transmission—totally displacing oil-derived petrochemicals is technically impossible.

On the whole, the aggressive development of unconventional gas has the potential to enhance supply adequacy, affordability, economic growth, and environmental sustainability, if environmental impacts can be carefully managed. But the magnitude of the resource that can be developed is uncertain, as is the rate at which it can be produced in Asia. Serious issues of environmental and population disruption need to be tackled. While not a truly clean resource, unconventional gas could provide a cleaner bridge to a future less dependent on fossil fuels.

Nuclear power

The proposition that nuclear power should be expanded in Asia is fraught with contention. But a responsible accounting of Asia's energy challenge is incomplete without a discussion of the pros and cons of initiating or extending a nuclear energy program, and of the challenges facing policy makers who must grapple with this thorny issue. Countries will reach their own conclusions based on their individual situations.

There are 437 reactors in commercial operation worldwide with a total installed capacity of 372,325 MW (IAEA 2013). The installed capacity share of Asia and the Pacific is 23.6%, and actual generation share is 18.6%. Asian countries with installed nuclear power capacity are Armenia with 375 MW, the PRC 12,816 MW, India 4,391 MW, Japan 44,215 MW, the Republic of Korea 20,754 MW, Pakistan 725 MW, and Taipei,China 5,018 MW.

As of the end of 2012, the construction of new nuclear capacity had swung heavily toward Asia, with over 57.5% of new generating capacity in developing Asia (Figure 2.3.10). Despite some Asian countries' reevaluating their nuclear programs in the aftermath of the Fukushima disaster, most current construction of nuclear plants is in Asia.

Nuclear power compares favorably with other options by measures of GHG gas emission and air pollution. While nuclear is not completely without GHG emission, it ranks with hydro and wind power as a low emitter (Figure 2.3.11). Nuclear power plants, like renewables, emit during operation virtually no air pollutants such as nitrogen oxides, sulfur dioxide, or particulates.

Nuclear is cost-competitive with fossil fuels and cheaper than present-day renewables. The major financial impediment is the typically very large upfront capital cost. This is often exacerbated by extended schedules for clearing regulatory and permit hurdles. Yet, when evaluated on a lifecycle basis that incorporates the costs of construction, interest during construction, fuel, operation, maintenance, waste management, and decommissioning, nuclear compares favorably with conventional power plants (Figure 2.3.12).

This evaluation sidesteps widespread public concerns about nuclear safety, especially in the wake of the Fukushima meltdown. Additional public concerns exist over the handling and disposal of radioactive waste and associated risks. Finally, the expansion of nuclear power creates worry about the proliferation of nuclear weapons.

Historically, the nuclear industry saw huge growth until the 1970s, when interest dampened because of deteriorating economies and mounting safety concerns in response to two serious accidents,

2.3.10 Distribution of nuclear power in major world regions (as of 31 December 2012)

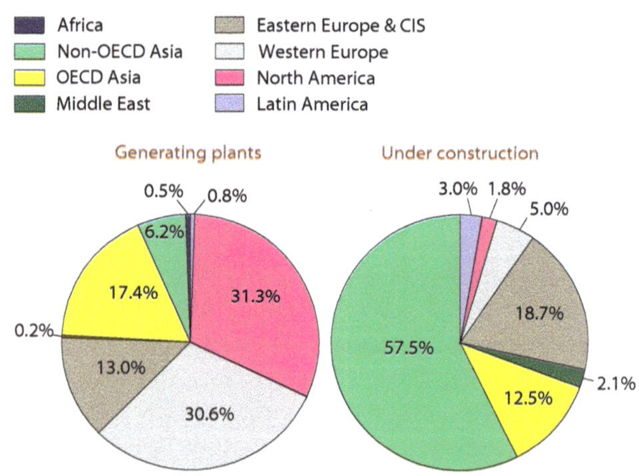

CIS = Commonwealth of Independent States, OECD = Organisation for Economic Co-operation and Development.

Source: IAEA 2013.

Click here for figure data

2.3.11 Life-cycle greenhouse gas emissions of electricity generating options

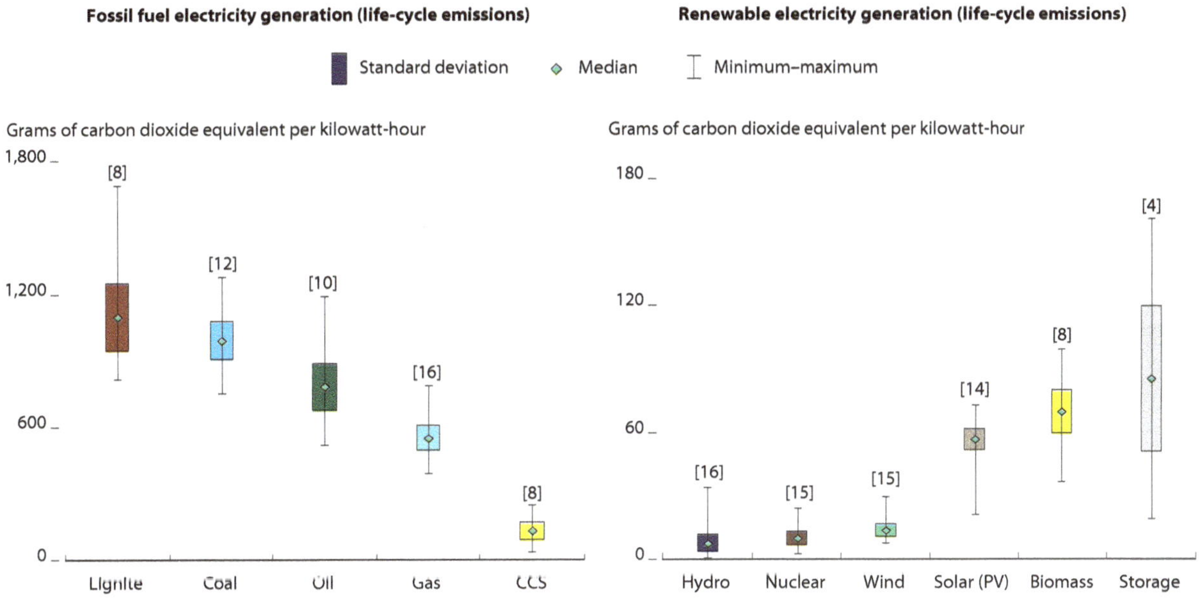

CCS = carbon capture and storage, PV = photovoltaic.

Source: Weisser 2007.

Click here for figure data

Three Mile Island in the US in 1979 and Chernobyl in what was then the Soviet Union in 1986. Interest in nuclear revived with the growing need to expand energy supply while limiting GHG emissions. Fukushima recently raised fresh concerns regarding safety, prompting Japan to conduct a full safety review of its nuclear plants, which continues today. The current situation is mixed, with some countries continuing to build nuclear plants, while others are more hesitant, and a few are pulling the plug on the nuclear option altogether. Germany, for one, plans to decommission all its nuclear power plants by 2022.

Phasing out existing nuclear power plants and not building new plants would necessarily create a power generation gap to fill. Without nuclear energy it would be more difficult for Asia to secure adequate, reliable energy supplies as it would remove one of today's commercially viable energy source from the energy equation. Just as importantly, removing nuclear power would raise environmental sustainability issues, as it is a relatively clean energy source (Box 2.3.2).

The International Atomic Energy Agency's action plan on nuclear safety, developed in response to the Fukushima disaster, aims to further strengthen the safety of nuclear operations globally; improve transparency and accountability along the entire nuclear chain; and enhance regulatory effectiveness, emergency preparedness, and the management of extreme accidents (IAEA 2011).

A contentious issue in nuclear power is how to manage radioactive waste. A number of planned repository projects have been assessed for potential radiation leakage for periods of up to 10 million years. These studies have shown low risk of serious radiation exposure. The design of nuclear reactors is also improving in terms of fuel cycling, which reduces the amount of waste needing disposal, and in terms of operational safety upgrades that alleviate the risk of accidents. Greater transparency and

2.3.12 Levelized cost of energy of generation options

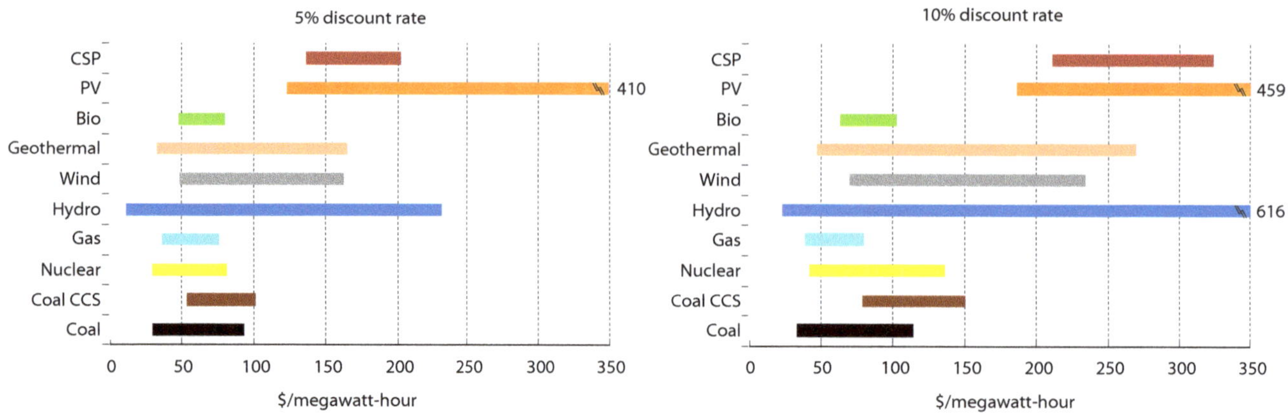

CCS = carbon capture and storage, CSP = concentrating solar power, PV = photovoltaic.
Source: IEA–NEA 2010.
Click here for figure data

closer scrutiny of licensing and operating procedures are additional safety-enhancing measures along with closer attention paid to disposal and decommissioning costs.

Completing the nuclear picture is the observation that experimental technologies have potential to overcome the difficulties of nuclear fission in the distant future (Box 2.3.3).

In sum, nuclear power holds the promise of minimizing GHG emissions and air pollution. It is cost-effective and becomes even more cost-effective if construction lead times can be shortened. Small modular reactors present a promising new development for speeding up construction. Safety risks arise from the possibility of nuclear accidents, and nuclear materials must be carefully handled and disposed of. There are some concerns about nuclear proliferation. Public opinion and geopolitical considerations will undoubtedly be key to determining the future of nuclear power in Asia.

Cleaner coal

Truly significant reductions in GHG emissions could be obtained by technologies that remove carbon and other GHG components from the emissions of coal- and gas-fired power plants. Asia's energy future would have far different GHG consequences if the coal used for generation were made more benign regarding GHGs within the forecast horizon.

GHG-benign coal requires carbon capture and storage (CCS) technology, which is at an early stage of development for power plants and thus very expensive. The CCS process has three key steps: carbon dioxide (CO_2) must first be captured from the furnace exhaust or from fuel during preparation, then transported, and finally safely stored so it never leaks back into the atmosphere. The natural gas industry has used CCS for some time, routinely separating CO_2 when treating natural gas. Norway has successfully stored CO_2 separated from its natural gas in subsea aquifers since 1996. This technology has to be scaled up considerably before it becomes available for power plants.

Several experimental projects have been announced in Australia, the PRC, Europe, the United Kingdom, and the US. However, progress

2.3.2 Greenhouse gas impact of phasing out nuclear power

Nuclear power plays a substantial role in Asia's energy sector, especially in Armenia, the PRC, India, Japan, the Republic of Korea, Pakistan, and Taipei,China. The continent had 116 nuclear power reactors in operation at the end of 2012 (IAEA 2013). Furthermore, nuclear power is expanding at a healthy pace throughout the region, which has 44 of the 67 reactors now under construction worldwide.

But the disaster at Japan's Fukushima nuclear power plant in March 2011 has called into question the future of nuclear expansion in Asia and elsewhere. It prompted the authorities in Japan and elsewhere to reconsider new projects and to review the design and safety systems of all nuclear power reactors. This will likely delay nuclear expansion in Asia, affecting those plants already commissioned for construction or in the approval pipeline. This slowdown and a possible phasing out of nuclear power programs in some countries could compromise the adequacy of the region's energy supply.

In response, governments need to accelerate the use of renewable sources, go back to fossil fuels, or both. However, renewable energy may not be an option in the short run, as it requires huge investments before it is ready for large-scale cost-competitive use. Issues regarding resource intermittency have to be resolved as well. Using fossil fuels to make up the shortfall would exacerbate Asia's high dependence on fossil fuels, force up Asian energy bills, and heighten Asia's exposure to supply disruptions.

A hypothetical phasing out of nuclear power over the forecast period would cause a significant increase in fossil fuel use for power generation. If no new nuclear plants were built and existing plants were retired, the capacity lost by 2035 would be offset mostly by coal and gas. Renewables would make at best a modest contribution.

This phaseout is assumed to follow the pattern shown in the box figure.

Projected phaseout of Asia's nuclear capacity

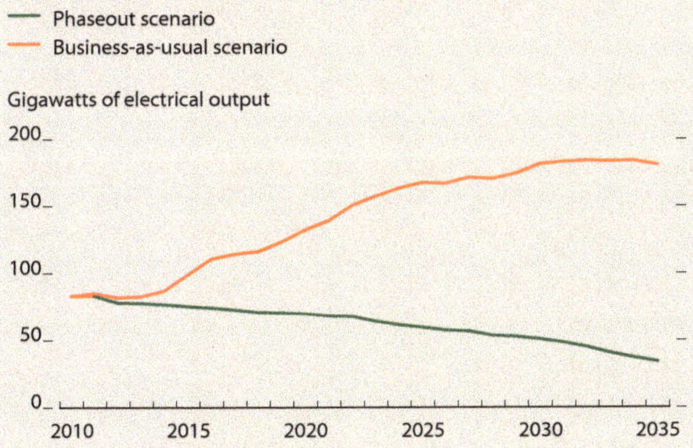

Sources: ADB estimates, IAEA 2012a,b.

Click here for figure data

If the nuclear phaseout were compensated using only one fossil fuel—coal, oil, or gas—the added emissions would be as shown in box table 1.

1 Estimates of increased carbon dioxide emissions (million tons of CO_2 equivalent)

	2025	2035	2010–2035
Coal	574.2–957.1	779.8–1,299.6	10,853.9–18,089.8
Oil	382.8–918.8	519.8–1,247.6	7,235.9–17,366.2
Gas	336.9–597.2	457.5–811.0	6,367.6–11,288.1

Source: ADB estimates.

According to the IEA's *World Energy Outlook 2012*, the actual mix of fossil fuel-based power generation was as follows in 2010: coal 78%, oil 4%, and gas 17.5%. Based on this mix, the range of carbon dioxide (CO_2) emission from the three sources are 523.7–891.5 million tons of CO_2 equivalent (MTCE) in 2025, 711.2–1,210.5 MTCE in 2035, and 9,898.8–16,849.6 MTCE in 2010–2035. By comparison, power generation in 2010 emitted 3,625 MTCE in the PRC and 872 MTCE in India (IEA 2012c). Therefore, a nuclear phaseout in Asia from 2010 to 2035 would increase carbon emissions by 220%–375% more than the combined emissions of the PRC and India in 2010.

World CO_2 emissions from power generation in 2010 amounted to 12,495 MTCE. Asia emitted 6,084 MTCE and thus accounted for 49% of the global total (box table 2). Based on the World Energy Outlook's new policy scenario, phasing out nuclear would increase the world power sector's CO_2 emissions by 3.6%–6.1% in 2025 and by 4.8%–8.1% in 2035. And it would increase the Asian power sector's emissions by 8.6%–10.8% in 2025 and 7.8%–13.3% in 2035. The region's ability to achieve sustainable growth with low GHG emissions would be uncertain without nuclear power.

2 Carbon dioxide emissions from power generation (million tons of CO_2 equivalent)

	2010	2025	2035
World	12,495	14,545	14,952
Asia	6,084	8,251	9,107

Source: IEA 2012c.

has been very slow. Some Asian countries have shown interest and are studying the status of the technology, how CCS could be used to reduce industrial CO_2 emissions, and what types of geological options exist for sequestering CO_2. The Global CCS Institute in Australia has provided grants to several countries to undertake initial geological investigations. In 2012, the Republic of Korea opened the Carbon Capture and Sequestration Research Center to develop new CCS technologies (*Korea Times* 2012). Asia can be envisioned becoming a hub of technological leadership in developing CCS. After all, Asia is the world's biggest user of coal, and CCS technology will help address its main drawback.

International cooperation between technology leaders and Asian utilities and research centers can allow the implementation of multiple experimental CCS projects, and international financial assistance can help lower the cost burden of initial projects. Early development and deployment is a global public good, and burden sharing will reduce the time—and very likely the cost—of switching to this new, cleaner coal technology.

Carbon taxes or a market-based carbon pricing mechanism can provide the incentive to accelerate the development of CCS technology. Because technologies to economically store CO_2 released by the burning of coal and gas would greatly curtail GHG emissions, promoting research, development, and demonstration projects that improve both the technology and its economics would present a major opportunity. The IEA projects the existence of 22 GW of CCS capacity worldwide by 2020, growing to 1,140 GW by 2050. Of this, the IEA projects 2.5 GW in the PRC and India by 2020, rising to 365 GW by 2050 (IEA 2009).

CCS technology, when available commercially, will have potential to eliminate nearly all CO_2 emissions from power plants using fossil fuel. In the meantime, ongoing incremental design improvements reduce such emissions. Designing boilers and steam turbines to operate at higher temperature and pressure packs more energy into the steam, improves efficiency, and thus reduces the amount of coal burned. These are known as "supercritical" and "ultra-supercritical" boilers, "critical" referring to the temperature and pressure above which steam will not turn back into liquid water.

Supercritical and ultra-supercritical power plants have been in operation for some time in Japan and the PRC. Countries in Asia that plan a larger share of coal in their primary energy mix or have the capability to use related technologies include India, Indonesia, Viet Nam, Pakistan, the Republic of Korea, and Malaysia. These countries can lower their GHG emissions by using supercritical and ultra-supercritical technology for all new coal-fired power plants. Capital costs would increase marginally, by about 2%, but coal use and thus CO_2 emissions would decline by 10%–15%. And lower fuel cost improves the economic viability of such projects.

Considering the large and growing role of coal in Asia's energy mix, the need to progress toward cleaner coal technologies is clear. Unlike in developed economies where electricity demand has flattened out, Asia

2.3.3 Nuclear fusion in the distant future

Nuclear fusion is far from ready for commercialization and, barring a spectacular technological breakthrough, will not play a role in the time horizon considered here. But nuclear fusion could eventually redraw the entire energy picture. Nuclear fusion would make possible clean electricity production without hazardous radiation. Clean fusion-based electric power would enable the clean operation of electric vehicles. It would also enable the production of hydrogen from seawater, creating a clean fuel to replace natural gas in all its uses. Huge investments have been made in the US and Europe to explore the feasibility of nuclear fusion. The potential of this technology is colossal, but the technical challenges are similarly daunting.

will require expanded power generation. Given Asia's needs and technical capabilities, the development of clean coal technology potentially offers immense environmental benefits—and commensurately large commercial opportunities.

Summary: improved energy supply

The foregoing analysis lays out the opportunities and challenges associated with a wide range of energy supply sources—most of them depending on new technologies—that can help Asia achieve energy security.

Each new energy source has its merits and shortcomings. Individually, their contribution to improving Asia's energy security will be limited, but collectively the various sources can make a big difference, especially when combined with better demand management. Asia must therefore strive on all fronts to secure ample, affordable, and clean energy supplies. More specifically, Asian countries must aggressively explore and invest in a good mix of supply sources and technologies, in line with each country's specific needs and comparative advantage. Developing these future technologies will often require government support in the early stages when they are a long way from commercial viability. While each source has its limits, every drop—every watt—counts.

The different endowments—different comparative advantages—across the region suggest scope for gains from trade, if arrangements for cross-border energy trade can be devised. Coordination across the region can make the most of individual countries' efforts to boost their energy security.

Fostering regional market synergies

Aggressive action to both manage demand and promote new, clean supply technologies can advance the cause of Asian energy security. But these advantages will not be fully realized without measures to bring demand and supply together more efficiently. Achieving Asia's energy security will thus require cooperative programs that integrate energy delivery systems on a regional scale.

Such programs have precedents, notably in Europe. And regional cooperation and integration is on the rise in Asia, as countries respond to a multitude of common challenges by pursuing closer links. This is true especially within Asian subregions. Growing regional ties are most visible in trade. East and Southeast Asian countries have formed a regional production network that has transformed the two subregions into "factory Asia." This brought the share of trade between member states of the Association of Southeast Asian Nations (ASEAN) to 21% of ASEAN's total trade in 1998 and to 25% by 2010. Finance and labor market integration is more limited but also growing. After the 1997 Asian financial crisis, the governments of ASEAN+3 (adding the PRC, the Republic of Korea, and Japan) joined forces in the Chiang Mai Initiative, a multilateral currency swap arrangement with a foreign exchange reserve pool of $240 billion. Subregional transport connectivity is also intensifying, as evident in transport initiatives in the Greater Mekong Subregion and Central Asia Regional Economic Cooperation.

But cross-border energy markets and infrastructure connectivity have so far been largely ignored in regional cooperation and integration. This is unfortunate in light of rapidly rising energy demand in Asia, which makes energy security a region-wide challenge that would benefit greatly from a collective regional response. The lack of regional cooperation and integration is all the more glaring as jointly promoting energy savings and energy security would not require new technology or pose the high cost and financial risk developing it might entail. But it does require the political will to cooperate and the mutual confidence that makes cooperation possible.

Connected electricity and gas grids can create large regional energy markets whose economies of scale enable improved efficiency. Closer energy links can deliver a lot of gains even in the short term. Demand management and the expansion of clean, affordable energy supply become more effective with regional cooperation and integration. Asian countries' complementary comparative advantages in the energy sector mean that the construction of energy trade infrastructure such as pipelines offers potentially huge benefits. This is evident in cooperation already achieved. Hydropower resources in the uplands of Bhutan, the Lao PDR, and Myanmar have been developed to provide clean, inexpensive energy to energy markets downstream in South and Southeast Asia. A natural gas pipeline supplies energy to Singapore from Indonesia. These regional projects have benefited energy buyers and sellers alike and have helped to constrain dependence on fossil fuels. Central Asia still benefits from the interconnected power grid it inherited from the Soviet Union in terms of system reliability.

Realizing cross-border synergy is technologically and commercially viable. What is missing is political commitment in Asian countries to cooperate in energy markets and build the necessary infrastructure.

Integrating electricity and gas delivery systems

The potential benefits from cross-border coordination of electricity and natural gas networks are immense. Power system failures and gas supply disruptions have major consequences that can be mitigated by properly designing collective electricity and gas delivery systems. Designing them from the outset to optimize delivery without undue concern about borders enables cost minimization and energy efficiency gains.

Interconnected electricity systems

The incentives to interconnect electric power systems are strong in terms of improved reliability, more effective fuel conservation, and broader economic benefits. Larger systems typically deliver power at lower cost per kilowatt-hour than do smaller ones, owing to economies of scale and diversified generation mix. Interconnected systems reduce capital costs by sharing backup generation capacity. And larger systems generally use less primary energy per kilowatt-hour of electricity delivered.

Similarly, interconnection advances the cause of energy efficiency. Larger systems can generally accommodate larger baseload-generation units, which typically enjoy greater fuel-conversion efficiency than do smaller units. The larger and more interconnected the power systems, the greater the energy-efficiency gains. Large interconnected systems make it practical to implement large hydropower projects, as is evident in Central Asia, where building large dams for power generation in the Kyrgyz Republic or Tajikistan could not be justified if only for a small national system.

Cross-border connections enable high-voltage transmission lines and direct connections that improve energy efficiency. Less electricity is lost in transit when it is transmitted at higher voltage. However, high-voltage lines are expensive to build and therefore economic only for transmitting large loads over long distances—often larger and longer than an isolated market can accommodate. High-voltage direct current connections improve grid stability and, by minimizing transmission losses, energy efficiency (Box 2.4.1).

Regional cooperation and integration is already under way but has scope for expansion. Asia is a long way from having unified region-wide power grid as in Europe, but there is no reason why it cannot entertain this ambition. In the short run, most cooperation and integration is taking place in Asia's subregions and among close neighbors.

Bhutan's exports of hydroelectric power are an example of win–win regional cooperation and integration. By virtue of its upstream location in the Himalayas, with rivers plunging rapidly down deep gorges between towering mountains, Bhutan has abundant hydroelectric potential. That the large and fast-growing neighboring Indian economy has a robust appetite for energy provides plenty of scope for mutually beneficial energy

2.4.1 Efficient transmission in interconnecting power grids

Most electricity worldwide is transmitted as alternating current (AC), the form of power produced by all electric generators and needed by end users for lighting, appliances, industrial processes, and other uses. The catch is that AC suffers from serious technical challenges related to synchronizing AC generation (all generators must be "locked" together in precise dynamic unison). In contrast, high-voltage direct current (HVDC) transmission overcomes this problem. The downside is that it has high capital costs because of the need to convert the original AC power into DC power for transmission and then back again to AC for distribution to customers. The high price tag on converters—called "rectifiers" for converting AC to DC and "inverters" for converting DC back to AC—can be justified economically only if the potential technical loses incurred transmitting large AC loads over long distances are high enough to cover the investment. That requires a big grid.

Other technical considerations can tilt the field in favor of HVDC transmission. In addition to lower transmission losses, HVDC transmission significantly improves the stability to the grid because energy flow over an HVDC interconnection can be precisely regulated. Further, the two AC systems at either end of an HVDC interconnection need not be synchronized with matching alternating frequency. This flexibility allows interconnection between countries using 60 alternating cycles per second (measured in hertz)—as in the Republic of Korea, the Philippines, Taipei,China, and parts of Japan—to neighbors using 50 hertz, as in the rest of Asia. Flexibility is further valuable in light of utility operators' need to match supply to ever-changing and sometimes unpredictable demand.

cooperation and integration. In fact, India started helping Bhutan develop its hydropower potential in the early 1960s. India financed through a mix of grants and loans several large hydropower projects such as at Chukha with 336 megawatts (MW), Tala with 1,020 MW, and Kurichu with 60 MW.

Much of the power generated by these hydroelectric projects was exported to India, providing India with much-needed energy and Bhutan with much-needed revenues. When northern India was hit by its worst power outage in a decade in July 2012, the Indian government turned to Bhutan for assistance. Bhutan responded by releasing additional power from its hydroelectric stations to kick-start India's fossil fuel-based power plants. Today, Bhutan meets 1% of India's electricity needs, and it entered into a deal to sell India 5.48 billion kilowatt-hours in the year from April 2012 to March 2013. Bhutan has 30,000 megawatts of hydropower potential, equal to about a fifth of India's hydropower potential.

The Greater Mekong Subregion (GMS) is an illustrative example of large scope for cooperation and integration. The sheer diversity of the subregion's resource base multiplies the huge potential gains achievable from regional energy integration. The GMS has enormous energy resource endowments. Realizing just half of its hydropower potential would generate 450 terawatt-hours, or almost double the subregion's total electricity generation from all sources in 2010. In addition, the region is endowed with abundant coal deposits and promising gas and petroleum reserves. However, these energy resources are unevenly distributed across the subregion. Hydropower potential is abundant in the PRC's Yunnan and Guangxi provinces, Myanmar, the Lao PDR, and Viet Nam, which together control 94% of hydropower resources in the GMS. Hydropower potential in Myanmar and the Lao PDR is huge relative to the countries' populations and expected electricity needs. Myanmar, Thailand, and Viet Nam have natural gas; Viet Nam has most of the subregion's oil; and Yunnan has the main coal deposits.

Cambodia, Thailand, and the PRC are net energy importers, while the Lao PDR, Myanmar, and Viet Nam are net exporters. In the GMS, regional cooperation and integration in energy have seen the most concrete progress in expanded hydropower trade among member economies. Thailand purchases hydropower that the Lao PDR generates at its Nam Theun 2, Nam Leuk, Nam Ngnum 2, and Theun Hinboun 1 and 2 power plants. The Lao PDR has more plants under construction or in the pipeline.

However, the growth of trade has been constrained by the failure to allow third party access to the transmission lines. One option is to develop a publicly owned high-voltage backbone line that various independent power producers could use to transfer power in exchange for paying so-called wheeling fees to the transmission owner. An example would be to construct a 500 kilovolt line in the Lao PDR connected with Thailand and Viet Nam toward optimizing the power systems of the three countries. To illustrate the advantages with an example outside the GMS, the 275 kilovolt transmission line on Borneo enables the export of 230 MW of hydropower generated in the Malaysian state of Sarawak to the Indonesian province of West Kalimantan, where generation largely uses far more expensive and polluting oil. The arrangement improves the environment in West Kalimantan and mitigates greenhouse gas emissions. Cheaper electricity supply reduces central government power subsidies to West Kalimantan by $100 million/year.

If GMS members similarly invested in regional energy infrastructure and institutionalized and systematized subregional cooperation and integration, they would be able to reap even greater benefits from their energy synergies and interdependence. A recent GMS study toward drawing up an energy master plan estimated that integrating power transmission in the subregion would save $14 billion over 20 years by substituting hydropower for power generation using fossil fuels. Further, it would reduce carbon dioxide emissions by 14 million tons per year by 2020 (ADB 2012).

Interconnected gas systems

Similar economies and efficiencies are realizable by connecting natural gas systems. Where gas endowments exceed domestic energy demand, interconnected energy markets would allow idle natural resources to be used like any other exportable commodity to create a revenue stream to help meet developmental needs. Cross-border gas pipelines also offer the opportunity to create gas distribution networks that economically serve the needs of communities along the route—communities that might otherwise not be served. As seen in the section on demand management, cooktops and furnaces can run on gas to avoid losing energy in electricity generation. Large pipeline networks operating at high pressure also provide storage capacity to help maintain a reliable supply during small technical interruptions.

One prominent example of mutual benefit through regional interconnection is the gas pipeline running from Turkmenistan to the PRC, which was completed in December 2009. For the PRC, imports of Turkmen gas have augmented supply by an amount equal to half of domestic production, boosting the share of gas in PRC energy consumption by 2 percentage points. This has replaced domestic coal and its higher emissions of greenhouse gases and pollutants, so the environmental benefits are sizable. For Turkmenistan, the pipeline has diversified its export market away from overly heavy dependence on the Russian Federation. More broadly, the pipeline will help to quench the PRC's fast-growing thirst for energy while giving gas-rich Turkmenistan access to a large and growing energy market.

Another example is the pipeline supplying gas from South Sumatra in Indonesia to Singapore for power generation. Singapore's economy relies on services and high-tech industry, both of which place very high value on the reliability of power supply. Its diversification of suppliers to include Indonesia improved the city state's supply security, and Indonesia acquired an assured revenue stream to use for development. Interestingly, before this arrangement the gas was used only to enhance oil recovery in the Indonesian state of Aceh, which imposed a higher transportation cost for a use with lower economic value. Gaining access to the Singapore energy market thus allowed Indonesia to boost the value of its natural endowment. Myanmar is similarly reaping benefit from a gas line connection to Yunnan Province in the PRC.

'Smart grids' to integrate renewables

As renewable energy sources grow, so-called "smart grids" that integrate renewables into the electricity network will play a bigger role in regional cooperation and integration. The fundamental reason is that renewable energy endowments are often remote from demand centers with lots of people and economic activity. Meanwhile, there is no reason to expect readily paired supply and demand centers to be in the same country. Wind power from thinly populated Mongolia can provide electricity to the PRC. Similarly, hydropower from Myanmar can provide electricity to the Bangkok metropolitan area of Thailand. Cost-effectively linking areas that offer ample renewable supply potential with populous, economically active markets through smart grids can catalyze the development of renewable energy in Asia. Without smart grids, renewable potential in thinly populated areas of Asia would be unexploited and wasted.

As an energy system comes to depend more on renewables, it needs to become more intelligent. Solar and wind are intermittent resources that cannot be relied on to deliver power on demand. Solar is available only by day, and then unpredictably, depending on cloud cover. Wind is highly variable and likewise unpredictable. Wind barely correlates with times of high system demand, and solar correlates only somewhat better, so integrating these unpredictable renewables into the power grid poses significant technical challenges. Large intelligent systems can take advantage of time-of-day demand differences across time zones and swing power across large areas as solar systems' output rises and falls.

Attendant to this problem is the need to incorporate distributed generating systems, which generate electricity not in centralized power plants but from small local sources such as solar panels on buildings, small on-site generators and co-generators, and local biomass- and waste-based power systems. Sometimes local sources are joined together in micro grids that operate locally for the most part but with a connection to the main grid. Integration challenges the central grid operator to maintain appropriate voltage and phase synchronization—and, ultimately, system stability.

Intelligent systems that can adjust to accommodate decentralized generation and renewable generation can optimize the system toward maximizing generation from renewables, minimizing costs, and improving the reliability of service. This requires that smart grids in different countries be able to communicate with one another toward operating together seamlessly. System optimization in the service of Asian energy consumers depends on strong regional cooperation.

A promising cross-border smart grid application would be to install very large wind farms in Mongolia and connect them to transmission networks in the PRC or even the Republic of Korea and Japan. Mongolia has enough wind resources for 1 terawatt of installed capacity collected by about 200,000 wind turbines, each with 5 MW of capacity. Tapping these excellent year-round resources on such a scale would push the price of wind energy down. Domestic demand would not justify the investment, but regional interconnection would transform its economic viability. Such a large renewable energy system would require smart grid technology to optimize resource use while ensuring grid reliability. A similarly tricky job for a smart grid is to manage a cascade of hydropower dams along a single river in the mountains to supply electricity to neighboring countries.

The widespread use of electric-powered transport will introduce challenges along with opportunities. Smart interconnected power grids that tie together electric vehicles in interconnected markets can charge the vehicles when surplus renewable energy is available, store electricity in the vehicles' batteries, and, during high grid demand, draw power back from any idle vehicles that are plugged into the grid.

Obstacles to regional cooperation and integration

Interconnecting energy systems across international frontiers requires that participating states adopt compatible technical standards and regulatory regimes. The unified European electricity and gas markets illustrate how standardization can progress. Cooperation in Europe started in late 1980s with the liberalization of the British electricity industry, which broke up the state-owned electricity monopoly and replaced it with a competitive electricity market that allowed neighboring France to sell its surplus production of low-cost electricity in the United Kingdom. Several other Western European countries pursued similar liberalization toward diminishing the role of the state in utility service delivery. A green paper and European directive issued by the European Parliament in 1996 regarding electricity, and others for gas in 1998, set common rules for domestic electricity markets as the foundation for an energy market spanning the European Union (EU). The Lisbon Strategy, 2000 combined the electricity and gas markets and recognized that being competitive in energy was essential for promoting European competitiveness and knowledge-based leadership globally.

A mandate later in 2003 provided third-party access to all existing energy infrastructure, and another in 2009 integrated the EU's energy and environmental objectives.

Already well interconnected, the EU recognized the value of interconnecting its electricity and gas networks more completely. The European Commission stated in 2006 that efficient energy infrastructure was essential to allow the EU to achieve its targets for sustainable development, competitiveness, and secure energy supplies. The commission added that "improved efficiency required considerable investment in upgrading gas and electricity networks and in developing their interconnections" (European Commission 2007). It pointed out in particular that interconnected networks prevented the risk of short supply by diversifying sources and facilitating the introduction of a "green network" carrying electricity generated from renewable sources. This prompted the promulgation of a system-wide priority interconnection plan. As the EU already had well-established regulatory frameworks and contractual and pricing standards, the EU directive is strong indication that more could be done to make the most of its energy infrastructure.

How much more so will Asia be challenged by energy market integration? Yet, from purely technical and commercial perspectives, Asian countries have every reason to pursue wider and deeper regional cooperation and integration in the energy sector. Unlike new technologies developed in pursuit of uncertain, long-term payoffs, fostering closer energy ties promises concrete payoffs even in the short run.

Technical challenges to integration

Interconnecting electricity and gas grids requires standardized regulations, pricing practices, and contracts. Especially for electricity, technical standards need to be uniform, or at least compatible, for systems to work (though, as noted in Box 2.4.1, local grids using different frequencies of alternating current can draw supply from a common grid that transmits using high-voltage direct current).

Similarly, the smooth operation of a unified regional oil market requires standardized oil product specifications to ensure that suppliers compete on a level playing field. Common environmental standards eliminate distortions in production costs. In the longer term, the expansion of fleets of vehicles powered by electricity and compressed natural gas will require that filling and recharging stations be standardized so that cross-border transportation systems function smoothly.

Countries with established or planned nuclear energy programs stand to benefit from common standards for nuclear licensing, operation, and supervision. This would make the best use of available human resource capacity, shorten any delays, and contain costs. Because radioactive contamination respects no borders, coordination can buttress public confidence.

As the European experience of integrating power systems illustrates, the technical barriers to integration are readily surmountable. The larger challenge inhibiting energy integration in Asia is summoning the political will to coordinate policy.

Policy challenges to integration

Asian leaders, like others around the world, tend to view energy security as a vital component of national security, which makes them reluctant to relinquish control. Further, Asian governments intervene heavily in their energy markets, notably with consumer subsidies, which reinforces the reflex to retain full control. Because energy is a basic necessity of human life, it is to some extent a public good, which is why Asian governments subsidize prices for basic fuels. Any trade in energy, let alone free trade, challenges such extensive government involvement.

Bundled up with issues of national security is a strong element of international competition for energy that is often intense because energy resources are limited. Countries are willing to pay a premium to secure access that is reliable, long term, and exclusive. International competition can poison the well of regional cooperation, as when the operation of a cross-border oil or natural gas pipeline is complicated by disputes over transit fees. Narrow national self-interest often stands in the way of advancing region-wide public goods in the energy sector.

Within individual countries, powerful vested interests in the energy sector may stand in the way of regional cooperation and integration. To enjoy economies of scale, many Asian countries operate electric utilities as either state-owned monopolies or private monopolies heavily regulated by the government. Either way, utility firms and other sector players exert a great deal of political influence and are likely to view regional initiatives as potential threats to their accustomed dominant positions in their home markets. They may resist harmonized standards, regulations, and pricing for reasons of narrow institutional interest without regard for the broader national interest that regional efforts promote.

The integration of subregions is likely the first step along the path leading ultimately to a pan-Asian energy market. Even in the highly integrated EU energy market, competition is healthiest at the subregional level.

And, certainly, the integration of subregional energy markets in Asia has not lacked international support and expertise. All major development partners that work in the region see immense benefit from regional energy trade and have provided grants and expertise to advance the agenda. One recurrent obstacle is failure to liberalize energy markets sufficiently for energy to be competitively priced and for new investments to respond to market signals. Asian countries need to understand the EU experience better and become convinced that regional energy markets serve their strategic interests, not least because energy security is difficult for most individual countries to secure for themselves.

Regional leaders meet often to discuss regional trade, but these discussions have yet to include energy. Even though individual countries struggle to meet their energy demand, confidence in partnership with neighboring countries remains low, and transparency in the energy sector has not been possible because governments see it as compromising their national strategic interest. A broader view shows regional energy trade strengthening Asian countries' energy security.

A good point of departure would be to establish a ministerial-level pan-Asian task force on energy cooperation and integration. Moving regional integration forward requires authoritative political commitment.

A brighter Asian energy future: every watt counts

The foregoing analysis makes clear that developing Asia must urgently take aggressive policy action to turn away from the path leading to a decidedly stark energy future and toward a future in which Asians enjoy secure access to adequate supplies of clean energy that is affordable to all. To realize the vision of the Clean Asian Century, with its promise of robust economic growth and substantially rising incomes, Asia must adopt a broad program of policy prescriptions on several fronts.

A unified Asian energy market

Asia must aspire to create a pan-Asian energy market by 2030. When it comes to regionally integrated electricity and gas markets, thinking big maximizes benefits. Asia must aspire to the degree of regional cooperation and integration in energy that currently prevails in Europe. The first step is to set up a ministerial task force to study the European experience and promote the political will to share more openly information on national power sectors, toward better harmonizing regulations, standards, and pricing policies.

This will require that Asian countries make a concerted effort to repeat, with regional energy cooperation, the success they have achieved with regional cooperation in other areas. While Asia's regional cooperation and integration is moving ahead rapidly in trade and other areas, progress on regional energy markets and infrastructure lags far behind despite large potential synergies.

Even where the scope for, and gains from, closer energy links are clear, such as in the Greater Mekong Subregion (GMS)—linkages remain limited at best. The GMS is well endowed with energy resources. Its hydropower potential amounts to 900 terawatt-hours, or four times the subregion's total electricity generation in 2010. Integrating power transmission in the GMS would save $14 billion over 20 years by substituting hydropower for electricity generated using fossil fuels.

To achieve a pan-Asian energy market, Asian countries need to muster the political will to look beyond narrow self-interest and clear the political hurdles that stand in the way of energy integration that is technically feasible and commercially viable. Overcoming technical obstacles, such as differences in standards, regulations, and energy pricing, requires participating countries to build goodwill in their political relations. Goodwill lends countries the confidence to be open and equitable about sharing benefits. It enables neighbors to share information and allay one another's concerns about the reliability of supply.

Short of comprehensive energy cooperation, there is plenty that individual national governments can do in the meantime to curb demand, expand the supply of clean energy, ensure affordable access for the poor, and develop capacity for future innovation.

Containing burgeoning energy demand

Asia must immediately take concrete steps to curb demand. Replacing inefficient general fuel subsidies with targeted subsidies can be a politically acceptable approach to eliminating broad inefficiencies without leaving the poor out in the cold. Second-generation greenhouse gas emission taxes recycle tax proceeds to help reduce the cost of cleaner inputs, thereby limiting their adverse impact on economic activity while mitigating global warming. Planning for "green cities" is crucial for an increasingly urban Asia. Reducing demand not only reduces the risk of supply bottlenecks but also promotes a cleaner environment.

A good place to start with energy is getting the price right. Countries in developing Asia must eliminate or rationalize distortionary subsidies as rapidly as practical to reduce energy overuse and waste. Subsidies impose a tremendous burden on public budgets, exceeding 2% of GDP in India, Indonesia, and Viet Nam and 4% in Bangladesh and Pakistan. If countries around the world eliminated wasteful subsidies, global carbon dioxide emissions would be an estimated 2.6 billion tons lower in 2035. To cushion the impact on the poor, governments should replace general subsidies with programs targeting the poor.

Failure to factor in environmental impact artificially discounts energy use below its true cost and thus encourages consumption. However, environmental taxes increase the cost of production and constrain economic activity. One policy solution is to combine domestic carbon taxes with revenue recycling, by which the government uses tax proceeds to reduce the cost of other productive inputs. This would mitigate the impact of carbon taxes on total production costs and thus on economic activity.

Asian governments must take the lead in changing the public's attitude toward energy use. The value of behavioral change is underscored by Japan's success in curbing demand since the oil shocks of the 1970s and again following the Fukushima disaster. Japan's energy intensity has improved by 25% since 1980, such that the country leads the world in the value of output per unit of energy. More recently, in the wake of the Fukushima accident and the resulting temporary shutdown of nuclear power plants, the grassroots Setsuden ("save electricity") campaign dramatically deployed energy conservation to stave off power outages. Further, behavioral change can limit rebound effects that occur when improved energy efficiency perversely increases consumption.

Green, smart urbanization and new transportation technologies are great ways to improve energy efficiency. Many Asian cities have already begun to move forward toward more intelligent urbanization. A large waste collection and disposal system of Incheon, Republic of Korea, generates electricity from waste. Ulaanbaatar, Mongolia, is deploying a combined heat-and-power plant that allows homes and commercial buildings to be cooled and heated using waste heat from power generation.

Massive rural–urban migration in developing Asia gives the region opportunities to design new urban areas for extremely efficient energy use. Asia is well placed to become the global leader in such design, as most advanced countries now have more static populations. Satellite cities built from scratch allow planners to design electricity and gas delivery systems with minimal overlap and maximal orientation toward energy savings. Similar opportunities exist, albeit on a more modest scale, as electricity and gas utilities connect rural areas previously devoid of modern power infrastructure. Applying gas directly to end uses such as cooking, for example, avoids loses incurred when gas is used to generate electricity. Programs to replace diesel city buses with buses that run on cleaner natural gas are already demonstrating their worth through improved urban air quality.

Notwithstanding considerable progress, plenty of scope remains for developing the technological bases for green, smart urbanization. Additional programs are needed to research, develop, and demonstrate clean and cost-competitive electric- and gas-powered cars and other energy-saving technologies applicable to urban settings.

Tapping cleaner energy supply

Asia should strive to diversify and optimize its energy mix in the medium and long term. In particular, it should rein in its disturbingly heavy dependence on imported oil. The share of Asia's imports supplied from the Middle East rose from 33% in 1990 to 48% in 2010. Such deepening dependence on a single region, combined with the lack of close substitutes for oil in transportation and industrial uses, undermines the reliability and adequacy of Asia's energy supply.

Securing adequate and reliable supplies of clean, affordable energy is challenging but achievable. As energy sources vary across the region, each country's options to augment its energy supplies depend on its endowments and needs. Potential energy sources have their own merits and shortcomings, but every drop—every watt—counts! Developing future technologies requires government support in the beginning. Effort is required on all fronts, from each country according to its comparative advantages.

Because of their strong environmental and energy security advantages, renewable energy sources merit close examination from the start. Asia is fortunate to have rich renewable energy potential. The region has substantial endowments of hydro, solar, and wind power. Already, 542 gigawatts (GW) of hydropower capacity are installed or under construction, with potential to quadruple it to 2,204 GW. Wind and solar have made remarkable strides. In less than a decade, generating capacity rose from negligible to 82 GW for wind and to 20 GW for solar, and great potential exists to further expand both. Asian countries are among the world leaders in the manufacture of renewable energy plants. However, while wind and solar power are becoming cheaper, and are expected to reach grid parity in some countries in a few years, they currently require favorable policy and financial incentives like feed-in tariffs and tax credits. Hydropower, on the other hand, is highly cost-competitive, especially when constructed on a large scale, but projects pose environmental and social challenges commensurate with their size. Biofuels hold promise to replace substantial quantities of gasoline and diesel in transportation, reducing net GHG emissions with fuels that are secure because they are homegrown. However, like wind and solar, biofuels have a way to go before they become cost-competitive with the fossil fuels they are being developed to replace.

Asia's energy future needs renewable sources, but renewables are not enough. For this reason, Asia must make good use of its substantial nonrenewable resources, favoring cleaner options and refinements. The energy mix will evolve slowly as older investments in plant and equipment are retired, but Asia's environmental needs urgently require that nonrenewable energy sources be made cleaner and safer.

Asia needs to take stock of its substantial reserves of shale gas, which have potential to offset coal use. Asia's geology is incompletely investigated, but indications are that the PRC has as much as 20% of global reserves of shale gas, ranking it first in the world. Technically recoverable reserves in India are estimated at a more modest 1% of global reserves but still equivalent to 1.6 billion tons of oil. As shale gas recovery uses emergent technology, the environmental impacts of drilling and production need to be evaluated for potential risks.

Asia should also look at emerging technologies that make carbon-based fuels cleaner to use. In light of Asia's relative abundance of coal, these technologies hold a lot of promise for the region. Carbon capture and storage has potential to lower carbon dioxide emissions, and Asia is already investing heavily in this technology.

And then there is nuclear energy. While the Fukushima incident underscored the need to strengthen reactor safety, nuclear appears to have a permanent place in Asia's energy mix. Phasing nuclear power out would require Asia to increase its use of fossil fuels, at least in the short to medium term. Powering Asia's more prosperous future without nuclear energy in the mix would increase the region's carbon dioxide emissions by 8%–13% annually in 2035.

Ensuring affordable access

True energy security is not possible without addressing the energy needs of the poor and residents of low-income countries. Concrete steps to support Energy for All include establishing income policies to secure an adequate energy floor for the poor, selecting appropriate technologies for distributed and off-grid power generation, and promoting community participation. Narrowing differences between countries is critical. Low-income countries need international aid to help them build equitable energy infrastructure that protects the poor. Extending affordable access to the entire population and narrowing the wide gaps between Asian countries will promote inclusive growth across Asia.

A high priority should be expanding the delivery of affordable energy to the poor. Despite Asia's rising affluence, in 2012 almost 700 million Asians, or 18% of all Asians, still lacked access to basic energy services such as electricity or modern fuels. Further, some 2.8 billion Asians, or about 74% of the total, still relied for some uses such as cooking on traditional fuels that are dirty and unreliable. Most of the world's energy poor live in Asia. Energy is both a basic human need and a tool that empowers the poor to be more productive and make their own contribution to inclusive growth. Developing Asia must strive to achieve universal access to affordable energy as soon as possible.

This necessarily entails special programs that support the energy consumption of the poor. Unlike general energy subsidies, which disproportionately benefit the non-poor, means-tested assistance that targets the poor extends energy access without jeopardizing fiscal sustainability. Support needs to be carefully designed to avoid encouraging wasteful energy use. It may offer low-tariff lifelines only to households that use very little electricity or cover only to the first small tranche of consumption. Careful design will ensure better targeting.

Also important is exploring how to adapt new technologies to the energy needs of the poor. To reach the isolated rural poor beyond the reach of the grid, electricity can be generated on micro scales using locally available renewable sources such as hydro, solar, biomass, and wind. Gas captured from livestock manure can provide clean cooking fuel. Low-income countries need to innovatively adapt imported technology to suit local conditions and meet local needs. They will find some imported technologies more appropriate than others.

Just as it behooves comfortable citizens to bridge the energy divide by helping the poor among them gain access to affordable energy, richer Asian countries must help their poorer neighbors. Wide gaps in energy access within a country jeopardize inclusive growth, and wide gaps between Asian countries at different stages of development do the same. Assistance to energy-poor countries should transfer funding and technology. Globally, advanced countries share responsibility for helping developing countries, including those in Asia, as all stand to benefit from reduced GHG emissions wherever they occur. Asian countries rich and poor have equal incentive to contribute energetically to global efforts to mitigate climate change. After all, climate change affects everyone.

Building capacity for future innovation

Asia must broaden and deepen its intellectual capital to better support its physical investments in energy. A modern energy sector will come about only if the knowledge base is there to support it. As the biggest energy user, Asia must acknowledge its role as the lynchpin of climate change mitigation and strive to marshal research and development capacity equal to the task. Technology transfer from developed countries can accelerate the deployment of new technologies, but the region must aggressively invest more on researching and developing new energy technologies.

At the same time, Asia needs to engender an institutional and policy environment conducive to creating and adopting new technologies. A policy priority for the whole region is to invest more in educating and training energy specialists, scientists, and engineers. Asian countries should allocate more funds to education, especially at the tertiary level, to develop the human capital required to meet the energy challenge.

Individually, each new energy technology makes only a limited contribution to Asia's energy security. Collectively, though, they have the potential to make a big positive difference. Linking the contributions together intelligently and coherently—through, for example, smart grids that accept energy from distributed generation using renewables—is the top priority. Each technology may offer only a drop in the bucket, but together they flow as a river to power the Clean Asian Century.

Every drop and every watt count!

References

Arvizu, D., P. Balaya, L. Cabeza, T. Hollands, A. Jäger-Waldau, M. Kondo, C. Konseibo, V. Meleshko, W. Stein, Y. Tamaura, H. Xu, and R. Zilles. 2011. *Direct Solar Energy.* In O. Edenhofer, R. Pichs-Madruga, Y. Sokona, K. Seyboth, P. Matschoss, S. Kadner, T. Zwickel, P. Eickemeier, G. Hansen, S. Schlömer, and C. von Stechow, eds. *IPCC Special Report on Renewable Energy Sources and Climate Change Mitigation.* Cambridge, UK, and New York: Cambridge University Press.

Asian Development Bank (ADB). 2003. *Indonesian Coalbed Methane: Task 1b—CBM Pilots, Data Base, and in-Country Capabilities.* Final draft prepared by Advance Resources International, Inc. Manila.

________. 2006. *Energy Efficiency and Climate Change Considerations for On-road Transport in Asia.* Manila.

________. 2011. *Asia 2050: Realizing the Asian Century.* Manila.

________. 2012. *Green Urbanization in Asia.* In Key Indicators for Asia and the Pacific 2012. Manila.

BP. 2012. *Statistical Review of World Energy 2012.* http://www.bp.com/section bodycopy.do?categoryId=7500&contentId=7068481 (accessed 4 March 2013).

________. 2013. *Energy Outlook 2030.* http://www.bp.com/extendedsection genericarticle.do?categoryId=9048887&contentId=7082549

Brookes, L. 1979. A Low Energy Strategy for the UK by G. Leach et al.: A Review and Reply. *Atom.* 269. pp. 3–8.

Butkiewicz, L. 2012. *The Shale Gas Revolution: Implications for U.S. and Canadian Energy Policy and Asian Energy Security—An interview with James Slutz.* http://www.nbr.org/research/activity.aspx?id=270

Chakravarty, D., S. Dasgupta, and J. Roy. 2013. *Rebound Effect: How Much to Worry? Current Opinion in Environmental Sustainability.* Under review.

Dart Energy. India. http://www.dartenergy.com.au/page/Worldwide/India/ (accessed 5 January 2013).

Del Granado, J. A., D. Coady, and R. Gillingham. 2012. The Unequal Benefits of Fuel Subsidies: A Review of Evidence for Developing Countries. *World Development.* 40 (11). pp. 2234–2248.

Economist, The. 2012. *Daily Chart: Pricing Sunshine.* 28 December. http://www.economist.com/blogs/graphicdetail/2012/12/daily-chart-19

Energy Information Administration (EIA). 2011a. Appendix B. Metric and Thermal Conversion Tables. *Natural Gas Annual.* Washington, DC: United States (US) Department of Energy. http://www.eia.gov/naturalgas/annual/pdf/appendix_b.pdf

________. 2011b. *International Energy Statistics.* Washington, DC: US Department of Energy. http://www.eia.gov/cfapps/ipdbproject/iedindex3.cfm?tid=2&pid=33&aid=7&cid=r7,&syid=2006&eyid=2010&unit=MK (accessed 15 March 2013).

________. 2011c. Table A1. *World total primary energy consumption by region. International Energy Outlook 2011.* Washington, DC: US Department of Energy. http://www.eia.gov/forecasts/ieo/pdf/ieorefcase.pdf

________. 2011d. *World Shale Gas Resources: An Initial Assessment of 14 Regions Outside the United States.* April. http://www.eia.gov/analysis/studies/worldshalegas/

________. 2012a. *Annual Energy Outlook 2013 Early Release Overview.* Washington, DC: US Department of Energy. http://www.eia.gov/forecasts/aeo/er/pdf/0383er(2013).pdf

________. 2012b. *Electric Power Monthly.* February. http://www.eia.gov/electricity/data.cfm#sales

———. 2012c. Natural Gas Delivered Prices by End-Use Sector and Census Division. *Annual Energy Outlook 2012.* http://www.eia.gov/oiaf/aeo/tablebrowser/#release=AEO2012&subject=0-AEO2012&table=78-AEO2012&region=0-0&cases=ref2012-d020112c

———. 2013a. *Natural Gas Summary.* http://www.eia.gov/dnav/ng/ng_sum_lsum_dcu_nus_a.htm (accessed 14 March 2013).

———. 2013b. Table A6. Approximate Heat Rates for Electricity, and Heat Content of Electricity. *Monthly Energy Review.* March. http://www.eia.gov/totalenergy/data/monthly/pdf/sec13_6.pdf (accessed 18 March 2013).

Environmental Protection Agency. 2012. Notice of Data Availability Concerning Renewable Fuels Produced from Palm Oil Under the RFS Program. *Federal Register.* 77 (18). pp. 4300–4318. http://www.gpo.gov/fdsys/pkg/FR-2012-01-27/pdf/2012-1784.pdf (accessed 13 March 2013).

European Commission. 2004. *The Energy Taxation Directive.* http://ec.europa.eu/taxation_customs/taxation/excise_duties/energy_products/legislation/index_en.htm (accessed 27 February 2013).

European Union. 2007. Communication of 10 January 2007 from the Commission to the Council and the European Parliament entitled *Priority Interconnection Plan.* http://europa.eu/legislation_summaries/energy/internal_energy_market/l27081_en.htm (accessed 14 March 2013).

European Photovoltaic Industry Association. 2013a. *On the Road to Competitiveness.* http://www.epia.org/policies/sustainable-market-developmet/market-competitiveness/?L=0

———. 2013b. *100 GW of Solar PV Now Installed in the World Today.* http://http://www.renewableenergyworld.com/rea/news/article/2013/02/100-gw-of-solar-pv-now-installed-in-the-world-today

ExxonMobil. 2009. *Outlook for Energy: A View to 2030.* Irving, TX. http://www.exxonmobil.com/Corporate/Files/news_pub_eo_2009.pdf

Focus Reports. 2012. Indonesia: Re-energizing the Archipelago. *Indonesia Oil and Gas Report.* October. pp. 7–29. http://issuu.com/focusreports/docs/indonesia_oil___gas_report_october_2012

Fueyo, N., A. Gomez, and C. Dopazo. Forthcoming. *Energy Security, Sustainability, and Affordability in Asia and the Pacific.*

Goldstein, B., G. Hiriart, R. Bertani, C. Bromley, L. Gutiérrez-Negrín, E. Huenges, H. Muraoka, A. Ragnarsson, J. Tester, and V. Zui. 2011. Geothermal Energy. In O. Edenhofer, R. Pichs-Madruga, Y. Sokona, K. Seyboth, P. Matschoss, S. Kadner, T. Zwickel, P. Eickemeier, G. Hansen, S. Schlömer, and C. von Stechow, eds. *IPCC Special Report on Renewable Energy Sources and Climate Change Mitigation.* Cambridge, UK, and New York: Cambridge University Press.

Government of the Philippines, Department of Energy. 2011. *Electric Power: Power Statistics,* http://www.doe.gov.ph/EP/Powerstat.htm (accessed 13 March 2013).

Government of Western Australia, Department of Mines and Petroleum. Hydraulic Fracture Stimulation. *Gas Fact Sheet.* http://www.dmp.wa.gov.au/documents/121983_Gas_Fact_Sheet_Hydraulic_Stimulation.pdf (retrieved 3 January 2013).

Green Car Congress. 2006. *Seoul Mandates 100% CNG Buses by 2010.* http://www.greencarcongress.com/2006/09/seoul_mandates_.html (accessed 18 February 2013).

Institute of Energy Economics, Japan. 2011. Japan Rode Over Summer with Nationwide Power Saving. *Japan Energy Brief* No. 15. September. http://eneken.ieej.or.jp/en/jeb/1109.pdf (accessed 15 March 2013).

International Atomic Energy Agency (IAEA). 2011. *Draft IAEA Action Plan on Nuclear Safety.* GC(55)/14. Report by the Director General. http://www.iaea.org/About/Policy/GC/GC55/Documents/gc55-14.pdf

________. 2012a. Energy, Electricity and Nuclear Power Estimates for the Period up to 2050. *Reference Data Series* 1. http://www-pub.iaea.org/books/IAEABooks/10358/Energy-Electricity-and-Nuclear-Power-Estimates-for-the-Period-up-to-2050-2012-Edition

________. 2012b. Nuclear Power Reactors in the World. *Reference Data Series* 2. http://www-pub.iaea.org/books/IAEABooks/8954/Nuclear-Power-Reactors-in-the-World-2012-Edition

________. 2013. *Power Reactor Information System* (PRIS). http://www.iaea.org/pris

International Energy Agency (IEA). 2009. *Technology Roadmap: Carbon Capture and Storage.* Paris. http://www.iea.org/publications/freepublications/publication/name,3847,en.html

________. 2010a. *Energy Technology Perspectives 2010.* Paris. http://www.iea.org/publications/freepublications/publication/name,26100,en.html

________. 2010b. *The Contribution of Natural Gas Vehicles to Sustainable Transport.* Paris. http://www.iea.org/publications/freepublications/publication/name,3929,en.html

________. 2011a. *Energy for All: Financing Access for the Poor.* Paris: Organisation for Economic Co-operation and Development (OECD)/IEA. http://www.worldenergyoutlook.org/media/weowebsite/2011/weo2011_energy_for_all.pdf

________. 2011b. *Technology Roadmap: Biofuels for Transport.* Paris. http://www.iea.org/publications/freepublications/publication/name,3976,en.html (accessed 13 March 2013).

________. 2011c. *World Energy Outlook 2011.* Paris. http://www.worldenergyoutlook.org/publications/weo-2011/

________. 2012a. *Golden Rules for a Golden Age of Gas: World Energy Outlook Special Report on Unconventional Gas.* Paris. http://www.worldenergyoutlook.org/goldenrules/

________. 2012b. *Technology Roadmap: Hydropower.* Paris: International Energy Agency. http://www.iea.org/publications/freepublications/publication/2012_Hydropower_Roadmap.pdf?bcsi_scan_97e98328e2b67804=0&bcsi_scan_filename=2012_Hydropower_Roadmap.pdf

________. 2012c. *World Energy Outlook 2012.* Paris. http://www.worldenergyoutlook.org/publications/weo-2012/

________. 2013. *Hydropower: A Key to Prosperity in the Growing World.* http://www.ieahydro.org/uploads/files/hydropower_a_key_to_prosperity.pdf (accessed 15 March 2013).

International Energy Agency and Nuclear Energy Agency (NEA). 2010. *Projected Costs of Generating Electricity* (2010 Edition). Paris: IEA, NEA, and OECD.

International Institute for Sustainable Development, Global Subsidies Initiative. 2008. *Biofuels—At What Cost?* http://www.iisd.org/gsi/biofuel-subsidies/biofuels-what-cost (accessed 13 March 2013).

Isaak, D., D. Park, and M. Lee. Forthcoming. *Oil Security Issues in Asia and the Pacific.*

Jenkins, J., T. Nordhaus, and M. Shellenberger. 2011. *Energy Emergence: Rebound and Backfire as Emergent Phenomena.* Oakland: The Breakthrough Institute. http://thebreakthrough.org/archive/new_report_how_efficiency_can

Katakey, R., D. Sethuraman, and A. Guo. 2012. [People's Republic of] *China Shale Delay to Boost LNG Imports in Boon for Exxon: Energy.* Bloomberg. 14 February. http://www.bloomberg.com/news/2012-02-13/china-shale-delay-to-boost-lng-imports-in-boon-for-exxon-energy.html

Khazzoom, D. 1980. Economic implications of mandated efficiency standards for household appliances, *Energy Journal.* 1 (4). pp. 21–40.

Kim, A. and Z. Yu. 2012. [People's Republic of] China's Vast Shale Gas Potential Limited by Pipeline Infrastructure Obstacles. *Financial Times.* 15 March. http://www.ft.com/cms/s/2/5f383926-6edf-11e1-afb8-00144feab49a.html#axzz2KwLh1qVW

Korea Times. 2012. [Republic of] Korea Develops World's Most Efficient Carbon Capture Tech. 11 September. http://koreatimes.co.kr/www/news/tech/2012/09/129_119632.html

Kouvaritakis, N., L. Paroussos, T. Revesz, E. Zalai, and D. Van Regemorter. 2005. *Impacts of energy taxation in the enlarged European Union, evaluation with GEM-E3 Europe.* Final report. Study for the European Commission. http://master.e3mlab.ntua.gr/reports/energy_tax_study.pdf

Kuuskraa, V. A. 2009. *Worldwide Gas Shales and Unconventional Gas: A Status Report.* Paper prepared and presented at the United Nations Climate Change Conference, COP15, Natural Gas, Renewables and Efficiency: Pathways to a Low-Carbon Economy. Copenhagen. 17–18 December.

Lee, M., D. Park, and H. Saunders. Forthcoming. *Asia's Energy Adequacy, Environmental Sustainability, and Affordability: An Overview.*

Lelyveld, M. 2012. [People's Republic of] *China Debates Shale Gas Growth.* Radio Free Asia. 16 July. http://www.rfa.org/english/energy_watch/gas-07162012105003.html?searchterm=China%20Debates%20Shale%20Gas%20Growth

Li, L. and Y. Han. 2012. The Energy Efficiency Rebound Effect in [the People's Republic of] China from Three Industries Perspective. *Energy Procedia.* 14. pp. 1105–1110.

Lin, B. and X. Liu. 2013. Refined Oil Pricing Mechanism Reform and Energy Rebound for Passenger Transportation in [the People's Republic of] China. *Energy Policy* (in press).

McGlade, C., S. Sorrell, and J. Speirs. 2012. *A review of regional and global estimates of unconventional gas resources.* In I. Pearson, P. Zeniewski, F. Gracceva, P. Zastera, C. McGlade, S. Sorrell, J. Speirs, and G. Thonhauser, with C. Alecu, A. Eriksson, P. Toft, and M. Schuetz. *Unconventional Gas: Potential Energy Market Impacts in the European Union.* Luxembourg: Publications Office of the European Union.

Montgomery, J. *100 GW of Solar PV Now Installed in the World Today.* RenewableEnergyWorld.com. http://www.renewableenergyworld.com/rea/news/article/2013/02/100-gw-of-solar-pv-now-installed-in-the-world-today

Naess-Schmidt, S. 2012. Multiple Benefits of Energy Efficient Renovation of Buildings—Impact on Public Finances. Presented at the IEA Roundtable on the Macroeconomic Impacts of Energy Efficiency Improvements. Paris. 24–25 January.

Ojha, K., B. Karmakar, A. Manda, and A. K. Pathak. 2011. Coal Bed Methane in India: Difficulties and Prospects. *International Journal of Chemical Engineering and Applications.* 2 (4). pp. 256–260.

Organisation for Economic Co-operation and Development (OECD). 2010. *Cities and Climate Change.* OECD Publishing.

Owen, D. 2009. *Green Metropolis: Why Living Smaller, Living Closer, and Driving Less are the Keys to Sustainability.* New York: Riverhead Books.

Pena, N. 2008. Biofuels for Transportation: A Climate Perspective. *Solutions White Paper Series.* http://www.ialottery.com_www.pewtrusts.com/uploadedFiles/wwwpewtrustsorg/Reports/Global_warming/BiofuelsFINAL.pdf

Remo, A. R. 2011. DOE out to boost geothermal capacity by 75%. *Philippine Daily Inquirer.* 26 August. http://business.inquirer.net/15199/doe-out-to-boost-geothermal-capacity-by-75 (accessed 13 March 2013).

Rogner, H. H. 1997. An Assessment of World Hydrocarbon Resources. *Annual Review of Energy and the Environment.* 22. pp. 217–262.

Ross, M. Forthcoming. Diversification of Energy Supply: Prospects for Emerging Energy Sources.

Roy, J. 2000. The Rebound Effect: Some Empirical Evidence from India. *Energy Policy.* 28 (6–7). pp. 433–438.

Saunders, H. D. 1992. The Khazzoom–Brookes Postulate and Neoclassical Growth. *The Energy Journal.* 13 (4). pp. 131–148.

________. 2008. Fuel Conserving (and Using) Production Functions. *Energy Economics.* 30. pp. 2184–2235.

________. In press. Historical Evidence for Energy Consumption Rebound in 30 US Sectors and A Toolkit for Rebound Analysts. *Technological Forecasting and Social Change.* http://dx.doi.org/10.1016/j.techfore.2012.12.007

Schnettler, A., T. Dederichs, A.-K. Meinerzhagen, E. Szczechowicz, H. Duer, C. Rosenhagen, N. Lambert, E. van Sambeek, and J. Chu. 2012. *Renewable Energy Technology Deployment, Opportunities for the Use of Renewable Energy in Road Transport in Different Regions (Europe, North America,* [People's Republic of] *China).* Paris: IEA. http://iea-retd.org/archives/publications/retrans-regions

Shah, J. 2012. Mongolian Renewable Energy. Presented at the ADB Quantum Leap in Wind. 17–18 May. Ulaanbaatar, Mongolia.

Sorrell, S. 2007. *The Rebound Effect: An Assessment of the Evidence for Economy-wide Energy Savings from Improved Energy Efficiency.* London: UK Energy Research Centre. http://www.ukerc.ac.uk/Downloads/PDF/07/0710ReboundEffect/0710ReboundEffectReport.pdf

________. 2009. Jevons' Paradox Revisited: The Evidence for Backfire from Improved Energy Efficiency. *Energy Policy.* 37 (4). pp. 1456–1569. ISSN 0301-4215.

Sovacool, B. 2012. Environmental Issues, Climate Change, and Energy Security. Presented at the ADB ADO Theme Chapter Workshop, 13–14 December 2012. Manila.

Sovacool, B., I. Mukherjee, I. M. Drupady, and A. L. D'Agostino. 2011. Evaluating Energy Security Performance from 1990 to 2010 for Eighteen Countries. *Energy.* 36 (10). pp. 5846–5853.

Tokyo Electric Power Company. 2012. *Overview of Electricity Supply and Demand this Summer.* http://www.tepco.co.jp/en/press/corp-com/release/betu12_e/images/120914e0401.pdf (accessed 16 March 2013).

Tsao, J. Y., H. D. Saunders, J. R. Creighton, M. E. Coltrin, and J. A. Simmons. 2010. Solid-state Lighting: An Energy-Economics Perspective. *Journal of Physics D: Applied Physics.* 43 (35). pp. 1–17.

Turner, K. Forthcoming. Rebound Effects from Increased Energy Efficiency: A Time to Pause and Reflect. *The Energy Journal.* Cleveland: International Association for Energy Economics.

US Geological Survey. 2012. *An Estimate of Undiscovered Conventional Oil and Gas Resources of the World, 2012.* Denver. http://pubs.usgs.gov/fs/2012/3042/fs2012-3042.pdf

________. 2013. *Gas Hydrates Project.* http://pubs.usgs.gov/fs/gas-hydrates/

Wah, H. S. 2011. Indonesia's Opportunity in the Development of Unconventional Gas Resources. Presented at IndoGas 2011: The 5th International Indonesian Gas Conference and Exhibition, 26 January. Jakarta, Indonesia.

Weisser, D. 2007. A Guide to Life-Cycle Greenhouse Gas (GHG) Emissions from Electric Supply Technologies. *Energy.* 32 (9). pp. 1543–1559.

World Bank. 2011. 2008 Again? *Indonesia Economic Quarterly.* March. http://www-wds.worldbank.org/external/default/WDSContentServer/WDSP/IB/2011/03/18/000333037_20110318015637/Rendered/PDF/601520revised010IEQ1Mar2011english.pdf

World Health Organization. 2008. *Air Quality and Health.* Fact Sheet No. 313. Geneva.

Background papers

Fueyo, N., A. Gomez, and C. Dopazo. Forthcoming. Energy Security, Sustainability, and Affordability in Asia and the Pacific. *ADB Economics Working Paper Series.* Manila: Asian Development Bank (ADB).

Hong, J., C. Kim, and H. Shin. Forthcoming. Power Sector in Developing Asia: Current Status and Policy Issues. *ADB Economics Working Paper Series.* Manila: ADB.

Isaak, D., D. Park, and M. Lee. Forthcoming. Oil Security Issues in Asia and the Pacific. *ADB Economics Working Paper Series.* Manila: ADB.

Lee, M., D. Park, and H. Saunders. Forthcoming. Asia's Energy Adequacy, Environmental Sustainability, and Affordability: An Overview. *ADB Economics Working Paper Series.* Manila: ADB.

Lucas, N. Forthcoming. Energy Security in Asia: Prospects for Regional Cooperation. *ADB Economics Working Paper Series.* Manila: ADB.

Rogner, H. H. and K. Nam. Forthcoming. Nuclear Power Development in Asia. *ADB Economics Working Paper Series.* Manila: ADB.

Ross, M. Forthcoming. Diversification of Energy Supply: Prospects for Emerging Energy Sources. *ADB Economics Working Paper Series.* Manila: ADB.

Sharma, D. Forthcoming. Energy Efficiency Improvements in Asia: Macroeconomic Impacts. *ADB Economics Working Paper Series.* Manila: ADB.

Sovacool, B. Forthcoming. Environmental Issues, Climate Change and Energy Security in Developing Asia. *ADB Economics Working Paper Series.* Manila: ADB.

_________. Forthcoming. Energy Access and Energy Security in the Asia Pacific. *ADB Economics Working Paper Series.* Manila: ADB.

3

Economic trends and prospects in developing Asia

Central Asia

Armenia
Azerbaijan
Georgia
Kazakhstan
Kyrgyz Republic
Tajikistan
Turkmenistan
Uzbekistan

Armenia

The economy grew strongly in 2012. Prudent fiscal and monetary policies helped control inflation, narrow deficits in the budget and current account, and keep the ratio of external public debt to GDP manageable. Growth will likely continue over the medium term if the government implements plans to accelerate structural reform and mobilize revenues essential for prudent social and development expenditures.

Economic performance

Government estimates showed economic growth accelerating to 7.2% in 2012 from 4.7% in 2011, with all supply-side sectors of the economy expanding (Figure 3.1.1).

Industry (excluding construction) grew by 5.7%, reflecting favorable conditions in foreign markets and the government's efforts to stimulate exports. Growth in industry came mainly from mining, beverages, and building materials. Good weather and government programs offering farmers free seed and subsidized fuel, fertilizer, and credit helped agriculture expand by 9.3%. The construction sector, still reeling from the 2009 recession, inched up by a mere 0.5%, mainly reflecting renewed construction in the energy and transport sectors. Services, accounting for 45% of GDP, gained further steam and expanded by 8.4%, with the fastest growth rates in finance, insurance, entertainment, and recreation.

On the demand side, growth was driven mostly by higher private consumption, while total investment and net exports reduced growth. The negative effect of net exports eased somewhat, as exports grew more quickly than imports because of the relatively favorable external environment. Private consumption rose by an estimated 10.1%, fuelled by remittances, continued rapid growth in lending, and moderate growth in domestic earnings. Public consumption was flat in line with the government's conservative fiscal stance. Gross fixed capital formation contracted by 4.2% because of sluggish public and private investment.

Average annual inflation plunged by two-thirds, to 2.6% from 7.7% in 2011, mainly because of smaller price rises for food and services (Figure 3.1.2). Aided by higher food production, favorable global prices, and continued tight monetary conditions, the 12-month inflation rate (comparing December to December) declined to 3.6% in 2012 from 4.7% in 2011, within the central bank's target band of 2.5%–5.5%.

Fiscal policy was generally tight, aimed at gradually shrinking the deficit without derailing economic growth. As expenditures rose less than planned, the budget deficit narrowed to 1.5% in 2012, less than the programmed 2.6% (Figure 3.1.3).

This chapter was written by Grigor Gyurjyan of the Armenia Resident Mission, ADB, Yerevan.

3.1.1 Supply-side contributions to growth

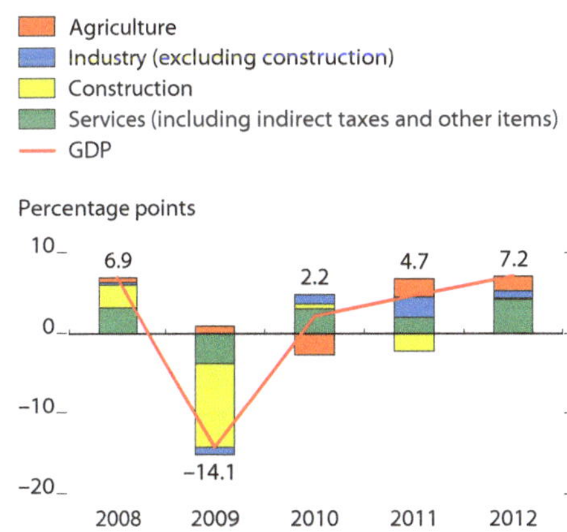

Sources: National Statistical Service of the Republic of Armenia. http://www.armstat.am; Central Bank of Armenia. http://www.cba.am (both accessed 12 March 2013).

Click here for figure data

3.1.2 Inflation

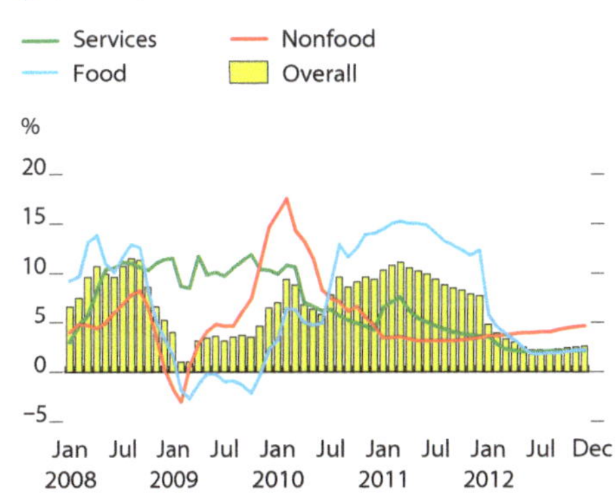

Source: National Statistical Service of the Republic of Armenia. http://www.armstat.am (accessed 12 March 2013).

Click here for figure data

Fiscal consolidation combined with economic growth and some improvements in tax collection lifted total government revenue by 6.6% in 2012. Expenditures grew by 1.5% in absolute terms—mostly to cover higher public spending on the social safety net, education, and health, which together claim nearly half of government expenditure—but edged down as a percentage of GDP. Meanwhile, undefined "other expenditures" and outlays for nonfinancial assets declined.

Despite rapid growth, careful debt management, and the government's conservative policy on external borrowing, public debt as a share of GDP expanded from 40.7% in 2011 to 44.1% at the end of 2012, still below the 50% ceiling that would trigger a deficit limit of 3% according to the Public Debt Law (Figure 3.1.4). In nominal terms, public external debt increased by $170 million to $3.7 billion, or 37.7% of GDP. Domestic public debt climbed by $70 million to $630 million, or 6.4% of GDP. Although total public debt is considerable, debt service remains manageable because most debt is on concessional terms.

Having peaked in 2009, the current account deficit again declined to an estimated 10.4% of GDP in 2012 from 10.9% in 2011 (Figure 3.1.5).

Exports surged by an estimated 7.0% to $1.7 billion, benefitting from generally benign global commodity prices, which boosted export values for the mining sector, and the strong performance of the food-processing industry. Imports climbed by 1.7% to $3.7 billion to meet domestic demand that was powered by higher remittances. Despite robust export growth, imports still dwarfed exports. The large trade imbalance was covered by growing remittances and official grants and loans. Net inflows of foreign direct investment, concentrated in mining and telecommunications, remained subdued at an estimated $420 million, down 6% from 2011. Remittance inflows from workers abroad, mainly in the Russian Federation, rose by 8.8% to $1.4 billion, returning to their 2008 peak (Figure 3.1.6).

Despite higher domestic demand, the refinancing rate has been kept at 8.0% since September 2011. Pushed by increased lending and a continued buildup in net domestic assets, the money supply (M2) rose by 19.5% in 2012. The central bank's efforts to dampen exchange rate volatility lowered foreign exchange reserves, despite strong remittances, by $108 million to $1.8 billion at the end of December 2012 (Figure 3.1.7).

Over the year, the dram depreciated by 4.4% in nominal effective terms and by 6.7% in real effective terms. While exports benefited from depreciation, they remained constrained by weak productivity and competitiveness and persistently high concentration in mining and metals.

Economic outlook

With the outcome of the February 2013 presidential elections signaling the maintenance of current policies, continued but more moderate growth is expected in 2013 and 2014. Assuming continued structural reform and no further worsening of global economic conditions, GDP growth is projected at 4.5% in 2013 and 4.6% in 2014 (Figure 3.1.8). Growth could be slower if external risks, including a further slowdown of growth in the Russian Federation and possible recession in the euro area, materialize.

3.1.3 Fiscal indicators

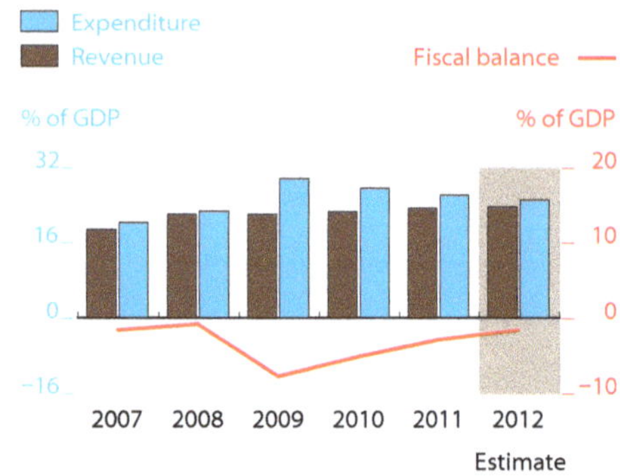

Source: National Statistical Service of the Republic of Armenia. http://www.armstat.am (accessed 12 March 2013).

Click here for figure data

3.1.4 Public debt

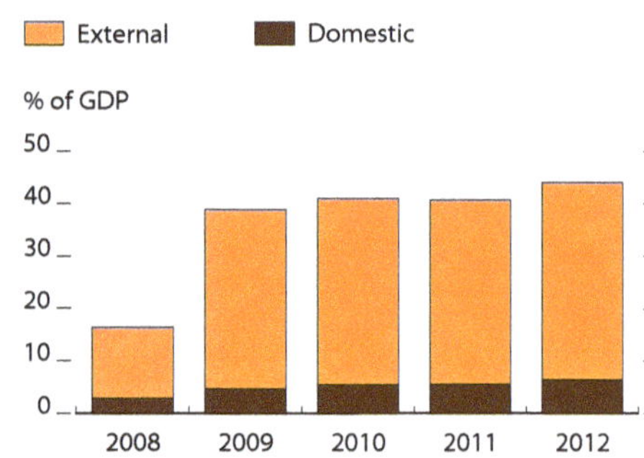

Source: National Statistical Service of the Republic of Armenia. http://www.armstat.am (accessed 12 March 2013).

Click here for figure data

3.1.5 Current account components

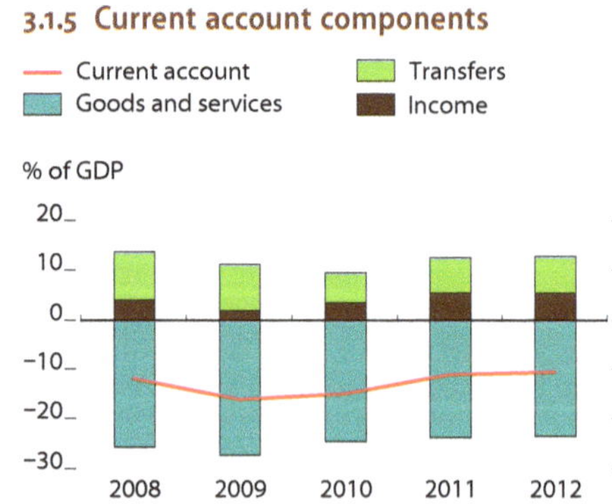

Source: National Statistical Service of the Republic of Armenia. http://www.armstat.am (accessed 12 March 2013).

Click here for figure data

Agriculture is expected to continue growing as productivity improves and the area under irrigation expands. Industrial expansion, led by mining and food processing, will further buttress growth. Services should also expand as higher remittances drive consumption. Lagging construction growth will be supported by the building of the North–South Road Corridor and other large infrastructure projects. Continued structural and public sector reform aiming to improve the business environment and private sector development could further strengthen the economic outlook and promote growth.

In the short run, service payments on the external debt of the government and central bank are expected to peak in 2013 at $423 million, including both principal and interest. This sum will pose a major drain on financial resources, equal to 15% of the value of exported goods and services, and could put pressure on the overall balance of payments. The government's share of this debt service is $225 million, which will equal 10% of government revenues in 2013, though this burden is projected to ease thereafter.

In the long run, the introduction of a mandatory funded pension system in January 2014 is expected to create a pool of long-term assets to help finance investment, which should foster growth and promote job creation. With continued tight monetary conditions and an assumed gradual upswing in agriculture, average annual inflation is projected at 3.6% in 2013 and 3.2% in 2014. During these 2 years, the 12-month inflation rate (December to December) is expected to remain within the central bank's target band of 2.5%–5.5%. Smaller price rises for food will reduce the impact of the higher price for imported natural gas planned in 2013.

The government is likely to maintain its policy of gradual fiscal consolidation, to allay concerns about the buildup of public and external debt. The fiscal deficit is projected to narrow further without constraining economic recovery. The 2013 budget aims for an overall deficit equal to 2.6% of GDP, as was programmed for 2012. The government's medium-term fiscal objective is to narrow this deficit to 2.3% of GDP in 2014 and 2.0% in 2015. Spending will continue to focus on strengthening social infrastructure and the social safety net. Sustained tax and customs reform and efforts to enhance economic competitiveness are expected to raise the tax-to-GDP ratio over time.

Monetary policy is expected to return gradually to a neutral stance over the medium term, to sustain growth while ensuring price stability. However, the financial sector remains highly dollarized in terms of both assets and liabilities, leaving the country vulnerable to exchange rate shocks and making monetary policy less effective. The authorities have discouraged further dollarization by imposing higher risk weights and provisions on foreign currency assets and higher reserve requirements on foreign currency deposits.

The trade deficit is expected to narrow moderately. Assuming no downward pressure on commodity prices, export growth should continue. The government's strategy to diversify exports, approved in 2011, is to develop 11 industrial subsectors selected for their export potential. This strategy is expected to help expand exports by 8.5% in 2013 and 9.0% in 2014, but lower world demand or prices for key commodity exports such as copper and other metals would constrain export growth.

3.1.6 Sources of remittance inflows

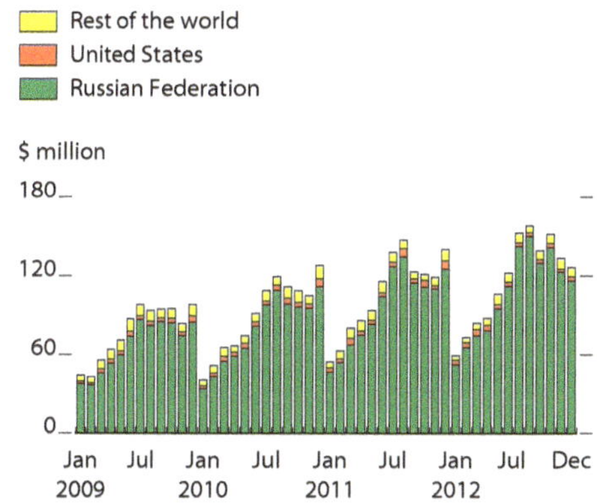

Source: Central Bank of Armenia. http://www.cba.am (accessed 12 March 2013).

Click here for figure data

3.1.7 Effective exchange rates and reserves

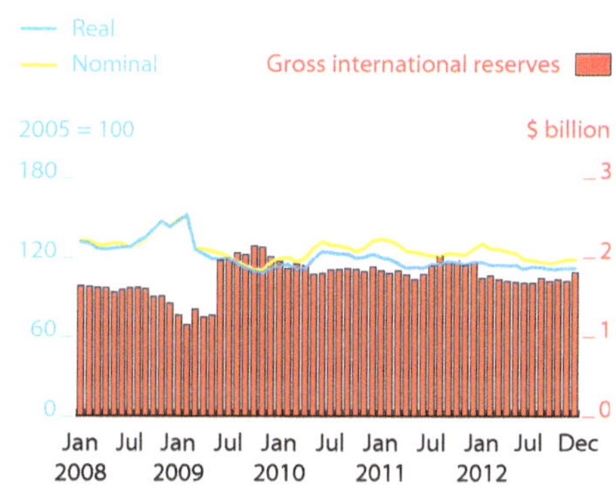

Source: Central Bank of Armenia. http://www.cba.am (accessed 12 March 2013).

Click here for figure data

3.1.8 GDP growth

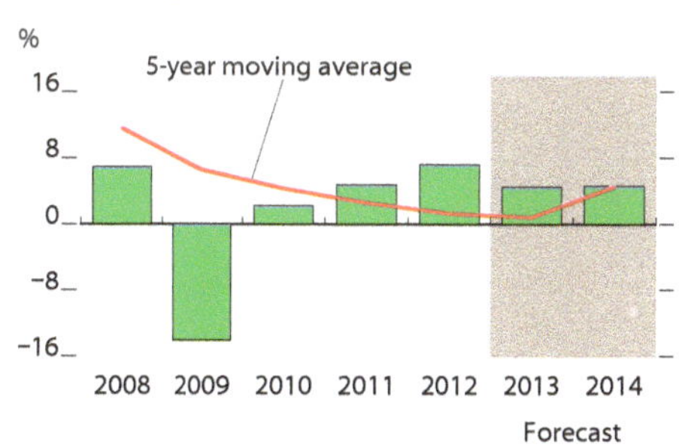

Sources: National Statistical Service of the Republic of Armenia. http://www.armstat.am (accessed 12 March 2013); ADB estimates.

Click here for figure data

Recent trends in domestic demand and investment—and large infrastructure projects that are seen as boosting domestic demand for imports—suggest that imports will grow by 6.5% in 2013 and 5.0% in 2014, which is somewhat less than projected export growth.

Backed by robust remittance inflows, the current account deficit is projected to narrow to 9.8% of GDP in 2013 and 9.1% in 2014 (Figure 3.1.9). Continued loan inflows and a modest rise in foreign direct investment are expected to help finance the current account deficit. Total external debt is expected to rise in the forecast period, but economic expansion will probably mean that external debt declines slightly as a percentage of GDP.

3.1.9 Current account balance

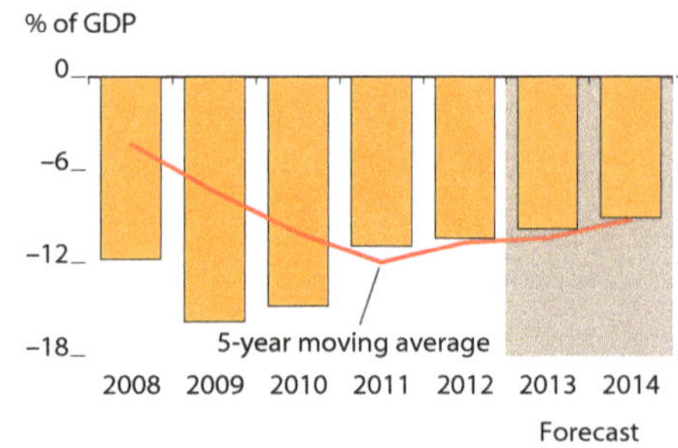

Sources: National Statistical Service of the Republic of Armenia. http://www.armstat.am (accessed 12 March 2013); ADB estimates.

Click here for figure data

Policy challenge—promoting poverty reduction

Despite impressive growth, much remains to be done to combat the rise in poverty that occurred after the sharp economic contraction experienced in 2009. Accelerating structural reform to develop the private sector, implement an export-oriented diversification strategy, and mobilize resources for higher outlays on social sectors could enhance growth, thereby facilitating job creation and poverty reduction.

While Armenia scores well in many international comparisons, further improvements in tax collection, contract enforcement, competitiveness, legal and judicial reform, governance, and anti-corruption measures are essential for the economy to achieve and sustain its growth potential. Pursuing structural reform will enhance Armenia's attractiveness to foreign investors and eventually improve the job market and living standards.

Disparity between the capital and the regions in incomes and economic development risks undermining long-term, inclusive growth. Promoting private sector development, especially of small and medium-sized enterprises outside the capital, is critical to narrowing the gap in living standards between the capital and the rest of the country.

Armenia's overreliance on mining and construction are emblematic of the lack of economic diversification that the 2008–2009 global financial crisis revealed as a major vulnerability. Seriously implementing measures to advance the export diversification strategy approved in 2011—and programs designed to build a knowledge-based economy, enhance productivity, and promote technological modernization—can diversify growth, strengthen competitiveness, and eventually stimulate sustainable growth in employment and incomes.

In this regard, government plans to establish an export lending agency and an industrial development fund in 2013 are encouraging, as are its commitments to earnestly enforce a law on free economic zones and a "regulatory guillotine" initiative adopted in 2011 toward eliminating excessive regulation. As evidenced by strong growth in information and communication technology since the early 2000s, investment in infrastructure and technology to support industries with high returns can catalyze economic growth.

Over time, expanding public infrastructure and targeted social spending should promote inclusive economic growth. Financing these outlays without worsening the ratio of public debt to GDP will require further increases in the tax-to-GDP ratio and curbs on other expenditure.

3.1.1 Selected economic indicators (%)

	2013	2014
GDP growth	4.5	4.6
Inflation	3.6	3.2
Current account balance (share of GDP)	–9.8	–9.1

Source: ADB estimates.

Azerbaijan

Growth reached 2.2% from near stagnation in 2011, as the oil sector contracted less and activity outside of the oil sector accelerated. Smaller oil exports narrowed the current account surplus, but foreign direct investment, mainly in oil and gas projects, rose by more than 20%. Higher public investment spending, supported by transfers from the State Oil Fund, is expected to help spur growth to 3.1% in 2013 and, as oil production increases, to 4.8% in 2014.

Economic performance

Growth improved to 2.2%, following near-zero growth in 2011. Oil output declined less, contracting by 5.0%, and expansion continued in the other sectors of the economy, which grew by 9.7% (Figure 3.2.1).

On the supply side, industry contracted by 1.9%, following the 3.4% increase in 2011 (Figure 3.2.2). The 2012 contraction mainly reflected poor performance in the oil sector, where output fell by 5.3% because of repairs at the main Azeri–Chirag–Ginashli oil platform. Other industrial output rose by 7.8%. Construction continued to grow, rising 18.8% on the back of the government investment program and private initiatives, including the construction of infrastructure linked to hosting the Eurovision Song Contest and the rehabilitation program following a major earthquake early in 2012. Government subsidies and concessional lending programs helped agriculture grow by 3.7%, with increases in both crop and livestock production. Through its agricultural leasing agency, the government continued to support farmers with machinery, imported breeding stock, and other agricultural inputs.

Services were a major source of growth, rising by 9.9%, with wholesale and retail trade growing by 9.6%. Growth also reflected strong performances in oil transportation, which grew by 5.0%, and in communications, which grew by 16.8%.

On the demand side, consumption and investment were the main sources of growth. Consumption rose by 2.9%. This was driven mainly by private consumption, which provides about 40% of GDP and grew by 2.5%, reflecting higher domestic bank lending and increased activity and incomes outside the oil sector. Total investment, at about 23% of GDP, grew by 20.9%, with most of the growth in public investment.

Inflation fell to 1.1% from the 7.9% recorded in 2011 and 4.8% at the start of the year, mainly reflecting slower food price increases. Government-managed food markets helped control food prices while providing farmers direct access to retail food markets. Continuing exchange rate stability helped limit price increases for imported goods (Figure 3.2.3).

3.2.1 Oil and non-oil GDP growth

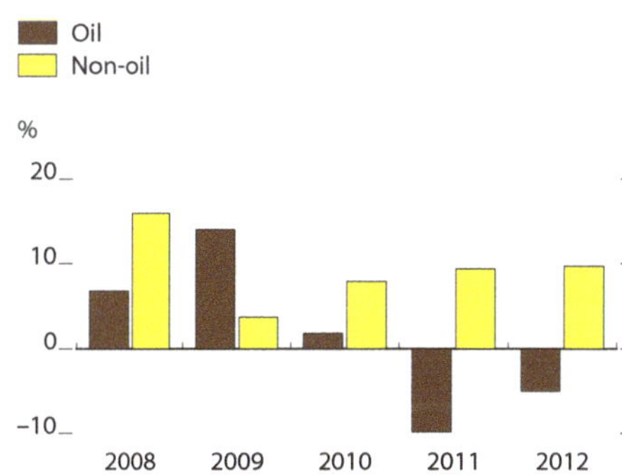

Source: State Statistical Committee of the Republic of Azerbaijan.
Click here for figure data

3.2.2 Supply-side contributions to growth

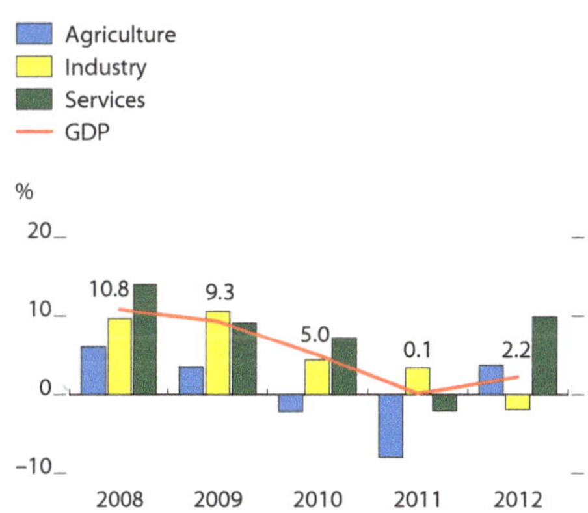

Source: State Statistical Committee of the Republic of Azerbaijan.
Click here for figure data

This chapter was written by Nail Valiyev of the Azerbaijan Resident Mission, ADB, Baku.

Fiscal policy turned more supportive in 2012 but remained hugely dependent on the oil sector. The surplus in the consolidated budget rose to 3.0% of GDP from 0.6% in 2011, because rising revenue greatly outpaced rising expenditure. Revenue grew by nearly 35%, to 29.0% of GDP, mainly reflecting increases in sovereign fund transfers and profits taxes. Transfers from the State Oil Fund—the sovereign wealth fund and a key source of revenue since 2009—provided 60% of budget revenues. Expenditures grew by 22% and totaled 25.8% of GDP. Public investment projects were the major driver of expenditures and absorbed 43% of total spending. The decision to begin repaying savings lost at the Soviet Depositary Bank after the collapse of the Soviet system helped increase social expenditures.

The central bank relaxed monetary policy in 2012 for the first time since May 2011, lowering the refinancing rate from 5.25% to 5.00% as inflation declined. To offset the impact of capital inflows and reflect lower demand for foreign currency, the central bank sold securities to banks to sterilize $1.5 billion of their foreign exchange inflows, prevent significant appreciation of the Azerbaijan manat, and make producers outside of the oil economy more competitive. These moves helped limit the appreciation of the manat against the US dollar to 0.19% in the year to the end of 2012 (Figure 3.2.4).

To strengthen the banking sector, the central bank continued its efforts to formulate a risk-based prudential supervision framework adhering to Basel III standards for banking supervision. In addition, following the bankruptcy of one bank, the central bank announced a fivefold increase in aggregate required capital, both core and supplementary, to AZN50 million, effective 1 January 2014. New banks must have this amount as paid-in capital.

Broad money (M3) grew by 20.7%, reflecting higher economic activity and bank loans to the private sector. Credit extended to the economy, primarily loans to the private sector, rose in 2012 by 24.1%, reflecting personal loans and trade finance. Credit quality improved, as the percentage of nonperforming loans fell to 6.3% in January–November 2012. Foreign currency savings and deposits dropped by 1.2%, while local currency holdings rose.

The current account surplus decreased to 22.6% of GDP from 25.7% in 2011, as exports declined more quickly than imports. Exports fell by 7.5% during first 9 months of 2012 as oil exports, which account for 94% of all exports, declined by 8.8%, mainly because lower oil production reduced export volume. Other exports, mainly of fruits and vegetables, chemical products, and metal, rose by 21.6% during January–September 2012. In addition, exports of services grew by 51.9% with a significant jump in tourism. Imports grew slightly, by 1.0% during January–September 2012, reflecting less need to import most kinds of food in light of higher domestic production, as well as lower demand for equipment and machinery at the early stage of new hydrocarbon projects. However, wheat imports rose sharply, as did imports of vegetable oil. Furniture imports also increased. Foreign direct investment rose by 23.4% in 2012 from 3.2% in 2011, mainly reflecting investments in the second phase of the Shahdeniz gas field and in new oil field exploration.

3.2.3 Monthly inflation

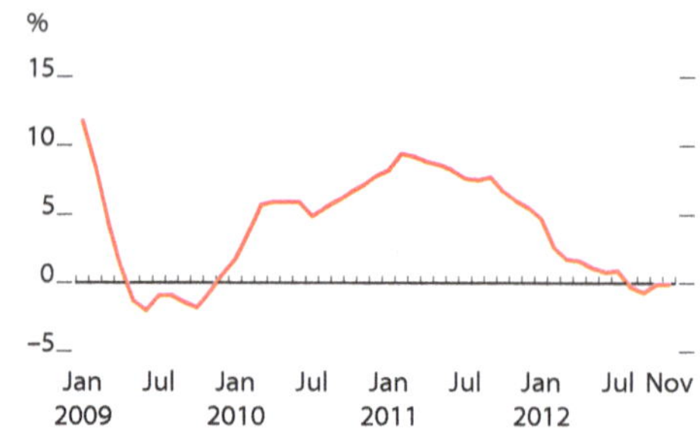

Sources: International Monetary Fund. International Financial Statistics online database (accessed 26 March 2013); Central Bank of the Republic of Azerbaijan.

Click here for figure data

3.2.4 Nominal exchange rate

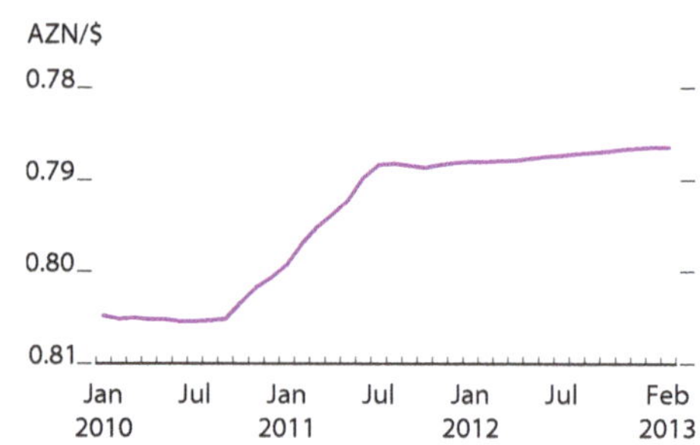

Source: Central Bank of the Republic of Azerbaijan.

Click here for figure data

3.2.5 International reserves

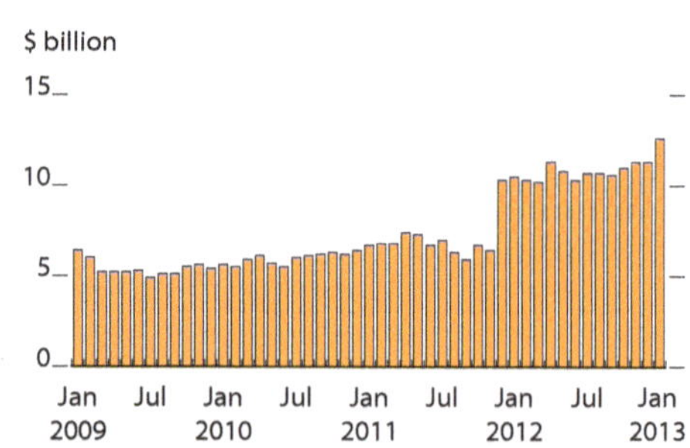

Source: International Monetary Fund. International Financial Statistics online database (accessed 26 March 2013).

Click here for figure data

Official reserves at the end of 2012 totaled $12.0 billion (Figure 3.2.5). Assets of the State Oil Fund totaled another $34.1 billion. Looking ahead, the government adopted a policy to limit external public and publicly guaranteed debt to 10.0% of GDP, which is well above the 6.0% of GDP reported by the Economist Intelligence Unit for end of 2012 (Figure 3.2.6). All external debt amounts to one-eighth of total official reserves.

3.2.6 External debt

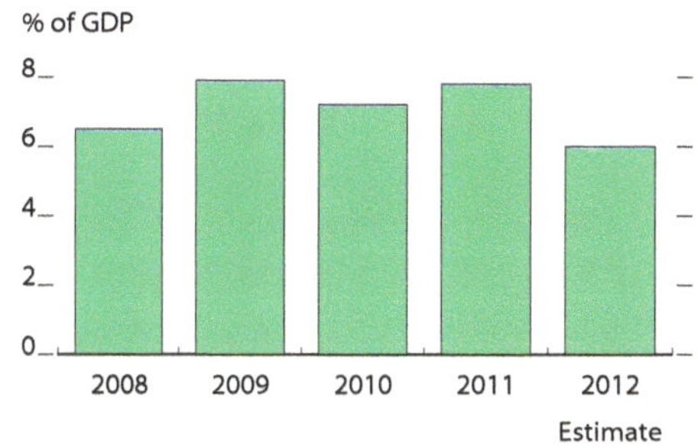

Sources: Central Bank of the Republic of Azerbaijan. http://www.cbar.az (accessed 27 March 2013); ADB estimates.
Click here for figure data

Economic prospects

The major driver of growth in 2013 and the next few years is expected to be activity outside the oil sector. Energy output will grow little through 2015 but is expected to expand more once gas field development is completed and the exploration of new oil fields proves successful, most likely after 2015. Planned public spending will boost public investment, while ongoing energy projects will increase foreign direct investment. New regulations on capital adequacy may allow increased lending to boost private investment.

Growth is forecast to accelerate to 3.1% in 2013 and climb further to 4.8% in 2014, mainly because of public spending outside the oil sector and, in 2014, some increase in oil production (Figure 3.2.7).

On the supply side, industry will contract slightly in 2013 as oil output falls, before it revives in 2014. The 2013 fiscal budget includes support for regional development diversifying away from oil. Higher public spending and private investment are forecast to drive annual construction growth of 18.0%. Agriculture is expected to grow by 5.0%–6.0% annually as irrigation projects and reclamation progress. The government's food security program aims to eliminate the need for wheat imports by 2015.

3.2.1 Selected economic indicators (%)

	2013	2014
GDP growth	3.1	4.8
Inflation	6.0	7.0
Current account balance (share of GDP)	13.0	17.0

Source: ADB estimates.

Inflation is projected to accelerate to 6.0% in 2013 and 7.0% in 2014, reflecting public investment programs and large increases in current public expenditures, as salaries increase and social spending expands. However, moderate food inflation will help offset price increases elsewhere (Figure 3.2.8).

Fiscal policy is expected to be more expansionary, with the budget recording small deficits of 1.1% of GDP in 2013 and 1.3% in 2014. Revenues are expected to grow each year by 20% and expenditures by 27%. State Oil Fund transfers should continue to provide about 60% of budget revenue. Salary increases, social development spending to support minimum living standards, the payment of pension plans inherited from the Soviet Union, and public investment outlays will be the main drivers of government expenditure. The 2013 presidential election may also raise spending.

Monetary policy will adjust to reflect how inflation develops. Open market operations and changes in the refinancing rate will guide broad money growth. New regulations on capital adequacy are expected to stimulate the consolidation of some smaller banks or else foreign investment in them. Regulations may require successful banks to diversify their portfolios. However, delays in privatizing the one state-owned bank—the International Bank of Azerbaijan, which holds at least 40% of all bank assets—will continue to constrain the banking sector, signaling a lack of progress in stimulating private sector activity.

3.2.7 Annual GDP growth

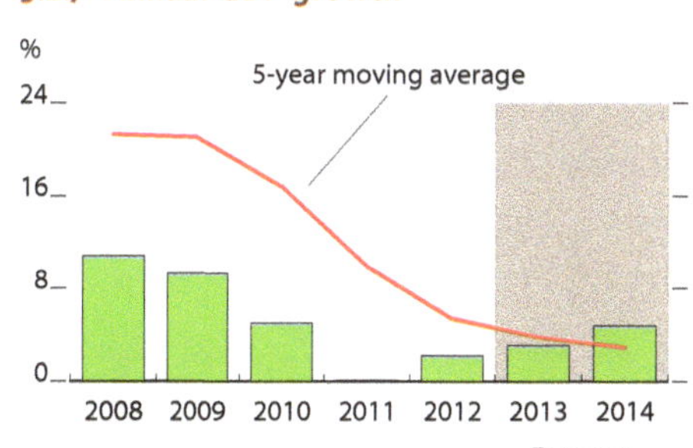

Sources: Central Bank of the Republic of Azerbaijan. http://www.cbar.az (accessed 27 March 2013); ADB estimates.
Click here for figure data

The current account balance is forecast to decline to 13.0% of GDP in 2013, reflecting rising imports of wheat, automobiles, home appliances, and equipment for ongoing energy projects. The services deficit may widen, reflecting rising demand for imported services in the hydrocarbons sector. In 2014, the current account surplus is expected to rise to 17.0% of GDP (Figure 3.2.9), as output in the main Azeri–Chirag–Ginashli oilfield is expected to increase slightly. In sum, exports, led by hydrocarbons, are expected to contract by 2.1% in 2013 before reversing direction to grow by 1.7% in 2014. Development in the hydrocarbons sector and investment will boost imports of machinery and equipment and keep inflows of foreign direct investment high, though lower than in peak years. Reserves are expected to grow further, reaching $42 billion. External debt is forecast to show little change, remaining at 7.0% of GDP.

3.2.8 Inflation

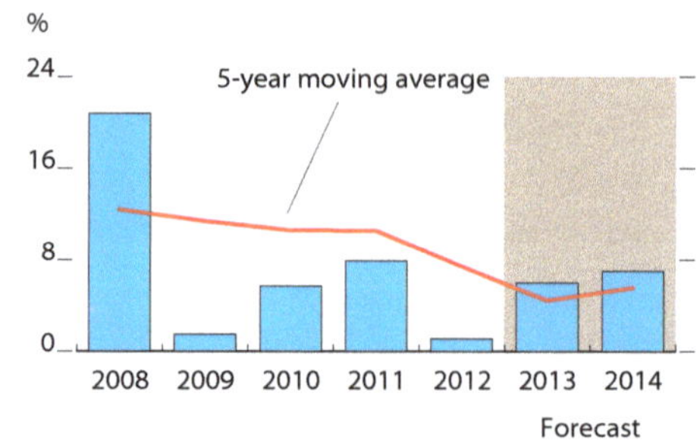

Sources: Central Bank of the Republic of Azerbaijan. http://www.cbar.az (accessed 27 March 2013); ADB estimates.
Click here for figure data

3.2.9 Current account balance

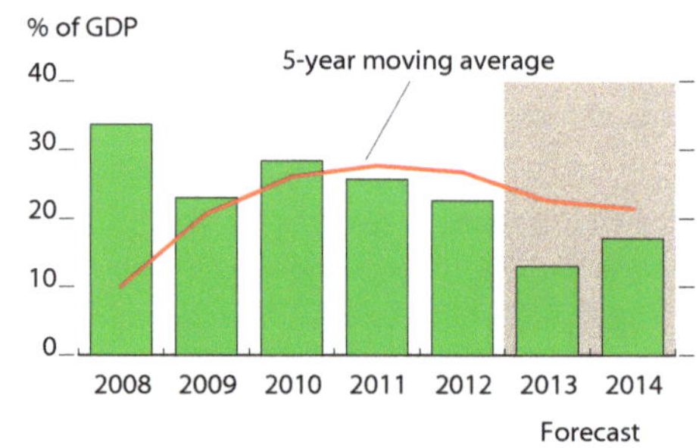

Sources: Central Bank of the Republic of Azerbaijan. http://www.cbar.az (accessed 26 March 2013); ADB estimates.
Click here for figure data

Policy challenge—diversifying the economy

The recent slowdown caused by declining oil production illustrates the risks arising from the economy's continued dependence on petroleum. Economic diversification is critical to maintaining stable growth. The government's recently issued Strategy 2020 aims to double growth in GDP per capita, mainly by expanding activity beyond oil, which is expected to grow at least 7% annually.

Achieving these targets will be difficult without improving the business environment and private sector initiatives. Although Azerbaijan ranks well in terms of starting businesses and registering property, according to the World Bank's *Doing Business 2013*, it ranks only 169th of 185 countries in dealing with construction permits, getting electricity, and trading across borders. Structural reforms in these and other areas, such as simplifying taxpaying and easing access to credit, will be important to encourage investment outside of the oil sector.

The new strategy is designed to promote regional development, mainly through government projects to improve regional infrastructure. Such intensive regional development programs will require careful public expenditure management and improved budget formulation. Private initiatives, including public–private partnerships, can help contain budget expenditures on public infrastructure and ensure their long-term sustainability if well managed. Securing such private initiatives will require an appropriate regulatory framework for public–private partnership, a better investment climate, and a more effective financial sector with deeper capital markets and more extensive banking services.

The new strategy targets diversifying the economy by encouraging innovation and expanding advanced technical facilities to enable a shift toward knowledge-based industries. Since 2008, growth in the information, communications, and technology sector has averaged 20% a year, reflecting the government's strong commitment to improve its products and e-services. Further development of the knowledge-based economy may encourage additional investments in human capital and capacity building.

Georgia

Growth slowed to 6.1% from 7.2% in 2011, reflecting uncertainties in an election year that brought in a new government. Planned fiscal consolidation and continuing uncertainty in the political and investment climate are expected to limit growth to 5.5% in 2013, but growth should rise to 6.0% in 2014. The current account deficit is expected to narrow as fiscal consolidation reduces imports and as structural reforms gradually raise exports.

Economic developments

Another year of strong growth nevertheless saw the rate decrease to 6.1% from the 7.2% of 2011, reflecting uncertainties surrounding the October 2012 parliamentary elections and the subsequent transition to a new government administration. Unemployment remains very high, at 15.1% as of 2011, with two-thirds of the labor force engaged in low-productivity subsistence farming. Youth unemployment, at 35%, is particularly high.

Georgia experienced a peaceful political transition in 2012. The new government has committed to promoting more inclusive growth with additional support for agricultural, rural, and small town development and increased social spending. The government aims to improve trade ties with the Russian Federation. While differences remain, a resumption of these ties should increase Georgia's exports in agriculture, light manufacturing, and services.

On the supply side, industry expanded by 9.9%, up from the 9.4% rise in 2011, led by construction and manufacturing (Figure 3.3.1). Agriculture contracted sharply in 2012, shrinking by 3.3% after the 8.0% growth in 2011 and reflecting smaller harvests of crops and livestock. Services grew by 5.8%, up from 5.7% in 2011, because of better performance in the financial sector, tourism, transport and communications, and wholesale and retail trade.

On the demand side, consumption expanded by 5.5%, less than half the 12.8% rise in 2011. Private consumption grew by 4.3%, versus 16.0% in 2011, possibly reflecting consumer uncertainty in the run-up to the October 2012 parliamentary elections. Public consumption rose by 10.8%, eight times the 1.4% rate in 2011. Spending on public salaries and social expenditure increased somewhat but still comprised only 42% of total outlays. Investment expanded by 28.8%, compared with 42.2% in 2011, driven by public spending on infrastructure in the run-up to the elections. Net exports declined by 22.0% from the 2011 figure.

Consumer prices fell by 0.9% in 2012, reversing the 8.5% rise in 2011 (Figure 3.3.2). Deflation reflected a 2.0% decline in prices for imported

3.3.1 GDP growth by sector

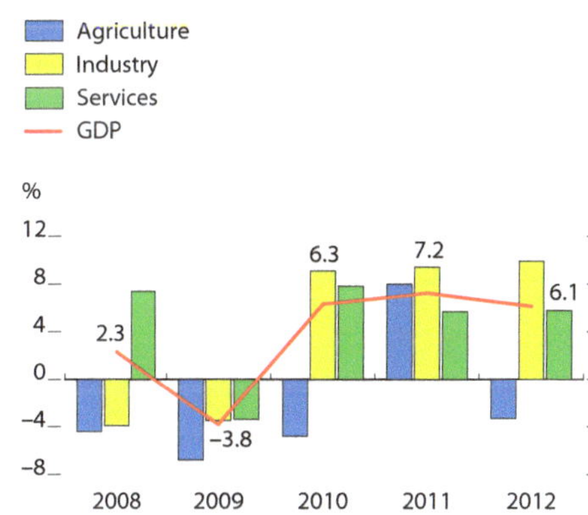

Source: National Statistics Office of Georgia. http://www.geostat.ge (accessed 20 March 2013).
Click here for figure data

3.3.2 Inflation

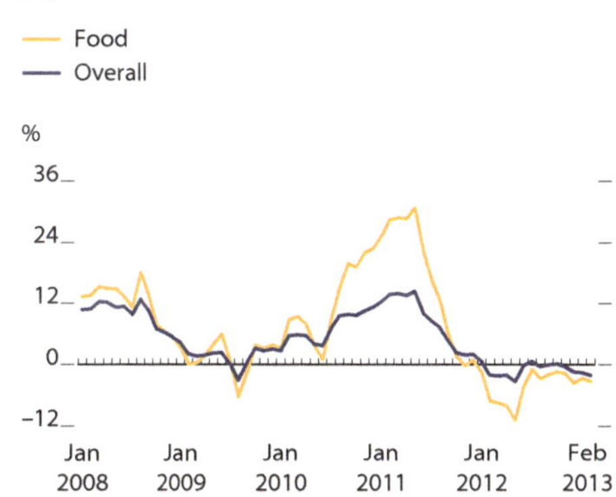

Source: National Statistics Office of Georgia. http://www.geostat.ge (accessed 20 March 2013).
Click here for figure data

This chapter was written by George Luarsabishvili of the Georgia Resident Mission, ADB, Tbilisi.

food and fuel and efforts to contain price increases for certain utilities, along with slower credit growth. Deflation was greatest for food and fuel but also affected other items such as clothing and footwear, furnishings, and recreational and cultural activities. Inflation during the 12 months ending in December was –1.4%, down from 2.0% in 2011.

Fiscal policy remained expansionary (Figure 3.3.3). The consolidated budget deficit narrowed to 3.0% of GDP from 3.6% in 2011. Revenues totaled 28.9% of GDP, slightly above the 28.2% of 2011, as larger nontax revenues supplemented higher receipts from value-added and corporate profits taxes. Total expenditure was 31.9% of GDP, up from 31.8% in 2011, despite higher public investment spending and continuing large outlays on untargeted subsidies, including the general food and energy voucher program initiated in 2011. Total government debt, mainly concessional external borrowing, declined marginally to 33.8% of GDP from 33.9% in 2011.

Monetary policy was relaxed, to combat deflation and support growth, as the authorities lowered the policy rate from 6.50% in January to 5.25% by the end of December and again in February 2013 to 4.75%, the lowest rate since 2008. However, the banking system remains highly dollarized, with foreign exchange deposits exceeding 60% of all deposits in 2012, so the decline in the policy rate had little impact on market rates. Average aggregate lending and deposit rates slipped only marginally, to 18.6% and 8.6%, respectively. The spread remained among the highest in the South Caucasus because of a shallow financial market, low saving, and lack of confidence in the domestic currency (Figure 3.3.4). Moreover, credit growth slowed from 20.5% in 2011 to 13.3% in 2012, reflecting a pre- and post-election slowdown in loan demand. The financial sector weakened, as bank profits fell by more than two-thirds, reflecting losses at several smaller, less-competitive banks. Nonperforming loans rose by about 1% to 9.3% at the end of 2012.

Given excess liquidity in banks, demand for refinancing loans fell in early 2012, weakening the interest rate transmission mechanism. Broad money growth slowed to 11.4% in 2012 from 14.5% in 2011, reflecting slow growth in domestic currency deposits that offset higher growth in foreign currency deposits (Figure 3.3.5). The exchange rate remained steady at about GEL1.7 = $1, but the real exchange rate saw the Georgian lari depreciate slightly because of deflation (Figure 3.3.6).

The current account deficit rose to 13.5% of GDP from 12.8% in 2011, reflecting a worsening trade deficit that was partly offset by a rise in net services (Figure 3.3.7). Exports grew by 8.1%, versus 32.2% in 2011, reflecting increases in vehicle re-exports, ferroalloys, minerals, and mineral fertilizers. Imports grew by 15.0%, versus 33.6% in 2011, fueled by heavy public spending on infrastructure and continued strong remittances. Services rose by 37.9%, following growth of 45.6% in 2011, as weaker performance in transportation, insurance, finance, and computer services offset strong gains in tourism. The deficit in the income account narrowed, reflecting lower interest payments and profit repatriation. Current transfers remained steady, with workers' remittances rising by 8.8% to $0.6 billion. Transfers from the Russian Federation, comprising 58.1% of all transfers, increased by 14.3%.

Portfolio inflows rose nearly sixfold to $847 million due to Eurobond issues, which helped finance the current account deficit. Foreign direct

3.3.3 Fiscal indicators

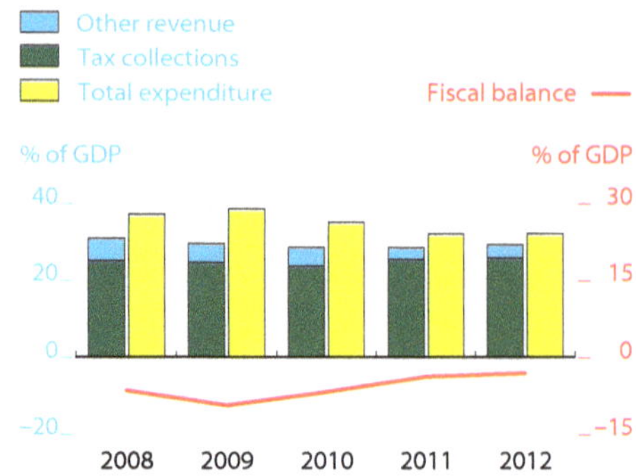

Sources: International Monetary Fund. 2010. *Country Report* No. 10/219. July; 2011. *Country Report* No. 11/146. June; 2012. *Country Report* No. 12/98. April. www.imf.org; Ministry of Finance of Georgia. www.mof.ge (accessed 20 March 2013).

Click here for figure data

3.3.4 Interest rates

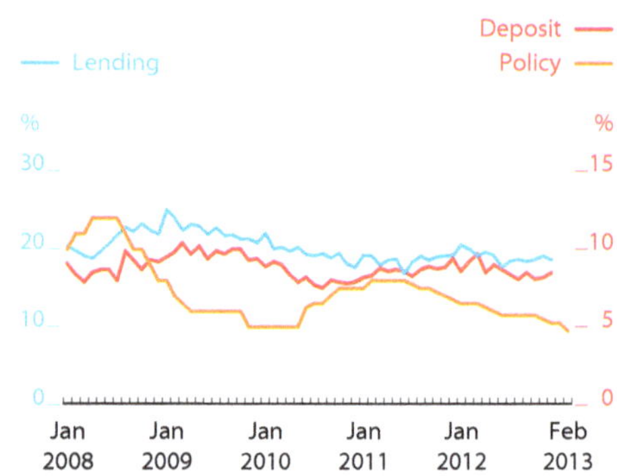

Source: National Bank of Georgia. http://www.nbg.gov.ge (accessed 20 March 2013).

Click here for figure data

3.3.5 Contributions to money supply growth

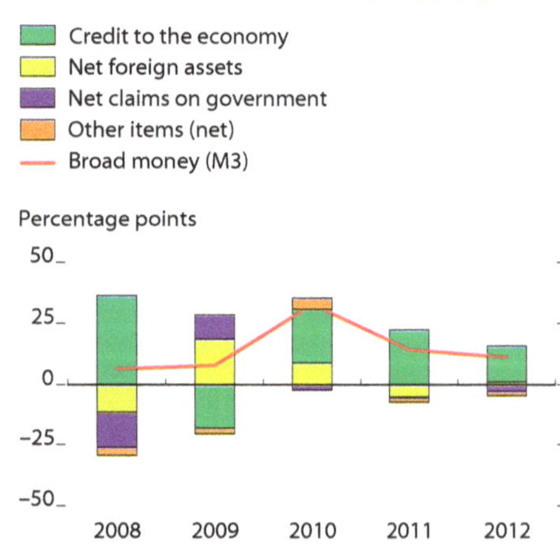

Source: International Monetary Fund. International Financial Statistics online database (accessed 15 March 2013).

Click here for figure data

investment amounted to an estimated $865.2 million, about 23% less than that in 2011, as inflows slowed, particularly in latter half of 2012, deterred by pre- and post-election uncertainties. Gross reserves rose to $2.9 billion.

Economic prospects

Growth is forecast to decelerate to 5.5% in 2013 and then increase to 6.0% in 2014, as planned fiscal consolidation and uncertainty in the political and investment climate slow domestic demand, despite anticipated growth in private consumption (Figure 3.3.8).

On the supply side, industry is forecast to expand, as structural reforms designed to achieve higher-quality public investment are expected over time to boost productivity, catalyzing growth in manufacturing and other tradable goods. Agriculture is expected to grow, reflecting improved expectations for key crops and livestock, assuming normal weather. Services are projected to expand, with strong growth in transport, communication, and financial intermediation. On the demand side, investment, net exports, and to a lesser extent consumption are all expected to expand in both years.

Inflation is projected to accelerate to 3.0% in 2013 and rise further to 4.0% in 2014, as higher social expenditure, including growth in pensions and teachers' salaries, create demand-side inflationary pressures.

Over the next 2 years fiscal policy is expected to tighten. The consolidated budget deficit is projected to shrink to 2.8% of GDP in 2013 and 2.5% in 2014. This reflects further cuts in government expenditure alongside a shift in spending toward social programs. Revenues are forecast to decline slightly as a share of GDP to 26.6% in 2013 before rising again to 27.4% in 2014. Total expenditure is forecast at 29.4% of GDP in 2013 and 29.9% in 2014, as the government implements measures intended to improve the quality of fiscal spending. Total government debt is projected to decrease to 32.1% of GDP in 2013 and 32.0% in 2014 as external debt declines (Figure 3.3.9).

Over the next 2 years, monetary policy is expected to support growth while achieving the central bank's medium-term inflation target. Broad money growth is projected to rise sharply, to 21.2% in 2013, and then fall again to 18.5% in 2014, reflecting higher growth in credit to the private sector. Exchange rate policy, while allowing some flexibility, is expected to focus on the stability of the national currency.

The current account deficit is forecast to narrow to 11.9% of GDP in 2013 and 10.7% in 2014, as slower growth resulting from fiscal consolidation and other factors reduce demand for imports, and exports rise as structural reforms in agriculture and other sectors begin to take hold. Exports are projected to grow by 11.5% in 2013 and 14.8% in 2014, while imports expand by 7.0% in 2013 and 7.5% in 2014. Services should be in surplus due to the continued strong performance of financial and computer services. The income account deficit is expected to narrow, reflecting a decline in profit transfers and higher portfolio investment income. Current transfers are forecast to increase to $1.3 billion in 2013 and $1.4 billion in 2014 on the back of higher worker remittances. Expected strong inflows of foreign direct investment, in excess of $1 billion each year, will help finance the current account deficit. Gross reserves are

3.3.6 Effective exchange rates and GEL/$ nominal exchange rate

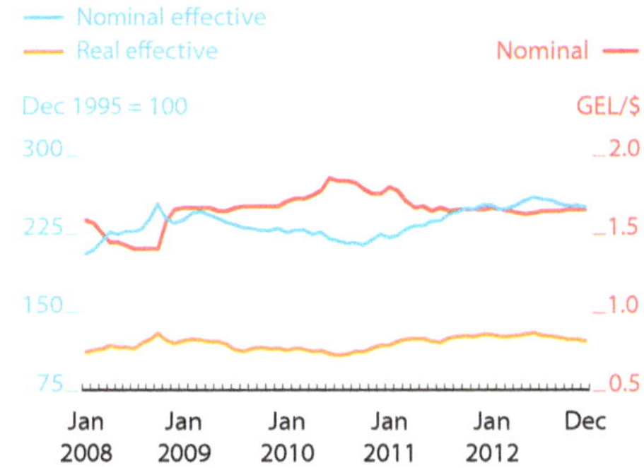

Source: National Bank of Georgia. http://www.nbg.gov.ge (accessed 20 March 2013).

Click here for figure data

3.3.7 Current account components

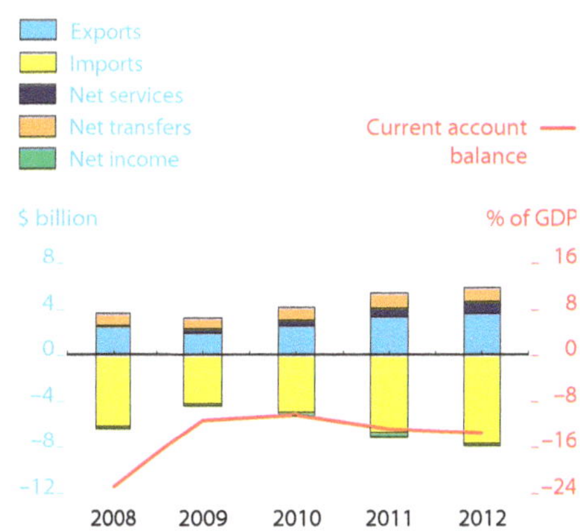

Source: National Bank of Georgia. http://www.nbg.gov.ge (accessed 20 March 2013).

Click here for figure data

3.3.8 GDP growth

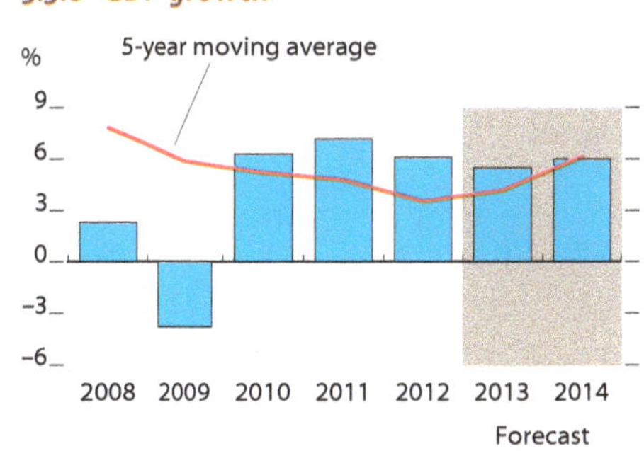

Source: ADB estimates.

Click here for figure data

projected to decline slightly to $2.6 billion in 2013 before recovering to $2.7 billion in 2014 (Figure 3.3.10).

Risks to the projections include slackening activity in the Russian Federation and the euro area, and possible problems in managing quasi-sovereign funds outside the state budget. Moreover, the high current account deficit remains a source of vulnerability and a risk to growth, given large external financing needs in a sluggish global environment.

3.3.1 Selected economic indicators (%)

	2013	2014
GDP growth	5.5	6.0
Inflation	3.0	4.0
Current account balance (share of GDP)	–11.9	–10.7

Source: ADB estimates.

Policy challenge—inclusive growth

Georgia's impressive growth has fallen short in achieving poverty alleviation, job creation, and balanced regional development. A key development challenge is to make growth more inclusive, which would generate productive employment opportunities of particular benefit to subsistence farmers and others in Georgia's poorer rural regions. Inclusive growth could also ease the current account deficit if it boosted domestic savings and exports. Future policies should tackle Georgia's infrastructure deficit, improve connectivity, make basic services more widely available and sustainable, and enhance the productivity and skills of labor.

Ultimately, raising domestic savings is essential to address external imbalances. Policies that reduce tensions between Georgia and the Russian Federation may boost investor confidence and respond to perceptions of country risk. Better protection of property rights through fair and impartial judicial processes is also essential, as are measures that discourage dollarization and reduce financial market risks. Despite Georgia's overall progress in various business climate surveys, progress in sectoral reform has lagged. Agricultural policies can be improved to promote economies of scale, enhance productivity, and spur value-chain development. Policy reform in the power sector is essential to foster the sustainable exploitation of Georgia's hydropower potential, enable efficient cross-border power trade, improve energy security, and generate sufficient government resources. Education policies should address pronounced skills gaps in key job-generating sectors.

The government aims to enhance development by instilling stronger planning and results orientation, including monitoring progress toward achieving targets. The government plans to increase investment in agriculture and industry, partly by establishing investment funds to attract private sector financing. Planned higher investment in social capital includes doubling the health-care budget, extending health insurance to uninsured citizens, and raising teachers' salaries.

3.3.9 Government debt indicators

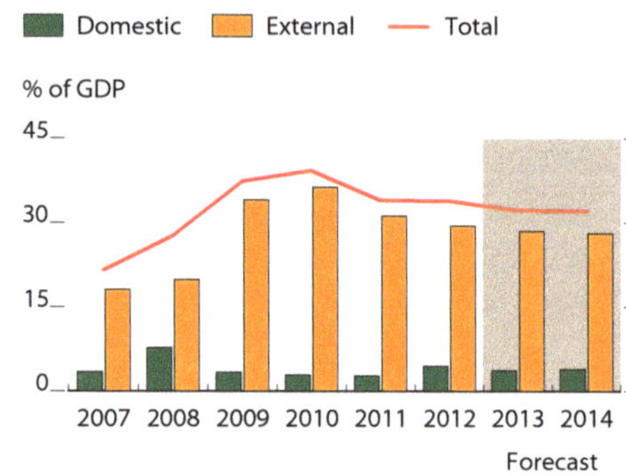

Sources: International Monetary Fund. 2012. *Regional Economic Outlook: Central Asia.* November. http://www.imf.org; National Bank of Georgia; ADB estimates.

Click here for figure data

3.3.10 Gross international reserves

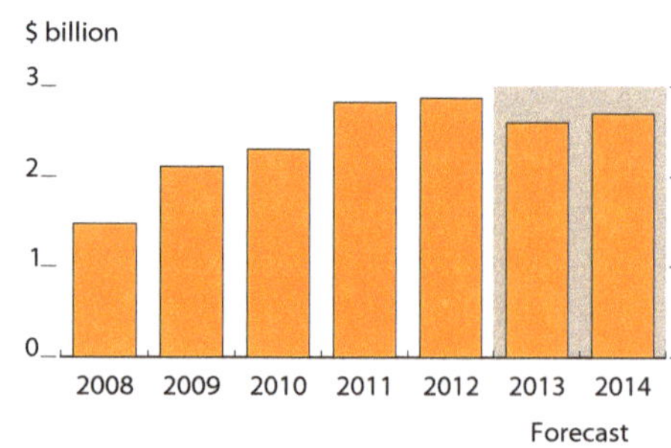

Sources: National Bank of Georgia. http://www.nbg.gov.ge (accessed 20 March 2013); ADB estimates.

Click here for figure data

Kazakhstan

Growth slowed to 5.0% from 7.5% in 2011, as industry largely stagnated and severe drought cut agricultural output by nearly 18%. Inflation also slowed. Rapid import growth, linked partly to public investment programs, narrowed the current account surplus to 4.3% of GDP from 7.2% in 2011, but assets in the country's sovereign wealth fund again increased. Growth is expected to recover slowly, to 5.2% in 2013 and 5.6% in 2014, as continued government investment spending boosts domestic demand.

Economic performance

After 2 years of strong recovery, economic growth slowed to 5.0% from 7.3% in 2010 and 7.5% in 2011 (Figure 3.4.1). The service sector was again the main source of growth, while the contributions of agriculture and industry fell to their lowest levels in 15 years.

Services, which generate more than half of GDP, rose by 9.8%, reflecting more than 14% growth in retail and wholesale trade and smaller gains in communications, transport, and hotels and restaurants. Professional services rose by 16.2% and public services by 12.2%.

Agriculture contracted by 17.8%, mostly from poor harvests. Severe drought almost halved grain output from the record high harvest in 2011, despite major investments and producer subsidies. Industrial production grew only marginally, by 0.5%, compared with 3.7% in 2011, reflecting weak growth in mining (0.2% versus 1.3% in 2011) and manufacturing (0.7% versus 6.2% in 2011), the latter reflecting a decline in metallurgical production. In the broad mining sector, crude oil output declined by 1.4%, while coal extraction grew by only 1.7% and natural gas by 3.1%. Construction expanded by 2.9% (about the same as in 2010 and 2011), again benefiting from state-led projects under a program to accelerate industrial and innovative development and incentives for residential construction.

On the demand side, consumption expanded by 11.4%, with public consumption growing more quickly than private consumption (Figure 3.4.2). Growth in net exports slowed to 10.0%, as imports grew much more rapidly than exports. Fixed capital investment grew by 3.8%, up from 2.8% in 2011, reflecting faster growth in investments by small and medium-sized enterprises.

Inflation slowed from 8.3% in 2011 to a post-independence low of 5.1%, reflecting a dramatic slowdown in food prices, mainly for grain products, to 4.5% from 11.9% in 2011, and a smaller decline in inflation for nonfood goods, to 4.3% from 5.4% in 2011. Prices for services rose by 6.8%, as in 2011, including double-digit increases for transport, telecommunications,

3.4.1 Supply-side contributions to growth

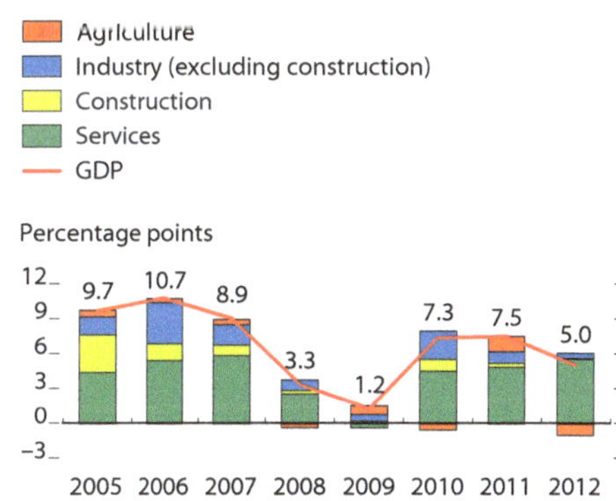

Source: Agency of Statistics of the Republic of Kazakhstan.
Click here for figure data

3.4.2 Growth of GDP demand components

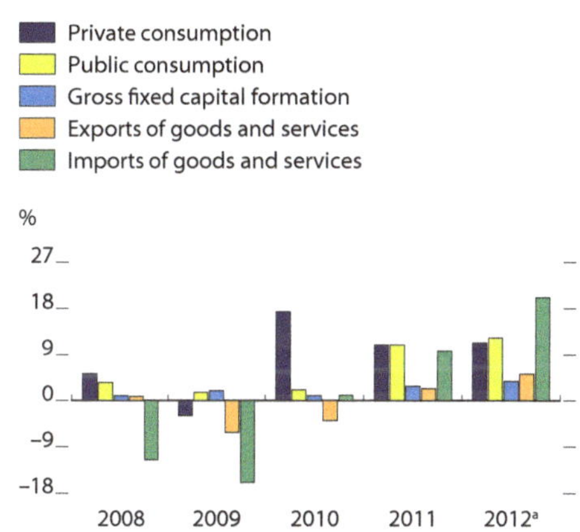

[a] Data for 2012 are for 9 months only.
Source: Agency of Statistics of the Republic of Kazakhstan.
Click here for figure data

This chapter was written by Manshuk Nurseitova of the Kazakhstan Resident Mission, ADB, Astana.

and postal services. Inflation accelerated somewhat beginning in August but remained moderate over the full year. The 12-month (December over December) rate decelerated to 6.0% from 7.4% in December 2011 (Figure 3.4.3).

Fiscal policy was more expansionary in 2012, as the deficit in the republican budget expanded to 3.0% of GDP from 2.1% in 2011. Receipts reached 15.5% of GDP, including 4.6% ($9.2 billion) in transfers from the National Fund of the Republic of Kazakhstan (NFRK, the sovereign wealth fund), down somewhat from total receipts of 16.1% of GDP in 2011. Expenditure amounted 18.5% of GDP, up from the 18.2% recorded in 2011. The adoption of several new social programs, including measures to develop small towns and build affordable housing, helped boost expenditures.

At the end of September 2012, public external debt stood at $30 billion, or 15% of GDP, 3 percentage points of which was government and government-guaranteed debt, the other 12 points being the debts of state-owned enterprises. Including the domestic debt of state-owned enterprises, estimated at 10%–12% of GDP, and that of the government and central bank, estimated at 12.2% of GDP, total public sector debt approached 37%–39% of GDP.

Monetary policy was eased in 2012, reflecting slower inflation. The central bank gradually reduced the policy interest rate from 7.5% in February to a post-independence low of 5.5% in August of 2012. Broad money growth slowed to 7.9% from the 15.0% in 2011, reflecting slower currency expansion and a decline in corporate deposits. The increased need for budget financing raised interest rates on short-term government notes to 2.14% from 1.63% in 2011. The tenge exchange rate fluctuated within the range of T147.8–T150.5 per $1, with an average rate of T149.1 for the year, depreciating from T146.6 in 2011 as the central bank avoided major interventions in the market (Figure 3.4.4). However, the real effective exchange rate against a basket of 34 currencies appreciated by 5.2%.

The banking sector is still beset by problems, despite efforts by the government and the central bank to improve the situation. The percentage of nonperforming loans has been growing since 2009, climbing to 37% by the end of 2012 from 35% a year earlier. A fifth of banks are losing money, with the largest losses at BTA Bank, which was nationalized in 2009 and underwent a second restructuring of its external debt in 2012. Several banks applied for assistance from the central bank's distressed assets fund established in April 2012. Some of the largest created subsidiaries to deal with nonperforming loans, which have made many banks risk averse, prompting them to invest excess liquidity in short-term government securities and central bank notes. This has suppressed rates on these assets.

The current account surplus diminished to 4.3% of estimated GDP from 7.2% in 2011, as faster growth in imports shrank the trade surplus (Figure 3.4.5). The services deficit expanded by $1.3 billion, or 20%, while outward transfers tripled to $1 billion from $0.3 billion in 2011. The deficit in the capital and financial account, including errors and omissions, narrowed to about $11.5 billion from $13.3 billion in 2011, largely reflecting a better position for short-term capital. Net foreign direct investment

3.4.3 Inflation

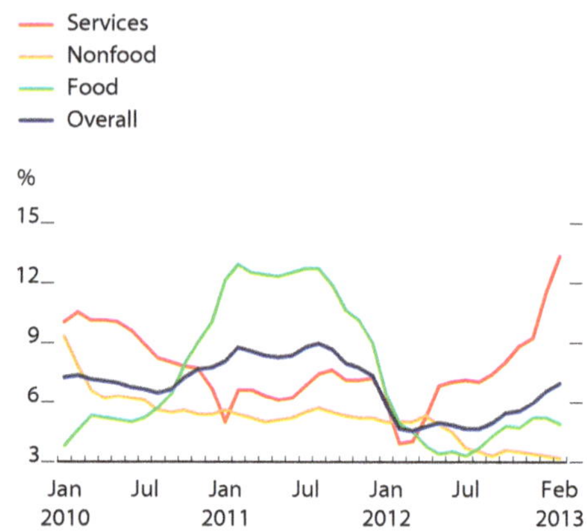

Source: Agency of Statistics of the Republic of Kazakhstan.
Click here for figure data

3.4.4 Central bank currency interventions

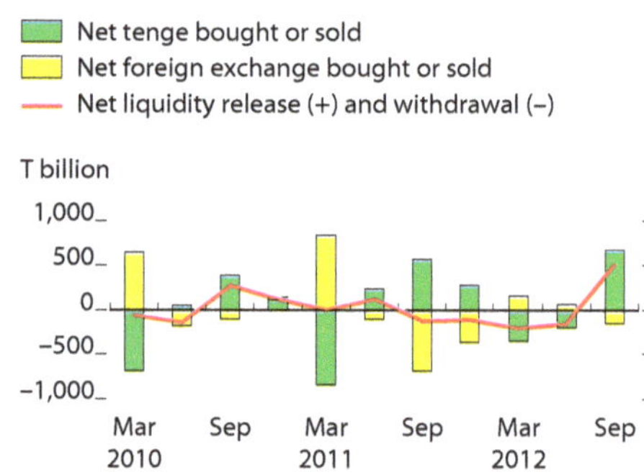

Source: National Bank of Kazakhstan. 2012. *Financial Stability Report.*
Click here for figure data

3.4.5 Current account indicators

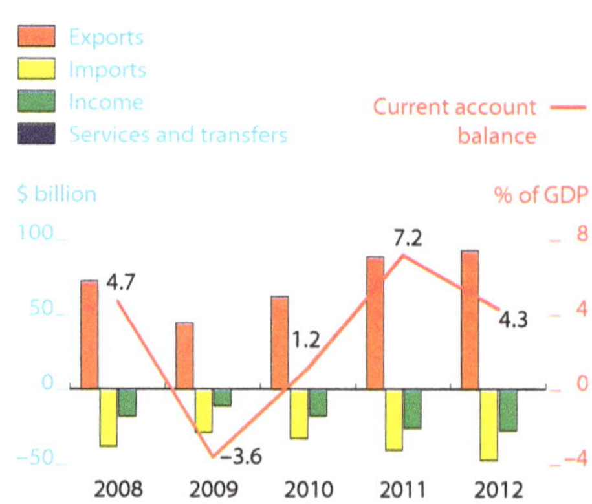

Source: National Bank of Kazakhstan.
Click here for figure data

grew by 40% to $12.7 billion from $9.1 billion in 2011, as investments abroad contracted from $4.6 billion to $1.4 billion and inward foreign direct investment rose modestly, from $13.7 billion to $14.2 billion. A net $16.7 billion outflow on portfolio investments was largely explained by the $14 billion rise in the NFRK's foreign assets and the almost $1 billion decline in Kazakh banks debt liabilities—and possibly a significantly greater decline with BTA Bank debt amortization.

The central bank's gross international reserves rose during the first half of the year but fell from August, as the central bank used part of its reserves to replenish the NFRK, ending the year at $28.3 billion, or $1.1 billion less than a year earlier. NFRK assets grew steadily, totaling $57.8 billion at the end of 2012 (Figure 3.4.6).

Total external debt—more than half owed by local subsidiaries to their parent multinational firms—was estimated at 67.3% of GDP at the end of September 2012, marginally down from 70% a year earlier. The country's net foreign position, including balances in the NFRK, contracted by $1.7 billion and stood on 1 January 2013 at $11.9 billion.

3.4.6 Foreign exchange reserves and fund assets

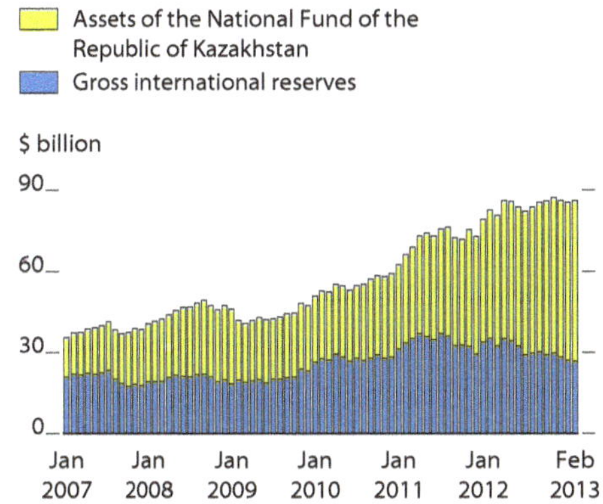

Source: National Bank of Kazakhstan.

Click here for figure data

Economic prospects

GDP is forecast to grow by 5.2% in 2013 and 5.6% in 2014, largely reflecting higher domestic demand, including investment spending under the industrialization program and the more active investment of NFRK assets (Figure 3.4.7). Some $1.5 billion of NFRK assets will be lent to the national oil company KazMunaiGas in 2013, and $2.5 billion more in 2014. Economic performance will also depend on demand from Kazakhstan's major trading partners: the European Union, Russian Federation, and People's Republic of China. Production from the Kashagan project, postponed again in 2012, is now expected to begin in the second half of 2013 with limited scope before expanding in 2014 to boost oil exports.

Construction and development for Kazakhstan's Expo 2017 will expand government investment but may also raise public debt unless the private sector participates. The adoption in February 2013 of a program to develop agribusiness will require a substantial $20 billion of public support during 2013–2020, potentially attracting three times as much in private investment. The government is initiating a new law on public–private partnership to finance and implement large social and infrastructure programs.

Inflation is expected to remain moderate but toward the middle of the central bank's 6%–8% target range, reflecting the continued administration of prices, the use of special food stabilization funds in the regions, and a conservative monetary policy. Tariffs for services, including transport and communal utilities, will continue to rise in 2013, affecting the cost of all goods.

Fiscal policy is expected to remain somewhat expansionary, with a bias towards spending for industrialization, social modernization programs, and social safety nets. However, the republican budget deficit is forecast to narrow to 2.1% of GDP in 2013 and 1.8% in 2014 (Figure 3.4.8). The budget deficit will be covered through internal and external borrowing, including about $1 billion in sovereign Eurobonds in 2013—$500 million in the first half of the year.

3.4.7 GDP growth

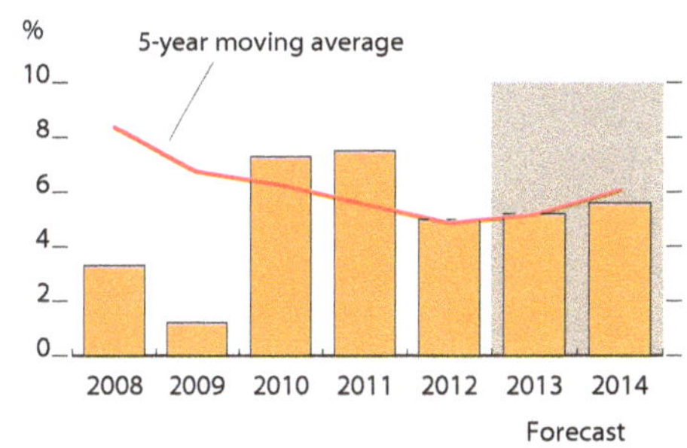

Source: Asian Development Outlook database.

Click here for figure data

3.4.8 Fiscal indicators

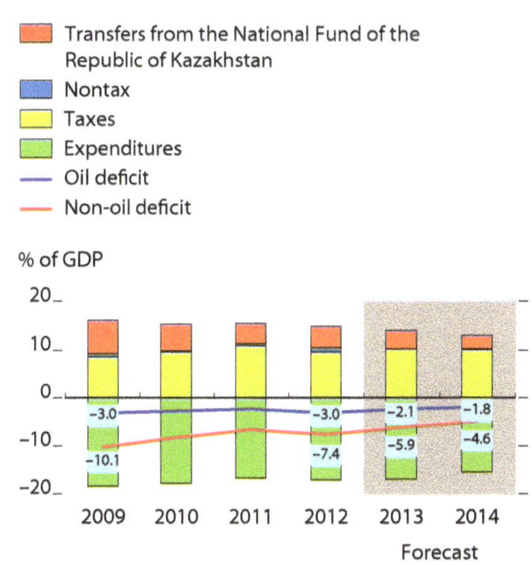

Source: The Ministry of Finance of the Republic of Kazakhstan.

Click here for figure data

Republican budget revenues, including transfers from the NFRK, are forecast to slide from 15.5% of GDP in 2012 to 14.8% in 2013 and 13.5% in 2014 (Figure 3.4.9). Tax receipts should gradually rise from 62% of revenue in 2012 to 74% in 2014, while transfers from the NFRK should remain unchanged in 2013 and decline in 2014. Revenue could be higher if the Kashagan and Karachaganak projects start operations in 2013. In addition, a new feature called "conditional financing," limited to 4% of republican budget expenditure, will be introduced in 2013, to fund more regional programs if current revenue improves.

Total expenditure is forecast to fall to 16.9% of GDP in 2013 and 15.3% in 2014. The planned reform of the pension system will merge 11 funds into one asset management fund and gradually align pension ages for women and men, which may help reduce outlays beginning in 2014.

Monetary policy is expected to remain conservative, with the central bank adjusting its policy rate as needed to contain inflation. Moderate inflation is anticipated, along with a low policy interest rate to encourage commercial banks to cut their interest rates. The central bank is expected to regulate the financial sector in a strong but low-profile manner, focusing in 2013 on cleaning the balances of commercial banks and improving access to finance for priority sectors of economy. As part of this policy the national holding company SamrukKazyna must dispose of its shares in three nationalized banks by the end of 2013. The central bank has enough capacity to keep the exchange rate relatively stable but is not expected to intervene against major trends in the exchange market, having lost over $6 billion in reserves during 2007–2008.

The current account balance could achieve surpluses of 2.5% of GDP in 2013 and 4.0% in 2014, if oil prices are stable (Figure 3.4.10). However, current forecasts anticipate some oil price declines in 2013 and no improvement in metals prices, so surpluses may be smaller. Exports in 2013 and 2014 are forecast to increase by 1%–2% of GDP, reflecting higher oil production. Imports are expected to grow much more quickly to maintain outlays for the program to accelerate industrial and innovative development. This will narrow the current account balance.

Ongoing projects to resolve transport bottlenecks, expand oil fields, and improve infrastructure will not take full effect in 2013 or 2014, possibly meaning further outflows in services and remittances. Reserves are expected to remain largely unchanged from the end 2012, while higher oil prices further build NFRK assets, now projected to reach $75 billion, or 30% of GDP, in 2014.

Policy challenge—energy efficiency

Although its primary energy reserves are among the largest in the world, Kazakhstan does not meet its domestic energy needs. In 2011 Kazakhstan had the world's third most energy-intensive economy, in terms of energy consumption per unit of GDP. Its emissions of greenhouse gases per unit of GDP are also very high. In addition, the energy system and its regional distribution companies face major risks from limited network capacity, outdated equipment, high losses, and inadequate or absent control systems, while tariffs set too low for cost recovery preclude network reconstruction or modernization. The current electricity market

3.4.9 GDP and national fund cash flows

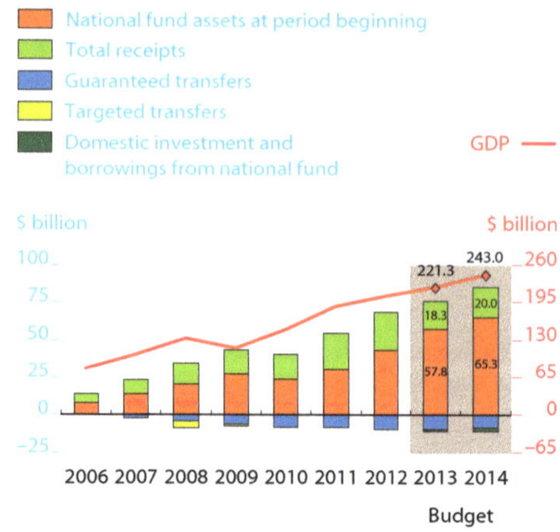

Source: The Ministry of Finance of the Republic of Kazakhstan.
Click here for figure data

3.4.1 Selected economic indicators (%)

	2013	2014
GDP growth	5.2	5.6
Inflation	6.7	6.5
Current account balance (share of GDP)	2.5	4.0

Source: ADB estimates.

3.4.10 Current account balance

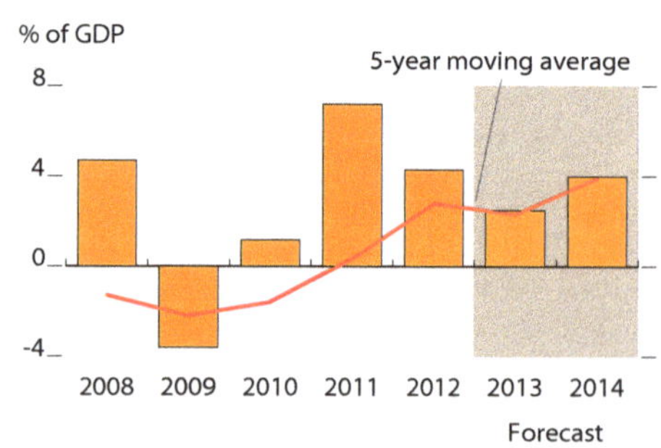

Source: Asian Development Outlook database.
Click here for figure data

and legislative and regulatory frameworks make constructing new power plants unattractive. The government has pursued several programs in recent years to involve the private sector in developing and operating energy facilities, but with mixed results.

High energy intensity reflects the predominance of energy-intensive industries and outdated energy infrastructure. Some 30 industrial enterprises consume over 70% of electricity, and comparisons with the European Union show that more than two-thirds of them could reduce their energy intensity. Moreover, almost 90% of electricity is generated by coal-fired plants with barely one-third of the efficiency of similar plants in advanced economies. Over 70% of the population gets district heating from 40 solid-fuel combined heat and power plants operating in 29 cities. These plants date from the 1960s to the 1980s, and almost all are past their service lives, as evidenced by network distribution losses and frequent failures. High energy intensity defeats coping with demand surges. Additional generation capacity could reduce the supply deficit, which would require new investment.

The government considers energy efficiency a critical pillar of its energy policy. A law on energy saving and energy efficiency came into effect in July 2012, to be followed by supporting legislation. The goal is to reduce energy intensity by 10% in 2015 from the 2008 level and by 25% in 2020. In addition, the government has launched its Green Economy Initiative, to reduce greenhouse gas emissions by 15% in 2020 from the 1992 level and by 25% in 2050.

Kazakhstan could benefit from revived energy trading within Central Asia, which would enable it to draw on its neighbors' hydropower through the regional electrical system that connects Kazakhstan, the Kyrgyz Republic, Tajikistan, Turkmenistan, and Uzbekistan. Drawing from pooled transnational assets would reduce the need for reserve power and allow the export of seasonal excess energy supplies to the People's Republic of China, India, Iran, and Pakistan. While transnational energy and water resources would need coordinated management, a study conducted under the Central Asia Regional Economic Cooperation estimates the potential regional economic benefits of energy trading in 2013–2015 could be $2 billion without major infrastructure or system investments.

Kyrgyz Republic

While the peaceful transfer of power in 2011 and the swift formation of a new government in 2012 laid the foundation for growth, low gold production nevertheless caused GDP to contract by 0.9%. In 2013 growth is expected to rebound to 5.5%. Meanwhile, the government will begin implementing its new Sustainable Development Strategy, 2013–2017, a blueprint for building a stable society, strengthening the rule of law, and improving the investment climate.

Economic performance

GDP declined during 2012 as adverse geological factors affected gold production. Despite some recovery in gold output toward the end of the year and 5.0% growth in other sectors, real GDP contracted by 0.9% (Figure 3.5.1). All sectors except gold and agriculture showed robust gains, reflecting growing public confidence. Agricultural growth was hurt by a poor grain harvest.

3.5.1 Supply-side contributions to growth

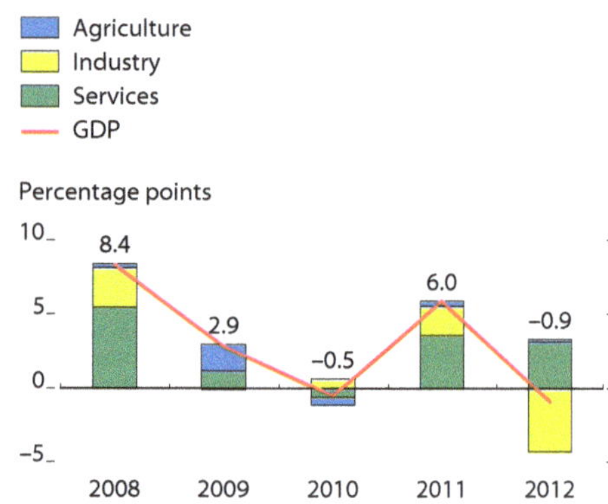

Source: National Statistics Committee of the Kyrgyz Republic. http://www.stat.kg (accessed 15 March 2013).
Click here for figure data

Industrial output fell by 13.8%, reflecting a 27.2% drop in manufacturing, which reflected in turn the decline in gold output and lower production of machinery and equipment. Growth in other key manufacturing subsectors averaged a robust 6.1%, driven by higher domestic consumption. Output of textiles grew by 12.5%, and chemical production by 22.7%, to supply growing trade with the Russian Federation and Kazakhstan. Mining output grew by 22.5%, reflecting higher extraction of coal, basalt, and other minerals. Construction grew by 17.3%, following the sluggish 2.5% growth of 2011, because of large investments in new buildings and repairs to existing structures.

Agriculture grew by only 1.2%, less than the 1.9% rise in 2011. Lower productivity and adverse weather caused a 10.0% decline in the grain harvest, which was offset by 2.4% growth in livestock production.

Services, which provide half of GDP, grew strongly for the second consecutive year, by 6.2%. The strongest gains were in transportation at 8.9%, trade 10.5%, and hotels and restaurants 11.7%, reflecting higher consumer demand and improved cross-border trade.

On the demand side, private consumption is estimated to have grown by more than 6%, as higher employment, wage increases averaging 16.5%, and a rise in remittances exceeding 17.0% fueled an 11.0% increase in retail sales.

Investment expanded by 21.5%, including a 30.2% rise in gross fixed capital formation, following the 3.1% investment decline in 2011. The increases, all in the private sector, reflected gains in energy, mining, processing, and trade but were partly offset by declines in

This chapter was written by Gulkayr Tentieva of the Kyrgyz Resident Mission, ADB, Bishkek.

communications, transport infrastructure, and housing. Government investment shrank by 4.8%, as austerity measures aimed to reduce lower-priority spending. Net exports declined, as export volumes fell by 13.1% while import volumes grew by 26.2%.

Measured as a year average, inflation slowed significantly to 2.8% from 16.6% in 2011, with a 3.9% decline in food prices largely offsetting a 10.1% rise in other prices. Inflation rose slightly during the second half of the year led by higher prices for wheat, which caused the 12-month (December over December) inflation rate to reach 7.5%, above the comparable rate of 5.7% for 2011 (Figure 3.5.2).

Despite improved tax collection, rapid growth in social expenditures caused the budget deficit to widen to 6.6% of GDP from 4.8% in 2011 (Figure 3.5.3). Government revenue rose to 28.6% of GDP from 27.2% in 2011, reflecting growth aside from gold and improved tax administration. However, higher wages, pensions, and spending on energy infrastructure caused expenditures to rise to 35.2% of GDP from 31.9% in 2011.

Public debt, equivalent to 47.9% of GDP at the end of 2012, rose slightly from 45.6% of GDP in 2011 but was far below the 55.2% of 2010 (Figure 3.5.4), partly because of agreements reached with Turkey and the Russian Federation to write off debt. The agreement with the Russian Federation, ratified in November 2012, provided for the immediate write-off of $189 million in debt and the phased write-off of the remaining $300 million over 10 years starting in 2016.

Extensive dollarization in the Kyrgyz Republic and a shallow financial sector limit the impact of monetary policy. During 2012 the central bank relaxed monetary policy as inflation slowed, steadily lowering the policy rate over the year from 13.6% at the beginning to 2.6% at year-end, in line with declining core inflation and growing confidence in the banking sector. The average deposit rate rose slightly, to 5.4% from 4.9% in 2011, while the lending rate fell to 23.0% from 23.8% in 2011.

During 2012, the deposit base grew by 36.1% and credit to the economy grew by 26.2%. The share of nonperforming loans at year-end fell again to 7.2% in 2012 from 10.2% in 2011 and 15.8% in 2010. The value of the Kyrgyz som remained relatively stable against the US dollar but depreciated slightly during the second half of the year, sliding from Som46.69 to the dollar in January to Som47.40 by 31 December 2012 (Figure 3.5.5). The central bank intervened in the foreign exchange market only to smooth short-term fluctuations.

The external current account deficit is estimated to have widened to 20.9% of GDP from 6.1% in 2011, reflecting lower export volumes and a slight fall in gold prices.

The trade deficit is estimated to have increased significantly, to $3.0 billion, as higher purchases of gasoline and diesel fuel caused imports to rise by 26.2%, while exports fell by 13.1%, mainly reflecting lower gold exports. Members of the Commonwealth of Independent States remained the Kyrgyz Republic's largest trading partners. Remittances rose to $1.8 billion from $1.5 billion in 2011 (Figure 3.5.6), reflecting positive developments in the Russian Federation and Kazakhstan. Investment inflows rose by 26.7%, largely reflecting new investments in the energy sector and elsewhere. Gross international reserves climbed by 12.7% to $2.1 billion.

3.5.2 Inflation

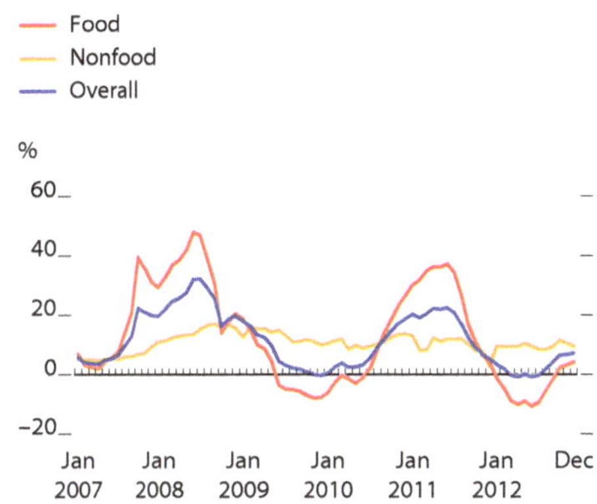

Source: National Statistics Committee of the Kyrgyz Republic. http://www.stat.kg (accessed 15 March 2013).
Click here for figure data

3.5.3 Fiscal indicators

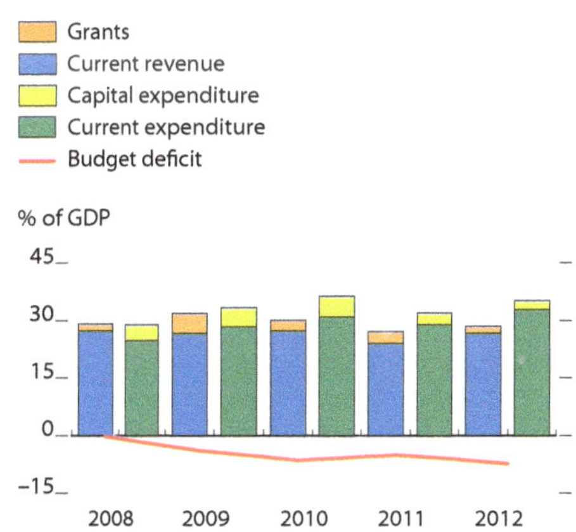

Sources: International Monetary Fund. 2009. *Country Report* No. 09/209. July; 2010. *Country Report* No. 10/336. October; 2011. *Country Report* No. 11-354. December; 2012. *Country Report* No. 12/111. May; 2012. *Country Report* No. 12/329. December. http://www.imf.org; Ministry of Finance.
Click here for figure data

3.5.4 External debt

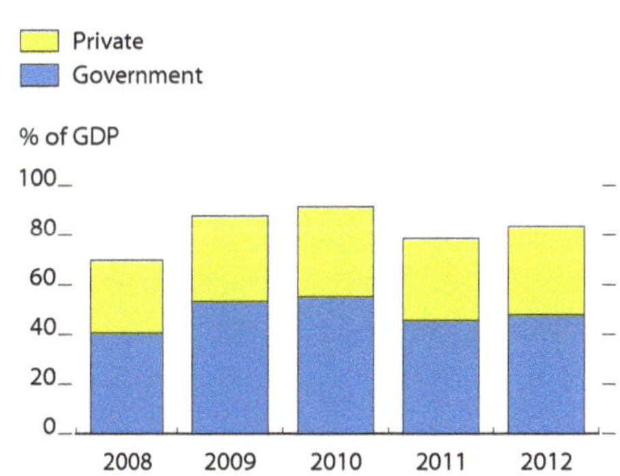

Note: Government debt refers to both government and government-guaranteed debt.

Sources: National Statistics Committee of the Kyrgyz Republic. http://www.stat.kg; National Bank of the Kyrgyz Republic. http://www.nbkr.kg (both accessed 15 March 2013); Ministry of Finance.
Click here for figure data

Economic prospects

Growth is expected to rebound to 5.5% in 2013 and 4.5% in 2014 (Figure 3.5.7) on the back of higher gold production and investments, mainly from the Russian Federation and the People's Republic of China, in energy and transport infrastructure projects. However, gold output could fall below expectations if the political environment deteriorates, weakening investment incentives. The restoration of public confidence and greater political stability should raise domestic demand, spurring growth in the private sector apart from gold. Good economic conditions in the Russian Federation and Kazakhstan will likely promote growth by generating higher remittances and external demand. Reform in state governance also holds promise.

The service sector will remain the major source of economic expansion, with growth expected at 5.0% each year. Transportation and communications should perform well, as major road networks and energy infrastructure are rehabilitated and communication networks are expanded. Industry is expected to grow by 10.0% each year, with metals and metallurgy the main drivers, gold remaining the principal output, and gold and energy showing the highest growth rates.

Inflation is expected to rise to 7.5% in 2013 with the rebound in gold output and infrastructure investments in the energy sector, and then ease to 5.5% in 2014. Substantial price hikes are not expected for food, which occupies 45% of the consumer price index, given current forecasts for declining global food prices.

The fiscal deficit should narrow to 5.5% of GDP in 2013 and 4.0% in 2014 as gold-related tax revenues rise. The government is committed to fiscal consolidation in the medium term and will be guided by conservative revenue forecasts, restrained expenditure on low priority items, and social considerations. Total revenue is expected to increase to 33.0% of GDP, as improving tax administration remains high on the government's agenda. Total expenditure is expected to rise to 38.3% of GDP, reflecting lower current expenditure but higher capital spending. Future pension increases will continue to be tied to changes in the income officially deemed necessary for subsistence.

Monetary policy is expected to remain cautious as the central bank works to absorb any excess liquidity caused by government spending. The central bank will likely raise the policy interest rate if inflation rises, as expected. Nominal interest rates are expected to stay in the 13.0%–15.0% range, helping the som to appreciate during 2013.

The current account balance is forecast to improve, with rapid export growth narrowing the deficit to 7.0% of GDP in 2013 and further to 5.0% in 2014 (Figure 3.5.8). Exports are forecast to grow by 20.0% in 2013 and 15.0% in 2014, mainly due to a rebound in gold exports during 2013 and higher exports of textiles and agricultural produce in 2013 and 2014. These exports should benefit from anticipated accession into the customs union with Belarus, Kazakhstan, and the Russian Federation in 2014, though trade may fall initially with countries outside the union. Imports are expected to grow steadily at 15.0% both in 2013 and 2014 because imported equipment, machinery, and fuel are needed for new infrastructure projects in energy, transport, and other sectors. External reserves are forecast to climb to $2.2 billion in 2013

3.5.5 Monthly exchange rate

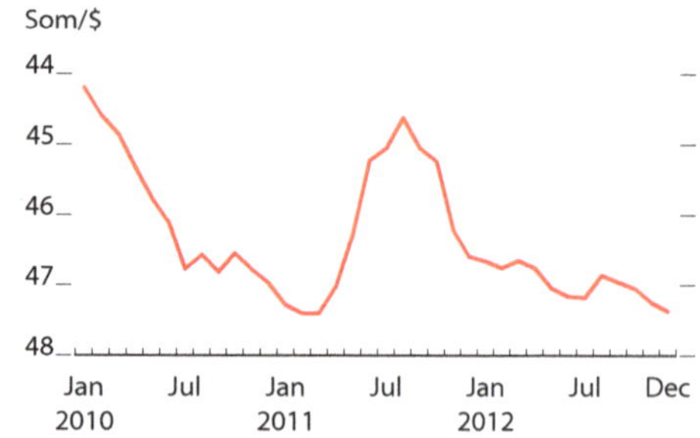

Source: National Bank of the Kyrgyz Republic. http://www.nbkr.kg (accessed 15 March 2013).

Click here for figure data

3.5.6 Remittances

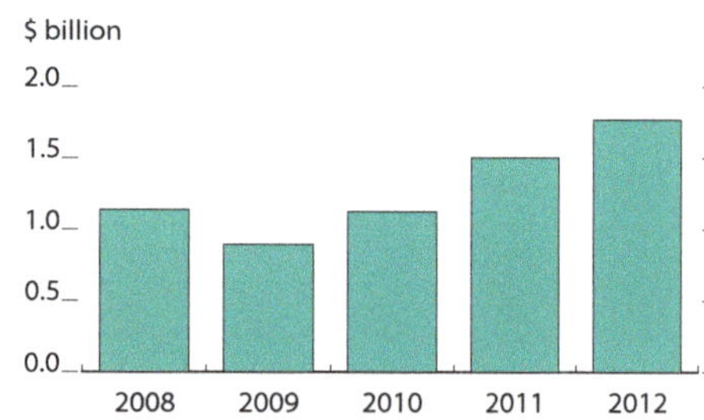

Source: National Bank of the Kyrgyz Republic. http://www.nbkr.kg (accessed 15 March 2013).

Click here for figure data

3.5.7 GDP growth

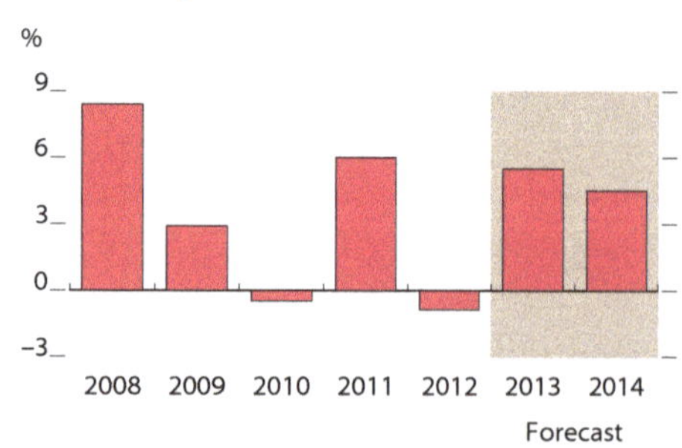

Sources: National Statistics Committee of the Kyrgyz Republic. http://www.stat.kg (accessed 15 March 2013); ADB estimates.

Click here for figure data

and $2.4 billion in 2014. Foreign direct investment inflows will depend largely on the government implementing its proposed structural reform and improvements to the investment climate. External government and government-guaranteed debt is forecast to subside to about 44% of GDP.

3.5.1 Selected economic indicators (%)

	2013	2014
GDP growth	5.5	4.5
Inflation	7.5	5.5
Current account balance (share of GDP)	–7.0	–5.0

Source: ADB estimates.

Policy challenges—energy security and reform

Increasingly unreliable electricity supply is among the binding constraints on growth that pose major risks to economic development.

The Kyrgyz Republic has the potential to expand hydropower capacity, which supplies more than 80% of all locally generated electricity. However, the sector is plagued by high commercial and technical losses, poor corporate governance, corruption, aging assets in serious need of rehabilitation and upgrading, and artificially low tariffs.

Energy security remains a primary concern. The country is a net energy importer, with 70% of its energy needs supplied by imported coal, oil, and gas. While Central Asia is rich in fossil fuels, the delivery of fuel imports, particularly of gas, is not always reliable. Because electricity generation exceeds domestic needs, the Kyrgyz Republic is a net electricity exporter. However, the seasonal nature of hydropower generation means that the country suffers from winter electricity shortages. Whether the Central Asian electricity grid, a legacy of the Soviet era, will continue to link countries in the region adds to uncertainty about energy security.

3.5.8 Current account balance

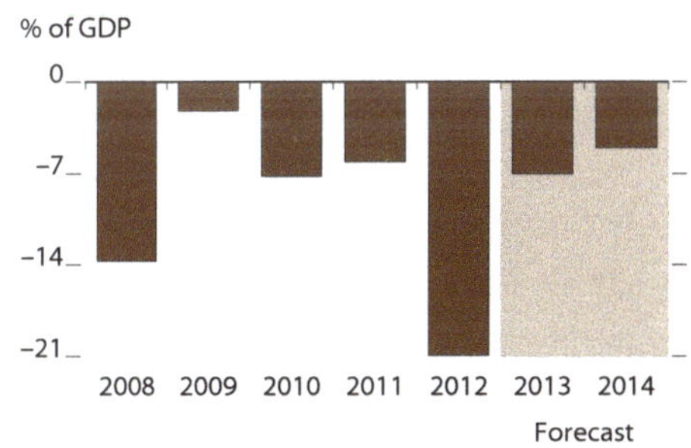

Sources: National Bank of the Kyrgyz Republic. http://www.nbkr.kg (accessed 15 March 2013); ADB estimates.

Click here for figure data

To resolve these challenges, in 2012 the government adopted a new energy sector strategy and developed its energy sector reform action plan. The plan aims to improve state regulation, strengthen the management of energy companies, make corporate activities more transparent, gradually raise tariffs, and expand production to increase exports of electricity and stabilize domestic electricity supply. To improve energy security in the short term, the government plans to complete a 500 kilowatt power substation and the 410 kilometer Datka–Kemin electricity grid. Over the longer term, the government has begun feasibility studies for two electricity grids connecting the country's system with that of Kazakhstan (Kemin–Almaty) and the People's Republic of China (Datka–Hudjent). Important but aging assets, especially the Toktogul hydropower plant, urgently need rehabilitation.

The government is negotiating several energy projects, including Kambar–Ata II and a cascade of smaller hydropower stations on the Naryn River. However, sustaining the energy system will require billions of dollars of investment in new projects and the rehabilitation of existing assets. Thus, improving the investment climate, protecting investor rights, and developing a new tariff policy remain as challenges to achieving a more secure energy supply that contributes to economic development.

Tajikistan

Growth accelerated slightly to 7.5% in 2012 as remittances hit record highs, but slightly slower growth is forecast for 2013 and 2014. Domestic income and investment remain low. Reforms promised to permit Tajikistan's accession to the World Trade Organization will be important to improve the business climate, increase foreign investment, and reduce excessive reliance on remittances.

Economic developments

Tajikistan achieved robust growth of 7.5%, slightly above the 7.4% recorded in 2011 (Figure 3.6.1), mainly reflecting strong domestic demand from record-high remittances, which equal about half of GDP. Meanwhile, domestic income and investment remained critically low.

On the supply side, services remained the main driver of economic growth, expanding by 14.5% and led by retail trade, which grew by 17.1%. Construction, industry, and agriculture also grew, but at more modest rates. Industry expanded by 10.4%, backed by continued growth in mining and light processing. Textiles grew by 30%, as weak external demand and lower international prices for cotton prompted firms to focus on local processing. Aluminum production grew by a modest 0.7%, constrained by aging technology and a reduced supply of natural gas from Uzbekistan, and discouraged by lower international prices. Agriculture grew by 10.4%, largely because of strong growth in agricultural processing. However, cotton production grew by only 0.5%, as sharp fluctuations in cotton prices discouraged farmers from following through on initial expansions in planted area. Despite slow growth, aluminum and cotton still represented 58% of total output, down from 70% in 2008.

On the demand side, consumption was the main driver of growth. Higher spending for social services, human development, and social protection raised private consumption, while increased outlays for education and health care boosted public consumption. However, public investment including outlays by state enterprises declined as investment in energy, transport, and communication fell by 20.2%. Private investment grew by only 1.0%, and the share of private investment in GDP remained below 5%. Despite the government's continued efforts to improve the investment climate, serious impediments such as an inefficient tax system, the high cost of financing, and weak property rights have kept private investment and income low.

Inflation slowed to 5.8% from 12.5% in 2011 (Figure 3.6.2). Food prices rose by only 3.5%, despite a sharp jump in wheat and flour prices caused

3.6.1 GDP growth by sector

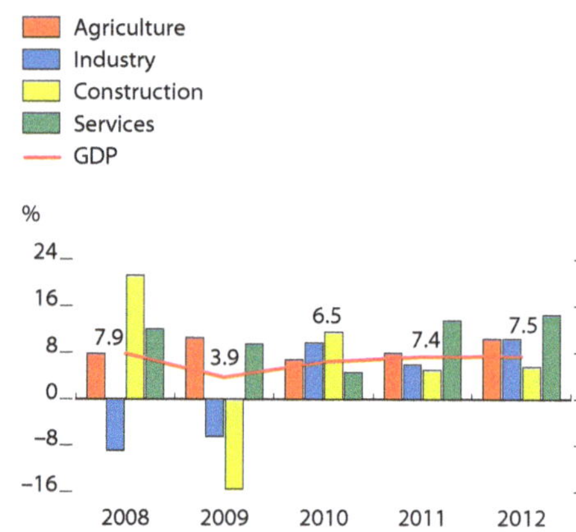

Sources: International Monetary Fund; Tajikistan State Statistics Agency. http://www.stat.tj (accessed 15 March 2013).
Click here for figure data

3.6.2 Monthly inflation

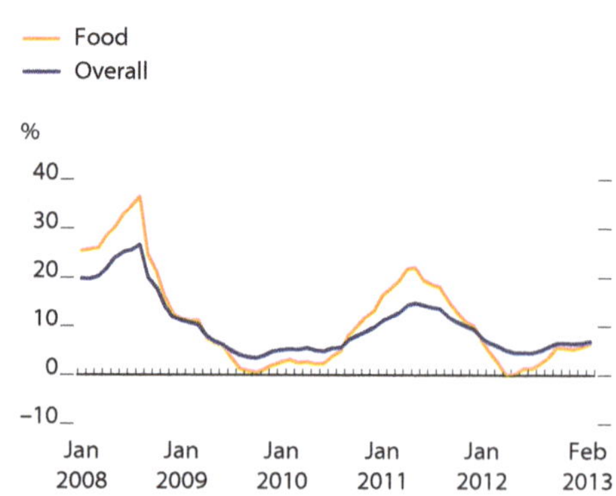

Source: Tajikistan State Statistics Agency. http://www.stat.tj (accessed 21 March 2013).
Click here for figure data

This chapter was written by Kakhorjon Aminov of the Tajikistan Resident Mission, ADB, Dushanbe.

by a drought in Kazakhstan and the Russian Federation. Inflationary pressures came mainly from services, where prices rose by 12.9%.

Fiscal policy tightened, leaving an overall budget surplus (including all investment spending) of 0.1% of GDP that reversed the 2.5% deficit in 2011 (Figure 3.6.3). The state budget surplus, which excludes foreign-financed investment, rose to 1.8% of GDP from 0.5% in 2011. Revenue performance was on track, reflecting a 22.6% rise in tax revenue and a more than 7.3% increase in nontax revenue as the restructuring of the government's tax committee and better tax administration improved collection. Total expenditure rose by 21.9%, reflecting a 21% increase in spending for social protection. Pensions increased by 30% and social sector wages by 30%–40%, reflecting the government's commitment to improve social services. However, infrastructure spending fell by 10.1% following the completion of projects commissioned to celebrate Tajikistan's 20 years of independence. Public and publicly guaranteed debt declined to 33.9% of GDP from 34.3% at the end of 2011.

Lower inflationary pressures allowed the central bank to pursue a more accommodative monetary policy. The refinancing rate was reduced repeatedly in 2012, from 9.8% to 8.0% in March, 6.8% in July, and 6.5% in September. Bank credit expanded by 9.2%, mainly driven by a 14% increase in short-term credit. However, the share of long-term credit diminished slightly, by 0.5%, particularly for local currency lending.

Overall, the banking system remains prone to risks from low profitability and a significant percentage of nonperforming loans, as 9.5% are 30+ days overdue. Microfinance, on the other hand, continued to expand. In 2012, the average somoni exchange rate remained stable at TJS4.8 = $1 (Figure 3.6.4), which helped moderate inflationary expectations through its impact on import prices.

The current account balance worsened, recording a deficit of 3.5% of GDP after the surplus of 2.3% in 2011, as the trade balance deteriorated. Exports rose by 8.2%, to an estimated $1.4 billion, while high remittances helped boost imports by 18.6% to $3.8 billion. Export growth reflected significant gains of 13.5% for cotton fiber and 11.6% for textiles. In addition, the expanding mining sector has made mineral exports increasingly important, with export earnings doubling in 2012. Electricity exports, though relatively small, grew nearly fourfold in 2012 as the supply of electricity to Afghanistan was sustained through the winter despite severe domestic electricity shortages, partly to keep the transmission system functional. Purchases of consumer goods were behind the 18.6% rise in imports. However, remittances, mainly from the Russian Federation and Kazakhstan, rose by more than 28% to a record of $3.6 billion, or more than 47% of GDP.

Continued government borrowing for investment projects helped boost capital inflows. Foreign direct investment edged up to an estimated $50 million in 2012 after hitting a trough in 2010 of less than $10 million. However, foreign direct investment remains very low at only 0.5% of GDP. Official reserves rose to $662 million at the end of 2012, equivalent to 2.2 months of imports, from $572 million a year earlier. Public and publicly guaranteed external debt was 31.2% of GDP, little changed from the 32.1% a year earlier (Figure 3.6.5).

3.6.3 Fiscal balance

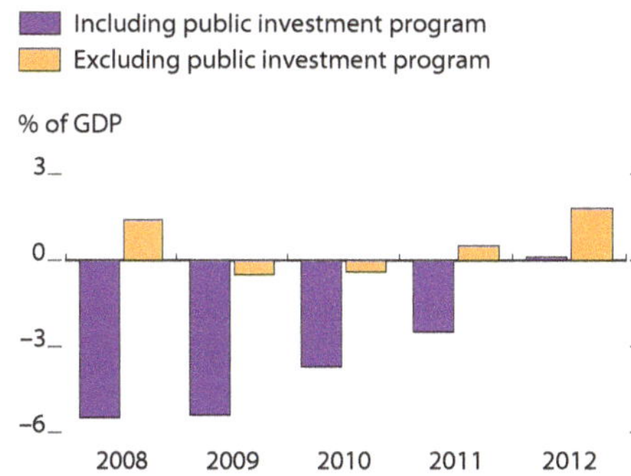

Sources: International Monetary Fund. 2011. *Country Report* No. 11/130. June; 2012. *Country Report* No. 12/110. May. http://www.imf.org

Click here for figure data

3.6.4 Nominal exchange rate

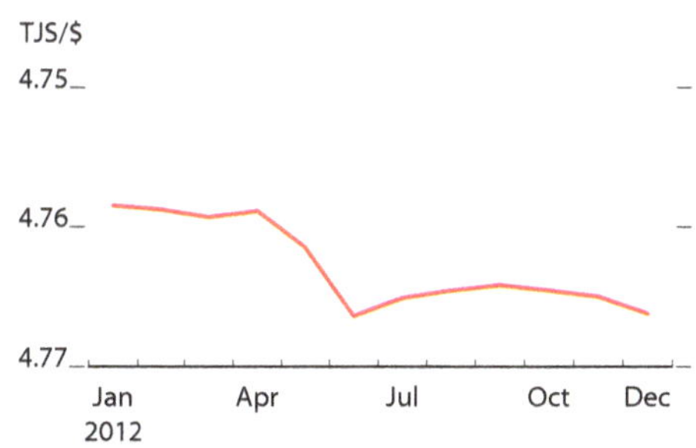

Source: National Bank of Tajikistan.

Click here for figure data

3.6.5 External public and publicly guaranteed debt

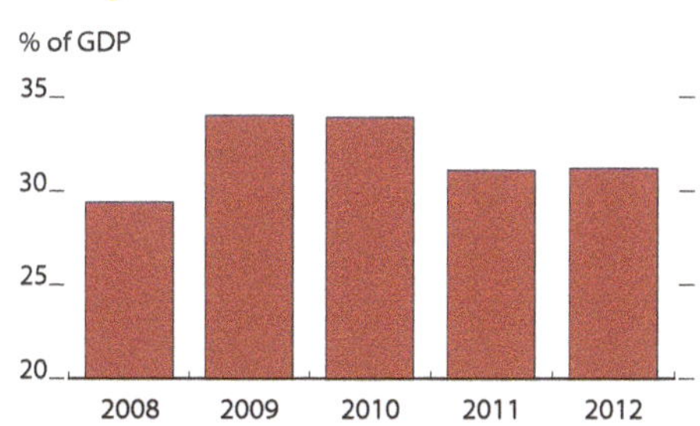

Sources: International Monetary Fund. 2011. *Country Report* No. 11/130. June; 2012. *Country Report* No. 12/110. May. http://www.imf.org.

Click here for figure data

Economic prospects

The economic outlook is cautiously optimistic, as healthy remittance inflows will continue to support Tajikistan's growth in 2013 and 2014, stimulating private consumption, imports, and budget revenues. More diversified industry and agriculture will result in more sustainable economic growth, which is forecast at 6.5% in 2013 and 6.0% in 2014 (Figure 3.6.6). However, the economy remains vulnerable because of heavy dependence on remittances.

Although continuing growth is expected, several factors heighten uncertainty or limit growth prospects. The aluminum industry is likely to slow further as production facilities continue to deteriorate and power problems and input restrictions persist. Moreover, the volume of cotton and aluminum exports will remain sensitive to international prices.

Growth will also depend on four factors: projected growth in the Russian Federation; stability in regional trade and cargo transit; the amount of precipitation, which is essential for agriculture and hydroelectric generation; and political and social stability.

In addition, Tajikistan suffers from a poor investment climate and a weak financial sector. Despite improvement in some areas, Tajikistan ranks among the bottom fourth of all countries worldwide in the World Bank's *Doing Business 2013*, with exceptionally low scores for dealing with construction permits, getting electricity and credit, ease of paying taxes, and trading across borders. When joining the World Trade Organization in March 2013, Tajikistan agreed to improve its trade regime and accelerate reforms to create a more transparent and predictable environment for trade and foreign investment. Implementing these reforms is essential to boost private investment.

Inflation is expected to stay relatively moderate in 2013 and 2014, in line with declining international food prices, though inflation could be higher if food and fuel prices exceed projections. The inflation rate is forecast to remain at 6.5% in 2013 and reach 7.0% in 2014 (Figure 3.6.7).

Tajikistan's fiscal stance will be somewhat more expansionary with planned higher expenditure, mainly for social spending and infrastructure. The budget deficit is expected to widen to 2.5% of GDP in 2013 and then narrow again to 2.0% in 2014, while the state budget deficit is projected at 0.5% of GDP in 2013 and 2014. Despite somewhat elevated public debt, the government is likely to continue borrowing externally for large infrastructure projects, mainly in energy and transport. The Public Debt Management Strategy for 2012–2014 reaffirms the government's commitment to keep public and publicly guaranteed debt below 40% of GDP, to ensure that new loans have a minimum grant element of 35%, and to undertake cost–benefit analyses of large investments.

Monetary policy will need to strike a balance between supporting Tajikistan's economic recovery and ensuring price stability. The refinancing rate is expected to remain between 6.5% and 7.5% in 2013 and 2014. Money growth is projected to slow moderately, from 23.2% in 2012 to about 18% a year in 2013 and 2014. The exchange rate is forecast to remain relatively stable, supported by remittances, despite downward pressure from weak export performance. Continued exchange rate flexibility and close coordination with monetary and fiscal policies will be important to maintain competitiveness and avoid shocks.

3.6.1 Selected economic indicators (%)

	2013	2014
GDP growth	6.5	6.0
Inflation	6.5	7.0
Current account balance (share of GDP)	–5.0	–4.8

Source: ADB estimates.

3.6.6 GDP growth

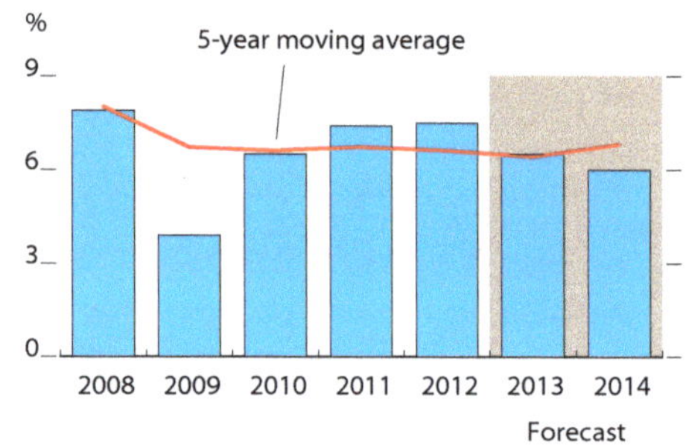

Sources: International Monetary Fund; Tajikistan State Statistics Agency. http://www.stat.tj (accessed 15 March 2013); ADB estimates.

Click here for figure data

3.6.7 Inflation

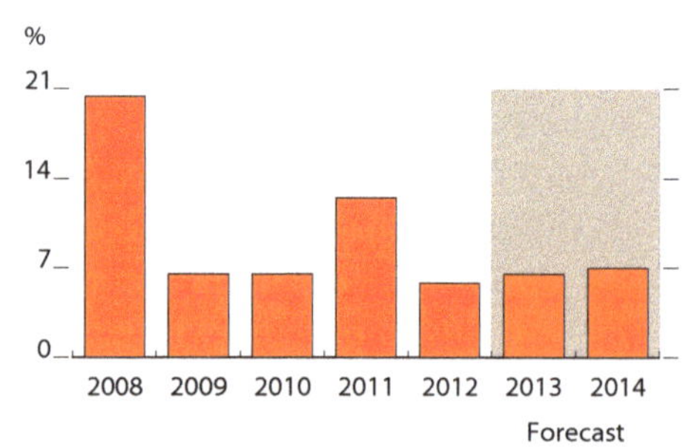

Sources: International Monetary Fund. 2011. World Economic Outlook database. September; Tajikistan State Statistics Agency. http://www.stat.tj (accessed 15 March 2013); ADB estimates.

Click here for figure data

The current account deficit is expected to widen to 5.0% in 2013 and then narrow slightly to 4.8% in 2014 (Figure 3.6.8). Despite declines in aluminum and cotton, total exports should rise because of gains in agricultural products, electricity, and textiles. Imports should also increase, because of rising remittances (Figure 3.6.9). Foreign direct investment inflows should continue to rise gradually, in line with ongoing reform. Most investments will likely involve several large infrastructure projects. External debt is forecast to reach 32.5% of GDP at the end of 2013 and 32.8% a year later. Reserves are expected to rise to $762 million by the end of 2013 and $862 million a year later, equivalent to less than 3 months of imports.

3.6.8 Current account balance

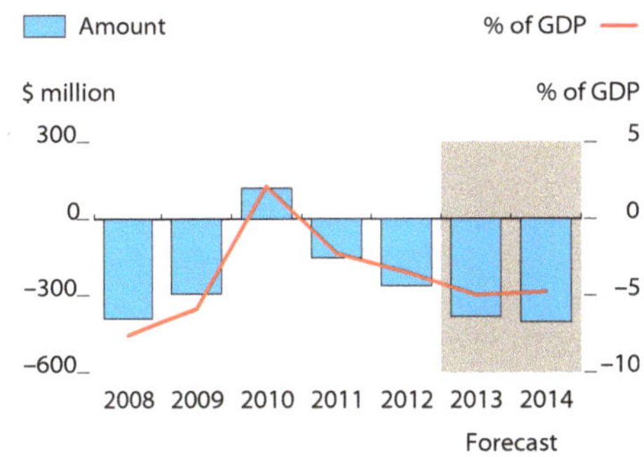

Sources: International Monetary Fund. 2011. *Country Report* No. 11/130. June; 2012. *Country Report* No. 12/110. May. http://www.imf.org; ADB estimates.

Click here for figure data

3.6.9 Net remittances

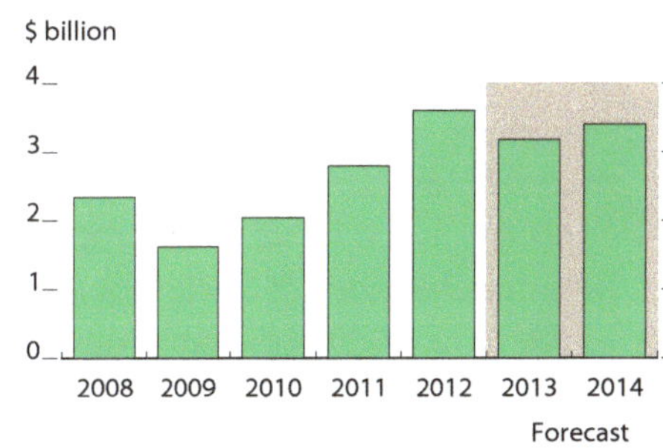

Sources: International Monetary Fund. 2011. *Country Report* No. 11/130. June; 2012. *Country Report* No. 12/110. May. http://www.imf.org

Click here for figure data

Policy challenge—addressing severe winter energy shortages

Persistent shortages of electricity in winter, causing severe blackouts for 70% of the population and most firms outside the capital, are Tajikistan's biggest growth constraint. These shortages, estimated at a quarter of winter electricity demand, create economic losses equivalent to 3% of GDP and cause significant hardship, especially in rural areas. The problem results from Tajikistan's overwhelming dependence on hydropower and limited flows during the cold winter months. Deteriorating generation plants, high transmission and distribution system losses, and poor operational and financial management in the sector compound the problem.

Reliable power supply is critical to sustained growth. Current disruptions deter investment and job creation, keep hospitals and schools from functioning properly, and create health hazards from wood burned for heating and cooking; most regions get only 5–8 hours of electricity per day from November to March. Increasing demand for fuelwood has caused extensive deforestation and loss of biomass, creating soil erosion, landslides, and other forms of land degradation. Currently, electricity is the cheapest and sometimes the only source of power for heating. Thus, homes and businesses depend heavily on electricity for heat, as well as for lighting and industrial processes. Electricity powers the production of Tajikistan's two largest exports, aluminum and cotton.

Despite seasonal shortages and other problems, Tajikistan was a key summertime power supplier in Central Asia before the 1990s and could produce more electricity now, both for domestic needs and to export to new markets such as Afghanistan and Pakistan. Achieving energy security is thus important for both domestic and regional economic growth and development. Improving governance in the energy sector can substantially enhance sector efficiency, and comprehensive reform is needed for energy sustainability and independence. Priorities for the government and development partners should include reforming Barqi Tajik, the national electricity monopoly, to strengthen its commercial viability; implementing national programs to help households and large industrial consumers use electricity more efficiently; rehabilitating existing capacity and creating new capacity; promoting regional power trade initiatives and investment in necessary infrastructure; exploring renewable energy sources such as solar and wind power; and designing and implementing programs to improve public understanding and garner support for energy reform.

Turkmenistan

Growth remained robust at 11.1%, led by strong gas exports and high public spending on infrastructure, with rising imports limiting the current account surplus to 1.5% of GDP. Even higher oil and gas production and exports are expected in 2013 and 2014, providing continued funding for the large public sector. However, growth is forecast to moderate to 9% in 2013 and 8% in 2014.

Economic performance

The economy grew by a strong 11.1%, a bit less than the 14.7% recorded in 2011 (Figure 3.7.1). With growth averaging 11% since 2007, Turkmenistan was reclassified by the World Bank in July 2012 as an upper-middle-income country.

On the demand side, strong gas exports and public investment in infrastructure were the main growth drivers. Gas exports, comprising 70% of total exports, have continued to rise because of long-term contracts with the People's Republic of China (PRC), which has steadily increased its purchases since 2009. Other importers, notably the Russian Federation and Iran, have continued to purchase gas in more moderate volumes. Investment, mainly in hydrocarbons and various public sector projects, surged by 38% over 2011 levels, reflecting programs guided by the National Program of Socioeconomic Development (NPSED), 2011–2030, which aims to diversify and modernize the country's industrial base, develop rural areas, and raise living standards.

On the supply side, the government reported all sectors growing in 2012. Industry contributed more than half of all growth, with the hydrocarbon subsector, which provides 75% of industrial output and 40% of GDP, growing by an estimated 19%. Government investment projects and social programs boosted construction, while growth in services came mainly from wholesale and retail trade, transport, and communications. Agricultural growth came from higher crop and livestock production, reflecting government subsidies and lending programs and improvements to grain and cotton cultivation. Larger harvests of cotton (up by 12.6% over 2011) and wheat (up by 2.7%) helped reduce agricultural imports.

Liberalized prices for certain items put upward pressure on consumer prices. However, officially measured inflation was limited to 5.3% with the help of government subsidies for utilities; low prices for gasoline and public transportation; and price controls on major foodstuffs (Figure 3.7.2).

Fiscal policy aimed to support growth through public investment. The state budget, which excludes what are believed to be substantial extrabudgetary expenditures, recorded a large budget surplus equal to

3.7.1 GDP growth

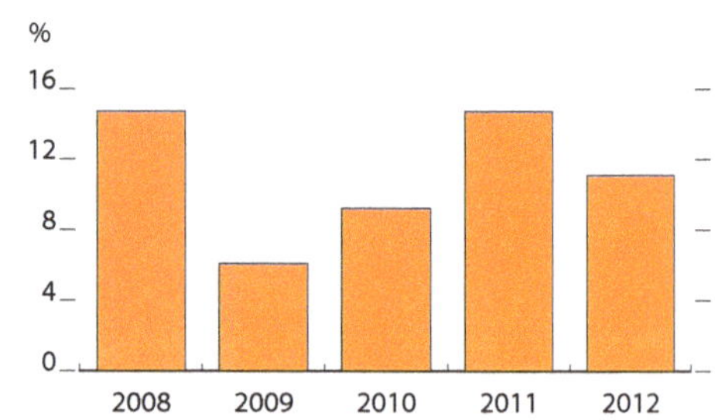

Sources: International Monetary Fund. 2012. *Regional Economic Outlook, Middle East and Central Asia.* November; ADB estimates.

Click here for figure data

3.7.2 Inflation

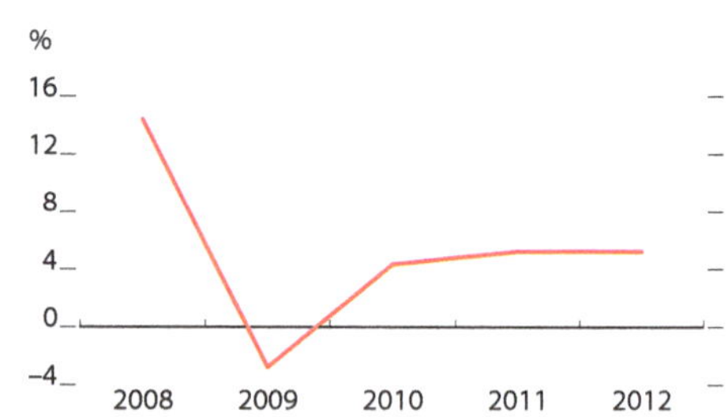

Sources: International Monetary Fund. 2012. *Regional Economic Outlook, Middle East and Central Asia.* November; ADB estimates.

Click here for figure data

This chapter was written by Jennet Hojanazarova of the Turkmenistan Resident Mission, ADB, Ashgabat.

6.0% of GDP, well above the surplus of 3.6% in 2011, as revenue grew much more quickly than expenditure (Figure 3.7.3). Rising hydrocarbon exports contributed to a 40% increase in revenue. Budget expenditure rose by 20.6% from 2011, reflecting greater spending for public investment projects, with socially oriented projects constituting over 70% of state budget allocations. As in previous years, the state budget surplus was transferred to a stabilization fund set up in 2008 to finance the country's development needs. The International Monetary Fund (IMF) estimated total public debt, all of it external, at 14.4% of GDP at the end of 2012.

Monetary policy remained broadly neutral in 2012, with the central bank's main instruments largely unchanged. Directed lending by the central bank slowed somewhat, as more liquidity from the stabilization fund became available through commercial banks and the recently established state development bank. Bank lending to state-owned enterprises—comprising 80% of total lending—rose by 32.6%, while lending to entities and individuals outside the public sector increased by 41.8%. The IMF estimates that broad money grew by 16.6% during 2012. Since the 2009 currency reform, the Turkman manat exchange rate has remained stable at TMM2.85 to $1. Rapid growth in reserves since 2011 has enabled the authorities to maintain this rate.

The current account surplus is believed to have slid from 2.0% of GDP in 2011 to 1.5% in 2012. Exports grew by 19.3%, according to government reports, reflecting higher exports of gas, crude oil, and oil products. However, export growth was offset by rising imports, reflecting growing demand for machinery and other equipment, and for foreign services in the hydrocarbon sector and construction. Turkmenistan received $12.6 billion in foreign direct investment during 2008–2011, including $3.2 billion in 2011, according to the United Nations Conference on Trade and Development, which listed Turkmenistan among the world's top 10 recipients of foreign direct investment (Figure 3.7.4). The Economist Intelligence Unit estimated that international reserves rose by 7% to $20.2 billion at the end of 2012.

Economic prospects

Growth is expected to slow somewhat, to 9% in 2013 and 8% in 2014. The drivers of growth will continue to be expansion in extractive industry and higher exports of gas and oil products. Rising earnings from hydrocarbon exports will support large public investments.

The government intends to expand hydrocarbon production (Box 3.7.1). The expansion is expected to stimulate output in power generation, oil refining, and chemicals, while the government's investment program should promote construction, transportation, and wholesale and retail trade. Government support for agriculture is expected to boost farm output and textile production, while support for private firms should promote agro-industrial processing.

Consumer price inflation is expected to rise to 6.0% in 2013 and 6.5% in 2014, despite price controls. The increases will reflect expanded public investment and rising consumption, both public and private, fueled by higher domestic credit, public sector salary increases of 10% and pension increases of 15% in 2013, and similar increases likely in 2014.

3.7.3 General government fiscal balance

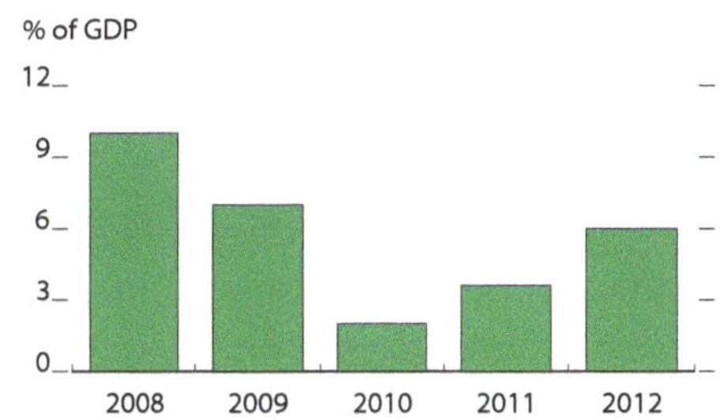

Sources: International Monetary Fund. 2012. *Regional Economic Outlook, Middle East and Central Asia.* November; ADB estimates.

Click here for figure data

3.7.4 Foreign direct investment

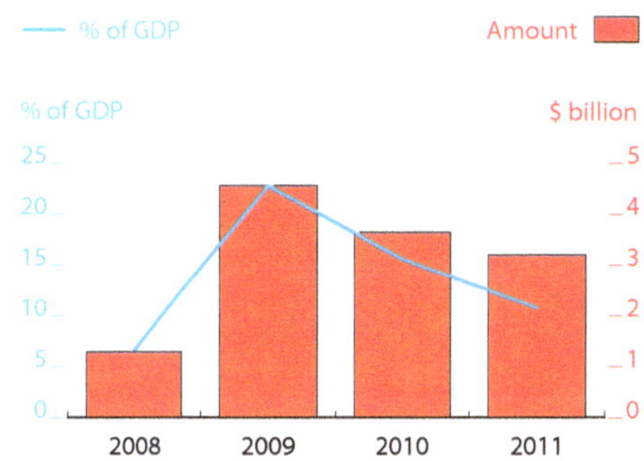

Source: UNCTAD. 2012. *World Investment Report.* Geneva.

Click here for figure data

3.7.5 Current account balance

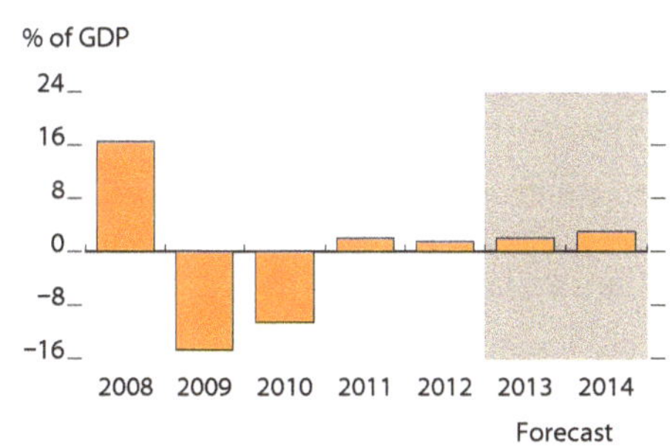

Sources: International Monetary Fund. 2012. *Regional Economic Outlook, Middle East and Central Asia.* November; ADB estimates.

Click here for figure data

Fiscal policy is expected to be more expansionary. The recently adopted budget for 2013 envisages a small deficit, with spending up by 29.8%, and revenues conservatively forecast to rise by only 18.7%. The IMF estimates that government gross debt will decline to 13.3% of GDP in 2013 and 11.9% in 2014.

The current account is expected to show surpluses of 2.0% of GDP in 2013 and 3.0% of GDP in 2014, based on anticipated growth in energy exports (Figure 3.7.5). With gross reserves expected to rise, Turkmenistan's external position should remain comfortable over the medium term.

3.7.1 Selected economic indicators (%)

	2013	2014
GDP growth	9.0	8.0
Inflation	6.0	6.5
Current account balance (share of GDP)	2.0	3.0

Source: ADB estimates.

Policy challenge—promoting diversification

The economy depends heavily on hydrocarbon exports, which provide more than 90% of exports. While the expansion of the energy sector is expected to substantially boost export earnings, energy price swings can create large fluctuations in export revenues, posing a risk to macroeconomic stability and financing for public investment. A stabilization fund created in 2008 has helped mitigate the adverse effects of external shocks. In the coming period of booming exports, the government will need to implement policies designed to contain inflation and avoid real exchange rate appreciation and excessive growth in the money supply, while promoting a more diversified economy.

The experience of the mid-1990s and 2008–2009, when sharp declines in demand for gas caused growth rates to plunge, has prompted efforts to reduce reliance on hydrocarbon exports. The NPSED highlights the need to diversify the economy beyond hydrocarbons and to add more value by shifting to high-technology and processed goods. The program aims to increase to 70% in 2020 the private sector's share of GDP not tied to hydrocarbons. Attaining this objective will require, however, many structural reforms and substantial investments in human capital and institutional capacity as well as clear supporting legislation.

Ensuring the efficient and rational spending of export revenues is also important. Much of the hydrocarbon wealth has accrued to the public sector through taxes and production-sharing mechanisms. Such inflows require highly developed institutional capacity to spend revenue wisely. The government aims to use the additional resources from hydrocarbon exports to spur growth, modernization, and economic diversification. Successful diversification will require that investments be prioritized and that support go to competitive industries that can thrive without continued subsidies in the future.

The authorities would do well to use the current favorable outlook and strong external position to deepen structural reforms and finance productive investment that promote diversification and encourage private sector development. They could support these measures by strengthening public financial management, developing the financial sector, and enhancing macroeconomic surveillance through further improvements in statistics and data collection.

3.7.1 Turkmenistan and global energy security

Turkmenistan is becoming an important energy hub. Its gas reserves are the second largest in the Commonwealth of Independent States and the fourth largest in the world, conservatively estimated by the petroleum transnational BP in 2011 at 24.3 trillion cubic meters (m^3), or 11.7% of the world total.

The Turkmen government has ambitious plans to develop the country's abundant oil and gas resources, and leading oil and gas companies have concluded long-term agreements. Targets set by the NPSED see gas production rising fourfold to 230 billion m^3 per year by 2030, 70% of it exported. Oil production is planned to rise sixfold to 66.6 million tons in the same period. During 2012–2016, annual average gas output is expected to rise to 90 billion m^3, 50% above current output.

The 7,000 kilometer pipeline across Uzbekistan and Kazakhstan to the PRC, built with PRC assistance in 2009, has annual capacity of 30 billion m^3, which will be expanded to 65 billion m^3 by 2020, raising Turkmen gas exports to a record high. According to government plans, the existing pipelines to the PRC, the Russian Federation, and Iran will be augmented with additional pipelines, including the Turkmenistan–Afghanistan–Pakistan–India natural gas pipeline and the Trans-Caspian gas pipeline across the Caspian Sea to Azerbaijan and on to Europe.

Uzbekistan

The economy grew by 8.2%, nearly as quickly as in 2011, driven by strong performance in all production sectors, continuing public investment, and high remittances and public sector wage increases, which boosted private consumption. Growth is forecast to slow only slightly in 2013 and 2014, while the current account remains in surplus. A more sophisticated and diversified industrial and export base is needed to sustain growth and expand employment over the longer term.

Economic performance

Despite weaker external demand, the economy again performed strongly. GDP grew by 8.2%, according to official data, driven by public investment and private consumption. The main supply-side contributors to growth were services, which grew by 10.4%, and industry including construction, which grew by 8.0% (Figure 3.8.1).

Industry growth was driven mainly by machinery, fuel, and light industry. Services played a larger economic role, due to strong performances by information and communication technology, finance, and trade and catering. Agriculture grew by 7%, primarily reflecting a larger cotton harvest and expanded livestock breeding.

On the demand side, private consumption rose by 6.0%, as a result of higher public sector wages and pensions, expanded remittances, and increased domestic lending. Gross fixed capital formation increased by 11.6%. (Data for total investment are not available, because there is no information on changes in stock inventories.) Public investment rose by 16.7%, improving on the 11.3% increase in 2011, as the government further expanded investment to support ongoing industrial modernization and infrastructure development. Most public investment was to overhaul key industrial sectors and construct new housing.

The government reported that inflation in 2012 remained within the official target of 7%. An alternative estimate by the International Monetary Fund is 12.9%. Inflationary pressures mainly reflected currency depreciation, wage and pension increases, and higher administrative prices for fuel, utilities, and bread, which were instituted toward achieving cost recovery. The central bank responded by tightening monetary policy, especially in the second half of the year, through sales of certificates of deposit on the open market, though the policy rate remained unchanged. An increase in net foreign assets was offset by accumulating government deposits, including in the Fund for Reconstruction and Development (FRD), a sovereign wealth fund. As a result, broad money growth slowed to 25.0% from 32.3% in 2011 (Figure 3.8.2).

3.8.1 Supply-side contributions to growth

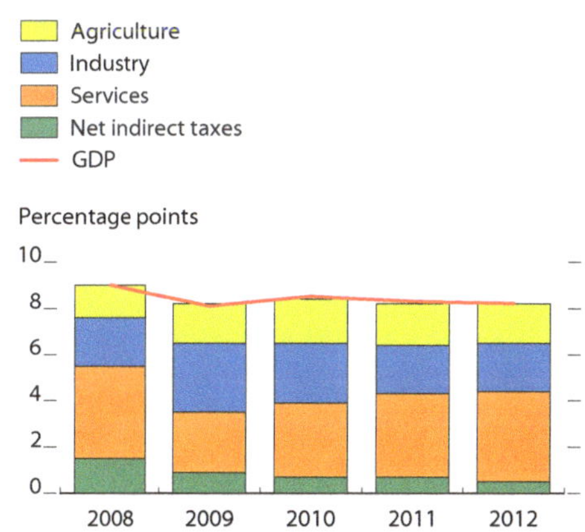

Sources: State Statistics Committee; Press service of the President; ADB estimates.

Click here for figure data

3.8.2 Inflation and broad money

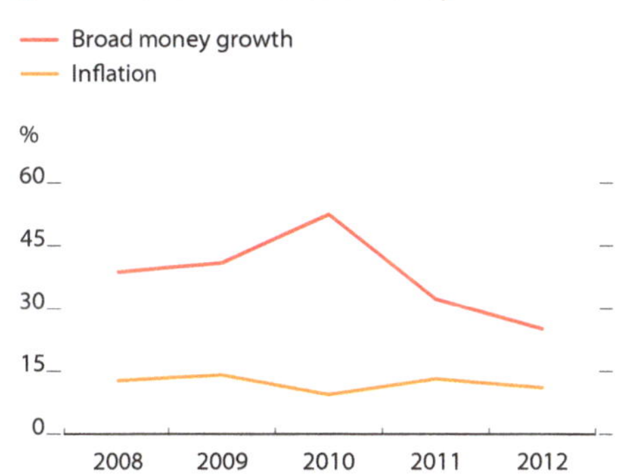

Sources: State Statistics Committee; International Monetary Fund; ADB estimates.

Click here for figure data

This chapter was written by Iskandar Gulamov of the Uzbekistan Resident Mission, ADB, Tashkent.

The central bank continued to intervene in the foreign exchange market with the aim of depreciating the local currency—the sum—to promote competitiveness. By year-end the sum had depreciated by almost 10% against the dollar.

Fiscal policy remained broadly unchanged in 2012. The consolidated budget, including large surpluses from the FRD, is again estimated to have recorded an overall surplus, equal to 3.1% of GDP. Revenue gains from historically high prices for key export commodities (mainly precious metals) and improved tax administration offset expenditures to cover wage and pension increases and higher social outlays. Revenues equaled 36.7% of GDP and expenditures 33.6% (Figure 3.8.3).

The current account surplus narrowed to an estimated 4.7% of GDP from 8.1% in 2011 as the trade surplus decreased (Figure 3.8.4).

Exports of goods and services declined by 5.1%, reflecting weaker external demand and declines in international prices for Uzbekistan's major export commodities: cotton, copper, and natural gas. Exports of cotton, foodstuffs, chemical, metals, and machinery all fell in 2012. However, an 81% rise in exports of energy products, primarily natural gas, limited the overall decline in exports.

Imports of goods and services rose by 9%, as continued state-led infrastructure development and industrial modernization required more imports of capital goods and services. Remittances and compensation from abroad, included in the income account, grew sharply, particularly from the Russian Federation, which totaled $5.6 billion. This was the highest amount since independence, reflecting strong demand for construction labor (Figure 3.8.5).

The government reported foreign investment inflows of $2.5 billion, mainly into oil and gas, petrochemicals, and automobile manufacturing. External debt is estimated to have increased modestly to 17.8% of GDP at the end of 2012 from 17.4% at the end of 2011, as the public investment program is increasingly being financed by foreign loans (Figure 3.8.6).

Economic prospects

GDP growth is forecast at 7.5% in 2013 and 8.0% in 2014, driven by state-led investment and domestic consumption. Industry and services will continue to be the main supply-side drivers of economic growth. Industrial output will be supported by higher domestic lending and foreign investment, while services will be driven by higher domestic demand, especially from the public sector. Agriculture is projected to post healthy growth, albeit less than the 8-year high observed in 2012.

Backed by a large FRD surplus, the government is expected to continue increasing public investment in infrastructure development, industrial modernization, and housing. The government investment program for 2013 envisages projects equal to 24.7% of GDP. Gross fixed capital formation is forecast to rise by 10% in 2013 and 11% in 2014.

The 2013 program will be implemented under the framework of the $47.3 billion Industrial Modernization and Infrastructure Development Program for 2011–2015, financed through a combination of external financing, domestic investment, and FRD resources. The program

3.8.3 Fiscal indicators and augmented budget

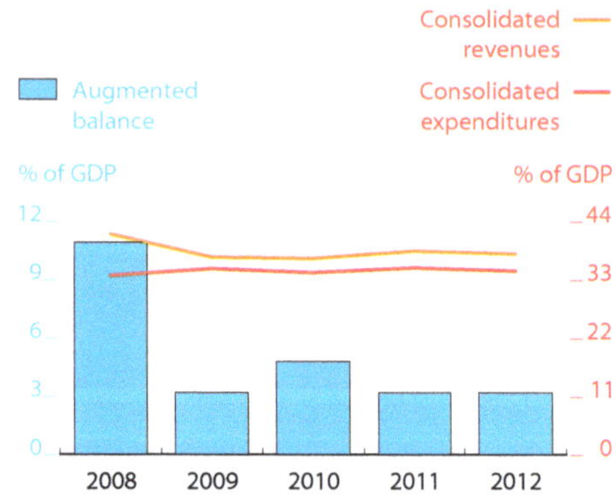

Note: Augmented budget includes the Fund for Reconstruction and Development.
Sources: International Monetary Fund; ADB estimates.
Click here for figure data

3.8.4 Current account components

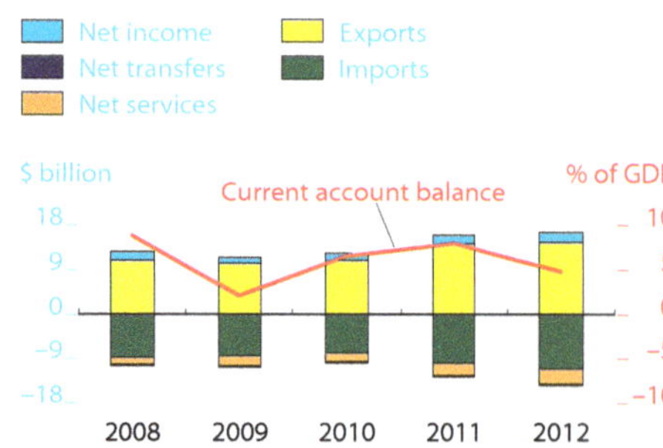

Sources: International Monetary Fund; ADB estimates.
Click here for figure data

3.8.5 Remittances and compensation from the Russian Federation

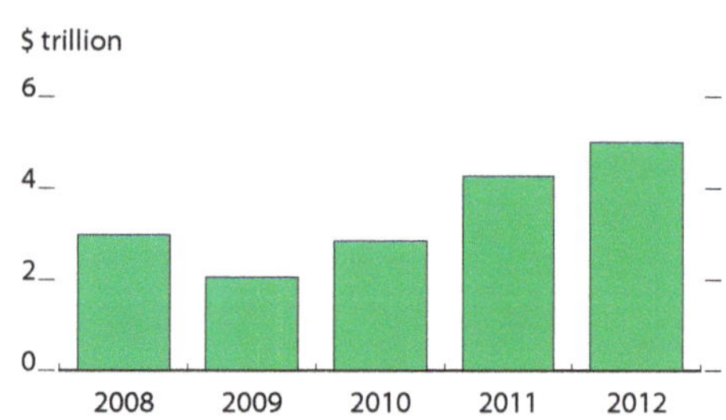

Sources: Central Bank of Russia; ADB estimates.
Click here for figure data

3.8.1 Selected economic indicators (%)

	2013	2014
GDP growth	7.5	8.0
Inflation	9.5	9.0
Current account balance (share of GDP)	4.3	3.2

Source: ADB estimates.

aims to add more value in manufacturing and raise exports of oil, gas, petrochemicals, and other chemicals. In addition to the ongoing $4.0 billion Surgill Natural Gas Chemicals Project, the program includes developing a $4.0 billion facility to liquefy natural gas in the Kashkadarya Region.

As in 2012, the government is expected to implement measures in 2013 and 2014 to augment consumption, most likely by raising public sector wages, welfare payments, and pensions. Private consumption is forecast to rise by 7.0% in 2013 and 8.0% in 2014, reflecting these developments, planned expansion of retail credit from banks, and the expectation of sustained remittances.

Inflation is forecast at 9.5% in 2013 and 9.0% in 2014. Anticipated declines in global food prices, lower import costs, the lagged effect of monetary tightening in 2012, and continued tight monetary policy are expected to slow inflation, despite planned wage and pension increases and further growth in net foreign assets.

Fiscal policy is expected to relax slightly in coming years, with the augmented budget surplus expected to decline to 2.9% of GDP in 2013 and 2.6% of GDP in 2014. Revenues from commodity exports will likely remain robust, albeit growing less rapidly than in 2011 and 2012. Revenues are forecast to equal 31.0% of GDP in 2013 and 30.2% in 2014. Supplementing these revenues will be FRD transfers projected at 5.5% of GDP in 2013 and 5.2% in 2014. On the expenditure side, the budget strongly emphasizes welfare and social development. Almost 60% of all expenditure is allocated to social security, welfare, health care, education, and culture. Augmented budget expenditure is forecast at 33.6% of GDP in 2013 and 32.9% in 2014.

Money supply growth is expected to remain at 25% in 2013 and 24% in 2014, as the government increases wages and pensions. Further build-up in the central bank's net foreign assets, at least to mid-2013, and continued foreign exchange intervention to depreciate the local currency will tend to raise foreign reserves. Nevertheless, the authorities are expected to keep monetary policy tight and continue the accumulation of government deposits and liquidity-mopping operations.

The current account surplus is forecast to shrink further, to 4.3% of GDP in 2013 and 3.2% of GDP in 2014, as the trade surplus dwindles (Figure 3.8.7).

Falling external demand and international prices for the country's main export commodities will adversely affect export performance. The key downside risks are economic slowdown in the European Union or the Russian Federation and, in the People's Republic of China, uncertain demand for imports. Weaker consumer demand in these countries would suppress trade and remittances. Merchandise exports should rise moderately, by 6.9% in 2013, before declining by 1.0% in 2014.

Merchandise imports are projected to rise gradually, by 9.1% in 2013 and 4.2% in 2014. Demand will come mostly from public infrastructure spending and the industrial modernization program. Lower global commodity prices will reduce import payments, as will greater import controls. Early in 2013 the government adopted a decree that effectively restricted imports by imposing additional procedures and controls on a number of consumer goods.

3.8.6 External debt and state investment program

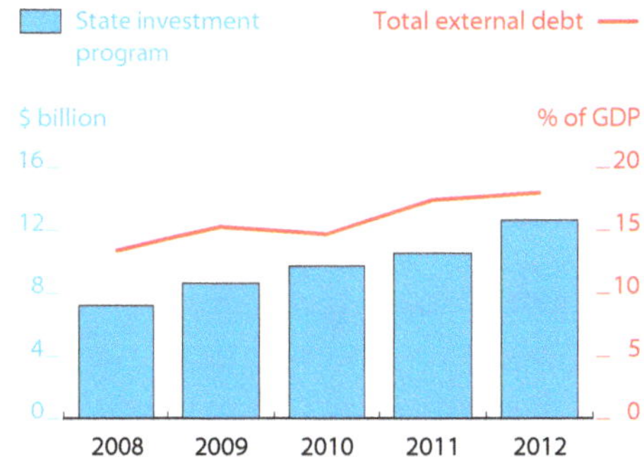

Sources: International Monetary Fund; ADB estimates.
Click here for figure data

3.8.7 Net exports and current account balance

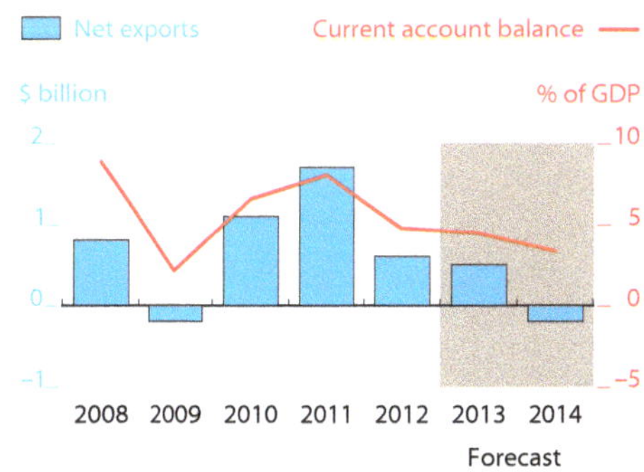

Sources: State Statistics Committee; International Monetary Fund; ADB estimates.
Click here for figure data

3.8.8 Export sophistication of Uzbekistan and selected Asian countries

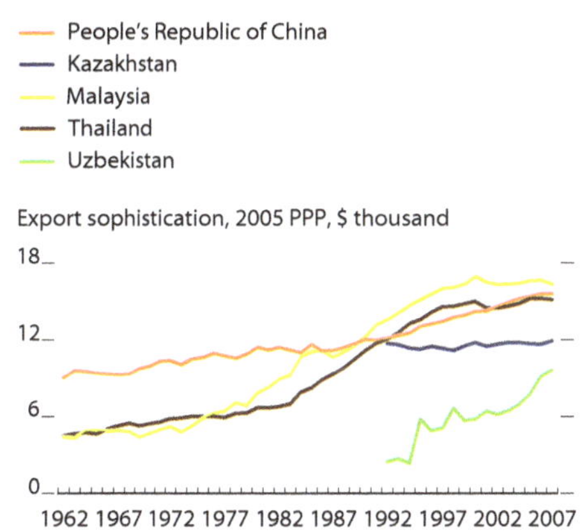

PPP = purchasing power parity.

Note: For details on this measure of productivity associated with a country's export basket, see R. Hausmann, J. Hwang, and D. Rodrik. 2005. What You Export Matters. http://www.nber.org/papers/w11905.pdf

Sources: United Nations. Comtrade database; Feenstra, R., R. Lipsey, H. Deng, A. Ma, and H. Mo. 2005. World Trade Flows: 1962–2000. *NBER Working Paper* No. 11040.
Click here for figure data

Reflecting higher foreign borrowing for industrial modernization and infrastructure development, external debt is forecast to reach 19.3% of GDP at the end of 2013 and 20.8% at the end of 2014—still modest by international standards.

Policy challenge—diversifying exports and liberalizing external trade

Although continued government investment in infrastructure and industrialization will promote growth, Uzbekistan needs to develop a more sophisticated and diversified industrial and export base to sustain growth and expand employment over the longer term. Moreover, infrastructure development and industrial modernization programs are themselves influenced in the long run by exports, as government investment is funded mainly by earnings from export industries, converted into FRD savings. Therefore, export diversity is crucial to the long-term sustainability of investment.

While export diversification has progressed, Uzbekistan's exports remain more concentrated and less sophisticated than those of other Asian countries. Figure 3.8.8 shows that, although the sophistication of Uzbekistan's export basket has improved notably, it remains far less sophisticated than that of middle-income Asian countries such as Malaysia and the People's Republic of China. The sophistication of Uzbekistan's exports also lags behind the norm for countries with similar per capita income (Figure 3.8.9).

Uzbekistan's export diversification is also very constricted (Figure 3.8.10), especially for sophisticated products in the core areas of metals, machineries, and chemicals. While the economy has expanded into somewhat more sophisticated products such as motor vehicles, they are still exported only to a few destinations, mostly to the Russian Federation. Uzbekistan therefore needs to expand its export markets for industrial products, as well as lift its product lines to those with higher value.

Policies and investments that improve the business environment, encourage private sector expansion, and strengthen infrastructure and logistics would promote a more diversified and sophisticated export sector. Uzbekistan is ranked last of 185 economies in the trading across borders category of the World Bank's *Doing Business 2013* report. Costs of exporting from and importing into the country average more than twice those of regional competitors. Liberalizing external trade through lower compliance costs, improved access to finance and foreign exchange, and simplified customs procedures would assist the private sector, which would in turn transform the economic landscape and promote growth. Structural reforms are especially important in view of continuing global uncertainty and the consequences for Uzbekistan's export prospects of advancing regional trade integration, as evidenced by the recent customs union involving the Russian Federation, Belarus, and Kazakhstan.

3.8.9 Export sophistication of countries with GDP per capita under $10,000

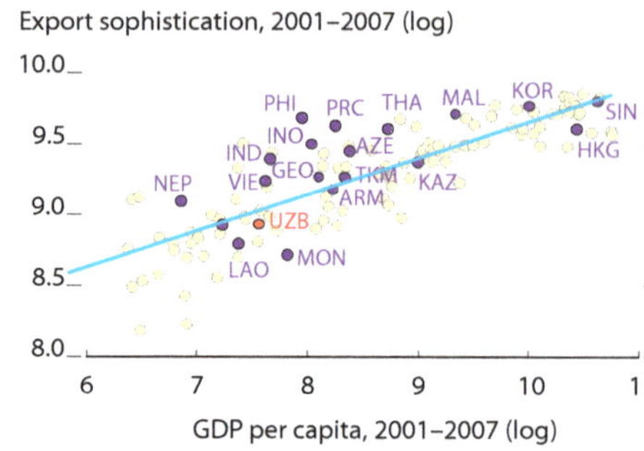

ARM = Armenia, AZE = Azerbaijan, GEO = Georgia, HKG = Hong Kong, China, IND = India, INO = Indonesia, KAZ = Kazakhstan, KOR = Republic of Korea, LAO = Lao People's Democratic Republic, MAL = Malaysia, MON = Mongolia, NEP = Nepal, PHI = Philippines, PRC = People's Republic of China, SIN = Singapore, TAJ = Tajikistan, THA = Thailand, TKM = Turkmenistan, UZB = Uzbekistan, VIE = Viet Nam.

Note: Countries with populations below 2 million were excluded.

Sources: United Nations. Comtrade database; Feenstra, R., R. Lipsey, H. Deng, A. Ma, and H. Mo. 2005. World Trade Flows: 1962–2000. *NBER Working Paper* No. 11040.

Click here for figure data

3.8.10 Export diversification and GDP per capita

a. Diversification of all industries, 2001–2007

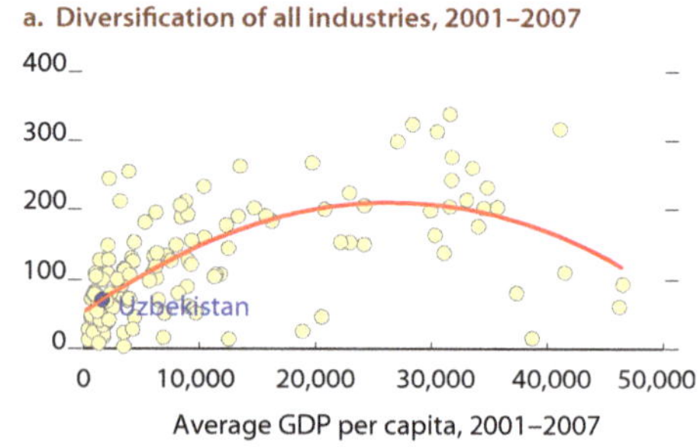

b. Diversification of core industries, 2001–2007

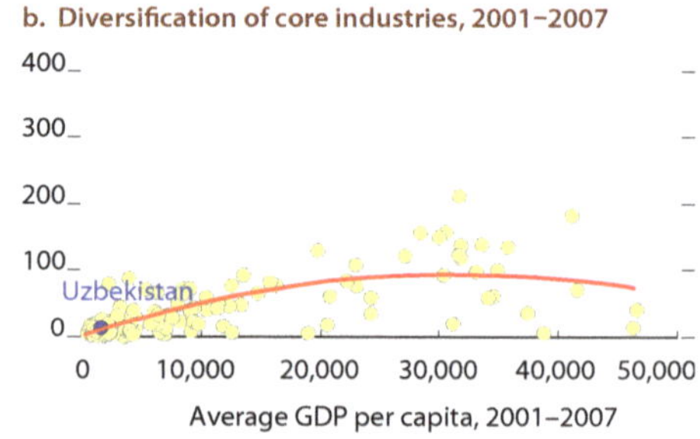

Note: Countries with populations below 2 million were excluded.

Sources: United Nations. Comtrade database; Feenstra, R., R. Lipsey, H. Deng, A. Ma, and H. Mo. 2005. World Trade Flows: 1962–2000. *NBER Working Paper* No. 11040.

Click here for figure data

East Asia

People's Republic of China
Hong Kong, China
Republic of Korea
Mongolia
Taipei,China

People's Republic of China

High growth and low inflation in 2012 are expected to continue in 2013. Growth slowed but continued to shine among large economies. Consumption outpaced investment to contribute the most to expansion. In line with the emphasis on domestic demand, the current account surplus continued to decline relative to GDP in a trend expected to continue in 2013 and 2014. The challenge is to implement ambitious reforms to restructure the economy toward domestic demand and inclusive growth.

Economic performance

Beset by a deteriorated external environment and a cooled real estate sector, economic growth in the People's Republic of China (PRC) slowed from 9.3% in 2011 to 7.8% in 2012, the lowest rate in the past 13 years but still higher than the government's target of 7.5%. Growth picked up late in 2012, boosted by stimulus measures adopted earlier in the year that included higher public spending, especially on infrastructure, and fiscal incentives. Economic activity—particularly manufacturing and other industry—started to rebound in September in a trend that has continued uninterrupted. Higher growth at 7.9% in the fourth quarter of 2012 ended deceleration that had persisted for 7 consecutive quarters. Higher salary and pension increases fueled real income growth—up by 9.5% in urban areas and by 10.7% in rural areas—lifting per capita income to $6,080 at the market exchange rate prevailing at the end of December.

Consumption expenditure growth slowed in 2012, reflecting lower economic dynamism, but nevertheless its contribution to growth surpassed that of investment (Figure 3.9.1). The slowdown in investment was due mainly to less-brisk growth of fixed asset investment, a major component of total investment (Figure 3.9.2), which in turn resulted from falling investment in real estate triggered by government restrictions on the purchase of investment property. A rebound in apartment sales since July 2012, driven by higher incomes and stable prices, suggests improved momentum in a key sector of the economy, which augurs well for higher growth in 2013.

Growth by economic sector varied from 8.1% in industry and services to 4.5% in agriculture. Growth in the industry sector—by far the largest component of GDP—declined by 2.2 percentage points year on year, contributing the most to GDP deceleration (Figure 3.9.3). Growth in services suffered less than industry, and growth in several high-end services including information, design, and creative industry outperformed traditional services, suggesting upward sophistication in the sector. Improved weather and government support to agro-services contributed to making agriculture the only sector in which growth accelerated.

3.9.1 Demand-side contributions to growth

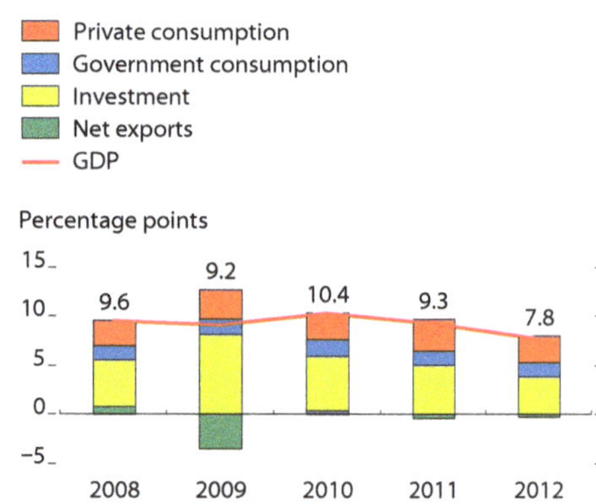

Sources: National Bureau of Statistics, People's Republic of China. http://www.stats.gov.cn/english/ (accessed 4 February 2013); ADB estimates.

Click here for figure data

3.9.2 Growth in fixed asset investment

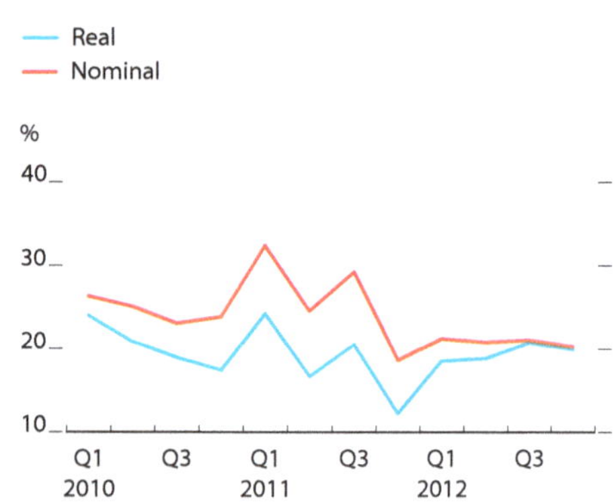

Source: ADB estimates based on data from CEIC Data Company (accessed 4 February 2013).

Click here for figure data

This chapter was written by Yolanda Fernandez Lommen, Niny Khor, and Jian Zhuang of the People's Republic of China Resident Mission, ADB, Beijing.

Measured by the consumer price index (CPI), inflation gradually slowed in 2012 from 4.5% year on year in January to 2.5% in December (Figure 3.9.4). For the year as a whole, CPI inflation declined to 2.6% from 5.4% in 2011. Improved supplies of food, mainly pork, and better weather contained the rise in food prices, the largest category in the CPI basket. The stabilization of housing prices also contributed to the moderating trend.

Fiscal policy supported growth through consumption subsidies and more favorable fiscal treatment of the service sector and small and medium-sized enterprises. In 2012 the consolidated fiscal deficit was modest at 1.6% of GDP, and bank borrowing to cover it raised total domestic public debt, including local government debt, to 54% of GDP.

Fiscal expenditure grew by 15.1% and revenue by 12.8%. A gradual shift in focus toward social expenditure was reflected in higher support to education, up by 28.3%. On the revenue side, corporate income tax collection increased by 17.2% in line with improved enterprise profitability, while individual income tax revenue declined by about 4% following the late 2011 raise in the income threshold at which individuals pay taxes.

With taxation at the forefront of the reform agenda, the government announced plans to expand property taxes piloted in Shanghai and Chongqing to other cities and gradually establish a nationwide property tax system to keep real estate from overheating and provide a steady income to local governments. Similarly, the trial replacement of the business tax with a value-added tax was extended to new provinces and municipalities. The program covers telecommunications, rail transportation, construction, and business services.

Monetary stance was accommodative in 2012. Lower inflation and declining growth prompted the central bank to cut both the 1-year benchmark interest rate and the reserve requirement ratio twice in 2012 (Figure 3.9.5). Nevertheless, money supply (M2) grew by 13.8%, in line with the government's target of 14.0%. Total social financing, a measure of liquidity outside M2, rose by 22.8% to CNY15.8 trillion at year-end, which is almost double the CNY8.2 trillion in new bank lending. The rise highlights the rapid development of such untraditional sources of liquidity as trust loans, bond issuances, entrusted loans, and bank acceptance bills, which do not fall easily under central bank control.

In 2012, the central bank began implementing a multiyear financial reform plan to liberalize exchange and interest rates, gradually open the capital account, and move from quantity-based to price-based tools of monetary policy. A deposit insurance scheme will complement plans to liberalize interest rates. Moreover, a special zone in Shenzhen will pioneer a direct cross-border yuan-denominated lending pilot with Hong Kong, China. Terms and interest rates will be set independently in line with efforts toward instituting greater interest rate flexibility and full convertibility. This measure—together with the doubling of the currency trading band to 1% in 2012, which introduced more flexibility in the country's exchange rate regime—will further boost the internationalization of the currency.

Reflecting the added flexibility, the renminbi appreciated in 2012 by an annual average of 2.4% against the US dollar and 10.6% against the euro.

3.9.3 Supply-side contributions to growth

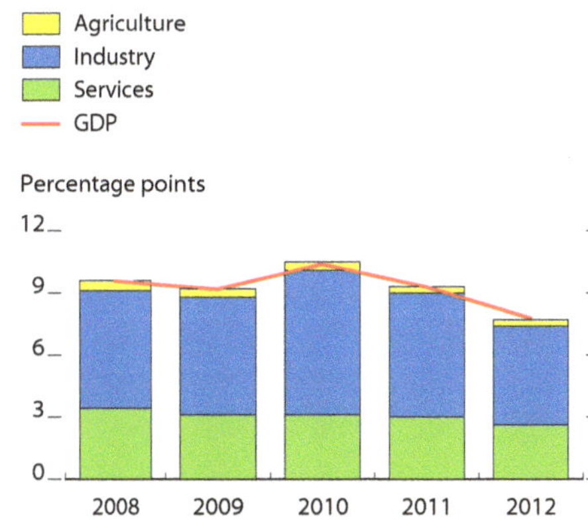

Sources: National Bureau of Statistics, People's Republic of China. http://www.stats.gov.cn/english/ (accessed 4 February 2013); ADB estimates.

Click here for figure data

3.9.4 Monthly inflation

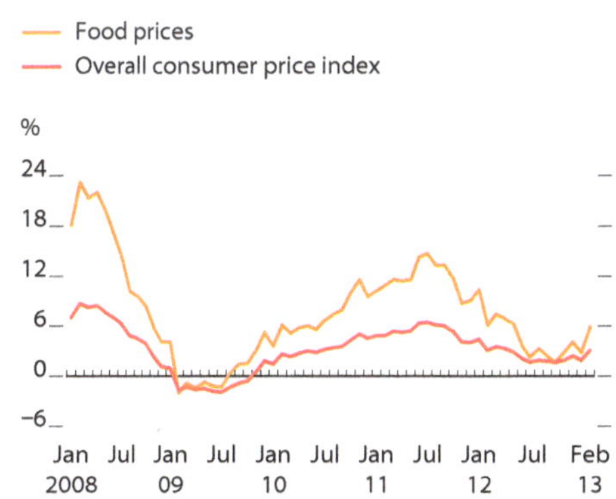

Source: CEIC Data Company (accessed 11 March 2013).

Click here for figure data

3.9.5 One-year benchmark lending rate and required reserves

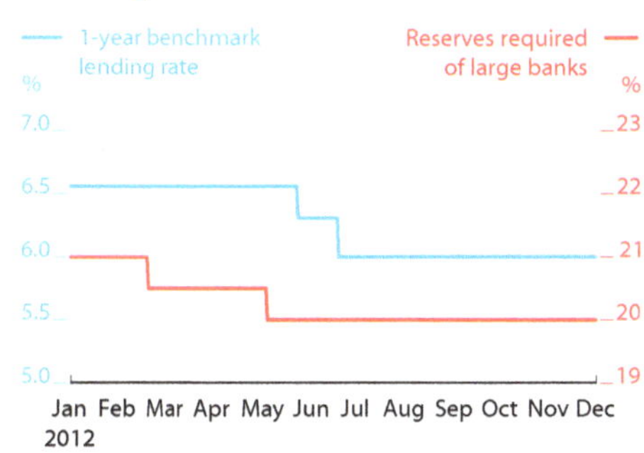

Source: CEIC Data Company (accessed 4 February 2013).

Click here for figure data

In real effective terms the currency appreciated by 5.9% in 2012 and by 9% since 2010, which may have implications for competitiveness (Box 3.9.1).

Trade flows grew more slowly in 2012, registering for the first time a slower increase than the government's target: 6.2% vis-à-vis 10.0%. Weaker demand from major trading partners depressed export growth to 7.9% based on customs data, down from 20.3% in 2011 (Figure 3.9.6). Exports nevertheless performed better than imports—which grew by only 4.4%, compared with 24.9% in 2011—widening the trade surplus to $233 billion from $158 billion in 2011, or below 3% of GDP. The services account remained in deficit as payments for tourism, transportation, and insurance exceeded receipts. These developments shrank the current account surplus to 2.6% of GDP in 2012 from 2.8% in 2011 (Figure 3.9.7).

Owing to the attractiveness of the Chinese market, foreign direct investment inflows were less affected than trade by the unfavorable external environment, declining by only 3.7% from a year earlier and reaching $112 billion. Gross foreign exchange reserves grew by 3.1% to $3.3 trillion in 2012.

3.9.6 Trade indicators, year-on-year growth

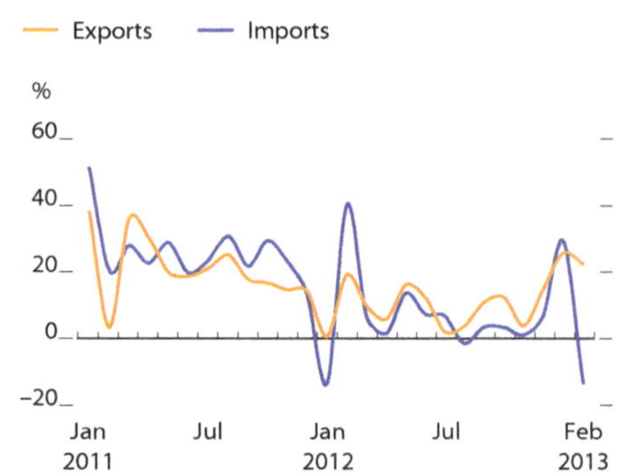

Source: CEIC Data Company (accessed 11 March 2013).
Click here for figure data

Economic prospects

The baseline outlook assumes that the US economy will continue its slow recovery, the euro area will avoid a worsening of the current crisis, and increased public spending in the PRC will improve living standards and boost consumption. Against this backdrop, and following the rebound in economic activity since September 2012, growth is expected to continue picking up in the first half of 2013 and stabilize for the remainder of the year, as the impact of stimulus implemented in mid-2012 fades.

Looking ahead, fixed asset investment will continue to drive growth, boosted by efforts to accelerate large infrastructure projects earmarked in the Twelfth Five-Year Plan, 2011–2015. Rising wages and pensions will support private consumption growth. The expected slow recovery of external demand suggests the contribution of net exports to growth will remain marginally negative in 2013 but turn modestly positive in 2014 as global trade picks up.

Export growth is projected at 10% in 2013, and import growth will reach 9% as domestic demand strengthens, commodity prices rebound, and the national currency continues to appreciate. The trade surplus will nevertheless be slimmer, narrowing the current account surplus to 2.5% of GDP in 2013 and 2.1% in 2014.

The accompanying policy stance will likely be supportive. Fiscal policy is expected to be more expansionary, with the overall fiscal deficit projected to widen to 2.2% of GDP in 2013 from 1.6% in 2012. The bias toward social expenditure will continue in accordance with government intentions to narrow the income gap and improve living standards through tax reform. Monetary policy will remain accommodative with broad money supply set to grow by 13% in 2013.

Under these assumptions, GDP growth is forecast at 8.2% in 2013. Greater efforts to comply with more stringent environmental targets, coupled with reforms to make growth more inclusive, will push growth down slightly to 8% in 2014 (Figure 3.9.8). Stable commodity prices will contain inflationary pressures in 2013, leaving the CPI up 3.2% on average,

3.9.7 Current account balance

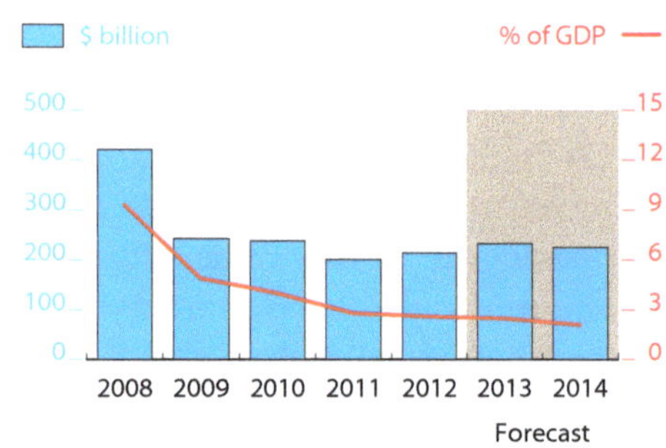

Sources: CEIC Data Company (accessed 4 February 2013); ADB estimates.
Click here for figure data

3.9.8 GDP growth

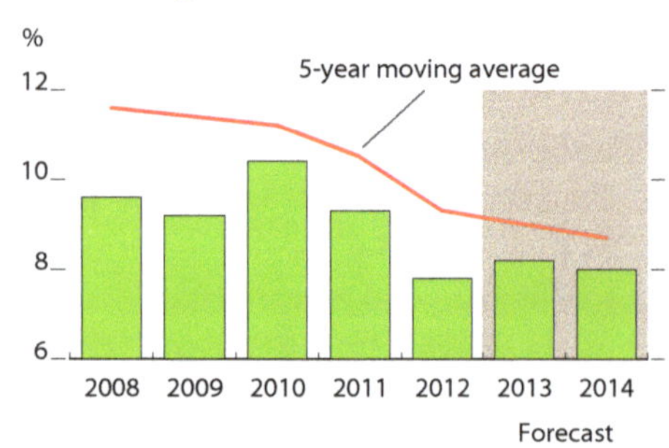

Sources: National Bureau of Statistics, People's Republic of China. http://www.stats.gov.cn/english/ (accessed 4 February 2013); ADB estimates.
Click here for figure data

slightly below the government target of 3.5%. However, higher labor costs and likely rises in food prices can be expected to drive the CPI up to 3.5% in 2014 (Figure 3.9.9).

The outlook is subject to several downside risks. First, in 2013 the economy will remain vulnerable to the sluggish global recovery, which could exacerbate weakness in external demand and hamper exports and employment. The main risk stems from the fragile economic outlook in the European Union, the PRC's largest trading partner and the only major market to which PRC exports shrank in 2012 (Figure 3.9.10).

Second, weather-induced food-price volatility, higher labor costs arising from tight market conditions, and planned measures to liberalize administered prices for utilities may generate inflationary pressures, albeit within government targets.

Third, local governments are under growing pressure to embark on large infrastructure projects to foster growth and employment. The trend may intensify as there is a historic pattern of investment growth accelerating during the second and third years of 5-year plans. This pattern, if repeated now, could rapidly expand local government indebtedness. Moreover, over half of the debt contracted by local government through investment platforms under the fiscal stimulus in 2009–2010 will mature in 2013. These factors could undermine debt sustainability for local governments and saddle banks with more nonperforming loans. However, systemic risk is unlikely to emerge in the banking sector. Not only is the current volume of nonperforming loans manageable at 1% (Figure 3.9.11), but overall loan-to-deposit and capital-adequacy ratios are within regulatory requirements. Further, effective banking supervision and more stringent regulations on untraditional lending channels are expected to be implemented as needed.

Fourth, the rapid aging of the population is taking its toll on the labor market, causing the size of the working-age population to decline in 2012 for the first time. Diminishing labor supply could create pressure to raise wages. Unless compensated by labor productivity growth, higher wages would erode the economy's competitiveness and growth potential, hampering government development plans.

These downside risks make 2013 a challenging year of transition for the new leadership. The new leaders have indicated their intention to focus on quality, efficiency, and the sustainability of economic growth, replacing the previous pursuit of fast-track growth. This welcome approach will help to rebalance over time the PRC's sources of growth in favor of domestic demand and shrink the income gap. However, in implementing its program, the new government will be challenged by the risks enumerated above and by the complexity of the reforms needed for the PRC to successfully raise incomes, as highlighted in the next section.

3.9.9 Inflation

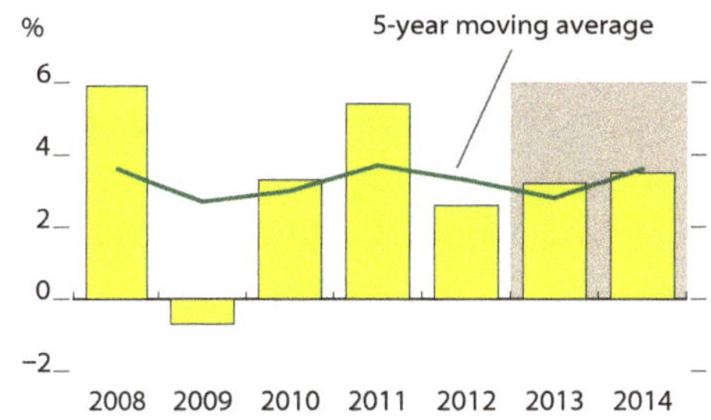

Sources: National Bureau of Statistics, People's Republic of China. http://www.stats.gov.cn/english/ (accessed 4 February 2013); ADB estimates.

Click here for figure data

3.9.10 Growth in exports by destination, 2012

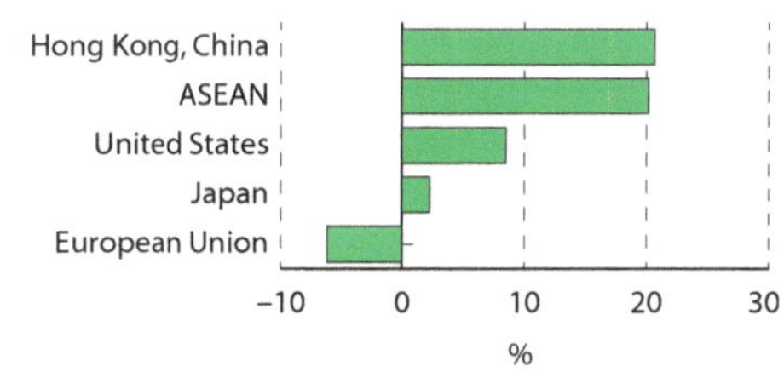

ASEAN = Association of Southeast Asian Nations.

Source: CEIC Data Company (accessed 14 March 2013).

Click here for figure data

3.9.1 Selected economic indicators (%)

	2013	2014
GDP growth	8.2	8.0
Inflation	3.2	3.5
Current account balance (share of GDP)	2.5	2.1

Source: ADB estimates.

Policy challenge—fiscal reform for inclusive growth

The greatest challenge arising from the new leaders' reform agenda is stepping up efforts to restructure the economy toward domestic demand and making growth more inclusive. Against this background, the new leadership has announced a reform plan with three pillars: financial market reform to liberalize interest rates and accelerate bond market developments, fiscal reform to support economic restructuring and narrow the income gap, and deregulation to support greater private sector participation in the economy. Among the three, the fiscal component stands as the most crucial and challenging reform to be addressed in the coming years.

In its transition toward a market-oriented economy, the PRC introduced only limited taxation, and central government transfers for education, health, housing, and pensions declined. A wide income gap and low consumption resulted, constraining the enormous potential of domestic demand as an engine of growth. In recent years, the government has adopted a range of measures to reverse the trend. In particular, social spending has increased. Even so, it remains low, with government expenditure on education and health care amounting to only 5.5% of GDP (Figure 3.9.12), less than half of the average of 12.5% allocated by countries in the Organisation for Economic Co-operation and Development. Moreover, reforms have focused on expanding benefit coverage rather than revamping the benefits themselves.

Recent income tax changes have reduced the number of individual tax payers to less than 3% of the population and their payments to 6% of fiscal revenue. The narrow base leaves policy makers with no powerful tool with which to improve income distribution. The direct income tax base can be broadened by shifting the informal sector into the formal economy, strengthening tax administration, and curtailing tax evasion.

The regressive bias of the taxation system needs to be corrected. It would be more equitable to move away from the current emphasis on indirect taxation, which is highly regressive, toward a progressive tax system that shifts the tax burden from low-income households to high earners. Taxing capital gains and property would also help to improve income distribution. Property tax is a potentially significant source of stable tax revenue for local governments, allowing them to mitigate their heavy reliance on revenue from land sales and improve their provision of basic social services.

A shift in public spending away from investment and toward social transfers would allow people to save less against an uncertain future and consume more now. Similarly, higher provisions for education and pensions would reduce life-cycle savings and free up household resources for consumption. Improving tax collection, further liberalizing energy and resource prices, introducing environmental taxes, and channeling state-owned enterprises' dividends into social expenditure would allow higher spending without straining public finances.

Also needed are reforms to make central government transfers to poorer provinces larger and more effective toward achieving more equitable delivery of local public services. Although transfer payments from the central government have increased, the capacity of local governments to provide public services has not improved in tandem, and fiscal and institutional capacity disparities remain large in governments at the sub-provincial level. In this context, revenue and expenditure responsibilities need to be better shared between the central and local governments.

To ensure fiscal sustainability and efficiency, the PRC should further strengthen fiscal management by consolidating central and

3.9.11 Nonperforming loans, commercial banks

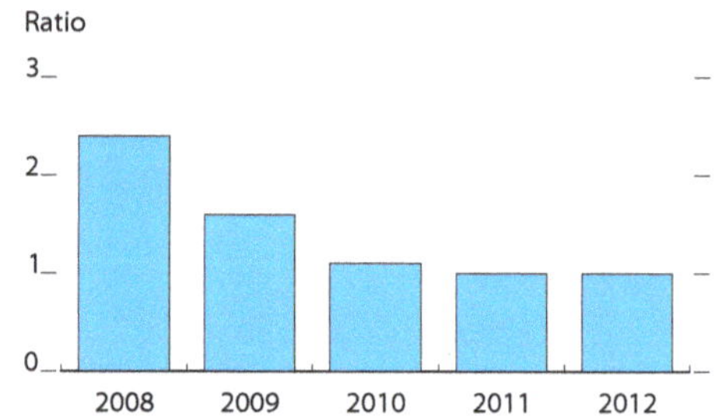

Source: CEIC Data Company (accessed 14 March 2013).

Click here for figure data

3.9.12 Government spending on health and education

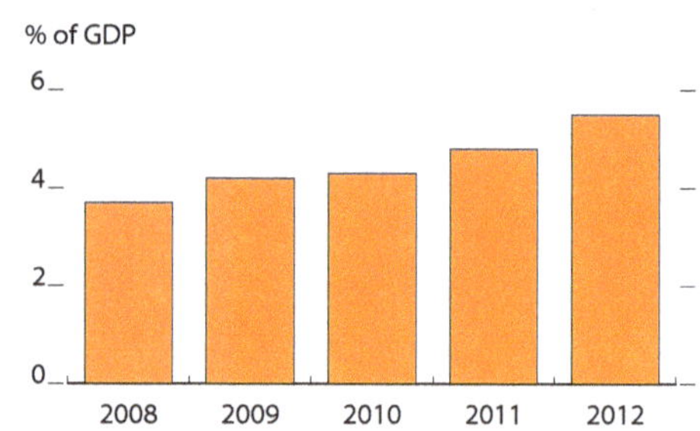

Sources: CEIC Data Company (accessed 14 March 2013); ADB estimates.

Click here for figure data

local government budgets, the social security budget, and income and expenditure associated with state-owned assets. It should adopt multiyear budgeting to better align longer-term expenditure needs with development goals.

Finally, to highlight the importance of the environmental challenge, the PRC should accelerate its introduction of green taxes. The PRC's rapid development has come at significant environmental cost. Notwithstanding the authorities' commendable efforts already undertaken to combat climate change, additional actions are required to improve energy efficiency and the management of water and land.

3.9.1 Wages and competitiveness in the People's Republic of China

In recent years the spotlight in the PRC has been on employment generation and economic competitiveness in light of concerns over the rapid increase in unit labor costs, stemming partly from dramatic increases in minimum wages. A major structural transformation of the labor market has amplified wage gains, causing them to outstrip labor productivity growth. Higher labor costs challenge the PRC's competitiveness and the ability of its economy to generate adequate jobs.

Structural changes in the PRC's labor market have occurred at a speed unprecedented in history. As recently as 1990, more than 80% of urban workers were still employed by state-owned enterprises and other collectives. Today, the private sector is the main provider and creator of jobs in urban areas, such that state-owned and collective units accounted for only 45% of all urban jobs in 2010. In rural areas, the changes are no less striking. Most rural employment is no longer agricultural, and legions of rural workers have migrated to urban areas.

During this period of structural transformation, labor productivity in the PRC has been growing more quickly than in the rest of the world, but it nevertheless remains low. In the most recent years for which data are available, annual labor productivity in the PRC was $3,700 per worker in 2005 dollars adjusted for purchasing power parity, far below the Republic of Korea's $27,800 and Singapore's $51,200.

At the same time, even after adjusting for inflation, average real wages for urban workers more than tripled in a decade. Minimum wages grew even more quickly than average wages, increasing by an average of 17% across the country in 2011 alone. In addition, nonwage costs such as for hiring and firing have increased with the introduction in 2008 of the Labor Contract Law. The impetus for higher wages has also come from the shrinking labor pool. In 2012, the working-age population aged 15–59 years old contracted by 3.5 million. In coastal areas, the decline is even more pronounced, as the inflow of migrant workers diminishes with rising standards of living and higher expectations among potential migrants in areas away from the coast. This trend is exacerbated by limitations long imposed on workers' mobility through household registration (*hukou*) restrictions.

There are signs that these developments and the appreciation of the real exchange rate have eroded the competitiveness of the economy. Low-cost and labor-intensive manufacturers have been relocating to cheaper locales, helping Southeast Asia in particular realize a sharply increased share of global investment. Moreover, the most recent ranking of global competitiveness reported by the World Economic Forum in September 2012 saw the PRC's ranking slip for the first time in 7 years, from 26th to 29th. According to the report, the PRC has become globally less competitive with respect to the goods market, firm-level technological readiness, the availability of on-the-job training services, flexibility in wage determination, hiring and firing practices, and redundancy costs. Improved competitiveness in these areas is essential to sustaining growth in the future.

Looking ahead, a number of measures are needed to keep competitiveness from eroding further. First, the authorities should ensure that increases in the minimum wage do not outpace productivity growth or, to avoid hindering job creation, the absorptive capacity of the labor market. Second, the public goal of reducing the income gap should entail transfers to low-income households. Third, productivity growth should be fostered through on-the-job training initiatives and by government incentives for firms to invest in new technologies. Finally, to improve market flexibility and job matching, steps are needed to reduce migration and transaction costs in the labor market. Key to reducing labor rigidity is reforming the *hukou* system, coupled with school subsidies in areas that are the main sources of migrant workers to reduce dropout rates as unskilled wages rise. These steps matter most in rural and less-developed areas, where improvements in human capital are indispensable to future growth.

Source: ADB. 2013. *Wages and Competitiveness in the People's Republic of China.* Observations and Suggestions No. 2013-2. Beijing.

Hong Kong, China

Fragility in the global economy dampened trade, but resilient domestic demand ensured modest growth. A rebound is expected in the next 2 years as the global economy gains momentum and trade picks up. Inflation will remain at around 4%, fuelled by rising property prices, and the current account surplus will widen. A liquidity glut and low interest rates entail the risk of asset price bubbles. Ample fiscal reserves provide flexibility to implement corrective measures against shocks.

Economic performance

Growth in Hong Kong, China was slow in the beginning of 2012. Global trade weakened as the fragile international economy failed to pick up because of the unresolved financial crisis in the euro area, lingering fiscal uncertainties in the US, and moderating growth in the People's Republic of China (PRC), strongly affecting this small, open economy. Encouraging developments in the fourth quarter, however, helped to push economic performance for the full year to modest 1.4% growth.

Domestic demand was the main engine of growth, with private consumption continuing to make the largest contribution, albeit substantially less than a year earlier (Figure 3.10.1). Consumer sentiment was cautious, despite low unemployment at 3.3% and increasing wealth with rising asset prices and real income, as measured by changes in the payroll index. The contribution of government consumption to growth improved but remained small.

Stronger investment in 2012 also contributed to growth, as construction and the private acquisition of machinery and equipment expanded. Net exports declined.

On the supply side, manufacturing contracted, but growth was spurred by the service sector, which provided more than 90% of GDP and accelerated by 2% in 2012, down from 5.2% a year earlier. Growth in the sector was driven by real estate and business services, public administration, social and personal services, and information and communication services (Figure 3.10.2). The other components of the sector posted more subdued growth. Retail sales grew more slowly than in 2011, despite the steady stream of visitor arrivals. The number of tourist arrivals grew by 16%, about the same as in 2011.

Exports and imports both contracted in the early part of the year but recovered somewhat in the second half. Much of the city's merchandise exports are re-exports, which moved in tandem with slower global trade, resulting in a larger increase in imports than in exports. Net service exports lost some of the dynamism of previous years, growing at 40%

3.10.1 Demand-side contributions to growth

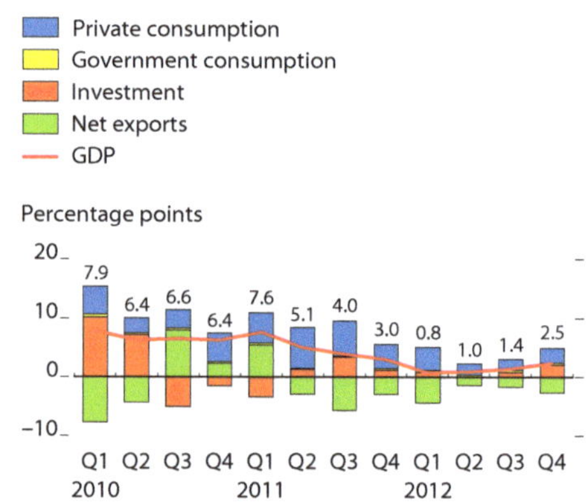

Source: Census and Statistics Department. http://www.censtatd.gov.hk/ (accessed 25 March 2013).
Click here for figure data

3.10.2 Components of the service sector

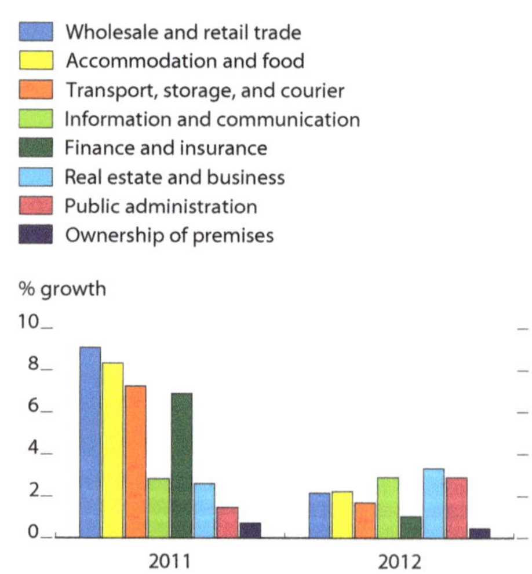

Source: Census and Statistics Department. http://www.censtatd.gov.hk/ (accessed 25 March 2013).
Click here for figure data

This chapter was written by Arief Ramayandi and Aleli Rosario of the Economics and Research Department, ADB, Manila.

compared with 192% in 2010 and 62% in 2011 and barely managing to overcome the deficit in merchandise trade.

Reflecting these developments, the current account recorded a small surplus of 1.1% of GDP in 2012, down from 4.8% in 2011 (Figure 3.10.3). The overall balance of payments was still in surplus, and foreign reserves amounted to $317.3 billion, equivalent to over 7.5 months of imports.

Inflation moderated but remained elevated as property prices rose on low interest rates. Moderated food prices, electricity subsidies, and 2 months of free rent for public housing tenants contained the price rise to 4.1% in 2012, down from 5.3% in 2011 (Figure 3.10.4).

The budget for FY2012 (ended 31 March 2013) is estimated to have recorded a surplus of 3.2% of GDP (Figure 3.10.5). Although only a meager 2.9% higher than in FY2011, estimated revenues far exceed the budgeted amount. Expenditures grew by 3.9% but also fell short of the budgeted amount by HK$13.1 billion because of lower social spending. Larger-than-budgeted surpluses in the past few years have led to the accumulation of fiscal reserves equal to 23 months of average government expenditure. The ample size of the reserves has prompted calls for the government to spend more on social welfare programs.

With the exchange rate pegged to the US dollar under the currency board, interest rates in Hong Kong, China track the policies of the US Federal Reserve. Accommodative monetary policy in the US meant low interest rates and ample liquidity, with broad money expanding by 11.1%. Bank credit grew by 9.6% as banks' exposure to the property sector rose to around 30% of loans outstanding. Low interest rates fueled demand for real estate and a 26% surge in residential property prices. Amid concerns regarding the risk to the banking sector posed by overheating in the property market, the Hong Kong Monetary Authority required banks to tighten underwriting criteria for mortgage loans on borrowers who already own at least one property.

The Hong Kong dollar real effective exchange rate rose at a moderate pace compared with Asian counterparts, preserving export competitiveness (Figure 3.10.6). The expansion of transactions denominated in PRC renminbi continued in 2012, with renminbi deposits amounting to 9.1% of the all deposits in the banking system. The number of banks engaged in the renminbi business is growing, and their services are broadening.

Economic prospects

Growth in the forecast period is expected to fall short of the 5-year average prior to the global financial crisis but will accelerate to 3.5% in 2013 and 3.8% in 2014, benefiting from expanded trade, robust domestic demand, and increased government support for industry and lower-income groups (Figure 3.10.7). Higher anticipated growth in the PRC will benefit Hong Kong, China in particular through increased trade and expanded renminbi business and payments.

Private consumption will grow with rising wages reflecting a tight labor market and an increase in the minimum wage to HK$30/hour from HK$28/hour on 1 May 2013 (Figure 3.10.8). The wealth effect from rising property prices is also expected to buoy consumer spending. Investment

3.10.3 Current account indicators

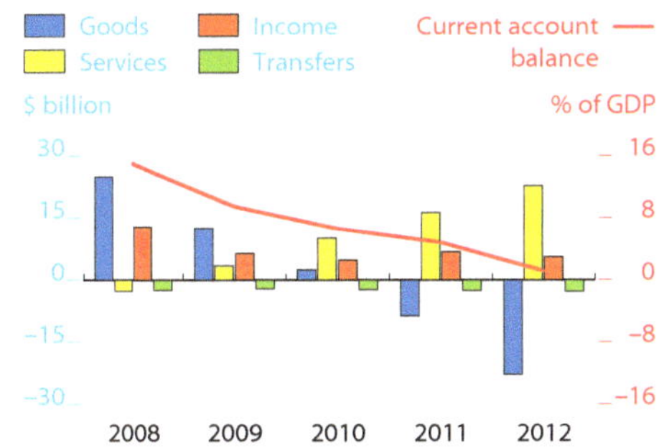

Source: CEIC Data Company (accessed 25 March 2013).

Click here for figure data

3.10.4 Sources of inflation

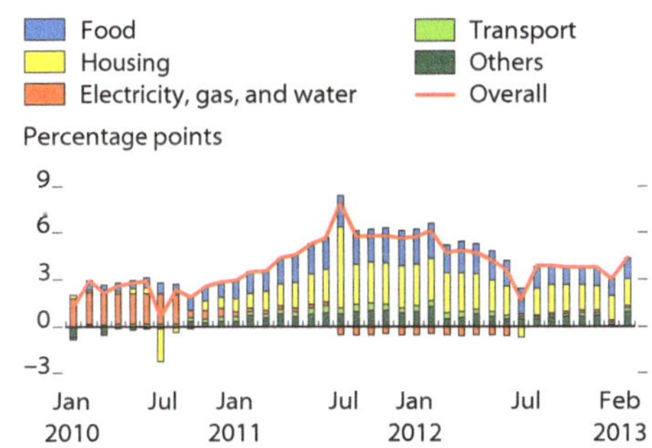

Source: CEIC Data Company (accessed 25 March 2013).

Click here for figure data

3.10.5 Government budget

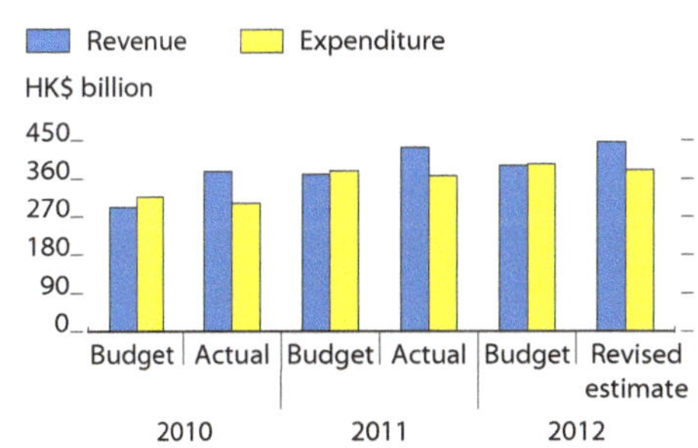

Sources: Hong Kong Monetary Authority; Government of the Hong Kong Special Administrative Region of the PRC. Various budgets. http://www.budget.gov.hk/

Click here for figure data

3.10.6 Real effective exchange rates, selected economies

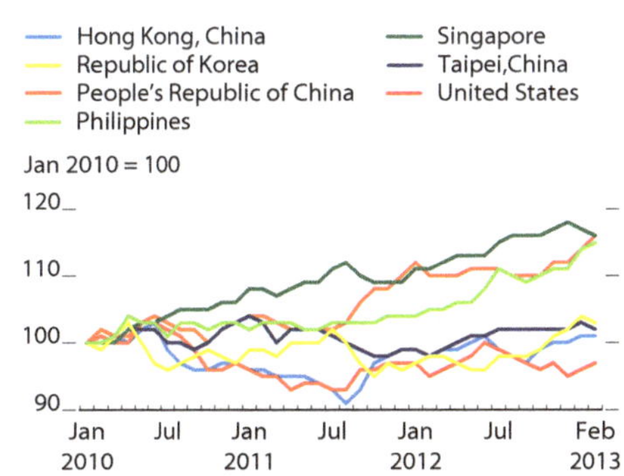

Source: Bank for International Settlements, http://www.bis.org/statistics/eer/index.htm (accessed 17 March 2013).

Click here for figure data

should continue to grow as public construction intensifies further and private construction picks up.

The four industry pillars—financial services, business and professional services, tourism, and trading and logistics—are expected to pick up during the year with support from the government. The proposed doubling of the government bond program from $100 billion to $200 billion and the lowering of profits tax on the offshore business of insurance companies will benefit the financial sector. Other sectors will gain from plans to attract large international events and meetings, develop Hong Kong's logistics services, provide additional funding for universities to facilitate technology transfer and innovation, and enhance special concessions for small and medium-sized enterprises.

With the expansion of external trade, exports are expected to grow more quickly, but the trade deficit will remain. Services receipts should pick up, supported by vibrant tourism and a recovery in transport services. The current account surplus is expected to widen to 4% of GDP in 2013 and 5% in 2014.

Inflation is unlikely to moderate substantially during the forecast period. It is expected to fall marginally to 3.9% in 2013 from 4.1% in 2012 as international food prices ease (Figure 3.10.9). However, expected wage increases could rekindle inflationary pressure, as could likely food price increases in the PRC, from which Hong Kong, China imports much of its food. Echoing the policies of the US Federal Reserve, low interest rates can be expected to prevail in the next 2 years, pushing up property and other asset prices and requiring tighter macroprudential measures to curb speculative demand and tame inflation to 4.3% in 2014.

Fiscal policy in FY2013 and FY2014 will be geared toward stimulating economic growth and supporting the development of established and emerging industries, while maintaining a prudent fiscal stance. A small deficit of 0.2% of GDP is projected for this fiscal year. Despite repeated revenue outcomes above budget in previous years, revenues for FY2013 are conservatively projected at HK$435 billion, lower than the revised estimate in FY2012. Expenditures are to increase to HK$440 billion on both higher capital outlays and increased current expenditure.

The growth scenario will be threatened if the PRC or US economy weakens or the euro area financial crisis deepens. Less likely but possible, a sudden reversal of the interest rate trend could derail growth prospects and adversely affect the health of banks. The availability of ample fiscal reserves provides the government with flexibility to implement corrective measures if any of these risks materialize.

Policy challenge—providing adequate and affordable housing

The rise of property prices has been a major concern in Hong Kong, China. Supply shortages and high and growing demand combine to stir up a vibrant property market. The low interest rate environment and improved income prospects have contributed to a widening demand-supply imbalance. Appetite for investment in housing units in all segments of the market continues to grow in response to abundant

3.10.1 Selected economic indicators (%)

	2013	2014
GDP growth	3.5	3.8
Inflation	3.9	4.3
Current account balance (share of GDP)	4.0	5.0

Source: ADB estimates.

3.10.7 GDP growth

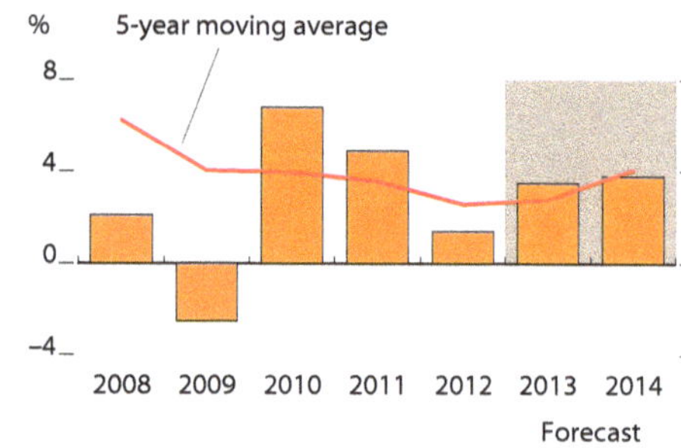

Source: *Asian Development Outlook* database.

Click here for figure data

3.10.8 Unemployment and earnings

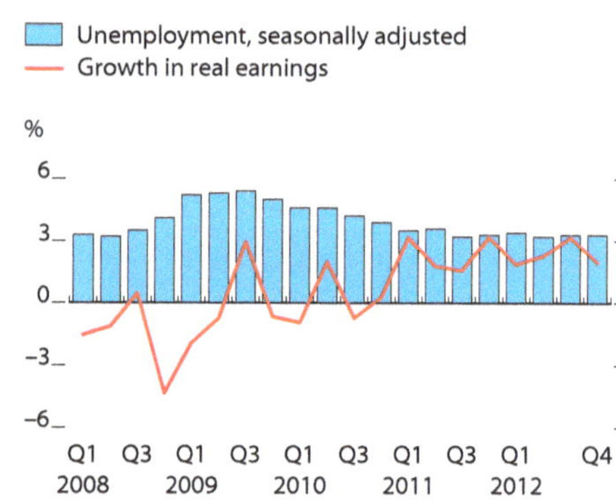

Source: Census and Statistics Department. http://www.censtatd.gov.hk (accessed 27 March 2013).

Click here for figure data

3.10.9 Inflation

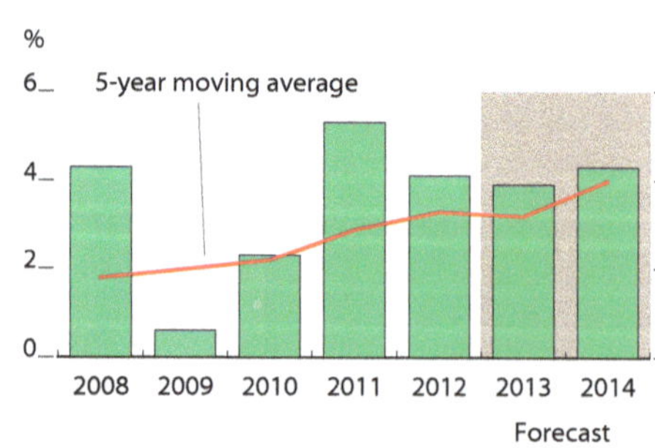

Source: *Asian Development Outlook* database.

Click here for figure data

liquidity and low interest rates, despite the macroprudential measures applied to curb speculative demand and protect the stability of the financial sector. As the rise in flat prices continues to outpace income growth, the affordability ratio had risen to nearly 50% by December 2012 (Figure 3.10.10).

Housing supply has perennially fallen short of demand largely because of inadequate land made available for residential use. For the medium term, the government has announced that it will make land available for the private development of about 20,000 housing units each year and the public development of 79,000 rental flats over 5 years starting in FY2012. It also plans to build for sale to the public about 17,000 flats over 4 years starting in FY2016. Given the time required for implementing a housing project, however, the mismatch between supply and demand can be expected to linger at least for the next 2 years.

The government's plan to develop a long-term housing strategy toward promoting the development of a healthy and stable property market is welcome, especially as land premiums and stamp duties are important sources of budgetary revenue. A strong commitment to act as necessary to protect the market from the risks of a property bubble is also essential. Indeed, policies implemented in 2012 and early 2013 have had some success in curbing speculation (Box 3.10.1), though property prices remain elevated. Housing prices are unlikely to stabilize as long as excess demand prevails and interest rates remain low. The challenge for the authorities is to maintain the stability of the property and financial markets, while meeting in a timely manner the needs of a changing population for affordable housing.

3.10.10 Housing affordability and growth of property prices

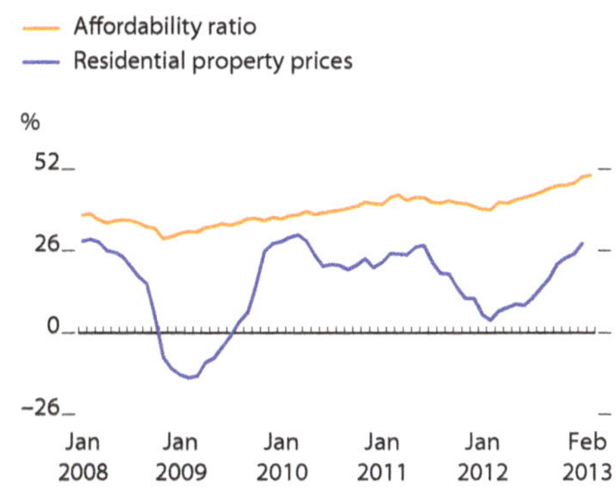

Note: The affordability ratio refers to mortgage payments for a 45-square meter apartment as a percentage of median household income.

Source: CEIC Data Company (accessed 28 March 2013).

Click here for figure data

3.10.1 Selected measures on the property market, 2012

In September 2012, the Hong Kong Monetary Authority tightened the maximum loan tenor to 30 years for all new property mortgages and reduced the following ratios for borrowers with multiple mortgages:

- the maximum debt servicing ratio from 50% to 40%,
- the maximum stressed debt servicing ratio limit from 60% to 50%,
- the loan-to-value ratio to 30% for mortgage loans, based on applicants' net worth, and another 10 percentage points lower for those with income derived mainly from outside Hong Kong, China.

In October 2012, the government enhanced the duty rates and extended the holding period in respect of the special stamp duty imposed on residential properties resold within 3 years of acquisition. The applicable special stamp duty rates are 20% of the property value for resale within 6 months, 15% for resale within 6–12 months, and 10% for resale within 12–36 months. A 15% buyers' stamp duty was also introduced on residential properties acquired by buyers who are not Hong Kong permanent residents.

The measures applied in 2012 helped reduce the transaction volume from a high of 14,306 in March 2012 to 9,129 by the end of December 2012, according to the records of the Land Registry.

Sources: Financial Secretary's Office. *2012 Economic Background and 2013 Prospects.* February 2013; Hong Kong Monetary Authority.

Republic of Korea

The adverse global outlook took its toll on exports, investment plummeted, and growth disappointed at 2% in 2012. Meanwhile, inflation abated, and the current account surplus widened. Modest improvement in external conditions will sow the seeds of recovery, and growth will pick up gently to 2.8% in 2013, with inflation remaining low and the current account surplus narrowing. Fiscal and monetary policy will broadly accommodate growth. Preventing and mitigating old-age poverty poses a high-priority policy challenge.

Economic performance

Last year was greatly challenging, in particular because weaker demand from the advanced economies and the People's Republic of China (PRC), the Republic of Korea's biggest market, dealt a double blow that knocked the wind out of exports and growth momentum. The adverse external outlook had knock-on effects on domestic demand, especially plant and equipment investment. Mildly accommodative monetary and fiscal policy provided some relief, but growth slowed significantly from 3.7% in 2011 to 2.0% in 2012. In parallel with global outlook trends, in particular the evolution of the euro area crisis, growth momentum weakened from the first quarter to the second and third quarters before picking up somewhat in the fourth quarter (Figure 3.11.1).

Feeble domestic demand provided little relief from the fragile external environment. Plant and equipment investment, heavily dependent on exports and sensitive to the global business cycle, contracted by 1.9% after expanding by 3.6% in 2011. Construction also contracted because of the stagnant housing market and feeble private sector demand overall. Private consumption growth moderated from 2.4% in 2011 to 1.7% in 2012, as large household debt and the stagnant housing market combined to outweigh the influence of a healthy employment gain of 440,000, which kept the unemployment rate at 3.2%.

Except for government consumption, all components of aggregate demand made smaller contributions to growth in 2012 than in 2011 (Figure 3.11.2). The contribution of net exports fell by half from 1.8 percentage points in 2011, and that of investment plummeted into negative territory from 0.4 percentage points in 2011. In short, the uncertain global outlook precipitated slower exports and an outright contraction of investment. Disappointing performance in 2012 marks a further deceleration from the 6.3% growth of 2010 and is fueling broader concerns about growth prospects over the medium and long term.

The persistent softness of demand from advanced economies, combined with the palpable slowdown of the PRC economy, made 2012 especially difficult for exporters. Year on year, merchandise exports grew

3.11.1 Quarterly GDP growth

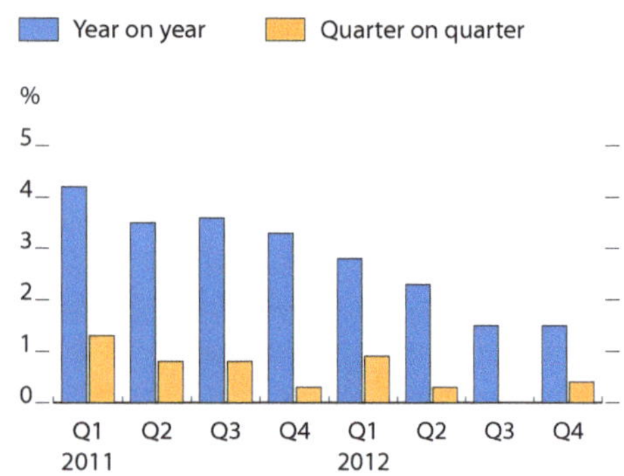

Source: Bank of Korea. Economics Statistics System. http://ecos.bok.or.kr/EIndex_en.jsp (accessed 27 March 2013).
Click here for figure data

3.11.2 Demand-side contributions to growth

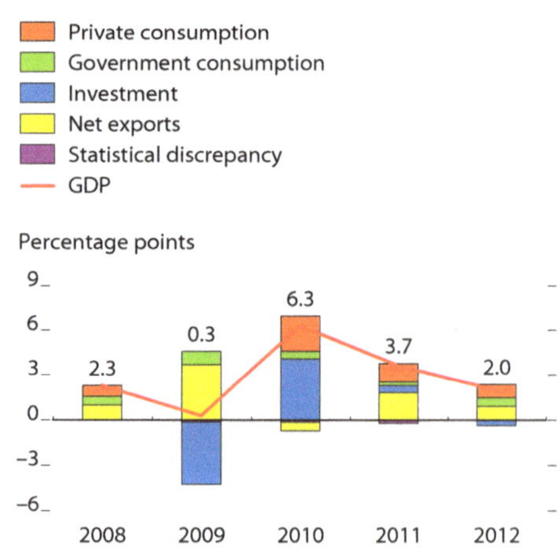

Source: Bank of Korea. Economics Statistics System. http://ecos.bok.or.kr/EIndex_en.jsp (accessed 27 March 2013).
Click here for figure data

This chapter was written by Donghyun Park of the Economics and Research Department, ADB, Manila.

by a mere 0.1% in 2012, a sharp decline from the 19.6% of 2011. Export growth was muted throughout the year (Figure 3.11.3). The one bright spot in an otherwise grim export environment was the robust market in the Association of Southeast Asian Nations (Figure 3.11.4).

Mirroring the fragility of domestic demand, imports of goods plummeted by 1.1% in 2012 from the 23.4% growth in 2011, leaving a yawning trade surplus. At the same time a sizeable surplus in construction services combined with smaller deficits in tourism and business services to reverse the chronic services trade deficit to a record surplus. These developments added up to a record current account surplus of $43.1 billion, or 3.8% of GDP, even though the won strengthened somewhat, rising from 1,146 to the dollar in January to 1,077 in December.

Inflation as measured by the consumer price index averaged 2.2%, down sharply from the 4.0% of 2011 but remaining within the central bank's inflation target band of 3.0% ±1 percentage point. Inflation decelerated during the course of the year as aggregate demand progressively softened (Figure 3.11.5). The lack of inflationary pressures and concerns about growth prodded the central bank to gradually loosen monetary policy during 2012, cutting its benchmark policy rate from 3.25% to 3.00% in July and further to 2.75% in October.

Fiscal policy was also mildly expansionary but well short of a full-fledged stimulus. The fiscal deficit was 2.9% of GDP, somewhat similar to the previous 2 years, and the ratio of public debt to GDP edged up slightly to 34.8% from 34.0%. Reflecting positive fiscal developments, all three major credit rating agencies—Moody's, Fitch, and Standard and Poor's—upgraded the Republic of Korea's sovereign credit rating in 2012.

Economic prospects

Looking forward, 2013 will see the beginning of a recovery, which will gain traction as the global recovery finds its footing in 2014. GDP growth is likely to improve modestly to 2.8% in 2013 from 2.0% in 2012. A full-fledged recovery will have to wait until 2014, when GDP growth will strengthen to 3.7% (Figure 3.11.6). While domestic demand will contribute to growth in 2013, it will be nowhere near robust enough to qualitatively change the gradual and limited nature of recovery in 2013. Uncertainties in the global outlook regarding the advanced economies will continue to cast a dark cloud over global trade during the first half. But those uncertainties are expected to ease during the second half. The Republic of Korea's performance will mirror the expected trajectory of the world economy, with growth in the second half of the year slightly outperforming expansion in the first half.

Merchandise export growth is set to rise modestly from 0.1% in 2012 to above 7% in 2013, as factors contributing to faster growth are likely to outweigh those depressing it. Stronger export growth since the fourth quarter of 2012 buttresses such cautious optimism. Exports to the PRC stand to benefit from that country's widely expected stronger growth. On the other hand, limited fiscal stimulus in developing countries and fiscal austerity in the advanced economies will firmly cap aggregate export demand (Figure 3.11.7). Export growth will thus be muted overall—unlike the V-shaped rebound after the global financial crisis—but will

3.11.3 Merchandise export growth

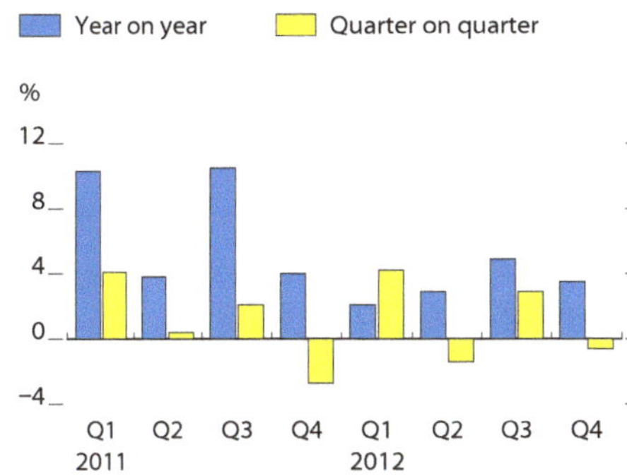

Source: Bank of Korea. Economics Statistics System. http://ecos.bok.or.kr/EIndex_en.jsp (accessed 22 February 2013).
Click here for figure data

3.11.4 Monthly exports to the Association of Southeast Asian Nations

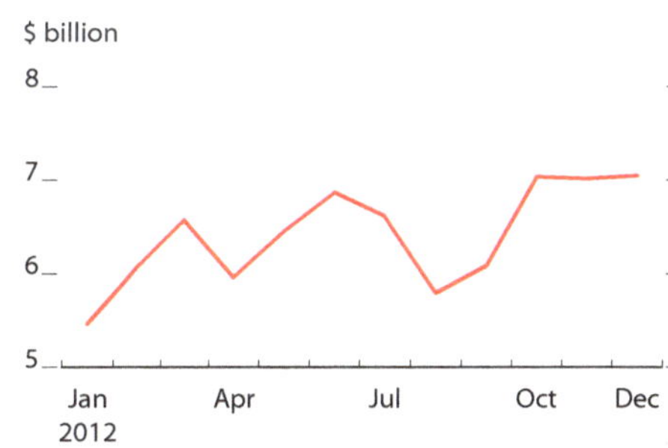

Source: CEIC Data Company (accessed 8 March 2013).
Click here for figure data

3.11.5 Inflation

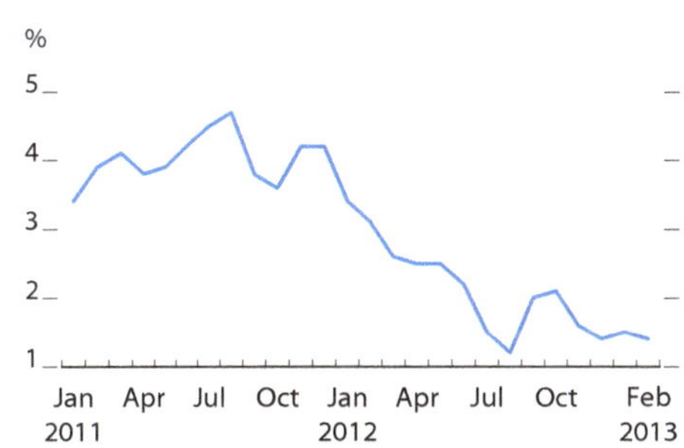

Source: Bank of Korea. Economics Statistics System. http://ecos.bok.or.kr/EIndex_en.jsp (accessed 8 March 2013).
Click here for figure data

mark an exit from the export distress of 2012. Meanwhile, imports are likely to rise in 2013 and 2014, reflecting strengthening domestic demand, and shrink the current account surplus to 3.0% of GDP in 2013 and 2.5% of GDP in 2014.

In line with the trajectory of the global outlook, investment will contract in the first half but grow at a healthy pace of 3.0% or better in the second half, on the back of growing outlays in export-oriented industries and sectors. The effect of exports on equipment investment, traditionally high for this export-dependent country, is likely to be acute. Uncertainty in the post-crisis period encouraged firms to base their investment decisions more on visible short-term export trends than on highly uncertain long-term prospects. Looking forward, while business confidence remains fragile, low interest rates, the strong won, and tightening capacity utilization in recent months will provide impetus to investment (Figure 3.11.8). As a result, plant and equipment investment is likely to bounce back gradually in tandem with export recovery. Construction investment, which has contracted for 3 consecutive years, is set to grow by 2.0%. The modest turnaround will center on public works and nonresidential buildings, while the sluggish housing market will continue to stymie residential construction. Private consumption growth is projected to strengthen from 1.7% in 2012 to close to 3.0% in 2013, in light of the expected pickup in exports, relative price stability, healthy employment gains, and moderating uncertainties.

In line with the modest pickup of growth, consumer price index inflation will rise slightly from 2.2% in 2012 to 2.5% in 2013 and 2.8% in 2014. This outcome reflects the evolution of several factors affecting prices. Since the Republic of Korea's potential GDP growth rate is estimated to be between 3.5% and 4.0%, a deflationary gap, which emerged during the second quarter of 2012, will persist well into 2013 (Figure 3.11.9). Feeble domestic demand, fierce competition among recently proliferating self-employed service providers, the projected moderation of global oil prices, and the appreciation of the won will all alleviate inflationary pressures. On the other hand, an exceptionally cold winter may trigger higher food prices, and long-frozen fees for some public services are due to be raised this year. In addition, incomes will grow as employment rises by an estimated 300,000 jobs. This employment expansion, while less than in 2012, continues a long-term trend of healthy employment growth.

Monetary policy aims to lower inflation to a rate like those experienced in advance countries. To this end, the central bank lowered and tightened the inflation target band from 3.0% ±1 percentage point to 2.5%–3.5%. However, this policy is likely to be tempered by a desire to support growth, so the central bank is likely to cut interest rates in the first half of 2013.

The basic stance of fiscal policy in 2013 and 2014 will be to support economic growth in the face of feeble aggregate demand. To this end, the budget will likely record a deficit of 0.3% of GDP in 2013. This is less than the 2.9% of 2012 and shrinks the ratio of public debt to GDP from 34.8% to 34.3%, but the government will nevertheless adopt a concerted countercyclical fiscal approach in the short run by frontloading 60% of its budget during the first half of the year, gearing the composition

3.11.6 GDP growth

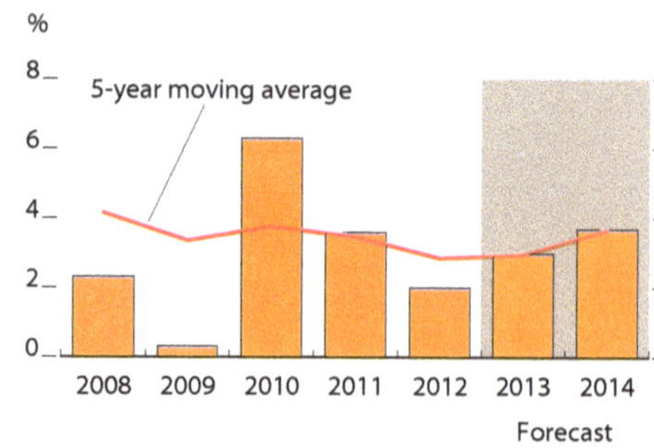

Sources: Bank of Korea. Economics Statistics System. http://ecos.bok.or.kr/EIndex_en.jsp (accessed 27 March 2013); ADB estimates.

Click here for figure data

3.11.7 Monthly exports to the European Union

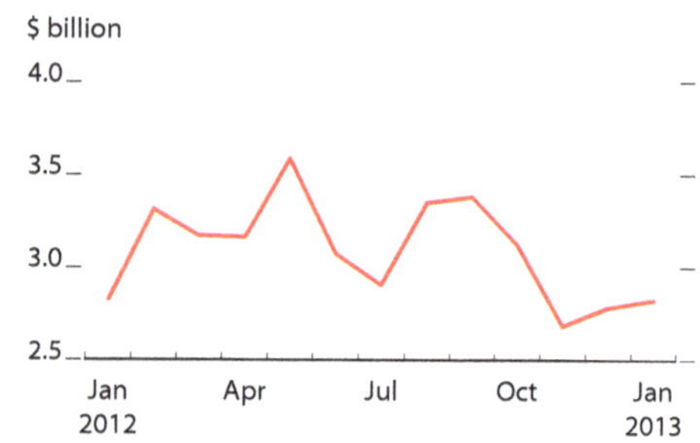

Source: CEIC Data Company (accessed 8 March 2013).

Click here for figure data

3.11.8 Monthly capacity utilization ratio

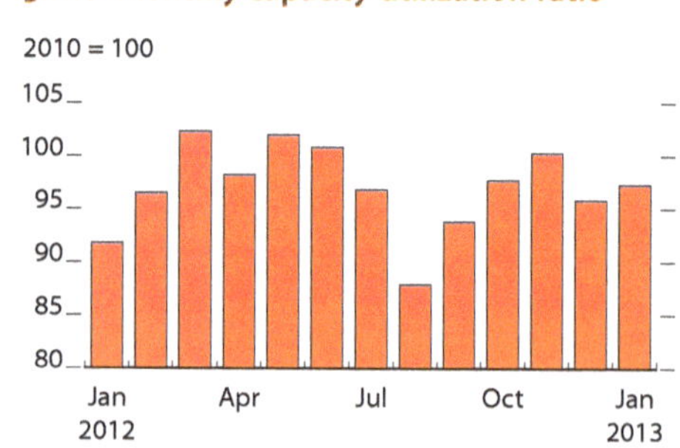

Source: CEIC Data Company (accessed 8 March 2013).

Click here for figure data

of expenditures toward maximizing support for growth. In particular, budget items targeted for significant expansion are social overhead capital investment, assistance to small and medium-sized enterprises, and job creation programs.

This baseline economic outlook is subject to a number of risks. GDP forecasts are fraught with uncertainty arising from persistent uncertainty in the global outlook. The upside and downside risks are finely balanced, however, with the short-term performance of the US and euro area economies constituting the main sources of both upside and downside risk for the Republic of Korea.

Protectionism, including competitive depreciation stemming from quantitative easing, is another potential risk. In this context, the sharp depreciation of the yen is of special concern because Japan and the Republic of Korea compete in many export industries (Figure 3.11.10). However, this concern is tempered by the likely positive impact of the weaker yen on the economy's competitiveness, as the Republic of Korea imports large amounts of capital and intermediate goods from Japan.

There is also political risk arising from the unpredictability of the Democratic People's Republic of Korea, which can shake the financial markets and have spillover effects on the economy in the south.

On the domestic front, the high and growing household debt—the perennial domestic risk—continues to weigh on private consumption even as it becomes less of a systemic financial and economic risk. There has been no noticeable uptick in consumer confidence. The average propensity to consume—the ratio of consumption to disposable income—fell from 78% before the crisis to 76% in 2012. For low-income groups, anxieties about possible unemployment in a weak economy seem to constrain consumption. For higher-income groups, their deleveraging to reduce household debt burdens, compounded by stagnant housing prices, limit the propensity to consume (Figure 3.11.11). These risks suggest that private consumption may not grow as assumed under the baseline outlook. More broadly, the economy's visibly slower and more volatile growth during the past 5 years has raised concerns about growth prospects over the medium and long term.

On the positive side, there are no major, high-probability systematic risks to financial stability. Even worst-case estimates of the impact of large household debt on banks' balance sheets are deemed manageable. The risk from the mounting bad loans of savings banks—second-tier financial institutions—has also been addressed through extensive restructuring. Moreover, prudent fiscal policy has created sufficient fiscal space should there be a crisis that demands a large stimulus. Indeed, rating agencies' sovereign credit rating upgrades reflect a market vote of confidence in the government's ability to tackle a crisis without sacrificing fiscal sustainability.

Policy challenge—mitigating old-age poverty

The Republic of Korea needs to find ways to deliver affordable, adequate, and sustainable income support for its elderly population, which is one of the fastest growing in the world (Figure 3.11.12). The country introduced

3.11.9 Output gap

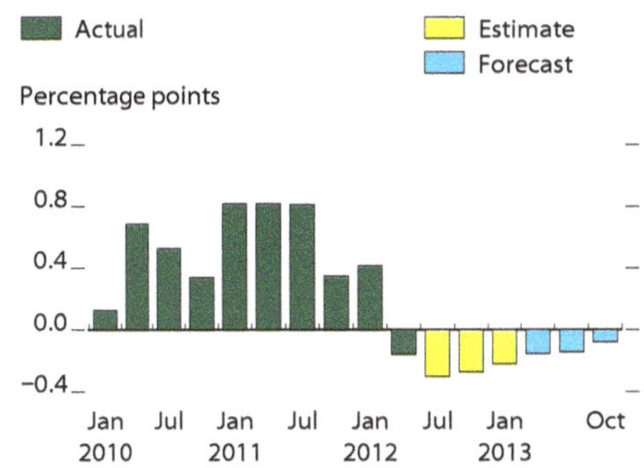

Source: LG Economic Research Institute. 2012. *LG Business Insight*. September.

Click here for figure data

3.11.10 Won–yen exchange rate

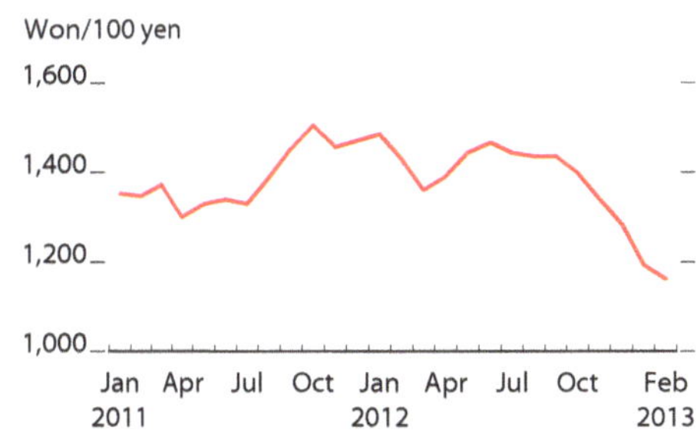

Source: Bank of Korea. Economics Statistics System. http://ecos.bok.or.kr/EIndex_en.jsp (accessed 8 March 2013).

Click here for figure data

3.11.1 Selected economic indicators (%)

	2013	2014
GDP growth	2.8	3.7
Inflation	2.5	2.8
Current account balance (share of GDP)	3.0	2.5

Source: ADB estimates.

a public national pension system only in 1988, and, among members of the Organisation for Economic Co-operation and Development, it ranks second, after Mexico, for its meager share of GDP devoted to social spending. At the same time, traditional reliance on families is being eroded by extensive socioeconomic change. Most worryingly, rates of poverty and extreme poverty among the elderly rose from 2006 to 2011. The risk of widespread old-age poverty has thus emerged as a major social and economic concern in recent years (Table 3.11.2). This issue was arguably the hottest subject of debate during the December 2012 presidential election, in which all candidates promised to devote more resources to mitigating old-age poverty.

The Basic Old-Age Pension (BOAP) is a noncontributory social scheme introduced in 2008 that uses general revenues to pay pensions to the elderly poor. Its central objective was to provide a safety net for many elderly who were at risk of falling into poverty because they were not covered by either the national pension system or the anti-poverty social security system unrelated to age. This coverage gap, while narrowing, is expected to remain substantial for years to come.

As designed, the BOAP suffers some serious flaws that ill-suit it to mitigating old-age poverty. First, as 30%–40% of the elderly live with their children, a lot of the assistance ends up in the hands of relatively well-to-do elderly who live with well-to-do children. According to KDI, an autonomous development institute set up by the Republic of Korea, 54.2% of the households in the wealthiest 10% of households with elderly members received BOAP benefits, suggesting that a substantial share of benefits flow to the better off. Second, the BOAP targets the poorest 70% of the elderly, which includes many higher-income elderly who do not actually need support. Third, many elderly poor, especially those not living with their children, fail to apply for the BOAP for lack of information. Fourth, owing to its noncontributory nature, the BOAP can blunt incentives to join the national pension system because it requires a contribution, thereby raising budgetary costs.

In February 2013, the incoming administration announced a plan to extend BOAP coverage to the entire elderly population and double the benefits paid out to the poorest 70%. Among other equity concerns, the proposed plan favors non-contributors over contributors, thereby making it very controversial, throwing its passage by the legislature into doubt, and undermining its efficacy in mitigating old-age poverty.

To reduce inequities and budgetary costs and make the BOAP more effective, benefit amounts and eligibility should be carefully designed to minimize disincentives to joining the national pension system. In particular, BOAP eligibility should depend on a well-defined measure of poverty, rather than on an arbitrary percentage of poor elderly. For the elderly living with their children, eligibility should take into account children's income. The primary, longer-term objective of pension reform must be to extend coverage under the main national pension system to the entire population.

3.11.11 Change in housing prices, Seoul metropolitan area

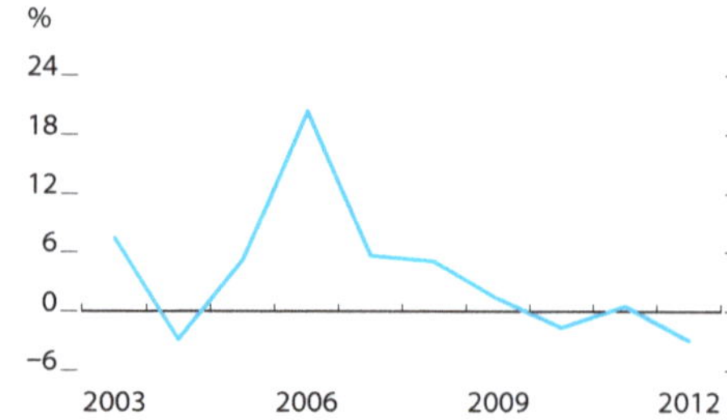

Source: Korea Appraisal Board. 2013. *Korea National Housing Price Trends*. Seoul.

Click here for figure data

3.11.12 Ratio of population aged 65+ to population aged 15–64

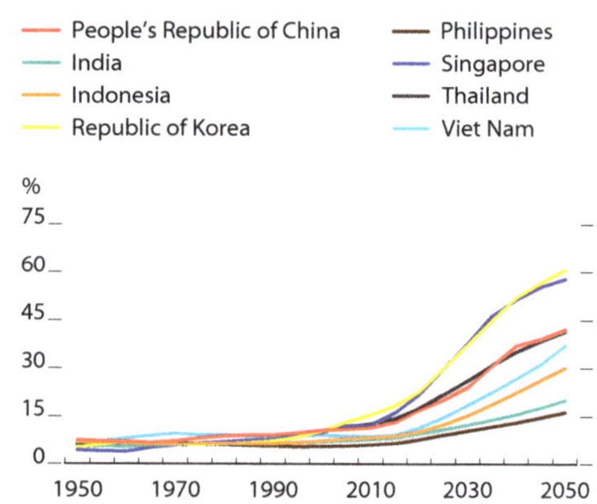

Source: United Nations. Department of Economic and Social Affairs, Population Division. 2011. *World Population Prospects: The 2010 Revision*. http://esa.un.org/unpd/wpp/index.htm (accessed 21 February 2013).

Click here for figure data

3.11.2 Poverty rates among the elderly, 2006 and 2011 (%)

Age	2006	2011
65–69	38.0 (9.4)	40.0 (15.2)
70–74	45.2 (13.0)	52.3 (21.4)
75–79	53.7 (22.6)	57.8 (27.6)
80+	45.4 (18.3)	51.4 (28.8)
60+	43.8 (14.0)	48.8 (21.4)

Note: Numbers inside parentheses indicate extreme poverty rate. Poverty rate refers to the share of the population with income below 50% of the median income. Extreme poverty rate refers to the share of the population with income below 25% of the median income.

Source: Korea Development Institute.

Mongolia

Continuing economic trends feature high growth and inflation, procyclical fiscal policy, and large current account deficits. GDP growth decelerated to 12.3% in 2012 from 17.5% in 2011, and inflation accelerated. Overly expansionary policies, including substantial off-budget spending, have caused internal and external macroeconomic imbalances. Over the longer term, sound public resource management and effective cooperation with private investors are needed to develop Mongolia's energy sector in a sustainable and environmentally friendly way.

Economic performance

Economic growth slowed to 12.3% in 2012, falling from 20.2% year on year in the fourth quarter of 2011 to 10.5% in the third quarter of 2012, after a slowdown in growth in the People's Republic of China (PRC) curbed demand for coal, Mongolia's biggest export. A driver of growth was infrastructure spending related to the mining boom, albeit to a lesser extent than in 2011, as the first phase of the Oyu Tolgoi copper and gold mine—among the five largest in the world—neared completion. As a result, gross capital formation, including equipment, buildings, and intermediate goods, increased by 24.0%, markedly down from the 69.9% of 2011 but still the largest contributor to GDP growth, followed by consumption (Figure 3.12.1).

While economic growth in 2012 originated in the mining sector, it was quite broadly based (Figure 3.12.2). Construction continued to boom, raising concerns about another bubble as in 2004–2008. Mining grew by 8.9% to generate 89.2% of exports, 17% of government revenue, and 18.6% of GDP, while employing less than 2% of the workforce. Agriculture, which provides more than one-third of employment, finally emerged from the devastating winter of 2009/10 that had decimated the country's livestock by nearly a fifth. However, growth in wholesale and retail trade slowed to 10.3% from 38.3% in 2011, as spending on investment and intermediate goods decelerated.

Inflation has remained high in Mongolia while declining in other Asian countries, owing mainly to rapidly rising government spending and higher food prices. In 2012, headline inflation increased to 14.3%, but core inflation (excluding food and energy prices) was more stable and averaged 10.5% (Figure 3.12.3).

Fiscal policy in 2012 continued to be procyclical, with the overall cash budget deficit rising to 7.7% of GDP from 4.8% in 2011 and the structural budget deficit rising to 8.3% from 6.9% in 2011. The initial government budget for 2012 projected revenue growth equal to 40%

3.12.1 Demand-side contributions to growth

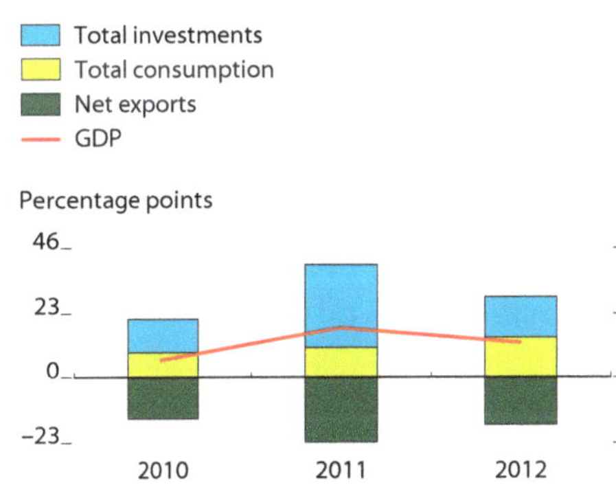

Source: National Statistics Office of Mongolia. 2012. *Monthly Statistical Bulletin.* December. http://www.nso.mn

Click here for figure data

3.12.2 Supply-side contributions to growth

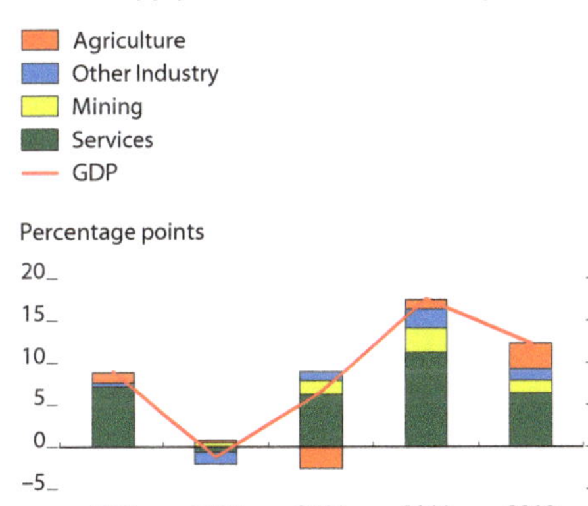

Source: National Statistics Office of Mongolia. 2012. *Monthly Statistical Bulletin.* December. http://www.nso.mn

Click here for figure data

This chapter was written by Jan Hansen and Amar Lkhagvasuren of the Mongolia Resident Mission, ADB, Ulaanbaatar.

of GDP, expenditure growth of about 32%, and a cash budget deficit of 1%. But cash revenues rose by only 11.2%, as value-added taxes and customs duties did not grow as expected. The government plans to issue $5 billion in bonds on the international market, of which $1.5 billion was sold in November 2012. The proceeds are expected to be transferred to the Development Bank of Mongolia (DBM), which is becoming a major source of public financing for infrastructure projects, corresponding to 3.6% of GDP in 2012. The Fiscal Stability Fund, mandated under the 2010 Fiscal Stability Law (FSL), held MNT328 billion in December 2012, which corresponds to 2.4% of GDP and is likely insufficient in case of a substantial shock (Figure 3.12.4).

Monetary policy has been mildly countercyclical in recent years. Mandated by law to pursue price stability, the central bank raised the policy rate in 2012 by 1 percentage point to 13.25%, as inflation rose substantially above the official target ceiling of 10%. This measure and a three-step increase in the reserve requirement ratio to 12% in April 2012 from 5% in February 2011 have contributed to a significant slowdown in money and credit growth. Broad money (M2) growth slowed from 37.0% in 2011 to 18.8% in 2012, and growth in bank credit almost halved in the same period. Although inflation remained above target, in January 2013 the central bank lowered the policy rate by 0.75 percentage points to 12.50%, citing a drop in inflation. Negative real interest rates and the recent cut in the policy interest rate indicate an expansionary monetary policy.

External trade slowed in 2012. The value of merchandise exports (mainly minerals) fell by 9% in response to a slowdown in PRC growth, while imports increased by 2.1%, widening the trade deficit. Meanwhile, a narrower deficit in the services account helped trim the current account deficit to 31.3% of GDP in 2012 from 31.5% in 2011. Foreign direct investment, largely in mining, decreased to 37.8% of GDP from 53.8% in 2011 (Figure 3.12.5). The resulting basic balance—the current account balance plus foreign direct investment—remained positive but smaller. At year-end, gross international reserves had accumulated to $4.09 billion, equal to 7 months of imports. These reserves included drawdowns from a swap line with the PRC, central bank deposit taking from the DBM, and the recent international bond issuance. Thus the share of borrowed reserves rose significantly.

In response to the 2008–2009 global financial crisis, the government adopted a broadly floating exchange rate regime toward instituting inflation targeting. However, during 2012, the central bank occasionally intervened to limit the togrog's depreciation. This eroded how effectively monetary policy could control inflation and the adverse effects of the Dutch disease. The official exchange rate of the togrog against the dollar has fallen by 8% since April 2012, while the real exchange rate continues its trend appreciation caused by high domestic inflation (Figure 3.12.6).

Economic prospects

Mongolia's medium-term economic prospects are favorable. The mining sector is expected to continue to be the main engine of growth in 2013 and 2014, with commercial production at the Oyu Tolgoi copper and gold mine starting in mid-2013. Growth is expected to accelerate to 16.5%

3.12.3 Monthly inflation

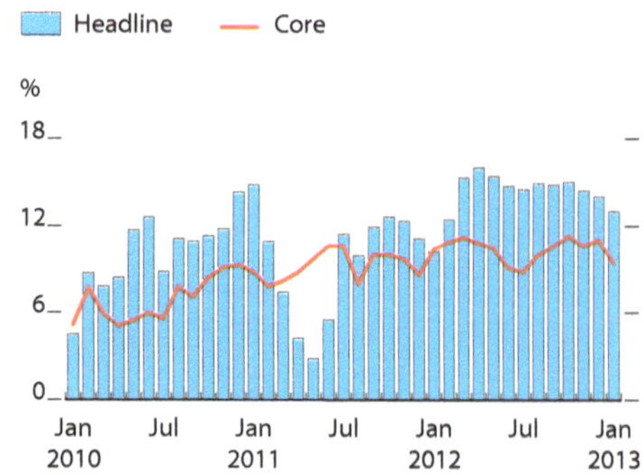

Source: Bank of Mongolia. 2012. *Statistical Bulletin*. December. http://www.mongolbank.mn

Click here for figure data

3.12.4 Fiscal indicators

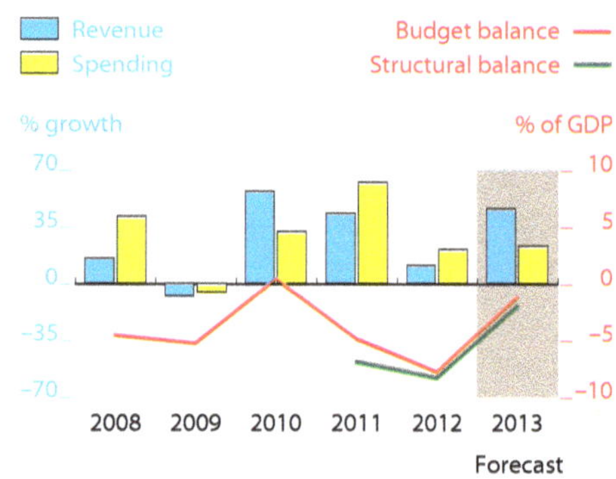

Source: National Statistical Office. 2012. *Monthly Statistical Bulletin*. http://www.nso.mn

Click here for figure data

3.12.5 External balance

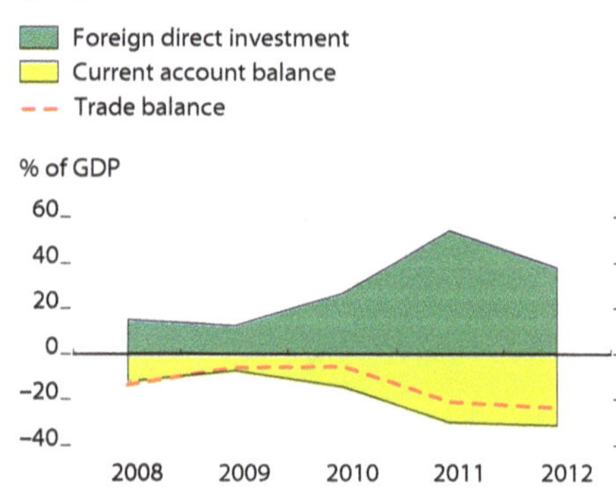

Sources: National Statistical Office. http://www.nso.mn; Bank of Mongolia. http://www.mongolbank.mn

Click here for figure data

in 2013, before being trimmed to 14% in 2014 by capacity constraints in public investment planning and project management, a tight labor market and skill shortages, and some tightening of monetary and fiscal policies including lower off-budget spending financed by the DBM (Figure 3.12.7).

Until that tightening takes place, inflation is expected to remain well into double digits, reaching about 13% in 2013 (Figure 3.12.8). Assuming more prudent fiscal policy and some tightening of monetary policy in 2014, inflation could be brought down to 10%.

The 2013 government budget is the first prepared under the full effect of the FSL, which sets ceilings on the structural deficit, debt, and expenditure growth. These ceilings function as fiscal circuit breakers and work together to ensure fiscal discipline.

The 2013 budget foresees overall revenue growth at 28.9%; expenditure growth at 17.9%, mainly reflecting a sharp increase in capital expenditure; and an overall budget deficit of 1.1% in cash terms and 2% structural, which is the maximum allowed under the FSL. The revenue projections are overly optimistic, however, as they are not based on actual revenue outcome in 2012 but on the much higher revenue projections of the 2012 supplementary budget, setting the stage for a significant revenue shortfall and a deficit violating the FSL ceiling. The government is expected, however, to tighten public expenditure as needed in 2013 to comply with the FSL and constrain lending by the DBM.

Under the assumption of stable global commodity prices (Figure 3.12.9) and continued high economic growth in the PRC, Mongolia's mineral-dominated exports will likely show very strong growth over the next 2 years, while imports will grow moderately in line with a slowdown in mining investments partly compensated by high growth in public investments, especially infrastructure. These developments are expected to drive the current account deficit down to 22% of GDP this year and 15% in 2014. The net effect of the start of Oyu Tolgoi operations on the balance of payments will be limited in 2013, as gross export proceeds will go mostly to repaying investment costs.

The outlook for 2013 and 2014 is subject to substantial risks. A renewed slowdown in the PRC, which absorbs almost all of Mongolia's exports (92.6% in 2012), is the biggest external risk. A worsening of the global economy, in particular in the euro area, could also be damaging. Internal risks are expansionary monetary and fiscal policy, including off-budget expenditure, and the possibility of renewed problems in the banking sector. The price stabilization program announced in October 2012, through which the central bank provides loans at subsidized interest rates through the commercial banks to specified industries, aims to contain supply-side inflationary pressure but may intensify those from the demand side and create macroeconomic risks and distortions. The program amounts to about 14% of GDP over a 3-year period. The DBM's operations undermine the integrity of the FSL and should be taken into account when judging the short- to medium-term macroeconomic impact and long-term sustainability of government spending. Without strong fiscal retrenchment, adherence to FSL requirements, and appropriate monetary management, inflation in the forecast period could be higher.

The fragile banking system has been reinforced, but vulnerabilities remain. Nonperforming loans fell to 4.3% of all loans in November 2012,

3.12.6 Exchange rate

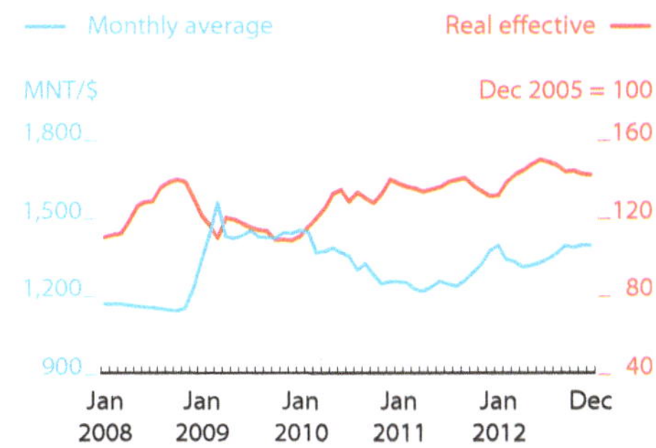

Source: Bank of Mongolia. http://www.mongolbank.mn (accessed 15 March 2013).

Click here for figure data

3.12.7 GDP growth

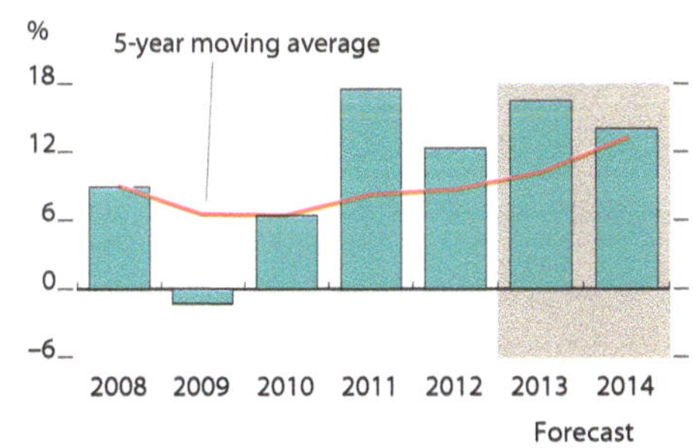

Source: Asian Development Outlook database.

Click here for figure data

3.12.8 Inflation

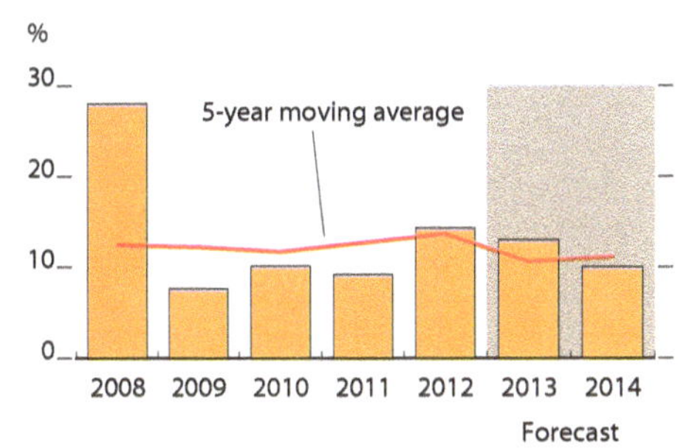

Source: Asian Development Outlook database.

Click here for figure data

3.12.1 Selected economic indicators (%)

	2013	2014
GDP growth	16.5	14.0
Inflation	13.0	10.0
Current account balance (share of GDP)	–22.0	–15.0

Source: ADB estimates.

and the capital adequacy ratio for systemically important banks was raised to 14%, among other measures. However, the banking system continues to suffer from structural weakness related to corporate governance and risk management. Moreover, the rapid acceleration of bank lending in 2011 has masked growing problems in asset quality that can leave banks exposed.

Policy challenge—energy security

Mongolia's growing demand for energy, heavy dependence on coal as its major energy source, and reliance on two big neighbors—the PRC and the Russian Federation—for increasingly important oil challenge its economic development. Rising demand for energy reflects rapid economic growth, the development of the mining industry, and the doubling of Ulaanbaatar's population since 1995. Oil imports—more than 90% from the Russian Federation—have risen by 44% since 2003 (Figure 3.12.10).

Mongolia has vast proven reserves of coal and some oil, but their exploitation has been either delayed or inefficient (Figure 3.12.11). Coal fuels 70% of electricity generation and 90% of heating but with poor energy efficiency. Facilities are old, and electricity tariffs below market rates put proper maintenance and investment in new plants beyond the reach of undercapitalized plant operators. Ulaanbaatar has no spare capacity for power and heat. Many households unconnected to the grid use coal stoves, polluting the air in Ulaanbaatar and other urban areas.

The government has a two-pronged approach to energy vulnerability. In the short-term, it attempts to stabilize energy prices to protect consumers. To this end, oil imports have been exempted from custom duties and excise taxes in autumn and spring.

Over the longer term, the government is considering using public–private partnership to expand electricity generating capacity. It is preparing an energy master plan that defines long-term priorities and intends to build a 450 megawatt combined heat and power plant in Ulaanbaatar. This project, if successfully implemented, will show the government to be a credible partner of the private sector, which is important for developing energy resources. The government has announced plans to finish constructing its first oil refinery by 2015. Meanwhile, Mongolia has huge potential for renewable energy resources. The country's first wind farm, at Salkhit, is expected to add 5% of national electricity supply while reducing carbon dioxide emissions. Solar resources are substantial, and there is potential for hydropower. Tapping these resources requires sound public planning and resource management and effective cooperation with private investors.

3.12.9 Global prices of main exports

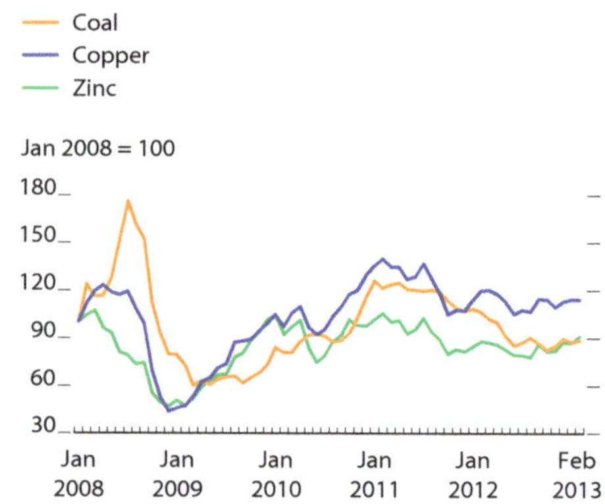

Source: World Bank. Commodity Price Data (Pink Sheet). http://econ.worldbank.org (accessed 22 March 2013).
Click here for figure data

3.12.10 Electricity production and import

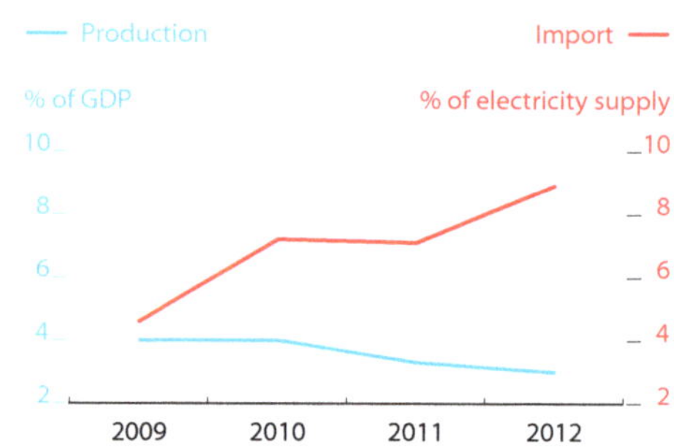

Source: National Statistics Office of Mongolia. 2012. *Monthly Statistical Bulletin*. December. http://www.nso.mn
Click here for figure data

3.12.11 Coal production and use

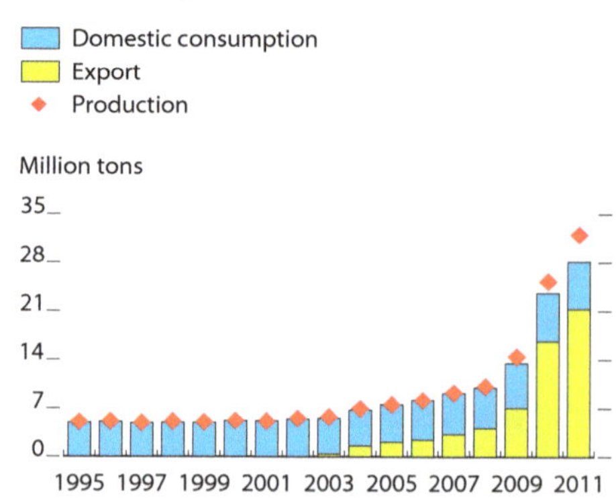

Source: Asian Development Bank. 2012. *Key Indicators for Asia and the Pacific*. http://www.adb.org
Click here for figure data

Taipei,China

Economic activity picked up in the second half of 2012, compensating for the slump in the first half to record growth at 1.3%. As external conditions improve, this tepid economic expansion is giving way to more robust growth in 2013 and 2014 without igniting inflation. The authorities should continue to maintain adequate policy flexibility to respond to economic challenges that may be posed by a slowdown across the strait or a weaker yen.

Economic performance

After registering 4.1% growth in 2011, Taipei,China's economy slowed to 1.3% expansion in 2012 (Figure 3.13.1). Exports of goods and services declined in the first half of the year owing to the slowdown in the People's Republic of China (PRC) and the continued weakness in major industrialized economies but eventually recovered and grew by 3.1% as demand for electronics and precision products picked up. Imports of goods and services declined by 1.9% as weak external demand dragged domestic investment. Net exports contributed 1.1 percentage points to real GDP growth.

Consumer unease caused lower retail sales, curbing growth in private consumption that, with a modest rise in government consumption, saw total consumption increase by only 1.3%. This narrowed consumption's contribution to growth to 0.84 percentage points. Total investments contracted by 4.2%, as the government stimulus measures had waned since 2009, and as the private enterprises trimmed their investment outlays.

Growth was highly variable across sectors (Figure 3.13.2). Industry, the largest sector, contributed about a quarter of GDP growth, despite rising by a meager 0.9% owing to a slow 1% rise in manufacturing output. Mining and quarrying increased by a hefty 10.4% in 2012 but contributed little to growth because of their small share in GDP. Construction declined, and typhoons left agricultural output down by 5.8%. The service sector grew by a modest 1.0%, as the information, communications, tourism, and entertainment industries picked up and growth in wholesale and retail trade and real estate moderated. Tourist arrivals from the PRC increased dramatically in 2012, as visa requirements relaxed.

Average inflation rose to 1.9% from 1.4% in 2011, owing to acceleration in food prices and the reduction of fuel subsidies that had been in place for 16 months. Rising real estate prices decelerated to 5.7% from 9.9% in 2011, reflecting deteriorating economic conditions and central bank intervention to cool property speculation, which moderated private investments.

3.13.1 Demand-side contributions to growth

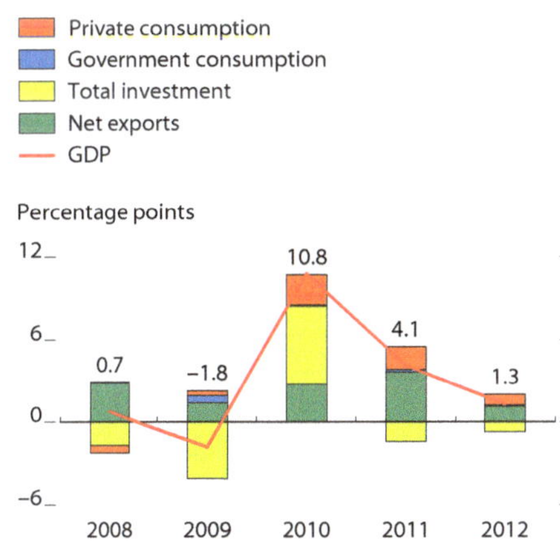

Source: Directorate-General of Budget, Accounting, and Statistics. http://eng.stat.gov.tw (accessed 14 March 2013).
Click here for figure data

3.13.2 Supply-side contributions to growth

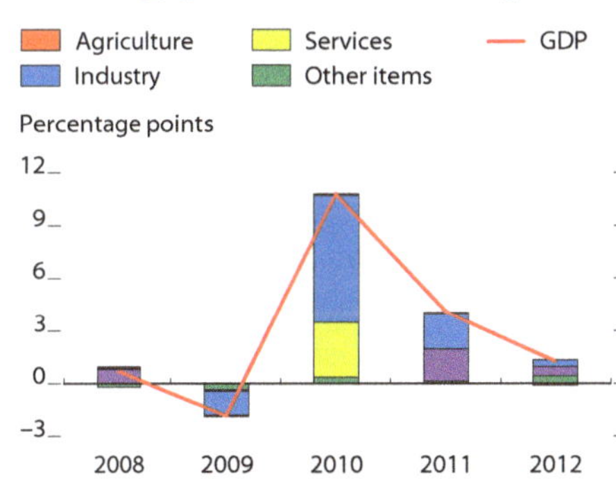

Source: Directorate-General of Budget, Accounting, and Statistics. http://eng.stat.gov.tw (accessed 12 March 2013).
Click here for figure data

This chapter was written by Akiko Terada-Hagiwara and Shiela Camingue of the Economics and Research Department, ADB, Manila.

Consistent with the government's policy of narrowing the fiscal deficit, growth in expenditures slowed to 1.5% despite substantial rises in social welfare payments and development spending. Revenues increased by 3.5% as tax receipts grew, bringing the fiscal deficit for the year down to 1.6% of GDP.

The central bank kept the rediscount rate unchanged at 1.875% (Figure 3.13.3), in the face of the continued downside risks arising from the global economic situation and moderating inflation. The money supply (M2) grew by 3.5% in 2012, more slowly than in 2011, reflecting smaller increases in net foreign assets and in bank credit as lending to the private sector grew more slowly and net claims on government enterprises contracted.

Merchandise exports and imports shrank in 2012 (Figure 3.13.4). Merchandise exports fell by 2.4%, despite a rebound in the second half of the year, when exports increased to the US; the euro area; the PRC; Southeast Asia; and Hong Kong, China. The ASEAN-6 trade bloc within the Association of Southeast Asian Nations took 18% of exports. Imports declined by 3.7%, mainly because of subdued investment.

Buoyed by the tourism boom, services recorded a surplus of $6.1 billion, a 58% rise from 2011, and repatriated profits and dividends into the country remained elevated. Thus, despite slowing exports, the current account surplus climbed to 10.5% of GDP from 8.9% in 2011 (Figure 3.13.5). The balance of payments surplus reached $15.5 billion, triple that of 2011, despite a net capital outflow of $31.6 billion owing to greater investment in foreign debt securities.

Economic prospects

Economic growth is projected to rebound to 3.5% in 2013. Industrial activity is expected to ramp up as demand recovers in the PRC, with which warming ties could boost the service sector through tourism. Private investment is expected to be notably stronger in 2013, benefitting from government plans to encourage investment in high-technology manufacturing and lower barriers to foreign investment, as well as an "invest at home" program aimed at local companies that have moved production capacity to the PRC over the past 2 decades. An improving outlook for information technology exports, indicated by increasing orders from developing Asia and the euro area, bodes well for private sector investment. Public investment may not grow, however, and current expenditure may fall as the government intends to further narrow the fiscal deficit to 1.3% in 2013.

The continued recovery in exports, driven by growing momentum in the major industrialized economies including the euro area, could be the main engine of economic expansion in 2014. Improved external demand should encourage private investment and employment, help sustain private consumption, and elevate economic growth to 3.9%.

Inflation is projected to ease to 1.6% in 2013, as international raw material prices stabilize, fruit and vegetable and global commodity prices moderate, and a planned increase in electricity prices is postponed. A tighter labor market may create upward pressure on inflation, mainly in 2014, when inflation will likely edge up to 1.8% on the average.

3.13.3 Credit indicators

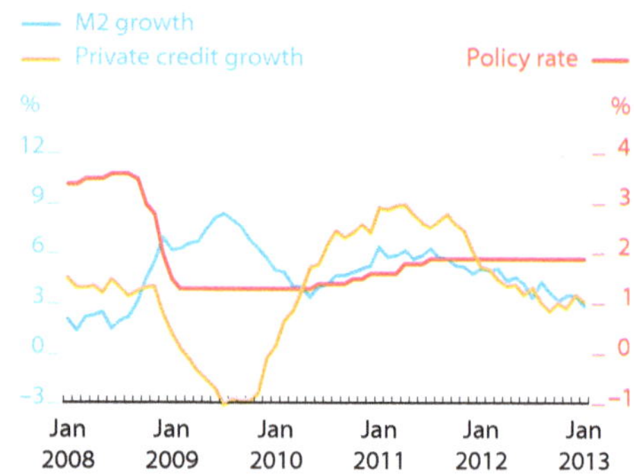

Source: CEIC Data Company (accessed 12 March 2013).
Click here for figure data

3.13.4 Trade indicators

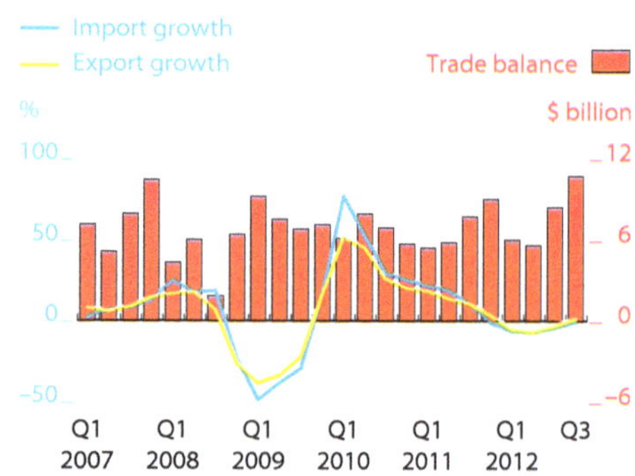

Source: CEIC Data Company (accessed 12 March 2013).
Click here for figure data

3.13.1 Selected economic indicators (%)

	2013	2014
GDP growth	3.5	3.9
Inflation	1.6	1.8
Current account balance (share of GDP)	11.0	12.0

Source: ADB estimates.

3.13.5 Current account components

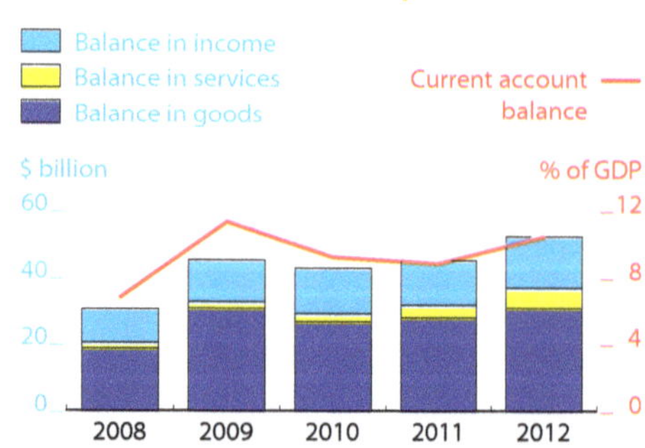

Sources: Directorate-General of Budget, Accounting, and Statistics. http://eng.stat.gov.tw; CEIC Data Company (both accessed 14 March 2013).
Click here for figure data

The central bank has not changed its policy rate since September 2011. Continuing weakness in global demand and the likelihood that the gap between actual and potential output will narrow only slowly will likely keep monetary policy accommodative.

Exports remain competitive as indicated by the real effective exchange rate (Figure 3.13.6), and yen depreciation is likely to have minimal effect, as suggested by the scenario analysis in Box 3.13.1. Exports are projected to improve in 2013 and 2014 with higher growth in the PRC and more geographically diverse export markets. Imports are also expected to increase, especially as tariffs on imported equipment and machinery are cut. The trade account will likely improve and tourist arrivals from the PRC rise. Taipei,China's current account surplus is expected to remain at about 12% of GDP during the forecast period, generating large surpluses in the balance of payments.

As a highly open economy, Taipei,China is vulnerable to fluctuations in external demand, all the more so because of its heavy reliance on electronics exports. Economic prospects in the euro area remain lackluster, and the PRC may tighten policy to rein in property prices and air pollution, constraining growth in Taipei,China. Exchange rate fluctuations, notably with Japan, could also affect economic prospects.

Policy challenge—response to external shocks

Taipei,China is affected by the global economy through changes in foreign demand, which affect its output gap; movements in foreign exchange rates; and the effect of interest rates overseas on the NT dollar. As regional supply chains have developed over the past decade, the economy of Taipei,China has become more interdependent with those of the rest of emerging Asia, which absorb 66% of its exports, the lion's share going to the PRC (Figure 3.13.7).

Simulations were conducted to gauge the impact of slowing external demand and the weakening of yen on Taipei,China's growth outlook (Box 3.13.1). They showed a much larger effect from a slowdown if it occurred in emerging Asia than in the euro area and little sensitivity to yen depreciation. These results, while indicative, point to the need for Taipei,China to continue to maintain enough policy flexibility to respond to the changing external environment, especially through monetary and fiscal initiatives.

3.13.6 Exchange rate movements

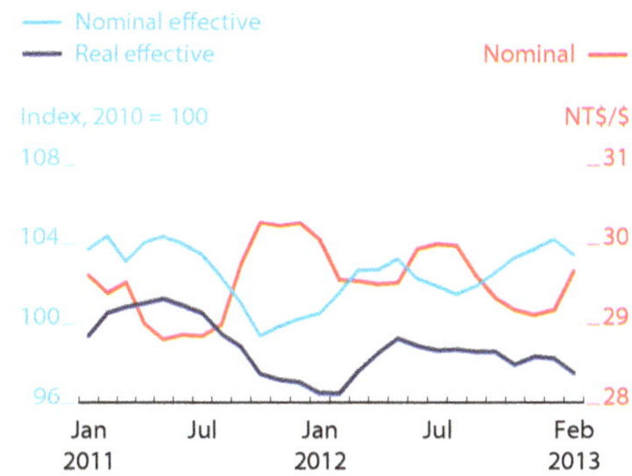

Source: Haver Analytics (accessed 19 March 2013).

Click here for figure data

3.13.7 Exports to countries in the global projection model

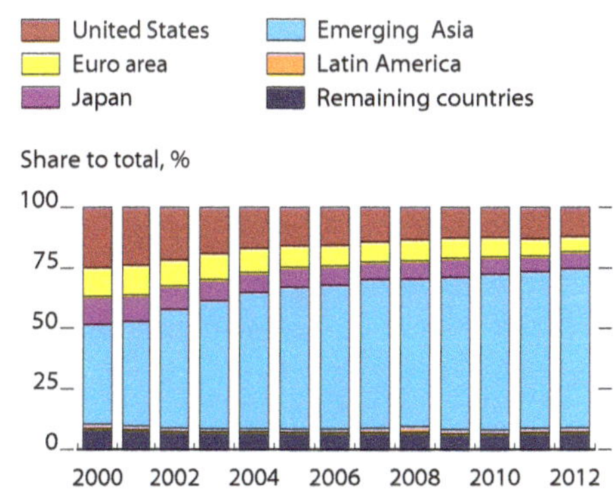

Notes: Euro area refers to euro area-17 excluding Estonia.

Emerging Asia = People's Republic of China; Hong Kong, China; India; Indonesia; Republic of Korea; Malaysia; Philippines; Singapore; Taipei,China; and Thailand.

Remaining countries = Argentina, Australia, Bulgaria, Canada, Czech Republic, Denmark, Estonia, Israel, New Zealand, Norway, the Russian Federation, South Africa, Sweden, Switzerland, Turkey, United Kingdom, and Venezuela.

Source: ADB estimates using the global projection and small, open economy models.

Click here for figure data

3.13.1 Impact of developments in trade partners

The impact of slowing external demand and the weakening of yen on Taipei,China's growth outlook were analyzed using the global projection model (GPM) as detailed in Carabenciov et al. (2013), and a small, open economy model (SOE). The GPM posits six regional blocks: the US, the euro area excluding Estonia, Japan, Latin America, emerging Asia, and a block of other countries. The SOE uses equations on output gap, inflation, real exchange rate, unemployment, and interest rates and links with the GPM through output gap and exchange rate equations. Two scenario analyses were done using the GPM, and the results were used as parameters for the SOE to determine impact on the Taipei,China economy. The results show output gap as the strongest channel for transmitting spillover effects and spillover effects strongest from emerging Asia (box table), with which the island has the strongest trade ties.

The first scenario looks at the impact of a shock that reduces GDP growth in the euro area by 1 percentage point below its baselines of –0.3 in 2013 and 1.2% in 2014 and compares it with the effect of the same development in emerging Asia (setting growth in emerging Asia 1 percentage point lower than the baselines for 2013 and 2014). GDP growth for other blocks remains at their baselines. A simulation is then conducted to see how other macroeconomic variables—output gap, inflation, interest rate, real exchange rate, and unemployment—respond to the assumed scenario.

The results suggest that a 1 percentage point slowdown in the rest of emerging Asia would shave Taipei,China's growth by 0.2 percentage points in 2013 and 0.4 percentage points in 2014. This is twice as large as the impact of the same developments in the euro area (box figure). There may be secondary and indirect spillover effects of the euro area slowdown, transmitted to Taipei,China through emerging Asia, but they would materialize only in later years and would not substantially change the results for 2013 and 2014.

The second scenario looks at the impact of the Japanese yen depreciating to an average of ¥100 per US dollar in 2013 and 2014 from the average 2012 rate of ¥79. Japan is the fourth-largest destination for Taipei,China exports, with a share of 7%, and it supplies more than 20% of imports, mainly capital goods for manufacturing. Therefore, other things being equal, a weaker yen would make Japanese products more competitive in Taipei,China's export markets, but it would also lower the cost of producing exports, with the net effect on the economy uncertain.

The simulation results suggest that Taipei,China's growth would not be affected by a weakened yen in 2013 but might decline marginally by about 0.05 percentage points in 2014. The growth rate would rise initially as manufacturing output increases owing to the lower cost of imported inputs but decline marginally later as competitiveness slightly weakens. The real effective exchange rate would gradually strengthen but only minimally. Factors that could amplify the impacts are the substitutability of products from Japan and Taipei,China and potential changes in the competitive landscape, such as the acquisition of Japanese brands by firms in the Republic of Korea.

Spillover from shocks in the euro area, emerging Asia, and Japan

Scenarios	Impact on GDP growth in Taipei,China (percentage points) 2013	2014
Scenario 1: 1 percentage point reduction in 2013 and 2014 GDP growth forecasts for the euro area and emerging Asia		
Euro area	–0.1	–0.2
Emerging Asia	–0.2	–0.4
Scenario 2: Japanese yen depreciation from ¥79 = $1 in 2012 to ¥100 = $1 in 2013 and 2014		
Japan	0.0	–0.05

Source: ADB estimates using the global projection and small, open economy models.

Spillover effects of shocks on Taipei,China's GDP growth

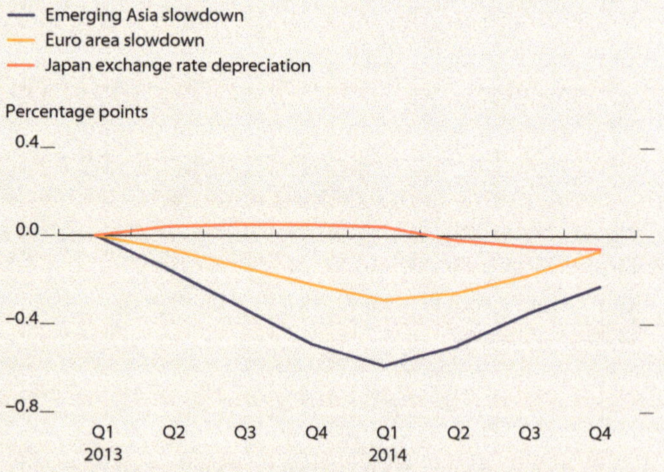

Notes: Euro area refers to euro area-17 excluding Estonia.
Emerging Asia = People's Republic of China; Hong Kong, China; India; Indonesia; Republic of Korea; Malaysia; Philippines; Singapore; Taipei,China; Thailand.
Source: ADB estimates using the global projection and small, open economy models.
Click here for figure data

Reference

Carabenciov, I., C. Freedman, R. Garcia-Saltos, O. Kamenik, D. Laxton, and P. Manchev. Forthcoming. GPM6—The Global Projection Model with 6 Regions. *IMF Working Paper.*

South Asia

Afghanistan
Bangladesh
Bhutan
India
Maldives
Nepal
Pakistan
Sri Lanka

Afghanistan

The next 2 years before the government assumes full responsibility for security in 2014 will be critical. Security and political uncertainties, including a presidential election, will weigh heavily on the direction the country takes. To ensure economic stability and a sound basis for transition, the government will have to fulfill commitments made under the Tokyo Mutual Accountability Framework and implement various policy and institutional reforms agreed under the current International Monetary Fund program.

Economic performance

GDP growth is estimated to have accelerated to 11.9% in 2012, following 7.2% expansion a year earlier, entirely due to the strong performance of agriculture, as weather improved from a drought in 2011 (Figure 3.14.1).

Private consumption buoyed by international aid flows, much of it related to security, remained the main source of growth. Aid fueled most of the demand for goods and services, especially in construction. Private investment increased slightly to 8.4% of GDP in 2012, as a 20% retrenchment by small and medium-sized enterprises was offset by a 26% increase in new investments in aviation, industry, agriculture, and real estate by large companies that began to shift their business focus from internationally funded security projects to enterprises catering to local demand.

Strong growth in agriculture, at 31.5%, reflected favorable weather, especially in the north. Wheat production, which accounts for three-fourths of cereal production, grew by 48%. Growth in industry slowed to 7.2% from 9.8% in 2011, mainly because of slower expansion in manufacturing and construction caused by protracted power shortages and spending cramped by the uncertain political and security situation. Growth in services, which accounts for about half of GDP, slowed to 7.3% from 12.7% in 2011, attributed to reduced spending by international security forces and by the local population because of uncertainty in the run-up to 2014.

Opium production fell from the equivalent of 7% of GDP in 2011 to 4% in 2012 as disease and unfavorable weather afflicted the main growing areas. The value of opium production is estimated to have halved from $1.4 billion in 2011 to $0.7 billion in 2012. Opium is not counted as part of GDP, but earnings generated by its sale that are retained and spent in Afghanistan boost domestic demand.

Average consumer price inflation almost halved to 6.2% in 2012 from 11.8% in 2011, mainly on account of a sharp drop in food prices, as the good harvest boosted domestic food supplies. Food inflation slowed to

3.14.1 Supply-side contributions to growth

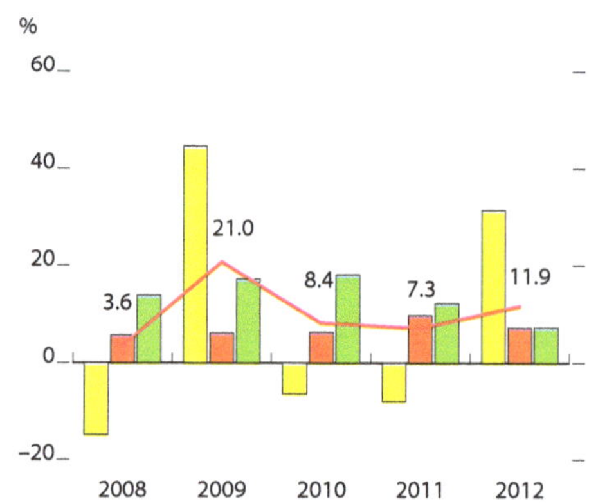

Sources: Ministry of Finance; ADB estimates.

Click here for figure data

This chapter was written by Rehman Gul of the Afghanistan Resident Mission, ADB, Kabul.

2.4% in August before rising to 4.4% in December, owing to increases in prices for imported goods such as milk, cheese, eggs, meat, spices, and nonalcoholic beverages (Figure 3.14.2). Nonfood inflation also declined over the year to 7.4% in December 2012, mainly reflecting lower international fuel prices and domestic transportation costs.

Fiscal policy in 2012 focused on revenue mobilization and budget management. The government was unable to fully achieve the domestic revenue target set in the current International Monetary Fund (IMF) program. Domestic revenue fell to 10.3% of GDP, mainly from a shortfall in custom duties, which account for one-third of total revenue (Figure 3.14.3). This took the government further away from its fiscal sustainability target, as domestic revenues financed 56% of the government's recurrent operating expenditures in 2012, down from 68% in the previous year. A number of grants and projects previously administered separately by development partners were added to the national budget during 2012. This resulted in development partners financing 44% of the recurrent expenditure and 65% of development expenditure.

The Da Afghanistan Bank, the central bank, primarily targets price stability using foreign exchange auctions and short-term capital notes as monetary tools. The monetary authorities succeeded in keeping inflation low by pursuing a tighter monetary policy in 2012. The policy slowed growth in broad money to 9.3% from 21.3% a year earlier, which, with improved domestic food production, succeeded in moderating inflation. The afghani depreciated by about 5% to AF51.8 = $1 in the 12 months to January 2013, apparently owing to foreign exchange being in tighter supply and higher demand (Figure 3.14.4).

The current account deficit excluding grants is estimated to have widened slightly to 42.7% of GDP in 2012, mainly reflecting higher imports (Figure 3.14.5). Including grants, the current account surplus improved to 4.0% of GDP from 3.0%, mainly from increased public transfers. Foreign direct investment rose to $405 million, largely on investment to develop oil in the Amu Darya Basin. Gross international reserves increased by 10.6% to $6.9 billion in FY2012 (ending 20 March 2013), enough to cover 7.3 months of FY2013 projected imports, excluding imports for re-export.

Economic prospects

GDP growth is forecast at 3.3% in 2013 and 5.1% in 2014. Unusually slow growth in 2013 reflects the expectation that food crop production will be substantially lower than in 2012, when weather was unusually favorable, this base effect dragging down GDP growth overall. Afghanistan will go through a period of political and security uncertainty that is expected to weigh heavily on economic growth. Private consumption will slow but remain as the main source of growth. Industry and services are expected to grow more slowly as smaller international security forces may spend less.

The FY2013 national budget focuses on domestic revenue mobilization, sustainable growth, and poverty reduction. The development of the extractive industry, social sectors, and agriculture will be top priorities alongside security. Total spending will increase by 26.5%, with

3.14.2 Inflation

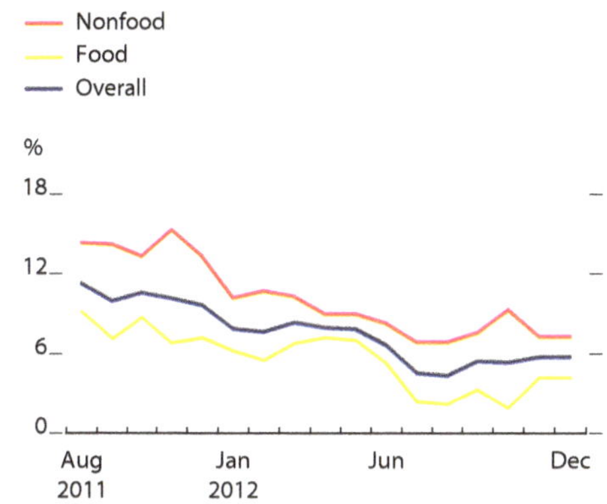

Note: March 2011 = 100.

Sources: Central Statistical Office. http://cso.gov.af/en (accessed 30 March 2013); ADB estimates.

Click here for figure data

3.14.3 Fiscal indicators

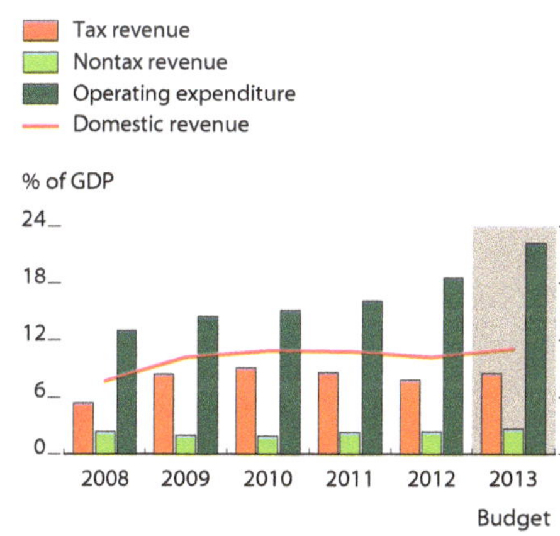

Sources: International Monetary Fund. 2012. *Country Report* No. 12/245. August; Da Afghanistan Bank. http://www.centralbank.gov.af (accessed 4 March 2013).

Click here for figure data

3.14.4 Nominal exchange rate

Source: Da Afghanistan Bank. http://www.centralbank.gov.af (accessed 4 March 2013).

Click here for figure data

development partners to finance 60% of the $6.6 billion national budget, or 49% of the recurrent budget and 66% of the development budget. Domestic revenue will increase by 18.0% but slide to 50.1% of recurrent operating expenditure. The planned value-added tax will, if approved and implemented by 2014, help bridge the gap between recurrent budget and domestic revenues. On-budget grants will increase in 2013 and 2014, as the budget is extended to cover more external grants heretofore administered by development partners and new pledges made at conferences in Tokyo and Chicago are realized.

Inflation during 2013 and 2014 is forecasted to be around 6.0% on the assumption of good harvests, easing international commodity prices, and the maintenance of tight monetary and fiscal policies. Afghanistan will continue to manage a floating exchange rate.

The current account deficit excluding grants is projected to widen to 44.0% of GDP in 2013 as imports rise and exports slip slightly. In 2014, the deficit will fall to 42.2% of GDP as the growth in nominal GDP continues while the dollar value of imports, the trade deficit, and public transfers are broadly unchanged from a year earlier. Including grants, the current account surplus will dwindle to 0.3% of GDP in 2014.

3.14.1 Selected economic indicators (%)

	2013	2014
GDP growth	3.3	5.1
Inflation	6.1	5.8
Current account balance (share of GDP)	1.6	0.3

Source: ADB estimates.

3.14.5 Current account balance

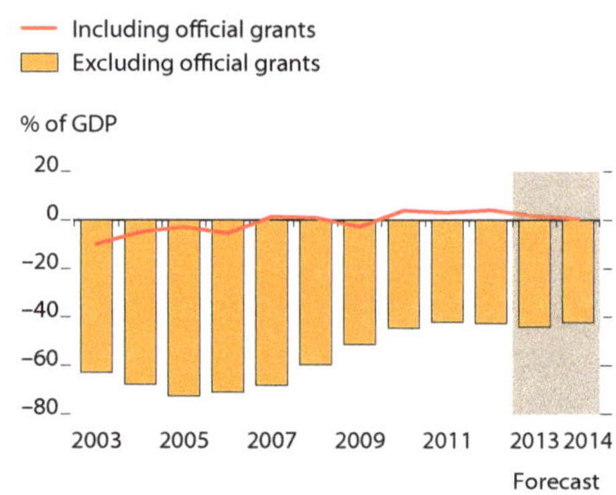

Sources: World Bank. 2011. Economic Update for Afghanistan. October; International Monetary Fund. 2011. *Country Report* No. 11/330. November; Da Afghanistan Bank. http://www.centralbank.gov.af (accessed 4 March 2013).

Click here for figure data

Policy challenge—funding the transition

The withdrawal of international security forces by the end of 2014 and the transition to Afghans assuming full responsibility for security will put pressure on public expenditures and widen fiscal gaps. These pressures arise mainly from having to expand security and development expenditure that was previously provided by international forces, as well as covering the recurrent costs of public assets built by development partners. Consequently, IMF projections show public expenditures growing significantly to reach 39% of GDP by 2025. Domestic revenues, by contrast, are expected to reach only 17% of GDP by 2025, leaving a significant financing gap equal to 22% of GDP. To cover this gap initially, development partners at the 2012 conference in Tokyo pledged $16 billion for development through 2015, conditional on improved governance and transparency. They reconfirmed their commitment to channel half of aid through the budget and align 80% of their programs with national priority programs. In 2012, members of the North Atlantic Treaty Organization pledged $4.1 billion a year to fund security costs after 2014.

Afghanistan has large mineral resources potentially worth about $1 trillion, according to the US Geological Survey. If developed, these resources could provide a solid base for economic development. The government has agreed with international companies to establish large projects to mine copper and iron ore. However, implementing these projects will require a substantially improved security environment. Government revenue from an oil production project in the Amu Darya Basin is estimated to be $64 million in 2013 and $90 million in 2014, which is an encouraging start.

Bangladesh

Growth slowed, inflation quickened, and exports weakened, but the current account surplus nearly doubled on strong remittances. The authorities began implementing a program of macroeconomic and structural reforms to correct emerging imbalances and foster sustained, rapid growth. Weak external and domestic demand are projected to slow growth this year but leave the current account in surplus. Political instability in the run-up to elections is a risk. Improving the business climate and infrastructure, deepening the financial sector, and liberalizing trade are needed to boost investment and competitiveness.

Economic performance

GDP growth slowed to 6.3% in FY2012 (ended June 2012) from 6.7% in the previous year (Figure 3.15.1). Agricultural growth halved to 2.5% from 5.1% in FY2011, as crop growth dropped to 0.9% from 5.7%. Higher power, fuel, and fertilizer prices, and reduced area for the monsoon season (*aman*) rice crop, weakened performance. Industry growth was strong at 9.5%, up from 8.2% in FY2011, as manufacturing expanded by 9.8% and construction and power both turned in somewhat better performances. Domestic market-oriented small-scale manufacturing benefited from new tax incentives and greater access to financing. Services growth slowed slightly to 6.1%, mainly because of lower exports and imports.

On the demand side, private consumption benefited from a marked expansion in workers' remittances and higher bank credit. Reflecting the global economic slowdown, growth in exports and imports alike decelerated sharply, with net exports subtracting from growth. At 25.4% of GDP, investment was slightly higher than the previous year's 25.2%. Public investment improved to 6.3% of GDP from 5.6% in FY2011 but was mostly offset by the decline in private investment to 19.1% of GDP. Although new foreign direct investment (FDI) rose to $1.0 billion because of larger inflows into the banking, telecommunications, energy, and garment industries, FDI was still less than 1% of GDP and 5% of total investment.

Year-on-year inflation steadily worsened to 11.6% in January 2012 because food prices remained elevated while nonfood prices rose in response to rapid growth in credit, upward adjustments in government-administered fuel and power prices, and sharp taka depreciation. However, inflation declined from February, reaching 8.6% in June 2012, as food prices dropped with improving market supply following the harvest and as monetary policy tightened (Figure 3.15.2). Inflation averaged 10.6% in FY2012, up from 8.8% in FY2011.

3.15.1 Supply-side contributions to growth

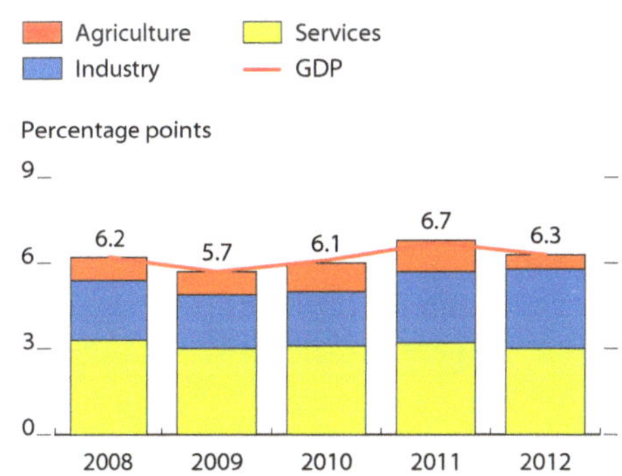

Source: Bangladesh Bureau of Statistics. 2012. *National Accounts Statistics.* May.

Click here for figure data

3.15.2 Monthly inflation

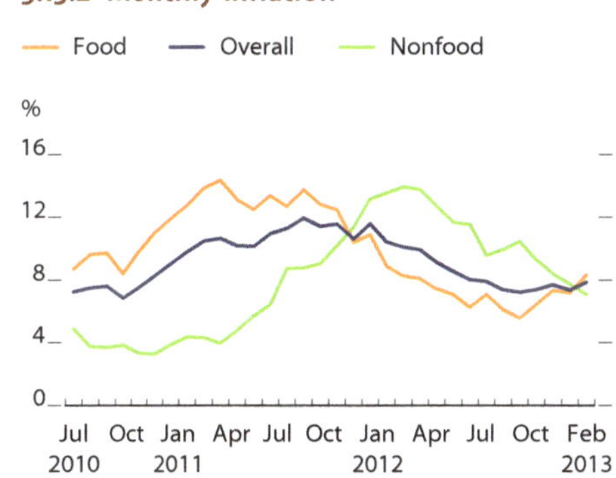

Source: Bangladesh Bank. 2013. *Monthly Economic Trends.* February. http://www.bangladesh-bank.org

Click here for figure data

This chapter was written by Mohammad Zahid Hossain, Md. Golam Mortaza, Shamsur Rahman, and Barun K. Dey of the Bangladesh Resident Mission, ADB, Dhaka.

Money supply and credit growth slowed as the year progressed (Figure 3.15.3) and the central bank's midyear tightening of monetary policy took hold. By June 2012, year-on-year growth in broad money was brought down to 17.4% from 21.3% a year earlier. Private credit growth slowed to 19.7% from 25.8% in the same period of the previous year. Expansion in net credit to the government was slashed to 25.2% by June 2012, down from 73.5% in December 2011, as higher mandated prices for fuel and electricity reduced the need to finance subsidies.

The central bank tightened monetary policy in FY2012, lifting repo and reverse-repo policy rates by 100 basis points to 7.75% and 5.75%. Moreover, in January 2012, it withdrew the 13.0% interest rate cap on commercial bank lending rates and stepped up its monitoring of liquidity conditions in the interbank call money market to foster better transmission of its policies. Reflecting these steps, short-term rates adjusted rapidly, with the weighted average yield on 91-day Treasury bills climbing to 11.4% by June 2012 from 6.8% in June 2011. Higher rates on new bank lending were reflected in the system's overall average lending and deposit rates, the former rising to 13.8% from 12.4% and the latter to 8.2% from 7.3%.

Budget revenues rose strongly to 12.5% of GDP from 11.7% in FY2011 as tax compliance improved (Figure 3.15.4). Income tax receipts rose by 22.8%, and indirect taxes grew by 22.9%. Current spending advanced slightly to 10.0% of GDP in FY2012 from 9.7% the previous year. Despite improved utilization of its allocation, annual development program spending still fell short of the budget allocation; this helped to limit the fiscal deficit to 5.1% of GDP, marginally above the budget target of 5.0%.

Export growth braked sharply to 6.2% in FY2012 from 39.2% in FY2011, as demand in the euro area and the US weakened for the mainly low-end garments on offer and per-unit prices fell. Exports of ready-made garments—accounting for nearly four-fifths of total earnings—grew by only 6.6%, down from 43.4% a year earlier. Exports of other products also slowed. Imports grew by only 5.4% in FY2012, markedly slowing from 41.8% in FY2011, which mainly reflected moderation in imported inputs for the garment industry, including capital equipment, and lower prices for cotton and other raw materials. Food grain imports declined because of higher stocks, though imports of consumer goods—about 10.0% of total imports, mainly sugar, edible oil, and milk—grew rapidly. Remittances strengthened by 10.2% in FY2012, up from 6.0% in the previous year, because of a larger number of Bangladeshi workers going abroad, taka depreciation since early 2011, and better banking services.

Despite the widened deficit in trade and services, larger workers' remittances raised the FY2012 current account surplus to $1.6 billion, or 1.4% of GDP, from $885.0 million (0.8%) in FY2011 (Figure 3.15.5). The combined capital and financial accounts recorded a smaller deficit of $486.0 million in FY2012, a significant narrowing of the $1.3 billion deficit in FY2011 because of higher FDI and much smaller net repayments of trade credit. The overall balance of payments showed a surplus of $494.0 million in FY2012, a significant rise from the deficit of $656.0 million in the previous year.

Earlier pressure on the exchange rate abated in the second half of FY2012, as import demand slowed and remittances rose. In nominal

3.15.3 Growth of monetary indicators

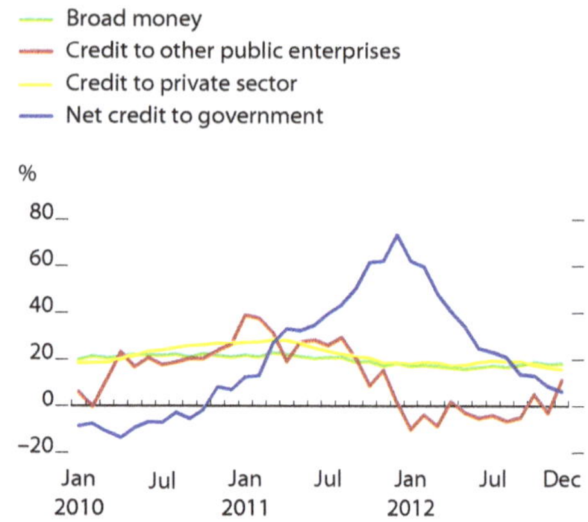

Source: Bangladesh Bank. 2013. *Monthly Economic Trends.* February. http://www.bangladesh-bank.org
Click here for figure data

3.15.4 Fiscal indicators

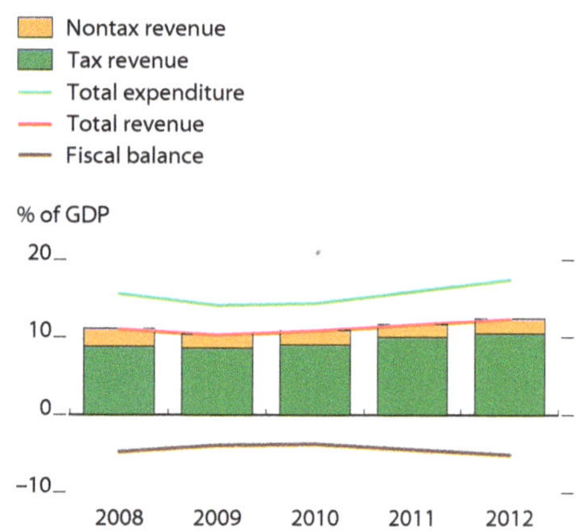

Source: Asian Development Outlook database.
Click here for figure data

3.15.5 Current account components

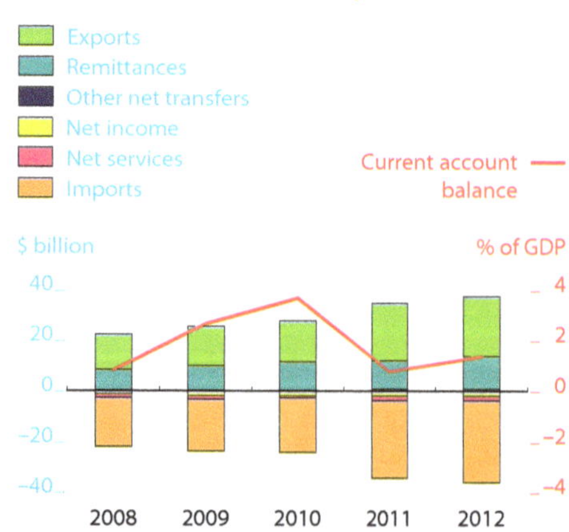

Source: Bangladesh Bank. *Annual Report 2011–2012.* http://www.bangladesh-bank.org
Click here for figure data

terms, the taka nonetheless depreciated by 9.4% against the US dollar in FY2012, reflecting developments in the first half (Figure 3.15.6). The real effective exchange rate rose by 2.2% year on year at the end of June 2012 because domestic inflation outpaced that of trading partners, indicating some erosion in export competitiveness. In the first 7 months of FY2013, the real effective rate rose further by 9.1%, as the nominal exchange rate remained broadly stable and an adverse inflation differential persisted.

Economic prospects

Economic forecasts for FY2013 and FY2014 rest on four assumptions: First, the central bank's slight easing in monetary policy announced in January 2013 will not stoke inflation, given the declining trend in international commodity prices and a favorable domestic crop outlook. Second, the government will contain subsidies by continuing to raise fuel and electricity prices and thus keep in check its need for bank borrowing. Third, though political activity is expected to be volatile, social stability will be maintained. And, finally, weather will be favorable.

GDP growth is projected to edge lower in FY2013 to 5.7% (Figure 3.15.7). Export demand, a major contributor to GDP growth, is expected to slacken slightly, reflecting the *Asian Development Outlook* baseline assumptions that the euro area economy stagnates and the US recovery remains frail. Despite higher remittances, growth in demand for private consumption is expected to weaken as households adopt a cautious approach to spending because of political uncertainties ahead of parliamentary elections expected by early 2014, depressing production in industries oriented to domestic markets. Lower rice prices will further dampen consumer demand through reduced agricultural income. Ongoing decline in imports of capital equipment and slow import growth for raw materials indicate lower utilization of existing production capacity and a lull in investment. A drop in import letters of credit opened for machinery and industrial raw materials signals weak economic activity in the coming months. With some strengthening of economic activity expected in the euro area and the US in 2014, GDP growth is projected to recover moderately to 6.0% in that year on the back of gradual rises in exports, consumer spending, and investment.

Industry growth is expected to slow to 6.5% in FY2013, reflecting slack demand externally and domestically. The Monetary Policy Statement released in January—which cut repo and reverse-repo rates by 50 basis points to 7.25% and 5.25%, effective 1 February 2013, and slightly raised the targets for private credit growth—signaled greater emphasis on sustaining growth while maintaining the 7.5% target for average inflation for the year. However, these measures are unlikely to spur much more private borrowing as long as prevailing consumer and investor sentiment remains subdued. Headwinds to growth include worsening power shortages as new supply lags growing demand, the inability of new industrial units to get natural gas connections because of supply limits, increased fuel and electricity prices along with wage pressures adding to production costs, and sluggish activity in the real estate market and construction. With expected improvements in external and domestic demand, industry growth is projected at 7.5% in FY2014.

3.15.6 Exchange rates

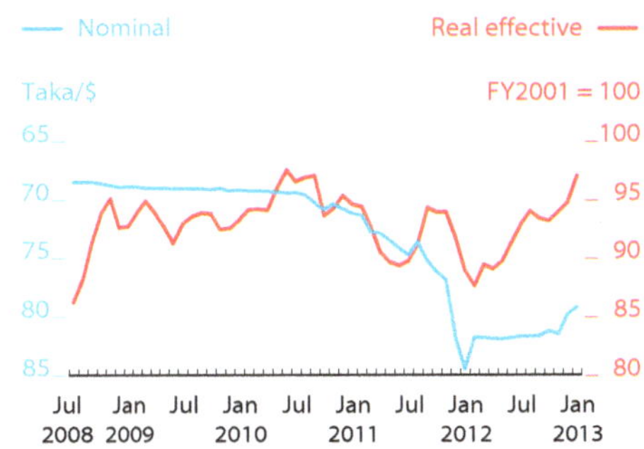

Source: Bangladesh Bank. 2013. *Monthly Economic Trends*. February. http://www.bangladesh-bank.org
Click here for figure data

3.15.1 Selected economic indicators (%)

	2013	2014
GDP growth	5.7	6.0
Inflation	7.8	7.0
Current account balance (share of GDP)	2.0	1.0

Source: ADB estimates.

3.15.7 GDP growth by sector

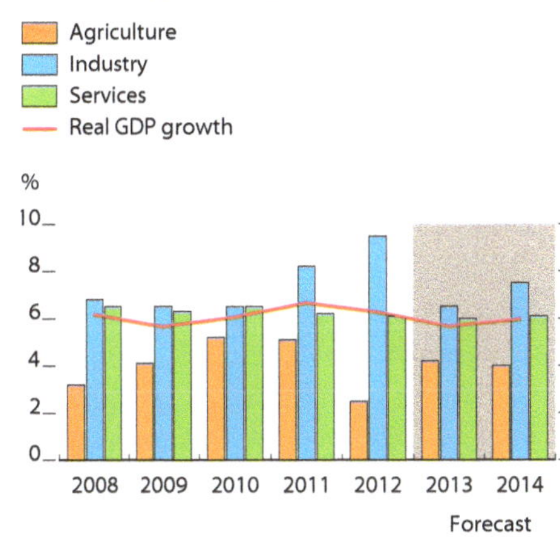

Sources: Bangladesh Bureau of Statistics. 2012. *National Accounts Statistics*. May; ADB estimates.
Click here for figure data

Favorable rainfall during planting and expanded acreage sown to the winter rice crop should help agricultural output in FY2013 recover to 4.2% growth. Greater access to credit resulting from central bank initiatives is expected to bolster output from livestock, aquaculture, and non-cereal crops. In FY2014, agricultural growth is projected to ease to 4.0%, returning to trend following the previous year's high base. Services growth in FY2013 is expected to slow to 6.0%, reflecting weaker economic activity, and then expand by at least 6.1% in FY2014 on moderate recovery in overall demand.

Average annual inflation is projected to slow to 7.8% in FY2013 (Figure 3.15.8). Inflation decelerated year on year from 11.6% in January 2012 to 7.9% in February 2013 because of easing nonfood prices in conjunction with broadly stable food inflation. Although the January 2013 increase in various fuel prices by 5.3%–11.5% will put pressure on prices, higher crop production and lower international food and commodity prices are expected to dampen inflation. The continuation of appropriate monetary policies is expected to ease inflation to 7.0% in FY2014.

Export growth is expected to slow slightly to 6.0% in FY2013, reflecting economic doldrums in the euro area and slow recovery in the US (Figure 3.15.9). Garment exports rose by 10.1% in the first 8 months of the fiscal year but are expected to slow again. Earnings from other exports have been mixed, showing little change. Export growth is expected to rise to 8.0% in FY2014 on slightly better demand.

Recent serious fires in garment factories have prompted the government, employers, and buyers to consider how to improve worker safety and working conditions, and some steps in this direction have been announced. Bangladesh's share of the global garment market has been growing. It is the second-largest exporter to the European Union, with a 12.0% market share in FY2012, when exports surged by 21.6%, substantially benefiting from a change in Generalized System of Preferences rules of origin that became effective in January 2011. Bangladesh also had a significant 4.6% share of the US market. Exports of high-end garments are rising, and garment sales to Australia, Canada, the People's Republic of China, India, Japan, Turkey, and other emerging markets in Asia and South America are expanding briskly.

Imports declined by 3.3% in the first 7 months of FY2013, mainly reflecting reductions in capital goods, rice, and other food items. Lower export growth stemmed imports of inputs to export industries. Although the import bill is expected to rise in the remainder of the year, mainly for fuel, imports are still expected to decline overall by 2.0% in FY2013, before growing again, by 6.0%, in FY2014.

Remittances grew by 17.3% to $9.9 billion in the first 8 months of FY2013. More workers going to the Middle East in 2011, substantial sales of government bonds to expatriate Bangladeshis, and better banking services contributed to the large gain. Remittance growth is expected to decelerate in the remainder of the year and stand at 12.0% in FY2013 and 10.0% in FY2014 as fewer workers go overseas, their numbers down by 31.8% in the first 8 months of FY2013 (Figure 3.15.10).

The current account is projected to show a larger surplus of 2.0% of GDP in FY2013 as the trade deficit narrows (Figure 3.15.11). Foreign

3.15.8 Inflation

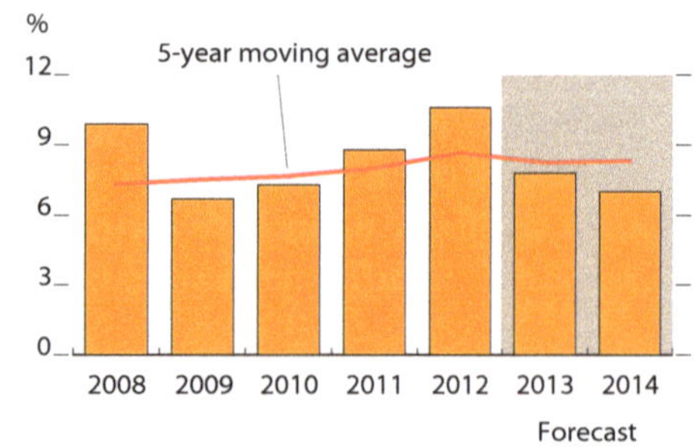

Sources: Bangladesh Bank. 2013. *Monthly Economic Trends.* February. http://www.bangladesh-bank.org; ADB estimates.

Click here for figure data

3.15.9 Contributions to export growth

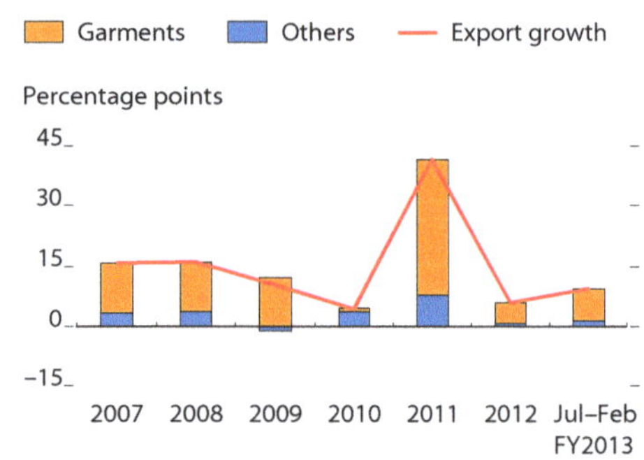

Sources: Export Promotion Bureau; ADB estimates.

Click here for figure data

3.15.10 Overseas employment growth

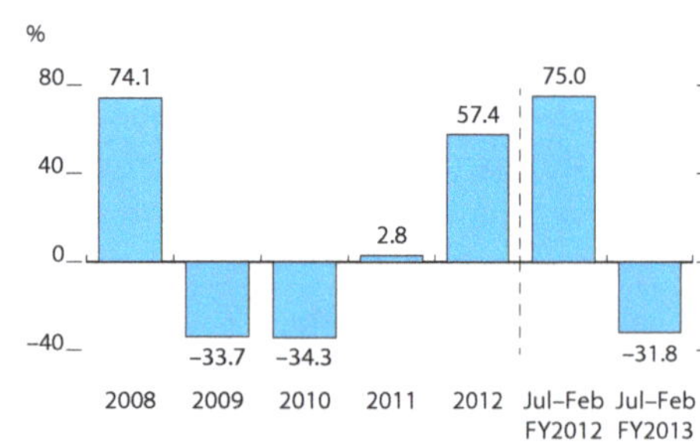

Source: Bangladesh Bank. 2013. *Monthly Economic Trends.* February. http://www.bangladesh-bank.org

Click here for figure data

3.15.11 Current account balance

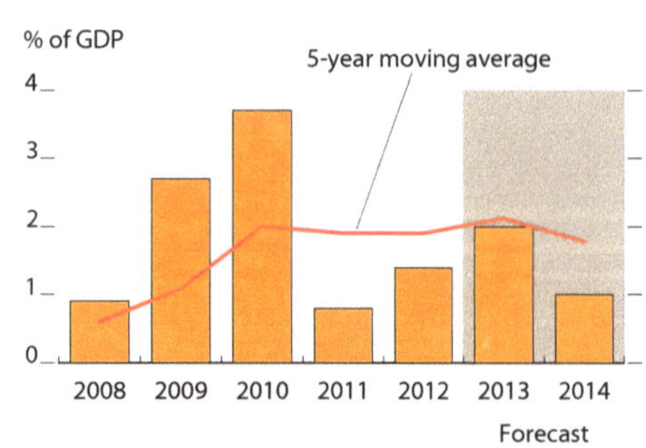

Sources: Bangladesh Bank. *Annual Report 2011–2012.* http://www.bangladesh-bank.org; ADB estimates.

Click here for figure data

exchange reserves rose to $13.8 billion at the end of February from $10.4 billion at the end of June 2012 (Figure 3.15.12), as the current account balance moved from a large deficit in the first 7 months of FY2012 to a sizeable surplus in the same period of FY2013 and the combined capital and financial account balance also rose slightly from $2.0 billion to $2.1 billion. Net inflows of foreign assistance rose sharply and FDI inflows improved. Pressure on the balance of payments will remain low in FY2014, though the current account surplus is expected to shrink to 1.0% of GDP as economic recovery revives imports.

Revenue collection grew by 15.1% in the first 7 months of FY2013, probably too slowly to meet the budget's target improvement of 21.6%. The budget set public spending growth at 18.9%. Annual development program spending will rise as the government seeks to address infrastructure deficits ahead of the elections but will nonetheless remain below the budget target. The government is holding current spending on subsidies in check by setting fuel and electricity prices higher. The overall deficit is expected to stay within the targeted 5.0% of GDP (Figure 3.15.13). Domestic financing, mainly from banks, will cover 2.7% of GDP, and foreign sources the remaining 2.3%.

Under the 3-year extended credit facility agreed with the International Monetary Fund, the government plans to pursue sound fiscal and debt management through reform to tax policy and administration, public financial administration, and debt management. Parliament passed a value-added tax law in November 2012 for implementation by 2015, which will help modernize the tax system and boost revenues to support Bangladesh's medium-term development priorities. To contain subsidy costs, a formula to automatically adjust fuel prices will be introduced.

There are downside risks to projections. Economic developments in the euro area and the US may prove to be much weaker than assumed in the *Asian Development Outlook* baseline, materially affecting exports from Bangladesh. Another risk is budget revenues weakening if political unrest intensifies enough to markedly disrupt economic activity. Extreme spending policies to brighten reelection prospects could compromise monetary and fiscal discipline. Natural disasters pose perennial risks.

Development challenge—removing constraints on growth

Bangladesh needs to give priority to enhancing its business climate, which the World Bank's *Doing Business 2013* shows deteriorating in the past year (Figure 3.15.14). The country also lags in South Asia in terms of infrastructure quality, as seen from the World Economic Forum's *Global Competitiveness Report 2012–2013* (Table 3.15.2). In addition to improved infrastructure and trade logistics, the trade regime needs to become more open to force manufacturers to improve their productivity and global competitiveness. This would accelerate economic growth and create more and better jobs. The depth and efficiency of the financial sector needs to be developed more fully to expand private access to financing and create a source of long-term lending for infrastructure.

3.15.12 Foreign exchange reserves

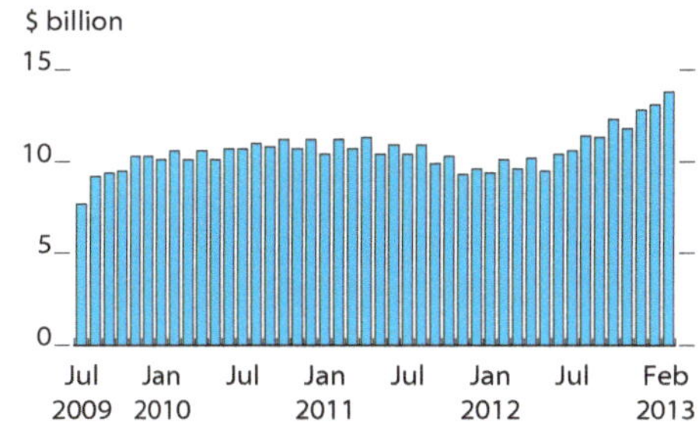

Source: Bangladesh Bank. 2013. *Monthly Economic Trends.* February. http://www.bangladesh-bank.org

Click here for figure data

3.15.13 Budget deficit financing

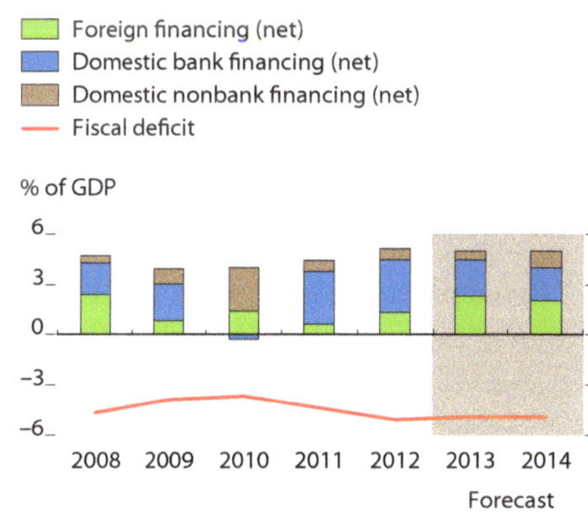

Source: Asian Development Outlook database.

Click here for figure data

3.15.14 How Bangladesh ranks on *Doing Business 2013* indicators

Note: Numbers in parentheses show ranking out of 185 countries worldwide. 1 = best, 185 = worst.

Source: World Bank. Doing Business database. http://www.doingbusiness.org/data (accessed 13 March 2013).

Click here for figure data

3.15.2 Comparison of infrastructure quality, 2012

Country ranking[a]		Overall infrastructure	Electricity	Roads	Railroads	Ports	Air transport
Bangladesh	131	2.8	1.8	2.8	2.5	3.3	3.5
China, People's Rep. of	69	4.3	5.2	4.4	4.6	4.4	4.5
India	87	3.8	3.2	3.5	4.4	4.0	4.7
Pakistan	105	3.4	2.3	3.9	2.6	4.4	4.3
Sri Lanka	50	4.8	5.3	4.6	3.8	4.9	5.0

[a] Ranking out of 142 countries.

Note: 1 = extremely underdeveloped, 7 = extensive and efficient by international standards.

Source: 2012 World Economic Forum, *Global Competitiveness Report 2012–2013*.

Bangladesh's acute shortage of skills constrains productivity growth in manufacturing and limits economic diversification. With 30% of the population younger than 15 years old, Bangladesh is poised to reap a strong demographic dividend. A major challenge, however, is to transform the vast young population into a trained human resource base in short order by boosting education quality and developing the specific skills industry demands.

Land shortage is emerging as a major constraint on infrastructure and industrial development. Unplanned urbanization is compounding the problem of finding suitable locations for enterprises, which are excessively concentrated in the capital. Dhaka generates over a third of the country's GDP with less than a tenth of its population, and congestion in Dhaka and Chittagong, the country's second city, hampers international competitiveness. The absence of developed connectivity and basic services in other cities and towns robs them of favorable production opportunities and attractive living conditions.

Policy makers need to identify new growth drivers, notably promoting labor-intensive manufacturing for export and expanding industry to serve domestic markets. With the country's abundant supply of low-cost labor and advantageous location, strong potential exists for a number of sectors: pharmaceuticals, shipbuilding, electronics, leather, textiles, home furnishings, ceramics, agro-processing, jute, footwear, light engineering, plastics, information and communication technology, and business processes outsourcing.

Climate change poses huge risks for this low-lying, flood-prone country. An emerging challenge is to expand capacity and mobilize financing to cope with and help mitigate climate change.

Bhutan

Growth moderated last year as the authorities tightened credit to address a rupee liquidity crunch caused by both cyclical and structural factors. The Royal Monetary Authority implemented significant monetary reforms including the introduction of policy and base rates. Looking ahead, growth is expected to pick up, propelled by exports of hydropower and higher tourist arrivals.

Economic performance

Economic growth moderated to 7.5% in FY2012 (ended 30 June 2012) from 10.0% a year earlier (Figure 3.16.1). The slowdown reflected credit measures taken by the Royal Monetary Authority (RMA) to curb an escalating balance of payments deficit with India and alleviate the rupee liquidity crunch. Both general and specific credit restrictions were implemented to constrain imports that are a large component of consumer and investment spending. Reflecting the measures, growth in consumption, which accounts about three-fifths of GDP, slowed to 7.8% in FY2012 from 10.0% in FY2011.

The measures had their greatest impact on construction and transport and communications services. Construction growth slowed to 9.1% from 17.4% in FY2011, and transport and communications slowed less sharply to 12.7% from 16.6%. Hydropower output, which contributes about 20% of GDP, grew by 7.6% on better water storage after being broadly flat a year earlier. The construction of large ongoing power projects was not subject to tightening.

Consumer price inflation reached an all-time high of 13.6% from a year earlier in the fourth quarter of FY2012 (Figure 3.16.2). Food inflation was 18.7% and nonfood inflation 10.7%. Local prices broadly follow prices in India because the Bhutanese ngultrum is pegged to the Indian rupee. However, scarce supplies appear to have bid local prices to a premium in the second half of FY2012. Average inflation was 10.2% for the fiscal year.

The average annual growth of broad money (M2) slowed to 5.8% in FY2012 from 23.6% in FY2011. Short-term liquidity concerns arising from asset–liability mismatches in the banking sector has led the RMA to create a short-term liquidity adjustment facility and to reduce its cash reserve ratio twice, taking it from 17% to 5%.

The RMA implemented significant reforms by introducing monetary policy rates and a base-rate system for Bhutanese financial institutions. The policy rate, set at 6%, will act as the main monetary policy instrument, supplemented by the cash reserve ratio. The base rate will set the floor for lending by financial institutions and also be the reference rate for floating-rate products. Bank base rates were set between 10.4% and 12.7%, while a uniform base rate of 13% was applied to nonbanking institutions.

3.16.1 Supply-side contributions to growth

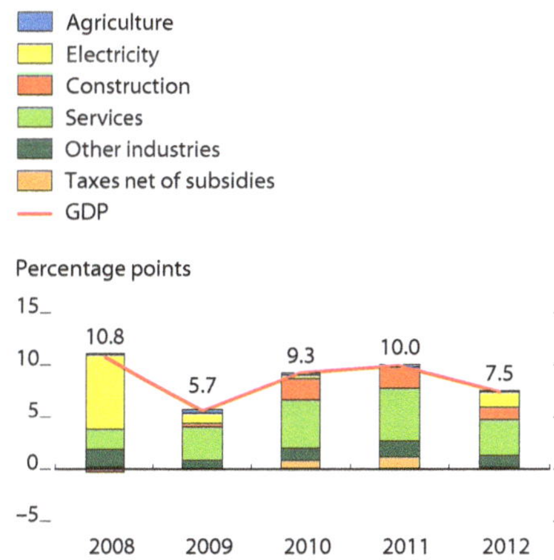

Source: National Statistics Bureau. *National Accounts Statistics 2012.* http://www.nsb.gov.bt

Click here for figure data

3.16.2 Contributions to inflation

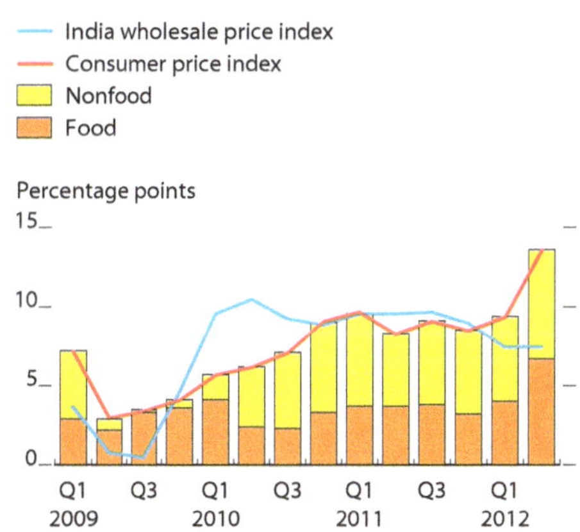

Source: Royal Monetary Authority of Bhutan. 2013. *Annual Report FY2011/12.* http://www.rma.org.bt

Click here for figure data

This chapter was written by Sabyasachi Mitra , Yoko Niimi, and Ruzette Mariano of the South Asia Department, ADB, Manila.

Bhutan aims to diversify economic activity and is expanding and upgrading its hotel industry with a target to attract 100,000 tourists by the end of 2013. The total revenues of the tourism sector reached $52 million in October 2012, improving on the $48 million in earnings realized in calendar year 2011.

Labor market conditions have improved with a steady decline in the unemployment rate in recent years. Total unemployment fell to 2.1% of the labor force in FY2012 from 4.0% in FY2009, while the youth unemployment rate was brought down to 7.2% from 9.4% a year earlier, which is much lower than 12.9% recorded in FY2009 (Figure 3.16.3). However, youth unemployment still accounts for about half of total unemployment, and addressing youth unemployment remains a key challenge in Bhutan.

The current account deficit in FY2012 is estimated at 18.9% of GDP, down from 23.5% in FY2011 (Figure 3.16.4). The imposition of credit measures and foreign exchange restrictions caused a slight narrowing of the trade deficit to 26% of GDP from 30%. Exports shrank by 10.6% year on year, while imports fell by 9.5%. India continues to be a major trading partner, receiving over 80% of all exports from Bhutan and providing over 70% of Bhutan's total imports.

The overall balance of payments recorded a deficit of 5.9% of GDP, down from a surplus of 5.5% in FY2011. This reflected declining capital transfers, foreign direct investment, and government loans. Gross international reserves fell by $136 million to $770 million in FY2012, enough to cover 9.9 months of imports (Figure 3.16.5). External debt reached $1.4 billion (73.4% of GDP), down by 1.8 percentage points from the previous year. About three-fifths of the debt is denominated in Indian rupees. Most borrowings from the Government of India were earmarked for hydropower development.

Economic prospects

Growth is expected to recover in FY2013 and reach 8.6%, driven mainly by hydropower and tourism. The contribution of the service sector to growth is expected to improve as the government develops the country's tourism potential. As this trend is likely to continue, 8.5% growth is expected in FY2014.

Inflation is expected to moderate to 9.3% in FY2013, as the government has adopted a tight fiscal stance and clamped down on growth in credit, especially for home construction and personal loans, in response to the rupee liquidity crunch. Inflation is expected to ease further to 7.4% in FY2014 as the foreign exchange position relaxes.

Continued shortage of electricity in India will support Bhutan's hydropower exports. However, a widening of current account deficit is likely to persist at about 20% of GDP in FY2013 and FY2014, driven by strong demand for imports related to hydropower development.

The government aims to limit the fiscal deficit to 1.5% of GDP in FY2013 by cutting capital expenditures, which are expected to contract by 22.9% in FY2013 after expanding by 30.8% in FY2012 (Figure 3.16.6). Current expenditures are expected to expand by 5.3% in FY2013 from 17.7% last year. The cutback in fiscal outlay follows the fiscal rationalization measures announced in the budget.

3.16.3 Unemployment

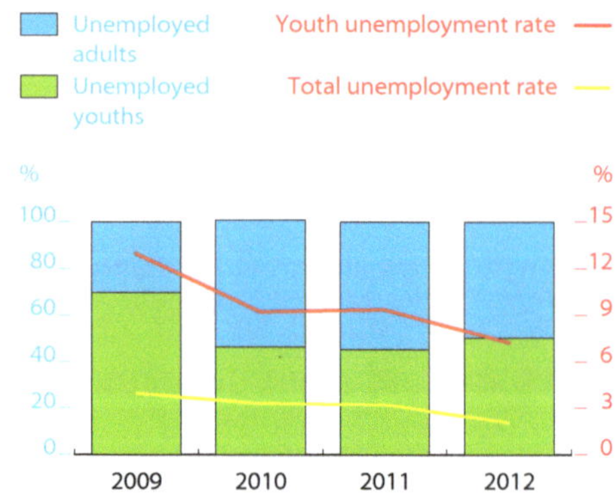

Source: Ministry of Labor and Human Resources. Various years. *Labour Force Survey Report.* http://www.molhr.gov.bt
Click here for figure data

3.16.4 Balance of payments

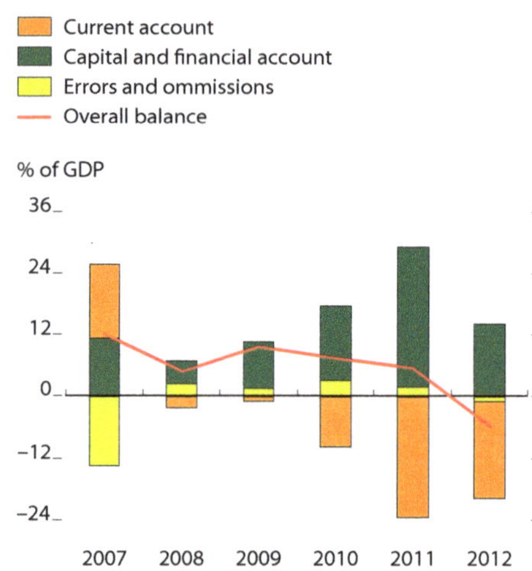

Source: Royal Monetary Authority of Bhutan. 2013. *Annual Report FY2011/12.* http://www.rma.org.bt
Click here for figure data

3.16.5 Gross international reserves

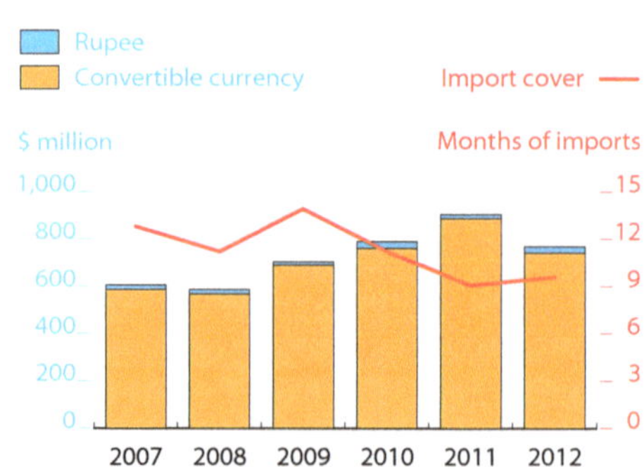

Source: Royal Monetary Authority of Bhutan. 2013. *Annual Report FY2011/12.* http://www.rma.org.bt
Click here for figure data

Policy challenge—sustaining high economic growth

Bhutan has achieved remarkable economic performance and made significant progress in reducing poverty and advancing social development over the past decade. However, sustaining high and inclusive economic growth remains a major challenge. The tight overall balance with India has recently placed great pressure on Indian rupee liquidity in Bhutan. The RMA's small rupee working balances over the past few years have been maintained by the sale of convertible currencies and borrowing on lines of credit with Indian banks; as of June 2012, outstanding net liabilities on this account were Rs9.6 billion (about $174 million).

The ongoing rupee liquidity problem has been caused by both structural and cyclical factors, which can be attributed to weak economic management. The lumpy nature of hydropower-related imports and the long gestation between construction and operation make managing the trade balance in the medium term a challenge. Lumpy debt payments and high seasonality in hydropower generation and electricity exports contribute to volatility in net rupee inflows. This highlights the need for enhancing capacity to manage debt.

The rupee shortage also reflects the rapid growth of the economy. Rising per capita income has fuelled domestic demand for consumption goods and launched a housing boom, both of which have contributed to the large import bill from India. Limited ability to contain public spending has widened trade deficits and put further pressure on the balance of payments with India. On the financial side, rapid growth in private consumption has been fed by excessive growth in credit. Indeed, loans to the private sector grew by 30.1% in FY2012, greatly outpacing nominal GDP growth of 17.7%. The limited effectiveness of monetary and liquidity management instruments in stabilizing inflation and avoiding asset price buildup has also contributed to the problem.

The Ministry of Finance and the RMA have undertaken a number of measures to address the rupee liquidity issue. For instance, the RMA has clarified that, while the rupee serves to anchor the nominal value of the ngultrum, there should be no presumption of unlimited convertibility. The RMA has made it mandatory to use the banking system to settle Indian rupee transactions, especially for cross-border purchases between India and Bhutan. In addition, it has sought to improve liquidity management by introducing policy rates and the base-rate system, as well as the liquidity adjustment facility. The Ministry of Finance's tighter fiscal policy, aiming to reduce the fiscal deficit to 1.5% of GDP in FY2013, is a welcome step.

While Bhutan has been the fastest-growing economy in South Asia, the recent rupee shortage has revealed structural imbalance in the economy and Bhutan's weak economic management. As the large spending on hydropower development is expected to continue in the medium term, Bhutan must strengthen in a timely way its macro-financial management to sustain high growth without exacerbating domestic and external economic imbalances.

3.16.1 Selected economic indicators (%)

	2013	2014
GDP growth	8.6	8.5
Inflation	9.3	7.4
Current account balance (share of GDP)	–20.0	–20.0

Source: ADB estimates.

3.16.6 Fiscal indicators

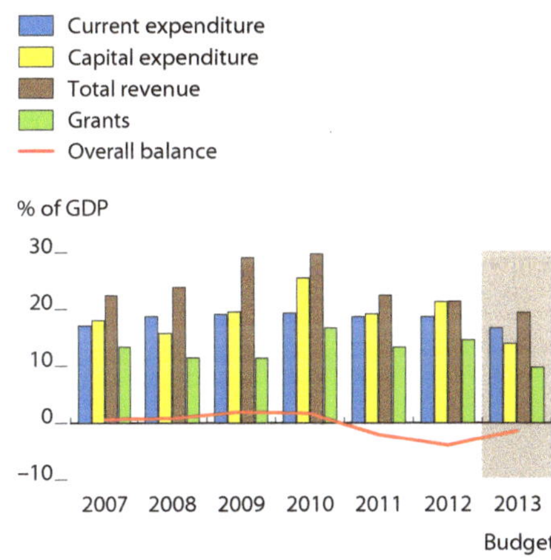

Source: Royal Monetary Authority of Bhutan. 2013. *Annual Report FY2011/12.* http://www.rma.org.bt

Click here for figure data

India

Growth further decelerated as a slump in industry and investment spread to consumption and exports. Though inflation and the fiscal deficit were reined in, the current account deficit rose to a record high. Delays in resolving structural impediments to growth were compounded by a global trade slowdown. Boosting investment is critical for a return to high growth but requires reforms to eliminate bottlenecks that are stalling projects. Recent steps to address some of these challenges are expected to help growth pick up modestly.

Economic performance

Economic growth in FY2012 (ended 31 March 2013) decelerated to 5%, its lowest rate in a decade, from 6.2% in FY2011 (Figure 3.17.1). While tepid industrial growth and a downdraft in investment continued from FY2011, the downturn was exacerbated by a slump in services activity, weakening consumption, and contracting exports.

Growth in consumption expenditure halved from the previous years' average to 4.1% as private and public spending both dropped. Subdued economic activity, high inflation, a weak currency, and steep interest rates dented consumer confidence. The slowdown in public consumption reflected the containment of government expenditure in the second half of FY2012 to restrain the budget deficit.

Supply bottlenecks such as the lack of fuel for power generation, difficulty in acquiring land and environmental clearances, contentious tax policies, and procedural delays continued to stifle investment, causing growth in fixed investment to drop to 2.5% (Figure 3.17.2).

Industry in FY2012 weakened further, driven by a slump in manufacturing and mining. At 1.9%, manufacturing registered one of its weakest expansions in the post-1991 reform era as capital goods production contracted for a second year in a row. Delays over land and environmental clearances continued to hamper mining operations, keeping growth tepid at 0.4% despite a low base. Dwindling production of natural gas at a large new field caused by pricing and technical issues, and a lack of new discoveries in recent years, drove natural gas production down by 13.3%. Electricity production also moderated as thermal generation was hampered by inadequate coal supplies and hydro generation was affected by depleted reservoirs following deficient rains. Power shortages have raised firms' costs and hampered production. Construction, helped by a delayed monsoon and the resulting long dry spell, expanded by 5.9%.

The late onset of the southwest monsoon and its subsequent unfavorable progress cut agriculture growth by half to 1.8% in FY2012. Grain production is estimated to be 3.5% lower than in the previous year, reflecting a drop in the production of rice, wheat, pulses, and coarse cereals.

3.17.1 GDP growth by sector

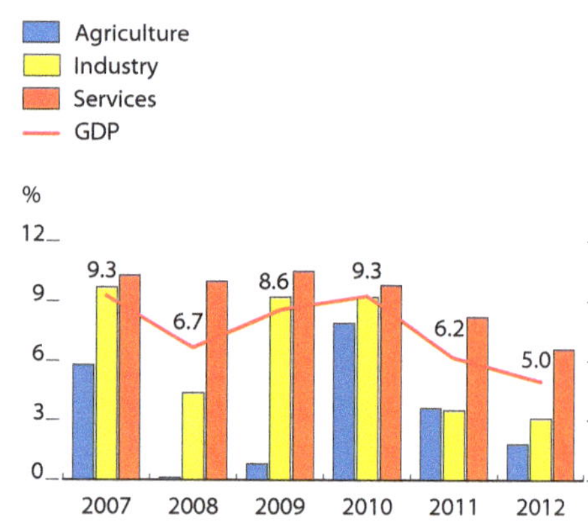

Source: CEIC Data Company (accessed 23 March 2013).
Click here for figure data

3.17.2 Fixed investment growth

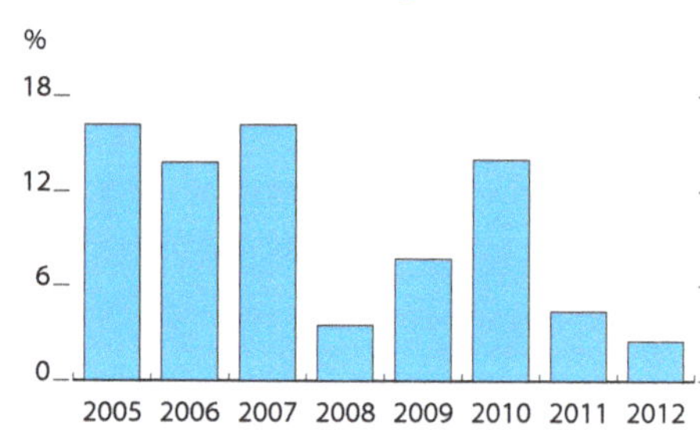

Source: CEIC Data Company (accessed 23 March 2013).
Click here for figure data

This chapter was written by Abhijit Sen Gupta of the India Resident Mission, ADB, New Delhi.

Services, which had largely held out against the slowdown in FY2011, decelerated sharply to 6.6% in FY2012, its lowest growth rate in more than a decade. This weak performance reflected the effect of the downturn on incomes, confidence, and consumer spending.

While wholesale price inflation moderated from highs in previous years, it remained elevated, averaging 7.4% in FY2012. Tight monetary policy and a slowing economy brought down inflation in nonfood manufactured goods to below 5% as the year progressed (Figure 3.17.3). However, food inflation persisted near double digits from the impact of a deficient monsoon on production and a weak farm supply response for high-protein items. Inflation based on consumer prices continued to trend at a higher level of about 10%, since food prices have a much greater weight in the index.

After maintaining a tight monetary stance to contain high inflation and inflation expectations, the Reserve Bank of India, the central bank, cut policy interest rates by 100 basis points in FY2012 to promote growth with the expectation of a less expansive fiscal policy and steps to remove impediments that have stifled a supply-side response (Figure 3.17.4). However, it cautioned against inflation risks emanating from the delayed monsoon, weak currency, and sustained wage pressures. Further, since September, the central bank has cut the cash reserve ratio by 75 basis points to 4% to alleviate liquidity shortfalls in the banking system.

High interest rates, slackening economic activity, and slowing business and consumer demand combined to decelerate credit growth. At the same time, there was a deterioration in credit quality. Nonperforming and restructured loans are estimated to have increased to 9.5% of total loans and advances in September 2012 from 5.5% in March 2011 (Figure 3.17.5). The fall in asset quality increased banks' risk aversion and prompted portfolio switching from credit creation to investments in government securities, facilitated by large market borrowing by the government.

Despite the economic slowdown, the central government budget deficit for FY2012 was contained at 5.2% of GDP, well below the deficit of 5.7% in FY2011 but marginally above the 5.1% target. However, the quality of the fiscal consolidation is a concern. In a bid to rein in the deficit, capital expenditure was compressed and grew by only 5.8%, against the original target of 29.2%. Thus, even though the overall deficit nearly reached its target, the revenue deficit—the excess in current expenditure over tax and nontax revenue—exceeded the budgeted target by 0.5% of GDP. This reflected slippage in meeting budgeted objectives for higher tax revenues and lower subsidies.

Despite several increases in diesel prices and a cap on the number of subsidized cooking gas cylinders, petroleum subsidies were more than double the original estimates. Even food and fertilizer subsidies exceeded their budgeted targets as a weak currency increased import costs and minimum support prices for grains were raised. Consequently, subsidy payments were estimated at 2.5% of GDP, well above the target of bringing them below 2% of GDP.

On the revenue side, tepid industrial activity and stagnant imports left corporate tax and customs and excise duty collections short of their targets, though this was partly offset by higher personal income and service tax collections. Moreover, revenue from disinvestment in public sector corporations was lower than planned.

3.17.3 Inflation

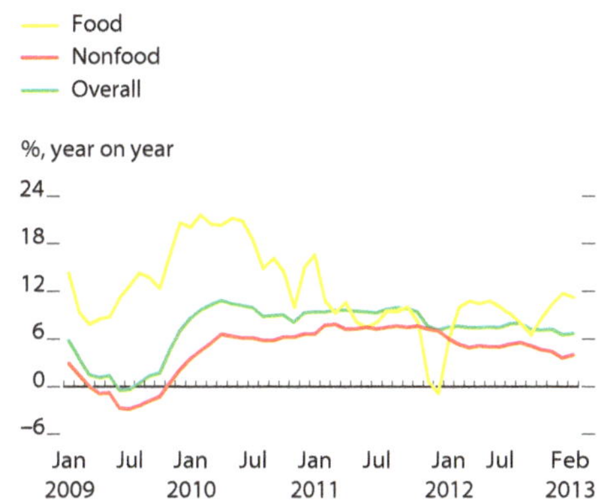

Note: Based on the wholesale price index.
Source: Ministry of Industry and Commerce.
Click here for figure data

3.17.4 Policy interest rates

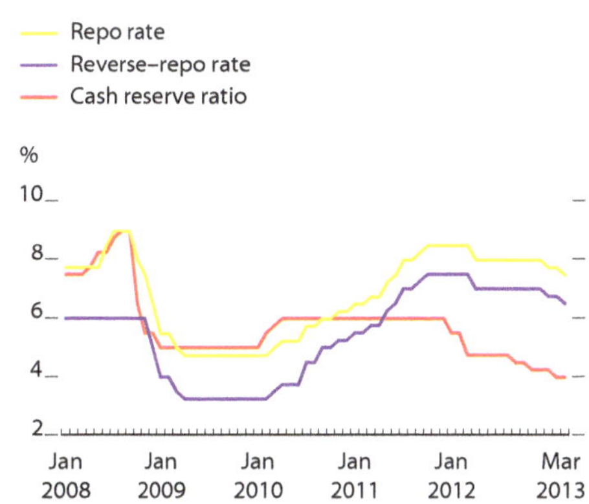

Source: CEIC Data Company (accessed 23 March 2013).
Click here for figure data

3.17.5 Nonperforming and restructured loans

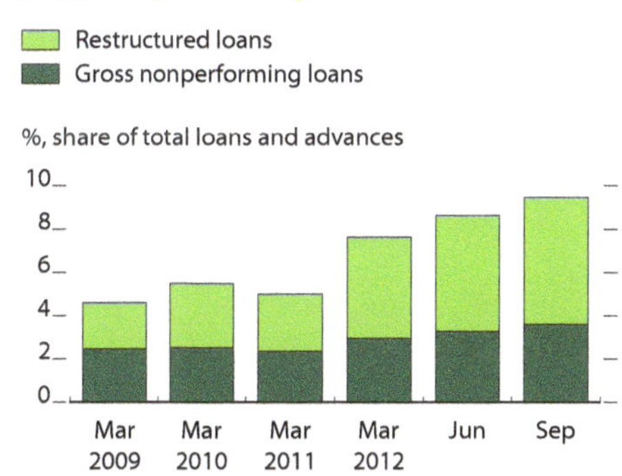

Source: Reserve Bank of India http://www.rbi.org.in/scripts/BS_SpeechesView.aspx?id=732
Click here for figure data

The current account deficit for FY2012 is estimated at 5% of GDP, significantly higher than last year's record, driven by a deteriorating trade balance (Figure 3.17.6). Despite a weak currency, merchandise exports contracted by 4%, because of weak global demand, down to $297.4 billion. However, imports remained nearly static, declining by only 1% to $494 billion despite the slowdown in growth, largely due to inelastic oil demand and large gold imports. While in previous years the worsening trade deficit was cushioned by improvement in invisibles, FY2012 witnessed moderation in the invisibles' surplus, driven by anemic expansion in software and business services exports and remittances, and higher investment income payments.

Spurred by announcements of various reform initiatives, portfolio flows picked up in the second half of the year to reach an estimated $26 billion in FY2012. This helped the Indian rupee to strengthen after June 2012, but it nevertheless depreciated in FY2012 by 7.5% against the US dollar, and the real effective exchange rate fell by about 5% (Figure 3.17.7). The increase in portfolio investment helped to lift stock prices, with the Bombay Stock Exchange Sensex up by about 8% for the year (Figure 3.17.8). With robust portfolio investment and moderate increases in foreign direct investment (FDI) and commercial borrowing covering the current account deficit, the central bank refrained from intervening much in the foreign exchange market. Foreign exchange reserves remained broadly stable over the year at around $295 billion.

Economic prospects

The slowdown in domestic investment will need to be reversed for growth to trend upward in a sustained manner. However, recent data from the Centre for Monitoring Indian Economy on planned capital expenditures are not encouraging, as they continue to show a downward trend in announced new projects and an increase in the number of shelved projects (Figure 3.17.9). Clearly, turning this trend around will be a major challenge.

Recent reforms include the creation of the Cabinet Committee on Investment to expedite government clearances for large projects and cabinet clearance of a land acquisition bill. However, these are only first steps toward improving the investment climate, and further measures will have to be undertaken for the investment cycle to turn around. These would include tough economic and politically difficult policy decisions related to delays in environmental clearances, parliamentary approval of the land acquisition bill that involves complex issues, improving the availability of fuel sources and infrastructure linking fuel sources with power generating plants, and attaining fiscal consolidation without sacrificing capital expenditure.

Various business survey indexes present a mixed picture, indicating the need for further action to restore confidence. The central bank's business expectation index in January deteriorated in comparison with the previous year, though there was some improvement over the previous quarter (Figure 3.17.10). The latest reading of HSBC Markit purchasing managers' index for manufacturing and services is no higher than average levels earlier in FY2012 (Figure 3.17.11).

3.17.6 Trade indicators

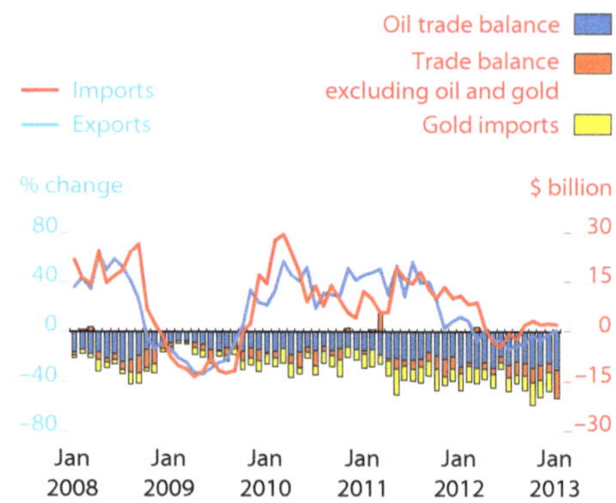

Source: CEIC Data Company (accessed 24 March 2013).

Click here for figure data

3.17.7 Exchange rates

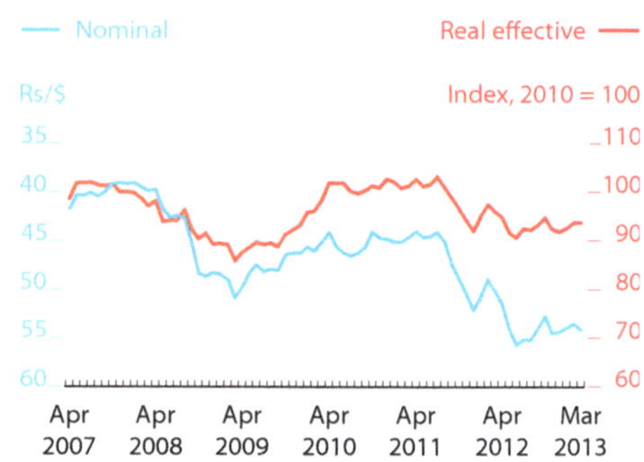

Source: CEIC Data Company (accessed 23 March 2013).

Click here for figure data

3.17.8 Stock price indexes

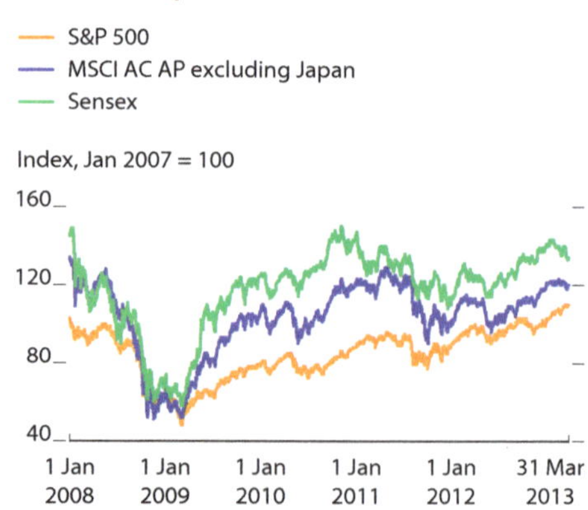

Source: Bloomberg (accessed 2 April 2013).

Click here for figure data

Progress on reforms in FY2013 is expected to improve business and consumer confidence sufficiently to underpin a moderate improvement in investment and consumer spending. An upturn in global trade volume and greater budgeted government spending would further add to total demand. With results demonstrated from planned measures to reduce the budget deficit, especially progress on reducing fuel subsidies, the central bank would further ease monetary policy, which would help to sustain and build demand momentum.

A normal monsoon is expected to substantially boost agriculture growth from the depressed base a year earlier. This will strengthen rural consumer demand and ease price pressures. Industry growth should improve on better domestic and external demand, but unresolved structural issues will continue to constrain investment, mining, and power. Services are expected to see a stronger pickup in activity than industry, though growth will continue to be restrained by the limited demand. However, community services could see an uptick with increased government spending in the run-up to an election.

In this scenario, GDP growth nudges up to 6% in FY2013. Improved global prospects, some easing of price pressures, and forward movement in resolving structural bottlenecks would allow growth to increase to 6.5% in FY2014.

Core inflation pressures have receded considerably, reflecting the lagged impact of monetary tightening and the slowdown in economic activity. At less than 5%, core inflation is in line with the central bank's target. A normal monsoon, fiscal consolidation, and easing global commodity prices will allow some reduction in price pressures. However, some elements of wholesale price index inflation will remain sticky. Rising input costs, robust agricultural wage growth, higher minimum support prices for crops, and continuing undersupply of protein-rich products, fruits, and vegetables will keep food inflation elevated. The direct and indirect effects of the decision to allow diesel prices to be raised in a series of small steps until losses are eliminated will exert upward pressure on prices. Consequently, average inflation is expected to decline only slightly in FY2013 to 7.2%.

Inflation in FY2014 is expected to moderate to 6.8% with the effort to raise diesel prices completed and having worked through the economy, and with some forward movement in addressing supply-side bottlenecks affecting agriculture.

While monetary policy is likely to be eased further in FY2013 and beyond, as progress is made on bringing down inflation, the extent of easing will be conditioned on progress in reducing the current account and budget deficits.

The central government plans for its budget deficit to fall to 4.8% of GDP in FY2013, mainly through enhanced revenue collection (Figure 3.17.12). However, with the tax structure remaining largely unchanged, apart from higher surcharges on earnings above a threshold and higher excise and custom duties on select items, revenue targets depend heavily on growth picking up. Similarly, revenue from disinvestment and spectrum allocation is set well above the average of previous years. Meeting these magnitudes would depend on favorable market conditions.

3.17.9 New projects and projects shelved

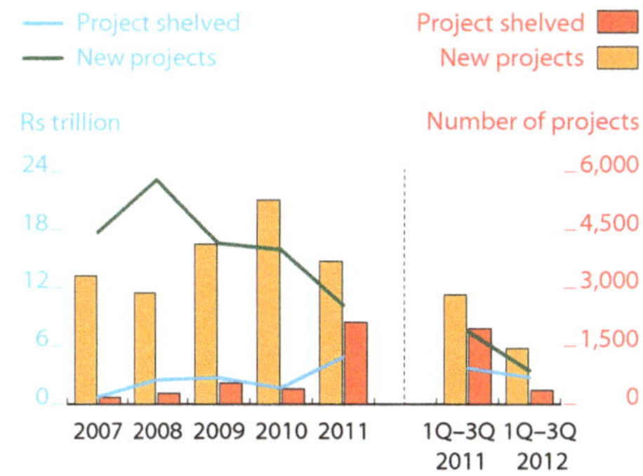

Source: Centre for Monitoring Indian Economy.
Click here for figure data

3.17.10 Industrial outlook survey

Source: Reserve Bank of India. http://www.rbi.org.in (accessed 25 March 2013).
Click here for figure data

3.17.11 HSBC Markit India purchasing managers indexes

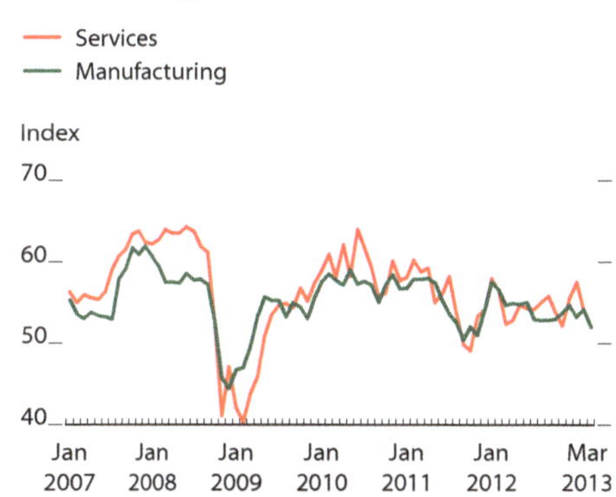

Source: Bloomberg (accessed 24 March 2013).
Click here for figure data

Budget expenditure is set to rise sharply by 16.4% in FY2013, while subsidies are expected to fall by 10.4%. The adequacy of the allocation for subsidies depends critically on the government's willingness to continue regular revisions of diesel prices and to adjust the price of urea (Figure 3.17.13). Adverse developments from baseline assumptions on global prices of crude oil and fertilizers are risks, as is the exchange rate. Similarly, the actual requirement for food subsidies will be determined by the extent of increases in minimum support prices, the timing of the introduction of entitlements under the proposed National Food Security Act, and its scope.

Despite sluggish growth in the advanced economies, global trade volume is expected to revive and grow by 4% in 2013. The first signs of this were seen in increases in India's exports in January and February after 9 months of declines measured year on year. Given the low base and a record of taking advantage of market opportunities, exports are projected to grow by 8% in FY2013. Despite economic growth picking up marginally in FY2013, import demand will continue to be strong at 6% given India's growing dependence on imports of crude oil, coal, metals, and fertilizer. With no major improvement expected in net services and remittances, rising income payments will continue to limit the invisibles surplus. Accordingly, the current account deficit is forecast to improve to 4.4% of GDP in FY2013.

An uptick in domestic growth will boost imports by 16% in FY2014. At the same time, stronger growth prospects in the advanced economies is expected to support further expansion in exports by 14%, facilitating an improvement in the current account deficit to 3.7% of GDP.

With the current account deficit estimated to persist significantly above trend in FY2013 and FY2014, the sustainability and financing of the deficit is becoming a rising concern. The deepening dependence on debt and portfolio flows to finance the deficit has made the economy vulnerable to an oscillating risk of an on/off global macro environment and changes in sovereign ratings. Overall, the current account deficit is expected to be adequately financed by capital flows with some drawdown of reserves in case of a shortfall.

These forecasts are subject to several risks. Weak monsoons would shave agriculture growth and dent rural consumption. Delays in fiscal consolidation and slow progress in addressing some of the structural bottlenecks would damage confidence and hamper growth prospects. Finally, the global recovery continues to be weak, and significant risks arise from unresolved fiscal issues in the US and the possibility of financial shocks in euro area.

Policy challenge—financing the current account deficit

With the current account deficit breaching 4% of GDP in recent years, India has become increasingly reliant on external capital to finance the deficit. The worsening of the current account deficit has been mainly on account of a deteriorating trade deficit, which has exceeded 10% of GDP in recent years (Figure 3.17.14).

With external demand remaining tepid, exports in the near future are unlikely to grow at the robust rates experienced during FY2003–FY2007.

3.17.1 Selected economic indicators (%)

	2013	2014
GDP growth	6.0	6.5
Inflation	7.2	6.8
Current account balance (share of GDP)	−4.4	−3.7

Source: ADB estimates.

3.17.12 Fiscal indicators

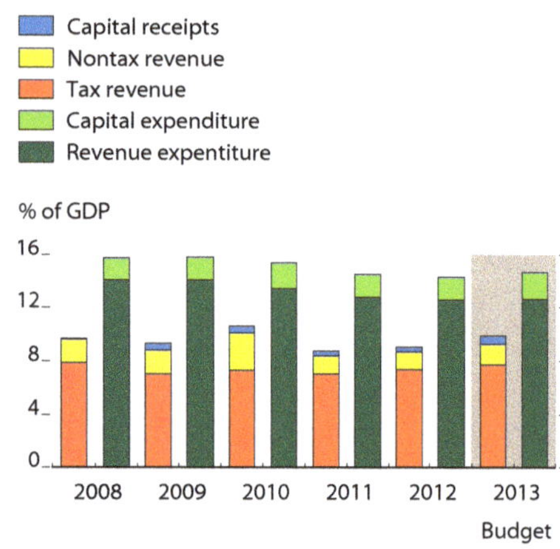

Source: Ministry of Finance.
Click here for figure data

3.17.13 Subsidies

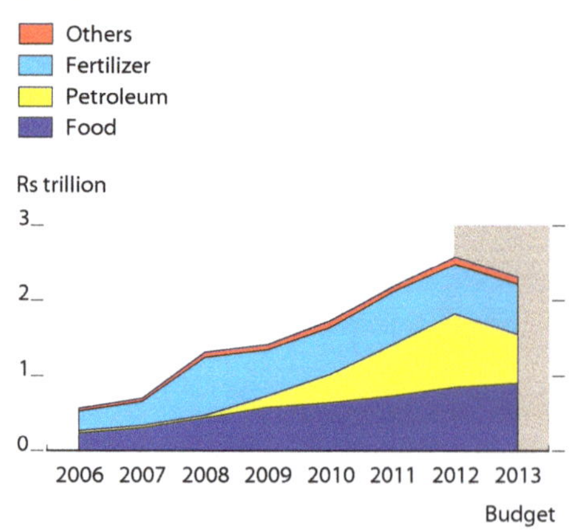

Source: CEIC Data Company (accessed 25 March 2013).
Click here for figure data

Further, the supply side constraints and policy disarray that have stalled domestic industrial and investment activity have also hindered exports. Fiscal subsidies provide little incentive to ration demand for commodities, and structural bottlenecks hamper the production of goods such as coal, fertilizers, and iron ore, inducing growth in imports that are relatively inelastic in response to price and currency movements. Moreover, high inflation in recent years has made gold an attractive form of savings, causing imports to surge.

The invisibles surplus, which previously cushioned the trade deficit, is likely to moderate with weak recovery in advanced economies and low incremental spending on items such as software and business processing services. Investment income outflows, including interest payments, profits, and dividends, will remain elevated, reflecting the rising stock of FDI, portfolio investments, and external loans. Consequently, the current account deficit is expected to remain elevated.

Financing a high current account deficit will be a challenge in an environment of global uncertainty and sluggish domestic growth. In fact, from FY2008 to FY2012, cumulative net capital flows fell short of financing the deficit, causing reserves to stagnate (Figure 3.17.15).

Moreover, there is concern over the pattern of financing the current account deficit, as the share of financing occupied by stable FDI inflows has fallen below 30% since the global financial crisis, from over 80% earlier. Debt flows have become the main source of financing, responding to large interest rate differentials and relaxed controls. Relaxation has included deregulated interest rates paid on the deposits of nonresident Indians, increased limits on external commercial borrowings, higher quotas for foreign investment in government and corporate bonds, and more types of long-term investors being allowed to participate in the market. Buoyed by these measures, the stock of external debt rose from $172.3.5 billion in March 2008 to $365 billion in September 2012, as short-term debt increased from 16.3% to 23.1% of total debt. While short-term debt is not excessive by conventional standards, the existence of large amounts of nonresident Indian deposits and foreign equity holdings would amplify potential damage to the economy in case of a major global financial shock or a marked weakening of domestic fundamentals.

The increasing reliance on debt flows has meant that debt service payments will rise to an annual average of $24.9 billion during FY2011–FY2015 from $16.2 billion during FY2006–FY2010. This and a high current account deficit have made India susceptible to a sovereign rating downgrade. However, recent reforms aimed at rejuvenating investment and advancing fiscal consolidation have mitigated this risk.

The high current account deficit, elevated external debt, and stagnant reserve holdings have worsened measures of reserve adequacy, though they remain robust by international standards.

Reverting to a sustainable current account deficit that can be financed by a stable mix of capital flows would require resolving the structural issues that are limiting investment and preventing a return to rapid growth that is needed to foster a dynamic export sector. At the same time, cutting the fiscal deficit will help raise domestic savings and encourage private investment. Further progress on liberalizing the FDI regime would help attract a more stable source of capital.

3.17.14 Current account components

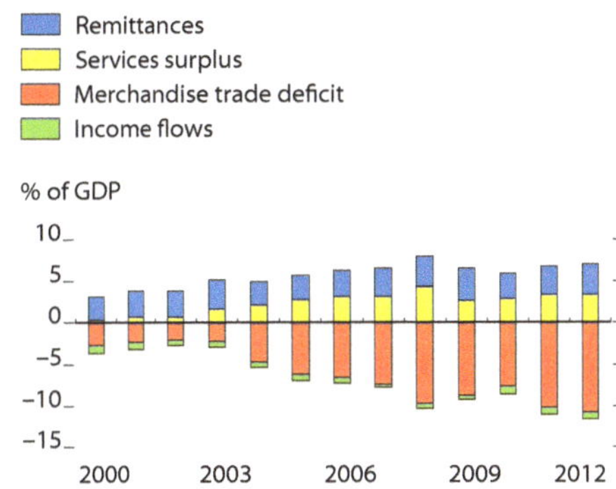

Source: Reserve Bank of India www.rbi.org.in (accessed 18 March 2013).

Click here for figure data

3.17.15 Financing of current account deficit

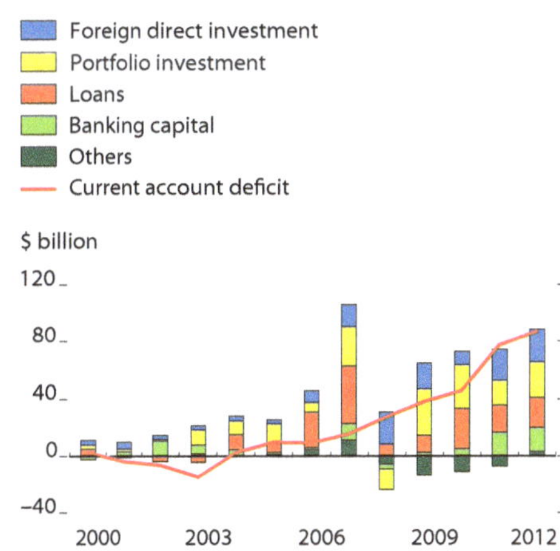

Source: Reserve Bank of India www.rbi.org.in (accessed 18 March 2013).

Click here for figure data

Maldives

A sharp slowdown in tourist arrivals dragged down economic growth. Fiscal and external imbalances intensified. The outlook is for a modest recovery on limited improvement in tourism, the economic mainstay. Inadequate political backing for implementing decisive fiscal measures in recent years and the difficulty of achieving economic diversification and generating employment threaten to restrain rapid and inclusive growth.

Economic performance

GDP growth in 2012 slowed to 3.4% from 7.0% in 2011 as tourism and related activities, which directly provide 28% of GDP, sharply decelerated (Figure 3.18.1). Other related tertiary sectors such as wholesale and retail trade, transportation, and communications are also affected. Growth in tourist arrivals slumped to 2.9% in 2012 from 17.6% in 2011, as recession in Europe and the slowdown in the global economy combined with uncertainty created by domestic events to stymie the industry (Figure 3.18.2). The continued influx of visitors from the People's Republic of China, up by 15.6%, was the bright spot in the market, while growth in arrivals from other Asian countries slowed to 1.5%. Tourist arrivals from Europe fell by 3.7%, slashing the European market share to 54% from over 70% only 5 years earlier, as the Asian share nearly doubled to 38%. Tourist spending edged up a miniscule 0.3% in 2012, stalling from 9% growth a year earlier.

Strong growth in important areas of the economy—manufacturing (4.7% of GDP) up by 17.5%, construction (9.3%) up by 16.1%, and fisheries (the main employer in the atolls) up by 9.7%—was insufficient to offset the headwinds from tourism and related industries.

The sudden resignation of President Mohamed Nasheed on 7 February 2012 under disputed circumstances set off major political unrest that affected tourism. Since then his Maldives Democratic Party has organized protest rallies and blocked the parliament for several weeks. A presidential election is scheduled for September 2013, but it is unclear if the former president will be qualified to run. If not, political unrest is expected to intensify.

Inflation remained high despite falling global commodity and food prices. Inflation eased to an average of 10.9% in 2012 (Figure 3.18.3). Upward pressures on prices included the introduction of a general goods service tax in the first quarter of 2011 and pressures from limited foreign exchange availability and the exchange rate. The rufiyaa, which since April 2011 has been allowed to move within a band 20% above and below Rf12.8 to $1, has remained near the upper bound.

3.18.1 Supply-side contributions to growth

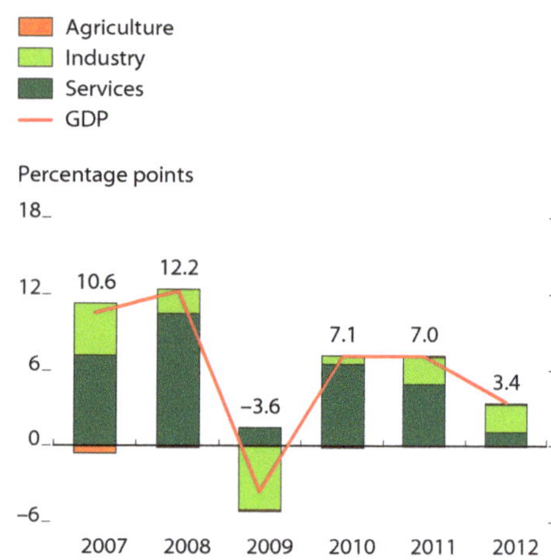

Source: Maldives Monetary Authority. 2013. *Monthly Statistics.* March. http://www.mma.gov.mv

Click here for figure data

3.18.2 Tourist arrivals

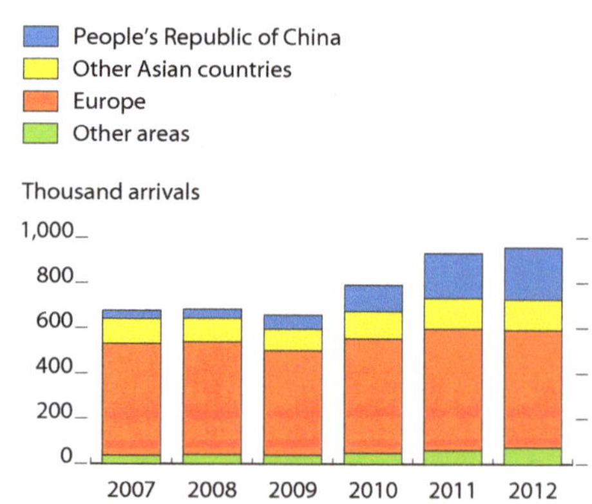

Source: Maldives Monetary Authority. 2013. *Monthly Statistics.* March. http://www.mma.gov.mv

Click here for figure data

This chapter was written by Sabyasachi Mitra, Huiping Huang, and Ruzette Mariano of the South Asia Department, ADB, Manila.

The central bank maintained the reverse–repo rate at 7% to curb inflation despite the economic slowdown. Net credit to the government rose by 12.9% in 2012, much more slowly than the 27% increase in 2011, as the government relied heavily on foreign borrowing to finance its widening deficit. Credit to the private sector fell by 9.1%, with about half of the falloff affecting the tourism sector, mainly a reduction in loans for working capital and resort renovation. Broad money growth consequently slowed to 5.0% in 2012 from 20% a year earlier.

The budget deficit in 2012 is estimated to have widened substantially to 12.6% of GDP from 7.5% in 2011 (Figure 3.18.4). Government revenue fell by 0.7% despite marked increases in goods and service taxes, both general and for tourists, because import duties dropped by nearly half, owing to the decline in imports for tourism and some duty reductions. Total revenue fell to 28.8% of GDP, a drop of 2.7 percentage points from a year earlier. This accounted for just over half of the 5.1 percentage point increase in the deficit in relation to GDP. Expenditure increased by 2.4 percentage points to 41.4% of GDP, the rise entirely owing to a 15.9% increase in current expenditure to 30.8% of GDP, as there was relatively little increase in capital spending or net lending to public enterprises. The bulk of the deficit was financed through foreign borrowings and grants, with about one-fifth coming from the central bank. Total public external debt was 38.2% of GDP in 2012.

The current account deficit widened to 26.3% of GDP from 21.4% in 2011 (Figure 3.18.5). The deterioration reflected an increase in the trade deficit on weaker exports, stagnation in income from tourism, and higher remittances made by expatriate workers. The trade deficit, at 63.6% of GDP in 2012, illustrates the country's substantial reliance on imports, especially for the tourist industry. The bulk of the large current account deficit was financed by unrecorded financial inflows and the errors and omissions item in balance-of-payments accounting, indicating weakness in data currently available. The overall balance of payments was in deficit by $37.4 million, equivalent to 1.6% of GDP. Gross official reserves at the end of 2012 were $304.6 million, enough to cover only 2.1 months of projected imports of goods in 2013.

Economic prospects

The economy is forecast to recover modestly to grow by 4.3% in 2013 and 5.5% in 2014, as the anticipated gradual global economic recovery boosts tourism. Higher spending ahead of the planned August 2013 national elections is expected to add a fillip to growth. In 2014, the new government may initiate the implementation of its intermediate macroeconomic policy, and the direction thus provided may improve local investment in the tourism sector.

In light of an expected surge in pre-election expenditures and recent experience, the budget deficit is expected to be 7.9% of GDP in 2013, or more than double the official budget deficit estimate of 3.6%. To achieve the official estimate, the government would have to commit to fiscal consolidation measures such as streamlining the civil service and improving tax administration. In the past, implementing similar policies has entailed lengthy administrative and legislative procedures, making

3.18.3 Contributions to inflation in Malé

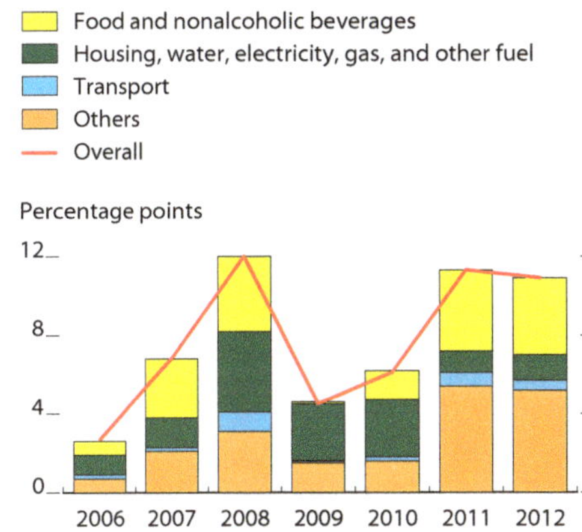

Source: Maldives Monetary Authority. 2013. *Monthly Statistics.* March. http://www.mma.gov.mv

Click here for figure data

3.18.4 Fiscal indicators

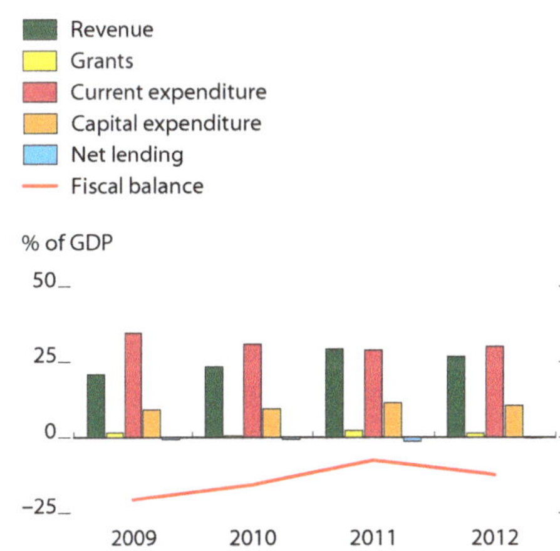

Source: Maldives Monetary Authority. 2013. *Monthly Statistics.* March. http://www.mma.gov.mv

Click here for figure data

3.18.5 Balance of payments

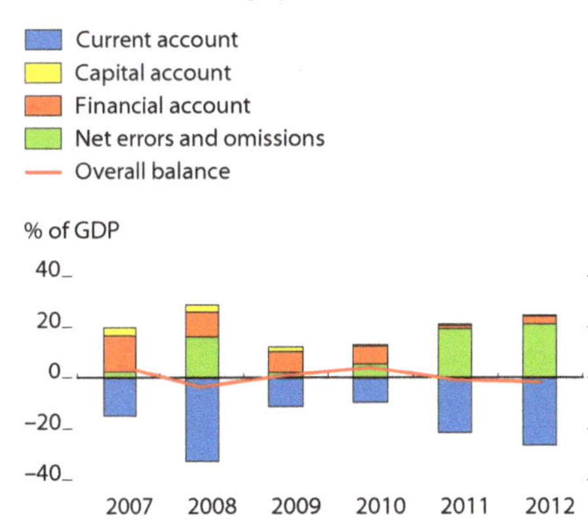

Source: Maldives Monetary Authority. 2013. *Monthly Statistics.* March. http://www.mma.gov.mv

Click here for figure data

these developments unlikely to materialize within the year. Nevertheless, stabilizing the huge public debt, which now is near 80% of GDP, will become daunting unless forceful measures are quickly adopted.

Inflation will likely ease to 9.3% in 2013 and 8.5% in 2014 because of base effects and the improved availability of foreign exchange—and despite spending ahead of the elections sustaining inflation pressure in the first half of 2013. The modest pickup in tourism may improve the current account balance somewhat, but the deficit is expected to remain wide, even deteriorating slightly to 27.8% of GDP in 2013 before improving to 22.0% in 2014.

3.18.1 Selected economic indicators (%)

	2013	2014
GDP growth	4.3	5.5
Inflation	9.3	8.5
Current account balance (share of GDP)	–27.8	–22.0

Source: ADB estimates.

Policy challenge—fostering inclusive growth

The Maldives faces a slew of medium-term development challenges. Worrisome youth unemployment causes social problems and political instability. High unemployment reflects the narrow employment base and the mismatch between the youths' skills and labor market requirements. Many jobs are therefore filled by expatriate workers. A substantial investment in skills development is a pressing need. Creating jobs requires developing new industries beyond fishing that are viable in a small, dispersed island nation. A key challenge is lifting the economy's overreliance on tourism and thereby alleviating the country's vulnerability to external shocks. The 2004 tsunami and 2008–2009 global financial crisis devastated tourism and sent the economy into a tailspin.

An extremely dispersed population in small island communities has long been recognized as a challenge to sustainable social and economic development. Communities must be consolidated to foster the creation of new industries and diversify the economy beyond tourism. Developing a stronger economic base is essential to cope with the country's heavy reliance on imports and persistently large current account deficits.

The Maldives also faces challenges to the environment and from climate change. The pollution caused by the untreated wastes of the dispersed population can undermine the archipelago's blue economy and image as a tourist paradise. Overdependence on imported oil for segmented and inefficient power generation adds to the challenge of the Maldives' becoming carbon neutral by 2020. The lack of economies of scale poses severe challenges to attracting finance for water and sanitation, waste treatment, and power projects, as well as for their proper operation and maintenance.

Population consolidation may be a long-term process, but action today is critical. The selection of large islands must be based not only on geographic convenience but also on business potential in areas such as shipping, trade and financial services, fish processing, and manufacturing. Islands that will serve as regional centers can be developed on a pilot basis to accommodate the scattered surrounding islands in that region. Gradually, these islands will become, like Malé, significant population centers.

Nepal

Growth picked up with a favorable monsoon and robust services growth. Inflation moderated on declining food prices, and the current account posted a large surplus on a surge in remittances and modest imports. Political uncertainty intensified with the dissolution of the Constituent Assembly, affecting budget operations and government policies. Growth is expected to slow following a poor monsoon. Improving economic performance depends on resolving political uncertainty and creating an enabling environment for business and investment.

Economic performance

GDP growth rebounded to 4.6% in FY2012 (ended 15 July 2012), boosted by a favorable monsoon and robust services growth despite a slowdown in industry and lingering political uncertainties (Figure 3.19.1). Agricultural output grew by 4.9%, the highest rate in 4 years, while the 5.1% advance in services reflected a pickup in tourism and consumer spending of remittances. Industry continued to perform poorly, growing by a mere 1.7%, because of an unfavorable business and investment climate caused by labor disputes, persistent electricity shortages, and the prolonged and disruptive political transition.

Inflation eased slightly to average 8.3% in FY2012, as food prices declined during most of the year because of good harvests in FY2011 and FY2012 (Figure 3.19.2). Stubbornly high inflation is increasingly driven by rising prices for nonfood items that echo inflation in India, which is Nepal's largest trading partner by far and to whose currency the Nepalese rupee is pegged. Other drivers are upward adjustment to administered fuel prices, depreciation of the Nepalese rupee against the currencies of third countries, rising wages, and persistent supply-side constraints.

The budget deficit narrowed marginally to 2.2% of GDP, owing to lower capital expenditure and greater revenue mobilization (Figure 3.19.3). Improved efficiency in tax administration and a wider tax base boosted tax revenue by an impressive 22.5%, lifting it by a percentage point to 13.6% of GDP. However, the ratio of total revenues including grants to GDP improved by only half a percentage point to 18.3%. Total expenditure amounted to 20.4% of GDP, from 20.2% in the previous year. Recurrent expenditure jumped by 42.7% to cover large fuel subsidies and ad hoc expenditure programs, while capital expenditure contracted sharply from a year earlier due to lower project disbursements arising from lack of political consensus on a timely budget.

A sharp drop in real estate prices in FY2011 caused a liquidity squeeze and credit problems at financial institutions, whose property lending had substantially expanded in recent years. Several required emergency

3.19.1 Supply-side contributions to growth

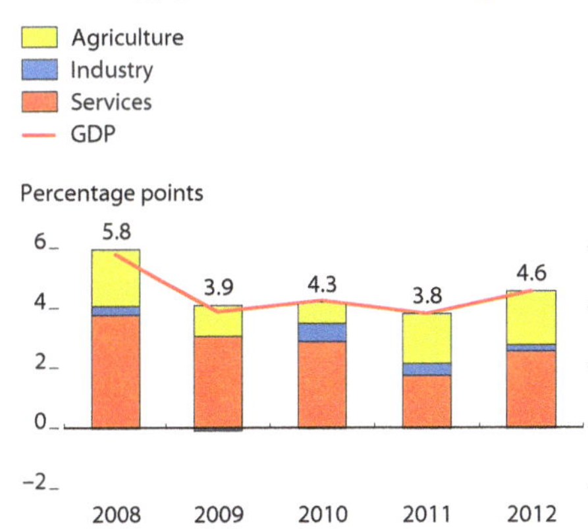

Source: Central Bureau of Statistics. 2012.

Click here for figure data

3.19.2 Inflation

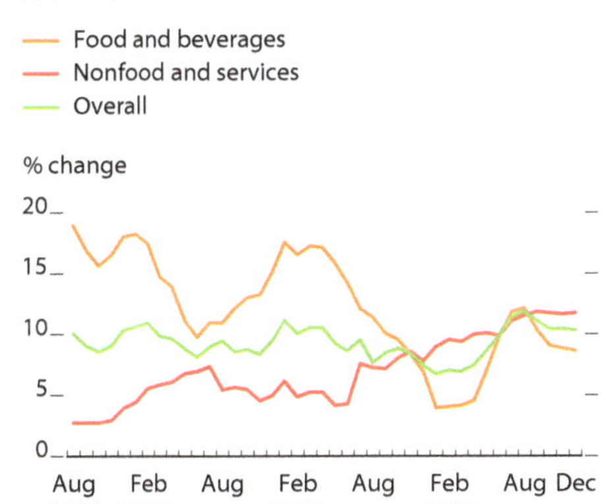

Source: Nepal Rastra Bank. 2013. *Recent Macroeconomic Situation.* http://www.nrb.org.np

Click here for figure data

This chapter was written by Chandan Sapkota and Neelina Nakarmi of the Nepal Resident Mission, ADB, Kathmandu.

lending from the central bank, as the amount of nonperforming loans rose and depositor confidence eroded. In FY2012, banking stress eased as robust remittance inflows boosted deposits and strengthened bank liquidity to comfortable levels. Interbank rates dropped to 1.1% from 8.1% in FY2011 (Figure 3.19.4). Regulatory lending caps on certain sectors and the lack of bankable projects kept credit growth moderate, as the central bank intensified its supervision and monitoring.

The current account balance recorded a large surplus of 4.9% of GDP in FY2012, mainly reflecting a large gain in worker remittances bolstered by an earlier marked increase in workers going abroad (Figure 3.19.5). Though merchandise exports grew modestly by 5.4%, to equal 5.2% of GDP, import growth of 4.5%—also modest partly because of low demand for construction materials and equipment—marginally widened the trade deficit to 24.0% of GDP. The overall balance of payments reached a record surplus of \$1.6 billion, and foreign exchange reserves grew to \$4.2 billion, equivalent to 7.9 months of imports of goods and services (Figure 3.19.6).

Economic prospects

The economic outlook hinges on how political uncertainties are resolved, the weather, and remittance inflows. Investor confidence is depressed by concerns over the political transition, now in its fifth year, following the dissolution in May 2012 of the Constituent Assembly, which failed to agree on a constitution. Recently, the political parties agreed to form a caretaker government led by the Chief Justice, which is expected to hold a Constituent Assembly election by 21 June 2013.

In view of the unfavorable monsoon, the shortage of fertilizers during the peak paddy planting season, low business confidence, the lack of a parliamentary-approved full budget, and subdued growth in India, GDP is projected to slow to 3.5% in FY2013. Production of paddy is projected to fall by 11.3%, maize by 8%, and millet by 2%. The lack of a full budget is causing funding shortages for ongoing development activities. While the industry sector performance is expected to remain weak, services growth is expected to continue to grow at around 5.4%. With a favorable monsoon, adequate fertilizer supplies, the timely adoption of a budget, and moderate expansion of remittances, GDP growth would rebound to 4.2% in FY2014.

Prospects for a lower agricultural harvest, wage pressures, further upward adjustment of administered fuel prices, continued power shortages, and other supply-side constraints are expected to push inflation to 10.5% in FY2013, above the central bank's midyear estimate of 9.5% but below the inflation average of 10.7% in the first half of the fiscal year. Assuming instead a good harvest and cautious monetary policies, inflation in FY2014 is projected to ease only slightly to 9.0% as most of the underlying pressures of the previous year persist.

On the external front, the trade deficit is expected to markedly widen in FY2013. Given subdued growth in India, sluggish activity in the euro area and the US, and the rising cost of domestic production, export growth is projected to slow to 0.2% in FY2013. Allowing for the usual lag between remittance growth and spending on imports, imports are expected to markedly expand by 18.7%. With the large increase in the

3.19.3 Fiscal indicators

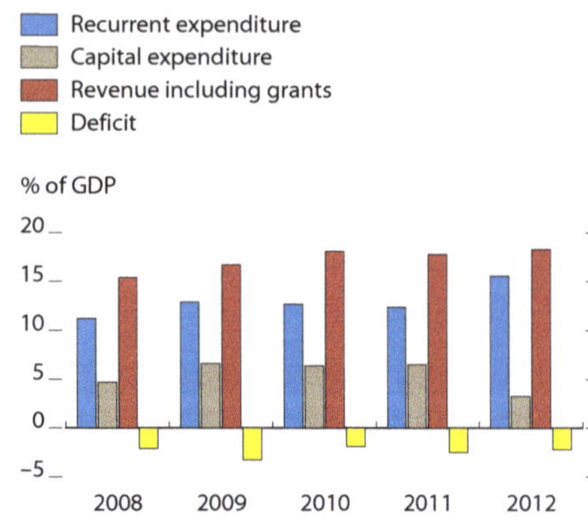

Sources: Ministry of Finance. *Economic Survey 2012* and *FY2012 Annual Statement of Income and Expenditure.*

Click here for figure data

3.19.4 Credit to the private sector and interbank rate

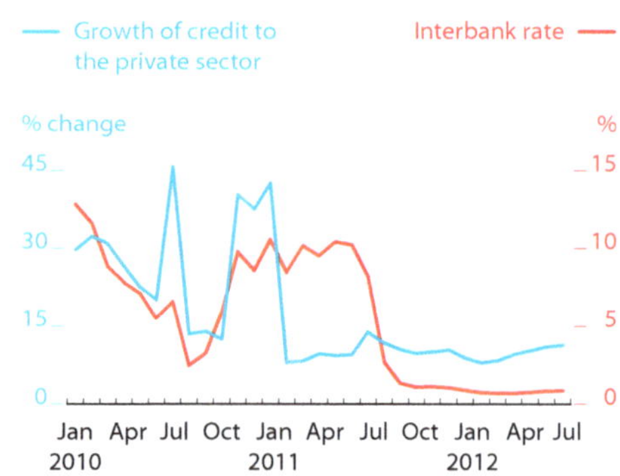

Source: Nepal Rastra Bank. 2013. *Recent Macroeconomic Situation.* http://www.nrb.org.np

Click here for figure data

3.19.5 Trade, tourism, and workers' remittances

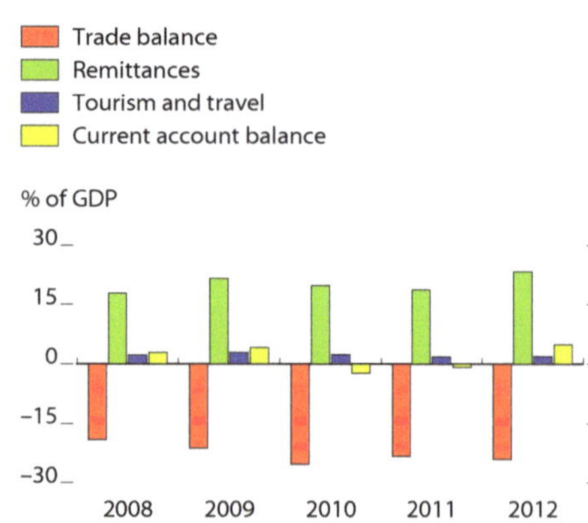

Source: Nepal Rastra Bank. 2013. *Recent Macroeconomic Situation.* http://www.nrb.org.np

Click here for figure data

trade deficit and more moderate remittance growth, the current account surplus will likely contract sharply to a deficit of 0.5% of GDP in FY2013 and then slide more slowly to a 1.8% deficit in FY2014 as high import demand moderates and stepped up exports reflect somewhat improved economic conditions in trading partners.

Without a budget for FY2013, revenue policy is guided by the Finance Act, 2012, meaning that rates of taxes, duties, fees, and other charges remain unchanged while actual expenditure should not exceed previous levels. With the widened tax base and improved collection capacity, revenues will likely be largely sufficient to cover expected total expenditure, which will again show low capital spending. The budget deficit is expected to be around 2.5% of GDP.

The budget continues to suffer stress from subsidies, including on diesel and liquefied petroleum gas. Prices should be rationalized, making provisions for the welfare of the poor. The FY2014 budget needs timely passage to allow the revision of tax rates, authorization for domestic borrowing, and provision of funding to accelerate development activities. Further, legislators need to address the quality of public spending, effective utilization of foreign aid, and governance issues.

Policy challenge—financial sector vulnerability

The sharp drop in real estate and housing prices and slowdown in remittances in FY2011 caused a series of problems for banks and other financial institutions (BFIs), which fall into three categories: commercial banks, development banks, and finance companies. Commercial banks dominate these deposit-taking institutions, holding 80% of the system's deposits and loans (Figure 3.19.7). The problems included more nonperforming loans and a liquidity squeeze as depositors lost confidence in the safety of their deposits. The balance sheet of BFIs deteriorated, and a number of development banks and finance companies sought assistance from the central bank.

In response to BFIs' difficulties (apart from offering emergency assistance and allowing forbearance), the central bank rolled out a number of regulatory and monitoring directives to deal with banking sector issues. It directed banks to limit real estate and housing loans to 25% of total loans, and it stiffened capital adequacy requirements. Commercial banks were able to comply with the directive and brought real estate lending down to 16.9% of total lending in FY2012. To diversify loan portfolios and direct credit to more productive sectors, the central bank directed banks to extend at least 10% of total loans to agriculture and/or energy. Moreover, banking institutions were required to publish base interest rates to improve transparency and competition in their operations and policies. Further, separate departments are being established in the central bank to supervise development banks and finance companies.

While prompt central bank action managed to handle the sector's immediate problems, issues that remain unaddressed include structural changes needed to shield the banking sector and the economy from internal and external shocks. The first unresolved issue is the liberal licensing regime that created an excessive number of BFIs—213 BFIs by

3.19.6 Gross international reserves

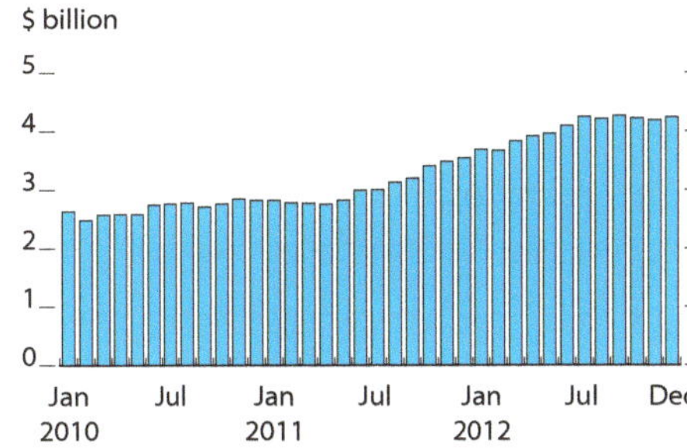

Source: Nepal Rastra Bank. 2013. *Recent Macroeconomic Situation.* http://www.nrb.org.np

Click here for figure data

3.19.1 Selected economic indicators (%)

	2013	2014
GDP growth	3.5	4.2
Inflation	10.5	9.0
Current account balance (share of GDP)	–0.5	–1.8

Source: ADB estimates.

3.19.7 Deposits, lending, and number of institutions, 2012

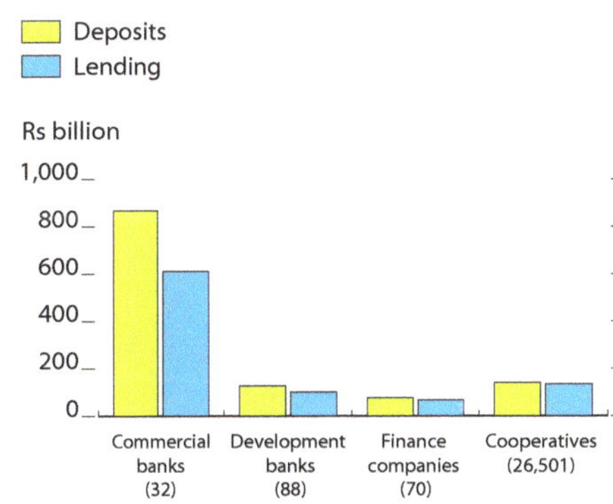

Sources: Department of Commerce; Nepal Rastra Bank. 2013. *Monthly Statistics.* February. http://www.nrb.org.np

Click here for figure data

FY2012—and thereby fomented unhealthy competition and fueled the bubble. BFIs need to be significantly consolidated in the coming years to ensure a sound financial sector.

Second, ensuring sound corporate governance should be priority, as many of the troubles in development banks and finance companies emanated from their managers' and directors' misuse of credit, often for personal gain. This issue calls for strengthening central bank monitoring, supervision, and regulatory capability.

Third, apart from diversifying lending, BFIs need to strengthen internal project and loan analysis, innovate loan products, and enhance their operational efficiency. At the macro level, the government needs to improve the business and investment climate, which would underpin loan quality.

Fourth, BFIs are still vulnerable to large fluctuations in remittance inflows that make deposit and lending flows volatile, which points to the need for more effective monitoring and control over developments in banking system liquidity. Notably, a recent stress test the central bank conducted on 32 commercial banks revealed that a routine credit shock would push capital holdings in 20 banks below the regulatory minimum.

Fifth, the activities of the largely unregulated cooperatives, which fall under the purview of Department of Cooperatives, need to be better understood and monitored, as does the nexus between these cooperatives and the banking system. Any major shock to the deposit and lending practices of cooperatives, whose combined deposits and lending portfolios are larger than those of either development banks or finance companies, would likely harm the entire banking system and economy. In this regard, the International Monetary Fund has estimated that a financial crisis in Nepal could cause GDP loss of 30% in the first 4 years before growth recovered to the baseline trend, reserves to fall by 50% in the first 2 quarters of the crisis, and a fiscal cost as high as 23% of GDP.

Pakistan

Growth picked up slightly, but for the fifth consecutive year low growth, falling investment, excessive fiscal deficits, high inflation, and a deteriorating external position weighed on the economy. While problematic security and natural disasters are endemic, a difficult political situation stalled effective policy response to macroeconomic and structural problems, especially regarding energy. As official reserves are steadily declining on low capital inflows and heavy debt repayments, downside risks color the outlook.

Economic assessment

Economic performance during the first half of FY2012 (ended June 2012) was driven by a rebound from the devastating floods a year earlier that was partly offset by record power outages from load shedding in the second half. Growth strengthened to 3.7% but again remained well below the 7% pace needed to absorb new workforce entrants (Figure 3.20.1).

Agriculture recovered to grow by 3.1%, as better weather favored the production of major crops, though minor crops in parts of the country were hurt by floods. Industry expanded by 3.4%, mainly from post-flood reconstruction. The impact of the higher load shedding was apparent as large-scale manufacturing reversed early gains, tapering off to 1.2% expansion for the year, even lower than the flood-induced slowdown to 1.8% in FY2011. Output of intermediate goods declined for the third year in a row as Pakistan's steel, petroleum refining, and fertilizer industries continue to operate well below capacity. The large service sector, growing by 4.0%, continued to account for most GDP expansion.

Private consumption expenditure expanded by 11.6% in FY2012 to provide nearly all GDP growth (Figure 3.20.2). As in past years, it benefited from rising remittances and government salary increases. Fixed investment fell for the fourth year in a row, to 10.9% of GDP, the lowest share since 1974 and the lowest among major Asian countries (Figure 3.20.3). This downdraft is being driven by prevailing security issues, worsening power shortages, and growing concern over the general direction and outlook for the economy.

Clearly, the steady decline in investment, coupled with reliance on consumption for growth, is unsustainable and undermines future growth prospects. Investment subtracted 1.4 percentage points from growth in FY2012. Net exports subtracted 3.8 percentage points partly because energy outages frustrated producers efforts to reliably meet export schedules and partly because demand was slack from the global slowdown.

Food inflation eased in FY2012, allowing consumer price inflation to slow from the 13.7% average pace of FY2011 to 11.0% in FY2012.

This chapter was written by Dawn Elizabeth Rehm and Farzana Noshab of the Pakistan Resident Mission, ADB, Islamabad.

3.20.1 Supply-side contributions to growth

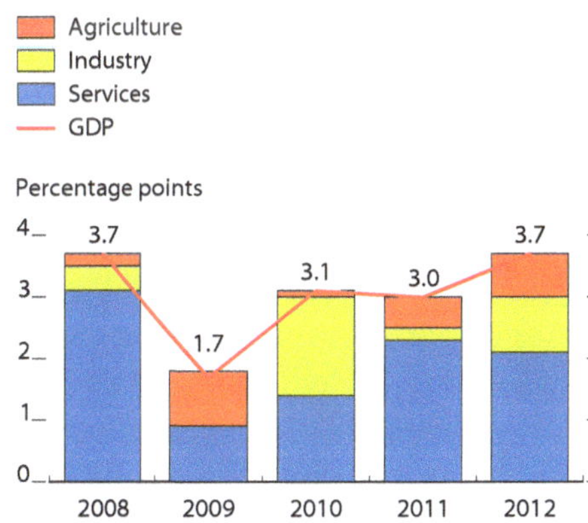

Source: Ministry of Finance. *Pakistan Economic Survey 2011–12.* http://www.finance.gov.pk

Click here for figure data

3.20.2 Demand-side contributions to growth

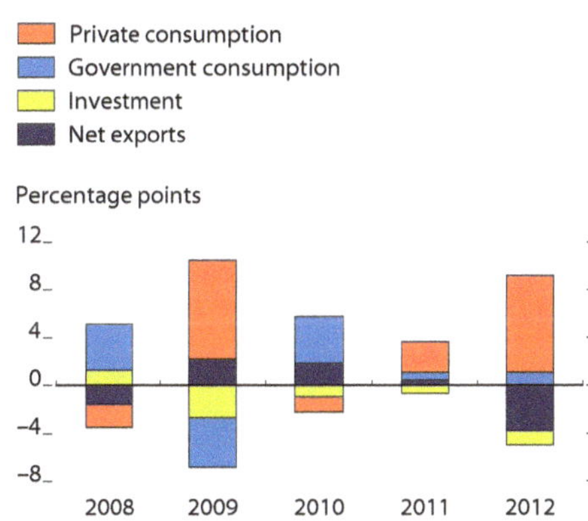

Source: Ministry of Finance. *Pakistan Economic Survey 2011–12.* http://www.finance.gov.pk

Click here for figure data

The persistence of inflation in nonfood components is evident in the observation that core inflation measures, which exclude food and energy, accelerated from 9.5% at the beginning of FY2012 to 11.4% by June 2012, as more items in the basket experienced double-digit increases.

The FY2012 budget deficit ballooned to 8.5% of GDP from 6.6% in the previous year, well above the 4% target (Figure 3.20.4). The bulk of the overrun was from recurrent outlays, mainly higher spending on power subsidies and funding to partly settle power sector arrears. Interest payments were also over budget, increasing to 4.0% of GDP and 42.2% of federal tax revenue, as domestic borrowing drove up the government's domestic debt by 27%.

Patterns from previous years continued, as outlays for wages and other expenses, pensions, subsidies, defense, and interest payments substantially exceeded federal tax revenues, leaving the government's current operations to be substantially financed through debt (Figure 3.20.5). Development expenditure, restricted by flooding in FY2011, bounced back and met its targeted 3.5% of GDP.

Tax revenues collected by the Federal Board of Revenue increased to 9.1% of GDP from 8.6% in FY2011 but still fell short of budget targets. The 20.8% growth in tax revenue reflected in part receipts from flood-related emergency measures, higher sales tax receipts on imports (particularly oil), and administrative improvements. There was also a significant shortfall on nontax revenues as Coalition Support Fund receipts and the auction of 3G mobile phone licenses were delayed. Collections under the petroleum development levy fell short as it was reduced to offset the impact of higher oil prices on consumers.

The magnitude of recent deficits worked against compliance with the Fiscal Responsibility and Debt Limitation Act, 2005. The provisions of the act called for a revenue surplus over current expenditure by FY2008 to ensure adequate capacity for public investment, doubling the share of spending allocated to health and education, and debt limits. While these goals appear distant at present, achieving them seemed feasible at the time, as FY2004–FY2007 fiscal deficits averaged a low 3.6% of GDP, there was near revenue balance, and foreign direct investment inflows to privatize state-owned enterprises were on the rise.

As external financing covered a scant 10% of the FY2012 deficit, the bulk of financing came from domestic markets, including PRs505.7 billion in borrowing from the State Bank of Pakistan, the central bank. A legal restriction calling for borrowing from the central bank to be zero at the end of each quarter fell by the wayside. The 27% increase in government domestic debt was mostly in short-term issues that eroded the government debt maturity structure and heightened rollover risk.

Public debt expanded to PRs1.6 trillion in FY2012, raising the ratio of government debt to GDP to 62.5% (Figure 3.20.6), which substantially exceeded the limit set under the Fiscal Responsibility and Debt Limitation Act. External public debt dropped from 27.6% of GDP to 25.6%, while domestic public debt including the debt of state-owned enterprises increased from 33.3% of GDP to 37.0%. Pakistan's debt is higher than the recommended 30%–40% of GDP for economies at a similar stage of development.

3.20.3 Gross fixed capital formation

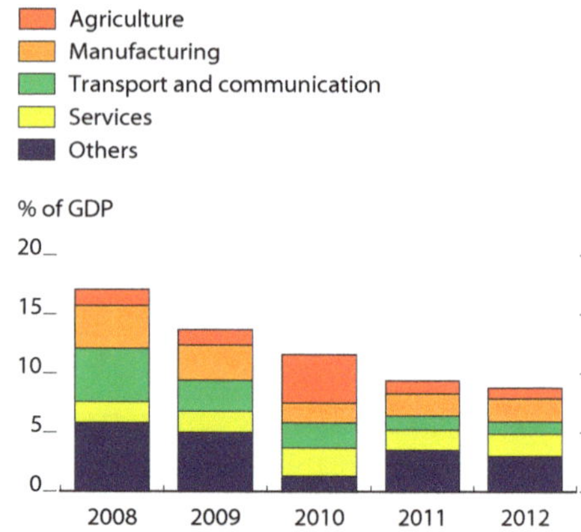

Note: Others include finance and insurance, electricity and gas, wholesale and retail, mining and quarrying, and ownership of dwellings.

Source: Ministry of Finance. *Pakistan Economic Survey 2011–12.* http://www.finance.gov.pk

Click here for figure data

3.20.4 Fiscal performance

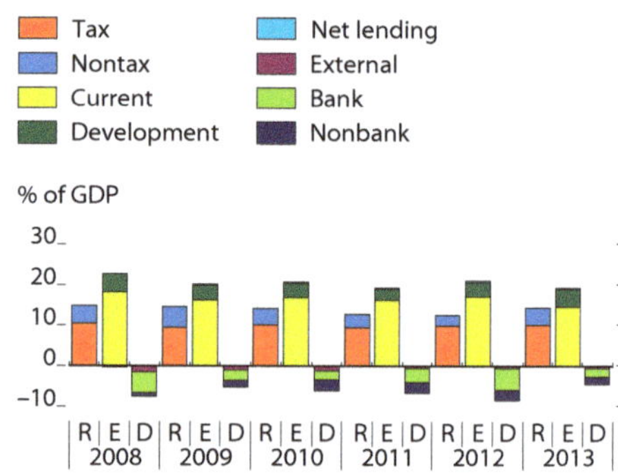

R = revenue, E = expenditure, D = deficit financing.

Notes: Data refer to consolidated federal and provincial governments. Net lending includes statistical discrepancy. Nonbank includes privatization proceeds.

Sources: Ministry of Finance. *Pakistan Economic Survey 2011–12;* Pakistan Fiscal Operations July–June 2011–12; *Federal Budget 2012–2013, Budget in Brief;* ADB estimates.

Click here for figure data

3.20.5 Current revenue and expenditure

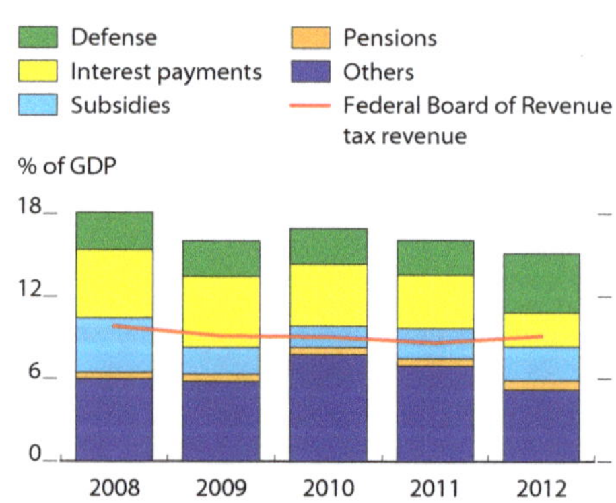

Sources: Ministry of Finance. *Pakistan Economic Survey 2010–11;* Pakistan Fiscal Operations 2011–12. www.finance.gov.pk

Click here for figure data

The central bank policy stance in FY2012 was generally accommodative. As inflation eased early in the year, it lowered the policy rate by 200 basis points to 12% to stimulate investment and strengthen growth. However, surging deficits made government debt readily available and more attractive than lending to the private sector in a risky business environment, which inhibited commercial banks' financial intermediation. Bank loans to private businesses did increase by PRs18.3 billion, or 0.8%, but this amount was dwarfed by banks' PRs692 billion in lending to the government (Figure 3.20.7).

Broad money growth of 14.1% in FY2012 was somewhat slower than in the year earlier, largely reflecting the drawdown of foreign exchange reserves, ensuring that money growth came entirely through an expansion of net domestic assets. The loss of foreign exchange reserves, combined with the large amount of government debt entering the market, caused liquidity shortages at banks that were met by weekly injections by the central bank of up to PRs600 billion, far larger than in the past.

The current account returned to a deficit of 2.0% of GDP in FY2012, after a marginal surplus in FY2011 (Figure 3.20.8). The reversal came mainly from an 11.9% increase in imports, as oil payments increased by nearly 17% and fertilizer imports doubled because of shortages of natural gas. Exports contracted by 2.8%, as textile exports stagnated, cotton prices fell, and food exports declined. Remittances continued to grow at a robust 17.7% pace, somewhat slower than a year earlier, but still providing an important cushion for the trade account deficit.

Inflows in the capital and financial accounts continued to decline, while debt amortization payments increased, reducing net liquid foreign exchange reserves by about one-quarter in FY2012, to $10.8 billion, or 2.6 months of import cover. Foreign direct investment fell to $821 million, and private portfolio investment recorded net outflow. Sustained inflation and pressure on the foreign exchange market induced a 9.1% depreciation of the Pakistan rupee against the US dollar.

Prospects

The end of the government's 5-year term in mid-March 2013 limited political scope for major policy or structural reforms. Economic developments in FY2013 are therefore unfolding along broadly similar lines as in FY2012 but with deepening concerns about sustainability and the adequacy of foreign reserves.

The economic situation weakened further in the first half of FY2013 as official reserves declined markedly, food and general inflation both reaccelerated in January following their earlier decline, and exports stagnated while imports contracted. Economic growth is expected to slow to 3.6% in FY2013, with risks on the downside from possible shortfalls in agricultural production, which may offset the modest improvement in large-scale manufacturing during the first half of the year. Production of petroleum products, iron, and steel picked up, but growth in textiles and food, which account for almost half of large-scale manufacturing production and the bulk of exports, remained negligible. Manufacturing performance for the year will hinge largely on limiting power outages during the hot season, when demand peaks. With little prospect for

3.20.6 Domestic and external debt

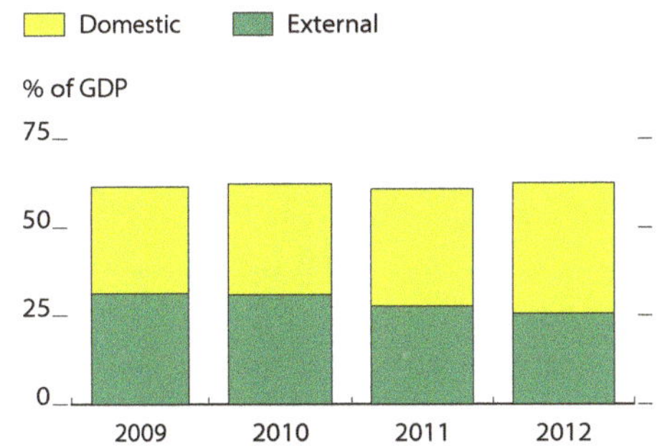

Source: State Bank of Pakistan. http://www.sbp.org.pk (accessed 6 March 2013).

Click here for figure data

3.20.7 Banking sector credit

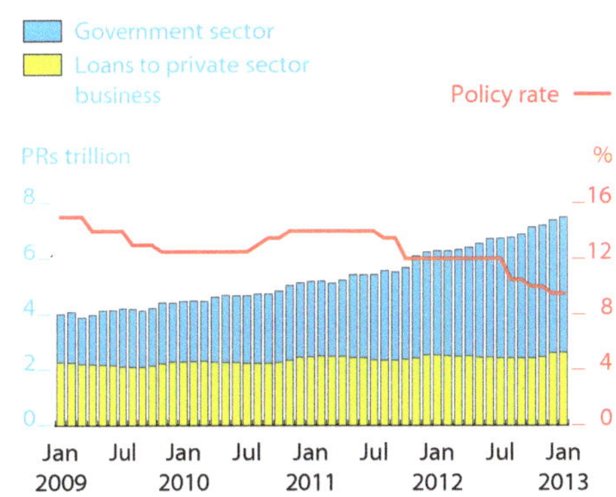

Source: State Bank of Pakistan, http://www.sbp.org.pk (accessed 6 March 2013).

Click here for figure data

3.20.1 Selected economic indicators (%)

	2013	2014
GDP growth	3.6	3.5
Inflation	9.0	9.5
Current account balance (share of GDP)	−0.8	−0.9

Source: ADB estimates.

3.20.8 Current account components

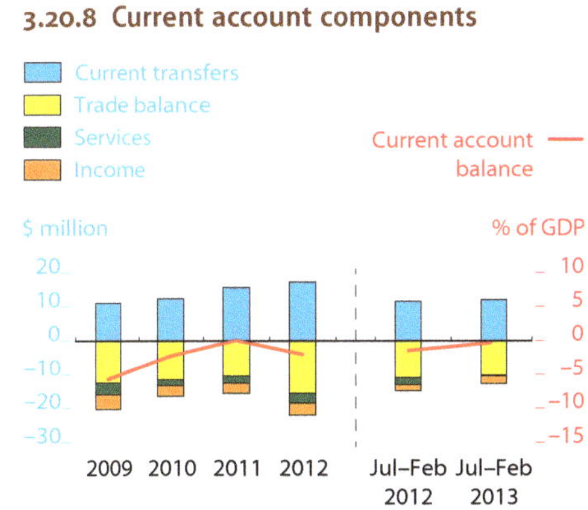

Sources: State Bank of Pakistan. Economic Data. http://www.sbp.org.pk (accessed 21 March 2013); ADB estimates.

Click here for figure data

improving energy supply or investment, growth is expected to remain weak at 3.5% in FY2014.

Consumer price inflation continued a downward trend during most of the first 8 months of FY2013 as food price inflation decelerated. However, year-on-year inflation at 7.4% in February 2013 was higher than the year low of 6.9% in November 2012 as food prices moved higher (Figure 3.20.9). Nevertheless, food inflation in this fiscal year is much slower than a year earlier, reflecting improved supply. Core inflation, excluding food and energy, also improved but, at 9.6% in February 2013, remains stubbornly high with many of its subcomponents staying in double digits, reflecting entrenched inflationary pressure in the economy. However, with slower growth in food and energy prices, inflation is expected to average 9.0% in FY2013, or 2 percentage points lower than in the previous fiscal year. On the expectation that there will be no substantive improvement in the country's fiscal and energy imbalances in FY2014, inflation is expected to edge up to 9.5%.

Easing inflation early in FY2013 prompted further reductions in the central bank's main policy rate by a total of 250 basis points, bringing it to 9.5% in December 2012 (Figure 3.20.10). While banks' weighted average rate on new loans in this period fell by about 200 basis points to 11.3%, overarching constraints coming from energy shortages and other uncertainties, such as law and order issues, will limit the impact of interest rate reductions on investment and business conditions in general. A modest increase in lending to private businesses in the first 7 months of FY2013 was mainly for working capital, with the bulk of lending going to textile firms.

A modest surplus in the current account during the first 7 months of FY2013, following inflows of $1.8 billion from the Coalition Support Fund, reverted to a deficit of $700 million in February 2013. As disbursements of the same magnitude are not expected during the second half of the year, it is expected that the current account will post a deficit on the order of 0.8% of GDP. Exports contracted by 0.9% during the first 8 months of FY2013, but a 3.5% contraction in imports was four times larger (Figure 3.20.11). Low export growth was largely the result of 2.7% lower textile exports, reflecting the impact of sustained energy shortages, difficulties in meeting production schedules, and slack global demand. The contraction in imports was mostly of food, transportation equipment, and petroleum.

Despite improvement in the current account, net liquid foreign exchange reserves declined further, dropping from $10.8 billion at the end of June 2012 to $7.9 billion at the end of February (Figure 3.20.12), reflecting higher debt amortization payments, including payments to the International Monetary Fund (IMF), and lower financial inflows. Low reserves adequacy, at less than 2 months of imports cover as of February 2013, raises concern over external sector sustainability. Pressure on reserves is expected to continue, with an additional $1.7 billion due to the IMF before the end of FY2013 and $3.2 billion during FY2014. The financial account was in deficit during the first 8 months of FY2013 (Figure 3.20.13) despite a modest revival in portfolio inflows as foreign direct investment stagnated. The nominal exchange rate depreciated by 4% in the first 8 months of FY2013.

3.20.9 Weighted contribution to consumer price index inflation

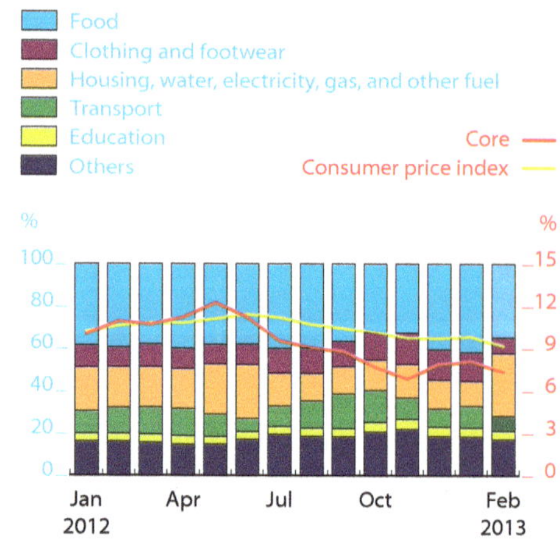

Source: State Bank of Pakistan. Economic Data. http://www.sbp.org.pk (accessed 5 March 2013).

Click here for figure data

3.20.10 Interest rates

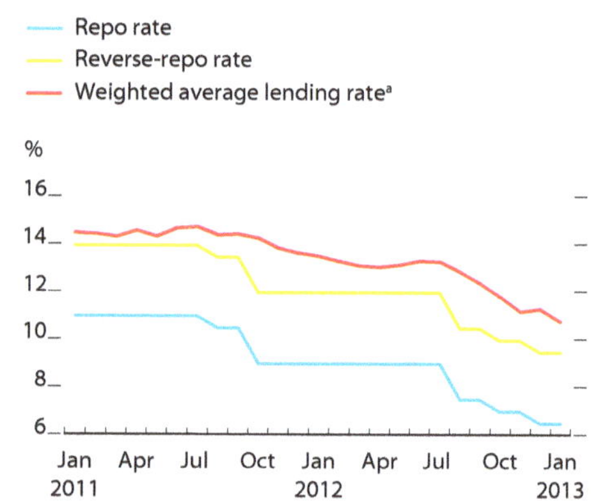

[a] On gross disbursements, the amounts disbursed by banks either in Pakistan rupees or foreign currency against loans during the month. Also includes loans repriced, renewed, or rolled over during the month. In case of running finance, the disbursed amount means the maximum amount received by the borrower at any point during the month.

Sources: State Bank of Pakistan. http://www.sbp.org.pk; CEIC Data Company (both accessed 21 March 2013).

Click here for figure data

3.20.11 Growth in exports and imports

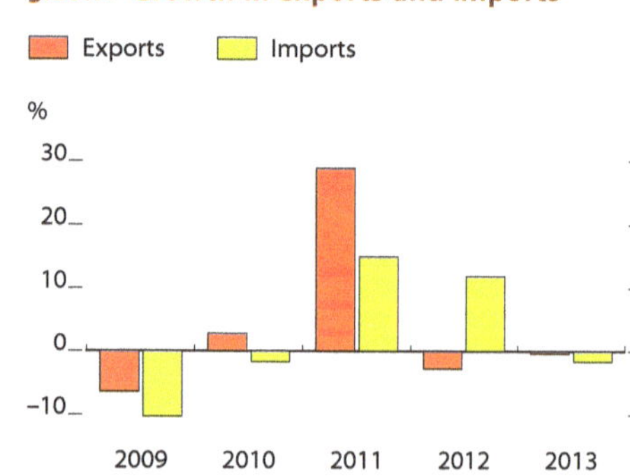

Note: 2013 data is from July 2012 to February 2013.

Source: State Bank of Pakistan. Economic Data. http://www.sbp.org.pk (accessed 17 January 2013).

Click here for figure data

Continued weak export prospects, combined with limited import demand held down by slow domestic growth and relatively stable global prices for oil, support a projection that the current deficit will increase marginally to 0.9% of GDP in FY2014. However, weak capital inflows and large debt repayments, including to the IMF, will put pressure on the official reserves and the exchange rate.

The fiscal outlook is largely unchanged from FY2012. Revenue targets announced with the FY2013 budget are unlikely to be met, as tax receipts have grown by only 12.0% in the first 6 months, well below the 23.7% increase needed to meet budget targets. On the expenditure side, overruns on interest outlays and subsidies are again expected, as subsidy allocations of PRs120 billion have already been exceeded and will reach at least PRs200 billion along with a further buildup of power sector arrears. The deficit for the first half of FY2013 is 2.5% of GDP, including the 0.7% of GDP from the Coalition Support Fund that is the single payment for the year. Given normal quarterly patterns for fiscal balances, the deficit for FY2013 is expected to breach the 4.7% target and is likely to come in at 7.0%–7.5% of GDP, excluding any payments to settle power sector arrears.

Government bank borrowing continued in the first half of FY2013. The government did acknowledge requirements under the State Bank of Pakistan Act by retiring PRs399 billion of the PRs505 billion borrowed from the central bank during the first quarter of FY2013, before borrowing back PRs183 billion in the second quarter in response to fiscal pressures, thereby breaching the act once again. Large government borrowing from commercial banks requires ever-larger injections from the central bank on a weekly basis to meet banks' liquidity requirements and keep money market rates anchored within central bank policy rates (Figure 3.20.14). Taming inflation would require shrinking these injections, which would require in turn lower government borrowing or else higher lending rates to further crowd out credit to the private sector.

3.20.12 Foreign reserves and exchange rate

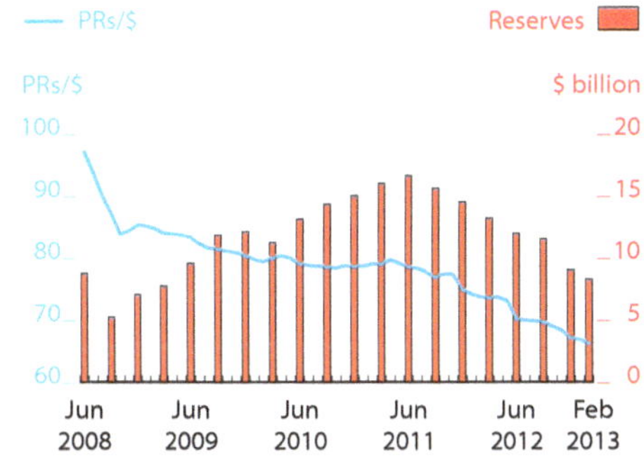

Sources: State Bank of Pakistan; CEIC Data Company (accessed 21 March 2013).

Click here for figure data

3.20.13 Foreign direct investment, portfolio, and financial account net flows

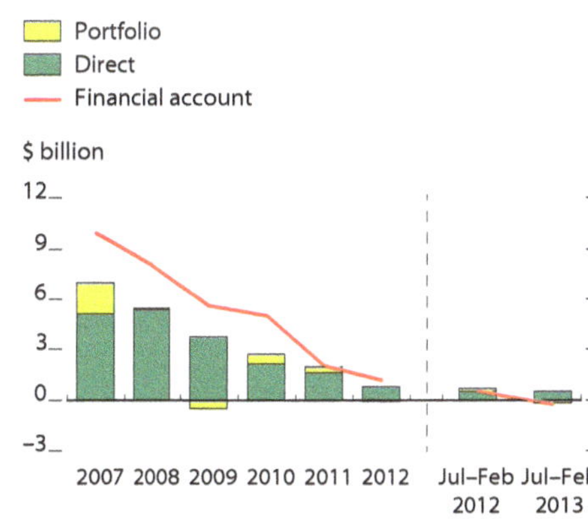

Source: State Bank of Pakistan. http://www.sbp.org.pk (accessed 6 March 2013).

Click here for figure data

Development challenge—lifting constraints on growth

The economy faces fundamental challenges to growth. The existing pattern of consumption-led growth with falling investment is unsustainable. In this context, macroeconomic sustainability and increasing investment go hand-in-hand with the improved growth prospects necessary to provide adequate employment. Unchanged policies marked by the lack of structural reform, high fiscal deficits, and accommodative monetary policies will mean continued slow growth, excessive inflation, and a weakening balance of payments that drains official reserves. Some drivers of the current situation, such as security challenges, are unlikely to change immediately. However, other factors, such as the energy deficit and the losses run up by public sector enterprises that drain fiscal resources needed for infrastructure development, are more malleable in the near and medium term.

Deterioration in the power sector is the main physical constraint on growth and a major cause of financial and economic instability. Power outages are estimated to cut growth by 2 percentage points annually,

3.20.14 State Bank of Pakistan open market operations

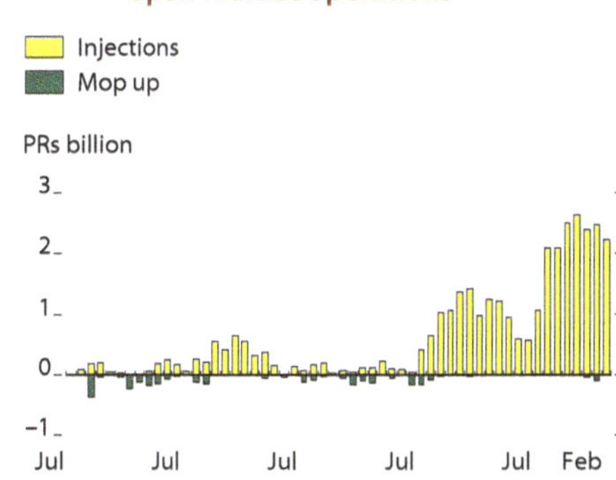

Source: State Bank of Pakistan. 2013. *Statistical Bulletin*. January.

Click here for figure data

making it unlikely that Pakistan will be able, without significant reform, to move toward the 7% growth rate needed to generate adequate employment and meaningful poverty reduction. The current environment in the power sector, in which receipts do not cover costs, means that for every unit of power sold there is a large loss that is either covered by a government subsidy or becomes part of the continuously accumulating arrears of the state-owned power companies. Growing arrears, which reached PRs450 billion at the end of December 2012, or about 2% of GDP, constrain the availability of cash needed to operate existing power-generation assets at full capacity. While it will take time to move to a more efficient system for generating, transmitting, and distributing electricity, improvements to collection, adjustments to pricing mechanisms, and improved management could enable higher power generation, lift the financial burden on the budget, and motivate private investment in the sector.

Large loss-making public sector enterprises absorb fiscal resources without any apparent improvement in their operations or financial viability. Explicit subsidies included in the budget for them are limited, as most assistance is in the form of sovereign loan guarantees that require lump sum payouts from the government at crisis points. The end result is the inefficient provision of services at prices that are higher than necessary. The framework for economic growth approved by the government in FY2011 identifies the restructuring of public sector enterprises as a key focus area. Its recent approval of corporate governance rules for public sector enterprises is a step in the right direction, but the rules will need to be rigorously applied in the face of long-standing resistance to change.

Finally, achieving the major challenge of boosting agricultural productivity and strengthening food security requires improving the management, storage, and pricing of water for irrigation. Anecdotal evidence suggests that agricultural productivity could be doubled with appropriate reform. Improved water management is critical to deliver sufficient water to the 80% of farmland in the country that is irrigated.

Pakistan is one of the most water-stressed countries in the world, not far from being classified as "water scarce," with less than 1,000 cubic meters per person per year. Water demand exceeds supply, which has caused maximum withdrawal from reservoirs. At present, Pakistan's storage capacity is limited to a 30-day supply, well below the recommended 1,000 days for countries with a similar climate. Climate change is affecting snowmelt and reducing flows into the Indus River, the main supply source. Increases in storage capacity to manage periods of low snowmelt and low rainfall are required, as well as the rehabilitation of the distribution system to reduce losses.

Sri Lanka

Policy measures in early 2012, including a tightened monetary stance and exchange rate flexibility, addressed emerging domestic and external imbalances. Weak external demand, drought, and floods slowed growth, but the balance of payments improved. Growth is expected to edge up, with some reduction in inflation and the current account deficit. High public debt means that sustaining rapid growth will require determined efforts to eliminate large losses in the energy sector and raise tax revenues to reduce budget deficits and borrowing.

Economic performance

Economic growth slowed in the second half of 2012 from a robust 7% in the first half to record annual expansion of 6.4% (Figure 3.21.1). This was the first time growth fell below 8% since the civil conflict ended, largely reflecting weak external demand, tight monetary conditions, and bad weather, as 15 of the country's 25 districts suffered drought that affected agriculture and hydropower generation.

Economic performance was underpinned by a strong showing in industry, which provides 30% of GDP and is estimated to have grown by 10.3%, as in 2011. A doubling of growth in construction accounted for the resilient performance, as expansion moderated in mining and quarrying, manufacturing, electricity, gas, and water.

In the service sector, which is the largest component of GDP, contributing some 59% to GDP, growth slowed to 4.6% in 2012, well below 8.6% a year earlier. Marked slowdowns in key subsectors such as wholesale and retail trade and transport and communications reflected subdued international trade and the impact of policy measures implemented in early 2012 for macroeconomic stabilization.

Agriculture, which contributes some 11% to GDP, performed well in the first half of 2012, reaching double-digit growth of 10%. However, severe drought followed by floods during the second half brought growth for the year to 5.8%—still recording a substantial recovery from the weak, weather-affected performance in the previous year.

Inflation, measured by the year-on-year increase in the Colombo consumer price index, continued to remain in single digits during 2012, averaging 7.6% for the year (Figure 3.21.2). However, inflation rose to around 9% in the second half with pressure on nonfood prices coming from increases in government-administered prices for fuel and electricity in February 2012 and the depreciation of the Sri Lankan rupee. Food inflation also increased during the year as import duties were increased on selected food items and domestic food supplies were disrupted by drought and flooding.

3.21.1 Supply-side contributions to growth

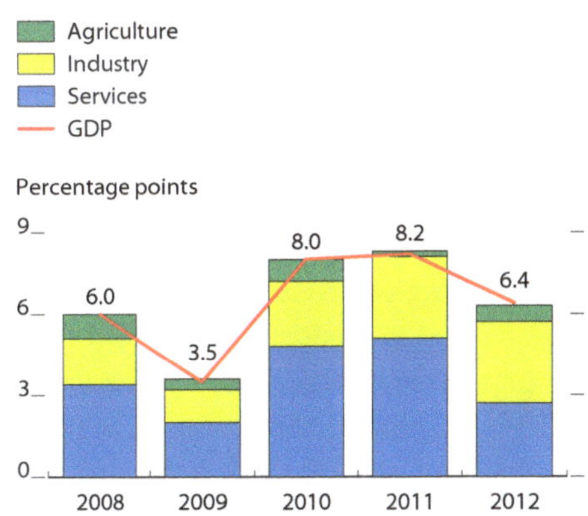

Sources: Central Bank of Sri Lanka. 2011. http://www.cbsl.gov.lk; Department of Census and Statistics of Sri Lanka. http://www.statistics.gov.lk (accessed 14 February 2013).
Click here for figure data

3.21.2 Inflation

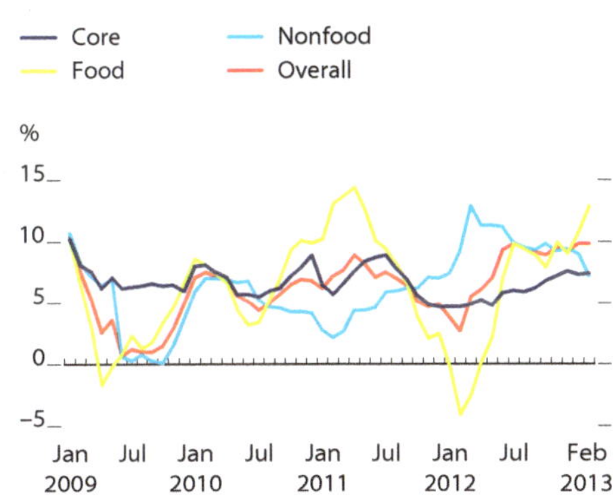

Source: Department of Census and Statistics Sri Lanka. http://www.statistics.gov.lk (accessed 14 February 2013).
Click here for figure data

This chapter was written by Tadateru Hayashi, Nimali Hasitha Wickremasinghe, and Savindi Jayakody of the Sri Lanka Resident Mission, ADB, Colombo.

The budget deficit is estimated to be 6.2% of GDP, exactly in line with the 2012 target (Figure 3.21.3). This was achieved, despite lower-than-expected revenues, by reducing budgeted current expenditure; capital expenditure was slightly lower than the targeted 6% of GDP. Revenue including grants is estimated to equal 14.2% of GDP, slightly lower than budgeted and less than in 2011. The shortfall was mainly due to lower value-added tax collections owing to slower growth.

The ratio of government debt to GDP rose to 82.6% in September 2012 from 78.5% at the end of 2011 owing to the impact of rupee depreciation on the value of foreign currency-denominated debt and increased borrowings, mainly through Treasury bills, to cover the budget deficit (Figure 3.21.4). Debt composition has changed with the gradual move toward more marketable instruments and foreign investment in government securities.

To counter external and internal imbalances that emerged during 2011, the central bank tightened monetary policy by raising policy rates in February and April 2012, and by imposing an 18% ceiling on licensed banks' credit growth in February. Repurchase and reverse-repurchase rates were increased by 75 and 125 basis points in total from those of 2011 (Figure 3.21.5). Active liquidity management by the central bank continued absorbing excess rupee liquidity in the domestic money market to underpin the tightened monetary stance. With these measures, banks' average lending rate on new loans rose by 300 basis points to just over 14%, and growth in credit to the private sector fell from about 35% in the first quarter to 17.6% by year-end. To address risks to growth, the central bank eased monetary policy in mid-December by reducing policy rates by 25 basis points and allowed the ceiling on credit growth to the private sector to expire at the end of 2012.

Exchange rate policy in 2012 moved toward greater flexibility by limiting central bank intervention in the foreign exchange market. The rupee quickly depreciated by about 15% against the dollar in the first half of the year, then slowly moved upward, appreciating by about 3% during the second half (Figure 3.21.6). Over 2012, the nominal and real effective exchange rates depreciated by about 11% and 6%, respectively.

Exports and imports both declined from the previous year after the second quarter, with exports contracting by 7.4% for the year and imports by 5.8%. Weak global demand and lower prices explained most of the drop in exports. Earnings from garments, the island's largest export, fell by 2.3%, mainly owing to slack economic conditions in the US and the European Union (EU) and the loss in 2010 of the Generalized System of Preferences Plus facility previously offered by the EU, which continues to cause garment factories to close. Agricultural exports, including tea, contracted by 7.8% due to the drought and weaker prices.

The performance of imports reflected currency depreciation, some higher tariffs, and central bank measures to restrict credit growth. Except fuel, machinery, and building materials, imports of all other import subcategories fell from a year earlier. Imports of consumer goods contracted by 18% and of intermediate goods by 6%, while imports of investment goods rose by 5%. Fuel imports increased by 5% as thermal power generation stood in for hydropower output constrained by drought. Despite the fall in export earnings, the trade deficit narrowed by 4% to $9.3 billion.

3.21.3 Fiscal indicators

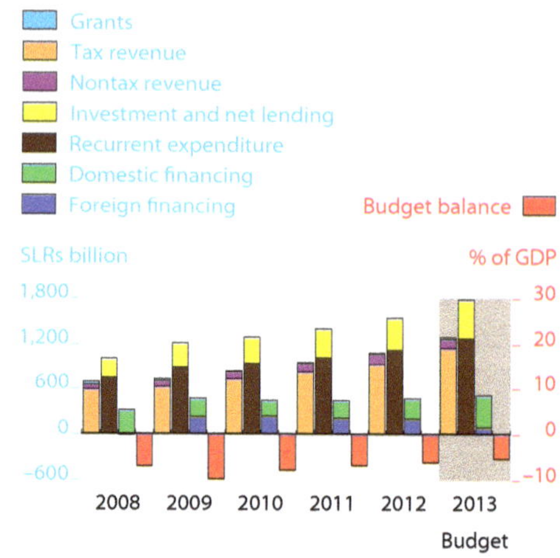

Sources: Central Bank of Sri Lanka. 2011. *Annual Report 2011.* http://www.cbsl.lk; Ministry of Finance and Planning and the Treasury of Sri Lanka. 2013. *Budget Speech 2013.* http://www.treasury.gov.lk

Click here for figure data

3.21.4 Government debt

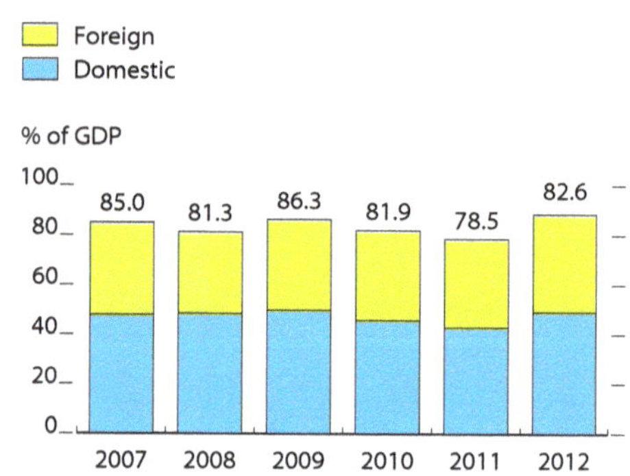

Note: 2012 data is up to the end of September.

Source: Central Bank of Sri Lanka. http://www.cbsl.lk

Click here for figure data

3.21.5 Credit growth and interest rates

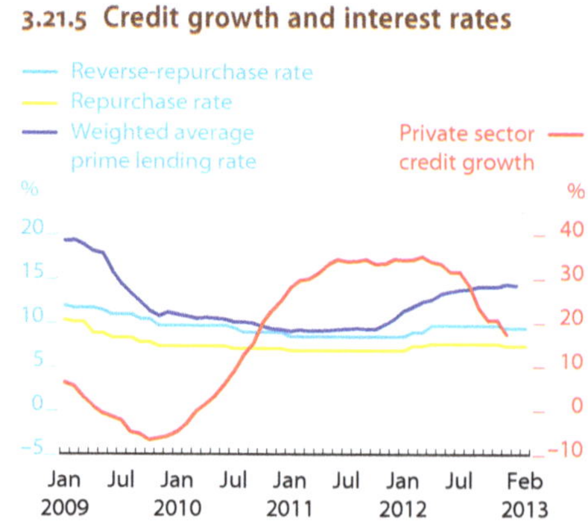

Source: Central Bank of Sri Lanka. http://www.cbsl.lk (accessed 20 March 2013).

Click here for figure data

The post-conflict tourism boom continued in 2012, with the number of tourists visiting Sri Lanka surpassing 1 million in 2012 and earnings from tourism expanding by 25.1% to reach $1 billion. Workers' remittances also expanded rapidly by 16.3% to $6 billion. Increased labor migration under the professional category and the expansion of formal channels for remitting money were the main factors boosting remittance inflows. These earnings held the current account deficit to an estimated $3.5 billion, about 5.8% of GDP, a marked improvement from 7.8% a year earlier (Figure 3.21.7).

Net foreign investments on the Colombo Stock Exchange increased to $305 million, and there was a significant increase in foreign purchases of government securities. Net inflows to the government in 2012 grew by 20.8%, in part reflecting the disbursement of foreign loans to finance major infrastructure development projects. Foreign direct investment of around $1 billion was, however, about the same as in 2011.

The proceeds of the fifth $1 billion sovereign bond issue and the final $415 million disbursement under the International Monetary Fund standby facility helped to buoy foreign exchange inflows. Gross official reserves increased by $0.9 billion to $6.9 billion, equivalent to 4.3 months of imports (Figure 3.21.8). In 2012, Fitch Ratings affirmed Sri Lanka's *stable* sovereign rating, and Standard & Poor's revised its foreign currency rating outlook from *positive* to *stable*.

Economic prospects

Private consumption expenditure, which accounts for about 70% of GDP, will remain the main engine of economic expansion, fuelled by rising incomes and remittances from Sri Lankans abroad. Investments are expected to expand further in 2013, with higher growth in construction buoyed by large infrastructure projects. Slow recovery in the euro area, Sri Lanka's largest export market, would continue to constrain growth potential somewhat. Exports will have to wait at least another year for a stronger recovery because weak external demand will continue in 2013. From the supply side, expansion is expected in services, led by hotels and other tourism-related businesses, along with growth in external and domestic trade. Agriculture is expected to improve with normal weather.

Economic growth will be subject to constraint from the balance of payments. Larger imports associated with high economic growth will worsen the trade deficit and—unless financed by exports, workers' remittance, and capital inflow—depreciate the currency. Because of the need to address inflation, the monetary policy stance set at the end of 2012 is not expected to be relaxed, which will restrain economic growth. As such, GDP growth is expected to edge up to 6.8% in 2013 and then advance by 7.2% in 2014 on better external conditions.

Fiscal policy will focus on further consolidation and the challenge of narrowing the budget deficit. The government projects a budget deficit of 5.8% of GDP in 2013, down from 6.2% estimated for 2012. The narrowing of the deficit is attributable to an expected 18.9% increase in tax revenue and grants, against a 15.9% increase in government expenditure. Expenditure as a share of GDP will be 20.5%, essentially unchanged from 2012. The ratio of current expenditure to capital expenditure will

3.21.6 Exchange rates

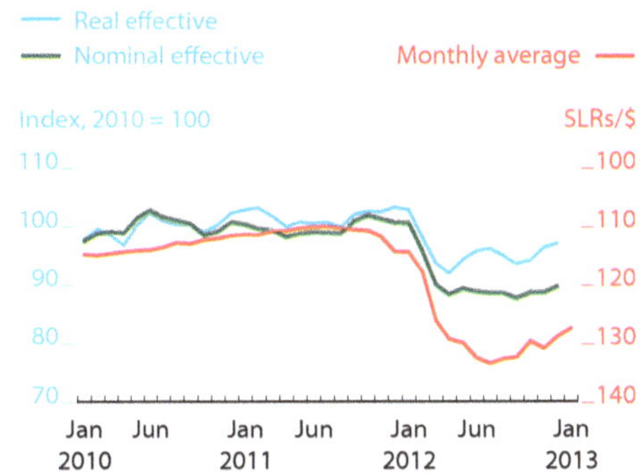

Source: Central Bank of Sri Lanka. http://www.cbsl.lk (accessed 8 March 2013).

Click here for figure data

3.21.7 Current account indicators

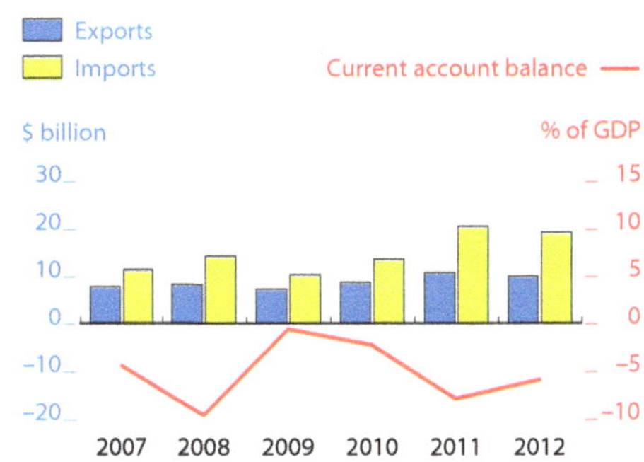

Sources: Central Bank of Sri Lanka. *Recent Economic Developments Highlights of 2012 and Prospects for 2013.* http://www.cbsl.gov.lk; ADB estimates.

Click here for figure data

3.21.8 Gross official reserves

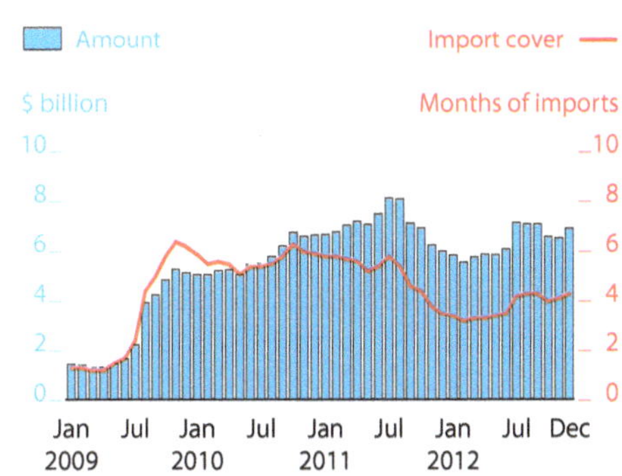

Source: Central Bank of Sri Lanka. http://www.cbsl.gov.lk (accessed 14 February 2013).

Click here for figure data

fall as the government increases public investments to a planned 6.1% of GDP, in line with its Mahinda Chintana development policy framework.

The planned expansion of revenue to 14.7% of GDP is to come mainly through higher collection of value-added tax and improved efficiency in tax collection, supported by higher economic growth and a better external trade performance. Increasing revenue is difficult. Revenue has been declining as a share of GDP, even in years with high economic growth (Figure 3.21.9). To decisively reverse this trend, tax efficiency would need to improve substantially and the tax base to widen.

Average inflation in 2013 is expected to be 7.5%, little improved from a year earlier, despite the base effect from the energy price adjustments in 2012 disappearing in the second quarter of 2013, expected declines in global commodity and oil prices, and expected exchange rate stabilization at current levels. Gas prices were adjusted upward by 2% and diesel by 5% in the last week of February 2013. Further price increases are required to address the current operating losses of the Ceylon Electricity Board (CEB), and to pay down debts to banks that funded previous years' losses. The estimated loss was about Rs89 billion (equal to 1.2% of GDP) for Ceylon Petroleum and Rs65 billion (0.9%) for the CEB. An increase in the national minimum wage is a risk that could top up inflationary pressures. Monetary policy will therefore need to remain tight to limit second-round effects and anchor inflation expectations in 2013.

External demand is expected to recover gradually in 2013. Merchandise exports are projected to grow at a slow 4% in 2013 and 5% in 2014. Meanwhile, worker's remittances will continue to expand rapidly. Services exports are expected to be boosted by growing tourism, the further development of business process outsourcing, and higher income from trade and shipping services partly derived from the opening of new port facilities.

Revenues from these items will allow imports to expand by 6% in 2013 and 10% in 2014 without widening the current account deficit as a share of GDP (Figure 3.21.10). Normal weather would increase the share of hydropower generation and contain the oil bill. The current account deficit is thus expected to be 5.0% of GDP in 2013 and 4.5% in 2014, both improvements on the estimated 5.8% in 2012. It is assumed that the current account deficit will continue to be financed by capital inflows.

Policy challenge—developing the power sector

Sri Lanka achieved remarkable progress in developing its power sector. The national electrification ratio grew from 29% in 1990 to an estimated 94% in 2012. Power supply is stable, and power cuts are very limited.

The cost of electricity supply is, however, high. Moreover, tariffs do not reflect full costs or adjust according to an automatic mechanism. The average cost of electricity generation is currently around SLRs21.0 per kilowatt-hour while the average selling price is SLRs16.4. The CEB's estimated loss of SLRs65 billion in 2012 occurred even with fuel supplied by Ceylon Petroleum at less than full cost. The CEB relies on bank loans to cover its operating costs. In January 2013 the regulator for the sector, the Public Utilities Commission, began preparing an assessment of the CEB's costs toward revising electricity tariffs based on a formula.

3.21.9 Government tax revenues

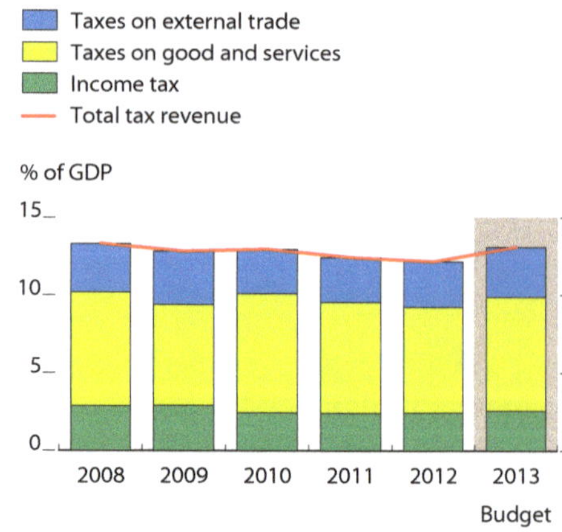

Sources: Central Bank of Sri Lanka. *Annual Report 2011.* http://www.cbsl.lk; Ministry of Finance and Planning and the Treasury of Sri Lanka. *Budget Speech 2013.* http://www.treasury.gov.lk

Click here for figure data

3.21.10 Current account components

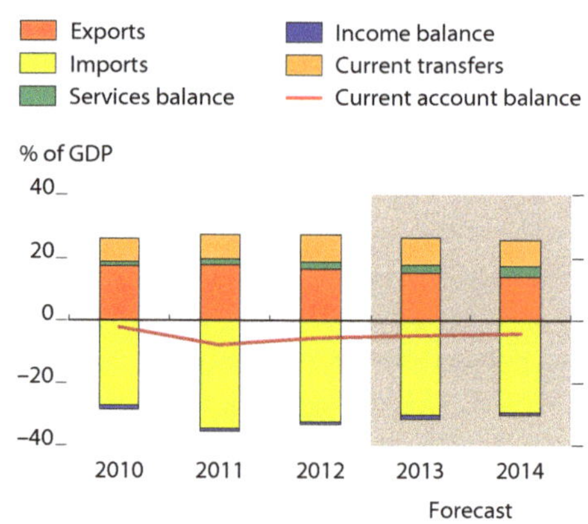

Sources: Central Bank of Sri Lanka. *Annual Report 2011.* http://www.cbsl.lk; ADB estimates.

Click here for figure data

The share of thermal power increased from 6% in 1995 to 60% during 2008–2012, as demand growth was met by oil-fired generation (Figure 3.21.11). The growing reliance on oil-fired plants, higher oil prices, and the delayed construction of new hydropower plants have significantly pushed up the cost of generation. The option now available for generating large base loads is traditional coal-fired plants, which are under development (Table 3.21.2). At present, unconventional renewable energy sources cannot contribute significantly because of their intermittent nature and other technical constraints. Another option Sri Lanka has to strengthen its energy security is to diversify into other forms of traditional generation and to build a cross-border connection with India, which is being planned.

Disparities still exist in electrification across the provinces. As demand grows, particularly in the former conflict areas, the transmission network must be continuously improved. The challenge is to obtain financial support to implement crucial transmission links.

The government's 10-year development framework, prepared in 2006, envisions the sustainable development of energy resources, access extended to the entire population, and reliable service delivery at a competitive price through commercially viable institutions subjected to independent regulation.

3.21.2 Long-term power generation expansion plan, 2011–2018

Year	Renewable additions (using hydro)	Thermal additions (using coal and furnace oil)
2011		Puttalam coal (stage 1) (315 MW)
2012	Upper Kotmale (150 MW)	
2013		Chunnakam furnace oil (24 MW)
2014		Puttalam coal (stages 2 & 3, 2 × 315 MW)
2015	Uma Oya (120 MW)	
	Gin Ganga (49 MW)	
2016	Broadlands (35 MW)	
2017		Trincomalee coal (2 × 250 MW)
2018	Moragolla (30 MW)	

MW = megawatt.
Sources: Ceylon Electricity Board. *Long-Term Transmission Development Plan 2011*; ADB estimates.

3.21.1 Selected economic indicators (%)

	2013	2014
GDP growth	6.8	7.2
Inflation	7.5	6.5
Current account balance (share of GDP)	–5.0	–4.5

Source: ADB estimates.

3.21.11 Average electricity generation, 2008–2012
100% = 10,761 GWh

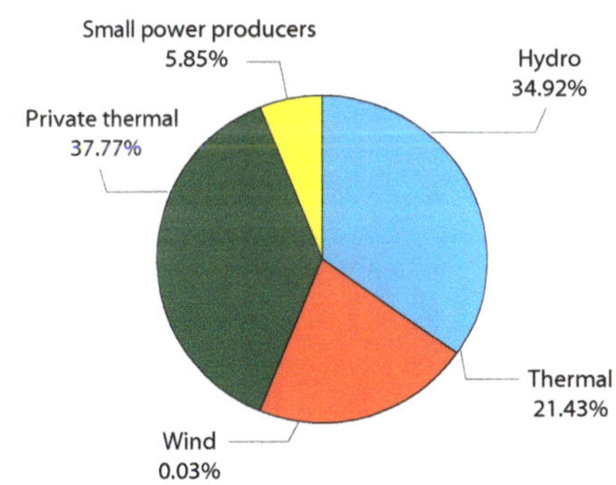

Source: Ceylon Electricity Board.
Click here for figure data

Southeast Asia

Brunei Darussalam
Cambodia
Indonesia
Lao People's Democratic Republic
Malaysia
Myanmar
Philippines
Singapore
Thailand
Viet Nam

Brunei Darussalam

Lower oil production and exports weighed on economic growth in 2012. Nevertheless, private consumption and fixed investment expanded. Growth in sectors unconnected to energy indicated the country's progress in its efforts to broaden its economic base. Modest GDP growth is projected for this year and next, accompanied by low inflation and substantial current account surpluses.

Economic performance

Economic growth slowed to an estimated 1% in 2012 owing to weakness in production and exports of crude oil (Figure 3.22.1). The latest official data put GDP growth at 0.6% in January–September from the same period in 2011.

Despite slight growth in GDP, private consumption increased by 4% in January–September, above the average of the past 5 years. Sales of new automobiles jumped by 28%. Increases in private consumption are underpinned by high employment, low inflation, and—thanks to strong government revenue flows from hydrocarbons—no taxes on personal incomes, goods and services, or capital gains. GDP per capita at $41,600 in 2012 was the highest in developing Asia after Singapore.

Fixed investment rose by nearly 3% and government consumption by 2% in January–September. While domestic demand increased in 2012, a decline in exports of hydrocarbons together with a rise in imports meant that net exports acted as a drag on GDP growth.

The oil and gas sector contracted by 2.4% in January–September. Oil production fell to 155,000 barrels a day from 166,000 barrels a day in 2011. Output has declined by about one-third since 2006, when it was 219,000 barrels a day (Figure 3.22.2). Natural gas production at mid-2012 showed a slight decline from a year earlier.

Encouragingly, economic activity unconnected with energy grew by 3.4%, indicating progress in the government's drive to diversify the economy before hydrocarbon reserves dwindle. These sectors have gradually increased their combined share of real GDP to 54.4% over recent years (Figure 3.22.3). Services grew by 3.3% and agriculture by nearly 9%. Manufacturing and construction recorded only slight growth. In a further positive sign, the privately owned part of the economy outside the energy sector grew by a healthy 4.6% in the third quarter.

Merchandise exports, mostly oil and liquefied natural gas, increased by 9.4% to $9.9 billion on a customs basis in January–September, supported by higher prices. Exports of methanol were interrupted in April 2012 when production was shut down temporarily for maintenance.

3.22.1 GDP growth

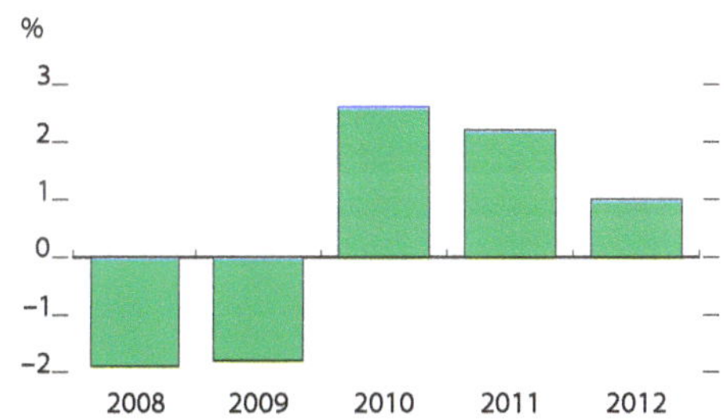

Sources: Asian Development Outlook database; ADB estimates.

Click here for figure data

3.22.2 Average daily production

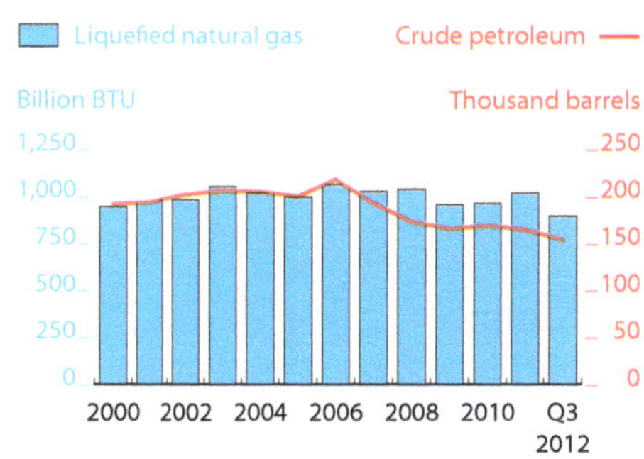

BTU = British thermal unit.

Sources: CEIC Data Company (accessed 23 March 2013); Department of Economic Planning and Development. 2012. *Brunei Economic Bulletin 3Q 2012.* http://www.depd.gov.bn/download/BEB_Q32012.pdf

Click here for figure data

This chapter was written by Mohammed Parvez Imdad of the Southeast Asia Department, ADB, Manila.

Imports rose much more quickly than exports, by 21.8% to $2.7 billion, on the back of firm domestic demand. Most capital and consumer goods are imported, as is most food. A substantial trade surplus produced another large current account surplus, estimated at 47% of GDP in 2012. International reserves rose by a third to $3.3 billion, cover for 11.9 months of imports of goods.

Inflation decelerated from 1.2% year on year at the start of 2012 to 0.5% in December (Figure 3.22.4). Prices of food, particularly meat and cooking oil, rose but this was mostly countered by lower prices for clothing, education, and transport. Price controls and subsidies help to keep inflation low. A firm exchange rate contributed by dampening imported inflation. The Brunei dollar, which is pegged to the Singapore dollar through a currency board arrangement, appreciated by 6.3% against the US dollar in 2012.

Income taxes, dividends, and royalties from hydrocarbons provide the government with substantial revenue to fund the large public sector, invest in public infrastructure, and provide a range of services and subsidies. Revenue in FY2011 (ended 31 March 2012) increased by 7.0% and government spending by only 1.4%, with the fiscal surplus remaining at over 20% of GDP.

3.22.3 Share of oil and other sectors in the economy

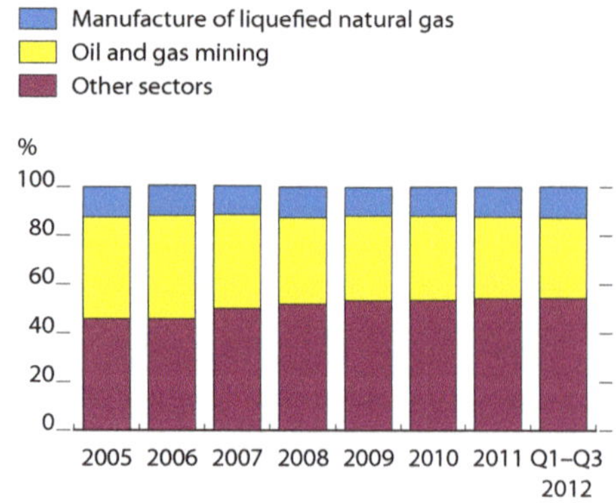

Source: CEIC Data Company (accessed 16 March 2013).
Click here for figure data

3.22.4 Monthly inflation

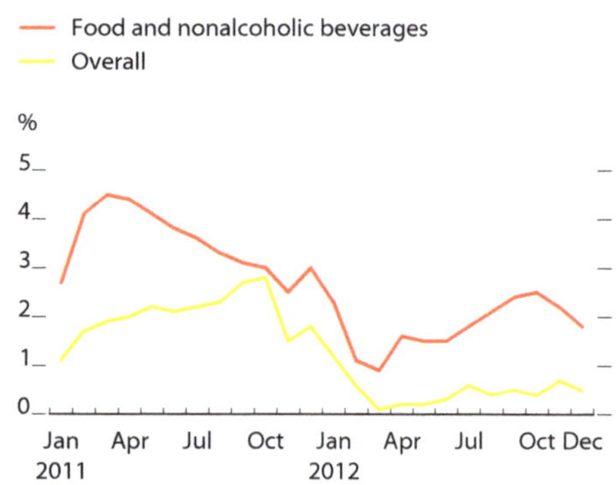

Source: CEIC Data Company (accessed 16 March 2013).
Click here for figure data

Economic prospects

The government aims to extend the productive life of hydrocarbons until other pursuits can play a much larger role in the economy. This is to be achieved by enhanced recovery and managed production from existing oil and gas fields and exploration for new ones. Forecasting GDP is hampered by uncertainty over the timing of new production and production stoppages for maintenance, as well as by limitations and delays affecting economic data. The projections below assume a modest recovery in hydrocarbons production and continued growth in the rest of the economy in the forecast period. On this basis, GDP is projected to increase by 1.8%–2.0% in 2013–2014.

More important for longer-term development are gains made toward broadening the economic base. The government has identified several industries for development, principally downstream petrochemicals, tourism, Islamic businesses including halal products and financial services, and information and communication technology services.

Infrastructure projects under way to attract these industries include the Pulau Muara Besar port and industrial zone supported by a bridge and roads to the port, an expanded international airport, upgraded power transmission lines, a high-speed broadband network with fiber-to-the-home connections, and an industrial park to research and develop agricultural products including halal food. A joint venture with a foreign company is establishing a helicopter and aircraft pilot training center that has ambitions to be a regional training facility.

Given the small size of the domestic market serving a population of only about 400,000, the government is pursuing export-oriented projects. Since foreign companies completed a $450 million plant to produce and export methanol in 2010, the government has approved plans for a $2.8 billion petrochemical project using natural gas and a $2.5 billion oil refinery and aromatics cracker, both of which are proposals from foreign companies. These projects are in the design and engineering phase.

Domestic institutions are being brought into play in the push for economic diversification. Last year the government established an investment holding company—Darussalam Assets—to improve the financial performance of government-owned firms and to take a strategic role in diversification efforts. The monetary authority started preparations to establish a national payment and settlement system, in part to develop the Islamic finance industry and promote the country as an Islamic finance hub.

Soft global oil prices cloud the outlook for growth in export receipts. Merchandise exports are projected to increase slightly in value in 2013–2014, while imports will likely maintain strong growth. Nevertheless, the current account surplus will remain substantial given the relatively large export base and income from the country's overseas investments.

Inflation is seen at about 1% through the forecast period. Subdued global food prices and the government's domestic subsidies and price controls should largely counter inflationary pressures that could emerge from expansion in domestic demand.

3.22.1 Selected economic indicators (%)

	2013	2014
GDP growth	1.8	2.0
Inflation	1.0	1.2
Current account balance (share of GDP)	45.0	47.0

Source: ADB estimates.

Policy challenge—attracting new industries

Brunei Darussalam ranks 28th of 144 countries in the World Economic Forum's *Global Competitiveness Report 2012–2013*, better than other countries in Southeast Asia except for Singapore and Malaysia. One factor that hurts competitiveness is the small market, for which reason the country ranks only 130 in the category of domestic market size.

To address this issue, the government is building transport, power, and communications infrastructure so that companies can serve foreign markets. It has implemented liberal policies on trade, investment, and labor—such that, for example, foreign workers comprised 74% of all private sector employment in 2010. The country is a member of the Trans-Pacific Partnership, which proposes further liberalization of trade and investment between members. Moreover, the government has lowered the corporate tax rate to 20% and offers other tax concessions and incentives.

Brunei Darussalam moved up four places to 79th of 185 countries in the World Bank's *Doing Business 2013* ranking. Moving into this ranking's top 20 is a government ambition that will require intensified efforts to, among other actions, upgrade training and labor regulations, develop capital markets, and streamline procedures for starting businesses.

Cambodia

Higher inflows of foreign direct investment contributed to strong economic growth in 2012. Outcomes exceeded expectations in agriculture, construction, and tourism. The forecast is for further robust growth, with the trajectory expected to steepen slightly in 2014 as recovery in major export markets takes hold. Inflation subsided in 2012 and is projected to remain modest through the forecast period. Although poverty has declined, persistently high child malnutrition remains a critical development challenge.

Economic performance

GDP growth picked up to 7.2% in 2012, driven by robust consumption and investment (Figure 3.23.1). Consumption expanded by an estimated 9.5% and made the biggest contribution to GDP growth from the demand side. Gross fixed investment increased by 30%, spurred by a surge in foreign direct investment (FDI) and higher bank lending. However, net exports dragged on GDP growth as they fell, partly reflecting elevated imports needed for power-generation projects.

The service sector expanded by an estimated 8% and was the main source of GDP growth from the production side. Strong growth in tourism and resurgence in real estate activity bolstered this sector. Assisted by more direct flights, tourist arrivals rose by 24.4% to 3.6 million and tourism receipts grew by 15.6% to $2.2 billion (Figure 3.23.2).

Growth in the industry sector moderated from the previous year's pace to just over 9% in 2012. Exports of garments and footwear to the US, Cambodia's top export market, fell by 1.8% to $2.6 billion, though those to the European Union (EU) rose by 10.8% to $1.8 billion. Industry sector growth was supported by a 5% increase in exports of milled rice to 187,000 tons, mostly to the EU. Construction accelerated as building project approvals nearly doubled to $2.1 billion last year.

Agricultural production increased by an estimated 4%, despite floods in some provinces and dry weather in others. Output of crop production, mainly paddy rice, rose by 4.3%, and fishery yields increased by 6%.

A moderation in food prices brought down inflation from 5.8% in January 2012 to 2.6% in December (Figure 3.23.3). Food comprises 43% of the consumer price index. Year-average inflation decelerated to 2.9%.

The government continued to rein in its fiscal deficit, which had widened sharply in 2009 to 8.6% of GDP. The fiscal gap, excluding grants, narrowed last year to an estimated 5.2% of GDP. Domestic revenue increased to 14.5% of GDP from 13.2% in the previous year, thanks to improved revenue collection and buoyant economic activity. Government spending was contained at 19.7% of GDP, down from 20.7% in 2011. Income from external grants and concessional loans amounted

3.23.1 Demand-side contributions to growth

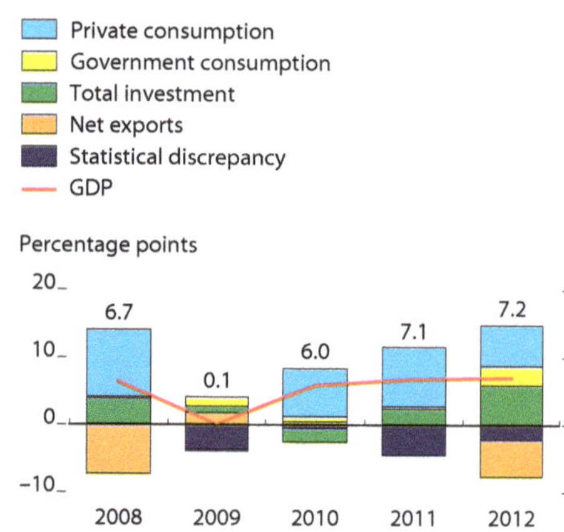

Sources: National Institute of Statistics; ADB estimates.

Click here for figure data

3.23.2 Tourism

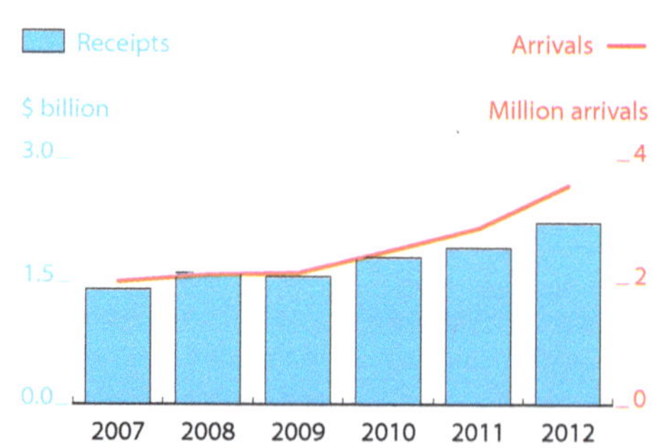

Source: Ministry of Tourism.

Click here for figure data

This chapter was written by Peter Brimble and Poullang Doung of the Cambodia Resident Mission, ADB, Phnom Penh.

to 5.8% of GDP, so the government was able to replenish its savings by the equivalent of 0.6% of GDP after running down its deposits over the previous 3 years.

Growth in credit to the private sector accelerated to 34.1% last year (Figure 3.23.4). Concerned about this rapid pace, the central bank raised the reserve requirement for foreign currency deposits in commercial banks by 50 basis points to 12.5% in September 2012. The ratio of private sector credit to GDP jumped to 41.6%, well above the median for low-income countries. Reflecting a deepening of the financial system, the ratio of broad money to GDP rose to 50.5% from 45.4% in 2011. The Cambodian riel appreciated by an average of 0.8% against the US dollar last year.

Merchandise exports, mainly garments, footwear, and rice, rose in US dollar terms by an estimated 11.4%. Imports, bolstered by purchases of construction materials for power plants and other projects, rose by 17.0%. As the merchandise trade gap widened, so did the current account deficit, to 11.6% of GDP if official transfers are excluded. The deficit was fully financed by FDI and official loans and grants. Net FDI surged by 75% to $1.5 billion (Figure 3.23.5), contributing to an increase in gross official reserves to $3.5 billion, which covers 4.4 months of imports.

An International Monetary Fund analysis of debt sustainability published this year saw Cambodia at low risk of debt distress. It cautioned that structural reform and revenue mobilization, as well as the careful management of potential contingent liabilities from power-generation projects, will be important to ensuring long-term debt sustainability.

Poverty incidence likely fell below 20%, surpassing the official target to reduce poverty by half from levels in the early 1990s. This reduction has been achieved through sustained economic growth, with particularly good performance in agriculture.

Economic prospects

Economic growth is forecast at 7.2% in 2013, picking up to 7.5% next year as recovery in Europe and the US takes hold (Figure 3.23.6).

European demand for Cambodian garments and footwear is expected to maintain good growth, supported by duty-free access to the EU. Shipments to the US will likely be subdued this year but should pick up after that. Increased foreign investment is funding new industries, including the manufacture of automotive parts and processing of agricultural products, as well as diversifying garment production into higher-value products. Last year's surge in building approvals bodes well for construction. The timing of offshore oil exploitation is unclear. Industry as a whole is expected to expand by 10.5% in 2013.

The service sector is seen growing by 7%. Growth in tourism is benefiting the hotel, restaurant, retailing, and transport and communications subsectors. Buoyant property development stimulates growth in finance and real estate services. Agriculture will likely grow by about 4%, assuming favorable weather. The government is supporting paddy production and exports of milled rice.

Fiscal consolidation looks set to continue in 2013, as the government targets a narrower fiscal deficit at 5.1% of GDP, to be funded by external grants and loans. Nevertheless, public spending could pick up ahead of

3.23.3 Monthly inflation

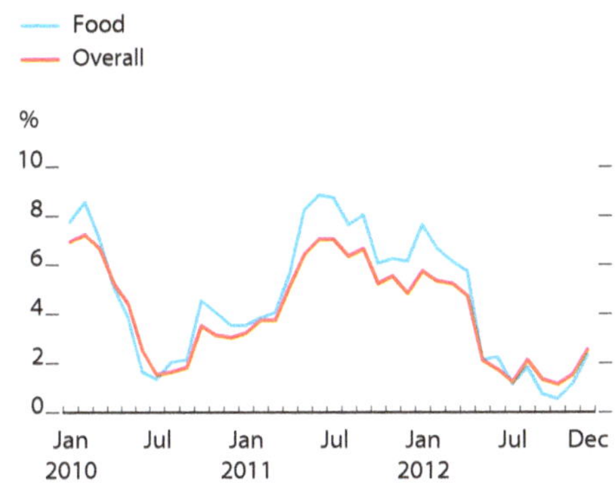

Source: National Institute of Statistics (accessed 14 March 2013).

Click here for figure data

3.23.4 Money supply and private sector credit

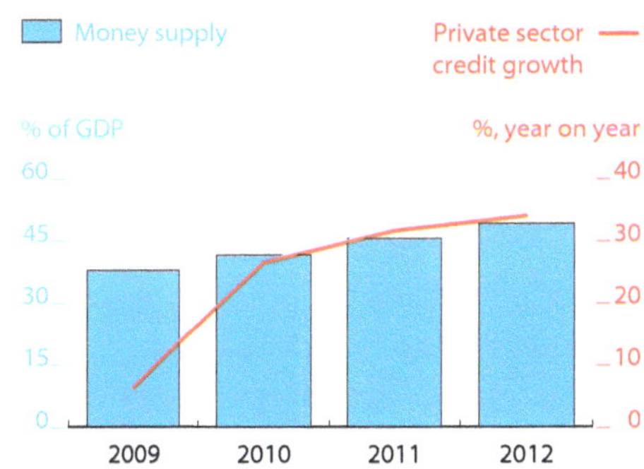

Source: National Bank of Cambodia.

Click here for figure data

3.23.5 Net foreign direct investment

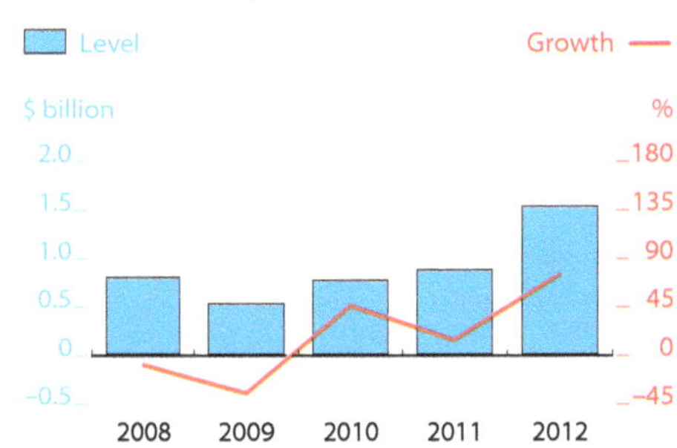

Source: National Bank of Cambodia.

Click here for figure data

3.23.6 GDP growth

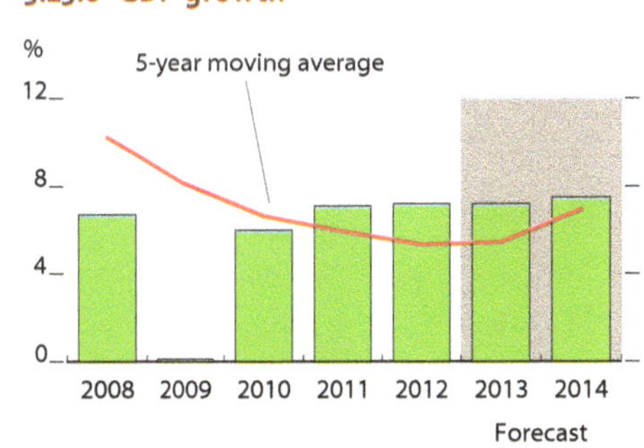

Source: Asian Development Outlook database.

Click here for figure data

national elections scheduled for July 2013, making fiscal consolidation more difficult. The stock of government deposits in the banking system—the country's buffer to deal with shocks—is likely to increase to 4.6% of GDP, compared with 8% in 2008.

In light of the rapid growth in credit and excess liquidity at some banks, additional increases in bank reserve requirements may be required to reduce risks to financial stability. In this regard, the authorities are considering such macroprudential measures as imposing higher capital requirements for banks, or tightening permitted ratios of loans to value or loans to deposits. The central bank plans to develop the interbank market by introducing negotiable certificates of deposit, moving toward more market-based monetary policy operations. To reduce the heavy use of the US dollar for local transactions, the government will continue to encourage the use of the riel. Last year, the ratio of US dollar deposits to total deposits was 95.7%, down only marginally from 97.0% in 2008.

Good domestic harvests and relatively stable global food prices suggest that inflation this year will be on average similar to that in 2012 (Figure 3.23.7). Inflation is seen quickening in 2014 as continued robust domestic demand likely encounters some supply constraints. These inflation forecasts will be at risk if bad weather pushes up food prices.

Merchandise exports are projected to pick up during the forecast period while growth in imports moderates after the completion of large power projects. Receipts from tourism will keep the services account in surplus. The current account deficit, excluding official transfers, is projected to narrow (Figure 3.23.8). FDI and other capital flows are expected to maintain international reserves at levels that cover more than 4 months of imports.

Developments that enhance the environment for the private sector included the initial public offering of shares in the Phnom Penh Water Supply Authority, the first listing on the Cambodia Securities Exchange. An arbitration center was launched to provide businesses with a faster and less expensive way to resolve commercial disputes, and a credit bureau started to provide banks with better information on potential borrowers. To tackle corruption the government issued lists in January 2013 showing the official fees for public services including customs, taxation, business and trading procedures, and other activities related to investment. Finally, the authorities are strengthening the environment for public–private partnership (Box 3.23.1).

3.23.1 Selected economic indicators (%)

	2013	2014
GDP growth	7.2	7.5
Inflation	3.0	3.5
Current account balance (share of GDP)	–11.1	–10.1

Source: ADB estimates.

3.23.7 Inflation

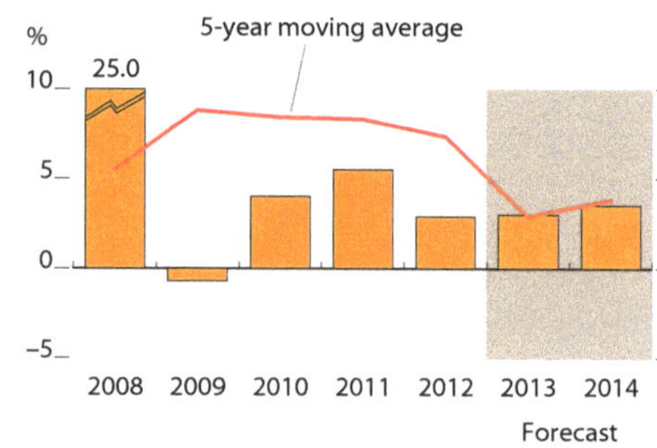

Source: Asian Development Outlook database.
Click here for figure data

3.23.8 Current account balance

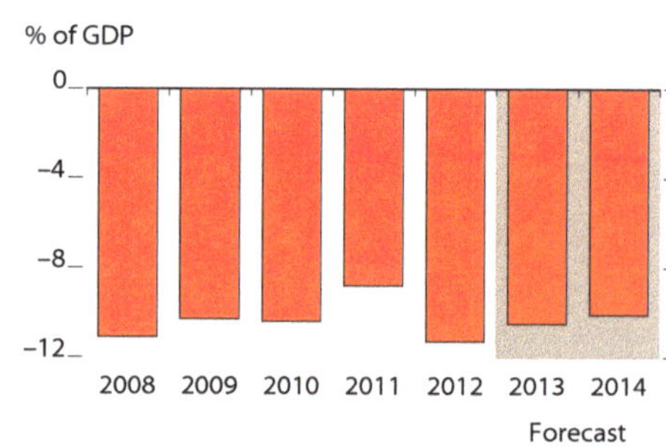

Source: Asian Development Outlook database.
Click here for figure data

Policy challenge—child malnutrition

The high incidence of child malnutrition in Cambodia is a critical development challenge. Poor nutrition in the 1,000 days from conception to the second birthday causes long-term damage to physical and cognitive development. Functional losses in this period can never be fully recovered. In addition to impacts on child health and mortality, malnutrition has adverse health and economic consequences that persist throughout the individual's lifetime and can be handed down to harm the next generation.

Chronic poor health and malnutrition stunt the growth of 40% of Cambodian children. Demographic surveys show 28% of children under 5 years of age underweight in 2005—and no improvement 5 years later.

Indeed, severe malnutrition increased, with the incidence of wasting among children rising from 8.4% to 10.9% (Figure 3.23.9). The incidence of anemia was at epidemic proportions, affecting 55% of children under 5 in 2010.

The World Health Organization estimated in 2011 that Cambodia loses $146 million in GDP each year from the impacts of vitamin and mineral deficiencies alone. While the full economic impact of malnutrition in the country has yet to be assessed, international evidence cited by the United Nations Development Assistance Framework suggests that a 1% decrease in adult stature translates into a 1.4% decrease in productivity.

Risk factors for child malnutrition include poverty (although child malnutrition also affects higher-income families in Cambodia), lack of toilets, unsafe water supply, inadequate breast feeding, and poor maternal nutrition. The 2010 demographic survey found that 57% of Cambodian households had no toilet and therefore defecated in the open, 26% of infants under 6 months were not exclusively breastfed, and 44% of women suffered some degree of anemia.

The good news is that addressing child malnutrition early can avoid long-term damage to health. Further, the solutions are highly cost-effective. The 2012 Copenhagen Consensus, a meeting of economists to establish cost-effective priorities to improve global welfare, found that fighting malnourishment should be the top priority and that the benefits in terms of improved health, schooling, and productivity would be significant.

Child malnutrition can be countered by

- targeting social transfers, fortifying foods, and improving local food production to overcome seasonal food shortages and ensure food supplies of sufficient quantity, quality, and variety;
- promoting breastfeeding and appropriate complementary feeding practices for young children;
- improving pregnant women's dietary intake through nutrition education and communication;
- providing to women and children improved basic health services and micronutrient supplementation; and
- reducing nutrient loss through improved hygiene, sanitation, parasite control, and food processing and storage.

The key is to develop mechanisms to scale up existing and future small-scale pilot initiatives that are designed to address these issues, thereby converting them into a government-led, integrated package of interventions for better food security, nutrition, sanitation, and hygiene. This requires a program with active community participation and a concerted strategy to change parental behavior that hinders child nutrition. Malnutrition issues could be addressed under the umbrella of social protection, for example through cash transfers, or through innovative public–private partnership.

3.23.1 Building public–private partnership

Cambodia needs investment of $12 billion–$16 billion to build infrastructure for its growing economy. In view of this substantial funding need, the government is putting more emphasis on public–private partnership in its development strategy. With development partner support, it has an ambitious range of initiatives under way to strengthen the legal, regulatory, and institutional environment for public–private partnership.

These changes should improve the transparency and quality of public–private partnerships. The first projects under the new program are expected to take shape in 2013 and 2014, for implementation soon after.

3.23.9 Child malnutrition

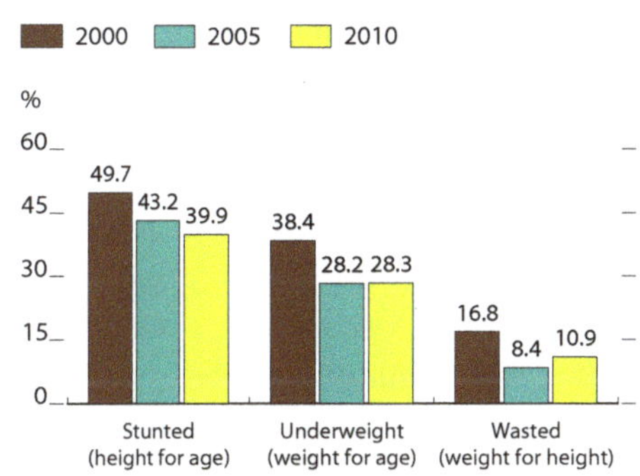

Note: Children under 5 years of age.

Source: Cambodia Demographic and Health Surveys.

Click here for figure data

Indonesia

Southeast Asia's biggest economy achieved another year of 6%-plus growth in 2012, despite falling exports. Sluggish external demand combined with stronger domestic demand to shift the current account into deficit. Inflation fell to a 12-year low. GDP growth is forecast to quicken in the next 2 years. Near-term challenges are to manage risks associated with the current account deficit and keep inflation moderate.

Economic performance

GDP growth at 6.2% in 2012 was based on robust private consumption and a better performance in fixed capital investment (Figure 3.24.1). Net exports fell, acting as a drag on GDP growth. Private consumption picked up to increase by 5.3%, the strongest pace in 4 years, and it contributed almost half of total GDP growth on the expenditure side. Consumption got a lift from increases in employment and wages as well as lower inflation. Sales of automobiles rose by nearly 25%, even though Bank Indonesia, the central bank, raised minimum downpayments on loans to buy cars and motorcycles.

Fixed investment accelerated to 9.8% in 2012, building on the previous year's increase of 8.8%, and was the source of 2.4 percentage points of GDP growth. Driving factors included an improved investment climate, a record of solid economic growth over recent years, and the expansion of credit. Outlays on buildings and infrastructure rose by 7.5%, and investment in machinery and equipment increased by a strong 12.7%. Renewed efforts to improve public infrastructure saw the central government's capital spending rise by 18.9%. As a result, the ratio of fixed capital formation to GDP rose to 33.2%, the highest in at least 20 years (Figure 3.24.2).

Realized foreign direct investment (FDI) surged by 26.1% to $23.6 billion, nearly half into manufacturing and 17% into mining (the data exclude investment in oil and gas). Investment in inventories also rose sharply.

The service and manufacturing sectors were key drivers from the supply side. Services expanded by 7.7%, contributing more than half of total growth (Figure 3.24.3). Telecommunications continued to record double-digit expansion owing to buoyant demand for mobile telephone and internet services.

Growth in manufacturing decelerated to 5.7%, reflecting weaker export markets. Mining output was lackluster, showing growth of just 1.5%, largely a result of declining crude oil extraction. Oil production fell by 42,000 barrels a day to 860,000 barrels a day last year, the outcome

3.24.1 Demand-side contributions to growth

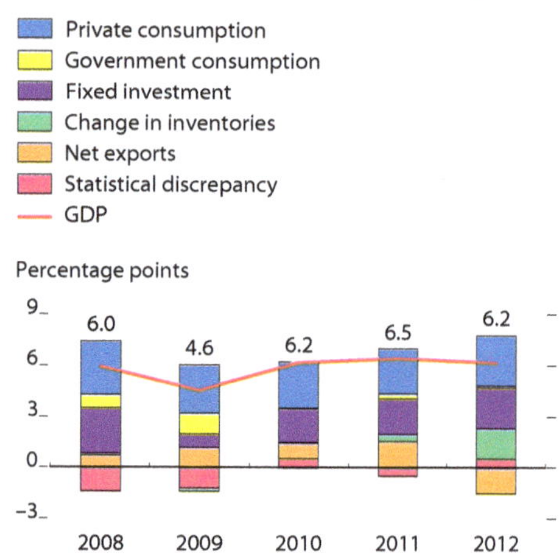

Sources: *Asian Development Outlook* database; CEIC Data Company (accessed 1 March 2013).

Click here for figure data

3.24.2 Fixed investment

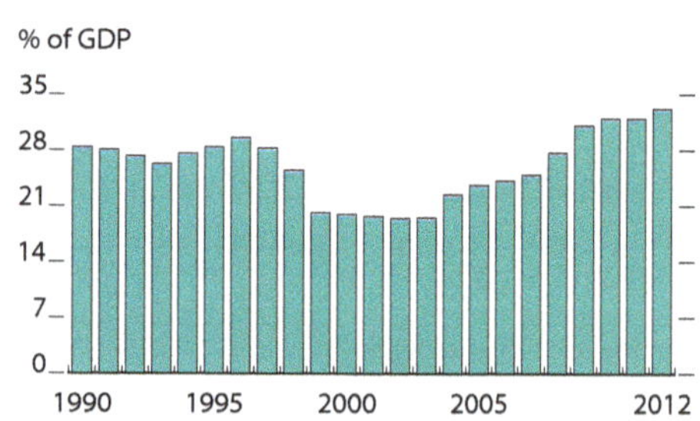

Sources: *Asian Development Outlook* database; CEIC Data Company (accessed 1 March 2013).

Click here for figure data

This chapter was written by Edimon Ginting and Priasto Aji of the Indonesia Resident Mission, ADB, Jakarta.

of aging oil fields and low investment over many years. (A decade ago production was more than 1.1 million barrels a day.) Construction recorded solid expansion of 7.5% in 2012. A good harvest of food crops lifted growth in agriculture to 4.0%. Paddy production rose by 5.5% to 68.9 million tons, which generated rice surpluses estimated at 5.7 million tons.

Merchandise exports fell by 6.3% in US dollar terms (Figure 3.24.4), weighed down by sagging demand in major markets and lower prices for export commodities. Exports of manufactured goods declined by 6.7%. Shipments of commodities including coal and palm oil fell when measured by value despite higher export volumes. Merchandise imports, in contrast, rose by 8.3%, reflecting buoyant fixed investment, which requires imported capital goods, and growth in imported inputs for the expanding manufacturing industries. Imports of consumption goods were virtually flat, discouraged by a depreciating rupiah.

These developments—lower exports and higher imports—narrowed the trade surplus by 76% to $8.4 billion. The current account shifted into deficit, equivalent to 2.8% of GDP, the first deficit since 1997. This put downward pressure on the rupiah, which depreciated by 8.0% against the US dollar in 2012.

Strong inflows of portfolio investment and FDI produced a substantial surplus in the capital and financial account. Portfolio investment nearly tripled to $9.2 billion last year, and net FDI inflows were a record at $19.9 billion. Foreign holdings of government bonds jumped by $3.4 billion to $28.0 billion (Figure 3.24.5). The balance of payments recorded a small surplus, and gross international reserves had increased by year-end to $112.8 billion, which is cover for 6.1 months of imports and government payments on foreign debt.

The good harvest, lower global food prices, and the postponement of increases in government-controlled fuel prices brought down inflation to an average of 4.3% in 2012, the lowest in 12 years. Inflation generally has trended down over recent years, reflecting the adoption of inflation targeting in 2005 and improved management of supply-side price pressures through an official inflation task force. Food prices started to edge up late in 2012 (Figure 3.24.6).

New jobs generated last year exceeded the number of entrants into the labor market. The unemployment rate fell from 6.6% to 6.1% in the 12 months to August 2012, though the rate of underemployment was barely changed at 29%. In a positive development, employment in the formal sector rose by 6.4%, or 2.7 million jobs, in this period, mostly in manufacturing and construction. Informal-sector employment fell by 2.3%, or 1.5 million jobs, as workers left agriculture. Poverty declined by 0.7 percentage points to 11.7% in the 12 months to September 2012 (Figure 3.24.7). Contributing factors were lower food price inflation, higher wages for agricultural and construction workers, and better incomes for farmers.

In the context of subdued inflation and a sagging global economy, Bank Indonesia lowered its policy interest rate by 25 basis points to 5.75% in February 2012 and reduced its overnight deposit facility rate by 25 basis points to 3.75%. Although the central bank later reversed the cut in the overnight deposit rate to drain excess liquidity, it maintained the policy

3.24.3 Supply-side contributions to growth

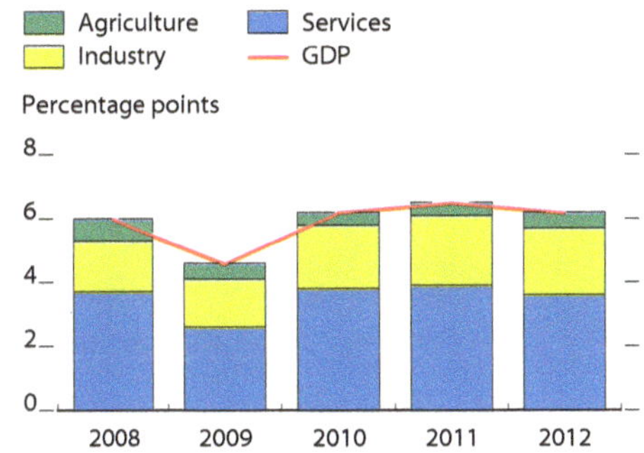

Sources: *Asian Development Outlook* database; CEIC Data Company (accessed 1 March 2013).

Click here for figure data

3.24.4 Trade indicators

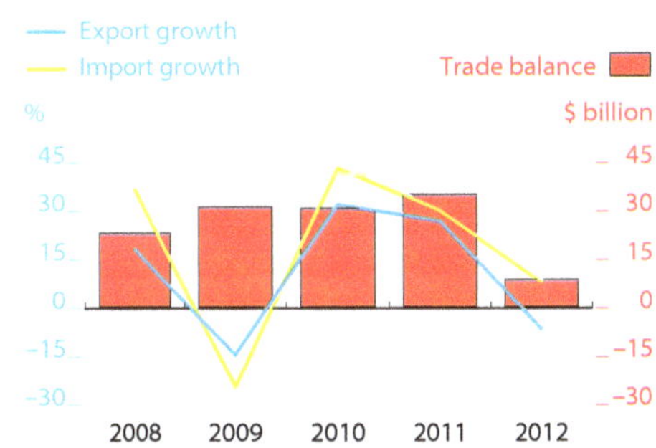

Sources: *Asian Development Outlook* database; CEIC Data Company (accessed 1 March 2013).

Click here for figure data

3.24.5 Foreign ownership of tradable government securities

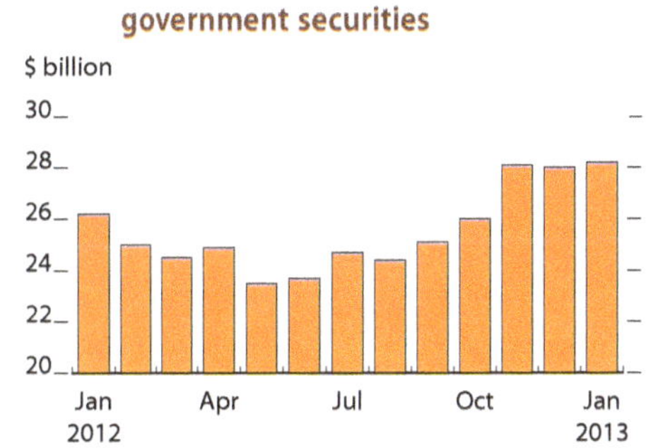

Source: CEIC Data Company (accessed 16 March 2013).

Click here for figure data

3.24.6 Monthly inflation

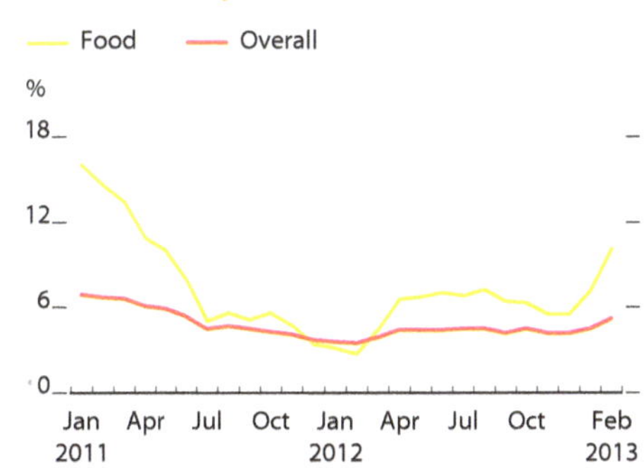

Source: CEIC Data Company (accessed 16 March 2013).

Click here for figure data

rate at 5.75%. A requirement since March 2011 that banks disclose base lending rates to the public helped to bring down lending interest rates in 2012 (Figure 3.24.8). Growth in credit remained high at 23.1%, with loans for investment up by just over 27% (Figure 3.24.9).

Fiscal policy was also set to counter the impact of the global slowdown on the domestic economy. The government raised spending and widened the budget deficit target to 2.2% of GDP in 2012, double the actual deficit in 2011 of 1.1%. As it turned out, shortfalls in government spending held the budget deficit to 1.8% of GDP. Central government debt fell to 24.0% of GDP, maintaining a downward trend (Figure 3.24.10).

Reflecting the country's better performance over recent years, Moody's raised Indonesia's rating to investment grade Baa3 in January 2012, and Fitch reaffirmed its investment grade rating BBB– in November 2012.

Economic prospects

Economic growth is forecast to pick up to 6.4% this year and 6.6% in 2014 (Figure 3.24.11), underpinned by robust private consumption, the improving investment performance, and a gradual pickup in world trade. Growth of 6.6%, projected for 2014, would be the highest in 15 years.

Private consumption is expected to quicken in 2013, fueled by rising employment, a 30% increase in average minimum wages, a 7% rise in public service wages, and a tax break from January 2013, when the government raised the income threshold at which income tax is payable. With parliamentary elections scheduled for April 2014 and a presidential election in July 2014, election-related spending is likely to contribute to consumption from the second half of 2013. A consumer survey conducted by Bank Indonesia in February 2013 showed an upturn in consumer confidence from a dip late last year (Figure 3.24.12).

Investment, both private and public, looks likely to maintain healthy expansion. Support for this projection comes from the upgrades in sovereign credit ratings, lower interest rates, increased budget allocations for infrastructure, and a lengthening record of good GDP growth. A $2.7 billion expansion by the auto maker Toyota over the next 4 years is one of several large FDI-funded investments. Businesses planned significant increases in investment in the first half of 2013, according to a survey late last year.

Public investment will benefit from a 55% increase in the 2013 budget allocation for infrastructure, even though the outcome will likely fall short of that target because of chronic delays in the execution of budget projects. With this in mind, the government is directing state-owned enterprises to become more involved in building infrastructure and is making concerted efforts to accelerate budget execution.

The government took two other steps last year to overcome obstacles to infrastructure development: First, it issued implementing regulations for the new land-acquisition law passed by Parliament in December 2011, which provides more certainty in the resolution of land acquisition for infrastructure. Second, it established a viability gap fund to support public–private partnership. This year, officials are reviewing investment regulations, including the list of industries currently closed or only partly open to foreign investment.

3.24.7 Poverty and unemployment

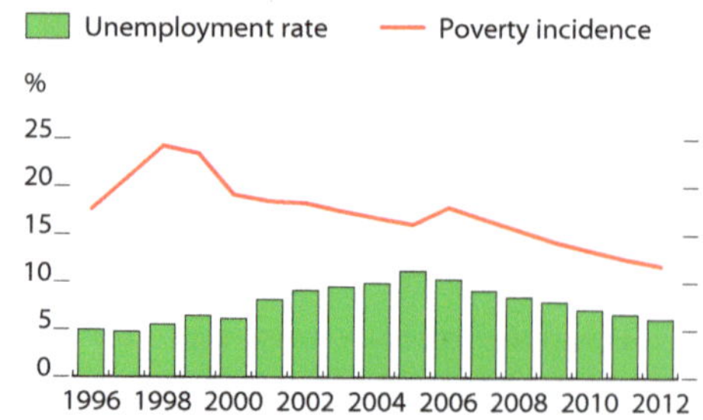

Sources: Statistics Indonesia. http://www.bps.go.id; CEIC Data Company (both accessed 16 March 2013).

Click here for figure data

3.24.1 Selected economic indicators (%)

	2013	2014
GDP growth	6.4	6.6
Inflation	5.2	4.7
Current account balance (share of GDP)	–2.3	–1.8

Source: ADB estimates.

3.24.8 Interest and inflation rates

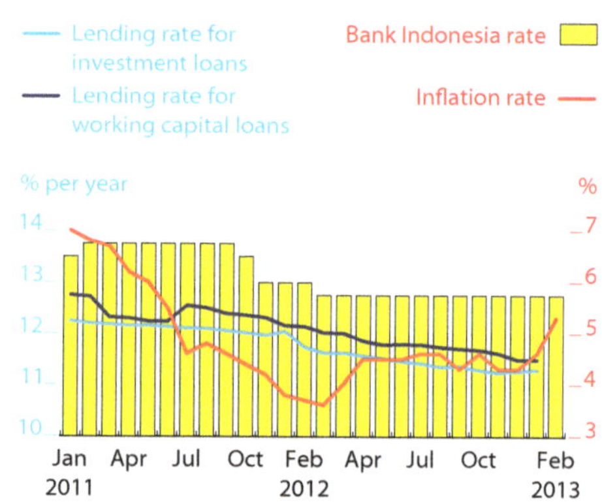

Note: Refers to rupiah credit.

Sources: Asian Development Outlook database; CEIC Data Company (accessed 21 March 2013).

Click here for figure data

3.24.9 Credit growth

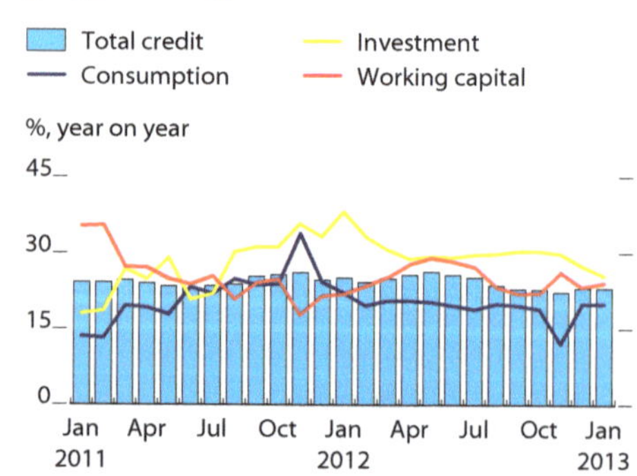

Sources: Asian Development Outlook database; CEIC Data Company (accessed 26 March 2013).

Click here for figure data

Exports are projected to improve in light of stronger growth in the People's Republic of China and some other markets in 2013. Next year, the export recovery should gather pace as prospects brighten for growth in major industrial economies. The drag on GDP growth from net exports is expected to moderate. Monthly data indicate that the decline in exports bottomed out in August 2012 (Figure 3.24.13). Prices for export commodities have firmed. Merchandise exports are forecast to rise by 7% in 2013. Robust investment will keep imports of capital goods relatively high, though imports of consumption goods will likely be curtailed by the rupiah's depreciation.

The trade surplus is projected to rise and the current account deficit to narrow (Figure 3.24.14). Inflows of direct and portfolio investment are seen keeping the balance of payments in surplus. Downward pressure on the rupiah is expected to abate as the current account deficit shrinks.

Inflation is forecast to average 5.2% in 2013, rising since last year because of a 15% increase in electricity tariffs, the depreciation of the rupiah, and a boost in minimum wages. Higher food prices lifted inflation to 5.3% in the first 3 months of this year. Upward pressure from this source should ease as the harvest season gets under way in April. Inflation in 2014 is expected to average 4.7%, taking into account base effects from the pickup this year. These forecasts assume the government does not raise fuel prices in 2013 or 2014. Inflation would be higher if fuel prices were increased to ease the high cost to the budget of fuel subsidies or if food supplies are disrupted by bad weather.

The government targets a budget deficit this year equivalent to 1.6% of GDP, narrowing slightly from last year's outcome of 1.8%. The budget contains incentives for oil and gas exploration, the production of low-emission motor vehicles, and manufacturing with higher value added, plus the boost in infrastructure spending.

Inflation within Bank Indonesia's target range of 3.5%–5.5% suggests that monetary policy will be accommodative to economic growth. If the government were to increase fuel prices, the central bank might need to quickly lift the policy rate to dampen inflationary expectations and bolster market confidence. Nevertheless, bank lending interest rates will likely stay relatively low this year and stimulate credit growth.

External risks to this outlook involve the global economy and capital inflows. Slower-than-projected growth in major export markets would delay the recovery in exports and hold down GDP growth. The shift of the current account into deficit has made the country more dependent on capital inflows. A sharp slowdown in inflows, or a reversal to outflows, would put pressure on the balance of payments and could disrupt the financing of the budget. The government has taken steps to manage this risk by establishing a bond stabilization fund and arranging for a $5 billion standby loan from development partners, among other precautionary measures.

Domestic risks involve investment and inflation. It will be important to maintain efforts to improve the investment climate to safeguard the uptrend in fixed investment. An unexpected spike in inflation, perhaps caused by tight food supplies or a large increase in fuel prices, would hurt consumption, investor sentiment, and capital inflows.

3.24.10 Central government debt

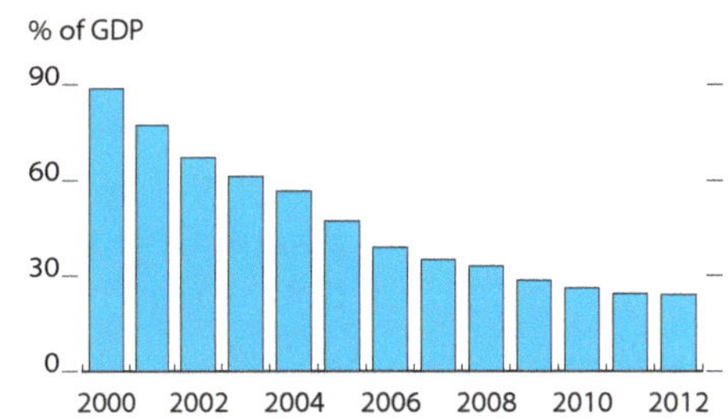

Sources: Asian Development Outlook database; Indonesia Debt Management Office. http://www.dmo.or.id (accessed 16 March 2013).

Click here for figure data

3.24.11 GDP growth

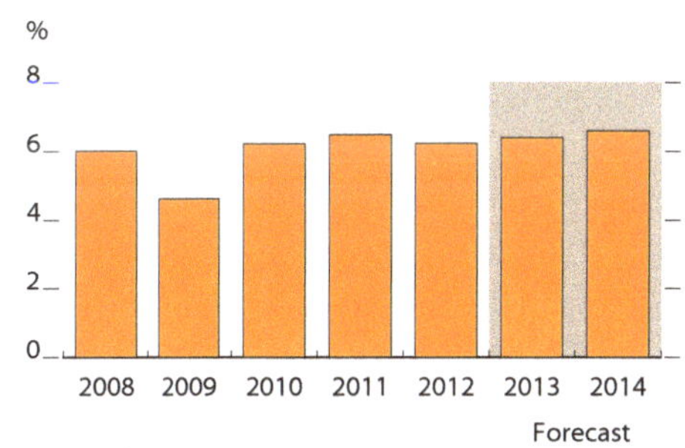

Source: Asian Development Outlook database.

Click here for figure data

3.24.12 Business and consumer confidence indexes

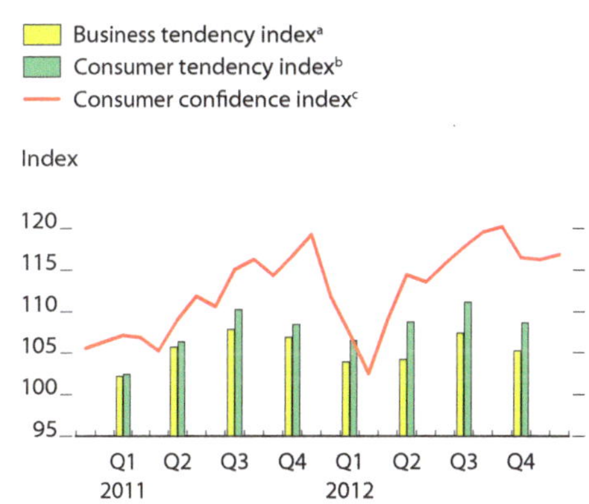

[a] From a quarterly Statistics Indonesia survey of business executives.

[b] From a quarterly Statistics Indonesia survey of middle- and upper-income households.

[c] From a monthly Bank Indonesia survey of households.

A score above 100 means that respondents are optimistic.

Source: Asian Development Outlook database.

Click here for figure data

Policy challenge—building infrastructure for inclusive growth

Economic growth averaging about 6% over the past 6 years has helped to lift 8.6 million people out of poverty. Yet 29 million Indonesians continue to live below the government's poverty line, and another 30 million would join them in the event of even a small reduction in their incomes. Of those employed, 60% work in the informal sector, where incomes are low. Further, income inequality as measured by the Gini coefficient has worsened from 0.35 in 2008 to 0.41 in 2011 (Figure 3.24.15).

Improved public infrastructure would make a significant contribution to reducing poverty and closing gaps in income inequality.

Toward reducing poverty, better infrastructure, particularly for transportation and generating electricity, would support growth in manufacturing, which generates jobs in the formal sector. The performance of manufacturing has been lackluster since the late 1990s and started to improve only in the past 2 years.

Congested ports and rising logistic costs are major constraints on the expansion of manufacturing. The average time cargo containers spend at Tanjung Priok, the country's main port, stretched to 6.7 days in January 2012 from 4.9 days in 2010. This compares with 1–2 days at Asia's most efficient ports (Figure 3.24.16). It costs $750 to transport a container 56 kilometers from the Cikarang industrial zone to Tanjung Priok port, almost 70% more than moving a container a similar distance in Malaysia. The difference is primarily caused by road congestion in Indonesia.

Toward closing income gaps, investment in infrastructure is needed to address high poverty rates in rural areas, which average 14.7% compared with 8.6% in urban areas. Surveys suggest that 41% of district roads and 24% of provincial roads throughout Indonesia are in bad condition. Development prospects are poor for rural areas that lack good connections with towns and markets. Finally, poverty in some eastern provinces is even higher—at 24.1% in Maluku and Papua. Weak infrastructure there hinders economic activity, the growth of employment, and access to services such as education and health care.

The government's master plan to accelerate economic development, known by its Indonesian abbreviation MP3EI, has three main pillars: developing six economic corridors, improving connectivity both within the country and internationally, and strengthening human resource capacity and technology. Acting to support these goals, the government has increased its budget for infrastructure, with a large share allocated to eastern provinces. Substantial additional funding could become available if the government redirected huge budget allocations for fuel subsidies, equivalent to 2.6% of GDP in 2012, toward infrastructure and social development. The fuel subsidies benefit mainly higher-income households.

Progress on infrastructure is being achieved. Work started last year on 182 infrastructure projects valued at $65 billion under the MP3EI program. Funding came from private companies (44%), state-owned enterprises (20%), governments (19%), and public–private partnerships (17%). Nearly 40% of this amount was allocated to eastern provinces. More projects are scheduled for this year.

3.24.13 Merchandise exports

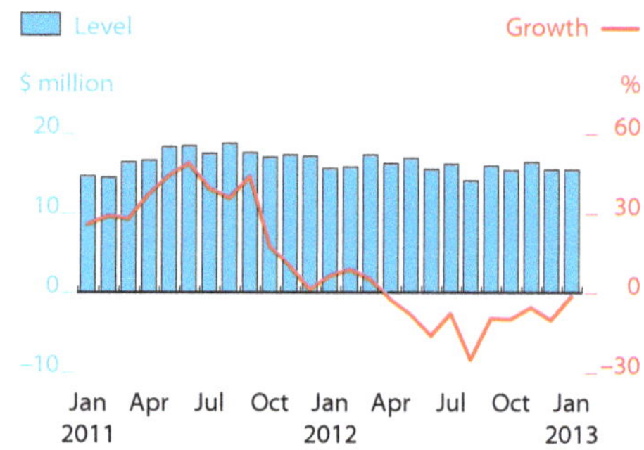

Source: CEIC Data Company (accessed 26 March 2013).
Click here for figure data

3.24.14 Current account balance

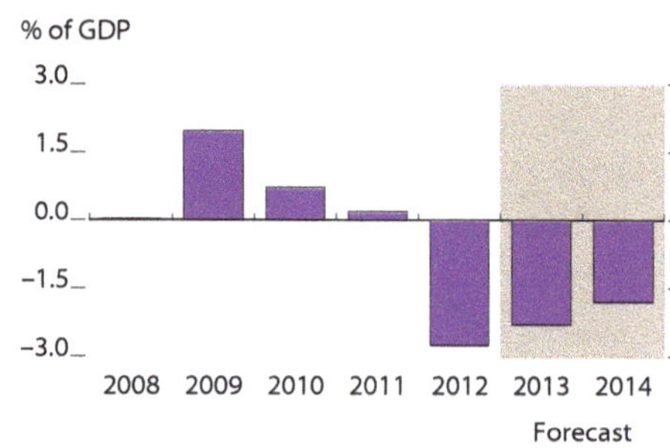

Source: Asian Development Outlook database.
Click here for figure data

3.24.15 Income inequality

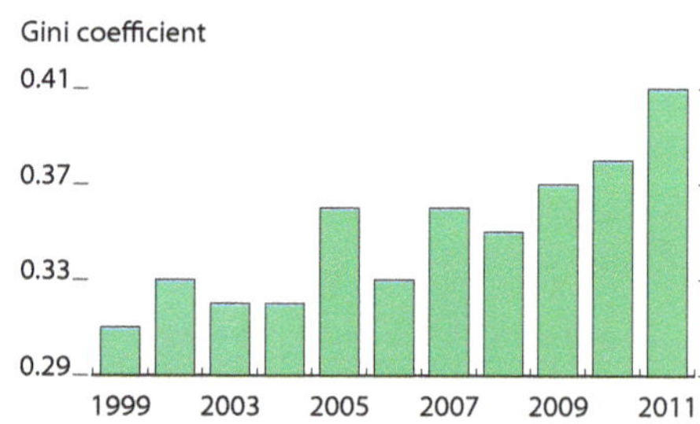

Source: Statistics Indonesia. http://www.bps.go.id/ (accessed 2 March 2013).
Click here for figure data

3.24.16 Dwell time in selected countries

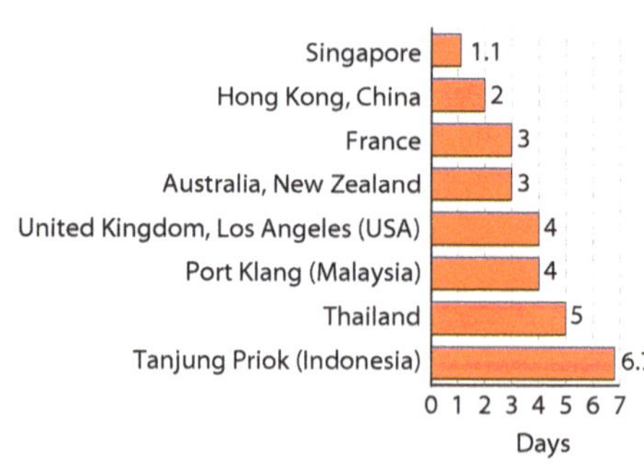

Note: Dwell time is the number of days on average that a cargo container stays in a port.

Source: Indonesia Infrastructure Initiative. 2012. *Journal of the Indonesia Infrastructure Initiative PRAKARSA*. Issue 10. April.
Click here for figure data

Lao People's Democratic Republic

Last year's economic outcomes—solid growth and moderate inflation—are likely to be repeated this year and next. Foreign direct investment has doubled in the past 2 years. However, rising domestic demand, stimulated by credit expansion, is putting pressure on foreign reserves. Concerns over the management of land and other natural resources are still to be addressed.

Economic performance

Growth in 2012 benefited from developments in agriculture, construction, hydropower, mining, and services. GDP increased by 7.9%, slightly above the average rate over the past 10 years (Figure 3.25.1).

The industry sector grew by an estimated 14% to remain a major driver of GDP. Mining production was boosted by the start of the Ban Houayxai gold and silver mine and the expansion of existing minerals projects. Copper output from the two largest producers, which together generate more than 90% of total production, rose by 8% to 149,500 tons, with gold production climbing by 61% to 206,240 ounces, and silver production up by 15% to 616,680 ounces.

Hydropower output jumped by 29% to 13.8 billion kilowatt hours. The country's biggest hydropower project, Nam Theun 2, raised production close to full capacity. Ample water in reservoirs enabled other plants to operate at higher capacity. New hydropower projects commissioned in 2012 increased national output by more than 650 megawatts. About 70% of all hydropower generated is exported, mainly to Thailand.

Major construction projects under way last year included the $3.7 billion Hongsa lignite thermal power project, seven new hydropower projects, and expanded facilities in the capital, Vientiane, to handle a major international meeting and the Association of Southeast Asian Nations (ASEAN) University Games toward the end of 2012. Cement production rose by an estimated 42.4% in 2012, reflecting buoyant construction. However, the garment industry suffered from weaker external demand and shortages of skilled labor. Garment exports fell by 25% to $173 million (Figure 3.25.2).

In agriculture, higher production of rice, cassava, maize, poultry, and livestock lifted the sector's output by 2.5%.

The service sector expanded by 8%, underpinned by a 22% boost in tourist arrivals to 3.3 million supporting hotels, restaurants, and transportation (Figure 3.25.3); growth in wholesale and retail trade; and the deepening of financial services. The increase in tourist arrivals from Asian countries outpaced declines from Europe and the US.

3.25.1 Supply-side contributions to growth

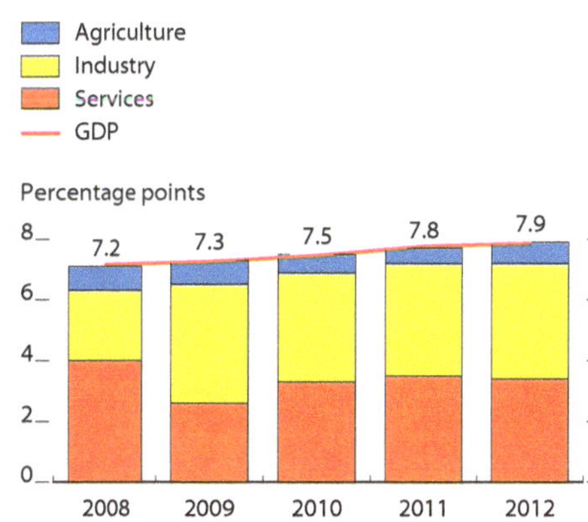

Sources: Lao Statistics Bureau; *Asian Development Outlook* database.

Click here for figure data

3.25.2 Exports of garments and footwear to the European Union and United States

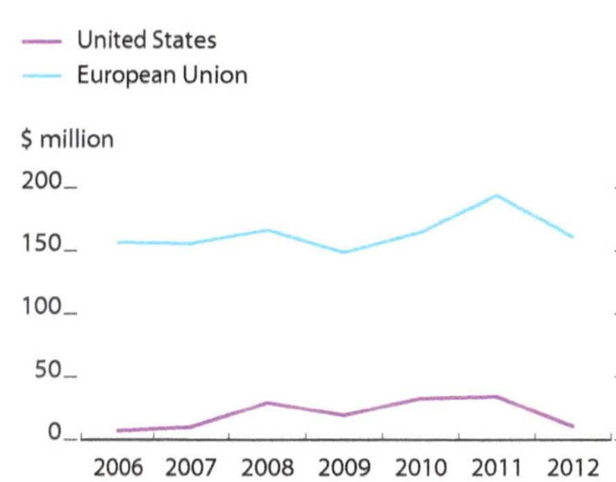

Notes: Import data from US OTEXA and Eurostat. Data from Eurostat were converted to US dollars using the euro/dollar average exchange rate for the year.

Sources: Office of Textiles and Apparel. http://otexa.ita.doc.gov; Eurostat. http://epp.eurostat.ec.europa.eu (both accessed 14 March 2013).

Click here for figure data

This chapter was written by A. Barend Frielink and Soulinthone Leuangkhamsing of the Lao Resident Mission, ADB, Vientiane.

Decelerating food and fuel prices brought down inflation to 2.9% year on year in July, at which point inflation started to edge up again (Figure 3.25.4). The year-average inflation rate of 4.3% was 3 percentage points below that of 2011.

While growth in M2 money supply remained strong at 31%, and in credit at 36.2%, credit expansion moderated from the very high rates of previous years (Figure 3.25.5). The central bank reduced its direct lending for infrastructure and slowed the registration of new commercial banks to dampen growth in credit. Foreign exchange policy focused on keeping the Lao kip broadly stable against the US dollar and the Thai baht. The kip appreciated by 0.3% against the dollar and by 2.4% against the baht in 2012. Dollarization declined to about 44% of M2, maintaining a gradual downtrend.

Fiscal accounts benefited from buoyant revenue from mining and hydropower, coupled with rising income from a value-added tax introduced in 2010 and external grants. The fiscal deficit, including grants and excluding off-budget spending, narrowed to 1.5% of GDP in FY2012 (ended 30 September 2012).

Growing credit and domestic demand propelled merchandise imports up by an estimated 17% to $5.4 billion in 2012. Exports rose by a relatively sedate 9% to $3.4 billion, resulting in a trade deficit of $2.1 billion. Receipts from tourism rose, but so did payments abroad of interest and income by resource-based companies, so that the current account deficit widened to an estimated 22.6% of GDP. Foreign direct investment increased to $1.4 billion last year, doubling since 2010. However gross international reserves of $708 million provided cover for just 1.6 months of goods and services imports.

Structural reforms in 2012 included improvements to trade and investment regulations instituted to satisfy commitments made to join the World Trade Organization (completed in early 2013) and the ASEAN Economic Community at the end of 2015. The government established the State Accumulation Fund to finance its responses to future natural disasters, economic downturns, and revenue shortfalls when global mineral prices slide. Fund resources are to come from additional mining revenue and any budget savings.

The International Monetary Fund and the World Bank analyzed debt sustainability in the Lao People's Democratic Republic (PDR) and consequently reclassified its risk of debt distress to moderate from high. The country's stock of external public and publicly guaranteed debt was, at $3.7 billion in 2011, equivalent to 44.4% of GDP, showing a decline from 50.3% in 2010 because of economic growth and the appreciation of the kip against the US dollar. However, the share of non-concessional debt has expanded over recent years.

Economic prospects

The outlook is for further solid growth during the forecast period, just below the 8% growth target in the government's Seventh National Socioeconomic Development Plan, 2011–2015 (Figure 3.25.6).

Substantial investment flowing into hydropower and mining, coupled with the construction of hotels, offices, and housing, will drive GDP

3.25.3 Tourism

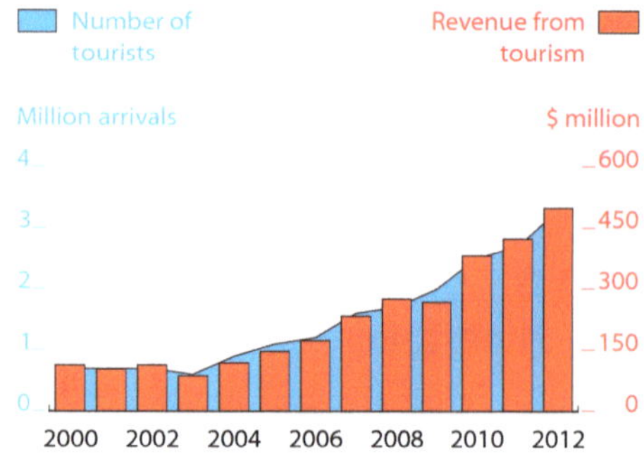

Source: National Tourism Administration.

Click here for figure data

3.25.4 Monthly inflation

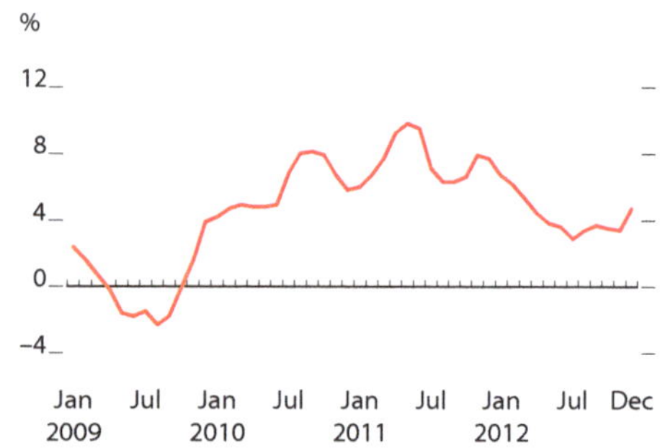

Source: CEIC Data Company (accessed 15 March 2013).

Click here for figure data

3.25.5 Monetary indicators

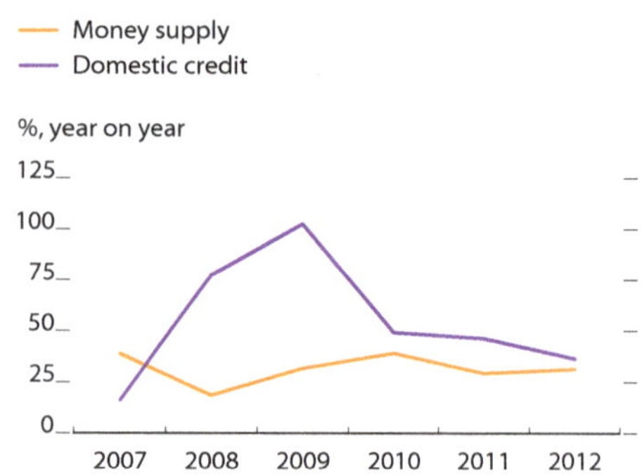

Note: Available data for 2012 is from January to November only.

Source: Bank of Lao PDR.

Click here for figure data

growth. In addition to the large Hongsa lignite power plant, which is about 40% completed, work has started on the $3.5 billion Xayaburi dam and hydropower project, scheduled for commissioning in 2018 with capacity to generate 1.3 gigawatts of electricity. Five smaller hydropower projects are under development. Some new commercial–residential projects in the capital involve investments of several hundred million dollars, largely funded by foreign investment.

The hydropower plants brought on line last year will contribute to an expected 12% increase in power generation in 2013. Gold and silver production is expected to increase, but copper output is likely to be little changed. The mining and processing of potash for fertilizer is an expanding industry, with one project starting last year and another scheduled to produce fertilizer this year. Coal production is expected to rise.

Agriculture, which employs more than 60% of the workforce, is expected to grow at a slightly faster pace in 2013.

Tourist arrivals are projected to rise by 5%–10% in 2013. Other service industries likely to maintain good growth include financial services, wholesale and retailing, and transport and communications. Manufacturing industries will benefit from the government's promotion of food and beverage processing, cement production, and garments, which aims to reduce imports of these products.

Fiscal policy may be more expansionary in FY2013, given that the target for the fiscal deficit is 3.1% of GDP, taking grants into account. The government is raising salaries for the civil service, police, and military by 165% in steps over 3 fiscal years, starting in FY2013.

Monetary policy could tighten during the forecast period if the strong growth in the money supply and credit over several years is considered to undermine banking system stability, contribute to the problem of low international currency reserves, or pose other macroeconomic risks. The government targets holding growth in the money supply below 30% in 2013, and the central bank aims to keep the kip broadly stable against the dollar and the baht.

Inflation is projected to edge up to 5.5% on average in 2013 in light of buoyant domestic demand and higher salaries for government employees (Figure 3.25.7). Prices for meat and cooked food picked up early this year.

Rising imports of consumer and capital goods will maintain pressure on the external position. Merchandise imports are forecast to increase by 15% this year and exports by 14%, widening the trade gap to $2.4 billion. The current account deficit will continue to exceed 20% of GDP (Figure 3.25.8).

Poverty incidence has likely declined from 27% in 2008, the last official survey. Projected economic growth and government social programs should further reduce poverty, but additional efforts are needed in remote regions, where high concentrations of poverty persist. Moreover, rates of child malnutrition are still high, as 41% of children under 5 years of age suffer chronic malnutrition. The country will be challenged to meet some Millennium Development Goals by 2015, including improvements in maternal mortality and access to safe drinking water and basic sanitation.

Risks to economic prospects come from increasingly volatile weather patterns, which can have severe impacts on agriculture. Viet Nam's

3.25.1 Selected economic indicators (%)

	2013	2014
GDP growth	7.7	7.7
Inflation	5.5	5.0
Current account balance (share of GDP)	–21.5	–23.6

Source: ADB estimates.

3.25.6 GDP growth

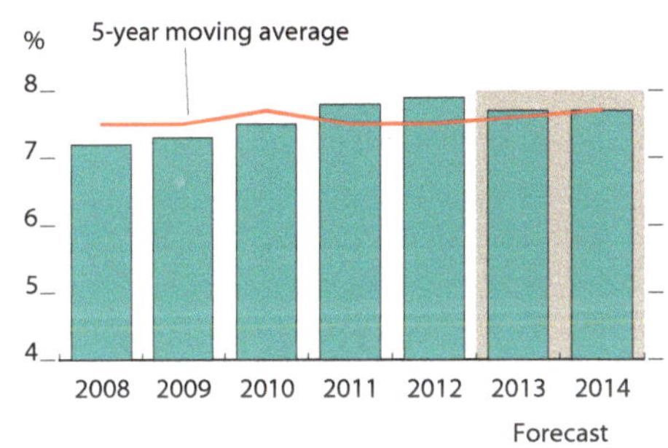

Source: Asian Development Outlook database.
Click here for figure data

3.25.7 Inflation

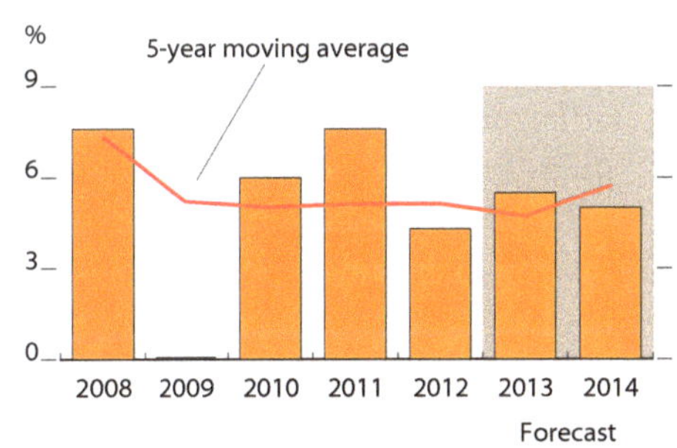

Source: Asian Development Outlook database.
Click here for figure data

3.25.8 Current account balance

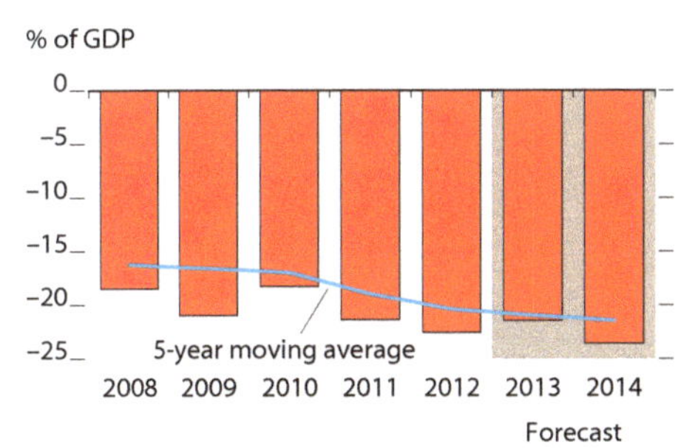

Source: Asian Development Outlook database.
Click here for figure data

economic slowdown poses risks because Vietnamese companies are major investors in the Lao PDR.

Policy challenge—managing land and other natural resources

The government has granted land concessions over a significant area in the past decade to encourage investment. During this period the country has attracted investment into agriculture; tree plantations; commercial, residential, and tourism property development; hydropower; and mining.

Investors, mostly from abroad, were awarded 1.1 million hectares of land from 2000 to 2009, according to a report prepared last year for the government (Figure 3.25.9). This area, which excludes land concessions for logging, mineral exploration, contract farming, and hydropower, is about 5% of the country's total land area, more than is dedicated to wet season rice, the main crop. Most foreign investors holding land concessions are from the People's Republic of China, Thailand, and Viet Nam.

While the report found that land concessions have contributed to economic growth and government revenue, it noted weaknesses in the management of concessions and the governance of land and natural resources.

Much of the investment in agriculture is directed to lowland areas that are accessible to towns and cities, with little going to poorer remote areas. Land concessions for agriculture and forestry are dedicated to a handful of mostly exotic crops, such as rubber and eucalyptus, endangering biodiversity and local food security. The narrow range of crops makes only a limited contribution to the goal of diversifying exports. Tracts of farmland on urban fringes are being converted for housing, manufacturing, and other property developments.

In some cases, local populations have lost access to the land and forests upon which they depended for subsistence. Inadequate compensation for land and the resettlement of displaced people in areas where they struggle to earn a livelihood have become major concerns for affected communities.

The land-concession system could be improved by better monitoring the allocation and development of land and by ensuring that displaced people receive fair compensation and resettlement in areas that enable them to maintain their livelihoods. Further, strengthening the land title system would provide people in rural areas with legally protected access to land for their livelihoods and enable the enforcement of existing land titles.

It would be helpful to establish a system for settling disputes over land, which would shorten the time taken and lift the burden on the courts.

3.25.9 Area allocated for investment, 2000–2009

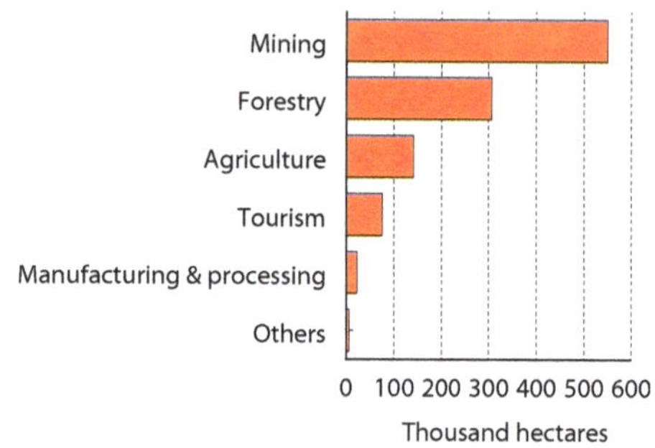

Note: Excludes logging concessions, contract farming, hydropower projects, and mining exploration.

Sources: Ministry of Natural Resources and Environment Natural Resource; Environment Information Center.

Click here for figure data

Malaysia

A surge in fixed investment combined with buoyant private consumption underpinned stronger economic growth in 2012, overriding weakness in exports. Government cash transfers and spending on infrastructure contributed to domestic demand. GDP growth is forecast to ease this year before picking up in 2014, while inflation is seen edging up from last year's low rate. Rising imports and subdued exports have eroded the surplus in the current account.

Economic performance

Strong expansion in private consumption and fixed investment lifted GDP growth to 5.6% in 2012, close to the average growth rate in the 5 years before the global financial crisis. Growth accelerated to 6.4% in the fourth quarter.

Private consumption increased by 7.7% and made a major contribution to GDP growth (Figure 3.26.1). It was driven by a robust labor market, growth in credit, and several government decisions during the year. Employment grew by 3.6%, mostly in domestic-oriented sectors such as services, and the unemployment rate declined to 3.0%. Average wages in the private sector rose by a robust 5.0%. The government's contribution to private consumption came from a 13.0% increase in public sector wages in March 2012 (directly benefitting 10% of the workforce), higher public sector pensions, and a range of cash transfers to low- and middle-income households.

Fixed investment surged by 19.9%, its best performance in 12 years (Figure 3.26.2). Much of the investment was related to the government's Economic Transformation Programme, which aims to lift Malaysia into the ranks of high-income nations by 2020 by upgrading industry and infrastructure. Private sector investment was particularly strong, climbing by 22.0%, while public sector investment rose by 17.1%. Major investment projects under way in 2012 included an $11.5 billion mass rapid transit rail system in Kuala Lumpur, expansion of oil and gas processing and other energy projects, and a high-speed broadband network. This surge in investment was an important source of GDP growth last year.

The ratio of fixed capital investment to GDP was, at 25.6% in 2012, the highest in 14 years, though still well below the 40% pace of the mid-1990s.

Government consumption spending decelerated from 2011 but still made a small contribution to economic growth last year. However, the external sector acted as a drag on GDP growth, as weak global demand flattened exports of goods and services in real terms while buoyant domestic demand fueled growth in imports.

3.26.1 Demand-side contributions to growth

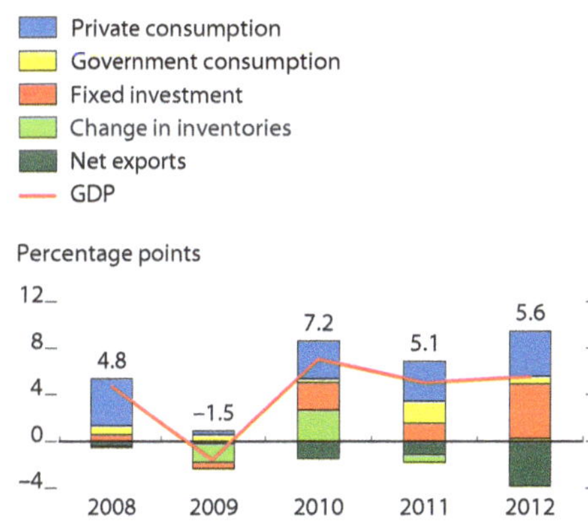

Sources: Department of Statistics Malaysia. http://statistics.gov.my; CEIC Data Company (both accessed 2 March 2013).

Click here for figure data

3.26.2 Fixed investment

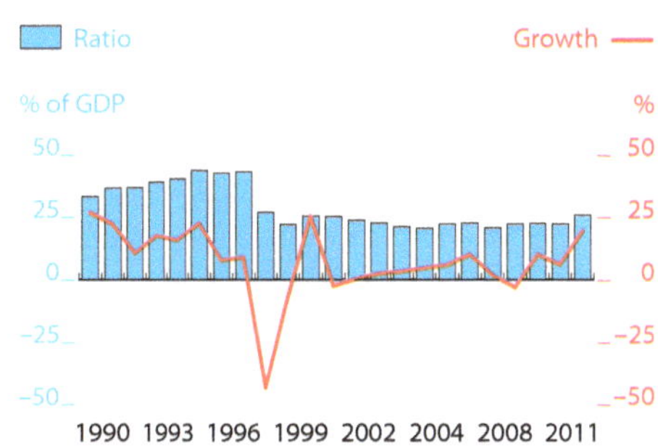

Source: CEIC Data Company (accessed 20 March 2013).

Click here for figure data

This chapter was written by Gary Krishnan of the Southeast Asia Department, ADB, Manila.

From the supply side, services grew by 6.4% such that the sector, which provides 55% of GDP, made the biggest sector addition to total growth. Major contributors were wholesale and retail trading and financial services. Construction soared by 18.5% as government-led infrastructure and industrial projects gained momentum. Residential construction was also buoyant. Manufacturing grew by a relatively modest 4.8%, weighed down by weakness in global demand for electronics. Mining rebounded after a contraction in the previous year to grow by 1.4% in 2012 on higher oil production.

Agriculture, by contrast, had a poor year owing to declines in the production of rubber because of bad weather and of palm oil that reflected a steady decline in yield. The agriculture sector grew by just 0.8%.

Fiscal policy stimulated the economy with the cash transfers and other benefits for consumers and incentives for business expansion. The government introduced a supplementary budget in June to fund additional spending, which rose by 9.5% from 2011. High global oil prices contributed to an 11.8% increase in government revenue. The fiscal deficit narrowed slightly to 4.5% of GDP in 2012, which was the fifth consecutive year of deficits above 4% of GDP (Figure 3.26.3). Federal government debt has increased over the past 5 years from 40.1% of GDP to 53.5%.

Bank Negara, the central bank, kept its policy interest rate at 3.0% through last year and into 2013 as it balanced buoyant domestic demand and fiscal stimulus on the one hand against low inflation and a subdued global outlook on the other. Credit to the private sector picked up to grow by 12.5% on average in 2012. The weighted average lending interest rate of commercial banks declined over the year to 4.7%. The Malaysian ringgit appreciated by 3.9% against the US dollar.

Inflation slowed as prices of food and fuel decelerated in 2012 (Figure 3.26.4). On a year-average basis, inflation was almost halved to just 1.7%. Subsidies on fuel, staple foods, and electricity, which cost the government the equivalent of 4.5% of GDP in 2012, helped to curb inflation.

Merchandise exports fell marginally to $227.6 billion as a consequence of sluggish demand in global markets and soft prices for export commodities such as rubber and palm oil. Exports of electronics fell, but not as steeply as in 2011. Commodity exports declined by about 7%. By contrast imports rose by 4.3% to $187.0 billion, reflecting the strength of private consumption and investment. These developments lowered the trade surplus by 16.2% to $40.5 billion (Figure 3.26.5). The deficit in services trade widened sharply, mainly due to a higher deficit in transportation services and slower growth in tourism, and the income deficit deteriorated on higher payments of dividends and interest to foreign companies. Consequently, the current account surplus fell to $19.4 billion, or 7.9% of GDP, the lowest share since 2001.

The capital and financial account recorded net outflows last year. Inward foreign direct investment totaled $9.4 billion, coming off an unusually high level in 2011. The balance of payments recorded a small surplus, and international reserves rose 4.8% to $139.7 billion, cover for 7.3 months of goods and services imports.

3.26.3 Fiscal performance

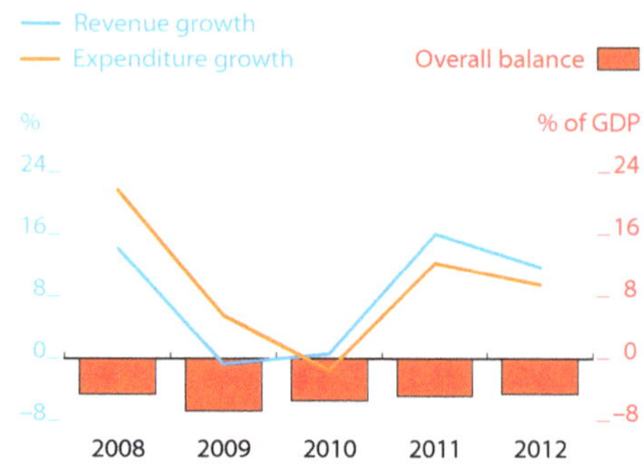

Source: Asian Development Outlook database.
Click here for figure data

3.26.4 Inflation and policy interest rate

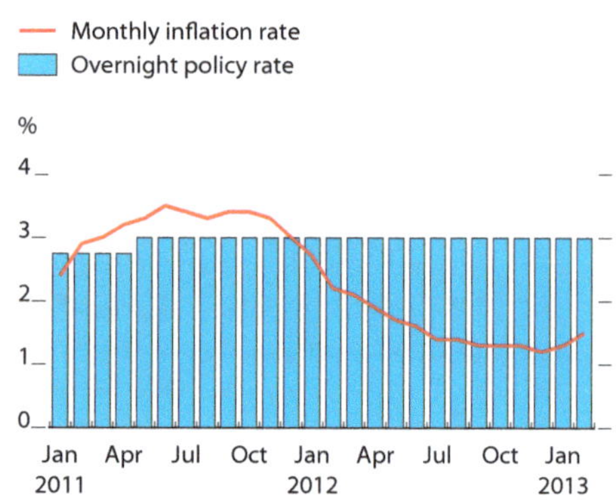

Source: CEIC Data Company (accessed 20 March 2013).
Click here for figure data

3.26.5 Trade indicators

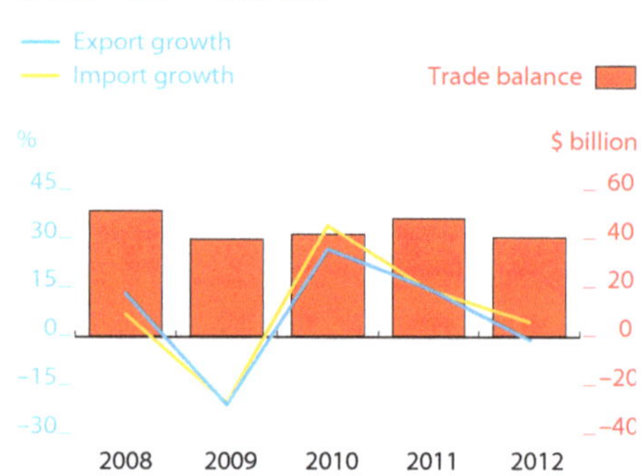

Source: Asian Development Outlook database.
Click here for figure data

Economic prospects

Forecasts assume that national elections to be held in May 2013 go smoothly and that the government pursues prudent economic and fiscal policies.

Private consumption will get support from robust labor market conditions, low inflation, higher incomes, and, from the 2013 budget, further transfer payments and tax concessions. New minimum wages of RM900 a month for Peninsular Malaysia and RM800 for East Malaysia came into effect from January 2013 and benefit 27% of all workers. The tight labor market suggests that job losses resulting from the new minimum wage will likely be temporary.

Nevertheless, growth in private consumption will likely moderate from 2012. Softer global commodity prices will weigh on incomes and consumption spending, particularly in rural areas. Further, the government is expected to resume phasing down subsidies on fuel and other items or move to a system that better targets subsidies. A proposed broad-based consumption tax that aims to reduce the government's reliance on the oil sector for public revenue could also dampen consumption growth temporarily if introduced.

Consumer sentiment remains positive: the index of consumer sentiment compiled by the Malaysia Institute of Economic Research edged higher in the fourth quarter of 2012 (Figure 3.26.6). However, the business conditions index compiled from a survey of manufacturers declined on concerns about the outlook for domestic and export sales.

Investment, too, is expected to moderate this year. Private investment is forecast to grow at a double-digit pace, but below last year's 22.0%. Large investments are planned for the oil and gas industry, for property developments, and to expand services. Credit to the private sector accelerated to 12.3% in January 2013 (Figure 3.26.7). As for public investment, the government is pushing ahead with its Economic Transformation Programme while also proposing to gradually rein in its fiscal deficit. The result is expected to be somewhat slower growth in public investment in the forecast period.

On the production side, solid growth in private consumption will boost the service sector, assisted by investments being made in high-speed broadband and wireless technologies, but the pace of growth is expected to decelerate from 2012. Manufacturing will get a lift, mainly in 2014 when recovery gathers momentum in major industrial economies. Production of natural gas and oil will increase this year as investment to develop new fields and enhance recovery at existing oil fields pays dividends. Agriculture is forecast to recover this year, but growth in construction will subside from last year's high rate.

Fiscal policy is expected to start to tighten later this year. The government has targeted a narrower fiscal deficit equivalent to an estimated 4% of GDP in 2013. The central bank will likely keep interest rates at levels supportive to economic growth into 2013 while standing ready to raise rates if price pressures gather steam.

Robust domestic demand and a foreseen gradual reduction of subsidies during the forecast period will nudge prices up, with moderating factors anticipated to be soft global food and fuel prices and a firm ringgit. The impact of the new minimum wage on companies' total costs is expected to be modest. Inflation is projected to pick up to average 2.2% in 2013 and

3.26.1 Selected economic indicators (%)

	2013	2014
GDP growth	5.3	5.5
Inflation	2.2	3.0
Current account balance (share of GDP)	5.8	5.6

Source: ADB estimates.

3.26.6 Business and consumer confidence indexes

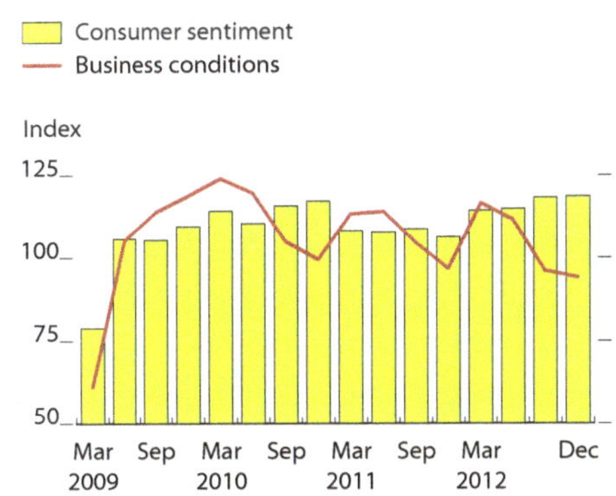

Note: Above 100 indicates expansion for manufacturing and optimism among consumers.

Source: CEIC Data Company (accessed 20 March 2013).

Click here for figure data

3.26.7 Credit to the private sector

Source: CEIC Data Company (accessed 4 April 2013).

Click here for figure data

3.0% next year (Figure 3.26.8). For the first 2 months of 2013 inflation was just 1.4%.

External demand is seen improving only gradually. A better outlook this year for the People's Republic of China and India, two important export markets, will benefit Malaysia's commodity exports though prices of commodities such as palm oil and liquefied natural gas will remain under downward pressure. The anticipated recovery in industrial economies in 2014 will improve prospects for electronics and other manufactured exports. Import growth will likely moderate in 2013 but still outpace growth in exports, given strong domestic demand. The drag on GDP growth exerted by net exports will lessen this year.

On the balance of these influences, GDP growth is forecast at 5.3% in 2013, accelerating a little to 5.5% next year as the global economic environment improves. The current account surplus is forecast to decline further as trade surpluses subside and deficits persist in the income and services accounts (Figure 3.26.9).

3.26.8 Inflation

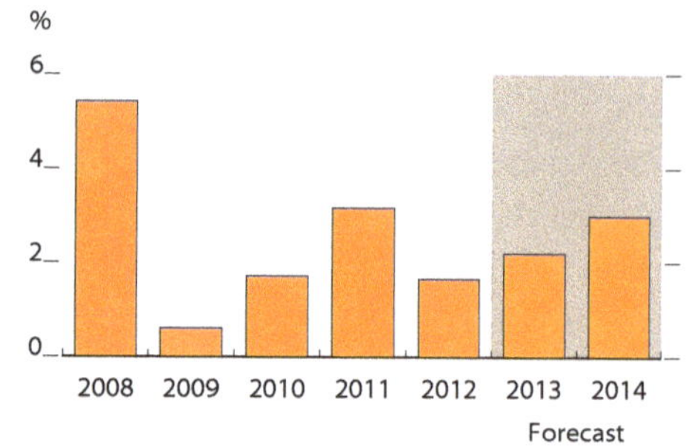

Source: Asian Development Outlook database.
Click here for figure data

Policy challenge—maximizing women's contributions

Women's rate of participation in Malaysia's labor force is well below that for males and the lowest in Southeast Asia (Figure 3.26.10). Only 48% of Malaysian women of working age reported that they were working, in either the formal or the informal sector of the economy, or looking for work in 2011.

Increasing the female participation rate to levels comparable with other countries would expand the workforce by at least 500,000 and perhaps by 2.3 million, the World Bank estimated in an economic report published in November 2012. It also estimated that Malaysia's GDP growth would have been 0.4 percentage points higher in 2000–2010 if the female participation rate had been lifted by 11 percentage points to 57%. Higher workforce participation would help overcome skills shortages, enlarge the pool of entrepreneurs, and improve the welfare of women.

One reason for the low participation rate is that Malaysian women generally find it difficult to reconcile family with work commitments. Fewer of them re-enter the workforce after childbirth than do women elsewhere. The 2013 budget introduced tax incentives to encourage more childcare centers to open, which should go some way toward addressing this issue. Another factor is the secondary education enrollment rate for Malaysian girls, which is relatively low compared with countries that have comparable income. The government is spending more on education, and it funds retraining women after a career break.

Policies that have produced results in other countries include more generous parental leave policies, encouraging part-time work, tax incentives, improved arrangements for childcare and tending to the elderly, raising the retirement age, and a greater focus on education and training for women. The government's 10th economic plan targets increasing the female workforce participation rate to 55% by 2015.

3.26.9 Current account balance

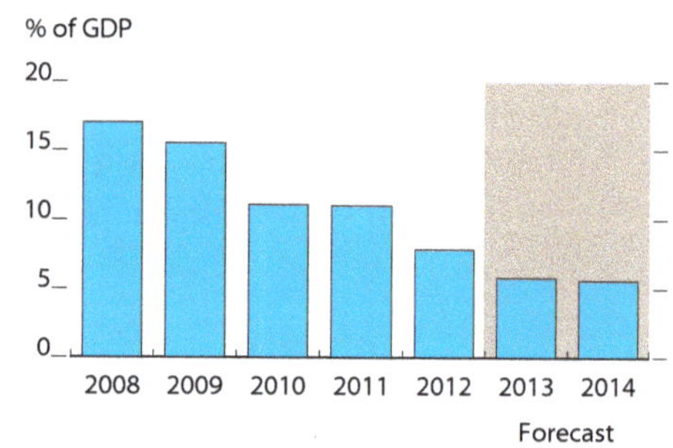

Source: Asian Development Outlook database.
Click here for figure data

3.26.10 Female labor force participation rate, 2011

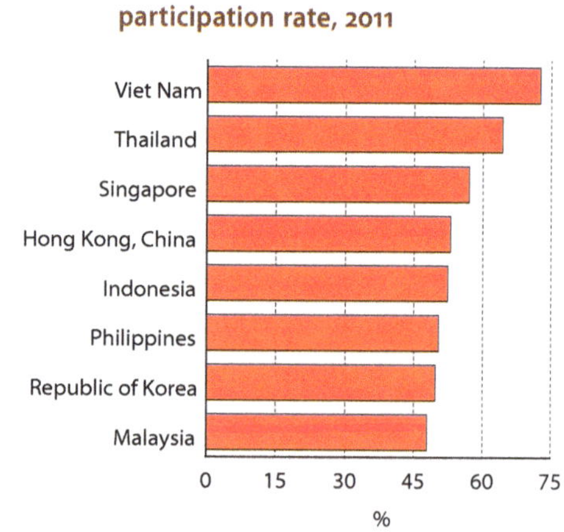

Source: ADB Statistical Database System (accessed 4 April 2013).
Click here for figure data

Myanmar

Policy reforms stimulated economic growth last year and are expected to drive further development during the forecast period. Inflation is projected to remain moderate. Improved economic prospects have sparked a surge of interest from foreign investors. Achieving the country's potential depends on maintaining momentum on the government's reform agenda.

Economic performance

GDP growth quickened to an estimated 6.3% in FY2012 (ended 31 March 2013) compared with an average of 5% in the previous 5 years. The pickup reflects business optimism buoyed by the government's steps since 2011 to liberalize the economy and prospects for further reform. A modest slowdown in agricultural growth in FY2012, partly reflecting floods in August 2012, was more than offset by increases in industrial output and services.

(Official national accounts data are available only on an annual basis with a 2-year lag and they show considerably higher rates of GDP growth that are inconsistent with correlates of growth such as energy use.)

The number of foreign firms granted investment approval rose to 62 in April–December 2012, well above the total for the 3 previous fiscal years (Figure 3.27.1). A sharp increase in approvals for manufacturing indicated a welcome diversification from the past focus on energy and mining. Investor optimism was also signaled by an almost 14-fold surge from FY2011 in the number of new foreign company registrations in the 10 months to January 2013, albeit from a low base and partly reflecting some domestic companies reclassified as foreign. New domestic company registrations have climbed in the past 2 years (Figure 3.27.2).

Inflation has subsided since 2008, when it exceeded 20%. This follows reduced monetization of the fiscal deficit and a stronger kyat exchange rate on the unofficial market. The consumer price index fell in early FY2012 with declining food prices. By December 2012, though, food prices were rising and inflation was 6.0% year on year (Figure 3.27.3).

The consolidated fiscal deficit of the central government and state economic enterprises narrowed to an estimated 5.4% of GDP in FY2012 from 6.0% a year earlier. Revenue benefited from the government's realignment in April 2012 of the fixed official exchange rate of the kyat, bringing it closer to the unofficial market exchange rate. As state enterprises are net exporters, the exchange rate realignment boosted budget receipts, including export tax income and customs duties. Higher revenue enabled the government to increase spending on health, education, and capital investment.

3.27.1 Foreign investment approvals

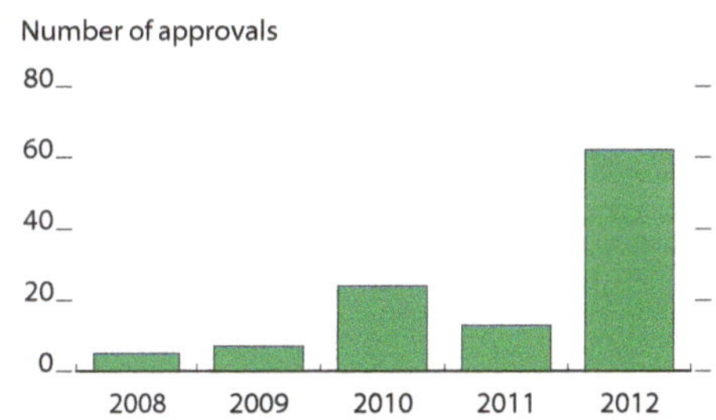

Note: Data in FY2012 cover April–December 2012 only.
Source: Central Statistical Organization.
Click here for figure data

3.27.2 Domestic business registration

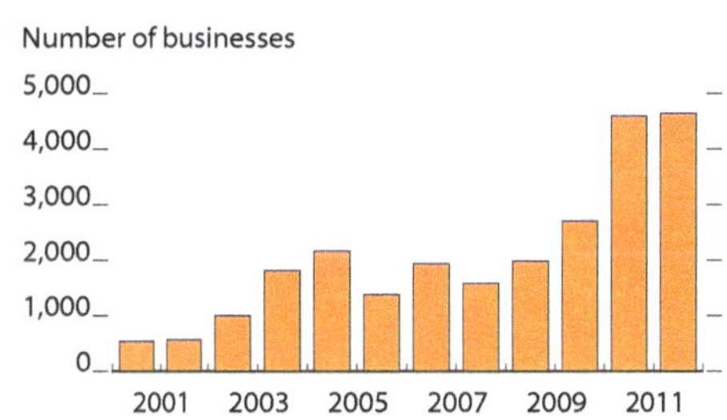

Note: Data in FY2012 cover April 2012–January 2013 only.
Source: Directorate of Investment and Company Administration.
Click here for figure data

This chapter was written by Sharad Bhandari of the Southeast Asia Department, ADB, Manila.

In external accounts, the current account deficit widened to an estimated 4% of GDP, with the trade balance in deficit owing mainly to a gradual liberalization of imports and higher investment. Customs data show a 3.6% decline in exports in April–December 2012 from a year earlier, likely caused by subdued demand in Thailand, the People's Republic of China (PRC), and India, as well as weaker international commodity prices.

Exports of natural gas, which comprise 38% of total exports, were flat, and agricultural exports mostly declined in April–December. Garment exports rose by 18% year on year, benefiting from greater access to global markets and low domestic wages. The general weakness in total exports underscores the importance of sharpening competitiveness with higher investment, new technologies, and improved access to finance, as well as an appropriate exchange rate. The kyat has appreciated in nominal and real terms on the unofficial market over the past few years.

Tourist arrivals and earnings from tourism have climbed as the country opened up after decades of isolation (Figure 3.27.4). Net foreign direct investment flows and renewed official development assistance supported an overall balance of payments surplus and increase in foreign exchange reserves to an estimated $5.1 billion in FY2012, equal to about 4 months of imports of goods and services.

Arrears to ADB and the World Bank were cleared in January 2013, allowing both banks to renew lending to the country. The Paris Club of creditors also reached an agreement to cancel or reschedule arrears.

Economic prospects

Economic growth is forecast to rise gradually to 6.5% in FY2013 and 6.7% in FY2014 (Figure 3.27.5). Projections assume the government will maintain momentum on policy reform over the medium term.

Growth will get a lift from the European Union's proposed reinstatement of preferential access for Myanmar's exports under the Generalized System of Preferences and the United States' suspension of its ban on imports from Myanmar. Two large gas fields, Shwe and Zawtika, are expected to come online in FY2013, more than doubling gas production and raising exports to the PRC and Thailand. Higher gas exports, greater access to international markets, and faster economic growth in key markets such as the PRC will support growth in exports. Visitor arrivals are likely to post further large gains.

Movement toward unifying multiple exchange rates and a managed float of the currency, along with licensing private banks to engage in international banking and to offer foreign exchange services, should shift more foreign exchange from informal to formal markets, increase liquidity, and facilitate the central bank's management of the exchange rate. The government is establishing a formal interbank market and plans to develop a secondary treasury securities market. A law to modernize and grant operational autonomy to the central bank has been submitted to the legislature.

Proposed fiscal reforms include simplifying the tax system, broadening the tax base, and eventually moving to a value-added tax to ease dependence on natural resources, which provide 23% of public revenue.

3.27.3 Monthly inflation

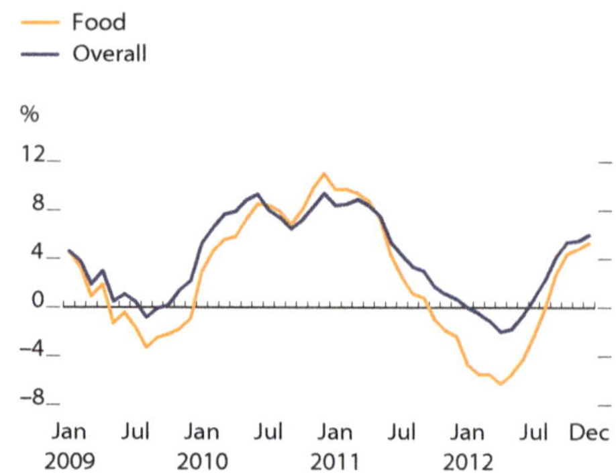

Source: Central Statistical Organization.

Click here for figure data

3.27.4 Tourism

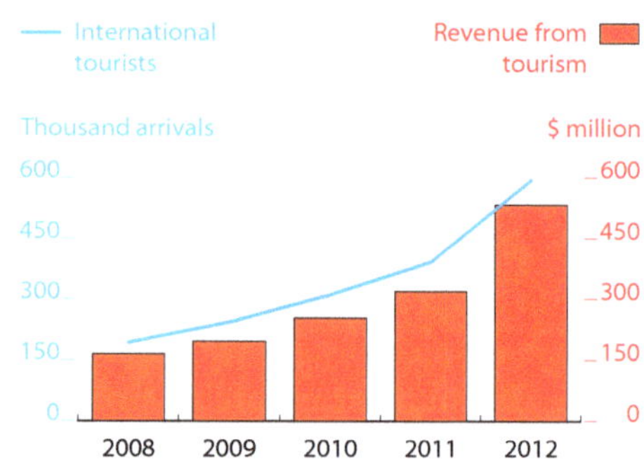

Note: Excludes border tourism.

Source: Ministry of Hotels and Tourism.

Click here for figure data

3.27.5 GDP growth

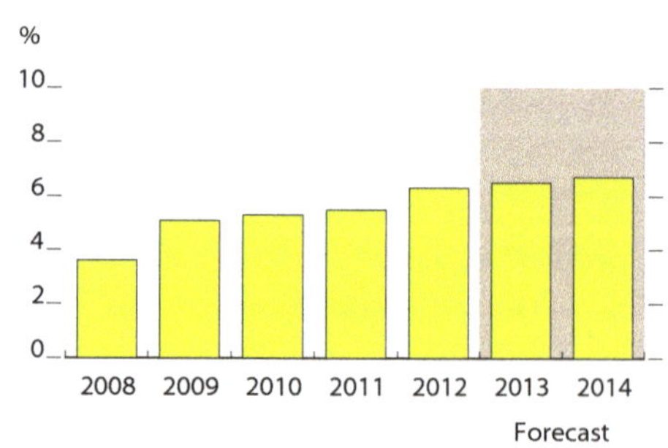

Sources: International Monetary Fund; ADB estimates.

Click here for figure data

Steps taken last year to give state enterprises more financial autonomy and demand more accountability should facilitate their corporatization and potential privatization. Coupled with higher net export receipts, primarily from gas, these fiscal measures allow the government to increase spending on health, education, and infrastructure while reining in the fiscal deficit to 5.2% of GDP in FY2013.

Inflation is forecast to average 5.1% this year and next (Figure 3.27.6). A lower fiscal deficit and reduced credit to the government from the central bank should dampen inflation over the medium term.

In spite of expected higher receipts from exports and tourism, the current account deficit is projected to widen as import growth accelerates, reflecting higher investment and measures to lift foreign exchange restrictions (Figure 3.27.7). Inflows of foreign direct investment, including from the award of new telecommunications licenses in 2013 and higher official development assistance, will likely keep the balance of payments in surplus.

Policy challenges—forward with reform

The government's ambitious reform agenda is commensurate with the catching up necessary to align policies with current international practice after long period of isolation. These reforms are outlined in the Framework for Economic and Social Reform, which sets out policy priorities until 2016 and guiding principles for longer-term development plans. The goal is higher, inclusive, and sustainable growth and reduced poverty, as 26% of the country's 60 million people live in poverty.

The framework identifies 10 priorities: (i) fiscal and tax reform, (ii) monetary and financial sector reform, (iii) trade and investment liberalization, (iv) private sector development, (v) improvements in health and education, (vi) food security and agricultural growth, (vii) governance and transparency, (viii) mobile telephony and internet, (ix) infrastructure investment, and (x) efficient and effective government.

While many of the reforms will take considerable time, several areas could yield results over the next 2–3 years. One is the underdeveloped finance system, in which credit to the private sector amounts to only 8% of GDP. With prudent regulation, easing controls on interest rates and restrictions on private bank lending would boost private sector access to credit.

Implementing important new laws on land ownership, labor, and foreign investment, as well as measures to simplify business registration, would improve the business environment. Relatively quick improvements to infrastructure would include rehabilitating roads, upgrading power systems to reduce transmission and distribution losses (Figure 3.27.8), and developing a sound regulatory framework for independent power producers and public–private partnerships.

Tourism has substantial potential to spur employment and inclusive growth, especially with simpler visa requirements. In agriculture, which contributes 36% of GDP and the majority of employment, near-term measures to improve access to finance and inputs, implement small irrigation projects, and expand agricultural extension would shore up inclusive growth and food security.

3.27.1 Selected economic indicators (%)

	2013	2014
GDP growth	6.5	6.7
Inflation	5.1	5.1
Current account balance (share of GDP)	–4.2	–4.4

Source: ADB estimates.

3.27.6 Inflation

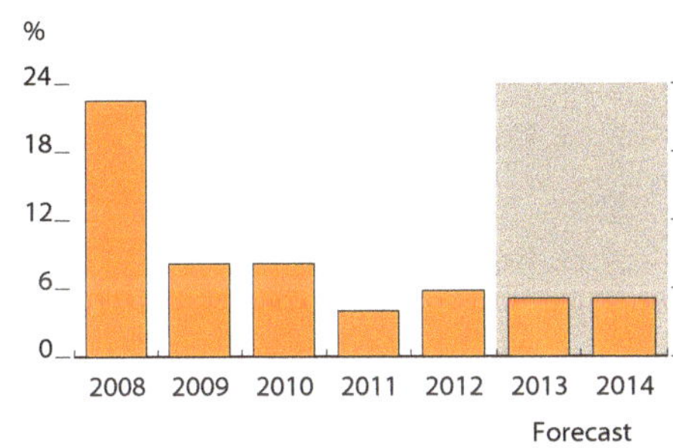

Sources: International Monetary Fund; ADB estimates.
Click here for figure data

3.27.7 Current account balance

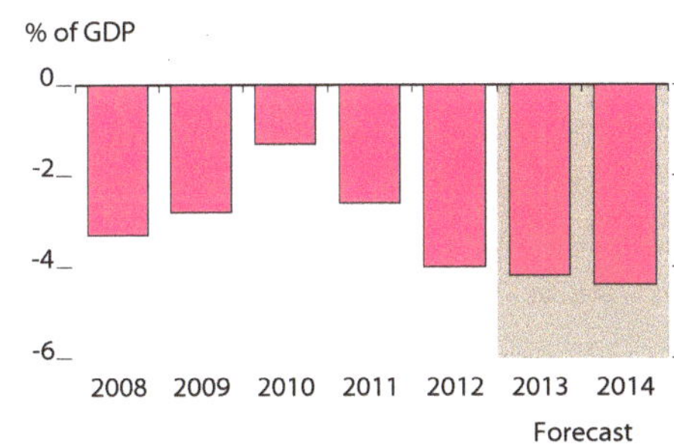

Sources: International Monetary Fund; ADB estimates.
Click here for figure data

3.27.8 Power transmission and distribution losses

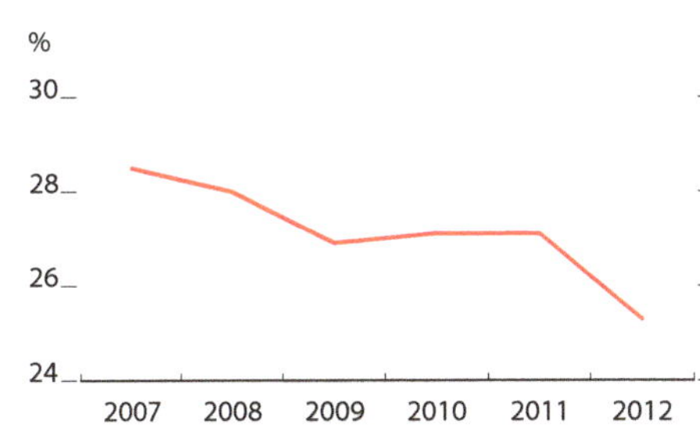

Source: Ministry of Electric Power.
Click here for figure data

Philippines

Buoyant private consumption and a rebound in government spending drove strong economic growth in 2012. A rise in net exports also contributed to GDP growth. Robust expansion is projected over the next 2 years, based on buoyant consumption and an improvement in investment. Inflation is moderate and expected to remain so. The challenge is to translate solid economic growth into poverty reduction by generating more and better jobs.

Economic performance

Sustained growth in private consumption, a recovery in government spending, and positive net exports lifted GDP growth to 6.6% in 2012, or 4.8% in per capita terms. Inflation eased to a 5-year low, and external accounts were healthy.

Private consumption rose by 6.1% and contributed the most to GDP growth from the expenditure side (Figure 3.28.1). Buoyant consumption was driven by higher remittances from overseas Filipino workers, a slight gain in employment, and low inflation. Remittances increased by 6.5% to $23.4 billion (up by 3.8% in strengthening Philippine pesos).

Government spending rebounded from the low levels seen in 2011, when governance reforms slowed budget disbursements. Higher spending on public infrastructure, alongside expansion in private construction and investment in equipment, pushed up fixed capital investment by 8.7% (Figure 3.28.2). Growth in investment was supported by improvements in the domestic business environment and declining interest rates. Fixed investment as a ratio to GDP edged up in 2012 but was still modest at 19.7%. A rise in net exports also contributed to growth, in contrast with 2011, when net exports fell.

From the production side, the service sector, accounting for over half the economy, remained the dominant growth driver. Its growth accelerated to 7.4%, which contributed nearly two-thirds of GDP growth. Retail trading accounted for one-fourth of services' growth, consistent with robust private consumption. Other key subsector contributors were finance and real estate services, business process outsourcing (BPO), and those associated with tourism.

Industry's performance improved last year. Manufacturing expanded by 5.4%, with strong growth in food processing in particular. However, the communications equipment subsector, which includes semiconductors, shrank owing to weak export demand. Construction and utilities expanded, so that industry as a whole accounted for one-third of GDP growth. Agricultural output rose by 2.7%, mainly a result of higher production of rice and maize.

3.28.1 Demand-side contributions to growth

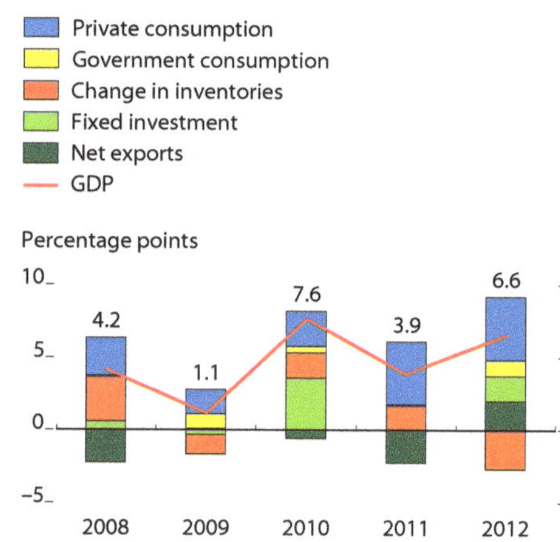

Sources: Asian Development Outlook database; National Statistical Coordination Board. http://www.nscb.gov.ph (accessed 1 February 2013).

Click here for figure data

3.28.2 Contribution to fixed capital growth

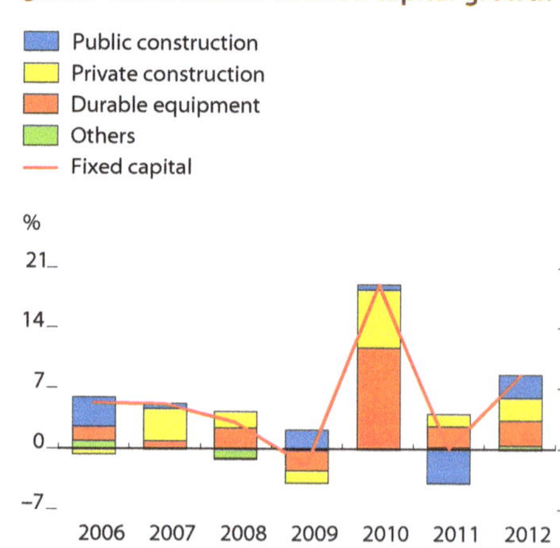

Source: CEIC Data Company (accessed 23 March 2013).

Click here for figure data

This chapter was written by Norio Usui and Teresa Mendoza of the Philippines Country Office, ADB, Manila.

Notwithstanding strong GDP growth, inflation eased in 2012 to average 3.2% (Figure 3.28.3). Better harvests tempered food inflation. Broadly stable global commodity prices and an appreciating peso helped to contain price pressures.

Modest inflation and the fragile international economy prompted Bangko Sentral ng Pilipinas, the central bank, to reduce policy interest rates by 100 basis points in 2012, trimming the overnight borrowing rate to 3.5% and the overnight lending rate to 5.5%. Bank lending interest rates eased and credit extended to the private sector increased by 17.8%.

Government spending on infrastructure jumped by 58%, after a decline of 29% in 2011 (Figure 3.28.4), but it still fell short of the budget target. Under-spending of budgeted allocations held the fiscal deficit to 2.3% of GDP (Figure 3.28.5), below the programmed level but a slightly wider deficit than in 2011. The ratio of tax revenue to GDP improved to 12.9%, though it, too, did not meet the government's target.

External accounts were in good shape. Merchandise exports rose by 8.5% in US dollar terms, a turnaround from a 6.3% fall in 2011. This recovery was driven largely by higher shipments of machinery and transport equipment, wood manufactures, furniture, fruit and vegetables, processed food, and beverages. Shipments of electronics continued to fall, though at a slower pace than in 2011. Imports grew by 5.1% in value so that the merchandise trade deficit narrowed by 5.3% to $14.8 billion. Trade in services produced a smaller surplus than in the previous year. After taking into account the substantial remittance inflows, the current account surplus rose slightly to $7.2 billion, equivalent to 2.9% of GDP (Figure 3.28.6).

Portfolio investment inflow rose by 14.9% to $4.7 billion and foreign direct investment by 9.8% to $2.0 billion—still low compared with other Southeast Asian countries. The overall balance of payments recorded a surplus of 3.7% of GDP, lifting gross international reserves to $83.8 billion at year-end. Reserves cover 12.0 months of imports and 10.5 times short-term external debt.

Remittances and capital inflows buoyed the peso, which appreciated by 6.6% against the US dollar to its highest rate in 5 years. In other financial markets, the Philippine Stock Exchange index climbed by 33% in 2012 to a record high; capital raised through the exchange doubled from 2011. Spreads narrowed between Philippine government bonds and US treasuries.

Economic prospects

The forecasts assume that the government makes further progress on reforms to improve the investment climate and that legislative elections in May 2013 go smoothly.

Private consumption is expected to remain a key driver of growth, underpinned by remittances and positive consumer sentiment (Figure 3.28.7). These transfers from overseas Filipinos have accelerated since the second half of last year. The number of deployed overseas workers in 2012 rose by 6.7%. Domestic employment is projected to increase this year, and election-related spending will lift consumption in the first half of 2013.

3.28.3 Inflation and policy rate

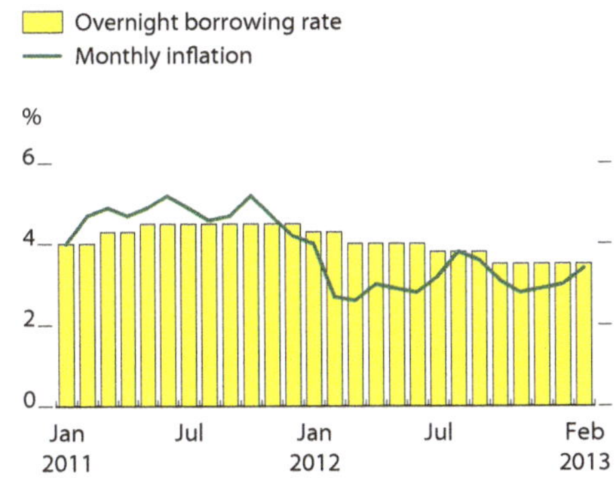

Source: CEIC Data Company (accessed 23 March 2013).
Click here for figure data

3.28.4 Government infrastructure outlay

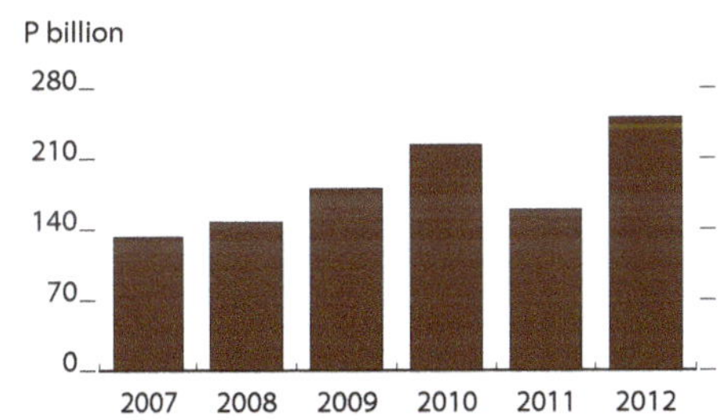

Note: Includes other capital outlays.
Sources: Department of Budget and Management. Various years. *Assessment of National Government Disbursements.* http://www.dbm.gov.ph (accessed 23 March 2013).
Click here for figure data

3.28.1 Selected economic indicators (%)

	2013	2014
GDP growth	6.0	5.9
Inflation	3.6	3.8
Current account balance (share of GDP)	3.0	3.2

Source: ADB estimates.

3.28.5 Fiscal indicators

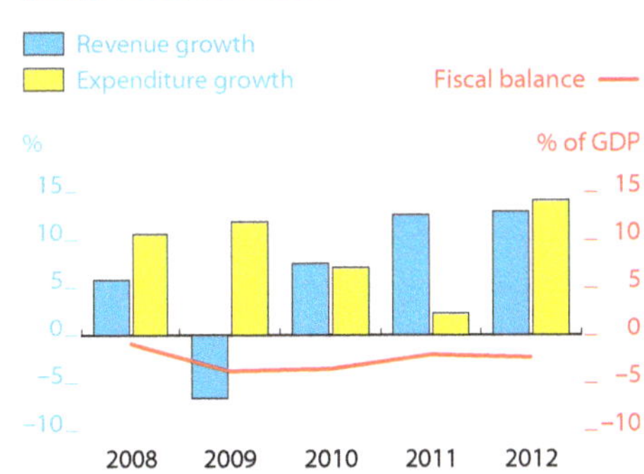

Sources: CEIC Data Company; Bureau of the Treasury. http://www.treasury.gov.ph (both accessed 16 March 2013).
Click here for figure data

As for private investment, a survey of businesses in February 2013 showed they were optimistic (Figure 3.28.7) and planned to increase hiring. Imports of capital goods rose by 14% in 2012, a sign of positive business sentiment. Bank lending for production rose by 15.2% in February 2013 from a year earlier (Figure 3.28.8), and the buoyant stock market has facilitated corporate expansion.

For the first time, the country achieved an investment grade credit rating in March 2013, bolstering the investment climate. Fitch raised its sovereign rating on long-term foreign-currency denominated debt to BBB– from BB+. It cited the Philippines' strong external balance sheet, resilient economy, improved fiscal management, and decline in government debt relative to GDP.

Fiscal spending will support economic growth, although not to the extent seen in 2012 when it rebounded from low levels. Government spending is programmed to rise by 13% in 2013, excluding interest payments. Reforms to speed up budget spending are making progress. Revenue is benefiting from higher taxes on tobacco and alcohol, effective January 2013, which will contribute to the goal of reining in the budget deficit to 2.0% of GDP in 2013–2016.

Robust consumption and investment and election-related spending bode well for expansion in the service sector. The BPO subsector is projected to grow by about 20% annually through 2016. The government is targeting large increases in tourist arrivals, from 4.3 million last year to 10.0 million by 2016. To support that aim, it is investing in tourism-related infrastructure and encouraging the expansion of air services.

Growth in manufacturing production quickened in the second half of 2012, and exports of semiconductors turned up late in the year. Construction is expected to maintain solid growth. High demand for housing and office space is spurring private construction, supported by low interest rates. The government has raised its budget for infrastructure in 2013 and a program to create public–private partnerships for infrastructure development, which started sluggishly, is gathering some momentum.

A projected pickup in exports of electronics will contribute to growth in merchandise exports in 2013. Rapidly growing Southeast Asian markets now buy 19% of the Philippines' exports, up from 13% in 2008. However, robust domestic demand suggests that imports will be considerably higher, so that net external demand weighs on GDP growth this year.

On the balance of these factors, GDP growth is forecast at 6% for this year, with a similar pace anticipated in 2014 (Figure 3.28.9). Growth in remittances and services exports will contribute to current account surpluses of around 3% of GDP.

Inflation is seen edging up to a moderate 3.6% this year owing to robust domestic demand and the higher taxes on tobacco and alcohol. These tax hikes added 0.5 percentage points to inflation recorded at 3.2% in the first 3 months of 2013. The firm peso and soft global commodity markets are expected to offset part of the upward pressure on prices generated by strong domestic demand in 2014, containing inflation to a forecast 3.8% (Figure 3.28.10). Inflation at these rates would be well within the central bank's target range of 3%–5%, giving it the option of keeping policy interest rates accommodative to growth.

3.28.6 Current account indicators

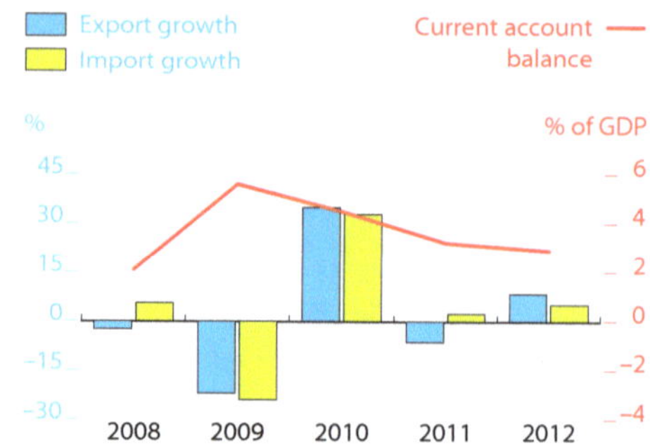

Sources: Asian Development Outlook database; CEIC Data Company (accessed 23 March 2013).

Click here for figure data

3.28.7 Business and consumer confidence indexes

Notes: The consumer or business outlook index is computed as the percentage of households or businesses that answered in the affirmative less the percentage of households that answered in the negative with respect to their views on a given indicator. A positive index indicates a favorable view.

Source: CEIC Data Company (accessed 4 April 2013).

Click here for figure data

3.28.8 Bank loans for production activities

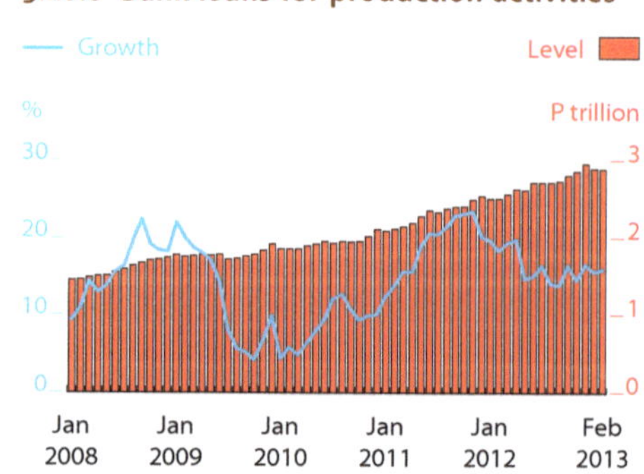

Source: CEIC Data Company (accessed 3 April 2013).

Click here for figure data

Concerned about risks associated with volatile capital flows, the monetary authorities last year moved to curb speculative inflows by prohibiting deposits from nonresidents in its special deposit account facility and cutting interest rates on these accounts. They also imposed a higher capital requirement for banks' holdings of non-deliverable forwards, which could be used for speculative purposes, and tightened rules governing these instruments. The central bank strengthened its oversight of bank lending for real estate to more closely monitor the impact of capital inflows. Bank balance sheets remain healthy overall: capital adequacy ratios are well above the 10% minimum statutory requirement (16.9% for universal and commercial banks in June 2012), and nonperforming loans are in the low single digits.

The government's credibility as an instrument advancing reform has been enhanced by the higher excise taxes on alcohol and tobacco, which will help to fund health care for the poor, and the passage of the Responsible Parenthood and Reproductive Health Act. Governance reform, too, has made progress, though much remains to be done. The 2012 Transparency International Corruption Perceptions Index ranked the Philippines 105th of 176 countries, still low but above Indonesia and Viet Nam, which had been ahead of the Philippines in 2011.

In its *Global Competitiveness Report 2012–2013*, the World Economic Forum elevated the Philippines by 10 places last year, to 65th of 144 economies, with marked improvement in terms of the macroeconomic environment. However, the country remained behind Malaysia at 25th, Thailand at 38th, and Indonesia at 50th, held back by low rankings notably on infrastructure, among other measures. Corruption and government bureaucracy remain concerns for investors, though there is a perception these issues are being addressed.

Progress achieved in the Bangsamoro framework agreement, a roadmap for a political settlement between the government and the Moro Islamic Liberation Front, could jump-start development on the large southern island of Mindanao.

Risks to the economic outlook include excessive portfolio capital flows. Portfolio investment registered with the central bank surged in the first 2 months of 2013 (Figure 3.28.11). Surging inflows risk sparking asset inflation, a rapid appreciation of the peso that would hurt export competitiveness and diminish the peso value of remittances, and excessive upward pressure on credit growth. A sharp reversal of the inflows would disrupt financial markets and business confidence.

Policy challenge—generating employment

Higher rates of economic growth over recent years have not made a serious dent in the employment problem in the Philippines. Unemployment at 7% in 2012 and underemployment at 20% understate how serious the problem is. The deployment of large numbers of workers overseas masks the full extent of the labor market weakness. An estimated 7 million Filipinos, equivalent to about 17% of the domestic labor force, have left the country to work, taking the total number of Filipinos living abroad to more than 10 million.

3.28.9 GDP growth

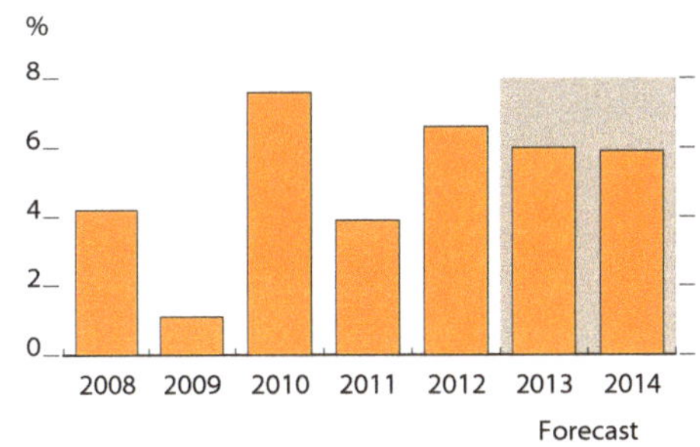

Sources: Asian Development Outlook database; National Statistical Coordination Board. http://www.nscb.gov.ph (accessed 1 March 2013).

Click here for figure data

3.28.10 Inflation

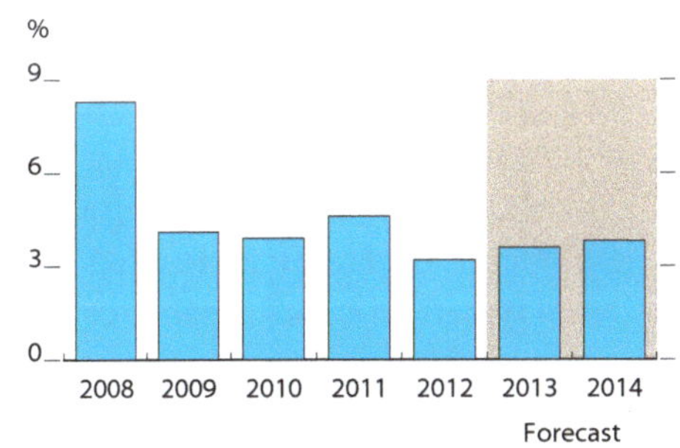

Sources: Asian Development Outlook database; National Statistics Office. http://www.census.gov.ph (accessed 15 March 2013).

Click here for figure data

3.28.11 Registered foreign portfolio investment

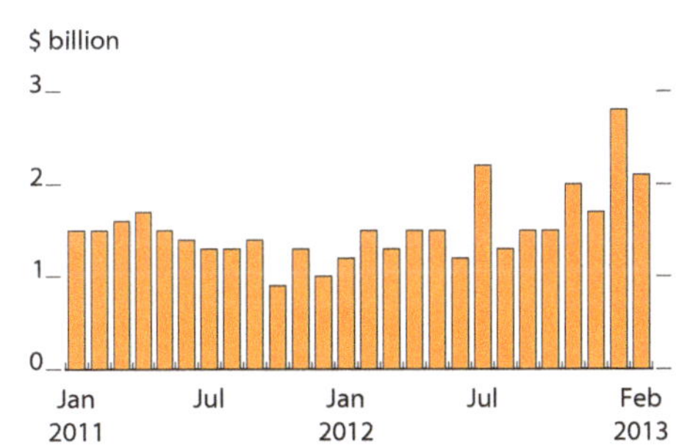

Source: CEIC Data Company (accessed 16 March 2013).

Click here for figure data

Further, 40% of those working within the country are classified as vulnerable—unpaid family workers and the self-employed, mostly in the informal sector.

A survey by the Social Weather Stations polling organization last year showed that 52% of respondents rated themselves as poor, the highest percentage since 2008. National poverty incidence in the latest family and income expenditure survey, conducted in 2009, was 26.5%, an improvement on 33.1% in 1991 but still high.

Despite the acceleration in GDP growth last year to 6.6%, employment growth slowed to 1.2%, with nearly all the new jobs generated by services (Figure 3.28.12). The Business Processing Association of the Philippines estimates that the rapidly expanding BPO industry will employ 926,000 full-time employees by the end of 2013, or 2% of the total labor force. BPO hires mostly skilled workers, however, which does not offer much hope to the large pool of unskilled labor. Tourism and related services employ 4 million people, or 10% of the labor force. Other services including finance and retailing also show consistent growth. Still, the service sector cannot absorb all new entrants to the workforce, which is growing by about 2% a year.

A stronger industrial base, particularly in manufacturing, could generate a wide range of jobs. But the development of manufacturing in the Philippines has lagged most other larger countries in Southeast Asia. The share of manufacturing in GDP declined to 22% in 2012 from 26% in 1990. Manufacturing in the Philippines provides only 8.3% of total employment, a much smaller contribution than in comparable countries (Figure 3.28.13).

Spurring industrial development requires broad-based reform to address the long-standing challenges of under-provision of infrastructure, an unfriendly investment and business environment, and poor governance. In the past 2 decades, steps have been taken on these fronts, as trade restrictions have been liberalized, the licensing system simplified, and a sound financial system established. More recently, governance reforms and gradual improvements in infrastructure have enhanced the investment environment.

While such reforms are crucial, by themselves they may not be enough to attract substantial new manufacturing investment in the near term. Targeted interventions aimed at manufacturers may be required. The challenge is to identify constraints on the development of particular industries and formulate policies to deploy against them. That requires considerable consultation with the industries concerned.

A window may be opening for the Philippines to pursue such a targeted policy, in light of renewed interest by some manufacturers to invest in Southeast Asia at a time that the improvements in the Philippines' investment environment are being recognized. Moreover, labor markets are tightening and wages rising more rapidly in several Asian countries that compete with the Philippines for manufacturing investment.

3.28.12 Employment growth

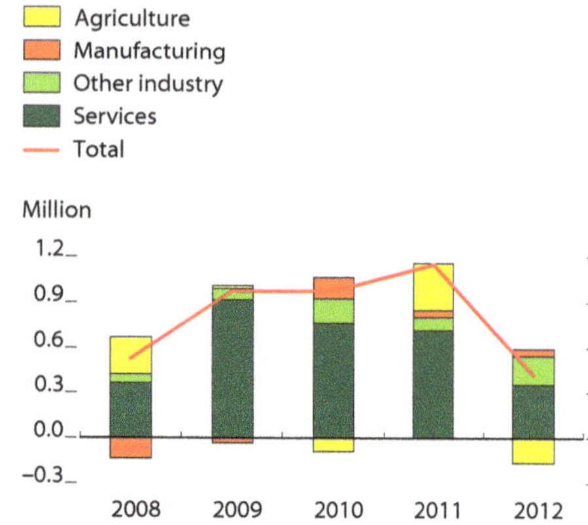

Sources: Bureau of Labor and Employment Statistics. *Current Labor Statistics*. Various years. http://www.bles.dole.gov.ph/

Click here for figure data

3.28.13 Employment in manufacturing, 2012

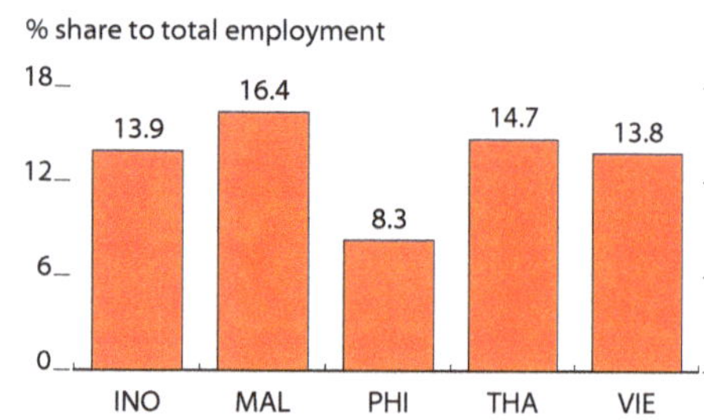

INO = Indonesia, MAL = Malaysia, PHI = Philippines, THA = Thailand, VIE = Viet Nam.

Note: Data for Viet Nam is for 2011.

Source: CEIC Data Company (accessed 16 March 2013).

Click here for figure data

Singapore

Growth will gradually accelerate over the next 2 years, with inflation moderating but still higher than average in the past decade and the balance of payments recording large but narrowing surpluses. Prudent economic policies, a flexible labor market, a sound banking system, and substantial foreign exchange reserves will counterbalance adverse developments overseas. As the government implements its growth strategy encouraging firms away from reliance on foreign labor, it should take measures to reduce the impact on small and medium-sized enterprises.

Economic performance

The economy expanded by 1.3% in 2012, down from 5.2% in 2011 in line with continuing challenges in the global economy. Demand slowed dramatically for externally dependent sectors, particularly manufacturing and wholesale and retail trade (Figure 3.29.1). Manufacturing growth was flat as electronics output dipped, owing to weaker demand for non-mobile technologies.

Domestically oriented sectors—construction and business services, in particular—were the main engines of growth in 2012, accounting for half of GDP growth. Construction expanded by 8.2%, supported by robust public and private demand. Sales of private houses jumped 40%, boosted by low interest rates. Strong growth in the business services sector depended heavily on the buoyant real estate market.

Domestic demand remained resilient, mainly due to inventory accumulation, while external demand weakened (Figure 3.29.2). However, consumption growth slowed to 2.2% from 4.6% in 2011 as spending on recreation and culture contracted and public consumption expenditure shrank by 3.6%. Weaker export growth and relatively faster import growth together narrowed net exports by 16.4%.

The economic slowdown took place amid ongoing economic restructuring. The government has adopted the recommendations of the Economic Strategies Committee that emphasize skills, innovation, and productivity as the main sources of growth. It limited the inflow of foreign workers by increasing the levies on nonresident foreign employees and lowering the ceiling on their allowed share in companies' total workforce. It initiated programs to encourage firms to raise their productivity by increasing the capital–labor ratio and through efficient workflow, rather than by relying on cheap labor. Coupled with low unemployment, these initiatives further tightened the labor market and put upward pressure on wages and inflation. As productivity gains will not happen overnight, slower expansion of the labor force will likely restrain growth.

3.29.1 Contributions to growth, by industry

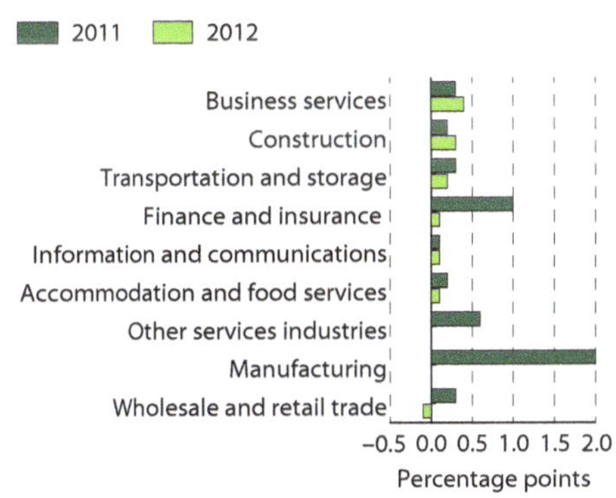

Source: Ministry of Trade and Industry. 2012. *Economic Survey of Singapore.* www.mti.gov.sg

Click here for figure data

3.29.2 Demand-side contributions to growth

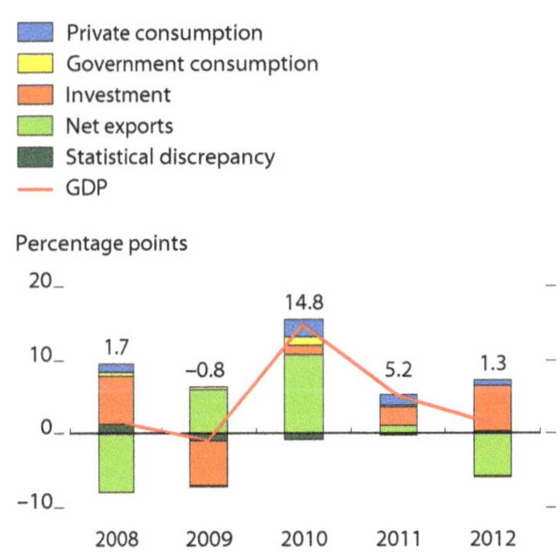

Source: CEIC Data Company (accessed 6 March 2013).

Click here for figure data

This chapter was written by Minsoo Lee and Arnelyn Abdon of the Economics and Research Department, ADB, Manila.

Inflation remained elevated but moderated somewhat to 4.6% in 2012 from 5.2% in 2011. The largest contributors to inflation in 2012 were housing and transportation, the latter driven by rising prices for vehicle quota premiums (Figure 3.29.3). Food price hikes eased as world prices declined and the Singapore dollar appreciated. Core inflation, which excludes the costs of housing and private road transport, averaged 2.6% in 2012, up from 2.2% in 2011.

Given Singapore's open capital account and its use of an undisclosed exchange rate band to execute monetary policy, interest rate and money supply developments are largely outside the control of the Monetary Authority of Singapore. To contain inflationary pressures, the authority has maintained a tightening bias since April 2010, leading to an appreciation of the nominal effective exchange rate by 5.9% in 2012, compared with 0.2% in 2011 (Figure 3.29.4). Money supply growth moderated to 7.2% from 10% the previous year as economic activity slowed. Credit expansion decelerated, with credit to the private sector expanding by 17% in 2012, down from 30% in 2011. Interest rates remain lower than those in the US (Figure 3.29.5).

Fiscal and macroprudential measures were tightened in 2012 to complement the central bank's contractionary stance and discourage speculation in the property market. Stamp duty tax on property purchases were raised from 10% to 15% for foreigners, and introduced at 5% for permanent residents; the loan-to-value ratio for mortgages was lowered from 60% to 50% for a second property.

The government's fiscal position remained strong in FY2012 (ended 31 March 2013) with revenue performing well and the overall fiscal surplus reaching 1.1% of GDP, almost the same size as in FY2011. Stamp duty collections were buoyed by the strong property market, and receipts from vehicle quota premiums swelled in response to government-imposed supply restrictions (Figure 3.29.6). Development expenditures expanded by 6%, reflecting higher spending on health, education, and transportation. Current expenditure contracted slightly, though the FY2012 budget introduced income support for households and financing facilitation for firms to ease the burden from economic restructuring.

Over the years, the economy has maintained a strong trade balance, with the current account surplus averaging more than 20% of GDP. In 2012, however, the current account surplus eased to 19% of GDP from 23% in 2011 as the surplus declined for both the trade balance and the services account. Overall, the balance of payments posted a surplus of 9% of GDP, up from 6% in 2011, largely due to a narrower deficit in the capital and financial account. Singapore maintains a strong external position, with international reserves covering 8 months of merchandise imports.

Economic prospects

GDP is forecast to grow by 2.6% in 2013, near the upper bound of the government's estimate of 1%–3%, and by 3.7% in 2014. For the rest of the decade, the Ministry of Trade and Industry projects GDP growth to be 3%–4%, which is a marked slowdown from the 6% average growth from 2000 to 2010.

3.29.3 Sources of inflation

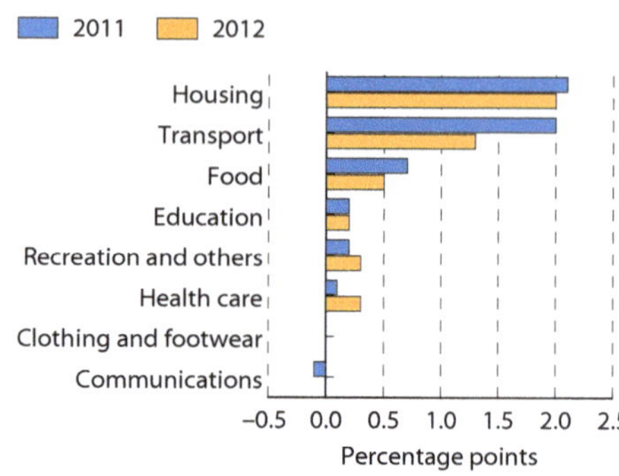

Source: Ministry of Trade and Industry. 2012. *Economic Survey of Singapore*. www.mti.gov.sg

Click here for figure data

3.29.4 Exchange rates

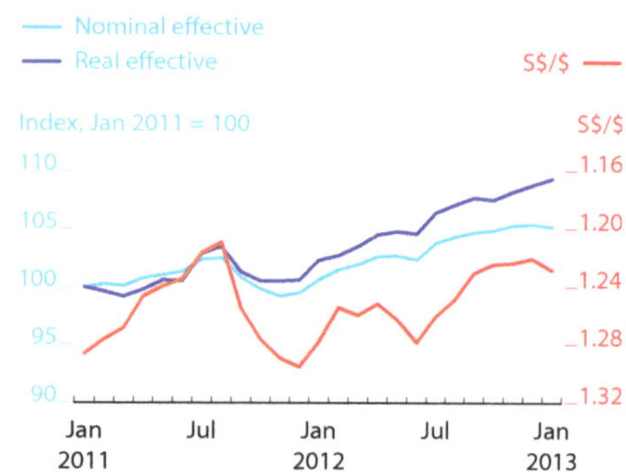

Sources: Bureau of International Settlements; CEIC Data Company (accessed 6 March 2013).

Click here for figure data

3.29.5 3-month deposit rates

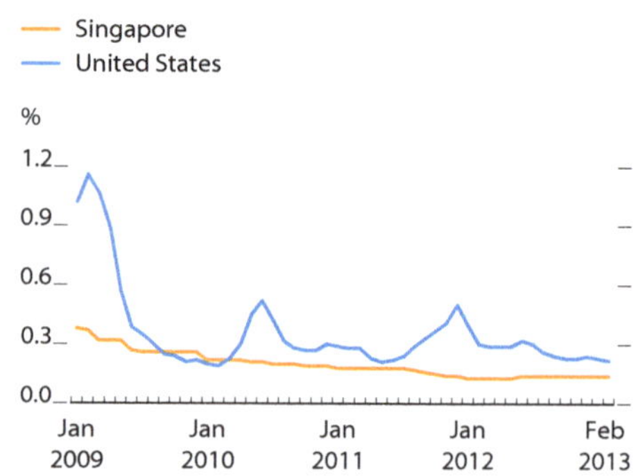

Source: CEIC Data Company (accessed 14 March 2013).

Click here for figure data

3.29.1 Selected economic indicators (%)

	2013	2014
GDP growth	2.6	3.7
Inflation	3.8	3.0
Current account balance (share of GDP)	16.0	15.0

Source: ADB estimates.

Domestic-oriented sectors will again be the primary drivers of growth this year and the next. Major infrastructure projects and residential construction will generate positive spillovers for other sectors. Cyclically sensitive industries such as manufacturing, wholesale trade, and financial services are expected to post modest growth, reflecting gradual recovery in external demand. Domestic demand will continue to be the main source of growth, on the back of improving fixed investment and a rebound in government expenditure.

Inflation will moderate further but remain above the historical average, owing to tight labor and housing markets (Figure 3.29.7). Overall inflation will likely slow gradually to 3.8% in 2013, within the range of the Monetary Authority of Singapore forecast of 3.5%–4.5% but double the 2% average over the past 2 decades. It is expected to ease to 3.0% in 2014. The forecast assumes that monetary policy will retain its bias toward Singapore dollar appreciation, that measures will be taken to cool the property market and expand housing supply, and that global commodity prices will moderate. Excessive capital inflows may also be a risk for inflation, but the authorities will likely introduce additional macroprudential measures, if necessary.

Singapore has a tradition of fiscal prudence with budget surpluses, except during recessions. Fiscal rules do not allow a cumulative deficit over the term of any one government. The budget for FY2013 estimates another overall fiscal surplus of S$2.4 billion, or 0.7% of GDP and lower than what was recorded in FY2012 (Figure 3.29.8). Authorities expect a slight decline in revenues, as receipts related to transport and the property market fall in the next 2 years. Expenditures are likely to be higher owing to increased outlays for higher education and health.

A slower pace of export growth and a relatively faster rise in imports—as domestic demand expands with government social spending—will likely narrow the current account surplus over the coming years. It is forecast at 16% of GDP in 2013 and 15% in 2014, down from 19% in 2012 (Figure 3.29.9).

The high degree of uncertainty over the global economy poses the highest risk to growth. As a trade-dependent city-state, Singapore will remain at risk from the patchy developments in the US, protracted sovereign-debt crisis in Europe, and moderation in economic growth in the People's Republic of China. A steep and abrupt correction in property values could cause substantial bank losses, as housing loans account for 31% of total loans. However, Singapore's strong fiscal position, flexible labor market, well-capitalized banking system, and substantial foreign exchange reserves can provide a buffer if any of these risks materialize.

Policy challenge—supporting small and medium-sized enterprises

Small and medium-sized enterprises (SMEs)—businesses with annual sales of up to S$100 million or up to 200 employees—are an integral part of the Singapore economy. SMEs account for 99% of all enterprises, more than 50% of output, and 70% of employment. Recent years have been particularly challenging for SMEs in Singapore. In addition to weak

3.29.6 Vehicle quota and premium

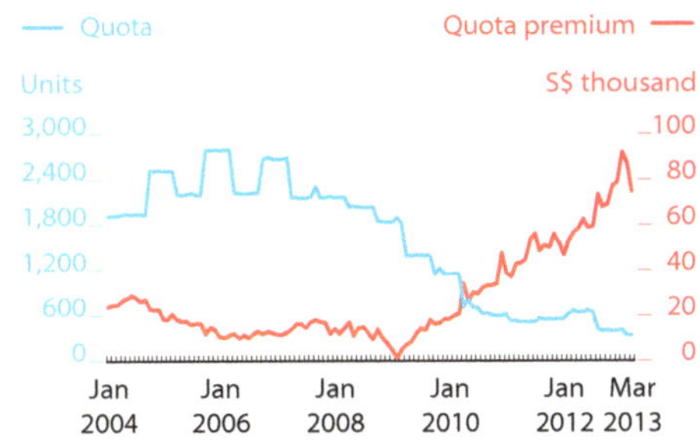

Note: First tender, for vehicles with engines 1,600 cubic centimeters and smaller.

Source: CEIC Data Company (accessed 18 March 2013).

Click here for figure data

3.29.7 Inflation

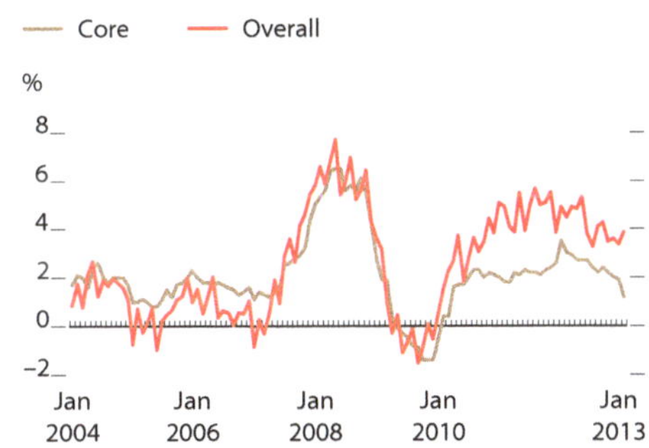

Source: CEIC Data Company (accessed 6 March 2013).

Click here for figure data

3.29.8 Fiscal balance

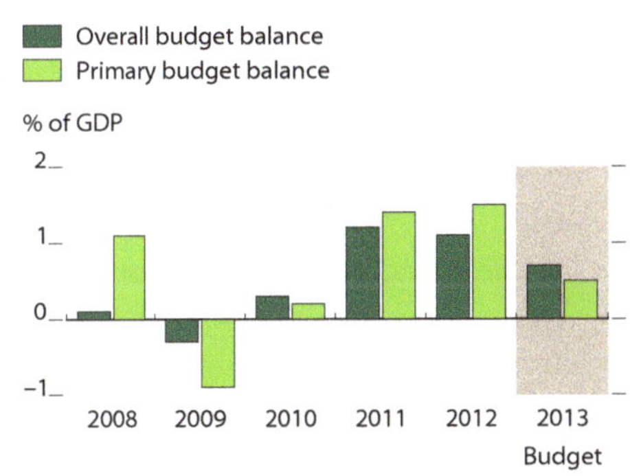

Source: Ministry of Finance. www.mof.gov.sg

Click here for figure data

3.29.9 Current account indicators

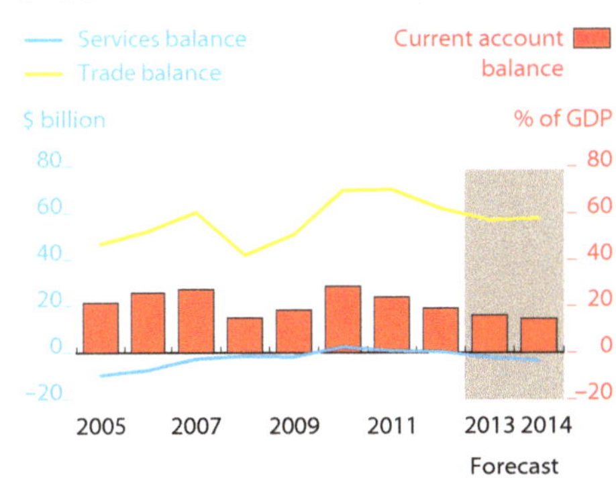

Source: CEIC Data Company (accessed 6 March 2013).

Click here for figure data

demand in the protracted global recession, SMEs face a labor supply squeeze and rising domestic costs, which are largely induced by the government's economic restructuring policy. SMEs feel the consequences of these shocks more strongly because of their limited access to finance and their less-developed financial and management capabilities. Recent surveys indicate that profits margins have narrowed, the number of SMEs reporting losses has risen, and enterprises are less optimistic regarding sales, profits, hiring, and capital investment in the coming months.

Recognizing SMEs' predicament, the FY2013 budget introduces a 3-year package worth S$5.35 billion to help businesses cope with rising costs (Table 3.29.2). It provides incentives for firms to invest in raising productivity and pay correspondingly competitive wages. Other programs specifically for SMEs are being implemented by a government agency facilitating the development and growth of indigenous firms. While these incentives will not fully offset costs in the short run, they provide a buffer for firms adjusting to the economic restructuring program.

The recent economic situation in Singapore, though not as severe as during the 2008–2009 global financial crisis, calls for more attention to the complex challenges that SMEs face. In the short term, SMEs must be willing to trim their margins and pay more for labor while building new business models. The measures announced in FY2013 will be helpful, but more needs to be done. Going forward, the government's policy of pushing firms toward less reliance on foreign labor, capital deepening, knowledge and systems upgrades, and innovation could be taxing for SMEs. Any shrinkage of the sector would have important unemployment and inequality consequences.

The challenge is to get the right balance such that restructuring toward higher productivity and sustainable growth does not happen at a very high social cost, while ensuring that policies do not encourage long-term dependency. This objective warrants well-targeted and incentive-compatible transfers to the most vulnerable firms, especially microenterprises. Rigorous evaluations of government support are necessary to assess actual impact on SMEs as a guide to policy makers. With a comfortable fiscal cushion, the government is well positioned, despite the sluggish global economy, to push for reforms toward a more sustainable and inclusive growth path that takes SMEs' requirements into account.

3.29.2 Selected budget 2013 measures for SMEs

Programs	Details
Wage credit scheme	• The government co-funding 40% of the wage increase for a Singaporean employee with a gross monthly salary of up to S$4,000
Productivity and innovation credit bonus	• A business spending at least S$5,000 on a credit-qualified activity receiving a matching bonus up to S$15,000
Corporate income tax rebate	• Each year, 30% of corporate income tax refunded, subject to a cap of S$30,000 per company
Helping SMEs upgrade productivity, innovation, and capability	• Enhanced productivity and innovation credit scheme • Collaborative industry projects • Technology adoption program • Land productivity grant • SME talent program • Workforce and training support
Helping SMEs tap opportunities for growth and others	• Market readiness assistance grant • Enhanced partnerships for capability transformation • Support to enhance companies' access to financing • Increase in central provident fund and lower contribution rates for low-wage workers • Lower tax on household benefits • Road tax rebate

SMEs = small and medium-sized enterprises.

Source: Standards, Productivity, and Innovation Board of Singapore.

Thailand

Policy stimulus supported a strong recovery last year after severe flooding devastated the economy in late 2011. While domestic demand rebounded in 2012, exports weakened on soft global demand and flood-related disruptions to manufacturing. GDP growth is seen moderating toward trend, with inflation forecast to remain modest. The country faces critical challenges in equity, public investment, and governance.

Economic performance

The economy rebounded last year from flooding that swamped industrial estates, farmland, and parts of the capital Bangkok in late 2011. GDP rose by 6.4% in 2012 compared with just 0.1% in the previous year (Figure 3.30.1).

Private consumption increased by 6.6% to contribute about half of total GDP growth. Consumption was stimulated by demand to replace household items after the floods and by several government policies. These included increases in minimum wages by up to 40% in seven provinces and in public service salaries, a tax rebate to first-time buyers of domestically made cars, which some 1.2 million car buyers took advantage of, tax breaks for first-time buyers of houses, and a government decision to buy unmilled rice from farmers at prices well above international levels.

Growth in employment and wages supported consumption, as average wages rose by 11.8% and employment by 1.2%. The unemployment rate fell to just 0.5% by year-end.

Fixed capital investment rose by 13.3%, propelled by the reconstruction of flood-damaged factories, houses, and other infrastructure and the replacement of capital equipment. Public construction was spurred by the building of mass rapid transit projects in Bangkok and mobile telecommunications networks.

However, external demand weakened last year due to sagging economic growth in major markets and disruption to export-oriented manufacturing caused by the floods. Net exports of goods and services acted as a drag on GDP growth.

Some manufacturers were able to return to full production relatively quickly, particularly those targeting the domestic market, but others—including makers of computers, hard drives, and semiconductors—took several months to rebuild and replace equipment. These industries also faced sluggish export demand.

Car and truck production jumped by 72%, reflecting the low base caused by the 2011 floods and additional demand stimulated by the rebate for first-car buyers. Manufacturing production rose by 7.0%,

3.30.1 Demand-side contributions to growth

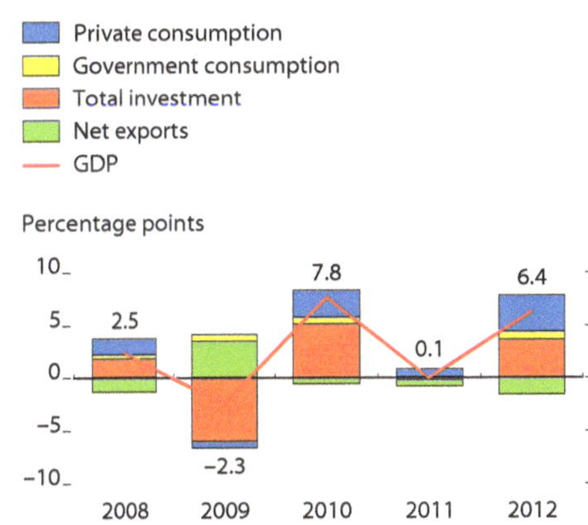

Source: National Economic and Social Development Board. http://www.nesdb.go.th (accessed 11 March 2013).

Click here for figure data

3.30.2 Supply-side contributions to growth

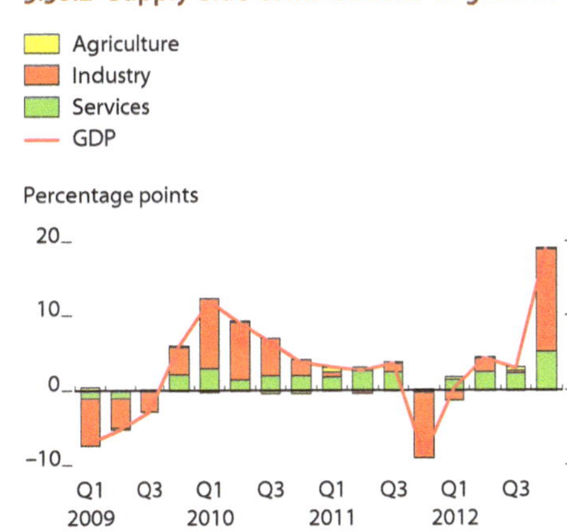

Source: National Economic and Social Development Board. http://www.nesdb.go.th (accessed 11 March 2013).

Click here for figure data

This chapter was written by Luxmon Attapich of the Thailand Resident Mission, ADB, Bangkok.

and the industry sector as a whole contributed 3.4 percentage points to GDP growth, the biggest sector contribution from the supply side (Figure 3.30.2).

The service sector grew by 5.8% and was also an important source of GDP growth. A 16% rise in tourist arrivals, to 22.3 million, contributed to 8.8% growth in the hotels and restaurants subsector. Financial services grew by 6.6%, with insurance benefiting from buoyant auto sales. Agricultural output increased by 3.1% with higher output of rice, cassava, natural rubber, and oil palm.

Food price inflation eased and fuel prices were fairly stable. Despite picking up in the fourth quarter because of an increase in electricity tariffs and higher excise taxes on alcohol and tobacco, inflation for 2012 was the lowest in 3 years (Figure 3.30.3).

The Bank of Thailand, the central bank, lowered its policy interest rate to 3.0% to assist economic recovery after the floods, and reduced the rate again in October 2012 to 2.75%, slightly below the inflation rate (Figure 3.30.4). Lending interest rates declined, and commercial bank lending expanded by 13.7% in 2012, with a 21.6% surge in consumer loans.

Fiscal policy also stimulated the economy. The fiscal deficit widened to 4.1% of GDP in FY2012 (ended 30 September 2012) from 1.3% in FY2011. About 90% of planned spending was disbursed, though this fell to 66% for the capital budget owing to delays in approving the FY2012 budget after a change of government in August 2011 and shortages of construction materials after the floods. The wider deficit reflects new government subsidies and tax breaks to support households, farmers, and businesses, including a cut in the corporate tax rate to 23% in 2012.

Moreover, considerable spending was funded off-budget. Parliament approved an emergency decree allowing the government to borrow the equivalent of $11.7 billion by June 2013 to be spent over several years on water management projects. About $100 million of this was spent in 2012.

Merchandise exports rose by just 3.2% in US dollars last year. The value of rice exports shrank by 28% because the subsidy on the domestic purchase price pushed Thai rice prices well above international levels. Exports of automobiles increased by 26%, but those of electronic products edged up by just 0.9%.

Imports outpaced exports, rising by 7.8% in US dollars, in part a result of capital equipment purchased to replace that damaged by the floods. Consequently, the trade surplus shrank by half to $8.3 billion (Figure 3.30.5). Insurance payouts after the floods contributed to a narrowing in the services trade deficit, but the sharply lower trade surplus meant the current account surplus fell to 0.7% of GDP.

The capital and financial account recorded a substantial surplus, largely because of net portfolio inflows and loans to businesses. The overall balance of payments remained in surplus, and gross international reserves rose by 3.7% to $181.6 billion, cover for 10 months of imports.

Higher capital inflows contributed to 6% appreciation of the Thai baht against the US dollar in 2012. The central bank indicated it would further liberalize outward foreign direct and portfolio investment, partly to take pressure off the baht. The Stock Exchange of Thailand index of share prices climbed by 35.8% over last year, and yields on government bonds generally declined. Housing prices showed modest gains.

3.30.3 Monthly inflation

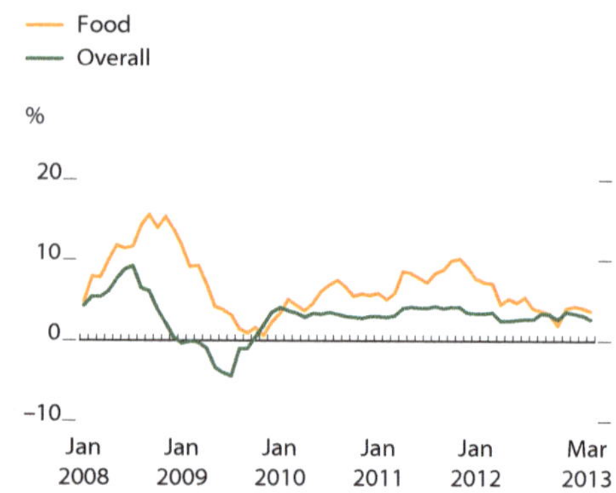

Sources: CEIC Data Company; Bureau of Trade and Economic Indices. http://www.price.moc.go.th (both accessed 2 April 2013).

Click here for figure data

3.30.4 Policy interest rate

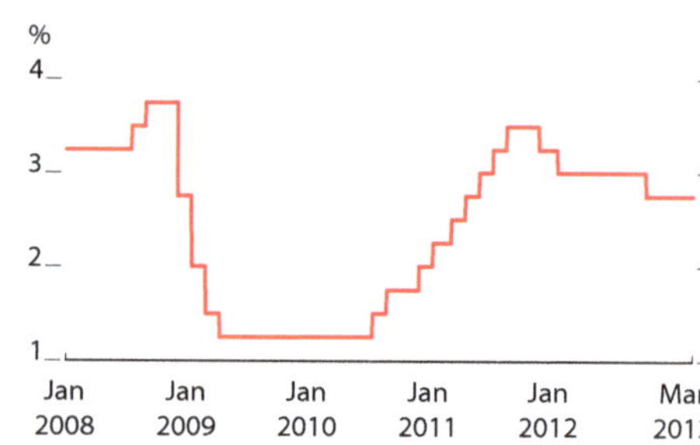

Source: Bloomberg (accessed 11 March 2013).

Click here for figure data

3.30.5 Trade indicators

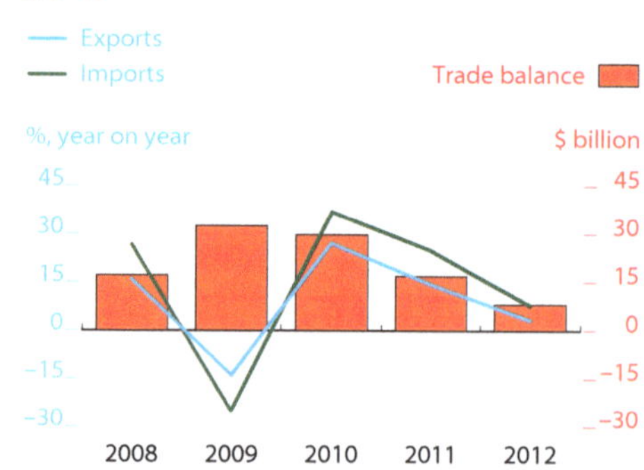

Source: Bank of Thailand. http://www.bot.or.th (accessed 11 March 2013).

Click here for figure data

Economic prospects

After the rebound in 2012, economic growth is expected to moderate to about 5% this year and next (Figure 3.30.6), the pace seen in the 3 years leading up to the global financial crisis. Projections assume the government follows through with large public investments it plans in water management and transport infrastructure during the forecast period.

Private consumption will continue to benefit from a tight labor market and the minimum wage increases, which were extended throughout the country from January 2013. A study by the Thailand Development Research Institute found that last year's 40% increase in minimum wages in seven provinces did not cause significant layoffs.

Despite concerns that the rice price subsidies may not be the most cost-effective option for raising rural incomes, the government extended the rice-purchase program into 2013. However, the impact of flood-relief payments and low-interest loans offered in 2011 will fade during 2013 and beyond. The tax break for first-time house buyers is scheduled to end in May 2013, while the incentive for first-time car buyers expired at the end of 2012. While consumer confidence rose in February to its highest level in 18 months (Figure 3.30.7), growth in private consumption is unlikely to match that in 2012.

Growth in private investment will also moderate as post-flood reconstruction winds down, though investment is likely to remain robust. Cement sales were strong early this year, suggesting that construction remains buoyant. The Board of Investments approved investment incentives for 2,262 planned projects valued at $330 million in 2012, double the value of the previous year. Business sentiment generally was high early in 2013 (Figure 3.30.7) and lending rates relatively low.

Government investment is expected to contribute more to economic growth, with public investment projected to rise by 12.5% this year. The water management program should gather momentum from the second half of 2013, with $1.3 billion projected to be spent this year. The government plans legislation under which it can borrow the equivalent of $67 billion off-budget over 7 years to invest in transport infrastructure: roads, railways, seaports, and airports. Investment in this program could start early next year. The fiscal deficit, including budget and off-budget spending, is projected to widen to 4.8% of GDP in FY2013.

Early in 2013 the central bank noted positive signs for continued economic growth, pointing to increases in indexes of consumption and investment, buoyant tourism, and an uptrend in exports in January.

Modest inflation—slightly above 3%—is projected for the forecast period (Figure 3.30.8). The government has extended a tax exemption on diesel fuel into 2013 and is expected to maintain controls on a range of consumer items. Global prices of oil and other commodities look likely to remain broadly stable. Rising domestic wages are anticipated to have a modest impact on inflation, which averaged 3.1% in the first 3 months of this year.

Monetary policy is expected to remain accommodative to growth for some time in light of low inflation and strong capital inflows. Higher government borrowing for public investment will likely drain some excess liquidity from the banking system. The monetary authorities have indicated they stand ready to take macroprudential measures to manage

3.30.1 Selected economic indicators (%)

	2013	2014
GDP growth	4.9	5.0
Inflation	3.2	3.1
Current account balance (share of GDP)	0.8	0.1

Source: ADB estimates.

3.30.6 GDP growth

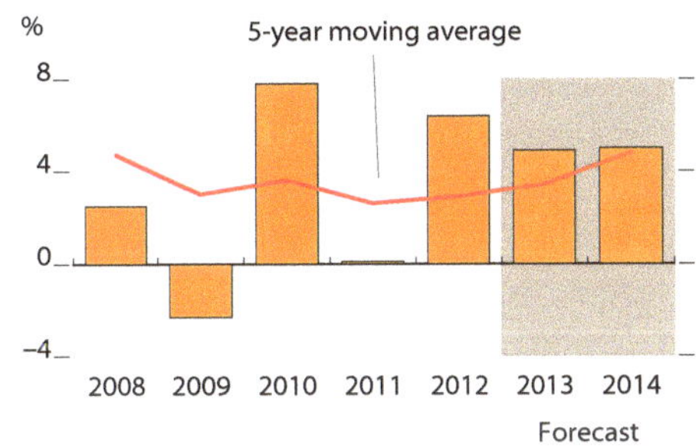

Source: Asian Development Outlook database.

Click here for figure data

3.30.7 Consumer confidence and business sentiment

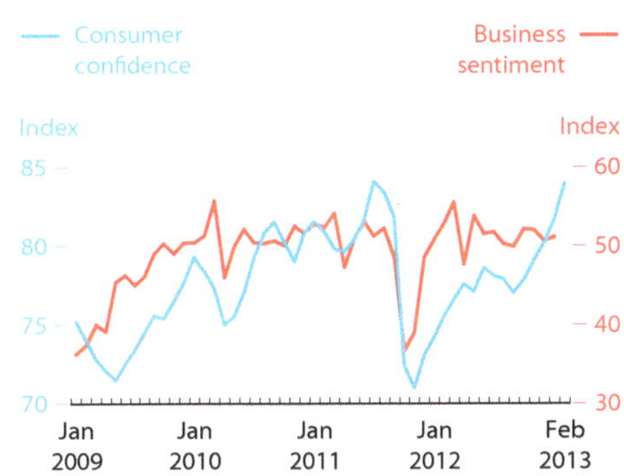

Sources: Center for Economic and Business Forecasting; Bank of Thailand. http://www.bot.or.th (both accessed 11 March 2013).

Click here for figure data

rising household debt if consumer lending continues at the high rate seen in 2012. The baht appreciated by 4.5% against the US dollar in the first 3 months of 2013 (Figure 3.30.9).

Stronger economic growth in some major export markets, including the People's Republic of China (PRC), and pickup in world trade indicate that growth in merchandise exports will quicken to about 10% in 2013, and step up again in 2014. Manufacturing industries' return to full production will support the increase in exports. Imports are forecast to increase by 11% this year, accelerating in 2014 when the government starts the new transport infrastructure projects. The current account is expected to record small surpluses (Figure 3.30.10).

Risks to this outlook include the challenges discussed below, potential significant delays affecting infrastructure projects, and capital inflows that maintain upward pressure on the baht, damaging the competitiveness of exports. Failure to address weaknesses in education is a longer-term risk to economic development.

The government is incurring substantial losses from its purchases of rice from farmers at prices above the international market. Thai rice inventories were estimated at 15 million tons early in 2013 as overseas buyers turned to lower-priced rice from India and Viet Nam (Figure 3.30.11). Losses could exceed the equivalent of 1% of GDP annually.

Policy challenges—equity, public investment, and governance

Thailand faces several critical policy challenges. One is inequality, which undermines social and political stability with associated risks to investor confidence. Inequality is reflected in large rural–urban and regional gaps in incomes and access to social and economic services (Figure 3.30.12). Such structural problems are unlikely to be resolved by ad hoc measures to boost incomes through subsidies and tax concessions. More effective targeting of public investment in social and physical infrastructure will be important to address these concerns.

A second issue is inadequate public investment, which dents the country's competitiveness. Public investment as a ratio to GDP has declined over many years (Figure 3.30.13). The World Economic Forum ranks Thailand 38th of 144 countries in its *Global Competitiveness Report 2012–2013*. However, Thailand's ranking sinks to 46th for infrastructure and lower still for railway, port, and telephone components of infrastructure. Also of concern is the country's lowly ranking on basic education, at 89th, and on adoption of technology, at 84th. A separate World Bank benchmark that measures the performance of logistics ranked Thailand 38th of 155 countries in 2012, below the PRC and Malaysia.

Public investment is needed in transport infrastructure to reduce logistics costs and in water management infrastructure to mitigate the social and economic impacts of climate change and flooding. Increased investment in social infrastructure is needed to ensure equitable improvements in skills and social capital that will boost creativity and productivity to generate sustained gains in living standards.

3.30.8 Inflation

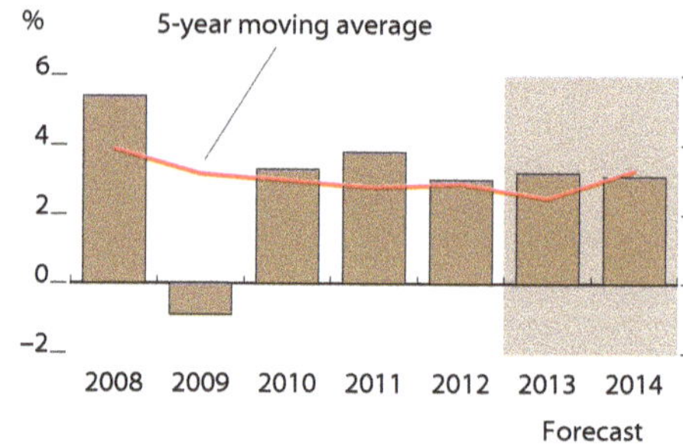

Source: Asian Development Outlook database.

Click here for figure data

3.30.9 Exchange rate

Source: Bloomberg (accessed 2 April 2013).

Click here for figure data

3.30.10 Current account balance

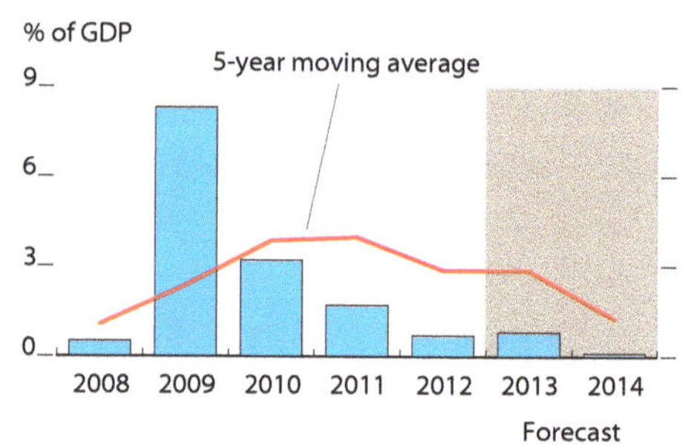

Source: Asian Development Outlook database.

Click here for figure data

3.30.11 Rice exports

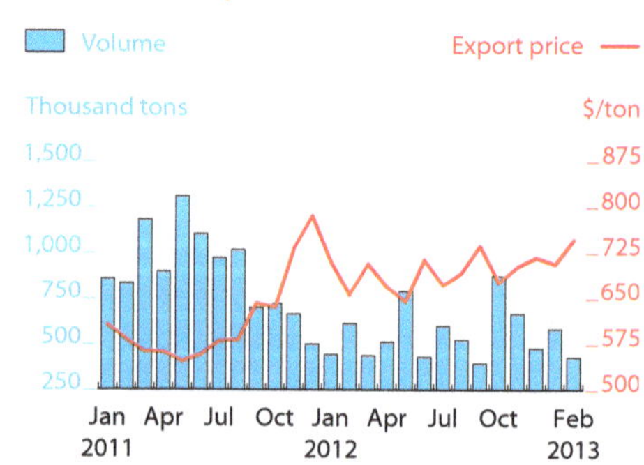

Source: CEIC Data Company (accessed 2 April 2013).

Click here for figure data

Mobilizing and effectively managing resources to ensure more equitable, efficient, and effective delivery of public services is one of Thailand's most pressing challenges. The government lacked resources for public investment following the 1997 Asian financial crisis. More recently, political instability has interrupted the planning and implementation of large public investment projects. Moreover, the government prioritized spending on fast-disbursing stimulus programs when the economy slumped during the global financial crisis in 2008–2009 and after the extreme flooding in 2011. Large public finance allocations were directed at incentives for first-time buyers of cars, pay rises for the public service, tax cuts for companies, popular measures such as the diesel fuel subsidy, and subsidized rice purchases from farmers.

The government is now beginning to address declines in public investment with significant multiyear programs for water management ($11.7 billion) and transport infrastructure (as much as $67 billion), funded off-budget. However, considerable uncertainty surrounds the pace of implementation.

Investment in transport infrastructure aims to reduce logistics costs by 2 percentage points, from about 15% of total production costs. Most of the investment in transport will go to rail networks to improve transport links within Thailand and to neighboring countries. The water management projects are designed to mitigate the social and economic impact of flooding and better manage water resources.

While the commitment to increased public investment is a positive development, off-budget programs have the disadvantage of compromising transparency. Instead, increases in budget funding for public investment could be generated by broadening the tax base or phasing out the economic stimulus programs. The government could also consider amending the Public Debt Management Act to raise borrowing limits while maintaining its fiscal sustainability framework to keep public debt below 50% of GDP.

This leads to a third challenge: the need to improve public sector management and accountability, and to fight corruption. This will become increasingly important as public investment expenditure rises.

3.30.12 Average real GDP per capita by region, 1995–2011

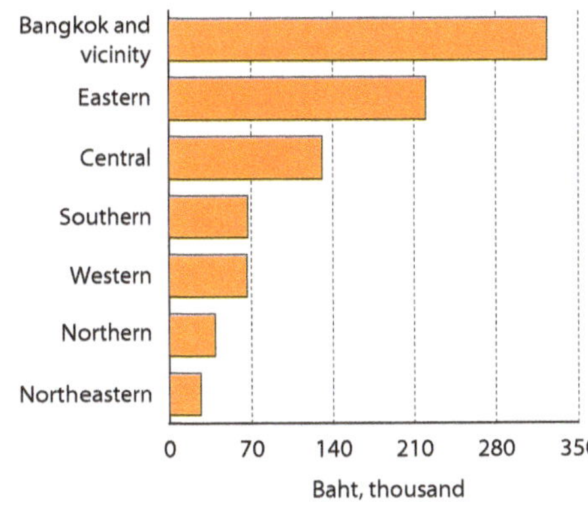

Source: CEIC Data Company (accessed 2 April 2013).
Click here for figure data

3.30.13 Public investment

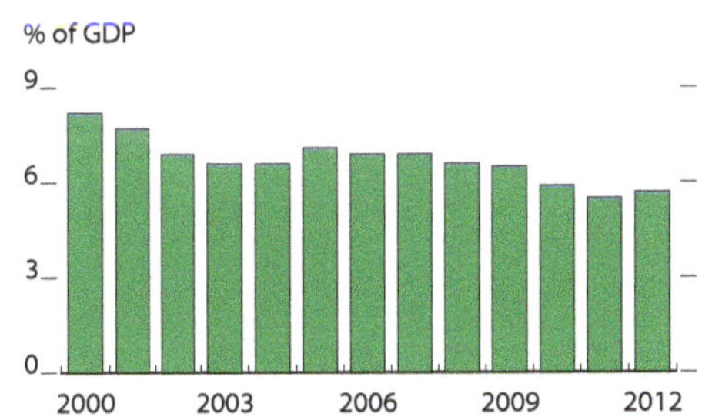

Source: National Economic and Social Development Board. http://www.nesdb.go.th (accessed 19 March 2013).
Click here for figure data

Viet Nam

The economy stabilized in 2012 as previous policy tightening suppressed inflation and bolstered external accounts. Subdued economic growth prompted an easing of monetary policy last year, but lending was constrained by problems in banks. GDP growth is forecast to edge up this year and next, with inflation in the high single digits. Sustaining foreign direct investment inflows and maintaining competitiveness requires intensified efforts to reform banking, state-owned enterprises, and the business environment.

Economic performance

GDP growth ebbed to 5.0% in 2012 (Figure 3.31.1), the slowest in 13 years, as fiscal and monetary tightening in 2011 continued to have an impact into last year. While the policies took a toll on growth, they achieved sharp reductions in inflation and a more stable exchange rate, and they contributed to a record current account surplus and to rebuilding foreign reserves.

All sectors—agriculture, industry, and services—recorded slower growth in 2012 than in 2011. Manufacturing decelerated to 4.5%, reflecting weak domestic demand, high inventories, and reduced bank lending. Construction grew by a modest 2.1% after contracting in 2011 when the government squeezed credit and cut public investment. Services expanded by 6.4% to make the biggest sector contribution to GDP growth last year. Tourism-related services benefited from 9.5% growth in visitor arrivals, though this was a slowdown from 2011. Agriculture grew by just 2.7%.

From the demand side, growth in private consumption eased to 3.4% owing mainly to a weaker labor market. About 116,000 businesses closed in the past 2 years. Investment grew by 2.2%, a turnaround from its contraction in the previous year. Foreign direct investment (FDI) inflows remained substantial, but private domestic investment was dampened by weak credit growth. The government brought forward some planned capital spending, which lifted public investment. Strong exports and sluggish imports meant net exports made a significant contribution to GDP growth for the second consecutive year.

The stabilization policies, together with good domestic harvests and soft global food prices, tamed inflation in 2012. It decelerated sharply from over 20% year on year in October 2011, bottoming out at 5.0% in August 2012 (Figure 3.31.2). On a year-average basis, inflation receded to 9.2%, half the rate of 2011.

Steep declines in inflation allowed the State Bank of Viet Nam, the central bank, to lower its refinancing and discount rates, and its caps on short-term deposit rates, by 600 basis points (Figure 3.31.3). It also increased its limit on credit growth for some banks and reintroduced,

3.31.1 Demand-side contributions to growth

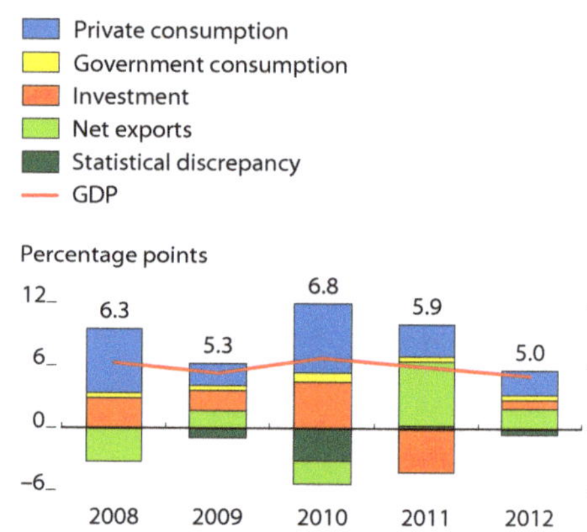

Source: General Statistics Office of Viet Nam.

Click here for figure data

3.31.2 Monthly inflation

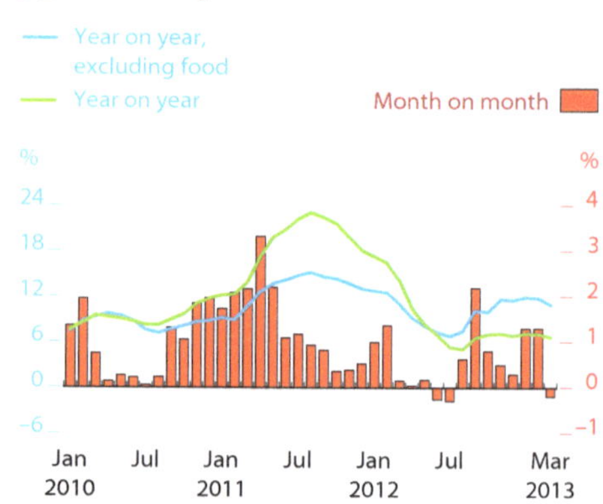

Source: General Statistics Office of Viet Nam.

Click here for figure data

This chapter was written by Dominic Mellor, Chu Hong Minh, and Nguyen Luu Thuc Phuong of the Viet Nam Resident Mission, ADB, Ha Noi.

then later lowered, a ceiling on bank lending interest rates for priority industries. Nevertheless, growth in credit estimated at 8.9% last year was the slowest for many years and fell short of the central bank's 15%–17% target (Figure 3.31.4).

Broad money supply (M2) increased by 22%, above the central bank's target of 14%–16%, suggesting sufficient liquidity but lack of demand for credit. Banks were cautious in extending credit due to their impaired balance sheets, illustrated by rising nonperforming loans (NPLs), and their concerns about the financial health of borrowers and other banks. Firms and individuals hesitated to take on debt at a time of weak domestic demand and a declining property market. Lending for consumption, real estate, and marketable securities was only 4% of total lending, well below the 16% cap on lending for these activities introduced by the central bank in 2011.

The Viet Nam dong, after depreciating against the US dollar for several years, traded within its official exchange rate band for most of 2012 (Figure 3.31.5). The more stable exchange rate mainly resulted from lower inflation, positive real interest rates, stronger external accounts, a cap on US dollar deposit interest rates, and lower domestic gold prices.

Fiscal stimulation of the economy was relatively modest in 2012. The government brought forward capital spending and made some concessions on taxes and fees. Budget spending relative to GDP was little changed from 2011 while tax revenue declined on this basis. The budget deficit widened slightly to 4.8% of GDP. On-budget capital spending as a share of total budget outlays fell from an average of 30% in 2008–2011 to 22%, in part a result of higher salaries in the public sector. Off-budget expenditures and lending was funded through domestic bond issuances.

High liquidity allowed the government to boost its net issuance of government bonds to the equivalent of about 3.6% of GDP, from 1.2% in 2011.

Strong growth in exports and subdued imports produced a record trade surplus estimated at $10 billion on a balance-of-payments basis. Merchandise exports rose by 18.2%, a much stronger performance than other countries in Southeast Asia. Viet Nam became the world's biggest exporter of rice and coffee in 2012. Manufactured exports rose steeply, reflecting the start of operations of foreign-invested factories making mobile phones, computers, and other electronics. Customs data show the proportion of high-tech products in total exports has climbed to 18% from 4% in the past decade (Figure 3.31.6).

Merchandise imports increased by 7.5% on sluggish domestic demand. The trade surplus, coupled with tourism receipts and remittance inflows, contributed to a current account surplus estimated at 6.4% of GDP, a huge turnaround from 4 years earlier, when the current account recorded a deficit of 11.9% of GDP. Together with higher capital inflows, these developments helped rebuild foreign reserves to an estimated 2.6 months of goods and services imports (Figure 3.31.7). FDI inflows rose by 11% to an estimated $8.4 billion, medium and long-term loans by 19% to nearly $4 billion, and portfolio investment by 36% to $2 billion.

The government continued to grapple with banking sector problems. Banks reported in October 2012 that NPLs were about 4.8% of total loans, but based on closer surveillance of the banking system the central bank estimated that the ratio of bad loans was 8.8% at midyear. It trimmed that

3.31.3 Interest rates

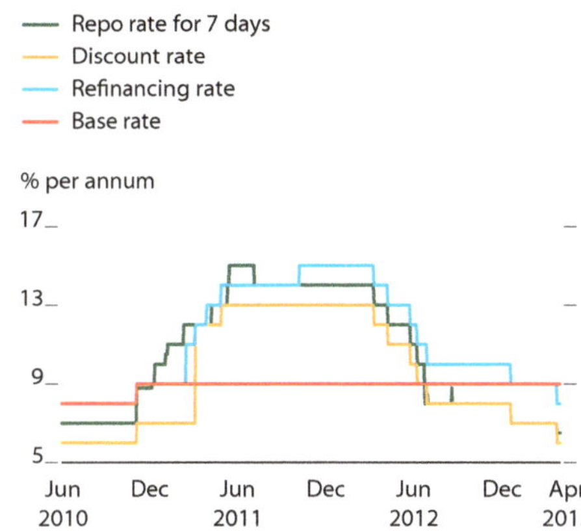

Source: State Bank of Viet Nam.
Click here for figure data

3.31.4 Credit and money supply growth

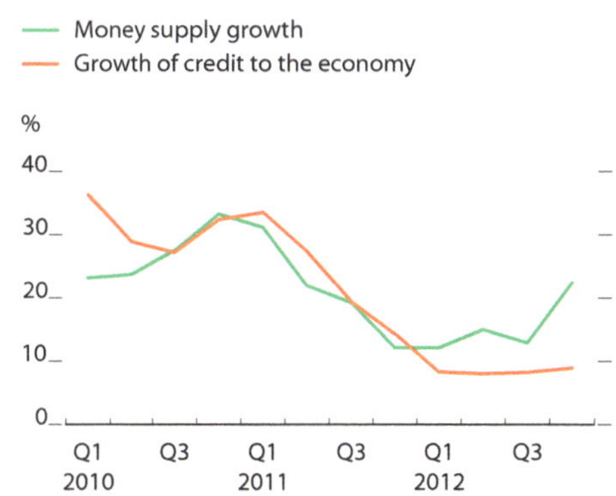

Sources: State Bank of Viet Nam; ADB estimates.
Click here for figure data

3.31.5 Exchange rate

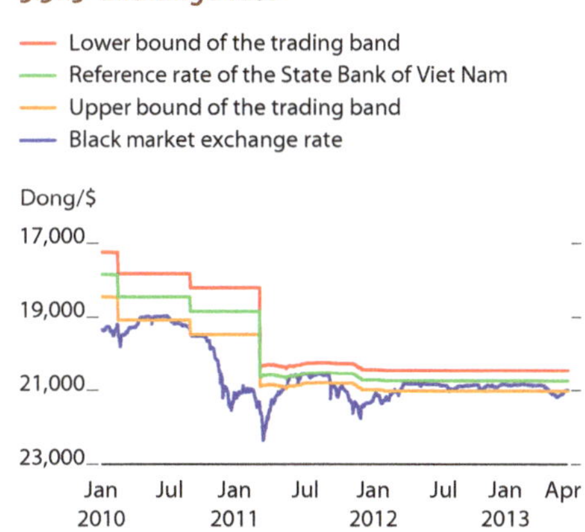

Sources: State Bank of Viet Nam; ADB observations.
Click here for figure data

estimate to 6.0% in February 2013. Independent analysts estimate that NPLs could be in double digits using international accounting standards (Figure 3.31.8). NPLs have proliferated because of rapid growth in lending over several years followed by the squeeze on credit in 2011, the downturn in the economy and property market, and poor performances by some highly leveraged state-owned enterprises (SOEs).

In March 2012 the government approved a reform plan to strengthen the banking system through mergers, recapitalization, the adoption of international prudential standards, and improvements in bank supervision. Several financially stressed banks were merged, and the authorities disclosed additional data on the health of the banking system. However, there was little progress on recapitalizing banks or resolving NPLs. The capital adequacy ratio of the banking system fell to 13.6% in January 2013 from 14.6% in April 2012. While this ratio is still well above the 9% floor set by the authorities, banks' capital positions may be weaker than reported if they have underestimated NPLs and not made adequate provision for them.

The government also outlined a plan to improve SOEs' disclosure, governance, and operations. More information on this strategy is scheduled to be disclosed in 2013.

Moody's downgraded Viet Nam's credit rating to B2 from B1 in September 2012, citing banking system weaknesses and lower economic growth. Standard & Poor's has a long-term rating for Viet Nam of BB− and revised its outlook to *stable* from *negative* in June 2012. Meanwhile Fitch, which has a B+ long-term rating, affirmed its *stable* outlook rating in January 2013.

Economic prospects

Government statements indicate that macroeconomic stability remains the main priority. The discussion below assumes policy stimulation to support growth during the forecast period will be moderate.

The central bank is targeting credit growth of 12%, stronger than the 2012 outcome of 8.9%, and M2 growth of 14%–16%, down from last year's actual growth of 22.4%. The central bank has removed restrictions on lending for consumption, real estate, and marketable securities. After inflation eased to 6.6% year on year in March 2013, the central bank lowered a number of interest rates, including its refinance and discount rates by 100 basis points to 8% and 6%, respectively. The impact of these lower rates on credit growth may be muted until the banking sector problems are addressed more decisively.

On the fiscal front the government has maintained the budget deficit target at 4.8% of GDP for 2013. In January it allowed small and medium-sized enterprises and labor-intensive manufacturers to defer corporate income tax and value-added tax payments, and it offered subsidies and tax breaks to revive the property market. Capacity to provide greater fiscal stimulation is constrained by public debt, which has increased to 55% of GDP, and contingent liabilities in SOEs and banks.

Private consumption will get support from the downtrend in inflation, though labor market weakness remains a dampener. The outlook for investment has improved with a surge in FDI commitments from Japan

3.31.6 High-technology exports

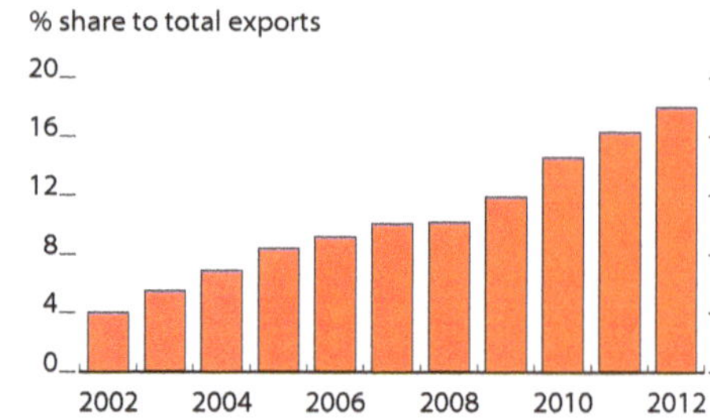

Note: Merchandise exports.

Sources: United Nations. Comtrade database. http://comtrade.un.org (accessed 1 April 2013) ; General Statistical Office; ADB estimates.

Click here for figure data

3.31.7 Gross international reserves

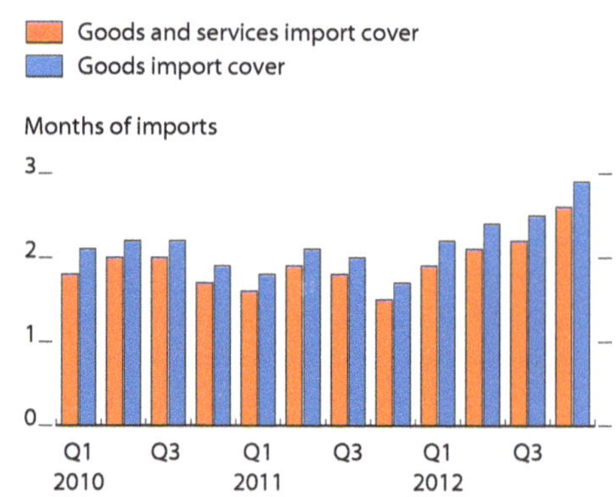

Note: Data exclude government foreign exchange deposits at the State Bank of Viet Nam and the foreign exchange counterpart of swap operations. Import data are on free-on-board basis.

Sources: State Bank of Viet Nam; International Monetary Fund; ADB estimates.

Click here for figure data

3.31.8 Nonperforming loans

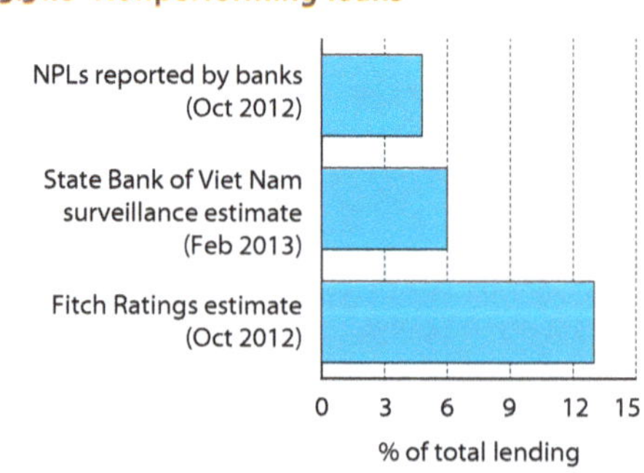

NPL = nonperforming loan.

Sources: State Bank of Viet Nam; Fitch Ratings.

Click here for figure data

last year and the policy decisions mentioned above. However, questions over the soundness of the banking system will continue to weigh on domestic private investment.

Exports are projected to maintain solid expansion, given higher economic growth in the PRC and some other markets this year, and the anticipated pickup in major industrial economies in 2014. Manufactured exports will continue to trend up as FDI-funded factories come into production. Imports also will increase, though, to meet domestic demand as it gradually recovers and to supply inputs for the export-oriented manufacturers.

GDP grew by 4.9% in the first quarter of 2013, marginally higher than the year-earlier period, and the purchasing managers' index trended up slightly as orders increased. On the down side, growth in industrial production at 4.9% and in real retail sales at 4.5% showed slight decelerations from a year earlier.

Taking these factors into consideration, GDP growth is forecast at 5.2% in 2013, picking up to 5.6% in 2014 (Figure 3.31.9) if progress is made in strengthening the banking sector and recovery in major industrial economies gathers momentum in 2014.

Inflation is seen easing to 7.5% on average this year before quickening to 8.2% in 2014. This view assumes reasonable weather for food production, a broadly stable dong exchange rate, and restrained policy stimulation. The trade surplus is expected to climb to a record $12.5 billion in 2013 and the current account surplus to increase further this year before easing in 2014 as imports accelerate in tandem with GDP growth (Figure 3.31.10).

Risks to the outlook center on the soundness of the banking system and the scale of NPLs. The NPL problem started spreading to the interbank money market from late 2011, when some banks were unable to recover funds provided to smaller banks with high NPLs. The central bank responded last year by, among other measures, restricting banks with interbank debts overdue by more than 10 days from borrowing through the interbank market. Those measures reduced interbank transaction risks but also restricted the functioning of the market (Figure 3.31.11). The central bank eased some restrictions at the start of this year.

A financial sector assessment, conducted by the International Monetary Fund and the World Bank with the agreement of the government, will be completed this year. Meanwhile, the authorities have introduced regulation that requires commercial banks to increase risk provisioning against NPLs and report on loan classification by June 2013. Compliance might take longer because banks need to upgrade their accounting systems. The central bank's supervisory and regulatory functions need to be strengthened to ensure compliance with the new regulations.

Cleaning up bank balance sheets would pave the way for a more robust expansion of lending. With this in mind the central bank intends to establish an asset-management company to acquire bad loans from banks. Adequate funding will be critical to the success of this plan, as will a transparent process by which assets are priced and an insolvency system with improved capacity to manage the resolution of distressed assets.

3.31.9 GDP growth

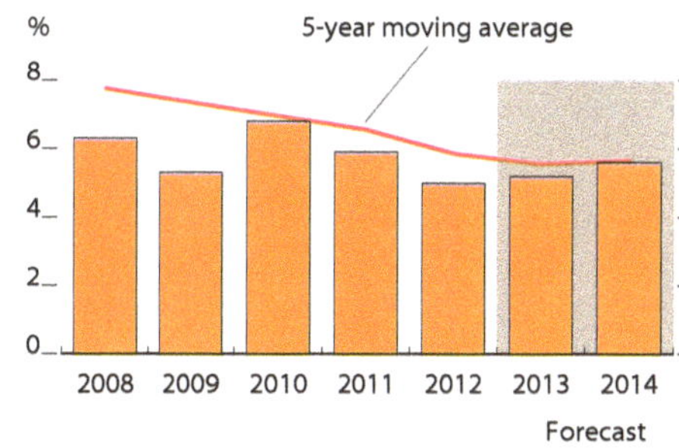

Source: Asian Development Outlook database.

Click here for figure data

3.31.10 Current account components

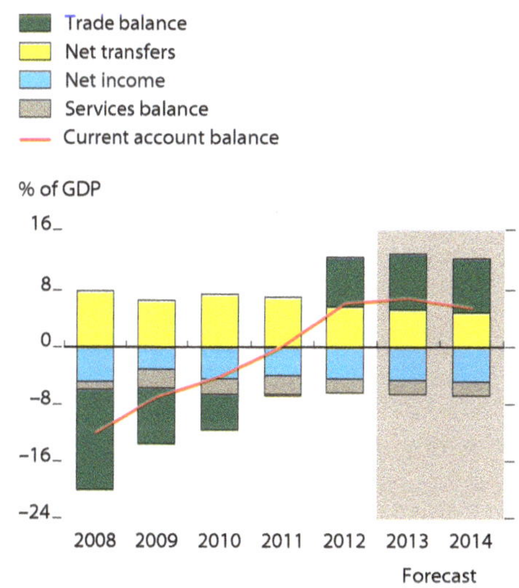

Sources: State Bank of Viet Nam; ADB estimates.

Click here for figure data

3.31.11 Interbank volume

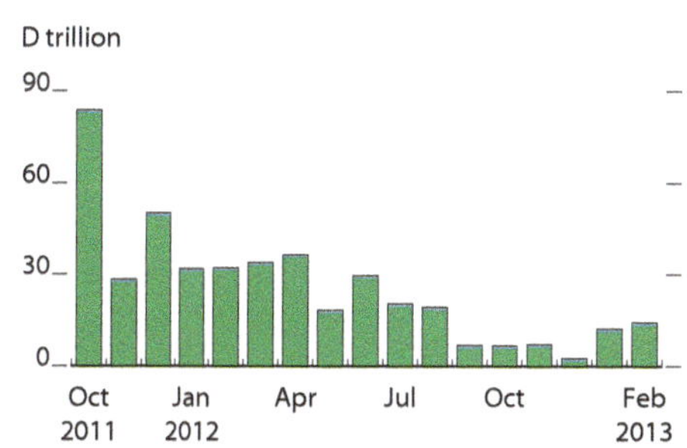

Source: Reuters.

Click here for figure data

A revival of the property market could ease pressure on the banks, at least temporarily. In this regard the government unveiled in January 2013 a package of measures that targets social housing projects with subsidized mortgage rates for low-income earners and public servants, reductions in state land rents, deferment of land use fees, and cuts in corporate income and value-added tax. The measures also involve a streamlining in the building permit process.

As a way to draw in foreign capital and expertise, the government is expected to increase the cap on foreign ownership in domestic banks by an institutional investor from 10% to 15%, and up to 20% for strategic investors, as well as allow more than 30% total foreign ownership in weak banks undergoing restructuring.

Plans for broader financial sector reform include the development of the bond market over the medium term as outlined in a government blueprint in February 2013. Policy actions will involve establishing credit rating agencies, a benchmark yield curve, a primary dealer system, and a legal framework to encourage investment in government bonds by voluntary pension funds and insurance companies. The government aims to increase the value of bonds outstanding from 18% of GDP in 2011 to 38% in 2020 and to raise the percentage of bonds held outside banks from 12% to 20% in that period.

As for the SOE sector, the government has committed to issuing a road map for reform by mid-2013. Implementation will require interagency coordination as SOE reform cuts across the mandates of several ministries. Restructuring plans have been approved for 24 large SOEs, and more such plans are expected, including equitization or partial privatizations through share offerings if market conditions allow. Equitization has slowed in recent years (Figure 3.31.12). One goal is to divest SOEs' noncore businesses by 2015, as many SOEs have accrued debts by investing in areas unrelated to their core businesses. The absence of an overarching regulatory framework for SOE reform could put at risk the implementation of restructuring plans developed through an ad hoc approach. For example, support for SOE restructuring will be difficult to muster until programs are put in place to support and retrain workers displaced during the shakeup of state firms.

Despite these concerns, Viet Nam has remained an attractive investment destination in light of its growing working-age population and low labor costs. This is illustrated by an increase in FDI from Japan. Nevertheless, the country faces increased competition for FDI in Southeast Asia, particularly from Indonesia (Figure 3.31.13). Viet Nam's ability to remain competitive and drive economic growth back up to 7%–8% will depend in large part on the timely and decisive implementation of structural reforms to the banking and SOE sectors and the improvement of other aspects of the business environment.

Indicating the extent of this challenge, Viet Nam's ranking in the World Economic Forum's *Global Competitiveness Report 2012–2013* fell by 16 places in the past 2 years to 75th of 144 countries (Table 3.31.2). That puts it below other larger Southeast Asian economies. Viet Nam scored poorly on several index components, including infrastructure (95), business sophistication (100), respect for property rights (113), irregular payments and bribes (118), and soundness of banks (125). The World

3.31.1 Selected economic indicators (%)

	2013	2014
GDP growth	5.2	5.6
Inflation	7.5	8.2
Current account balance (share of GDP)	6.9	5.6

Source: ADB estimates.

3.31.12 Number of equitized state-owned enterprises

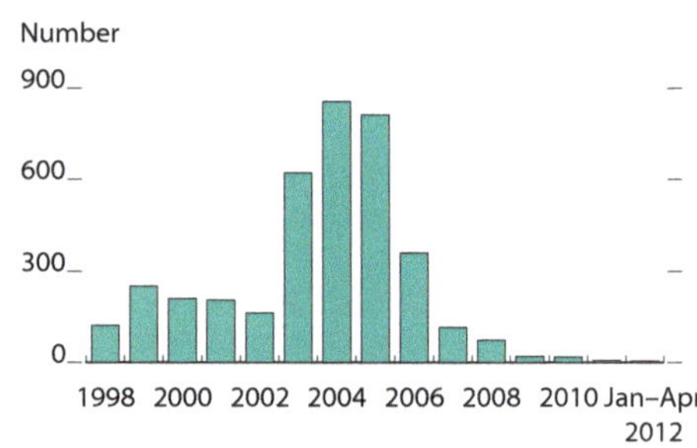

Sources: Ministry of Finance; ADB estimates.

Click here for figure data

3.31.13 Foreign direct investment from Japan

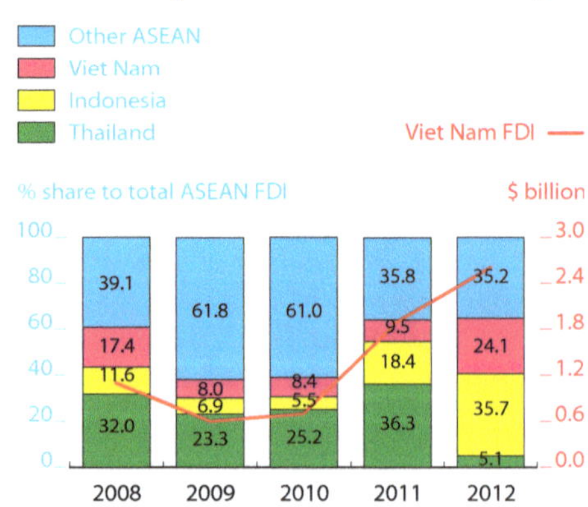

ASEAN = Association of Southeast Asian Nations, FDI = foreign direct investment.

Sources: Japan External Trade Organization; ADB estimates.

Click here for figure data

Economic Forum report noted that the country's relative strengths are its labor market (ranking 51) and large domestic market (32).

3.31.2 *Global Competitiveness Report, 2012–2013* rankings

	Rank
Singapore	1
Malaysia	25
Brunei Darussalam	28
China, People's Rep. of	29
Thailand	38
Indonesia	50
India	59
Philippines	65
Viet Nam	75
Cambodia	85

Source: World Economic Forum. http://www.weforum.org

Policy challenge—wastewater threat to water resources

Less than 10% of urban wastewater in Viet Nam is treated adequately. Most urban households use poorly maintained septic tanks or similar on-site systems that only partly treat sewage and can pollute freshwater resources. A study of water resources in 2009 found that the safety of water supplies in several river basins was at risk from the discharge of untreated and partly treated wastewater, including domestic sewage and industrial wastewater.

A rapidly growing urban population means the government will need to invest substantial amounts in wastewater collection and treatment to protect public health and guard against the pollution of freshwater resources. The government aims to connect 70% of the urban population, or about 35 million people, to central wastewater collection and treatment systems by 2025. Currently, only about 2.5 million people are centrally connected. The average per capita cost to connect to a new wastewater system with adequate treatment is \$200–\$600, suggesting the government will need to invest \$6.4 billion–\$20.0 billion over 12 years to meet its target (Figure 3.31.14).

Responsibility for urban infrastructure rests with local governments, but most do not have the financial or technical capacity to manage the scale, complexity, and cost of urban environment programs. Many wastewater utilities are not fully prepared to operate on commercial principles and attract private sector financing and expertise. Neither do they have access to capital markets. A sustained capacity-building effort is therefore required to implement urban wastewater management systems on a large scale.

While new wastewater treatment facilities have been constructed, a recent performance review found that legislation and regulations governing these projects need to be amended to ensure limited financial resources are directed to high-priority areas. Some investments were misdirected to unnecessarily costly treatment options or systems with high energy requirements. Local implementation of new sewer systems has on occasion resulted in poor coverage and failure to improve public health or the environment.

Looking further ahead, the government could supplement public funds by attracting private investment into wastewater management. This would require clarity on asset ownership, reliable information on existing infrastructure, clear assignment of responsibility for operation and maintenance, accounts and procedures that are consistent with international standards, and the timely imposition and enforcement of water and wastewater tariff increases to ensure at least cost recovery.

3.31.14 Urban population connected to wastewater system

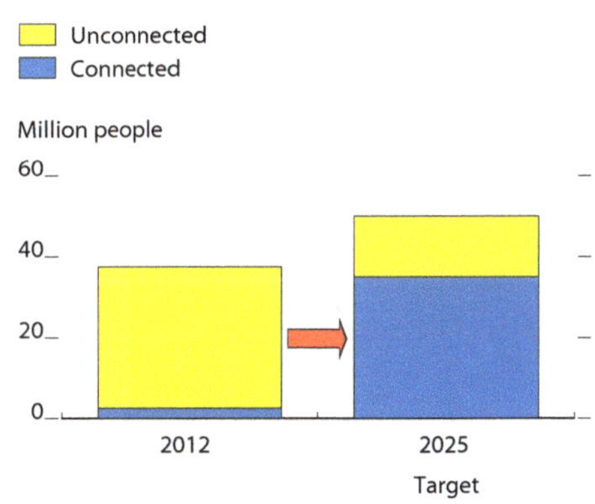

Source: ADB estimates.
Click here for figure data

The Pacific

Fiji
Papua New Guinea
Solomon Islands
Timor-Leste
North Pacific economies
South Pacific economies
Small island economies

Fiji

Stronger consumption and investment demand underpinned higher growth in 2012, despite the adverse impacts of three natural disasters and continuing weak global demand. Near-term growth is expected to be driven by tourism and public infrastructure investments. Longer-term economic prospects are likely to be influenced by political as well as economic developments.

Economic performance

According to the latest official estimate included in the 2013 budget, GDP growth rose to 2.5% in 2012 from 1.9% in the previous year as consumption demand strengthened (Figure 3.32.1). The Reserve Bank of Fiji, the central bank, reported that new consumption lending increased by 25.4% last year. Net value-added tax collection increased by 4.9% in real terms, reflecting higher consumption expenditure prompted by lower tax and interest rates. Lending for investment also increased, by 28.1%, according to the central bank. Increased loans to borrowers in real estate, tourism, and building and construction fueled the rise. Imports of capital goods showed an increase of 8.8% in the first 11 months of 2012. Sales of cement also trended upward over the year on the back of higher government capital spending.

However, the performance of some key sectors deteriorated during the year. Some agricultural output in 2012 was lost to flooding in January and March. Production of sugar, the country's primary agricultural export, fell by 7.1% during the year (Figure 3.32.2). Cyclone Evan caused damage estimated at $42 million, equal to 1% of GDP. Just under half of this loss was to agriculture outside of sugar. Despite the start of bauxite production in Naiwalevu, mining remained weak and the production of gold, Fiji's primary mineral resource, fell by 8%. Tourist arrivals declined by 2.1% relative to 2011, at least in part because of successive floods early in the year, with arrivals from Australia being down modestly (Figure 3.32.3). In December, flight cancellations caused by the cyclone drove down departures to Fiji that month from Australia and New Zealand—the two main markets—by 11% and 16%, respectively, year on year. Given these late developments, the official 2012 GDP growth estimate is likely to be revised downward, particularly when flow-through effects on other sectors are fully taken into account.

In 2012, inflation ran at 4.3%—less than half of the rate in 2011 (Figure 3.32.4). Floods in January and March disrupted the supply of locally produced fruits and vegetables, fueling higher inflation early in the year. Inflation then fell gradually as commodity prices stabilized.

This chapter was written by Caroline Currie of the South Pacific Subregional Office, ADB, Suva.

3.32.1 GDP growth

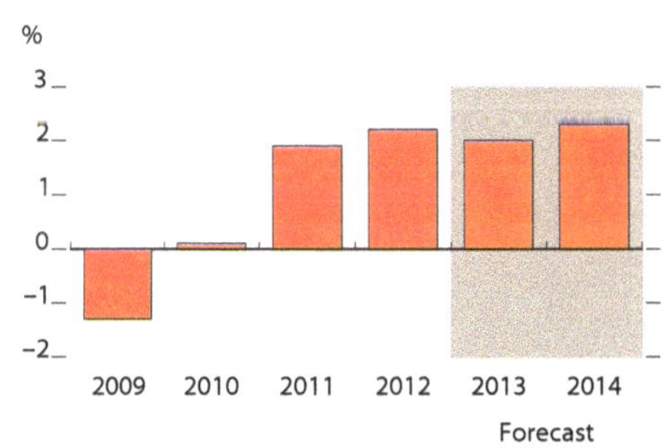

Sources: Fiji Bureau of Statistics; ADB estimates.
Click here for figure data

3.32.2 Sugar production

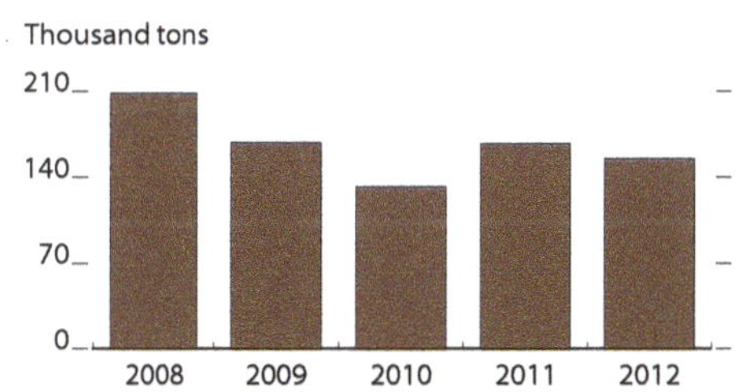

Source: Fiji Ministry of Finance. *Economic and Fiscal Update: Supplement to the 2013 Budget Address.*
Click here for figure data

3.32.3 Visitor arrivals

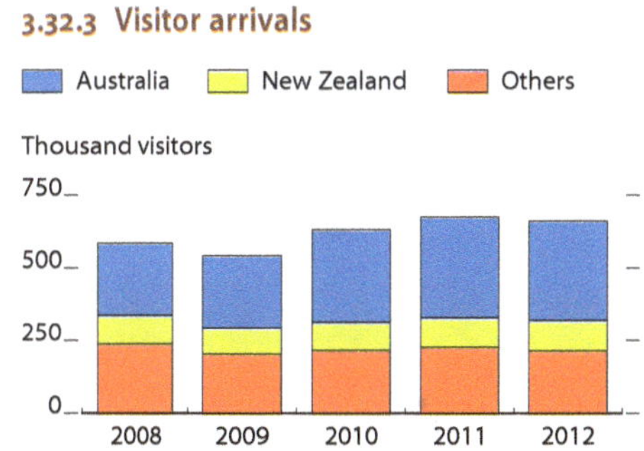

Sources: Reserve Bank of Fiji; ADB estimates.
Click here for figure data

Fiji's net budget deficit in 2012, excluding principal repayments on loans, was estimated to be equivalent to 1.6% of GDP. This was larger than the 1.4% of GDP recorded in the previous year, but on-target expenditure and unexpectedly high revenue collections—particularly corporate taxes following the adoption of an advance tax payment system for companies—brought the deficit down to below the target of 1.9% of GDP.

The central bank maintained an expansionary monetary policy, keeping its overnight policy rate at 0.5%, which it has maintained since October 2011. This contributed to low interest rates on loans and time deposits at commercial banks and kept liquidity high. In 2012, commercial banks' outstanding loans increased by 7.6% year on year. The central bank also loosened exchange rate controls in response to rising foreign reserves. Nonetheless, at the end of 2012, foreign reserves totaled $922 million, sufficient to cover 5.2 months of imports, up from 5.0 months in December 2011.

The 2013 budget reports Fiji's current account deficit as narrowing to 6.1% of GDP in 2012 from 7.0% in 2011. However, the actual current account deficit may widen because of a higher trade deficit late in the year reflecting lower sugar and gold export earnings, as well as lower tourism receipts. Merchandise exports, including re-exports, grew by only 5.1%, far short of the forecast 12.3%. Import growth estimates for 2012 have been revised upward to 5.4% from 4.7%.

3.32.4 Inflation

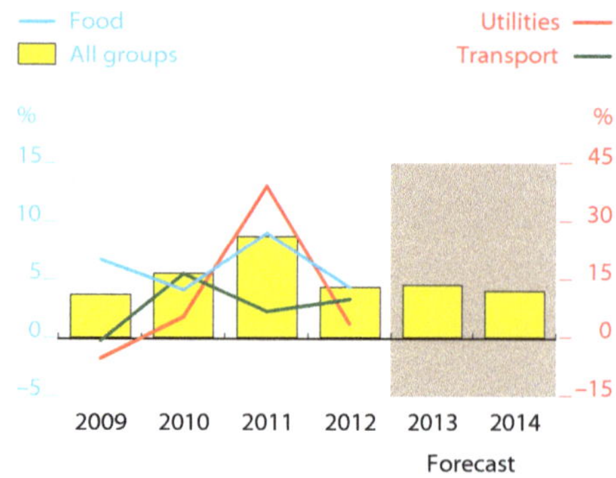

Sources: Fiji Bureau of Statistics; ADB estimates.

Click here for figure data

Economic prospects

Fiji's economy is forecast to grow by 2.0% in 2013, driven mainly by tourism and higher public capital expenditure. The increased public capital expenditure will focus on constructing new transport infrastructure, valued at more than $225 million, and infrastructure rehabilitation.

Consumption expenditure is expected to strengthen further in 2013, propelled by improved household disposable income from lower personal income tax rates, and the implementation of a 10% wage increase for public employees earning below F$10,000 per annum. Rising investment is expected to tighten the labor market and spur higher consumption. Investment is expected to reach 25% of GDP in 2013, up from 18% in 2012. The size of the investment expansion will raise fiscal risks and further stretch public fiscal resources.

Higher consumption, combined with public infrastructure work, election-related expenditure, and continued expansion in tourism in line with an improving global economy, support a prediction of growth rising to 2.3% in 2014.

Supply disruptions caused by Cyclone Evan are expected to accelerate inflation in 2013, particularly early in the year. Full-year average inflation is projected at 4.5%, as planned increases in capital spending push up prices, slowing to 4% in 2014 in line with declining international food and fuel prices.

Fiji's 2013 budget projects a net deficit equivalent to 2.8% of GDP, wider than the 1.6% recorded in 2012 (Figure 3.32.5). The government plans expansionary fiscal policy this year, with capital expenditure increasing to 32% of total spending, up from 29% in the previous year, to improve roads, water supply and sanitation, and information and communication

3.32.1 Selected economic indicators (%)

	2013	2014
GDP growth	2.0	2.3
Inflation	4.5	4.0
Current account balance (share of GDP)	–22.5	–7.0

Source: ADB estimates.

3.32.5 Net budget deficit

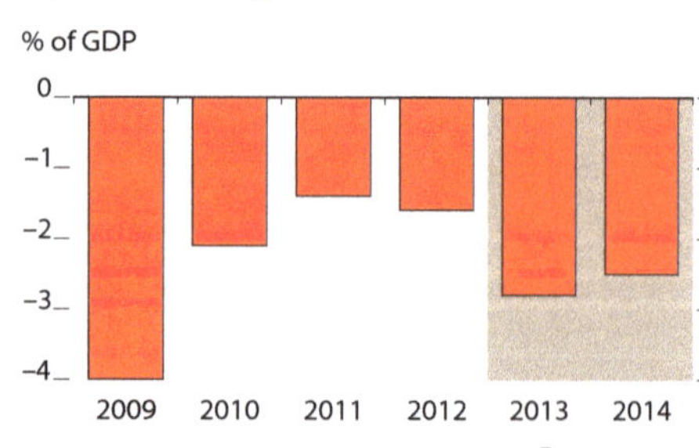

Source: Fiji Ministry of Finance. *Economic and Fiscal Update: Supplement to the 2013 Budget Address.*

Click here for figure data

technology infrastructure. This will entail deficit spending financed with domestic borrowing and loans from the export–import banks of the People's Republic of China and Malaysia. It will further tax the government's capacity to implement multiple projects.

The central bank plans to keep interest rates low to support domestic economic growth. The current account deficit is projected to widen to 22.5% of GDP in 2013 on the back of worsening terms of trade. Imports are expected to increase substantially as the national airline buys three new Airbus A330 aircraft this year, hoping to improve fuel efficiency, cargo capacity, and ultimately profitability. These developments are likely to put pressure on the country's foreign reserves.

Policy challenge—reinvigorating private sector growth

The current business regulatory environment and political uncertainty continue to weigh on Fiji's growth prospects. Barriers to higher growth include limited fiscal flexibility under current debt levels, challenging business and political environments, and a longstanding need for structural reform, particularly in the sugar sector.

The budget deficit could be larger than expected if economic growth below the government assumption of 2.7% reduces government revenues. Planned sales of government real estate to the Fiji National Provident Fund (FNPF) help finance the government's projected deficit. A larger deficit could prompt the expanded use of FNPF resources to finance it, which could raise concerns about the fund's long-term sustainability. Public debt is relatively high at 50.4% of GDP, about three-quarters of it in the form of government bond purchases by the FNPF (Figure 3.32.6).

Despite significant investment in recent years, the outlook for Fiji's sugar industry remains uncertain. The government's planned purchase of equipment to mechanize production and improve its efficiency may be insufficient to overcome the challenges the industry faces trying to compete internationally. Sugar production and its supply chain need deeper structural adjustment, the list of needs headlined by land tenure reform and an improved business environment. Such reforms would help revive the sugar industry and stimulate broader private sector development.

While new investments and signs of greater interest from investors are encouraging, the political situation will affect how much new foreign investment is realized. The process leading up to national elections scheduled in 2014 and the credibility of election results will be important determinants of Fiji's future economic performance. If a new democratically elected government is installed in a process that is acceptable domestically and internationally, renewed business confidence and development partner reengagement should follow. This would help harness the country's rich resource base and its natural position as a regional hub for the Pacific, shifting Fiji onto a higher growth path.

3.32.6 Public debt

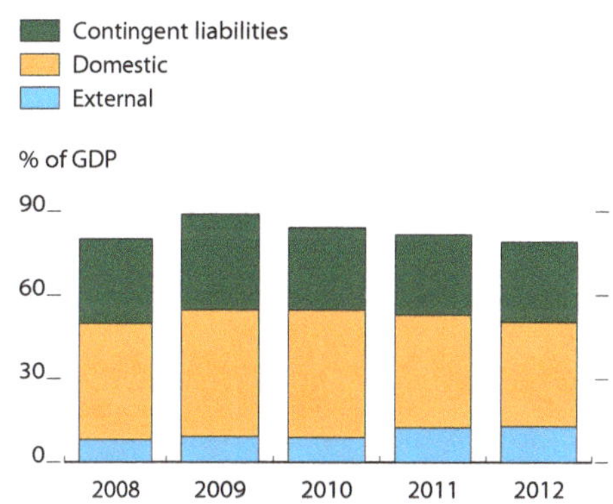

Source: Fiji Ministry of Finance. *Economic and Fiscal Update: Supplement to the 2013 Budget Address.*

Click here for figure data

Papua New Guinea

Growth in 2013 is expected to slow considerably as the construction of a liquefied natural gas project winds down. Deficit spending will offset some of this slowdown, but future spending growth must be contained to maintain macroeconomic stability. With growth increasingly dominated by mining and gas, a challenge for the government will be to stimulate other sectors offering more jobs and higher investment in the country's abundant renewable energy resources.

Economic performance

The largest developing economy in the Pacific maintained its position as one of the fastest-growing economies in Asia and the Pacific in 2012, with economic growth of 9.2%. Construction was the strongest performer, contributing 4.5 percentage points to growth, or nearly half of the outcome. Transport, finance, and retail trade added a further 2.8 percentage points on the strength of domestic demand created by the peak construction period of a new liquefied natural gas (LNG) project and government expenditure that was higher than expected. Mining output recovered from weather and technical disruptions experienced in 2011, adding a modest 0.3 percentage points to overall growth in 2012. Dragging on growth was falling oil output as reserves declined. Growth in agriculture, forestry, and fisheries output also slowed as the sector expanded by only 0.2% in 2012, down from 8.1% in 2011. Adding to this outcome were poorer growing conditions and moderating export prices, which depressed coffee, copra, and cocoa output. New investment in processing mills helped to support palm oil production (Figure 3.33.1).

The current account deficit grew to 17.5% of GDP in 2012 (Figure 3.33.2). This reflected moderation in agriculture and mining exports and higher imports tied to the construction of the LNG project. With rising imports financed largely by foreign direct investment, the large current account deficit poses little risk to macroeconomic stability. The central bank's foreign exchange reserves remained at near record highs throughout the year. At over $4 billion, reserves were sufficient to cover 11 months of imports.

The headline inflation rate fell to 4.1% in 2012, down from 8.5% in 2011 (though the outdated consumer price index basket likely underestimates inflation). Contributing to this official outcome was a significant rise in the value of the local currency due mostly to large inflows of foreign direct investment, which saw the exchange rate rise by 16% relative to the major import partners of Papua New Guinea (PNG). A higher exchange rate, declining commodity prices, and the government's ongoing tariff-reduction program reduced prices for tradable goods by 0.2%. Lower

3.33.1 Supply-side contributions to growth

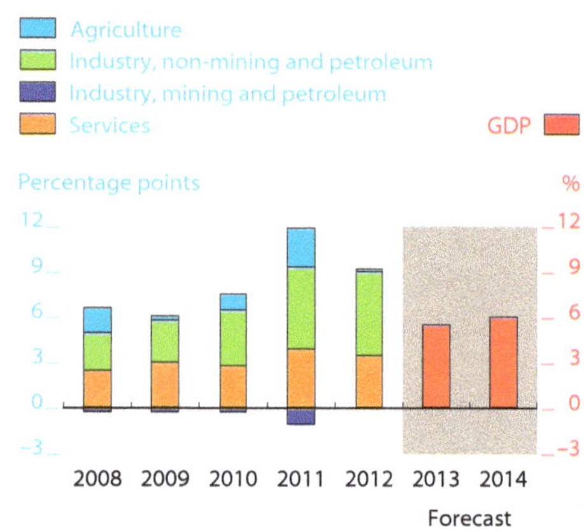

Sources: PNG Department of Treasury. 2012. *2013 National Budget*. December; ADB estimates.

Click here for figure data

3.33.2 Current account components

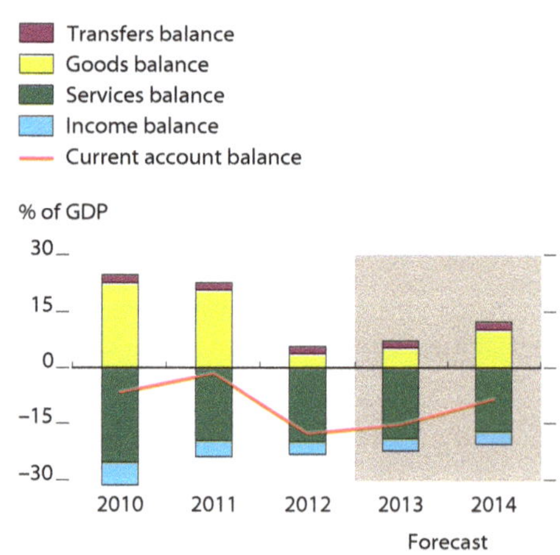

Sources: PNG Department of Treasury. 2012. *2013 National Budget*. December; ADB estimates.

Click here for figure data

This chapter was written by Aaron Batten of the Papua New Guinea Resident Mission, ADB, Port Moresby.

import prices late in the year flowed through to non-tradable or domestic inflation, causing it to slow to 4.2% in 2012 (Figure 3.33.3). Rising domestic prices were mostly attributable to locally produced meat, alcohol, and tobacco, as well as transport costs.

The budget outcome in 2012 was a deficit of 1.2% of GDP against an original forecast of a balanced budget (Figure 3.33.4). This reflected lower-than-expected revenue caused by unanticipated declines in international commodity prices, an appreciating currency that depressed the value in PNG kina of mining and petroleum taxes denominated in US dollars, and higher spending mainly related to national elections.

In response to lower inflation, the central bank lowered its target interest rate from 7.75% to 6.75% in September 2012, signaling easing monetary policy intentions. However, with the central bank unable to fully absorb the high liquidity in the commercial banking system, the impact of target interest rate movements on market interest rates and inflation continued to be limited. Private sector credit growth remained near 10% per annum during 2012, well off its peak of 40% in 2007 (Figure 3.33.5).

3.33.3 Inflation

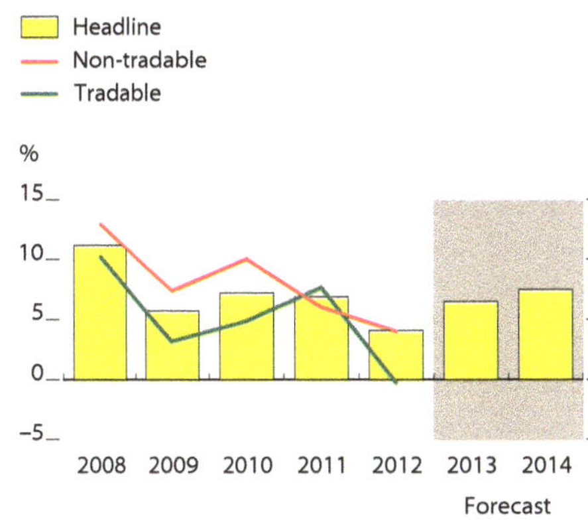

Sources: Bank of Papua New Guinea. http://www.bankpng.gov.pg (accessed 20 February 2013); ADB estimates.
Click here for figure data

Economic prospects

Economic growth is expected to slow to 5.5% in 2013 before picking up again to 6.0% in 2014. The non-mineral economy is expected to slow most sharply as the winding down of LNG project construction will dramatically curtail construction and transport activity, eventually spilling over into lower domestic consumption and retail and wholesale trade. Moderating international agricultural prices are expected to depress rural incomes derived from the sale of crops for export. A significantly increased national budget, which plans for large budget deficits of 7.2% of GDP in 2013 and 5.9% in 2014, will counter some of the effects of falling domestic demand on the non-mineral economy.

The mineral sector is expected to lead growth, expanding by 13.0% in 2013 as production bottlenecks clear at a number of gold and copper mines and production at the new Ramu nickel and cobalt mine ramps up. Continued declines in petroleum production, as reserves in major oil fields become depleted, will offset some of this growth in 2013, but the onset of LNG exports will greatly boost mineral output late in 2014, with overall growth in the sector expected to surpass 60% in that year.

In 2013, an expected easing of the kina exchange rate could fuel resurgence in imported inflation, while high government spending is likely to stoke domestic inflation. The winding down of LNG plant construction will be a counterinfluence subduing price growth later in 2013 and throughout 2014. This period will see up to 8,000 workers demobilized, easing a shortage of skilled labor and other private sector capacity constraints, particularly in construction and transport. Declining capital imports associated with the LNG project will relieve port congestion. On balance, inflation is projected to bounce back to 6.5% in 2013 and 7.5% in 2014.

The 2013 current account deficit is expected to narrow to 15.1% of GDP as lower LNG capital imports reduce the trade deficit. A rebound in production at existing mines and the ramping up of production at the

3.33.4 Budget balance

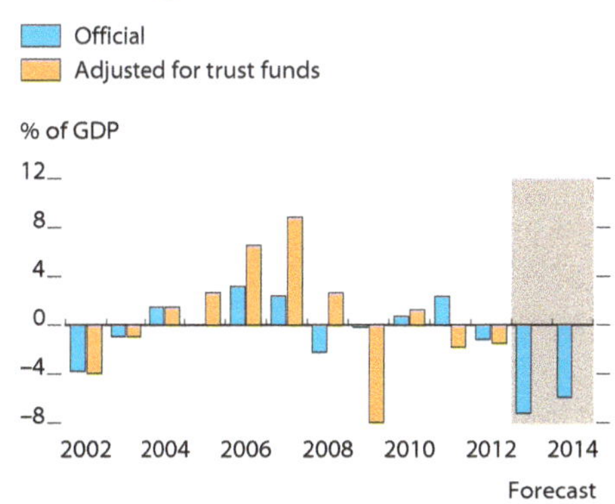

Sources: PNG Department of Treasury. 2012. *2013 National Budget*. December; ADB estimates.
Click here for figure data

3.33.5 Private sector credit growth and bank lending margin

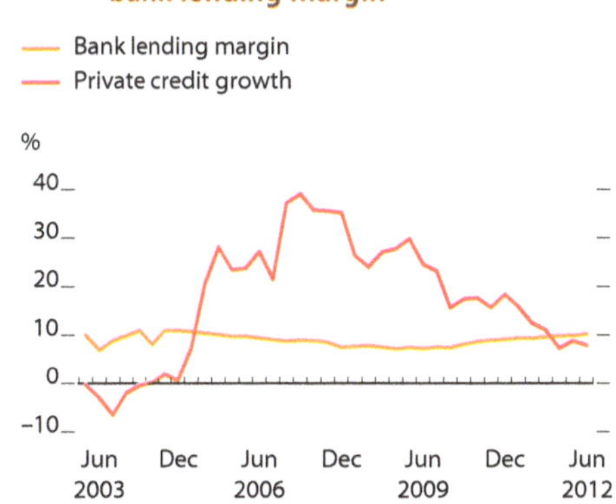

Source: Bank of Papua New Guinea. http://www.bankpng.gov.pg (accessed 20 February 2013).
Click here for figure data

Ramu facility will help boost export earnings. A further narrowing of the current account deficit to 8.4% of GDP is expected in 2014 as LNG exports begin.

Although large budget deficits are planned for 2013 and 2014, public debt is expected to remain low by historical standards, peaking at 35% of GDP in 2014. While such public indebtedness is moderate, PNG will need to ensure that higher spending does not undermine the fiscal buffers that have allowed it to withstand recent shocks (Figure 3.33.6).

Foremost is the need for spending to remain in line with the government's own deficit-reduction plan. To keep public debt below 35% of GDP, the 2013 budget plans for zero nominal growth in government wages and salaries and just 2.5% annual growth in spending on goods and services up to 2017. Such recurrent expenditure restraint will be difficult to achieve and risks starving service delivery by, for example, undercutting salaries for teachers and health workers. The government may therefore need to reprioritize spending away from capital investment and toward recurrent goods and services to ensure service delivery within designated spending limits.

The government faces growing challenges in financing its deficit spending. While domestic bank liquidity remains high, local commercial banks are approaching regulatory limits on their lending to the government. A result will likely be deficit financing sourced from international markets in 2013 and 2014, significantly increasing the government's cost of borrowing and exposure to exchange rate risk.

Fiscal risks arising from the budget must be better coordinated with those generated separately. The reduction in public debt over the past decade has been offset by a rise in off-budget liabilities, which now equal 15%–20% of GDP. Major components include borrowing to finance the state's equity in the LNG project, large unfunded superannuation liabilities, and contingent liabilities surrounding the successful completion of the LNG project. Progressively reducing these state liabilities will be important to taming fiscal risks.

In the medium-term, the outlook for growth remains strong and for public debt to remain low. While government plans to increase investment in critical national infrastructure and social services are commendable, this priority must be balanced against its need to maintain fiscal buffers against future shocks. Building up the country's economic resilience will be vital to avoiding any reprise of past boom–bust cycles.

Policy challenge—realizing energy potential and fostering employment growth

The last decade has witnessed dramatic growth in job creation, with the number of jobs in the formal private sector expanding by 70% since 2002. Underpinning this achievement has been broad-based growth across the non-mineral economy, with finance, retail and wholesale trade, transport, manufacturing, and construction all contributing strongly to employment (Figure 3.33.7).

As labor-intensive construction of the LNG project draws to a close and gas production begins in 2014, the main engine of growth will shift

3.33.1 Selected economic indicators (%)

	2013	2014
GDP growth	5.5	6.0
Inflation	6.5	7.5
Current account balance (share of GDP)	–15.1	–8.4

Source: ADB estimates.

3.33.6 Public debt sources

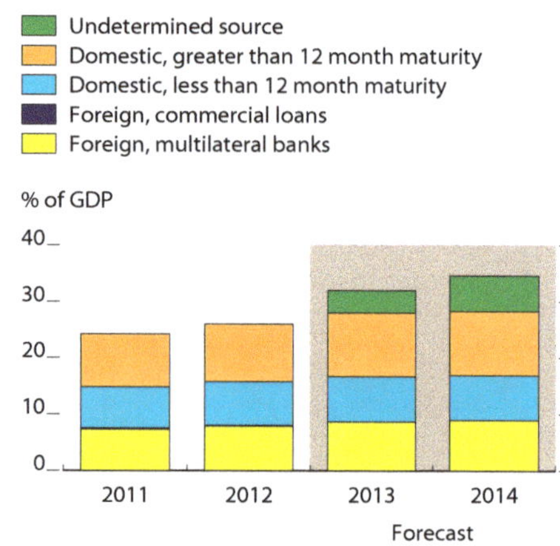

Sources: PNG Department of Treasury. 2012. *2013 National Budget*. December; ADB estimates.

Click here for figure data

3.33.7 Non-mineral GDP and employment growth

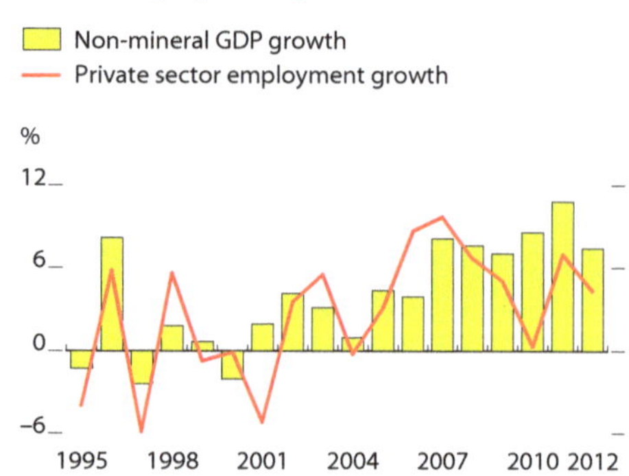

Sources: Bank of Papua New Guinea. http://www.bankpng.gov.pg (accessed 20 February 2013); PNG Department of Treasury. 2012. *2013 National Budget*. December.

Click here for figure data

toward mineral exports and away from the non-mineral economy. Unless new sources of non-mineral growth can be mobilized, private sector employment growth is likely to slow, potentially eroding inclusiveness in the country's economic prospects.

Central to meeting this challenge will be the government's ability to address structural constraints that discourage higher investment in the non-mineral economy. One critical constraint is the worsening adequacy of infrastructure for energy supply and distribution, which is now a major barrier to productivity, output, and employment growth, as well as to improving the welfare of the poor. Power outages are frequent, forcing many businesses to invest in generators instead of new machinery and technology. Schools and hospitals are unable to function efficiently, while the 11% household electrification rate leaves the overwhelming majority in the dark and without common appliances. As most private power is generated using diesel or gasoline, the portion of all electricity generated by hydropower fell from 76% in 1994 to 59% in 2011. This significantly raised the average cost of power production and nation's admirably low carbon emissions.

PNG has abundant energy resources. In addition to natural gas, it enjoys high rainfall over rugged mountains, but less than 5% of its hydropower potential is currently developed. Unlocking this potential will require the government to address a number of challenges through a coordinated policy response. For urban centers, PNG needs to upgrade deteriorating generation and distribution infrastructure while developing a more transparent and clearly defined access regime able to attract private investment. Promoting energy access in rural and remote areas presents additional challenges, as low population density raises supply costs. Current regulatory arrangements pose daunting disincentives for investment in new rural electricity infrastructure, as revenues tend to be insufficient to cover capital and maintenance costs. Achieving widespread rural electrification will thus require implementing a policy that entails community service obligations, clearly quantifies the cost of providing power in areas where cost recovery from the community is impossible, and compensates energy providers accordingly, be they private or public.

Focusing on reform priorities will be key to unlocking the vast potential for energy projects in PNG, expanding access to electricity in remote communities, and creating a business environment that can speed growth in the non-mineral economy, employment creation, and poverty reduction.

Solomon Islands

Growth moderated but remained strong in 2012, driven by ramped up mining activity. Further moderation in growth is expected over the next 2 years as forestry resources dwindle. To offset the decline of logging, the country needs to further develop other industries and revenue sources, as well as control the growth of government expenditure.

Economic performance

Growth slowed to 5.5% in 2012, from 10.6% in the previous year (Figure 3.34.1). The deceleration mainly reflected a much smaller increase in forestry sector output than in recent years. Logging provides 16% of output but, having reached record levels, grew by only 0.5% in 2012, compared with annual increases of around 36% in the previous 2 years (Figure 3.34.2). Agricultural output fell in 2012 with the production of cocoa falling by 33% and copra by 19% because of sluggish demand overseas. Palm oil and fisheries recorded small increases in production.

Industry (mostly mining, manufacturing, and construction) and services (mostly trade, transport, and communications) drove growth in 2012. Gold production from the Gold Ridge mine ramped up, and exports were 2.4 times higher in 2012 than in 2011. Solomon Islands' hosting of the Festival of Pacific Arts and higher foreign direct investment helped fuel growth outside of mining.

After a current account deficit in 2011 equivalent to 8% of GDP, the deficit for 2012 is estimated at 6% of GDP, as higher grants from development partners offset declines in export revenues (Figure 3.34.3). The country has seen a significant rise in its foreign reserves, bolstered by large inflows of grants and foreign direct investment. Higher fishing license revenues were also a significant source of foreign currency inflows in 2012. Foreign exchange reserves equaled 10.4 months of imports in December 2012, up from 8.9 months in December 2011.

Inflation declined from 7.4% in 2011 to 5.9% in 2012 because of slower economic growth, the revaluation of the domestic currency, and the Central Bank of Solomon Islands mopping up liquidity (Figure 3.34.4). In October 2012, the central bank replaced the Solomon Islands dollar peg to the US dollar with a peg to a basket of currencies. This was to enable the Solomon Islands dollar to respond more flexibly to market fluctuations.

The government incurred a fiscal deficit equivalent to 1.9% of GDP in 2012, reversing a surplus equivalent to 5.1% of GDP in 2011. It financed the deficit by running down fiscal reserves that had been built up as a buffer

3.34.1 GDP growth

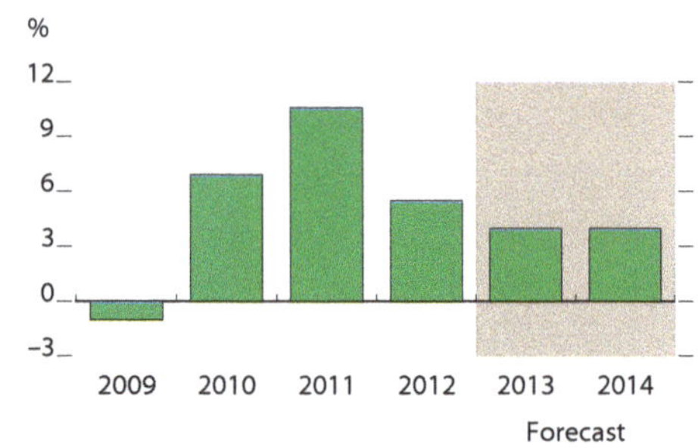

Sources: Central Bank of Solomon Islands; ADB estimates.

Click here for figure data

3.34.2 Log exports

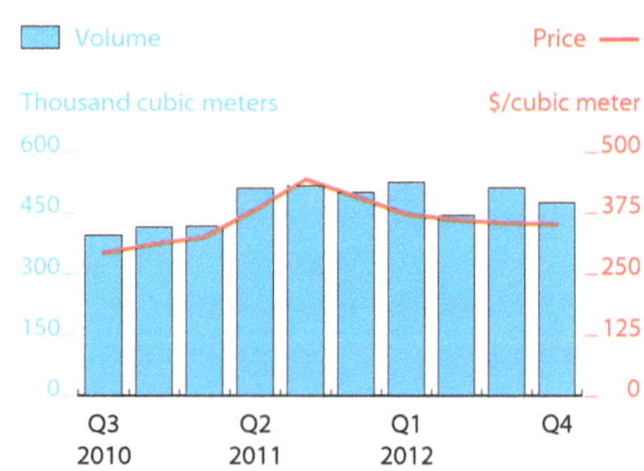

Sources: Central Bank of Solomon Islands; World Bank. Commodity Price Data (Pink Sheet). http://econ.worldbank.org (accessed 15 March 2013).

Click here for figure data

This chapter was written by Milovan Lucich of the Pacific Liaison and Coordination Office, ADB, Sydney.

against volatile revenue flows. The deficit reflected both lower revenues and increased spending. Revenue in 2012 increased by 17% over 2011 in line with strong nominal GDP growth, but this was less than the government budgeted, as lost revenues from doubling the income at which personal taxes are levied were higher than expected. Rises in spending were related to hosting the Festival of Pacific Arts—whose cost equaled 2.5% of GDP—and increasing constituency funds paid to members of Parliament, which have doubled in recent years to 4% of GDP.

Public debt continued to fall from the equivalent of 19% of GDP in 2011 to 15% in 2012 (Figure 3.34.5). The country resumed concessional borrowing in 2012 to finance the sovereign component of the Broadband for Development Project, which will connect the country to an undersea fiber optic cable.

Economic prospects

Growth is expected to slow further, to 4%, in 2013. Although agricultural production and gold output are projected to increase, log production is seen to decline. A scaling up of gold mining is expected as the Gold Ridge mine reaches full production capacity of 95,000 ounces per year, up from 79,400 ounces in 2012.

The Regional Assistance Mission to Solomon Islands will start to wind down in 2013 and thereafter focus largely on building the capacity of the Royal Solomon Islands Police Force. The mission's military component will be withdrawn from mid-2013 as the country transitions from post-conflict and crisis recovery to sustainable development based on the National Development Strategy, 2011–2020. The mission has also been a major development partner, but the effect of withdrawal on the economy will be minimized by transferring its development activities to the programs of other development partners, in particular Australia and New Zealand.

In 2014, growth is projected to remain at 4% with continued investment in mining and its spillover effects on the economy. Additional investment in telecommunications is expected to harness opportunities created by the broadband project.

Typical price lags in Solomon Islands mean international food price rises from mid-2012 are expected to affect inflation in early 2013 but dissipate by midyear. Over the full year 2013, average inflation is expected to ease to 4.5% as economic growth slows. Similar inflation is expected in 2014, in line with the modest growth forecast for that year.

The 2013 budget marks a return to fiscal consolidation with a balanced budget planned. Expenditure growth has been limited to 7% despite a planned increase in public wages. This compares with an average 22% annual increase in expenditure from 2004 to 2011. Revenue growth is estimated at 8% in 2013, creating a small budget surplus of $100,000—effectively a balanced budget.

The central bank is expected to continue to soak up excess liquidity through the sale of short-term bills. The exchange rate will continue to be managed against a basket of currencies, and the central bank may allow further appreciation if inflation accelerates.

3.34.3 Current account balance

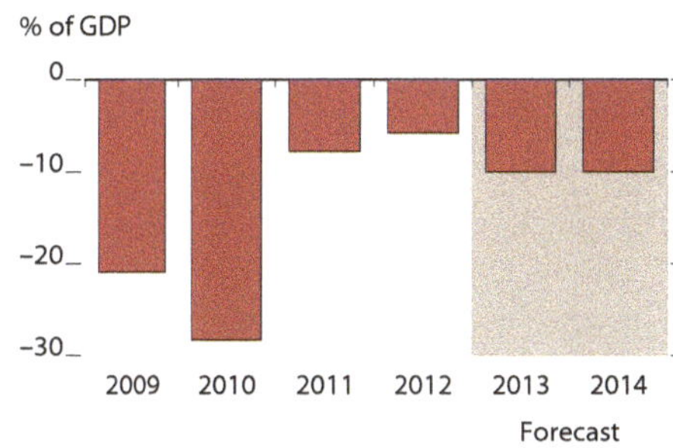

Sources: Central Bank of Solomon Islands; ADB estimates.
Click here for figure data

3.34.4 Inflation

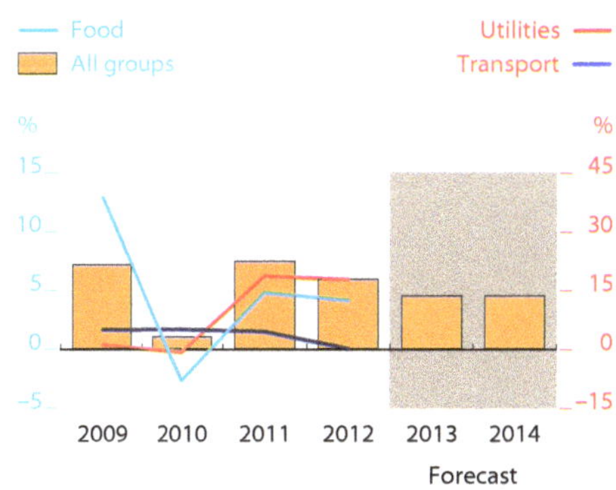

Sources: Central Bank of Solomon Islands; ADB estimates.
Click here for figure data

3.34.5 Public debt

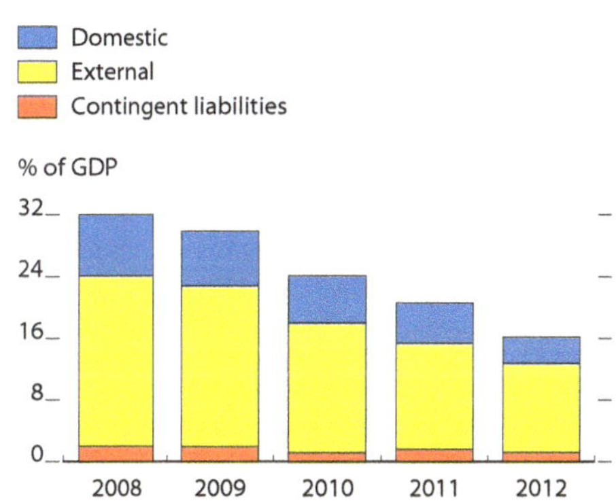

Source: Central Bank of Solomon Islands.
Click here for figure data

The current account deficit is expected to widen slightly to 10% of GDP in 2013, as the logging decline severely depresses export growth, and import growth—driven by construction and mining—remains firm. The deficit will be funded through continued inflows from development partners and foreign direct investment. Import cover is expected to remain comfortable at 7–8 months in 2013 and 2014.

3.34.1 Selected economic indicators (%)

	2013	2014
GDP growth	4.0	4.0
Inflation	4.5	4.5
Current account balance (share of GDP)	–10.0	–10.0

Source: ADB estimates.

Policy challenge—encouraging fiscal sustainability

Logging provides 15% of government revenue, 60% of exports, and 32% of foreign exchange earnings. It is the largest source of formal employment after the government, providing 5,000 jobs. Forests have been extensively exploited, with logging rates reaching several times the sustainable rate in recent years. One study warns that natural forest resources may be exhausted before 2020. A decline in logging would adversely affect the government's finances and require it to identify new sources of revenue, such as a new taxation regime for the mining sector, to support government expenditures.

In addition to developing alternative sources of revenue, the government will need to contain public expenditure growth and improve the quality of public spending. Despite a return to fiscal consolidation in the 2013 budget, the economy continues to face large fiscal risks. Major risks in the budget include the potential for overestimating domestic revenue, a greater-than-expected decline in logging, and expenditure pressures that may arise if the government needs to accommodate a fractious coalition. The large wage and salary bill will remain an ongoing fiscal strain, particularly with the planned increase in public wages, and could displace funding for investment and essential public services if the revenue outcome is lower than expected.

An issue that warrants particular attention is that of constituency development funds. Funds are given directly to members of Parliament for projects in their electoral areas. Amounts have increased substantially in recent years, growing to equal about 4% of GDP, and the use of these funds remains a part of government spending without accountability. The projects financed by these funds are not even enumerated in budgets or medium-term development plans. Capping and monitoring the use of constituency funds would be warranted. A welcome first step to improve the transparency and accountability of these funds is the drafting of a constituency development fund bill. The draft bill provides for establishing constituency development offices to help administer the funds in line with constituency development plans and brings the funds under the Public Finance and Audit Act, making them subject to audit and a complaints mechanism. Strengthening this bill to reduce the discretion available to parliamentarians, together with its passage and implementation, would significantly improve governance and public financial management in Solomon Islands.

Timor-Leste

Economic growth remained high in 2012, buoyed by a large increase in government spending. Growth in double digits is expected to continue in 2013 and 2014 with modest declines due to planned fiscal tightening. Inflation moderated from 2011 but remained above 10%, prompting the government to postpone some infrastructure initiatives. The biggest challenge facing leaders is to effectively channel petroleum revenues into ambitious plans to build infrastructure and human resources while sustaining the Petroleum Fund.

Economic performance

Strong economic growth continued in 2012, with non-oil GDP expanding by 10.6% (Figure 3.35.1). Government spending, particularly on public infrastructure, continued to drive the economy. This spending propelled growth both directly and indirectly through spillover effects on non-oil business investment and demand for the goods and services provided by private businesses. Government expenditure totaled $1.8 billion, up by 64.8% from 2011. The United Nations Mission in Timor-Leste departed at the end of 2012, but this appears to be having little impact on economic activity, as only 1% of GDP was linked to it and government spending has continued to rise.

Inflation in 2012 remained high at an annual average of 10.9% but moderated from 13.1% in 2011 (Figure 3.35.2). This reflected easing world food prices and lower import costs with the strengthening of the US dollar, which Timor-Leste uses as its official currency, against the currencies of some of Timor-Leste's important trade partners. Government spending in the face of persisting bottlenecks and spending linked to the midyear elections countered some of the deflationary impact of these external developments.

Capacity constraints on carrying out infrastructure development plans caused a significant portion of budgeted 2012 expenditures to be postponed amid implementation delays. Nonetheless, the ratio of government expenditures to non-oil GDP reached 192.7% in 2012, surpassing the previous high set in 2011. The largest increase was in capital expenditures, which grew by 78.4% over 2011. The vast majority of this spending went to national electrification. The system is being built to accommodate future electricity demand but currently has excess generating capacity. Despite rising Petroleum Fund returns and overall balance, the rise in spending has necessitated withdrawals from the fund that exceed what the Ministry of Finance estimates can be sustained over the long run.

3.35.1 Supply-side contributions to growth

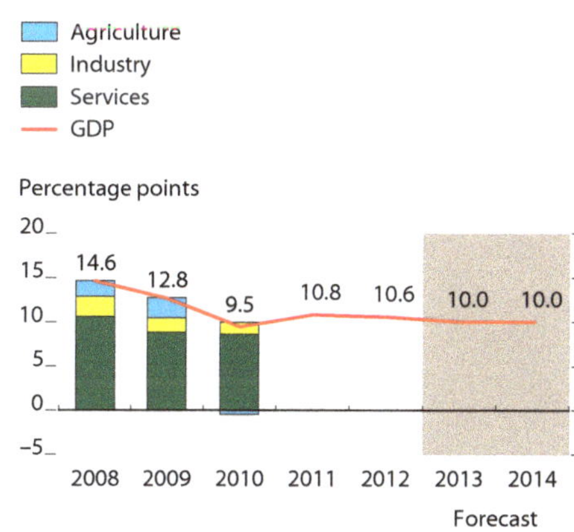

Sources: Timor-Leste National Statistics Directorate; ADB estimates.

Click here for figure data

3.35.2 Inflation

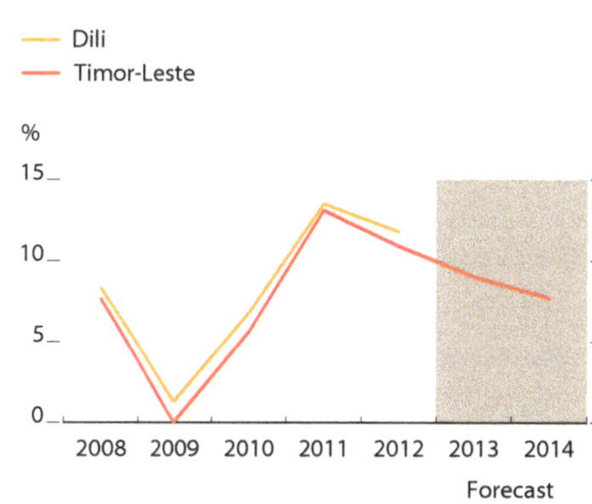

Source: Timor-Leste National Directorate of Statistics.

Click here for figure data

This chapter was written by Christopher Edmonds of the Pacific Department, ADB, Manila.

The government posted another large budget surplus of $1.8 billion, which was about 1.4 times non-oil GDP in 2012. However, the surplus was much smaller than in 2011 when it equaled 2.4 times non-oil GDP. The government received $3.0 billion in income from its oil concessions in 2012, down from $3.5 billion in 2011. As in recent years, these revenues dwarfed the government's domestic revenues of $146 million (Figure 3.35.3). Public savings, defined as the Petroleum Fund plus foreign exchange reserves, are $11.6 billion, which is more than 9 times annual non-oil GDP.

The value of goods and services imported into Timor-Leste in 2012 increased by 15%, but this was much lower than in the previous year, when there were particularly large imports of heavy construction equipment. Nonpetroleum exports, mostly coffee, increased by 10.9% but still covered only 4.4% of the cost of imported goods. The surplus in the income account from petroleum revenue continued to outweigh the wide trade deficit in 2012, providing a current account surplus equivalent to 1.7 times non-oil GDP.

3.35.3 Government revenue

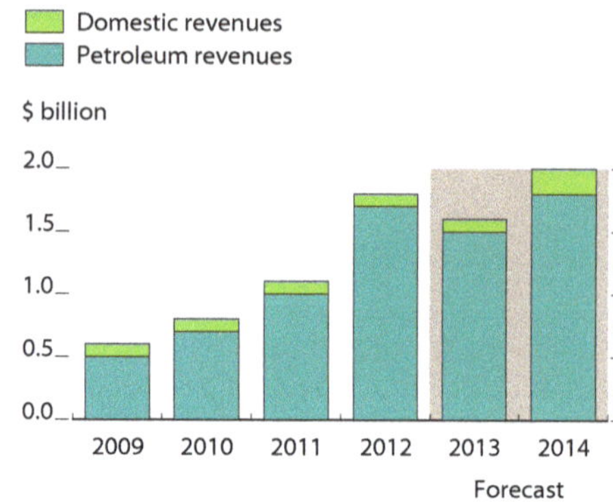

Source: Timor-Leste 2013 state budget.
Click here for figure data

Economic prospects

Strong economic growth is expected to continue in 2013 and 2014, driven largely by government expenditures and more modest rises in investment outside the petroleum sector. Total budgeted expenditures of $1.6 billion make the government's 2013 budget 8.8% lower than in 2012. However, economic growth is projected to continue at about the rate observed in 2012, as the budget, if fully executed, would push actual expenditure up 38% from 2012 actual expenditures. Actual government expenditures have been consistently below budgeted levels in recent years.

High inflation is consistent with the economy's high rate of growth. Inflation is projected to remain high at 9.0% in 2013, but this is lower than in 2012, reflecting some success in the government's efforts to stem inflation. These efforts include postponing planned expenditures on the Tasi Mane project and a new national development bank in 2012. Another factor seen to moderate inflation is the dissipation of inflationary pressures from one-time events that raised prices in 2012, including election-related spending and increased congestion at Dili's international port. Inflation is projected to continue to moderate to 7.7% in 2014, despite planned increases in government spending, as more public infrastructure comes online, supply chain bottlenecks are addressed, and the entry of new businesses increases competition in wholesale and retail markets.

The budget for 2013 has a large increase in government spending to $1.8 billion (Figure 3.35.4), or 200% of non-oil GDP, of which $1.6 billion will come from the Petroleum Fund and other sources of domestic revenue (with the remainder sourced from development partners). Capital expenditure, funded from the multiyear Infrastructure Fund, will remain prominent in the budget, with spending projected to rise to 100% of non-oil GDP. Outlays on the national electrification program are tapering off but will still be $280 million. Expenditure on the Tasi Mane project—intended to trigger development on the south coast—is budgeted at $1.32 billion. The budget also allocates $544 million for road upgrades over the next 5 years. World oil prices are projected to fall slightly in 2013 and 2014, which could reduce Timor-Leste's petroleum revenue and its

3.35.1 Selected economic indicators (%)

	2013	2014
GDP growth	10.0	10.0
Inflation	9.0	7.7
Current account balance (share of GDP)	102.8	66.0

Source: ADB estimates.

3.35.4 Government expenditure

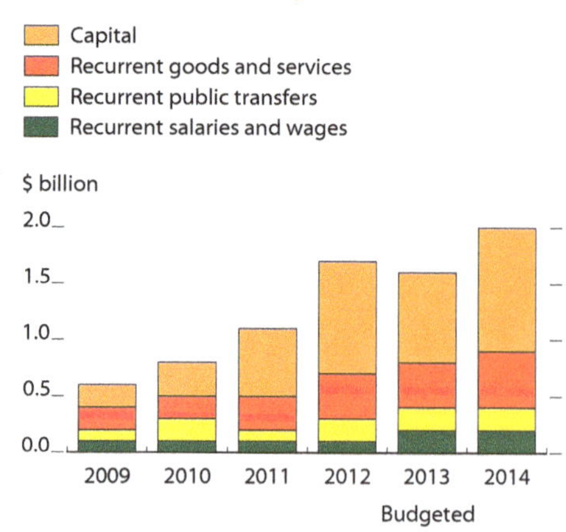

Note: 2009 to 2011 show actual expenditures, 2012 to 2014 show budgeted expenditures.
Source: Timor-Leste 2013 state budget.
Click here for figure data

budget and current account surpluses. Budget surpluses are projected to fall to about 100% of non-oil GDP in 2013 and 50% in 2014. The country's current account surplus is forecasted to fall to just over 100% of non-oil GDP in 2013 and 66% in 2014.

Policy challenge—spreading the benefits of energy exports

Balancing the policy objectives of achieving high economic growth and controlling inflation is an important policy challenge facing Timor-Leste's leaders. Although 2012 saw progress in bringing down inflation, high growth and persistent supply constraints mean inflation remains a concern. Inflation will likely decline in 2013 as some events that drove it in 2012 are unlikely to reoccur. If the US dollar continues to strengthen, that would lower import prices and reduce inflation. However, planned increases in government expenditure in 2014 and beyond are likely to renew price pressure. Measures to address supply constraints, such as developing public infrastructure to address bottlenecks in supply chains and encouraging new businesses to operate in Timor-Leste, offer the most promising avenues for stemming inflation in the long run.

Disagreement between the government and oil companies over tax payments raises concern about the prospects for developing the Greater Sunrise field. How this disagreement is resolved could have important implications for the country's long-term fiscal position. Projected balances in the Petroleum Fund—and the amounts that can be taken out of it to finance development without sacrificing the fund's long-term sustainability—take into account projected petroleum revenues only from areas currently being exploited (Figure 3.35.5). However, the finite nature of the country's petroleum reserves, the sensitivity of revenues to global price fluctuations, and events like the tax payment dispute highlight the need for the government to ensure that fiscal balances are kept in check and that scarce government resources are used efficiently.

The longer-term challenge facing Timor-Leste's leaders is steering the economy away from growth that depends primarily on oil revenues and public sector stimulus, and toward growth in which the private sector plays the lead role. The inaugural Business Activity Survey, covering 2010, illustrates the nascent state of the private sector. The survey confirmed the high concentration of formal sector businesses in Dili, which provide more than 80% of national employment and value added. It showed that retail and wholesale, construction, and accommodation and food service accounted for more than half of national employment and value added (Figure 3.35.6). The long-term prospects for the economy and private sector development are encouraging, as spillover from government spending should create business opportunities and successful past investments should encourage further investment. Economic diversification and private sector development would be fostered by further progress in improving the business environment. The government's One-Stop Shop initiative to simplify procedures for starting a new business, the passage of a public–private partnership framework, and progress toward developing a new law to govern land titles are promising steps.

3.35.5 Withdrawals from the Petroleum Fund

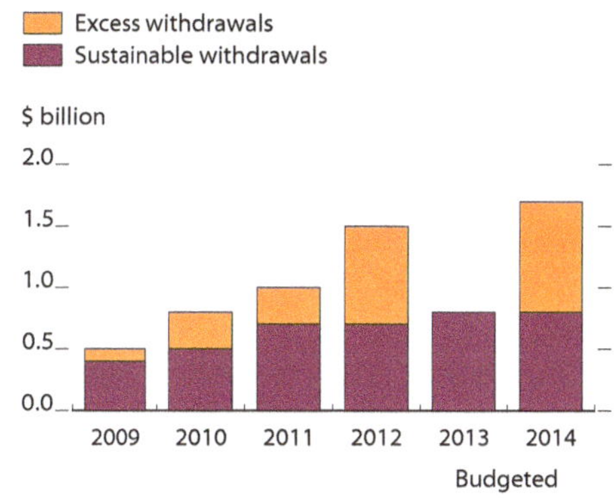

Note: Sustainable withdrawals are defined as the maximum amount that can be appropriated from the Petroleum Fund in a fiscal year and leave sufficient resources in the Petroleum Fund for an amount of equal real value to be appropriated in all later years. It is set at 3.0% of the petroleum wealth. The government can withdraw an amount from the Petroleum Fund in excess of this amount if a justification based on the long-term interest of Timor-Leste is provided to and approved by the National Parliament.

Source: Timor-Leste 2013 state budget.

Click here for figure data

3.35.6 The formal private sector in 2010

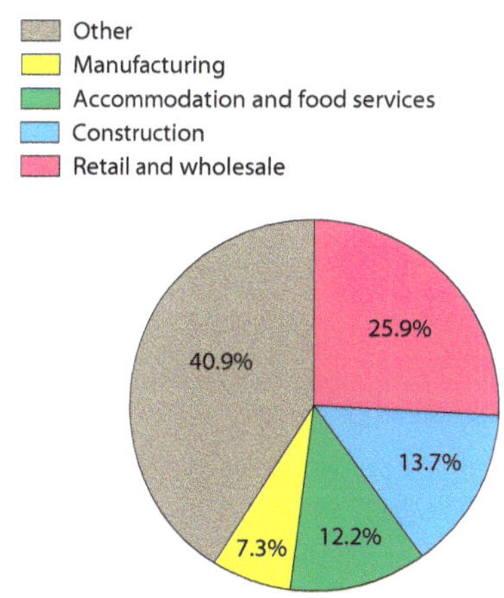

Employment

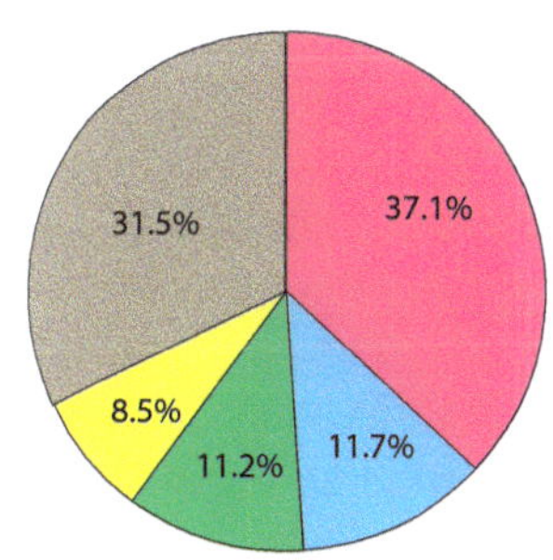

Value added

Sources: National Directorate of Statistics. 2012. *Business Activity Survey of Timor-Leste 2010*. Dili (January); Government of Timor-Leste. 2011. *2012 Budget Book No. 1*. Dili (November); National Statistics Directorate and United Nations Population Fund. 2011. Population and Housing Census 2010. *Suco Report*. Volume 4. Dili (July).

Click here for figure data

North Pacific economies

Slower growth has been set largely by infrastructure projects. In the Republic of the Marshall Islands, delays affecting a major airport upgrade held performance below expectations. Growth slowed in the Federated States of Micronesia as airport improvement reached completion, and in Palau as market saturation and infrastructure capacity constraints at peak periods moderated growth in visitor arrivals. Economic prospects depend on infrastructure projects in the near term, but longer-term growth could hinge on economic links with Asia.

Economic performance

North Pacific economies continued to expand in FY2012 (ended 30 September 2012 for all), but growth was generally more moderate than in previous years (Figure 3.36.1). In the Republic of the Marshall Islands (RMI) and the Federated States of Micronesia (FSM), growth was determined largely by movements in government spending, particularly on infrastructure projects. Economic growth in the FSM declined to 1.4% from 2.1% in FY2011 as infrastructure projects neared completion. In the RMI, a delay in the ongoing airport upgrade had held growth in FY2011 at only 0.8%, lower than expected, but resumed activity helped restore growth to 1.9% the following year. Another important contributor to growth in these economies has been earnings from fisheries. These rose as El Niño drove fish into colder, deeper waters such as those found in the exclusive economic zones of the RMI and the FSM.

Government spending, including outlays related to elections, contributed to Palau's 4.0% GDP growth in FY2012, but tourism was the main driver. Visitor arrivals increased by 13.4%, building on the 25.8% growth achieved in FY2011 and marking the third consecutive year of such double-digit growth following 2 years of declining tourist arrivals (Figure 3.36.2).

Inflation in all three North Pacific economies accelerated in FY2012, largely because of sharp increases in fuel prices in the last quarter of calendar year 2011. Inflation in the RMI increased slightly to 5.7% from 5.4% in FY2011, while inflation in the FSM rose to 5.6% from 4.7% in the same period, spurred by the higher availability of consumer loans. Prices in Palau similarly experienced additional upward pressure, in this case from robust tourism-related demand and possible capacity constraints in peak periods, as inflation soared to 6.0% from 2.6% in FY2011 (Figure 3.36.3).

The North Pacific states are consolidating expenditure to achieve long-term fiscal sustainability. This is especially important in light of the key role that public infrastructure projects play in driving economic

3.36.1 GDP growth

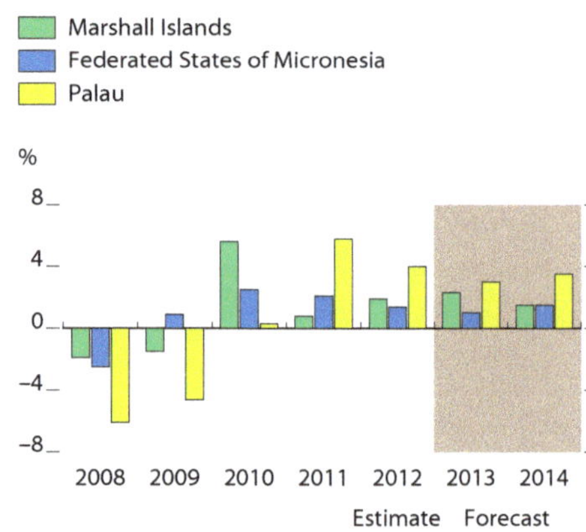

Sources: International Monetary Fund. 2012. Republic of the Marshall Islands, *Preliminary Conclusions of the 2012 IMF Staff Visit.* November; 2012. *2012 Staff Report with the Federated States of Micronesia, Concluding Statement of the IMF Mission.* November; 2012. Republic of Palau, *Country Report* No. 12/54. March; ADB estimates.

Click here for figure data

3.36.2 Visitor arrivals to Palau

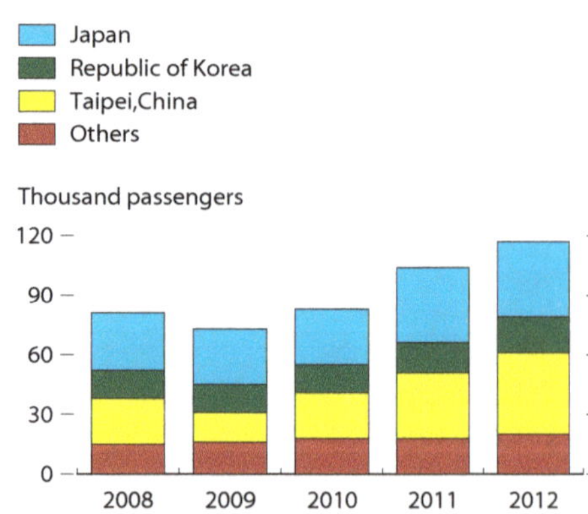

Source: Palau Visitors Authority. http://www.visit-palau.com

Click here for figure data

This chapter was written by Rommel Rabanal and Cara Tinio of the Pacific Department, ADB, Manila.

growth, and because grants under their compacts of free association with the US are ebbing annually and less available to fuel government spending. The RMI and the FSM compacts are set to expire in about a decade.

The FSM has in the past 4 years realized surpluses in its consolidated budget, which combines the accounts of the federal government and all four state governments. This trend continued with a consolidated surplus equal to 1.2% of GDP in FY2012, reflecting better revenue administration at the state level, economic growth, and more stable public wages. In contrast, the RMI realized a fiscal deficit estimated at 1.1% of GDP in the same period, reversing the 3.7% surplus recorded in FY2011. Unstable domestic tax collection and diminished foreign grants reduced government revenue and exacerbated the impact of off-budget expenditures arising from ad hoc directives. Palau recorded a fiscal deficit equal to 3.2% of GDP in FY2012, but this was a slight improvement from the FY2011 deficit of 3.5%, stemming mainly from higher revenue collection related to the strong economic performance driven by tourism.

Increased tourism also drove a current account surplus in Palau, which was equal to 6.0% of GDP in FY2012. Meanwhile, the RMI and the FSM continued to run current account deficits, equal to 6.3% of GDP for the RMI and 15.0% for the FSM. However, these deficits were narrower than in previous year, as the winding down of infrastructure projects, or delays in implementing them, cut imports of machinery and capital inputs.

3.36.3 Inflation

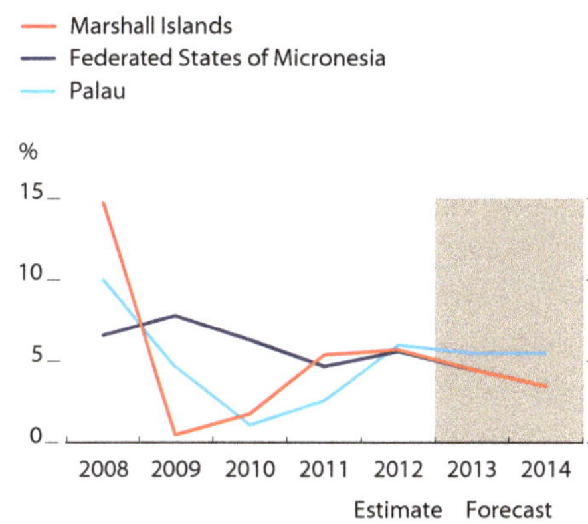

Sources: International Monetary Fund. 2012. Republic of the Marshall Islands, *Preliminary Conclusions of the 2012 IMF Staff Visit.* November; 2012. *2012 Staff Report with the Federated States of Micronesia, Concluding Statement of the IMF Mission.* November; 2012. Republic of Palau, *Country Report* No. 12/54. March; ADB estimates.
Click here for figure data

Economic prospects

Infrastructure development will remain a key driver of economic growth in the North Pacific, with construction providing short-term stimulus and the resulting capacity upgrades boosting longer-term prospects. Growth in the FSM is expected to moderate to 1.0% in FY2013 as most airport improvement projects are completed. In contrast, GDP growth in the RMI is projected to accelerate to 2.3% in the same period on the back of its recommenced airport rehabilitation project and spending related to the country's hosting of the Pacific Islands Forum. Because the growth outlook in Palau depends heavily on sustaining tourism's robust performance, it may slow as the limited capacity of tourism-related facilities and infrastructure imposes constraints during peak periods, and as recent high rates of growth translate into market saturation. Given these constraints, GDP growth in Palau is expected to moderate to 3.0% in FY2013.

Growth in the RMI is projected to moderate again to 1.5% in FY2014 as airport rehabilitation winds down. Conversely, the start in FY2014 of ADB-supported projects to upgrade ports in the FSM, and to improve water and sanitation in Palau, is expected to accelerate growth in the FSM to 1.5% and in Palau to 3.5%. Longer-term growth prospects are weighed down by outmigration, the lack of growth drivers from the private sector, and annual decrements in compact grants, particularly in the RMI and the FSM, where scheduled decrements are already taking place.

With international prices of food and fuel projected to decline over the next couple of years, inflation in the North Pacific is expected to

3.36.1 Selected economic indicators (%)

Marshall Islands	2013	2014
GDP growth	2.3	1.5
Inflation	4.5	3.5
Current account balance (share of GDP)	−2.5	−2.5
Federated States of Micronesia		
GDP growth	1.0	1.5
Inflation	4.5	3.5
Current account balance (share of GDP)	−14.3	−14.0
Palau		
GDP growth	3.0	3.5
Inflation	5.5	5.5
Current account balance (share of GDP)	7.5	7.5

Source: ADB estimates.

trend downward in the near term. In the RMI and the FSM, inflation is projected to moderate to 4.5% in FY2013 and 3.5% in FY2014. It is expected to remain higher in Palau because domestic activity is more robust and tourism facilities remain close to capacity. That said, a projected moderation in tourism-led growth is expected to push inflation slightly lower in FY2013 to 5.5%, a rate likely to be sustained in FY2014 by demand arising from the implementation of the large water and sanitation project.

The lower cost of food and fuel imports is also expected to affect current account balances across the North Pacific. The resulting savings, together with a sharp increase in grants, are seen to narrow the RMI's current account deficit from 6.3% of GDP to 2.5% in FY2013. The FSM's current account deficit is expected to improve to 14.3% of GDP from 15.0% in FY2012, in part because of lower imports of machinery and capital inputs as infrastructure projects are already completed. Current account deficits in the RMI and the FSM are generally financed through capital grants. High tourism receipts have supported current account surpluses over the past 3 years in Palau, and a lower merchandise import bill is projected to boost surpluses to 7.5% of GDP in both FY2013 and FY2014.

The governments of the RMI and the FSM have made good progress in controlling expenditure and generating more revenue. However, the International Monetary Fund estimates that the RMI must build up fiscal surpluses equivalent to 6.0% of GDP by FY2017, and maintain them at this level until FY2023, to generate sufficient replacement income for expiring compact grants (Figure 3.36.4). The FSM's fiscal adjustment is even more challenging, requiring surpluses equivalent to 6.4% of GDP by FY2016 (Figure 3.36.5). Recent fiscal surpluses are far below these goals. The FSM's consolidated budget surplus is projected to slim to 0.8% of GDP in FY2013, even with planned cuts to current and capital expenditure, because of the continuing decline in compact grants. The RMI's fiscal account is expected to remain in deficit despite anticipated cuts in current expenditure. While similar fiscal contraction is expected in Palau, its realization remains uncertain as the newly elected government, which assumed office in January 2013, has yet to submit a national budget. In the meantime, continuing budget authority legally allows expenditure up to the same amount as in FY2012.

3.36.4 Fiscal adjustment in the Marshall Islands

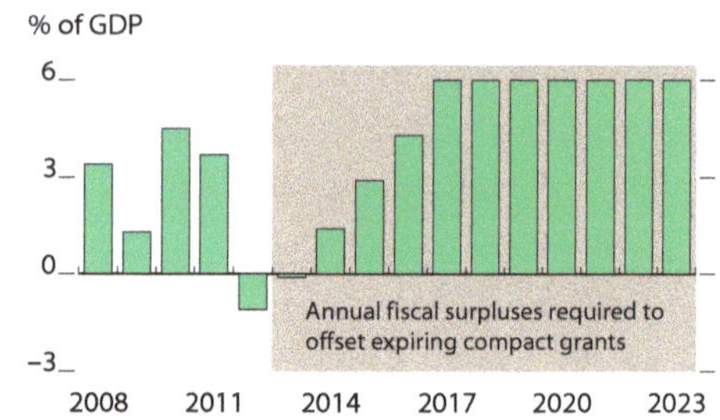

Source: International Monetary Fund. Republic of the Marshall Islands, *Preliminary Conclusions of the 2012 IMF Staff Visit.* http://www.imf.org

Click here for figure data

3.36.5 Fiscal adjustment in the Federated States of Micronesia

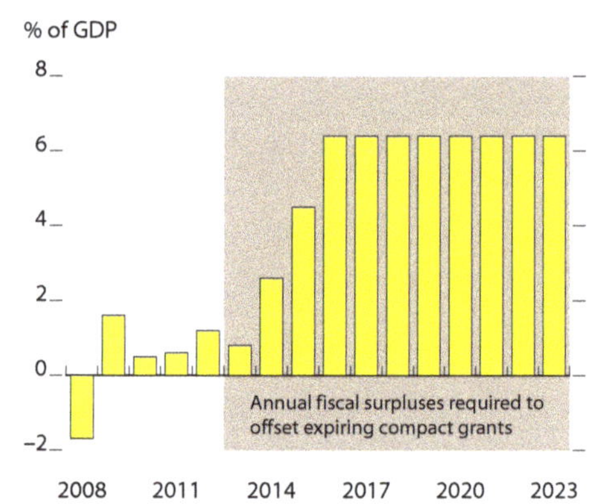

Source: International Monetary Fund. *2012 Staff Report with the Federated States of Micronesia, Concluding Statement of the IMF Mission.* http://www.imf.org

Click here for figure data

Policy challenge—stronger linkages with Asia

The end of the compact agreements will require comprehensive fiscal reform to ensure long-term fiscal sustainability. Revenue reform may include imposing value-added taxes. Cuts in current expenditure must reduce large public wage bills. Parallel improvements will need to improve tax administration. In addition, the end of payments under the compacts will mean that subsidies to state-owned enterprises and generous social security schemes will no longer be sustainable.

Asia's rising importance in the global economy presents opportunities for North Pacific economies to boost their growth potential by tapping into the region. The North Pacific's economic links with Asia have been gaining importance, and in some cases are already quite significant, as detailed by the article *Changing tides—evolving North Pacific economic linkages?* in the December 2012 edition of ADB's

Pacific Economic Monitor. For instance, Palau's merchandise trade is almost exclusively oriented toward Asia, at 99.8% for exports and 90.5% for imports in 2011, and over 80% of its visitor arrivals are from Japan, the Republic of Korea, and Taipei,China. The RMI's tuna exports reach a wide range of Asian countries such as the People's Republic of China (PRC) and Japan, its two biggest markets as of 2011, as well as the Philippines and Singapore. The FSM already imports key items from Asia, such as cars from Japan, fuel from the Republic of Korea, and household appliances from the PRC. Trade linkages with Asia are likely to continue expanding with cheaper transport costs to and from Asian markets, and lower production costs in the larger economies of developing Asia. Expanding such opportunities in a changing global economic landscape will help balance the group's economic ties, which remain heavily tilted toward the US. Stronger links with Asia are particularly relevant in the medium to long term as annual financial assistance from the US is scheduled to decline and eventually expire.

However, to fully benefit from Asia's rapid growth, the North Pacific should further develop these emerging economic links, particularly those in the areas of trade and investment. This requires substantial improvements to the business environment. In the World Bank's *Doing Business 2013* survey, North Pacific economies fared poorly, with the RMI ranked at 101 of 185, Palau at 111, and the FSM at 150—all weak in terms of protecting investors, enforcing contracts, and registering property, among other shortcomings (Figure 3.36.6). In particular, rigid investment and labor policies must be relaxed. Better business environments should help expand private sector sources of growth in these economies, particularly in sectors that can be viable even in small island economies. For example, a better business environment is likely to unlock the potential of underdeveloped tourism in the RMI, which receives only 3,500 arrivals annually, and in the FSM, with 15,000 arrivals, both dwarfed by the more than 100,000 annual arrivals to Palau.

3.36.6 *Doing Business 2013* rankings

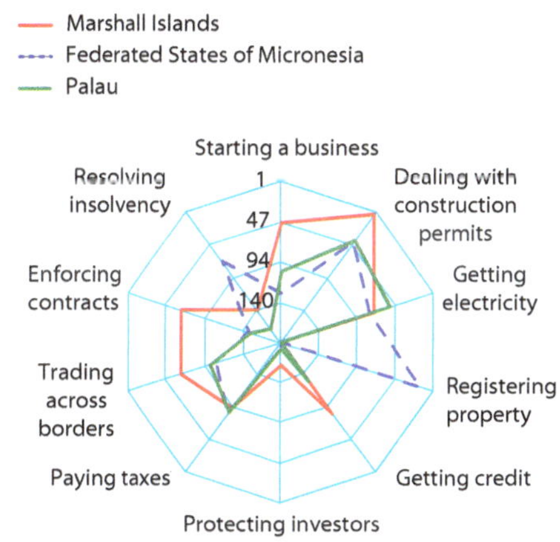

Note: Numbers in parentheses show ranking out of 185 countries worldwide. 1 = best, 185 = worst.

Source: World Bank. Doing Business database. http://www.doingbusiness.org

Click here for figure data

South Pacific economies

Public investments and tourism earnings continue to drive economies in the South Pacific. Increased visitor arrivals and public spending led economic expansion in the Cook Islands and Vanuatu, while growth decelerated in Samoa and Tonga as major infrastructure projects were completed. Growth in the South Pacific is expected to slow in the near term as construction on public investment projects continues to wind down.

Economic performance

South Pacific economies expanded in FY2012 (ended 30 June 2012 in the Cook Islands, Samoa, and Tonga, and coincided with the calendar year in Vanuatu). The rate of growth varied across countries (Figure 3.37.1). Growth in the Cook Islands accelerated to 3.3% in FY2012, from 1.0% in the previous fiscal year, driven by public spending on infrastructure projects and the continued strong performance of the tourism sector. Tourist arrivals in the Cook Islands have increased by an average of 8.0% over the past 2 years (Figure 3.37.2). Higher tourist arrivals were also a main reason why Vanuatu's economy expanded by 2.0% in FY2012, accelerating slightly from 1.4% in FY2011 (Figure 3.37.3).

Infrastructure spending funded by development partners has been the main determinant of fluctuations in economic growth in Samoa and Tonga. The Samoan economy expanded by 1.2% in FY2012, compared with 2.0% the previous fiscal year, as reconstruction and rehabilitation following the 2009 earthquake and tsunami were completed. FY2012 was the second consecutive year of modest expansion in private remittances, but, when adjusted for inflation, remittances have been nearly flat (Figure 3.37.4). Tourism in Samoa showed signs of recovery from natural disasters in 2009, but the sector was hit by Cyclone Evan in December 2012. The cyclone caused damage estimated at $210 million, equivalent to 30% of GDP.

Despite a slight improvement in tourism performance, Tonga saw growth decelerate to 0.8% in FY2012 from 2.9% in FY2011 as major projects wound down. Remittances continued to fall, totaling $67 million in FY2012, which was equal to 15.0% of GDP. This number is down from a high of $107 million, or 30.0% of GDP, in FY2008 (Figure 3.37.5).

Inflation in Tonga slowed to 4.6% in FY2012 from 6.1% in FY2011 as infrastructure projects wound down and weak domestic activity relieved pressure on domestic prices (Figure 3.37.6). These factors offset increases in international food and fuel prices recorded in calendar year 2011, which made accelerated inflation the rule elsewhere in the South Pacific.

3.37.1 GDP growth

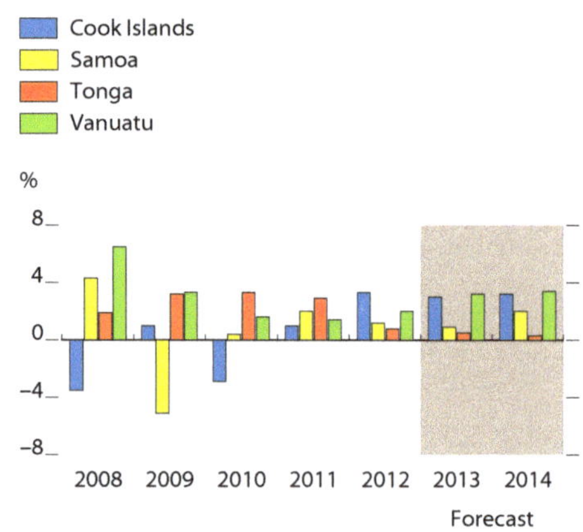

Sources: Cook Islands Statistics Office; Samoa Bureau of Statistics; Tonga Department of Statistics; and Vanuatu National Statistics Office.

Click here for figure data

3.37.2 Visitor arrivals to the Cook Islands

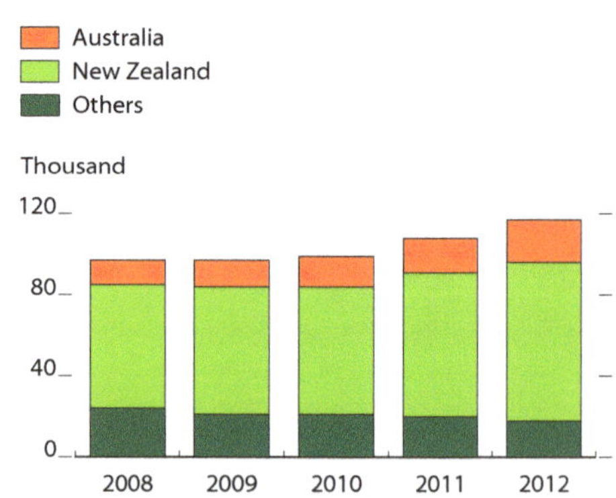

Source: Cook Islands Statistics Office.

Click here for figure data

This chapter was written by Caroline Currie, Malie Lototele, and Laisiasa Tora of the South Pacific Subregional Office, ADB, Suva; Milovan Lucich of the Pacific Liaison and Coordination Office, ADB, Sydney; and Cara Tinio of the Pacific Department, ADB, Manila.

In the Cook Islands, higher transport and utility costs worsened inflation to 2.8% during the period from 0.6%. Higher food prices in early 2012 drove up inflation in Samoa to 6.2% from 2.9% in FY2011, and in Vanuatu to 1.3% from 0.8%. However, lower international price rises for food and fuel in the latter part of calendar year 2012 caused consumer prices to trend lower in the Cook Islands, Vanuatu, and Samoa, the last of which experienced deflation.

Public expenditures over FY2012 caused fiscal deficits across the South Pacific, though fiscal consolidation has narrowed budget gaps in some economies. In the Cook Islands, infrastructure spending resulted in a fiscal deficit, but at 2.2% of GDP it was well within the 3.0% government target. As of September 2012, Vanuatu had incurred a deficit of 1.7% of GDP, compared with a 2.3% deficit for the whole of 2011. Election-related spending in Vanuatu and the introduction of subsidies to copra farmers fueled expenditure growth in the face of flat tax revenue collections and declining grants.

Fiscal consolidation has helped improve the fiscal positions of Samoa and Tonga. Although Samoa's FY2012 deficit of 4.5% of GDP exceeded government targets, it was an improvement over the 5.3% deficit incurred in FY2011. During the same period, Tonga's budget deficit narrowed to 2.9% of GDP from 7.4% a year earlier, mainly reflecting lower personnel costs and capital expenditure.

Monetary policy across the South Pacific has remained accommodative. Despite excess liquidity in the banking sector, the central banks of Samoa, Tonga, and Vanuatu have kept interest rates stable and low in a bid to stimulate credit growth. In addition, the National Reserve Bank of Tonga stopped requiring banks to pay interest on their exchange settlement accounts to encourage lending to the private sector. The Cook Islands has no central bank and uses the New Zealand dollar as its official currency.

Most South Pacific economies have continued to run current account deficits. Tonga's current account deficit widened to 17.9% of GDP in FY2012 from 11.1% in FY2011, as imports of goods and services grew more quickly than exports. Samoa's current account deficit also widened, to 10.8% in FY2012 from 9.2% in the previous fiscal year. In contrast, Vanuatu's current account deficit narrowed slightly to 6.0% of GDP in 2012 from 6.3% in 2011.

Economic prospects

Public investments and tourism will continue to drive growth in the South Pacific in FY2013 and FY2014. However, except in Vanuatu, growth will be slower than in recent years. Growth in the Cook Islands is projected to slow to 3.0% in FY2013 as infrastructure construction winds down and public spending declines, and as agricultural output slumps. Growth is expected to accelerate to 3.2% in FY2014 on the back of expected improving economic conditions in Australia and New Zealand. Future growth may be constrained if tourism service providers do not expand facilities. In Tonga, growth is projected at 0.5% in FY2013 and 0.3% in FY2014. The expected slowdown reflects the completion of public investment projects, weak business activity, and slow recovery in remittances and private sector credit.

3.37.3 Visitor arrivals to Vanuatu

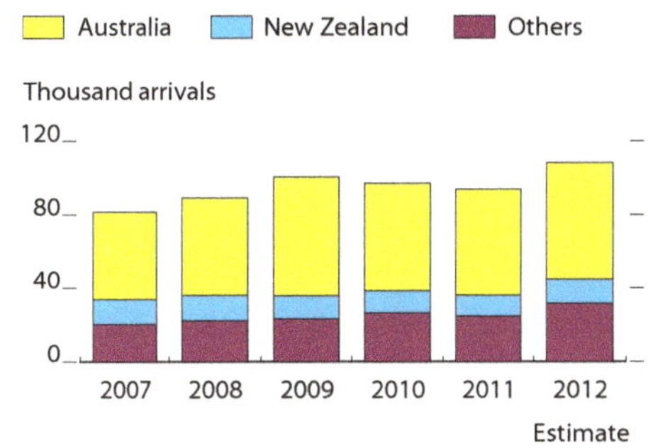

Sources: Vanuatu National Statistics Office; ADB estimates.
Click here for figure data

3.37.4 Private remittances to Samoa

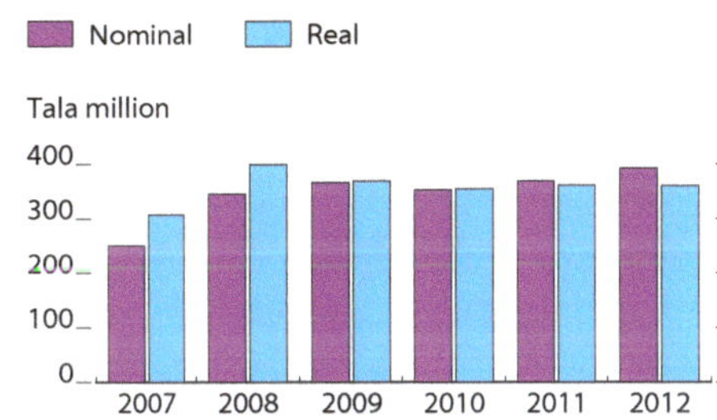

Source: Central Bank of Samoa.
Click here for figure data

3.37.5 Private remittances to Tonga

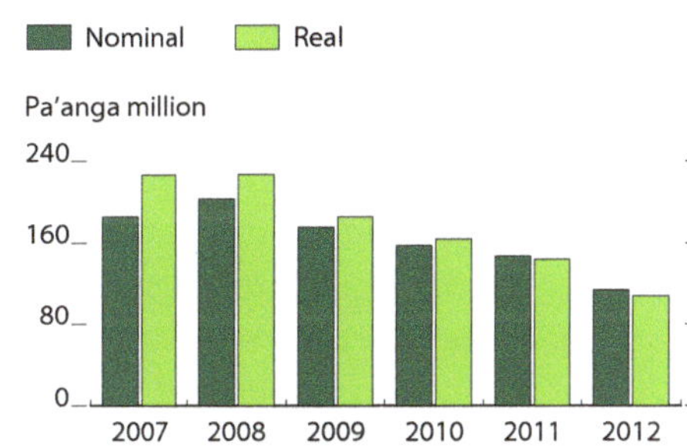

Sources: National Reserve Bank of Tonga; Tonga Ministry of Finance and National Planning.
Click here for figure data

3.37.6 Inflation

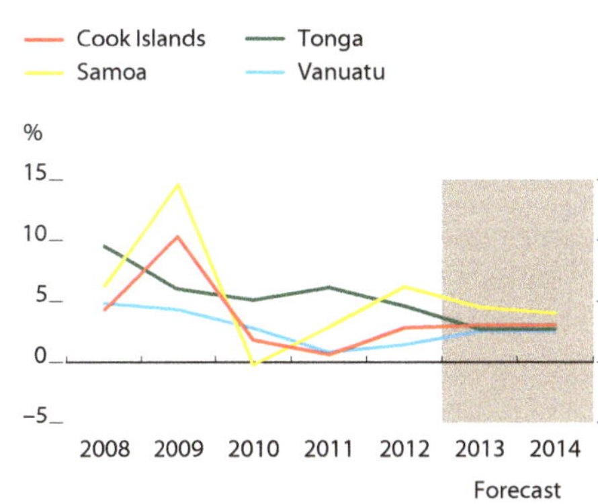

Sources: Cook Islands Statistics Office; Samoa Bureau of Statistics; Tonga Department of Statistics; and Reserve Bank of Vanuatu.
Click here for figure data

The Samoan economy is projected to grow by only 0.9% in FY2013 as infrastructure damage caused by Cyclone Evan depresses output from agriculture, tourism, and other productive sectors. Economic recovery efforts, once fully in place, are expected to have a positive impact on GDP in FY2014, with projected growth picking up to 2%. Restoring productive capacity and reconstructing essential infrastructure are expected to take 2–3 years.

In Vanuatu, growth is expected to pick up to 3.2% in 2013 and 3.4% in 2014, as delayed construction projects commence implementation and agricultural production likely recovers. Visitor arrivals are expected to increase modestly as tourists avoid destinations affected by Cyclone Evan and travel to Vanuatu instead.

The Cook Islands' fiscal deficit is expected to edge up to 2.3% of GDP in FY2013—still within government targets—as increases in personnel and capital expenditures are largely offset by higher tax collections and grant inflows. Samoa's fiscal deficit is forecast to increase substantially, to 11.8% of GDP, as the fallout from the cyclone severely depresses tax revenue collections and causes a spike in expenditures to restore essential infrastructure. Tonga's FY2013 budget plans a small surplus of 0.2% of GDP, in spite of a projected current expenditure increase. This is because the bulk of the increases will be covered by scheduled large project grants. Vanuatu has yet to pass its 2013 budget because the new government has not submitted an appropriation bill. However, a deficit of 2.6% of GDP is expected for the year as expenditure growth is seen to continue to outpace revenue growth, which is constrained by the country's narrow tax base.

International food and fuel prices are projected to decline over the next couple of years. In line with this, inflation in the Cook Islands is expected to remain relatively low at 3.0% through FY2013–FY2014. Tonga's inflation is seen to moderate to 2.7% in FY2013 and stabilize at that rate through FY2014 in light of the economy's low growth outlook and international price movements.

Despite experiencing deflation in the first half of FY2013, Samoa is expected to see inflation remain relatively high, at 4.5% for the full fiscal year, as cyclone-related supply disruptions push up domestic food prices. Inflation is expected to slow to 4.0% in FY2014 in line with declining international food and fuel prices, and as the domestic distribution network is restored.

In Vanuatu, prices are expected to rise by 2.5% in both 2013 and 2014 as the implementation of major construction projects and economic acceleration exert upward pressure on prices.

Central banks in the South Pacific are expected to retain their accommodative monetary policies to support economic activity. Inflation and international reserves are forecast to remain at acceptable levels, but sluggish private sector investment remains a concern.

South Pacific economies are expected to continue running current account deficits in FY2013. Imports of materials for post-cyclone reconstruction are seen widening Samoa's deficit to 13.4% of GDP, while stronger imports arising from growing domestic demand and construction projects funded by development partners will expand Vanuatu's current account deficit to 10.0% of GDP. In contrast, the current account deficit in Tonga is expected to narrow to 6.3% in FY2013. Weaker

3.37.1 Selected economic indicators (%)

Cook Islands	2013	2014
GDP growth	3.0	3.2
Inflation	3.0	3.0
Current account balance (share of GDP)	...	...
Samoa		
GDP growth	0.9	2.0
Inflation	4.5	4.0
Current account balance (share of GDP)	–13.4	–15.5
Tonga		
GDP growth	0.5	0.3
Inflation	2.7	2.7
Current account balance (share of GDP)	–6.3	–6.3
Vanuatu		
GDP growth	3.2	3.4
Inflation	2.5	2.5
Current account balance (share of GDP)	–10.0	–10.0

... = data not available.
Source: ADB estimates.

domestic demand arising from the completion of infrastructure projects and the slow growth outlook will depress imports.

Policy challenge—the burden of debt

Borrowing to finance development spending has worsened debt positions in the South Pacific. The resulting financial obligation could limit governments' fiscal flexibility and resulting ability to respond to future economic shocks. Exchange rate fluctuations could affect countries' capacity to repay debt involving large loans denominated in foreign currency.

Samoa's government has borrowed heavily to repair damage wrought by natural disasters. As a result, the economy's external debt reached 45.0% of GDP in FY2012 (Figure 3.37.7). This ratio was projected to increase to 54.0% in FY2013, but it may turn out to be higher because of the impact of Cyclone Evan on agricultural and tourism output, and thereby on domestic revenues, which may prompt higher actual borrowing to finance rehabilitation. For its part, Tonga has borrowed to finance reconstruction following civil unrest that took place in 2006. Its total public debt was estimated at 45.0% of GDP in FY2012, above the 40% maximum recommended by the International Monetary Fund for most low-income countries (Figure 3.37.8).

Most South Pacific countries plan fiscal consolidation toward reducing expenditure, improving fiscal balances, and easing public debt burdens. However, countries at high risk of debt distress must appropriately pace their fiscal consolidation to avoid disrupting governments' delivery of basic services or inducing economic contraction. Consolidation efforts must be complemented by structural reform to further ease fiscal pressures and help promote private sector-led economic growth. For economies receiving budget support, maintaining the implementation of these measures is central to the joint policy reform matrix agreed with development partners.

3.37.7 External debt of Samoa

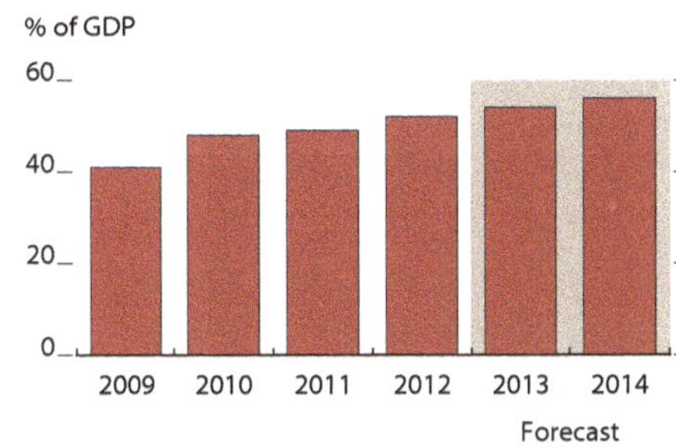

Source: Samoa Ministry of Finance. 2012. Fiscal strategy statement: Budget 2012/2013. May.

Click here for figure data

3.37.8 Public debt of Tonga

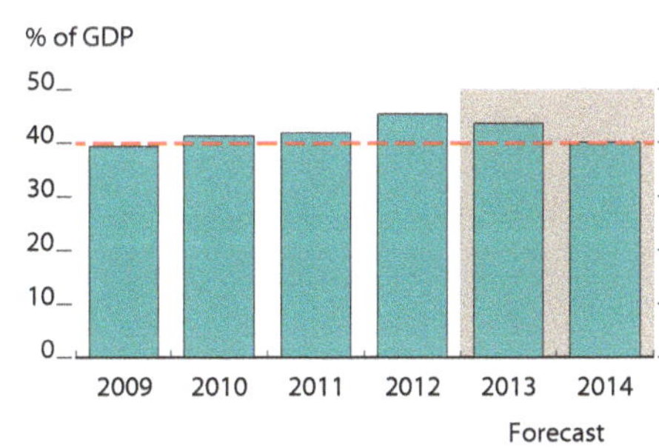

Note: The line denotes the International Monetary Fund's recommended maximum for public debt.

Source: International Monetary Fund. 2012. Tonga, *Country Report* No. 12/166. July.

Click here for figure data

Small island economies

Higher fishing revenues helped boost GDP growth and fiscal positions in the otherwise import- and aid-dependent small Pacific island economies of Kiribati, Nauru, and Tuvalu. Australia's reopened Regional Processing Centre in Nauru and externally funded projects in Kiribati and Tuvalu are expected to boost growth in 2013. Inflation is seen reappearing after a 3-year absence as growth accelerates and the impact of the stronger Australian dollar wanes. Paramount concerns are the longer-term sustainability of growth and intergenerational equity.

Economic performance

In 2012, inflows of development partner assistance, the positive effect of the El Niño weather pattern on fish stocks near the equator, and the introduction of a new fishing licensing scheme boosted government revenues and bolstered economic growth in Kiribati, Nauru, and Tuvalu. Conversely, continuing declines in seafarers' remittances stemming from weak global trade weighed down growth in Kiribati and Tuvalu.

Looking ashore, phosphate exports from Nauru reached 519,000 tons, the highest annual figure since the country recommenced production in 2007, and contributed strongly to economic growth of 4.9% in FY2012 (ended 30 June 2012). Expanded education and private retail services in Tuvalu helped restore growth of 1.2% in 2012 after 3 consecutive years of economic contraction. In Kiribati, development partner-funded seaport reconstruction and roadwork projects contributed to growth of 3.0% in 2012 (Figure 3.38.1).

All three countries use the Australian dollar as legal tender. None has its own central bank or an independent monetary policy or exchange rate flexibility. In recent years, the appreciation of the Australian dollar vis-à-vis the US dollar has effectively reduced the price of imports on average, greatly constraining consumer inflation (Figure 3.38.2). In Kiribati, consumer prices are estimated to have fallen by 1.8% in 2012, the second year of deflation in the past 3 years. Deflation has persisted in Nauru since FY2010. Tuvalu recorded inflation of 0.5% in 2011 and 1.4% in 2012. These low rates were held down by shifting trade patterns and stiffened retail competition (Figure 3.38.3).

Kiribati, Nauru, and Tuvalu are party to the Nauru Agreement, which recently implemented the Vessel Day Scheme, wherein fishing access and license fees are calculated using the number of days a foreign fishing vessel operates within a country's waters. This new policy combined with transitory catch improvement caused by El Niño to garner governments additional domestic revenue that improved the small island economies' fiscal positions.

3.38.1 GDP growth

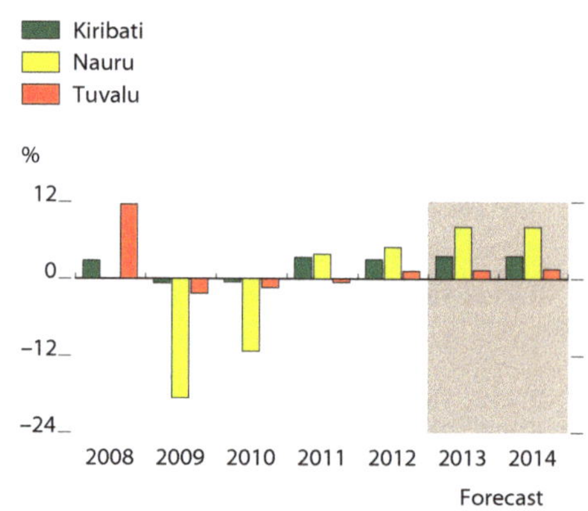

Sources: Kiribati National Statistics Office; Pacific Financial Technical Assistance Centre; Tuvalu Central Statistics Division; ADB estimates.

Click here for figure data

3.38.2 Australian dollar appreciation

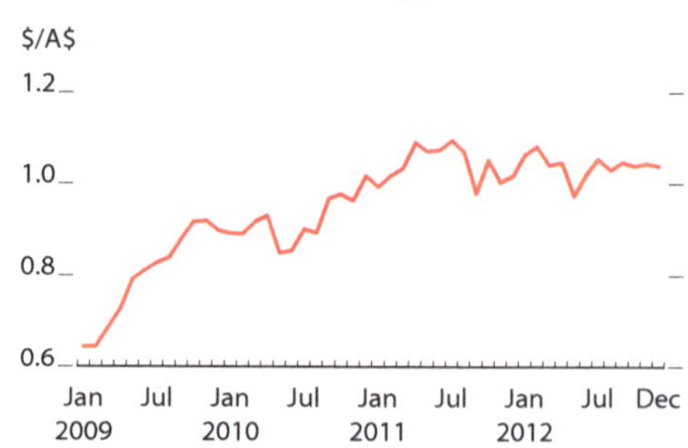

Source: Reserve Bank of Australia.

Click here for figure data

This chapter was written by Milovan Lucich of the Pacific Liaison and Coordination Office, ADB, Sydney; Malie Lototele of the South Pacific Subregional Office, ADB, Suva; and Rommel Rabanal of the Pacific Department, ADB, Manila.

Higher fishing fees and fish catches overturned original budget estimates that anticipated deteriorating fiscal balances in all three economies in 2012 (FY2012 for Nauru). Tuvalu posted a fiscal surplus, and the Kiribati and Nauru deficits were much smaller than expected, which at least temporarily eased perennial fiscal strains. It remains to be seen if higher fishing license revenues will become a permanent feature of government budgets. If the revenue increases are mostly attributable to licensing, higher collections may become permanent, but if they largely reflect El Niño-induced bumper catches, they can be expected to revert to historical levels.

Economic prospects

Infrastructure upgrades will likely be the primary drivers of growth over the next 2 years. The September 2012 reopening of the Regional Processing Centre (RPC) in Nauru for asylum seekers attempting to enter Australia without authorization is projected to boost economic growth to 8% in FY2013 and FY2014 through its impact on construction, hotels and accommodation, restaurants, and retail trade, as well as on government finances. The RPC, which currently holds around 400 refugees and directly employs 200 Nauruans in a population of 10,086, is expanding to a capacity of 1,500 asylum seekers. Partial repayment of government salaries in arrears, equivalent to 1.3% of GDP and funded by RPC-related revenues, will likely boost domestic consumption.

Meanwhile, the government expects phosphate production to slow from 519,000 tons in FY2012 to 450,000 tons in FY2013 because of poor weather and disruptions caused by the RPC's commandeering of mining equipment to clear land for construction (Figure 3.38.4). The phosphate industry employs about 700 Nauruans.

Kiribati's economy is projected to grow by 3.5% in 2013 and 2014 as construction picks up to implement projects funded by development partners: upgrading airports at Tarawa and Kiritimati, upgrading the South Tarawa Road, and extending Betio Port. In Tuvalu the airport upgrade, also funded by development partners, and continued retail expansion will drive economic growth of 1.3% in 2013 and 1.5% in 2014.

The recent trend of low inflation is expected to continue. Although the impact of a strengthening Australian dollar has probably ended, international food and fuel prices are expected to decline. Over 2013 and 2014, inflation is projected to remain at about 3% in Kiribati and 2% in Tuvalu. For Nauru, inflation is projected at a low 0.5% in FY2013, before rising to 2.5% in FY2014.

Island governments plan fiscal expansion to help support economic growth in the near term. In Nauru, the FY2013 budget already incorporates an expansionary stance supported by higher-than-expected revenues from fishing licenses and continued aid flows. As the reopening of the RPC will mean higher visa fees, fuel sales, and customs duty collections, the expansionary fiscal stance has been further amplified, and domestic expenditure will be almost double in FY2013. Fiscal expansion is also expected in Kiribati and Tuvalu, driven by planned increases in recurrent expenditures and by capital spending associated with ongoing infrastructure projects.

3.38.3 Inflation

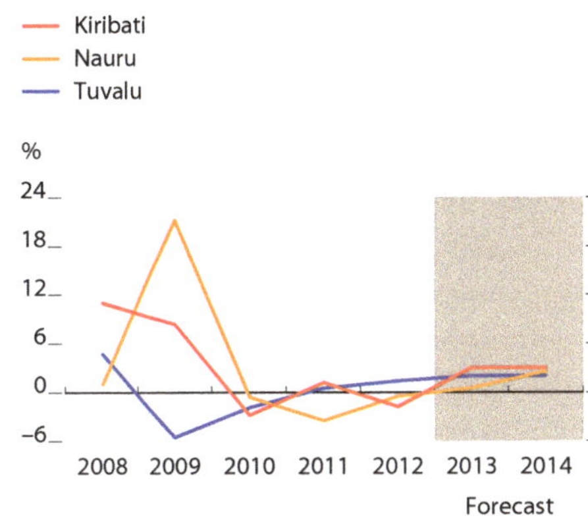

Sources: Kiribati National Statistics Office; Pacific Financial Technical Assistance Centre; Tuvalu Central Statistics Division; ADB estimates.

Click here for figure data

3.38.4 Phosphate exports from Nauru

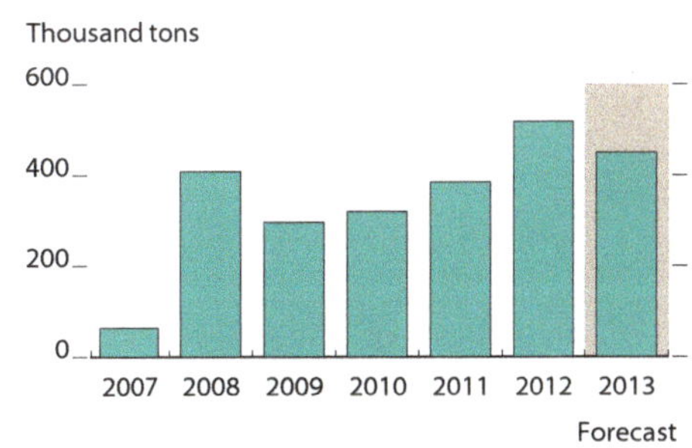

Sources: Republic of Nauru Phosphate Company; Nauru Bureau of Statistics.

Click here for figure data

3.38.1 Selected economic indicators (%)

Kiribati	2013	2014
GDP growth	3.5	3.5
Inflation	3.0	3.0
Current account balance (share of GDP)	–23.9	–20.0
Nauru		
GDP growth	8.0	8.0
Inflation	0.5	2.5
Current account balance (share of GDP)	...	...
Tuvalu		
GDP growth	1.3	1.5
Inflation	2.0	2.0
Current account balance (share of GDP)	–3.3	...

... = data not available.
Source: ADB estimates.

Policy challenge—sustainability and intergenerational equity

Limited resources and narrow economic bases give rise to reliance on aid flows, which account for as much as half of GDP in some of these small island economies. The pace of resource exploitation, the sustainability of growth, and intergenerational equity are therefore major issues. Financial resources from sovereign investment funds in Kiribati and Tuvalu, and phosphate reserves in Nauru, are being depleted at unsustainable rates to fund current expenditures, raising concerns regarding the tradeoff between supporting growth now versus ensuring that future generations share the benefits provided by finite and exhaustible resources.

The Government of Kiribati's target for drawing down the Revenue Equalization Reserve Fund is A$15.0 million annually from 2013 to 2015. The 2012 drawdown of an estimated A$37.5 million raises concerns about the fund's long-term sustainability. The real value of the fund per capita has been trending downward in recent years to well below the benchmark of A$4,500 (Figure 3.38.5).

The Tuvalu Trust Fund has languished below its target maintenance value since 2008 and been unable since then to transfer resources to the Consolidated Investment Fund, through which budget deficits are financed. The investment fund neared utter depletion in 2012, prompting an A$4 million contribution from Australia (Figure 3.38.6).

Nauru has recently ramped up its exploitation of secondary phosphate reserves, digging deeper to reach a production high in FY2012. The proper management of phosphate wealth and of revenues from the reopening of the RPC will largely determine Nauru's fiscal and economic sustainability over the long run. In addition to effects on local employment and construction, the RPC has the potential to increase visa fee revenues by as much as A$16 million per year when operating at full capacity. However, full scaling up depends on the government and landowners reaching agreement on the terms of the land lease for two of the three RPC sites. Like phosphate revenues, RPC earnings may be transitory, so the government could consider saving RPC-related revenues for future generations and investing in priority infrastructure projects and human capital development.

Prioritizing investments and building up savings will allow future generations to benefit from the current use of resources. In addition to equity concerns, such adjustments to fiscal policy would address issues affecting the sustainability of growth. Broadening the economic bases of these small islands through private sector development, the reform of state-owned enterprises, and other improvements to the business environment will help reduce reliance on foreign assistance and promote more inclusive growth over the longer term.

3.38.5 Revenue Equalization Reserve Fund of Kiribati, closing balance

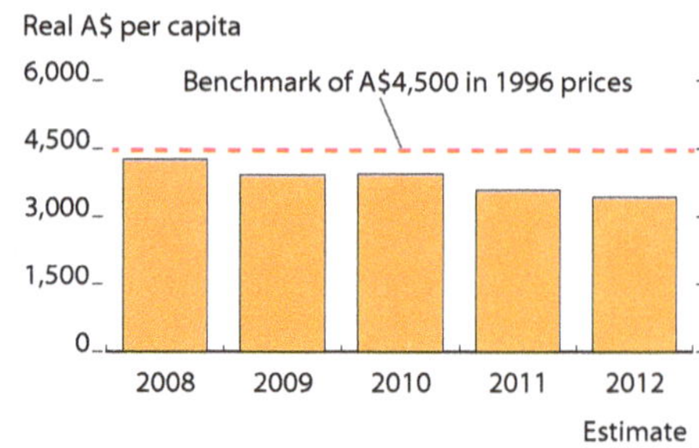

Source: ADB estimates using data from the Kiribati 2012 national budget.

Click here for figure data

3.38.6 Consolidated Investment Fund balance of Tuvalu

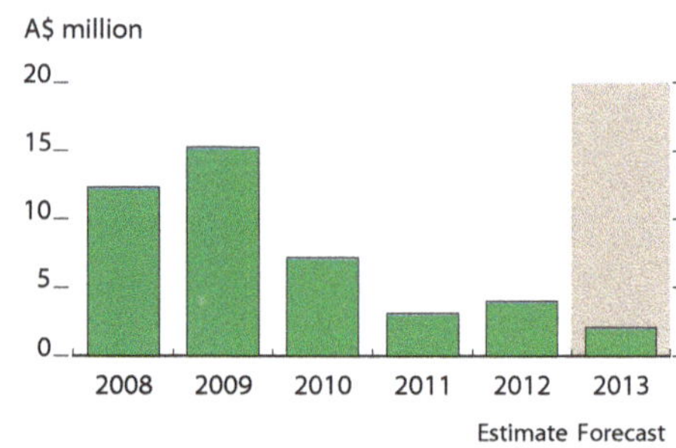

Source: International Monetary Fund. 2012. *Tuvalu, Country Report* No. 12/259. September.

Click here for figure data

Statistical appendix

Statistical notes and tables

The statistical appendix presents in 18 tables selected economic indicators for 45 developing member economies of the Asian Development Bank (ADB). The economies are grouped into five subregions: Central Asia, East Asia, South Asia, Southeast Asia, and the Pacific. Most of the tables contain historical data from 2008 to 2012; some have forecasts for 2013 and 2014.

The data were standardized to the degree possible to allow comparability over time and across economies, but differences in statistical methodology, definitions, coverage, and practices make full comparability impossible. The national income accounts section is based on the United Nations System of National Accounts, while the balance-of-payments data are based on International Monetary Fund (IMF) accounting standards. Historical data were obtained from official sources, statistical publications and databases, and documents of ADB, the IMF, and the World Bank. Projections for 2013 and 2014 are generally ADB estimates made on the basis of available quarterly or monthly data, although some projections are from governments.

Most countries report by calendar year. Some economies record their government finance data by fiscal year: Armenia; Azerbaijan; the Cook Islands; Hong Kong, China; Kazakhstan; the Kyrgyz Republic; the Lao People's Democratic Republic (Lao PDR); Samoa; Singapore; Taipei,China; Tajikistan; Thailand; and Uzbekistan. The Federated States of Micronesia, Nauru, the Republic of Marshall Islands, and the Republic of Palau report government finance and balance-of-payments data by fiscal year. Myanmar, Samoa, Tonga, and countries in South Asia except for the Maldives and Sri Lanka report all variables by fiscal year.

Regional and subregional averages and totals are provided in seven tables: A1, A2, A6, A11, A12, A13, and A14. In tables A1, A2, A6, and A14, the averages are computed using weights derived from gross national income (GNI) in current United States (US) dollars following the World Bank Atlas method. The GNI data for 2008–2011 were obtained from the World Bank's World Development Indicators online. Weights for 2011 were carried over through 2014. The GNI data for the Cook Islands were estimated using the Atlas conversion factor. Myanmar and Nauru have no GNI data. For tables A11 and A12, the regional and subregional averages were computed on the basis of a consistent sum, which means that if country data are missing for a given year, the sum of the prior year used for computing the growth rate excludes the corresponding country data.

Data for Myanmar and Nauru are excluded from the computation of all subregional averages and totals.

Tables A1, A2, A3, A4, and A5. These tables show related data on output growth, production, and demand. Changes to the national income accounts series for some countries have been made owing to a change in source, methodology, and/or base year. The series for Bhutan and India reflect the fiscal rather than the calendar year data, while those for Timor-Leste reflect gross domestic product (GDP) unrelated to oil or the United Nations mission.

Table A1: Growth rate of GDP (% per year). The table shows annual growth rates of GDP valued at constant market prices, factor costs, or basic prices. GDP at market prices is the aggregation of the value added of all resident producers at producers' prices including taxes less subsidies on imports plus all nondeductible value-added or similar taxes. Constant factor cost measures differ from market price measures in that they exclude taxes on production and include subsidies. Basic price valuation is the factor cost plus some taxes on production, such as property and payroll taxes, and less some subsidies, such as labor-related subsidies but not product-related subsidies. Most countries use constant market price valuation. Fiji, India, Pakistan, and Sri Lanka use constant factor costs, while the Maldives and Nepal use basic prices. GDP growth for 2008 is excluded for Nauru because of consistency issues.

Table A2: Growth rate of per capita GDP (% per year). The table provides the growth rates of real per capita GDP, which is defined as GDP at constant prices divided by the population. The series for most of the Pacific countries were revised to reflect a change in the source of population data. Also shown are data on per capita gross national product in US dollar terms for 2011, sourced from the World Bank's World Development Indicators online.

Table A3: Growth rate of value added in agriculture (% per year). The table shows the growth rates of value added in agriculture and its corresponding share in 2011. The agriculture sector comprises agricultural crops, livestock, poultry, fisheries, and forestry.

Table A4: Growth rate of value added in industry (% per year). The table provides the growth rates of value added in industry and its corresponding share in 2011. This sector comprises manufacturing, mining and quarrying, construction, and utilities.

Table A5: Growth rate of value added in services (% per year). The table gives the growth rates of value added in services, as well as its corresponding share in 2011. Subsectors generally include trade, banking, finance, real estate, public administration, and other services.

Table A6: Inflation (% per year). Data on inflation rates represent period averages. Except for India, which reports the wholesale price index, the inflation rates presented are based on consumer price indexes. The consumer price indexes of the following countries are for a given city or group of consumers only: Afghanistan is for Kabul until 2010, Cambodia is for Phnom Penh, Marshall Islands is for Majuro, Solomon Islands is for Honiara, and Nepal is for urban consumers.

Table A7: Growth in money supply (% per year). This table tracks the annual percentage change in the end-of-period supply of broad money as represented by M2 (for most countries). M2 is defined as the sum of M1 and quasi-money, where M1 denotes currency in circulation plus demand deposits and quasi-money consists of time and savings deposits including foreign currency deposits.

Tables A8, A9, and A10: Government finance. This set of tables refers to the revenue and expenditure transactions as well as the fiscal balance of the central government expressed as a percentage of GDP in nominal terms. For Cambodia since 2006, the People's Republic of China, India, Kazakhstan, the Kyrgyz Republic, Mongolia, and Tajikistan, transactions are those reported by the central government, while for Turkmenistan data are those reported by state governments. For Timor-Leste, government finance is compared with GDP unrelated to oil or the United Nations mission.

Table A8: Central government revenues (% of GDP). Central government revenues comprise all nonrepayable receipts, both current and capital, plus grants. These amounts are computed as a percentage of GDP at current prices. For the Republic of Korea, revenues exclude social security contributions. For Singapore, revenues refer to receipts credited to the three accounts listed for the previous table, including investment income, capital receipts, and investment adjustments. For Kazakhstan, revenues include transfers from the national fund. Grants are excluded in Cambodia, the Lao PDR, Malaysia, Singapore, and Thailand; revenues from disinvestment are included for India; and only current revenues are included for Bangladesh.

Table A9: Central government expenditures (% of GDP). Central government expenditures comprise all nonrepayable payments to both current and capital expenses, plus net lending. These amounts are computed as a share of GDP at current prices. For Thailand, expenditures refer to budgetary expenditures excluding externally financed expenditures and corresponding borrowing, while that for Tajikistan includes externally financed public investment programs. One-time expenditures are excluded for Pakistan.

Table A10: Fiscal balance of central government (% of GDP). Fiscal balance is the difference between central government revenues and expenditures. The difference is also computed as a share of GDP at current prices. Data variations may arise from statistical discrepancies, e.g., balancing items for both central and local governments, and differences in the concept used in the individual computations of revenues and expenditures as compared with the calculation of the fiscal balance. For Fiji, the fiscal balance excludes total loan repayments. For Thailand, the fiscal balance is a cash balance composed of the budgetary and nonbudgetary balances.

Tables A11, A12, A13, and A14: Balance of payments. This set of tables shows selected international economic transactions of countries as recorded in the balance of payments. These items cover annual flows, except that some countries show data as of a specified period only.

Tables A11 and A12: Growth rates of merchandise exports and imports (% per year). The annual growth rates of exports and imports, in terms of merchandise goods only, are shown in these tables. Data are in million US dollars, primarily obtained from the balance-of-payments accounts of each country. Exports are reported on a free-on-board basis. Imports are also generally reported on a free-on-board basis, except for

Afghanistan, Bhutan, Cambodia, India, the Lao PDR, Myanmar, the Philippines, Samoa, Singapore, Solomon Islands, Tajikistan, and Thailand, which value them on a cost, insurance, and freight basis.

Table A13: Trade balance ($ million). The trade balance is the difference between merchandise exports and merchandise imports. Figures in this table are based on the exports and imports levels used to generate Tables A11 and A12.

Table A14: Current account balance (% of GDP). The current account balance is the sum of the balance of trade for merchandise, net trade in services and factor income, and net transfers. The values reported are divided by GDP at current prices in US dollars. In the case of Cambodia, the Lao PDR, and Viet Nam, official transfers are excluded from the current account balance.

Table A15: Exchange rates to the United States dollar (annual average). The annual average exchange rates of each economy are quoted in local currencies per US dollar. The rate for 2012 for India is for the period April 2012–March 2013.

Table A16: Gross international reserves ($ million). Gross international reserves are defined as the US dollar value of holdings of foreign exchange, special drawing rights, reserve position in the IMF, and gold at the end of a given period. For Turkmenistan, gold is excluded from the computation. For the Marshall Islands and Taipei,China, this heading refers to foreign exchange reserves only. In some countries, the rubric comprises foreign assets and reserves of national monetary authorities and national oil funds, i.e., foreign assets of the Maldives Monetary Authority, net foreign reserves of the State Bank of Pakistan, assets of the National Oil Fund of Azerbaijan, and official external assets of Kiribati. The data for India are as of 15 March 2013.

Table A17: External debt outstanding ($ million). For most economies, external debt outstanding—public and private—includes medium- and long-term debt, short-term debt, and IMF credit. For Cambodia, Georgia, the Lao PDR, and Tajikistan only public external debt is reported. For Azerbaijan, India, Kazakhstan, and Singapore the figures for 2012 are as of the end of September.

Table A18: Debt service ratio (% of exports of goods and services). This table generally presents the total debt service payments of each economy, which comprise principal repayments (excluding on short-term debt) and interest payments on outstanding external debt as a percentage of exports of goods and services. For Cambodia and the Lao PDR, debt service refers to external public debt only. For Papua New Guinea, Samoa, and Viet Nam, exports of goods are used as the denominator in the calculation of the ratio; for the Philippines, exports of goods, services, and income are used as the denominator. For Bangladesh, the ratio represents debt service payments on medium- and long-term loans as a percentage of exports of goods, nonfactor services, and workers' remittances, while for Azerbaijan the ratio represents public and publicly guaranteed external debt service payments as a percentage of exports of goods and nonfactor services. For India, Kazakhstan, and Singapore data for 2012 are as of the end of September.

Table A1 Growth rate of GDP (% per year)

	2008	2009	2010	2011	2012	2013	2014
Central Asia	6.5	3.2	6.8	6.8	5.6	5.5	6.0
Armenia	6.9	-14.1	2.2	4.7	7.2	4.5	4.6
Azerbaijan	10.8	9.3	5.0	0.1	2.2	3.1	4.8
Georgia	2.3	-3.8	6.3	7.2	6.1	5.5	6.0
Kazakhstan	3.3	1.2	7.3	7.5	5.0	5.2	5.6
Kyrgyz Republic	8.4	2.9	-0.5	6.0	-0.9	5.5	4.5
Tajikistan	7.9	3.9	6.5	7.4	7.5	6.5	6.0
Turkmenistan	14.7	6.1	9.2	14.7	11.1	9.0	8.0
Uzbekistan	9.0	8.1	8.5	8.3	8.2	7.5	8.0
East Asia	7.3	6.8	9.8	8.2	6.5	7.1	7.1
China, People's Rep. of	9.6	9.2	10.4	9.3	7.8	8.2	8.0
Hong Kong, China	2.1	-2.5	6.8	4.9	1.4	3.5	3.8
Korea, Rep. of	2.3	0.3	6.3	3.7	2.0	2.8	3.7
Mongolia	8.9	-1.3	6.4	17.5	12.3	16.5	14.0
Taipei,China	0.7	-1.8	10.8	4.1	1.3	3.5	3.9
South Asia	6.4	7.7	8.5	6.0	5.0	5.7	6.2
Afghanistan	3.6	21.0	8.4	7.2	11.9	3.3	5.1
Bangladesh	6.2	5.7	6.1	6.7	6.3	5.7	6.0
Bhutan	10.8	5.7	9.3	10.0	7.5	8.6	8.5
India	6.7	8.6	9.3	6.2	5.0	6.0	6.5
Maldives	12.2	-3.6	7.1	7.0	3.4	4.3	5.5
Nepal	5.8	3.9	4.3	3.8	4.6	3.5	4.2
Pakistan	3.7	1.7	3.1	3.0	3.7	3.6	3.5
Sri Lanka	6.0	3.5	8.0	8.2	6.4	6.8	7.2
Southeast Asia	4.4	1.4	7.9	4.7	5.5	5.4	5.7
Brunei Darussalam	-1.9	-1.8	2.6	2.2	1.0	1.8	2.0
Cambodia	6.7	0.1	6.0	7.1	7.2	7.2	7.2
Indonesia	6.0	4.6	6.2	6.5	6.2	6.4	6.6
Lao People's Dem. Rep.	7.2	7.3	7.5	7.8	7.9	7.7	7.7
Malaysia	4.8	-1.5	7.2	5.1	5.6	5.3	5.5
Myanmar	3.6	5.1	5.3	5.5	6.3	6.5	6.7
Philippines	4.2	1.1	7.6	3.9	6.6	6.0	5.9
Singapore	1.7	-0.8	14.8	5.2	1.3	2.6	3.7
Thailand	2.5	-2.3	7.8	0.1	6.4	4.9	5.0
Viet Nam	6.3	5.3	6.8	5.9	5.0	5.2	5.6
The Pacific	6.1	4.3	5.5	8.3	7.3	5.2	5.5
Cook Islands	-3.5	1.0	-2.9	1.0	3.3	3.0	3.2
Fiji Islands	1.1	-1.3	0.1	1.9	2.5	2.0	2.3
Kiribati	2.8	-0.7	-0.5	3.3	3.0	3.5	3.5
Marshall Islands	-1.9	-1.5	5.6	0.8	1.9	2.3	1.5
Micronesia, Fed. States of	-2.5	0.9	2.5	2.1	1.4	1.0	1.5
Nauru		-18.6	0.0	3.8	4.9	8.0	8.0
Palau	-6.1	-4.6	0.3	5.8	4.0	3.0	3.5
Papua New Guinea	6.6	6.0	7.4	11.1	9.2	5.5	6.0
Samoa	4.3	-5.1	0.4	2.0	1.2	0.9	2.0
Solomon Islands	7.2	-1.0	6.9	10.6	5.5	4.0	4.0
Timor-Leste	14.6	12.8	9.5	10.8	10.6	10.0	10.0
Tonga	1.9	3.2	3.3	2.9	0.8	0.5	0.3
Tuvalu	11.6	-2.3	-1.4	-0.6	1.2	1.3	1.5
Vanuatu	6.5	3.3	1.6	1.4	2.0	3.2	3.4
Average	6.7	6.1	9.2	7.3	6.1	6.6	6.7

... = data not available.

Table A2 Growth rate of per capita GDP (% per year)

	2008	2009	2010	2011	2012	2013	2014	Per capita GNP, $, 2011
Central Asia	5.1	1.4	5.3	5.2	4.3	4.0	4.8	...
Armenia	6.7	-14.4	1.9	4.3	6.8	4.2	4.3	3,360
Azerbaijan	9.6	7.1	3.8	-1.1	0.8	1.8	4.3	5,290
Georgia	2.6	-3.9	5.0	6.4	6.8	4.8	6.0	2,860
Kazakhstan	1.8	-0.7	5.5	5.9	3.5	3.7	4.1	8,260
Kyrgyz Republic	6.8	0.7	-1.6	4.6	-2.9	3.9	2.9	880
Tajikistan	5.6	1.8	5.5	7.4	4.7	4.9	4.4	870
Turkmenistan	12.8	4.2	9.2	12.8	9.3	7.2	6.2	4,800
Uzbekistan	7.3	6.3	6.8	5.3	7.5	5.3	6.6	1,510
East Asia	6.8	6.3	9.3	7.7	6.1	6.7	6.7	...
China, People's Rep. of	9.0	8.7	9.9	8.8	7.3	7.7	7.5	4,940
Hong Kong, China	1.5	-2.7	6.0	4.1	0.5	2.8	3.1	36,010
Korea, Rep. of	2.0	0.0	6.0	3.4	1.8	2.6	3.6	20,870
Mongolia	7.1	-3.1	4.5	15.5	11.0	15.0	12.5	2,310
Taipei,China	0.4	-2.2	10.6	4.0	1.1	3.3	3.7	20,200
South Asia	4.8	6.2	6.9	4.5	3.7	4.3	4.7	...
Afghanistan	1.5	18.6	6.3	5.2	9.7	1.3	3.0	470
Bangladesh	4.8	4.4	4.7	4.1	5.0	4.3	4.6	780
Bhutan	8.7	3.8	7.3	8.1	5.7	6.7	6.7	2,130
India	5.2	7.1	7.8	4.8	3.7	4.7	5.2	1,410
Maldives	10.5	-5.2	5.3	5.3	1.7	2.6	3.7	5,720
Nepal	4.6	2.3	2.7	3.0	3.2	2.1	2.8	540
Pakistan	1.5	-0.4	0.9	0.9	1.6	2.2	1.7	1,120
Sri Lanka	4.9	2.4	7.0	7.1	9.2	2.6	3.0	2,580
Southeast Asia	2.5	0.1	5.8	2.8	4.6	4.2	4.5	...
Brunei Darussalam	-3.2	-3.1	0.8	0.5	-0.6	0.3	0.5	31,800
Cambodia	3.2	-1.4	4.8	5.2	5.7	5.0	5.8	820
Indonesia	4.7	3.3	3.4	3.6	6.0	5.4	5.6	2,940
Lao People's Dem. Rep.	4.9	5.0	5.3	5.7	6.5	5.9	6.1	1,130
Malaysia	3.5	-2.8	4.6	3.7	4.3	4.0	4.2	8,770
Myanmar	2.0	3.8	3.2	3.4	4.2	4.4	4.6	...
Philippines	2.0	0.5	6.1	1.9	4.8	4.3	4.3	2,210
Singapore	-3.5	-3.7	12.8	3.0	-1.1	0.4	1.5	42,930
Thailand	1.6	-3.1	7.2	-0.4	5.9	4.4	4.5	4,440
Viet Nam	5.2	4.2	5.7	4.8	4.0	4.1	4.5	1,270
The Pacific	4.2	2.6	3.6	6.4	5.4	3.0	3.3	...
Cook Islands	-3.9	0.7	-3.2	0.6	3.0	1.7	...	...
Fiji Islands	0.4	-1.9	-0.6	1.4	1.9	1.5	1.8	3,720
Kiribati	0.9	-2.5	-3.9	-0.3	1.4	1.9	1.9	2,030
Marshall Islands	-3.4	-1.8	4.9	-0.2	0.9	1.3	0.6	3,910
Micronesia, Fed. States of	-2.0	1.5	3.2	2.7	1.9	1.5	1.9	2,860
Nauru	...	-19.8	0.5	-0.7	4.9	8.0	8.0	...
Palau	-6.6	-5.2	-0.3	5.2	3.4	2.4	2.8	6,510
Papua New Guinea	4.3	3.8	5.1	8.7	6.9	3.3	3.7	1,480
Samoa	3.9	-5.5	0.1	1.8	1.0	0.7	1.8	3,160
Solomon Islands	2.9	-3.3	4.5	7.9	3.2	1.6	1.5	1,110
Timor-Leste	11.9	10.1	6.8	8.2	8.0	5.5	5.5	2,730
Tonga	1.3	2.9	3.0	2.6	0.6	0.2	0.0	3,820
Tuvalu	12.5	-2.8	-1.9	-1.1	0.7	0.8	1.0	4,950
Vanuatu	4.1	1.1	-0.8	-0.9	-0.3	0.9	1.1	2,750
Average	5.8	5.2	8.3	6.4	5.4	5.8	6.0	...

... = data not available.

Table A3 Growth rate of value added in agriculture (% per year)

	2008	2009	2010	2011	2012	Sector share, 2011, %
Central Asia						
Armenia	3.3	6.0	−16.0	13.6	9.3	20.7
Azerbaijan	6.1	3.5	−2.2	−8.0	3.7	5.4
Georgia	−4.4	−6.8	−4.8	8.0	−3.3	10.4
Kazakhstan	−6.1	13.5	−11.6	26.5	−17.8	6.1
Kyrgyz Republic	0.9	6.7	−2.6	1.9	1.2	18.7
Tajikistan	7.8	10.5	6.8	7.9	10.4	...
Turkmenistan	...	...	...	...	...	...
Uzbekistan	4.7	5.7	6.8	6.6	7.0	31.2
East Asia						
China, People's Rep. of	5.4	4.2	4.3	4.3	4.5	7.8
Hong Kong, China	−17.0	−4.6	3.8	0.8	−0.7	0.1
Korea, Rep. of	5.6	3.2	−4.4	−2.1	−0.6	2.9
Mongolia	4.7	3.6	−16.6	−0.5	21.3	16.6
Taipei,China	0.1	−3.0	1.7	7.2	−5.8	1.4
South Asia						
Afghanistan	−14.9	44.6	−6.4	−7.9	31.5	20.0
Bangladesh	3.2	4.1	5.2	5.1	2.5	20.0
Bhutan	0.8	1.7	1.5	0.9	0.8	14.4
India	0.1	0.8	7.9	3.6	1.8	14.1
Maldives	−3.4	−2.5	−0.9	1.1	4.9	3.3
Nepal	5.8	3.0	2.0	4.5	4.9	35.1
Pakistan	1.0	4.0	0.6	2.4	3.1	21.2
Sri Lanka	7.5	3.2	7.0	1.4	5.8	11.2
Southeast Asia						
Brunei Darussalam	3.8	5.6	−5.8	4.6	...	1.1
Cambodia	5.7	5.4	4.0	3.1	4.0	28.3
Indonesia	4.8	4.0	3.0	3.4	4.0	12.8
Lao People's Dem. Rep.	2.5	2.4	2.0	1.8	2.5	29.4
Malaysia	3.8	0.1	2.4	5.9	0.8	7.8
Myanmar	5.6	5.6	4.7	...	...	...
Philippines	3.2	−0.7	−0.2	2.7	2.7	11.5
Singapore	−4.6	3.1	3.9	3.2	1.2	0.0
Thailand	4.2	1.3	−2.3	4.1	3.1	8.6
Viet Nam	4.7	1.8	2.8	4.5	2.7	16.2
The Pacific						
Cook Islands	−9.9	7.2	1.5	−6.6	...	5.5
Fiji Islands	5.0	−13.0	−4.1	11.5	...	13.4
Kiribati	15.0	−8.2	−2.5	5.7	...	23.8
Marshall Islands	−1.8	12.7	24.3	4.8	...	12.9
Micronesia, Fed. States of	−0.2	−0.9	0.7	4.5	...	26.3
Nauru	1.7	1.7	...	...	...	...
Palau	−7.1	6.0	...	...	...	...
Papua New Guinea	4.3	0.7	2.9	8.6	0.2	32.7
Samoa	2.4	−10.8	−3.2	−1.4	−5.1	9.5
Solomon Islands	10.5	−1.3	...	...	...	...
Timor-Leste	7.6	8.5	−2.1	0.0	0.0	...
Tonga	−5.3	−1.4	0.5	2.0	0.5	18.9
Tuvalu	−0.6	0.7	2.2	0.5	...	20.1
Vanuatu	2.6	0.7	4.8	5.9	...	22.2

... = data not available.

Table A4 Growth rate of value added in industry (% per year)

	2008	2009	2010	2011	2012	Sector share, 2011, %
Central Asia						
Armenia	7.8	-29.6	5.8	1.0	3.5	35.6
Azerbaijan	9.7	10.6	4.4	3.4	-1.9	65.6
Georgia	-3.9	-3.5	9.1	9.4	9.9	27.2
Kazakhstan	2.6	1.4	7.2	3.4	1.2	38.6
Kyrgyz Republic	14.0	-0.3	2.5	7.0	-13.8	29.5
Tajikistan	-8.9	-6.5	9.7	5.9	10.4	...
Turkmenistan	...	...	...	...	...	...
Uzbekistan	6.5	9.7	8.3	6.7	8.0	35.0
East Asia						
China, People's Rep. of	9.9	9.9	12.3	10.3	8.1	59.9
Hong Kong, China	1.8	-5.1	7.6	8.8	5.6	7.2
Korea, Rep. of	2.0	-0.6	10.7	5.1	1.7	40.0
Mongolia	-0.8	-0.4	4.3	9.1	10.1	31.7
Taipei,China	0.2	-4.1	23.1	5.7	0.9	36.3
South Asia						
Afghanistan	5.7	6.1	6.3	9.8	7.2	26.6
Bangladesh	6.8	6.5	6.5	8.2	9.5	30.4
Bhutan	20.4	4.8	8.2	8.1	8.8	45.2
India	4.4	9.2	9.2	3.5	3.1	27.5
Maldives	9.5	-26.1	4.3	14.6	14.0	15.4
Nepal	1.7	-0.6	4.0	2.9	1.7	15.3
Pakistan	1.4	-0.1	6.1	0.7	3.4	25.5
Sri Lanka	5.9	4.2	8.4	10.3	10.3	29.3
Southeast Asia						
Brunei Darussalam	-5.4	-5.0	1.7	0.9	...	51.9
Cambodia	4.0	-9.5	13.6	14.5	9.2	30.6
Indonesia	3.7	3.6	4.9	5.3	5.2	40.7
Lao People's Dem. Rep.	10.2	17.4	14.5	14.2	13.7	28.6
Malaysia	0.1	-7.2	8.0	2.0	5.1	37.4
Myanmar	18.0	17.7	18.6	...	...	...
Philippines	4.8	-1.9	11.6	2.3	6.5	32.1
Singapore	-1.5	-1.3	24.7	7.4	1.2	33.5
Thailand	3.2	-5.0	12.8	-3.9	7.2	46.8
Viet Nam	6.0	5.5	7.7	5.5	4.5	41.8
The Pacific						
Cook Islands	2.5	-2.2	-8.7	8.7	...	9.4
Fiji Islands	-1.4	-0.4	5.7	1.4	...	18.7
Kiribati	-25.2	21.3	-9.9	11.8	...	8.6
Marshall Islands	3.3	-7.4	-6.2	-6.4	...	9.7
Micronesia, Fed. States of	7.6	36.3	16.2	12.8	...	8.9
Nauru	404.9	-41.1	...	...	...	...
Palau	-30.7	-11.6	...	...	...	...
Papua New Guinea	7.0	8.1	10.8	13.0	15.9	35.9
Samoa	5.9	-15.7	2.7	1.0	2.7	27.5
Solomon Islands	13.0	1.3	...	...	...	...
Timor-Leste	24.7	13.8	11.1	...	...	...
Tonga	0.7	12.9	11.6	5.5	1.2	21.2
Tuvalu	81.9	-14.4	-6.9	-28.7	...	12.1
Vanuatu	27.5	27.6	12.6	-20.9	...	9.4

... = data not available.

Table A5 Growth rate of value added in services (% per year)

	2008	2009	2010	2011	2012	Sector share, 2011, %
Central Asia						
Armenia	5.0	–3.6	4.6	5.9	8.4	43.7
Azerbaijan	14.0	9.1	7.2	–2.1	9.9	29.0
Georgia	7.4	–3.4	7.8	5.7	5.8	62.4
Kazakhstan	4.3	–1.1	7.1	9.0	9.8	55.3
Kyrgyz Republic	11.0	2.3	–1.1	6.9	6.2	51.8
Tajikistan	12.0	9.5	4.6	13.5	14.5	...
Turkmenistan	...	...	...	...	...	...
Uzbekistan	15.3	9.3	11.6	12.7	10.4	33.7
East Asia						
China, People's Rep. of	10.4	9.6	9.8	9.4	8.1	32.3
Hong Kong, China	2.4	–1.7	7.0	5.2	2.0	92.7
Korea, Rep. of	2.8	1.1	3.9	2.6	2.5	57.1
Mongolia	16.6	0.8	9.8	16.8	13.4	51.8
Taipei,China	1.3	–0.2	4.8	3.1	1.0	62.3
South Asia						
Afghanistan	13.8	17.2	18.1	12.7	7.3	53.3
Bangladesh	6.5	6.3	6.5	6.2	6.1	49.6
Bhutan	5.4	9.1	12.7	13.8	9.0	40.4
India	10.0	10.5	9.8	8.2	6.6	58.4
Maldives	13.5	1.7	8.0	6.0	1.4	81.3
Nepal	7.3	6.0	5.8	3.6	5.1	49.6
Pakistan	6.0	1.7	2.6	4.4	4.0	53.4
Sri Lanka	5.6	3.3	8.0	8.6	4.6	59.5
Southeast Asia						
Brunei Darussalam	2.6	2.1	3.8	3.7	...	47.0
Cambodia	9.0	2.3	3.3	5.0	8.0	41.1
Indonesia	8.7	5.8	8.4	8.5	7.7	46.5
Lao People's Dem. Rep.	9.5	6.2	8.0	8.5	8.0	41.9
Malaysia	8.6	2.9	7.2	7.0	6.4	54.8
Myanmar	11.6	12.2	11.6	...	...	...
Philippines	4.0	3.4	7.2	5.1	7.4	56.4
Singapore	4.5	–0.7	10.7	4.4	1.2	66.5
Thailand	1.3	–0.2	4.6	3.8	6.2	44.5
Viet Nam	7.4	6.6	7.5	7.0	6.4	42.0
The Pacific						
Cook Islands	–2.9	2.4	–2.5	0.4	...	85.2
Fiji Islands	0.9	0.9	–0.5	0.3	...	67.9
Kiribati	5.4	1.1	1.4	–1.2	...	67.6
Marshall Islands	–2.4	–0.5	3.2	0.9	...	77.4
Micronesia, Fed. States of	–3.5	–1.5	1.6	0.2	...	64.9
Nauru	32.8	1.0	...	...	...	...
Palau	–1.9	–1.8	...	...	...	...
Papua New Guinea	8.6	9.7	8.5	11.5	10.1	31.4
Samoa	3.9	1.5	0.0	3.0	1.5	64.3
Solomon Islands	1.3	–1.3	...	...	...	...
Timor-Leste	18.2	13.2	12.9	...	...	...
Tonga	4.1	0.8	1.0	1.8	0.5	59.9
Tuvalu	3.1	3.5	2.5	6.4	...	67.8
Vanuatu	5.0	3.3	3.1	3.6	...	68.4

... = data not available.

Table A6 Inflation (% per year)

	2008	2009	2010	2011	2012	2013	2014
Central Asia	16.4	5.9	7.0	8.9	5.3	6.7	6.7
Armenia	9.0	3.4	8.2	7.7	2.6	3.6	3.2
Azerbaijan	20.8	1.5	5.7	7.9	1.1	6.0	7.0
Georgia	10.0	1.7	7.1	8.5	–0.9	3.0	4.0
Kazakhstan	17.0	7.3	7.1	8.3	5.1	6.7	6.5
Kyrgyz Republic	24.5	6.8	7.8	16.6	2.8	7.5	5.5
Tajikistan	20.4	6.5	6.5	12.5	5.8	6.5	7.0
Turkmenistan	14.5	–2.7	4.4	5.3	5.3	6.0	6.5
Uzbekistan	12.7	14.1	9.4	13.1	12.9	9.5	9.0
East Asia	5.5	–0.1	3.1	5.0	2.6	3.1	3.3
China, People's Rep. of	5.9	–0.7	3.3	5.4	2.6	3.2	3.5
Hong Kong, China	4.3	0.6	2.3	5.3	4.1	3.9	4.3
Korea, Rep. of	4.7	2.8	3.0	4.0	2.2	2.5	2.8
Mongolia	28.0	7.6	10.1	9.1	14.3	13.0	10.0
Taipei,China	3.5	–0.9	1.0	1.4	1.9	1.6	1.8
South Asia	8.0	5.6	9.4	9.3	8.0	7.4	7.1
Afghanistan	26.8	–12.2	7.7	11.8	6.2	6.1	5.8
Bangladesh	9.9	6.7	7.3	8.8	10.6	7.8	7.0
Bhutan	6.4	7.1	4.8	8.6	10.2	9.3	7.4
India	8.1	3.8	9.6	8.9	7.5	7.2	6.8
Maldives	12.0	4.5	6.1	11.3	10.9	9.3	8.5
Nepal	7.7	12.6	9.6	9.6	8.3	10.5	9.0
Pakistan	12.0	20.8	10.1	13.7	11.0	9.0	9.5
Sri Lanka	–20.8	3.5	6.2	6.7	7.6	7.5	6.5
Southeast Asia	8.5	2.6	4.1	5.5	3.9	4.2	4.1
Brunei Darussalam	2.1	1.0	0.4	2.0	0.5	1.0	1.2
Cambodia	25.0	–0.7	4.0	5.5	2.9	3.0	3.5
Indonesia	9.8	4.8	5.1	5.4	4.3	5.2	4.7
Lao People's Dem. Rep.	7.6	0.0	6.0	7.6	4.3	5.5	5.0
Malaysia	5.4	0.6	1.7	3.2	1.7	2.2	3.0
Myanmar	22.5	2.3	8.2	2.8	3.5	5.1	5.1
Philippines	8.3	4.1	3.9	4.6	3.2	3.6	3.8
Singapore	6.6	0.6	2.8	5.3	4.5	3.8	3.0
Thailand	5.4	–0.9	3.3	3.8	3.0	3.2	3.1
Viet Nam	23.0	6.9	9.2	18.6	9.2	7.5	8.2
The Pacific	9.3	5.4	5.1	8.5	5.3	6.1	6.3
Cook Islands	4.3	10.3	1.8	0.6	2.8	3.0	3.0
Fiji Islands	7.8	3.7	5.5	8.7	4.3	4.5	4.0
Kiribati	11.0	8.4	–2.8	1.2	–1.8	3.0	3.0
Marshall Islands	14.7	0.5	1.8	5.4	5.7	4.5	3.5
Micronesia, Fed. States of	6.6	7.8	6.3	4.7	5.6	4.5	3.5
Nauru	1.0	21.2	–0.6	–3.5	–0.5	0.5	2.5
Palau	10.0	4.7	1.1	2.6	6.0	5.5	5.5
Papua New Guinea	10.8	6.9	6.0	8.4	4.1	6.5	7.5
Samoa	6.3	14.6	–0.2	2.9	6.2	4.5	4.0
Solomon Islands	17.4	7.1	1.0	7.4	5.9	4.5	4.5
Timor-Leste	7.6	–0.0	5.6	13.1	10.9	9.0	7.7
Tonga	9.5	6.0	5.1	6.1	4.6	2.7	2.7
Tuvalu	4.7	–5.5	–1.9	0.5	1.4	2.0	2.0
Vanuatu	4.8	4.3	2.8	0.8	1.4	2.5	2.5
Average	6.6	1.4	4.4	5.9	3.7	4.0	4.2

... = data not available.

Table A7 Change in money supply (% per year)

	2008	2009	2010	2011	2012
Central Asia					
Armenia	2.4	15.1	11.8	23.7	19.5
Azerbaijan	44.0	–0.3	24.3	32.1	20.7
Georgia	6.9	8.2	33.1	14.5	11.4
Kazakhstan	35.4	19.5	13.3	15.0	7.9
Kyrgyz Republic	12.6	17.9	21.1	14.9	23.8
Tajikistan	6.3	39.6	26.2	44.2	23.2
Turkmenistan	62.8	10.9	43.4	36.3	16.6
Uzbekistan	38.7	40.9	52.4	32.3	25.0
East Asia					
China, People's Rep. of	17.8	27.6	19.7	13.6	13.8
Hong Kong, China	2.6	5.3	8.1	12.9	11.1
Korea, Rep. of	12.0	9.9	6.0	5.5	4.8
Mongolia	–5.5	26.9	62.5	37.0	18.8
Taipei,China	7.2	5.8	5.4	4.8	3.5
South Asia					
Afghanistan	27.0	33.1	26.9	21.3	9.3
Bangladesh	17.6	19.2	22.4	21.3	17.4
Bhutan	2.3	24.6	30.1	21.2	–1.0
India	19.3	16.8	16.0	13.2	12.3
Maldives	21.8	14.4	14.6	20.0	5.0
Nepal	25.2	27.0	30.5	12.3	22.7
Pakistan	15.3	9.6	12.5	15.9	14.1
Sri Lanka	8.5	18.6	15.8	19.1	17.6
Southeast Asia					
Brunei Darussalam	21.6	–16.8	9.4	14.5	...
Cambodia	4.8	36.8	20.0	21.5	20.9
Indonesia	14.9	13.0	15.4	16.4	14.9
Lao People's Dem. Rep.	18.3	31.3	38.9	29.2	31.0
Malaysia	13.4	9.5	7.2	14.6	9.6
Myanmar	23.4	34.8	36.3	26.3	28.6
Philippines	15.6	8.3	10.6	6.3	10.6
Singapore	12.0	11.3	8.6	10.0	7.2
Thailand	9.2	6.8	10.9	15.1	10.3
Viet Nam	20.3	29.0	33.3	12.1	22.4
The Pacific					
Cook Islands	4.0	65.9	–2.3	–13.4	...
Fiji Islands	–5.4	7.4	4.2	14.8	6.3
Kiribati	...	...	...	...	...
Marshall Islands	...	...	...	...	...
Micronesia, Fed. States of	...	...	...	...	...
Nauru	...	...	...	...	...
Palau	...	...	...	...	...
Papua New Guinea	7.8	21.9	10.0	17.6	6.4
Samoa	5.8	9.1	7.1	–4.0	–6.4
Solomon Islands	8.0	16.8	16.6	15.6	...
Timor-Leste, Dem. Rep. of	34.1	29.6	18.2	9.3	26.2
Tonga	8.4	–1.9	5.1	2.7	...
Tuvalu	...	...	...	...	...
Vanuatu	13.2	0.5	–6.0	1.3	–0.6

... = data not available.

Table A8 Central government revenues (% of GDP)

	2008	2009	2010	2011	2012
Central Asia					
Armenia	22.0	22.0	22.6	23.3	23.6
Azerbaijan	26.8	29.0	26.9	30.1	32.0
Georgia	30.7	29.3	28.3	28.2	28.9
Kazakhstan	25.1	20.6	19.7	19.5	19.3
Kyrgyz Republic	29.9	32.2	30.5	27.2	28.6
Tajikistan	22.0	23.4	23.2	24.9	26.5
Turkmenistan	20.9	20.4	16.1	18.9	20.5
Uzbekistan	34.5	33.8	32.5	31.8	30.8
East Asia					
China, People's Rep. of	19.5	20.1	20.7	22.0	22.6
Hong Kong, China	18.5	19.2	21.2	22.6	21.8
Korea, Rep. of	21.2	20.4	19.1	19.9	21.6
Mongolia	33.1	30.3	37.1	40.3	35.6
Taipei,China	13.0	12.4	11.1	12.2	12.3
South Asia					
Afghanistan	17.5	20.6	22.0	20.6	25.0
Bangladesh	11.1	10.4	10.9	11.7	12.6
Bhutan	35.2	40.4	46.4	35.6	35.8
India	19.9	19.1	21.0	20.1	21.3
Maldives	30.8	22.6	24.0	31.5	28.1
Nepal	15.4	16.7	18.1	17.8	18.3
Pakistan	14.6	14.5	14.0	12.5	12.4
Sri Lanka	15.6	15.0	14.9	14.5	14.2
Southeast Asia					
Brunei Darussalam	60.2	39.4	51.9	46.8	...
Cambodia	13.3	11.9	13.2	13.2	14.5
Indonesia	19.8	15.1	15.4	16.3	16.2
Lao People's Dem. Rep.	14.4	14.9	15.7	16.4	17.7
Malaysia	20.8	22.3	20.1	21.0	22.1
Myanmar	13.5	11.7	13.0	13.0	19.8
Philippines	15.6	14.0	13.4	14.0	14.5
Singapore	16.8	16.9	16.9	17.7	18.2
Thailand	16.9	16.8	17.6	17.8	19.1
Viet Nam	29.3	28.1	30.1	26.6	25.1
The Pacific					
Cook Islands	32.1	33.7	29.0	28.7	41.6
Fiji Islands	25.1	24.7	24.9	26.8	...
Kiribati	69.3	79.0	81.5	82.9	74.1
Marshall Islands	70.1	69.2	66.9	63.7	60.8
Micronesia, Fed. States of	57.3	65.9	68.2	65.8	65.2
Nauru	61.7	80.7	49.5	62.1	85.3
Palau	39.5	40.4	43.0	37.1	37.5
Papua New Guinea	32.2	29.3	31.0	30.1	30.8
Samoa	31.2	34.5	36.2	37.5	34.3
Solomon Islands	33.6	34.1	34.1	43.3	40.3
Timor-Leste	381.6	275.5	308.4	354.4	276.7
Tonga	25.9	32.3	27.0	26.3	27.0
Tuvalu	74.6	83.2	69.9	82.7	88.0
Vanuatu	27.0	25.9	24.0	21.6	...

... = data not available.

Table A9 Central government expenditures (% of GDP)

	2008	2009	2010	2011	2012
Central Asia					
Armenia	22.7	29.6	27.6	26.1	25.1
Azerbaijan	26.6	29.7	27.7	29.6	31.7
Georgia	37.0	38.4	34.9	31.8	31.9
Kazakhstan	27.2	23.5	22.1	21.5	22.3
Kyrgyz Republic	29.3	36.1	36.6	31.9	35.2
Tajikistan	27.0	28.6	26.1	27.0	26.4
Turkmenistan	10.9	13.4	14.1	15.2	14.5
Uzbekistan	33.2	34.2	32.8	33.3	31.5
East Asia					
China, People's Rep. of	19.9	22.4	22.4	23.1	24.2
Hong Kong, China	18.5	17.6	17.0	18.9	18.7
Korea, Rep. of	22.9	25.2	21.7	22.2	24.5
Mongolia	37.6	35.5	36.6	45.1	43.3
Taipei,China	13.9	16.0	14.1	14.1	14.0
South Asia					
Afghanistan	21.7	22.1	21.1	21.2	25.1
Bangladesh	15.8	14.3	14.6	16.1	17.6
Bhutan	34.4	38.6	44.7	37.8	39.9
India	28.3	28.5	27.5	28.1	28.3
Maldives	42.0	43.1	39.6	39.0	40.4
Nepal	17.4	20.0	20.0	20.2	20.4
Pakistan	22.2	19.9	20.3	19.2	21.0
Sri Lanka	22.6	24.9	22.8	21.4	20.4
Southeast Asia					
Brunei Darussalam	30.0	33.4	27.2	23.3	...
Cambodia	15.9	20.5	21.3	20.7	19.7
Indonesia	19.9	16.7	16.2	17.4	18.0
Lao People's Dem. Rep.	20.2	20.7	24.6	24.4	25.6
Malaysia	25.4	28.9	25.5	25.9	26.6
Myanmar	16.0	16.9	18.4	16.9	25.3
Philippines	16.5	17.7	16.9	16.0	16.8
Singapore	16.8	17.2	16.6	16.5	17.1
Thailand	18.3	18.8	16.9	16.2	20.5
Viet Nam	32.4	37.4	37.4	31.6	32.0
The Pacific					
Cook Islands	28.8	35.9	28.8	28.0	43.7
Fiji Islands	29.0	33.4	30.7	35.7	...
Kiribati	88.9	91.8	92.0	97.1	94.2
Marshall Islands	61.0	61.4	54.7	60.0	61.9
Micronesia, Fed. States of	59.0	64.3	67.7	65.2	64.0
Nauru	71.8	80.4	43.5	61.4	86.5
Palau	43.2	46.5	44.5	40.6	40.7
Papua New Guinea	34.4	28.7	30.3	27.8	32.0
Samoa	32.6	37.6	42.8	42.7	38.8
Solomon Islands	39.6	50.2	32.8	38.2	42.2
Timor-Leste	110.8	104.7	116.9	112.3	139.7
Tonga	22.9	33.2	32.3	33.7	29.9
Tuvalu	74.3	91.9	99.3	90.0	80.4
Vanuatu	24.8	24.9	26.0	23.9	...

... = data not available.

Table A10 Fiscal balance of central government (% of GDP)

	2008	2009	2010	2011	2012
Central Asia					
Armenia	-0.7	-7.6	-5.0	-2.8	-1.5
Azerbaijan	0.2	-0.7	-0.9	0.6	0.3
Georgia	-6.3	-9.2	-6.6	-3.6	-3.0
Kazakhstan	-2.1	-2.9	-2.4	-2.1	-3.0
Kyrgyz Republic	0.0	-3.7	-6.3	-4.8	-6.6
Tajikistan	-5.5	-5.4	-3.7	-2.5	0.1
Turkmenistan	10.0	7.0	2.0	3.6	6.0
Uzbekistan	4.5	0.6	1.8	-1.5	-0.7
East Asia					
China, People's Rep. of	-0.4	-2.3	-1.7	-1.1	-1.6
Hong Kong, China	0.1	1.6	4.2	3.7	3.2
Korea, Rep. of	-1.7	-4.8	-2.6	-2.2	-2.9
Mongolia	-4.5	-5.2	0.5	-4.8	-7.7
Taipei,China	-0.8	-3.5	-3.0	-1.9	-1.6
South Asia					
Afghanistan	-4.1	-1.6	0.9	-0.6	0.0
Bangladesh	-4.7	-3.9	-3.7	-4.4	-5.1
Bhutan	0.8	1.9	1.6	-2.1	-4.0
India	-8.4	-9.3	-6.5	-7.9	-6.9
Maldives	-11.2	-20.5	-15.6	-7.5	-12.3
Nepal	-2.1	-3.3	-1.9	-2.4	-2.2
Pakistan	-7.6	-5.3	-6.3	-6.6	-8.5
Sri Lanka	-7.0	-9.9	-8.0	-6.9	-6.2
Southeast Asia					
Brunei Darussalam	30.2	6.0	24.7	23.6	...
Cambodia	-2.7	-8.6	-8.1	-7.5	-5.2
Indonesia	-0.1	-1.6	-0.7	-1.1	-1.8
Lao People's Dem. Rep.	-5.9	-5.8	-8.9	-7.9	-7.9
Malaysia	-4.6	-6.7	-5.4	-4.8	-4.5
Myanmar	-2.5	-5.2	-5.4	-3.9	-5.4
Philippines	-0.9	-3.7	-3.5	-2.0	-2.3
Singapore	0.1	-0.3	0.3	1.2	1.1
Thailand	-1.3	-4.8	-2.7	-1.3	-4.1
Viet Nam	-3.1	-9.3	-7.3	-5.0	-6.9
The Pacific					
Cook Islands	3.3	-2.2	0.2	0.7	-2.2
Fiji Islands	0.5	-4.0	-2.1	-1.4	-1.6
Kiribati	-19.6	-12.8	-10.6	-14.2	-20.0
Marshall Islands	3.4	1.3	4.5	3.7	-1.1
Micronesia, Fed. States of	-1.7	1.6	0.5	0.6	1.2
Nauru	-10.1	0.3	6.0	0.6	-1.2
Palau	-3.7	-6.1	-1.4	-3.5	-3.2
Papua New Guinea	-2.2	0.6	0.7	2.3	-1.2
Samoa	-1.5	-3.1	-6.6	-5.3	-4.5
Solomon Islands	-6.1	-16.1	1.4	5.1	-1.9
Timor-Leste	270.7	170.8	191.6	242.1	136.9
Tonga	3.0	-0.9	-5.3	-7.4	-2.9
Tuvalu	-0.7	-3.1	-30.0	-4.6	7.6
Vanuatu	2.1	1.0	-2.0	-2.3	...

... = data not available.

Table A11 Growth rate of merchandise exports (% per year)

	2008	2009	2010	2011	2012	2013	2014
Central Asia	42.6	-32.1	28.4	38.7	3.6	4.4	4.6
Armenia	-7.1	-32.7	57.0	34.4	7.0	8.5	9.0
Azerbaijan	43.8	-31.0	25.5	30.3	-4.1	-2.3	2.2
Georgia	16.3	-22.0	30.0	32.2	8.1	11.5	14.8
Kazakhstan	48.9	-39.0	40.2	43.7	4.4	5.0	5.0
Kyrgyz Republic	40.1	-9.6	5.0	27.7	-13.1	20.0	15.0
Tajikistan	-4.2	-28.2	18.3	5.2	8.2	8.5	7.5
Turkmenistan	29.3	-24.1	8.0	46.9	19.3	8.0	7.0
Uzbekistan	40.5	-4.2	4.7	31.3	2.2	6.9	-1.0
East Asia	13.4	-16.0	30.0	18.3	5.4	9.2	9.4
China, People's Rep. of	17.6	-16.1	31.4	20.4	8.0	10.0	9.0
Hong Kong, China	7.3	-10.8	22.8	12.5	6.4	9.8	10.8
Korea, Rep. of	11.6	-17.6	28.8	19.6	0.1	7.5	10.5
Mongolia	30.1	-25.6	54.3	65.6	-9.0	34.3	35.8
Taipei,China	3.4	-20.2	34.6	12.1	-2.4	5.5	8.0
South Asia	14.2	-3.3	31.1	24.6	-3.4	7.1	14.2
Afghanistan	34.4	2.1	12.3	-4.7	-3.0	-2.4	3.0
Bangladesh	17.4	10.1	4.2	39.2	6.2	6.0	8.0
Bhutan	4.4	-13.8	5.5	22.2	-10.6	-36.6	-30.8
India	13.7	-3.5	37.3	23.7	-4.0	8.0	16.0
Maldives	46.0	-49.0	16.8	75.4	-4.8	6.3	3.9
Nepal	9.3	-4.7	-6.3	11.7	5.7	0.2	5.5
Pakistan	18.2	-6.4	2.9	28.9	-2.8	1.0	3.5
Sri Lanka	6.2	-12.7	21.0	23.2	-7.4	4.0	5.0
Southeast Asia	12.1	-15.1	30.7	15.1	4.4	6.6	9.6
Brunei Darussalam	40.4	-33.0	29.8	32.5	1.5	2.2	3.2
Cambodia	7.6	-14.2	29.7	34.4	11.4	13.0	17.0
Indonesia	18.3	-14.3	32.1	27.0	-6.3	7.0	12.1
Lao People's Dem. Rep.	21.8	-5.5	44.4	42.0	9.0	14.0	13.9
Malaysia	13.0	-21.1	26.6	14.6	-0.0	2.0	7.0
Myanmar	12.3	-1.4	25.8	13.3	11.2	14.1	17.5
Philippines	-2.5	-22.1	34.9	-6.3	8.5	9.1	10.3
Singapore	6.7	-14.2	31.4	6.9	6.0	4.0	8.0
Thailand	15.9	-13.9	27.1	14.3	3.2	10.0	11.0
Viet Nam	29.1	-8.9	26.5	34.2	18.2	16.0	12.0
The Pacific	21.7	-24.4	31.7	24.6	-30.7	...	...
Cook Islands	83.5	-16.2	11.3	-2.3	-24.8	...	...
Fiji Islands	20.4	-32.1	38.9	29.0	5.1	...	...
Kiribati	-23.2	-26.7	52.4	22.9	9.3	6.2	5.8
Marshall Islands	10.4	2.7	55.2	55.2	...	...	...
Micronesia, Fed. States of	5.4	-8.8	17.2	37.9	6.9	8.8	...
Nauru	...	-31.4	...	...	...	...	...
Palau	12.4	-34.6	-13.3	-5.6	4.4	...	...
Papua New Guinea	21.4	-23.9	30.9	21.8	-36.7	33.7	20.0
Samoa	-18.8	-1.3	13.8	-13.9	-6.1	...	...
Solomon Islands	27.6	-21.4	35.6	84.6	...	...	...
Timor-Leste	0.0	-31.5	163.1	-18.5	0.0	22.7	...
Tonga	-9.6	-32.4	-8.1	38.0	7.3	6.0	8.1
Tuvalu	35.4	-18.2	-2.4	53.0	9.4	...	...
Vanuatu	41.6	33.2	-8.4	24.6	...	...	...
Average	13.9	-15.6	30.2	18.5	4.4	8.3	9.7

... = data not available.

Table A12 Growth rate of merchandise imports (% per year)

	2008	2009	2010	2011	2012	2013	2014
Central Asia	24.8	-16.4	6.8	27.5	14.2	12.7	5.8
Armenia	35.0	-25.0	13.4	14.0	1.7	6.5	5.0
Azerbaijan	25.3	-14.0	3.6	50.7	-3.6	45.9	-12.6
Georgia	25.6	-31.4	17.7	33.6	15.0	7.0	7.5
Kazakhstan	15.6	-24.7	13.6	23.2	16.5	10.0	10.0
Kyrgyz Republic	43.6	-25.0	5.9	32.0	26.2	15.0	15.0
Tajikistan	33.2	-21.4	3.5	19.9	18.6	9.0	6.5
Turkmenistan	41.9	50.5	-8.0	28.8	24.4	5.0	6.0
Uzbekistan	48.5	-2.7	-6.8	26.5	11.4	9.1	4.2
East Asia	16.6	-15.4	36.0	22.1	3.4	9.0	9.8
China, People's Rep. of	18.8	-11.2	39.1	25.1	4.4	9.0	9.0
Hong Kong, China	8.6	-7.9	27.1	15.4	9.4	10.9	11.1
Korea, Rep. of	21.9	-25.4	31.5	23.4	-1.1	8.0	11.0
Mongolia	57.4	-34.1	49.7	106.2	2.1	15.0	15.0
Taipei,China	9.4	-26.9	43.1	12.9	-3.6	7.0	10.0
South Asia	21.1	-3.8	-73.7	30.3	0.1	5.3	12.4
Afghanistan	14.7	-0.8	11.6	3.6	8.7	6.3	2.8
Bangladesh	25.6	4.2	5.4	41.8	5.4	-2.0	6.0
Bhutan	27.4	-9.6	39.0	40.5	-9.5	-20.5	-14.9
India	19.8	-2.6	26.7	31.1	-1.0	6.0	14.0
Maldives	26.4	-34.4	14.8	38.9	3.1	6.6	1.7
Nepal	24.1	8.3	35.5	8.9	4.7	18.7	13.7
Pakistan	31.2	-10.3	-1.7	14.9	11.9	0.0	2.2
Sri Lanka	24.7	-27.6	31.8	50.7	-5.8	6.0	10.0
Southeast Asia	18.4	-21.7	32.8	15.4	6.6	7.6	10.3
Brunei Darussalam	44.1	-20.3	2.0	19.3	20.5	25.0	28.5
Cambodia	12.4	-11.6	21.7	22.8	17.1	11.0	13.0
Indonesia	36.9	-24.0	43.7	30.3	8.3	6.7	11.2
Lao People's Dem. Rep.	31.5	2.0	23.5	29.7	16.8	15.2	19.5
Malaysia	6.6	-20.6	34.0	14.3	4.3	3.0	7.0
Myanmar	25.6	1.9	15.8	24.4	22.0	15.0	17.0
Philippines	5.6	-24.0	32.9	2.4	5.1	9.4	10.9
Singapore	15.1	-19.1	30.3	8.2	9.5	6.0	9.0
Thailand	26.7	-25.1	37.0	24.9	7.8	11.0	12.5
Viet Nam	27.9	-14.3	19.6	25.8	7.5	15.0	13.0
The Pacific	19.8	-16.1	20.7	22.3	-10.8	...	...
Cook Islands	-0.1	-27.9	-4.5	26.8	10.0	...	...
Fiji Islands	20.8	-37.3	24.7	23.6	2.2	...	...
Kiribati	5.3	-9.6	20.4	18.7	14.2	0.4	-2.1
Marshall Islands	2.4	4.8	41.1	-10.8	...	...	...
Micronesia, Fed. States of	14.4	2.9	4.3	9.1	1.0	0.6	...
Nauru	-1.3	11.0	...	...	...	...	...
Palau	21.1	-28.6	8.2	23.6	0.2	...	...
Papua New Guinea	18.6	-8.1	23.0	21.5	-23.1	52.3	2.6
Samoa	9.9	-8.0	14.1	2.5	-11.5	...	...
Solomon Islands	6.5	-14.1	50.8	15.4	...	...	...
Timor-Leste	61.7	9.9	2.8	87.3	15.0	13.0	...
Tonga	37.8	-13.2	-4.8	16.9	21.0	0.1	3.9
Tuvalu	63.2	-18.7	35.4	18.7	-6.9	-8.0	...
Vanuatu	38.9	-1.9	1.9	1.0	...	...	...
Average	17.7	-15.7	-10.2	21.6	3.9	8.3	10.1

... = data not available.

Table A13 Trade balance ($ million)

	2008	2009	2010	2011	2012	2013	2014
Central Asia	54,920	25,245	46,345	72,063	65,315	59,889	61,190
Armenia	–2,664	–2,081	–2,033	–2,078	–2,030	–2,128	–2,161
Azerbaijan	23,012	14,583	19,730	24,328	23,270	18,000	20,500
Georgia	–3,833	–2,399	–2,590	–3,494	–4,246	–4,385	–4,427
Kazakhstan	33,519	14,969	28,670	47,925	45,156	45,053	44,709
Kyrgyz Republic	–1,879	–1,120	–1,202	–1,665	–2,993	–3,344	–3,845
Tajikistan	–1,863	–1,559	–1,463	–1,930	–2,419	–2,643	–2,800
Turkmenistan	6,423	875	2,232	4,622	5,026	5,785	6,315
Uzbekistan	2,205	1,976	3,000	4,354	3,550	3,550	2,900
East Asia	408,594	330,269	322,848	292,680	367,147	407,922	435,210
China, People's Rep. of	360,646	249,511	254,179	243,549	323,100	372,749	406,296
Hong Kong, China	25,010	12,592	2,365	–8,596	–22,672	–30,000	–35,000
Korea, Rep. of	5,170	37,866	40,083	31,660	38,338	38,642	39,922
Mongolia	–710	–252	–292	–1,781	–2,354	–1,859	–913
Taipei,China	18,478	30,553	26,513	27,848	30,735	28,390	24,904
South Asia	–156,079	–148,752	–164,662	–231,609	–245,022	–251,269	–275,760
Afghanistan	–6,480	–6,355	–7,070	–7,559	–8,530	–9,298	–9,549
Bangladesh	–5,330	–4,710	–5,155	–7,744	–7,995	–5,928	–5,775
Bhutan	–72	–90	–299	–519	–477	–474	–464
India	–119,519	–118,202	–130,593	–189,759	–197,155	–203,036	–225,038
Maldives	–1,318	–913	–1,044	–1,379	–1,449	–1,546	–1,565
Nepal	–2,410	–2,733	–4,084	–4,422	–4,623	–5,672	–6,529
Pakistan	–14,970	–12,627	–11,536	–10,516	–15,481	–15,247	–15,258
Sri Lanka	–5,980	–3,122	–4,881	–9,710	–9,313	–10,067	–11,582
Southeast Asia	113,548	140,255	160,857	160,904	118,627	111,999	111,826
Brunei Darussalam	7,879	4,914	7,011	9,595	9,211	8,651	7,870
Cambodia	–1,584	–1,494	–1,582	–1,490	–2,043	–2,152	–2,169
Indonesia	22,916	30,932	30,627	34,783	8,417	9,545	12,426
Lao People's Dem. Rep.	–1,228	–1,372	–1,378	–1,516	–2,014	–2,361	–3,040
Malaysia	51,501	39,928	41,826	48,389	40,544	39,485	42,249
Myanmar	303	72	796	–10	–1,112	–1,376	–1,541
Philippines	–12,885	–8,842	–10,966	–15,652	–14,818	–16,350	–18,471
Singapore	42,080	51,105	69,907	70,267	62,221	57,052	57,557
Thailand	17,348	32,620	29,751	16,989	8,337	6,992	4,135
Viet Nam	–12,783	–7,607	–5,136	–450	9,884	12,512	12,810
The Pacific	139	–457	32	197	–1,299	–318	1,556
Cook Islands	–108	–78	–74	–95	–105	...	...
Fiji Islands	–1,106	–647	–723	–849	–838	...	...
Kiribati	–65	–60	–71	–83	–96	–95	–92
Marshall Islands	–70	–74	–101	–69	–69	–68	
Micronesia, Fed. States of	–122	–128	–131	–134	–133	–130	–129
Nauru	6	–8	...	...	...	...	...
Palau	–118	–85	–93	–118	–117	...	...
Papua New Guinea	2,655	1,524	2,221	2,712	1,132	901	1,956
Samoa	–238	–218	–249	–257	–227	...	...
Solomon Islands	–68	–74	–137	–3	...	...	...
Timor-Leste	–261	–295	–280	–565	–654	–736	...
Tonga	–145	–128	–123	–142	–173	–172	–179
Tuvalu	–15	–13	–17	–20	–19	–17	...
Vanuatu	–201	–182	–191	–181	...	...	...
Total	421,121	346,559	365,418	294,235	304,767	328,223	334,023

... = data not available.

Table A14 Current account balance (% of GDP)

	2008	2009	2010	2011	2012	2013	2014
Central Asia	8.1	0.4	4.9	8.1	5.3	3.1	4.5
Armenia	–11.8	–15.8	–14.8	–10.9	–10.4	–9.8	–9.1
Azerbaijan	33.7	23.0	28.4	25.7	22.6	13.0	17.0
Georgia	–22.8	–11.2	–10.2	–12.8	–13.5	–11.9	–10.7
Kazakhstan	4.7	–3.6	1.2	7.2	4.3	2.5	4.0
Kyrgyz Republic	–13.7	–2.2	–7.2	–6.1	–20.9	–7.0	–5.0
Tajikistan	–7.6	–5.9	2.1	–2.3	–3.5	–5.0	–4.8
Turkmenistan	16.5	–14.7	–10.6	2.0	1.5	2.0	3.0
Uzbekistan	8.9	2.2	6.6	8.1	4.7	4.3	3.2
East Asia	7.7	5.3	4.3	3.1	3.1	3.0	2.8
China, People's Rep. of	9.3	4.9	4.0	2.8	2.6	2.5	2.1
Hong Kong, China	15.0	9.5	6.6	4.8	1.1	4.0	5.0
Korea, Rep. of	0.3	3.9	2.9	2.3	3.8	3.0	2.5
Mongolia	–12.3	–7.5	–14.3	–31.5	–31.3	–22.0	–15.0
Taipei,China	6.9	11.4	9.3	8.9	10.5	11.0	12.0
South Asia	–3.0	–2.7	–2.2	–3.5	–4.3	–3.7	–3.2
Afghanistan	0.9	–2.8	3.9	3.0	4.0	1.6	0.3
Bangladesh	0.9	2.7	3.7	0.8	1.4	2.0	1.0
Bhutan	–2.2	–1.1	–9.9	–23.5	–18.9	–20.0	–20.0
India	–2.4	–2.8	–2.7	–4.1	–5.0	–4.4	–3.7
Maldives	–32.3	–11.1	–9.2	–21.4	–26.3	–27.8	–22.0
Nepal	2.9	4.2	–2.3	–0.9	4.9	–0.5	–1.8
Pakistan	–8.5	–5.7	–2.2	0.1	–2.0	–0.8	–0.9
Sri Lanka	–9.5	–0.5	–2.2	–7.8	–5.8	–5.0	–4.5
Southeast Asia	4.4	7.1	6.4	5.3	3.3	2.9	2.7
Brunei Darussalam	48.5	37.3	48.5	45.5	47.0	45.0	47.0
Cambodia	–11.1	–10.3	–10.4	–8.8	–11.6	–11.1	–10.1
Indonesia	0.0	2.0	0.7	0.2	–2.8	–2.3	–1.8
Lao People's Dem. Rep.	–18.5	–21.0	–18.3	–21.4	–22.6	–21.5	–23.6
Malaysia	17.1	15.5	11.1	11.0	7.9	5.8	5.6
Myanmar	–3.1	–2.6	–1.2	–2.5	–4.0	–4.2	–4.4
Philippines	2.1	5.6	4.5	3.2	2.9	3.0	3.2
Singapore	14.9	18.4	28.4	23.8	19.0	16.1	14.7
Thailand	0.5	8.3	3.1	1.7	0.7	0.8	0.1
Viet Nam	–11.9	–6.8	–4.0	0.2	6.4	6.9	5.6
The Pacific	47.7	15.6	21.5	41.7	15.0	4.8	4.4
Cook Islands	...	...	...	...	...	...	...
Fiji Islands	–17.4	–5.2	–7.5	–7.0	–6.1	–22.5	–7.0
Kiribati	–34.3	–30.5	–22.9	–27.2	–26.6	–23.9	–20.0
Marshall Islands	–1.8	–16.9	–28.1	–6.2	–6.3	–2.5	–2.5
Micronesia, Fed. States of	–16.8	–18.5	–16.5	–18.8	–15.0	–14.3	–14.0
Nauru	11.9	–7.0	...	...	...	...	...
Palau	–17.8	–1.5	2.0	4.1	5.9	7.5	7.5
Papua New Guinea	9.8	–7.1	–6.4	–1.3	–17.5	–15.1	–8.4
Samoa	–11.1	–6.2	–9.3	–9.2	–10.8	–13.4	–15.5
Solomon Islands	–17.8	–20.9	–28.3	–7.8	–5.8	–10.0	–10.0
Timor-Leste	297.8	164.0	201.3	261.5	153.5	102.8	66.0
Tonga	–11.9	–15.7	–13.4	–11.1	–17.9	–6.3	–6.3
Tuvalu	–26.6	15.1	–15.5	–39.8	–8.4	–3.3	...
Vanuatu	–6.6	–6.1	–5.5	–6.3	–6.0	–10.0	–10.0
Average	5.4	4.0	3.5	2.5	2.0	1.9	1.8

... = data not available.

Table A15 Exchange rates to the United States dollar (annual average)

	Currency	Symbol	2008	2009	2010	2011	2012
Central Asia							
Armenia	dram	AMD	306.0	363.3	373.7	372.5	401.8
Azerbaijan	Azerbaijan new manat	AZN	0.8	0.8	0.8	0.8	0.8
Georgia	lari	GEL	1.5	1.7	1.8	1.7	1.7
Kazakhstan	tenge	T	120.3	147.5	147.4	146.6	149.1
Kyrgyz Republic	som	Som	36.6	42.9	46.0	46.1	47.0
Tajikistan	somoni	TJS	3.4	4.1	4.4	4.6	4.8
Turkmenistan	Turkmen manat	TMM	2.3	2.9	2.9	2.9	2.9
Uzbekistan	sum	SUM	1,319.6	1,465.6	1,576.8	1,710.9	1,885.4
East Asia							
China, People's Rep. of	yuan	CNY	6.9	6.8	6.8	6.5	6.3
Hong Kong, China	Hong Kong dollar	HK$	7.8	7.8	7.8	7.8	7.8
Korea, Rep. of	won	W	1,100.5	1,275.0	1,155.4	1,107.4	1,125.7
Mongolia	togrog	MNT	1,165.8	1,437.8	1,357.9	1,265.2	1,359.2
Taipei,China	NT dollar	NT$	31.5	33.1	31.6	29.5	29.6
South Asia							
Afghanistan	afghani	AF	51.0	49.3	45.8	47.7	50.9
Bangladesh	taka	Tk	68.6	68.8	69.2	71.2	79.1
Bhutan	ngultrum	Nu	40.4	47.8	46.7	45.3	50.3
India	Indian rupee/s	Re/Rs	45.9	47.4	45.6	47.5	54.4
Maldives	rufiyaa	Rf	12.8	12.8	12.8	15.4	15.4
Nepal	Nepalese rupee/s	NRe/NRs	64.7	76.6	74.2	72.1	80.7
Pakistan	Pakistan rupee/s	PRe/PRs	62.5	78.5	83.8	85.5	89.2
Sri Lanka	Sri Lanka rupee/s	SLRe/SLRs	108.3	114.9	113.1	110.6	127.6
Southeast Asia							
Brunei Darussalam	Brunei dollar	B$	1.4	1.5	1.4	1.3	1.2
Cambodia	riel	KR	4,060.0	4,148.3	4,188.5	4,065.9	4,033.7
Indonesia	rupiah	Rp	9,699.0	10,389.9	9,090.4	8,770.4	9,386.6
Lao People's Dem. Rep.	kip	KN	8,734.9	8,501.0	8,248.6	8,011.4	7,994.0
Malaysia	ringgit	RM	3.3	3.5	3.2	3.1	3.1
Myanmar	kyat	MK	917.0	918.0	803.0	772.0	852.0
Philippines	peso	P	44.3	47.7	45.1	43.3	42.2
Singapore	Singapore dollar	S$	1.4	1.5	1.4	1.3	1.2
Thailand	baht	B	33.4	34.3	31.7	30.5	31.1
Viet Nam	dong	D	16,302.0	17,065.0	18,621.0	20,490.0	20,828
The Pacific							
Cook Islands	New Zealand dollar	NZ$	1.4	1.6	1.4	1.3	1.2
Fiji Islands	Fiji dollar	F$	1.6	2.0	1.9	1.8	1.8
Kiribati	Australian dollar	A$	1.2	1.3	1.1	1.0	0.9
Marshall Islands	US dollar	US$	1.0	1.0	1.0	1.0	1.0
Micronesia, Fed. States of	US dollar	US$	1.0	1.0	1.0	1.0	1.0
Nauru	Australian dollar	A$	1.2	1.3	1.1	1.0	0.9
Palau	US dollar	US$	1.0	1.0	1.0	1.0	1.0
Papua New Guinea	kina	K	2.7	2.7	2.7	2.3	2.1
Samoa	tala	ST	2.6	2.7	2.5	2.5	2.5
Solomon Islands	Sol. Islands dollar	SI$	7.8	8.1	8.1	7.6	7.4
Timor-Leste	US dollar	US$	1.0	1.0	1.0	1.0	1.0
Tonga	pa'anga	T$	1.8	2.1	2.0	1.7	...
Tuvalu	Australian dollar	A$	1.2	1.3	1.1	1.0	0.9
Vanuatu	vatu	Vt	101.4	105.9	97.2	94.6	...

... = data not available.

Table A16 Gross international reserves ($ million)

	2008	2009	2010	2011	2012
Central Asia					
Armenia	1,407	2,004	1,866	1,932	1,799
Azerbaijan	6,467	5,364	6,409	10,274	12,000
Georgia	1,480	2,110	2,264	2,818	2,873
Kazakhstan	19,872	23,091	28,275	29,328	28,280
Kyrgyz Republic	1,225	1,588	1,719	1,835	2,067
Tajikistan	150	278	476	572	662
Turkmenistan	...	...	...	...	...
Uzbekistan	9,534	12,226	14,580	19,780	23,000
East Asia					
China, People's Rep. of	1,966,200	2,453,200	2,914,200	3,255,800	3,352,300
Hong Kong, China	182,539	255,816	268,731	285,408	317,336
Korea, Rep. of	201,223	269,995	291,571	306,402	326,968
Mongolia	637	1,294	2,197	2,457	4,091
Taipei,China	291,707	348,198	382,005	385,547	403,169
South Asia					
Afghanistan	3,591	4,209	5,403	6,208	6,867
Bangladesh	6,149	7,471	10,750	10,912	10,364
Bhutan	589	704	792	906	770
India	252,326	277,042	303,482	294,398	292,317
Maldives	241	261	350	335	305
Nepal	2,477	2,872	2,759	3,003	4,238
Pakistan	8,577	9,118	12,958	14,783	11,901
Sri Lanka	1,753	5,097	6,610	5,958	6,877
Southeast Asia					
Brunei Darussalam	751	1,357	1,563	2,487	3,315
Cambodia	2,164	2,367	2,653	3,032	3,463
Indonesia	51,639	66,105	96,207	110,123	112,781
Lao People's Dem. Rep.	636	633	727	677	708
Malaysia	91,648	96,744	106,590	133,257	139,658
Myanmar	2,254	2,909	3,309	3,818	5,071
Philippines	37,551	44,243	62,373	75,302	83,831
Singapore	174,196	187,809	225,754	237,737	259,307
Thailand	111,008	138,418	172,129	175,124	181,608
Viet Nam	23,022	14,148	12,382	13,500	25,400
The Pacific					
Cook Islands	...	...	...	...	...
Fiji Islands	351	557	679	852	922
Kiribati	44	59	...	...	...
Marshall Islands	2	...	...	...	...
Micronesia, Fed. States of	45	53	57	77	77
Nauru	...	...	...	...	...
Palau	...	...	...	...	...
Papua New Guinea	2,095	2,623	3,092	4,323	4,296
Samoa	96	95	165	143	145
Solomon Islands	92	144	266	397	497
Timor-Leste	210	238	394	450	...
Tonga	48	64	87	120	140
Tuvalu	25	23	24	25	...
Vanuatu	128	137	155	172	...

... = data not available.

Table A17 External debt outstanding ($ million)

	2008	2009	2010	2011	2012
Central Asia					
Armenia	1,577	2,967	3,299	3,568	3,738
Azerbaijan	3,001	3,422	3,734	4,841	...
Georgia	2,691	3,658	4,219	4,506	4,820
Kazakhstan	107,933	112,867	118,270	125,153	134,878
Kyrgyz Republic	3,591	4,118	4,381	4,872	5,403
Tajikistan	1,498	1,692	1,911	2,093	2,260
Turkmenistan	606	485	2,347	2,049	4,820
Uzbekistan	3,748	5,022	5,753	7,899	9,100
East Asia					
China, People's Rep. of	390,161	428,648	548,938	694,997	850,000
Hong Kong, China	686,664	712,784	879,656	982,701	1,045,244
Korea, Rep. of	317,370	345,677	359,757	398,724	413,437
Mongolia	2,184	2,986	5,928	9,628	15,260
Taipei,China	90,361	81,963	101,581	122,528	124,325
South Asia					
Afghanistan	2,069	1,150	1,303	1,242	1,340
Bangladesh	20,266	20,859	20,336	22,086	22,095
Bhutan	820	795	873	1,312	1,358
India	224,500	260,935	305,852	345,357	365,315
Maldives	879	934	962	909	942
Nepal	3,197	3,495	3,442	3,658	3,863
Pakistan	46,161	52,331	57,363	61,844	65,833
Sri Lanka	15,107	18,662	21,438	24,466	...
Southeast Asia					
Brunei Darussalam	...	...	...	...	...
Cambodia	2,776	2,940	3,337	3,841	4,281
Indonesia	155,080	172,871	202,413	225,375	251,200
Lao People's Dem. Rep.	2,575	2,694	2,809	2,990	3,100
Malaysia	68,243	67,965	73,643	81,009	82,662
Myanmar	12,744	13,207	13,643	14,632	12,251
Philippines	54,328	54,856	60,048	60,442	60,337
Singapore	901,379	888,314	989,210	1,089,884	1,148,412
Thailand	76,102	75,306	100,561	105,957	130,500
Viet Nam	21,816	27,929	32,501	...	...
The Pacific					
Cook Islands	...	...	...	...	...
Fiji Islands	299	269	286	469	537
Kiribati	15	14	18	28	34
Marshall Islands	99	96	107	105	101
Micronesia, Fed. States of	74	85	84	87	87
Nauru	...	...	63	...	...
Palau	75	80	78	75	80
Papua New Guinea	1,040	1,028	922	979	1,260
Samoa	229	211	289	329	278
Solomon Islands	140	134	125	113	124
Timor-Leste	...	...	...	...	43
Tonga	86	95	121	166	186
Tuvalu	15	14	16	15	13
Vanuatu	100	102	111	...	...

... = data not available.

Table A18 Debt service ratio (% of exports of goods and services)

	2008	2009	2010	2011	2012
Central Asia					
Armenia	3.1	5.4	4.7	4.2	9.4
Azerbaijan	0.9	1.3	...	...	...
Georgia	3.4	5.2	4.9	7.5	...
Kazakhstan	41.7	63.2	32.1	24.2	21.3
Kyrgyz Republic	26.8	41.4	25.9	11.5	11.3
Tajikistan	10.5	20.3	7.5	5.1	...
Turkmenistan	1.4	1.1	0.9	0.6	...
Uzbekistan	5.7	5.4	7.9	9.7	10.7
East Asia					
China, People's Rep. of	1.8	2.9	1.6	1.7	2.0
Hong Kong, China	...	...	...	...	...
Korea, Rep. of	7.9	7.8	6.8	6.4	7.4
Mongolia	5.9	12.4	11.3	6.6	9.3
Taipei,China	3.9	2.6	1.2	2.2	1.6
South Asia					
Afghanistan	1.1	0.8	1.1	1.3	1.1
Bangladesh	3.2	3.2	2.9	2.5	2.4
Bhutan	17.3	30.5	29.7	52.3	117.5
India	4.4	5.8	4.3	6.0	5.9
Maldives	2.6	2.9	2.5	2.8	1.2
Nepal	9.6	10.2	11.6	11.1	11.1
Pakistan	13.0	17.2	16.7	11.3	14.6
Sri Lanka	15.1	19.0	15.9	12.6	...
Southeast Asia					
Brunei Darussalam	...	...	...	...	...
Cambodia	1.2	1.5	1.4	1.2	1.2
Indonesia	17.2	21.1	19.8	21.7	35.3
Lao People's Dem. Rep.	4.3	4.9	4.5	4.6	...
Malaysia	2.6	6.5	7.6	10.3	10.0
Myanmar	6.4	6.6	3.1	3.9	5.1
Philippines	9.7	10.4	8.7	10.2	7.4
Singapore	...	...	...	...	...
Thailand	8.3	7.6	4.7	3.5	4.3
Viet Nam	3.3	4.2	3.4	3.5	...
The Pacific					
Cook Islands	...	...	...	...	...
Fiji Islands	1.1	1.7	1.3	8.8	1.6
Kiribati	3.6	9.0	3.5	2.7	2.8
Marshall Islands	24.7	22.7	17.6	11.4	...
Micronesia, Fed. States of	5.4	6.7	6.6	6.9	6.6
Nauru	0.6	2.1	...	...	...
Palau	49.3	69.9	62.4	48.3	52.5
Papua New Guinea	1.8	0.5	0.3	0.4	0.3
Samoa	67.8	62.1	75.8	...	...
Solomon Islands	5.6	3.6	3.0	1.3	1.3
Timor-Leste	...	...	...	...	...
Tonga	10.1	5.7	10.6	8.7	9.0
Tuvalu	21.9	16.3	12.0	9.9	...
Vanuatu	1.3	1.5	1.4	...	...

... = data not available.